STUDY GUIDE TO ACCOMPANY SAMU

MICRO-
ECONOMICS

STUDY GUIDE TO ACCOMPANY SAMUELSON-NORDHAUS

MICRO-ECONOMICS

Fourteenth Edition

GARY W. YOHE

Wesleyan University

McGRAW-HILL, INC.

New York   St. Louis   San Francisco   Auckland   Bogotá   Caracas
Lisbon   London   Madrid   Mexico   Milan   Montreal   New Delhi   Paris
San Juan   Singapore   Sydney   Tokyo   Toronto

FOR LINDA, MARIELLE, AND COURTNEY

**STUDY GUIDE TO ACCOMPANY
SAMUELSON-NORDHAUS: MICROECONOMICS**

Copyright © 1992 by McGraw-Hill, Inc. All rights reserved.
This work is derived from the *Study Guide to Accompany
Samuelson-Nordhaus: Economics*, Fourteenth Edition, by
Gary W. Yohe. Copyright © 1992, 1989, 1985, 1980, 1976, 1973,
1970, 1967, 1964, 1961, 1958, 1955, 1952 by McGraw-Hill, Inc.
All rights reserved. Copyright renewed 1980, 1983 by Paul
A. Samuelson and Romney Robinson. Printed in the United
States of America. Except as permitted under the United
States Copyright Act of 1976, no part of this publication may
be reproduced or distributed in any form or by any means,
or stored in a data base or retrieval system, without the prior
written permission of the publisher.

1 2 3 4 5 6 7 8 9 0 MAL MAL 9 0 9 8 7 6 5 4 3 2

ISBN 0-07-054891-9

This book was set in Zapf Book Light by Publication Services.
The editors were James A. Bittker and Larry Goldberg;
the production supervisor was Al Rihner.
The cover was designed by Hermann Strohbach.
New drawings were done by Fineline Illustrations, Inc.
Malloy Lithographing, Inc., was printer and binder.

CONTENTS

To the Student   vii

PART ONE   BASIC CONCEPTS

1   Introduction   1
    Appendix 1   How to Read Graphs   6
2   Basic Problems of Economic Organization   17
3   Markets and Government in a Modern Economy   31
4   Basic Elements of Supply and Demand   39

PART TWO   MICROECONOMICS: SUPPLY, DEMAND, AND PRODUCT MARKETS

5   Supply and Demand in Individual Markets   53
6   Demand and Consumer Behavior   67
    Appendix 6   Geometric Analysis of Consumer Equilibrium   77
7   Production and Business Organization   85
8   Analysis of Costs   95
    Appendix 8   Production, Cost Theory, and Decisions of the Firm   108
9   Supply and Pricing in Competitive Markets   115
    Appendix 9   Special Cases of Competitive Markets: Supply and Demand at Work   129
10   Marginal Revenue and Monopoly   135
11   Oligopoly and Monopolistic Competition   145
12   Uncertainty and Games in Economic Behavior   155

PART THREE   WAGES, RENT, AND PROFITS: THE DISTRIBUTION OF INCOME

13   Incomes and the Pricing of Factors of Production   165
14   Wages and the Labor Market   175

| 15 | Labor Unions and Collective Bargaining | 185 |
| 16 | Land, Natural Resources, and Capital | 193 |

PART FOUR   EFFICIENCY, EQUITY, AND GOVERNMENT

17	Markets and Economic Efficiency	209
18	Government and the Economy	217
19	Government Taxation and Expenditure	229
20	Curbing Market Power: Regulation and Antitrust Policies	239
21	Income Distribution and the Struggle against Poverty	247
22	The Winds of Change: The Triumph of the Market	261

PART FIVE   INTERNATIONAL TRADE AND THE WORLD ECONOMY

23	International Trade and the Theory of Comparative Advantage	269
24	Protectionism and Free Trade	283
25	The Economics of Developing Countries	291
26	Exchange Rates and the International Financial System	299
	Answers to Quiz Questions: Multiple Choice	307

TO THE STUDENT

This *Study Guide* has one specific objective: to help you master the fundamentals of economic analysis as presented in the fourteenth edition of *Microeconomics* by Paul A. Samuelson and William D. Nordhaus. It has been prepared in close consultation with these authors to cover the material presented in the text and to involve you in deciphering that material. It is hoped that your work in the *Guide* will lead you to a deeper understanding of not only the content of each chapter of the text, but also of the rationale for anyone's ever worrying about such things. It will, however, accomplish this goal only if your reading is an active process. If you simply read the pages of the *Study Guide* as you would any other text, you will see another presentation of the same material. Your passive reading will have caused you to lose most of the value of your supplementary purchase. If, however, you read the pages more slowly with pencil and pen in hand and work through the various questions that they will pose, your active participation in exercising the fundamentals of economic analysis will generate a deeper understanding of what is going on and, I hope, a higher grade in your economics class.

Each chapter of the *Guide* begins with a list of learning objectives. These lists have been prepared to outline the major points of each chapter and appendix. After reading the text chapter, match them with a list that you draw up to see whether you (or I) have missed anything. You will, at that point, have a good idea of the material that the remainder of the chapter will exercise.

The second major part of each chapter in the *Guide* amounts to a collection of questions and problems designed to enhance your understanding of the learning objectives. Working through them one at a time (*before* looking at the answers provided in small print after each question) will test and extend your knowledge as you apply what the text has taught you. The process of learning economics is much like the one by which you might learn a new language. You can go to class and read textbooks to be exposed to the fundamentals of a new language, but it sinks in and becomes part of you only if you practice. With enough practice, you begin to think in the new language, and further progress becomes easier. Working through the question section of the *Guide*, you will similarly practice what you have learned in class and in the text, and eventually you might even begin to think like an economist.

Each chapter in the *Guide* concludes with a set of review concepts and a series of multiple choice quiz questions (with the answers provided at the end of the book). The review concepts are yet one more summary of the chapter's material, and the multiple choice questions are designed to tell you whether or not you have really mastered their content. You should, as you work through the questions, select one of the five alternative answers—the one that makes the most sense in context.

Some of the possible answers listed are correct statements but are irrelevant to the question being posed. Others are simply wrong. Still others are almost right, but nonetheless inferior to an alternative choice. The answers listed at the back of the book represent the best selections, and each is accompanied by a brief explanation of why. The multiple choice sections are as much a part of the *Guide* as other sections, and taking care in working through them should pay dividends.

One of the most successful ways of mastering the fundamentals of economic analysis is to try to summarize the material of each chapter or unit in successively shorter outlines. The prose that surrounds the questions in the middle of each chapter represents a first cut at such an outline. The list of learning objectives and/or the review concepts can, perhaps, represent a final stage. Use the *Guide* to look for threads of common thought and rationalization as you synthesize text material down to short lists of learning objectives. When you have reached the point of needing only the objectives lists to recall the content of any chapter, in particular, make sure that you have a firm understanding of their connection to each other *and* to material from other chapters. Having accomplished that understanding, you will be able to apply your knowledge to unfamiliar problems and contexts.

The real lessons of economics are ones of process—insights into the methods by which economists try to identify logically the essentials of a particular circumstance from a multitude of data. Equipped with insight into these processes and methods, you will be ready to proceed to subsequent economics courses and do well. Perhaps more importantly, though, you will be equipped with the mental skills necessary to deal with the myriad of economics-related issues and decisions that will face you all of your life. You may forget what opportunity cost is, for example, but you should continue to be able to identify essential tradeoffs and weigh them accordingly.

ACKNOWLEDGMENTS

Preparation of this *Study Guide* would not have been accomplished on schedule without the assistance of many people. I would like to formally recognize their contributions and express my gratitude.

My family, who missed another spring of my attention but supported my efforts anyway, certainly deserves a heartfelt "thanks." Their support makes these projects worthwhile. The appearance of Bonne Belle certainly provided a counterpoint of comic relief, as well.

Special thanks needs to be offered to Joan Halberg for her preparation of the manuscript. The scanner did some very odd things, and Joan figured it all out before I ever saw files.

In addition to thanking the hundreds of professors who responded to our questionnaire, I wish to thank the following reviewers who, through their comments and constructive criticisms, helped to strengthen the fourteenth edition *Study Guide:* Marion S. Beaumont, California State University—Long Beach; Philip Coelho, Ball State University; Thomas Mullen, University of Wisconsin—Whitewater; and Michael K. Taussig, Rutgers University.

Many people at McGraw-Hill also deserve grateful acknowledgment. Larry Goldberg, Ira Roberts, and James Bittker certainly fall into that category. A special thanks must, however, be extended to Elisa Adams. Her excellent work, good humor, and constant encouragement beginning with the twelfth edition were still felt this time around.

Finally, I express my sincere gratitude for the continuing opportunity, education, and friendship offered by Bill Nordhaus.

Gary W. Yohe

STUDY GUIDE TO ACCOMPANY SAMUELSON-NORDHAUS

MICRO-ECONOMICS

CHAPTER 1

INTRODUCTION

This introductory chapter is, above all, one which should be read with a view toward perspective. It has been designed to provide a rough outline of what the discipline of economics is all about. You need not worry particularly about the few details which are presented here. Try, instead, to get the "lay of the land." Try to get an idea of why people would ever want to concern themselves with the study of economics and how, in broad and general terms, such a study should be conducted. Keeping this in mind, you should be able to meet the following objectives after studying the text chapter and working through the *Study Guide* questions.

LEARNING OBJECTIVES

1. Understand the breadth of the study of economics by understanding how all the topics mentioned in the specialized definitions of economics fit into the umbrella definition: *Economics is the study of how societies use scarce resources to produce valuable commodities and distribute those commodities among various people.*

2. Distinguish between microeconomics and macroeconomics and between positive and normative economics.

3. Identify and describe the four major tools in the scientific approach to the study of economic issues: observation, economic analysis, scientific analysis, and experiments.

4. Identify and explain the many potential pitfalls in the study of economics: the fallacy of composition, the fallacy of *post hoc, ergo propter hoc*, the fallacy of failing to hold other things constant, and the danger of advancing individual subjective views of the world as generally valid descriptions of how the world operates. Explain how each might lead to faulty understanding of an economic system.

5. Understand that the *law of scarcity* lies at the heart of economics—that the scarcity of goods and resources requires that people and societies make decisions among economic goods, not free goods, and thereby immediately raises issues of economic efficiency and equity.

The text provides a very brief historical perspective by citing three individuals whose contributions represent landmarks in the development of economics as a scholarly discipline. Adam Smith published *The Wealth of Nations* in 1776, Karl Marx published *Capital* (*Das Kapital*) in three installments from 1867 to 1894, and John Maynard Keynes published *The General Theory of Employment, Interest and Money* in 1936. You will become increasingly familiar with these men and their thinking as you progress through your study of economics. It is enough, at this point, to be familiar with the broadest descriptions of their work and to note that the 1980s marked the rediscovery of the fundamental insights of Adam Smith—over 200 years after they were first published.

1. Indicate in the parentheses provided whether the following statements apply to the work of Adam Smith (S), Karl Marx (M), or John Maynard Keynes (K):

a. Capitalism is doomed, and its abuses will quickly be followed by business depressions, revolution, and socialism. . . . . ( )

b. Active fiscal and monetary management by federal governments can be used to avoid the worst downturns of the traditional business cycle. . . . . ( )

c. Markets can function quite well in the allocation of scarce resources if they are set free from heavy-handed governmental regulation and intervention. . . . . ( )

a. M **b.** K **c.** S

1 Introduction

Five alternative definitions of economics are cited in the text. Paraphrased slightly, they are:

1. Economics is the study of what goods are produced, how they are produced, and for whom.
2. Economics is the analysis of trends in the variables that summarize the performance of the overall economy—prices, output, employment, etc.
3. Economics is the study of how people choose to use scarce resources to produce various goods and to distribute those goods across society.
4. Economics is the study of commerce, broadly defined to include commerce among nations.
5. Economics is the study of money, banking, capital, and wealth.

Economics is, of course, all these things and much more. A single, umbrella definition is therefore provided to capture a common theme:

> Economics is the study of how societies use scarce resources to produce valuable commodities and distribute them among different groups of people.

2. Review the five more specialized definitions of economics cited above and try to see how each fits under the general umbrella. With all six notions in mind, which of the following seem to fall correctly (C) within the scope of economic investigation and which seem to fall outside (O) the general umbrella?

a. The first objective of economics as a science is to study the psychology of human performance in producing and selling goods in order to indicate to business how it can induce people to perform these activities more efficiently.
.... (C / O)

b. Economics is closely associated with the particular activities in which money is involved—the purchase and sale of goods and of securities, the employment of labor, and so on.
.... (C / O)

c. Economics is a study of the activities with which a nation acquires a high standard of income and of consumption.
.... (C / O)

d. In economics, we look at the processes of producing, selling, buying, and consuming goods in order to develop some theory with respect to these behaviors. .... (C / O)

e. Economics is a study of how people in a society decide what commodities and services they are going to produce, now and in the future, and how those commodities and services are to be distributed among members of the population.
.... (C / O)

---

a. O **b.** C **c.** C **d.** C **e.** C

Within the general rubric of economics, a significant distinction is made between the behavior of individual components of an economy (individuals, households, firms, industries, etc.), on the one hand, and the functioning of the economy taken as a whole, on the other. The former, called **microeconomics**, looks at the small building blocks of a larger system. How are vegetable prices set? How do people negotiate their employment contracts? How should people negotiate those contracts? Will some people work less hard if they are forced to pay higher income taxes? Will some save more if they are forced to pay higher sales taxes? These are the types of questions that are asked in the study of microeconomics.

By way of contrast, **macroeconomics** focuses on broader sorts of questions. How is national income determined? What is the relationship (if any) between the rate of unemployment and the rate of inflation? How should we expect the economy to respond to an enlarged supply of money? What should we expect to see as a consequence of enormous budget deficits at the federal level? These are all macroeconomic issues.

3. To exercise your understanding of the distinction between microeconomics and macroeconomics, consider the following list of publications. Each refers to topics studied in either microeconomics (MI) or macroeconomics (MA). Indicate, simply on the basis of the content suggested by the titles, which studies they might be related to.

a. Arthur Okun, *The Political Economy of Prosperity*
.... (MA / MI)

b. Orley Ashenfelter, "Union Relative Wage Effects," in Stone and Petersen (eds.), *Econometric Contributions to Public Policy* .... (MA / MI)

c. Edward Denison, "Is U.S. Growth Understated because of the Underground Economy? Employment Ratios Suggest Not," *Review of Income and Wealth* .... (MA / MI)

d. R. J. Gordon, "Inflation, Flexible Exchange Rates and the Natural Rate of Unemployment," in M. N. Baily (ed.), *Workers, Jobs and Inflation* .... (MA / MI)

e. Joseph Pechman, *Who Bears the Tax Burden?*
.... (MA / MI)

f. A. A. Berle, Jr., and Gardner Means, *The Modern Corporation and Private Property* .... (MA / MI)

a. MA **b.** MI **c.** MA **d.** MA **e.** MI **f.** MI

4. Economic knowledge is generally the result of research conducted according to what has been dubbed the **scientific approach**. List the four major tools of the scientific approach:

a. _____

b. _____

c. _____
d. _____

Of the four tools noted above, _____ is the process by which a multitude of data and seemingly unrelated facts are shaped into a coherent view of reality. It is a process that depends upon _____ for the generation of some initial hypotheses. Without careful review of what history tells us, we have no idea what to study. We have no hypotheses to investigate.

Validation of the hypotheses can be accomplished by one of at least two means. The most common is _____, in which mathematical methods are used to test whether or not the relationships suggested either by a preliminary review of history or by the logical implications of a theory or hypothesis hold water. With what degree of confidence can we put forward a correlation of economic variables as an interesting, causal connection? The answer to this question depends upon, among other things, the strength and accuracy of the purported connection, the quality of the data, and the degree to which the connection can be isolated.

In a few cases, though, _____ can be employed to serve the same function. Problems here involve designing and administering the exercise so that the data collected are useful, constructing and administering the control group so that statistical analysis of the data can be conducted with "other things being held equal," and maintaining interest over the long time required to generate undistorted data.

a. observation   **b.** analysis   **c.** statistical analysis   **d.** controlled experiments; analysis; observation; statistical analysis; controlled experiments

The distinction between microeconomics and macroeconomics can, to be sure, blur somewhat at their interface. When, for example, is an industry so large that an analysis of its response to a certain tax treatment is a question of macroeconomics and not microeconomics? When does a question of tax burden get so large that it has macroeconomic content? The list can be extended almost indefinitely. Recognizing this blurring is not, however, nearly as important as recognizing that macroeconomic and microeconomic views of how the world behaves must be consistent with each other. Sure, the economy taken as a whole is only a physical collection of individual economic agents operating in their own little environments. But how, in our study of economics, are we to add the actions of many agents to get a picture of an overall economy? The answer is, Very carefully.

The text includes a short section on potential pitfalls in economic reasoning; the **fallacy of composition** is a major concern of that section. This fallacy occurs when something that is known to be true for a part of an organization (or a microeconomy) is therefore assumed to be true for the whole organization (an overall macroeconomy). While our knowledge of how a macroeconomy works must be checked for consistency with our understanding of how its microeconomic components behave, it must also be developed in its own right if we are to make certain that we avoid this fallacy.

The distinction between micro and macro is far more than a semantic one. There are different tools and different modes of analysis used for the study of microeconomics than those used with macroeconomics.

Two other logical pitfalls are identified in the text. The first of these, linked with **failing to keep "other things equal,"** notes that the interdependencies of economic systems frequently make it difficult to study the single relationship in which you are interested. Failure to note these interdependencies can, however, prove fatal. Suppose, for example, that you noticed that sales of Japanese VCRs climbed throughout 1985 and 1986 even though a falling dollar made the machines increasingly expensive. You might conclude that more people wanted Japanese VCRs simply because the VCRs got more expensive, and you would be wrong. To draw such a conclusion, you would have to show that the increase in demand was not produced by other possible causes (e.g., higher incomes, an increase in the number of good movies available at video rental stores, reduced rental prices at those stores, an increase in the cost of hiring baby-sitters and going out to the movies, a perceived reduction in the quality of VCRs produced elsewhere in the world, etc.). Otherwise, we should expect that the normal relationship between price and demand held notwithstanding the experience of 1985 and 1986: all other things held constant, the observed higher prices for VCRs in 1985 and 1986 would have meant smaller demand.

The second fallacy, labeled *post hoc, ergo propter hoc*, is closely related to, but less subtle than, the "other things equal" pitfall. It warns that the fact that two events happen at the same time does not necessarily mean that one caused the other. People have noted that sunspot activity usually increases during times of recession in the United States. Do U.S. recessions cause sunspots? Hardly. Do sunspots cause recessions? Hard to swallow, too, unless you believe that increased sunspot activity increases some sort of radiation onto the earth's surface that somehow makes people less productive.

5. For each statement listed below, indicate whether the fallacy of composition (C), the fallacy of *post hoc, ergo propter hoc* (P), or the fallacy of failing to hold all other things equal (E) is involved. If none of the three applies, record (N).

a. The American economy remains essentially competitive as a result of diligent application of the antitrust laws. . ( )

b. All theories in social science are forced to simplify the real and complex world; because of this simplification, the conclusions of any such theory are inevitably distorted and inaccurate explanations. ( )

c. Workers in any single industry will benefit from higher wages; hence workers in all industries would benefit from a comparable wage increase. . . . . ( )

d. During the early stages of the energy-price shock of the late 1970s, lines at gasoline stations all across the United States typically extended well into the streets. It is clear, therefore, that the demand for gasoline increased dramatically as its price doubled. . . . . ( )

e. A recent report in the *New England Journal of Medicine* observed that gypsies in Boston all smoked too much but hardly ever died of lung cancer. Doubt is thus cast upon the purported link between excessive smoking and the incidence of lung cancer. . . . . ( )

f. The more the human brain masters a subject in social science, such as economics, the less room it has for comprehension of any quite different subject, such as physics.
. . . . ( )

g. If one firm in an industry benefits from a large-scale advertising campaign, this is an indication that if all firms in that industry were to advertise, they would all obtain comparable increases in sales. ( )

h. I can gain 15 minutes by driving my car to work instead of using public transportation; if everyone in my community were to follow my example, the total gain in time would run into hundreds of hours each day. . . . . ( )

---

a. P **b.** N **c.** C **d.** E **e.** P **f.** N **g.** C **h.** C

One final pitfall in the study of economics is cited in the text. Unlike the previous three, though, it does not relate to the logical construction of an economic investigation. It asks, instead, that we ponder how we interpret what we see. We are reminded that we all look at the world through glasses that are tinted by our own **subjective** impressions of how things are. Collecting the "facts" about a situation is thus not always an easy task. The raw elements of experience which our senses carry to the brain are meaningless until they are organized into a pattern. The brain's disposition in that process is to fit the material, if possible, into a familiar pattern even though, in the new situation, that pattern may be a false one.

When the ordinary business of living requires us to do so, we are forced to develop some workably valid interpretations of the behavior around us. In everyday experience, we can often discover quickly whether or not our conclusions are workably accurate. Interpret a person's behavior falsely, act on your conclusion, and you may soon learn that your interpretation was incorrect. There is, however, a broader range of human experience where this element of immediate verification is lacking, or where the degree of verification is uncertain. When the verification of a theory is difficult, the familiar theory may survive regardless of its veracity until it can be supplanted by a clearly superior theory. The risk involved in this process should be clear. If an unsatisfactory theory is used so frequently that it becomes entrenched in the canonical view of the world, then the development of a new, potentially superior theory will become highly unlikely—nobody will think to question an ingrained theory, so nobody will try to develop a new one.

6. If all goods were free goods, then issues of choice would be moot because the question of scarcity (*must have been solved by well-established markets* / *must have been eliminated*). All needs and wants would be (*eliminated* / *automatically satisfied without sacrifice* / *satisfied with only minimal sacrifice*). In the real world, however, resources are (*scarce* / *infinitely plentiful in a global perspective*). People must choose, therefore, whether to (*produce one good or another* / *purchase and consume one good or another* / *allocate a specific item to one person or another*).

---

must have been eliminated; automatically satisfied without sacrifice; scarce; All three choices apply.

7. A distinction is often raised between normative and positive economics. Positive economics is descriptive—a relating of facts and circumstance based upon observation. Normative economics is prescriptive—a relating of solutions and actions based upon ethics and value judgment. Economists disagree (*more* / *less* / *about the same*) on issues of positive economics than they do on issues of normative economics. Indicate which of the following are statements of normative (N) or positive (P) character.

a. Taxes should be progressive. . . . . (N / P)

b. Taxes discourage work effort. . . . . (N / P)

c. Inflation tends to be high when unemployment is low.
. . . . (N / P)

d. Inflation is less harmful than unemployment. . (N / P)

e. Pollution restraints cost jobs. . . . . (N / P)

f. Pollution restraints are worth the cost. . . . . . (N / P)

---

less **a.** N **b.** P **c.** P **d.** N **e.** P **f.** N

The above should not be construed as a statement that economists agree on all issues of positive economics. There could, for example, be considerable debate over whether periods of low inflation need to be accompanied by high unemployment. This would be a different debate from the one over whether or not inflation is as harmful to the economy at large as unemployment.

REVIEW CONCEPTS

We return now to the Learning Objectives listed earlier in the chapter; they appear here, paraphrased and expressed more succinctly, to serve as Review Concepts. Each was covered both in the text and in the *Guide*, so refer to the appropriate section(s) if anything listed below is unfamiliar.

1. Economics is the study of how societies use scarce resources to produce valuable commodities and distribute those commodities among various people. Scarcity is at the core of economics.

2. The terms "microeconomics" and "macroeconomics" divide the discipline according to the size of the economic agents and issues being considered; the terms "positive" and "normative" economics divide the discipline according to whether or not an evaluating norm is being applied.

3. Application of the scientific approach to the study of economics involves four tools: observation, economic analysis, scientific analysis, and a few controlled experiments.

4. Careful study of economics avoids the fallacy of composition, the fallacy of *post hoc, ergo propter hoc*, the fallacy of failing to hold other things constant, and the danger of advancing individual subjective views of the world as generally valid descriptions of how the world operates.

5. The scarcity of goods and resources requires that people and societies make decisions among economic goods, not free goods, and thereby immediately raises issues of efficiency and equity.

SUGGESTED ANSWERS TO QUESTIONS IN THE TEXT: Chapter 1

1. They are recorded in both text and the *Guide*. Most generally economics is the study of how to cope with scarcity, expressed in many forms by many people with many perspectives.

2. Refer to the given definitions, but interpret each in your own words. For example:
    a. *Post hoc, ergo propter hoc:* Correlation does not necessarily imply causality.
    b. Other things being equal: To focus upon the relationship between two variables, everything else that might affect either of them is held constant.
    c. Positive economics studies how things are.
    d. Normative economics studies how things ought to be, according to some norm (Shea Stadium analysis: "Baseball the way it oughta' be!"—at least until Strawberry went west).

3. Economic goods are scarce, to some degree, and so have a price. Sand on a beach is a free good, at least most of the time; sand at a construction site for concrete is not.

4. Normative: c and d; positive: a, b, and e.

5. Positive analysis lends itself to objectivity; normative analysis does not.

The fallacy of composition is not involved in the smoking-cancer debate because the correlation is being shown to be dependent upon human characteristics that are typical of all of us; there are therefore general explanations of why a higher frequency of cancer among smokers leads us to conclude that smoking would make any person more likely to contract cancer. The same explanation should rule out consideration of the *post hoc, ergo propter hoc* fallacy, but that is nonetheless the basis of the defense offered by the tobacco companies.

In the farmer case, something that might make one farmer better off (increasing productivity), as long as all the other farmers continue to do what they have always done (not increasing yields), can hurt all farmers if they all do it together (increasing productivity at some increase in cost, thereby increasing the supply of farm product, reducing its price, reducing the total value of farm output even though more product is produced, and ultimately lowering farm profitability).

6. The *post hoc, ergo propter hoc* fallacy is involved; causality is not implied by the data in the table. Additionally, all other things were *not* held equal; income (e.g.) increased.

7. What do you think? It might be fun to return to this question at the end of your course.

APPENDIX 1

HOW TO READ GRAPHS

Economics makes extensive use of graphs and charts. They appear in nearly every chapter of the text, and the appendix to Chapter 1 is included to provide the reader with a basic review of their foundation. This associated appendix extends that review.

Graphs and charts are tools with which the fundamental notions of economic reasoning can be illustrated, exercised, and stretched. They provide an easy context within which to explore many economic phenomena that would otherwise require pages of prose. To proceed without a minimal understanding of graphs would be to proceed at a great disadvantage; it would be like playing defense in basketball with both hands tied behind your back.

This appendix is designed to present both a brief review of the basics of graphical analysis and some small insight into its usefulness. If you are already comfortable with graphs, you may still want to scan this appendix for a glimpse of things to come; but then again, you may have better things to do. In either case, you should know that graphs are used in economics, most fundamentally, to illustrate simply how two sets of numbers are related to each other.

First Example: Study Hours and Leisure Hours

Suppose that you decide to plan your working day. A considerable part of each 24 hours must be given over to sleep, meals, and class attendance. Suppose that these matters take up 14 hours per day. This leaves the remaining 10 hours to divide between study, on the one hand, and leisure and recreation, on the other.

That 10 hours could be divided in an infinite number of ways. At one extreme would be 10 hours for leisure and 0 hours for study. This particular time allocation must be considered unsatisfactory in the sense that its pursuit tends to lead to unpleasant interviews with the dean of students or other people of similarly limited imagination. It is, nonetheless, a possible allocation of time. At the other extreme would be 10 hours for study and 0 for leisure and recreation, i.e., the week-before-examinations allocation. Between the two extremes is a wide selection of alternatives. Among these choices are the allocations indicated in Table 1A-1.

Table 1A-1

	A	B	C	D	E	F	G
Leisure hours	10	8	7	6	4½	2½	0
Study hours	0	2	3	4	5½	7½	10

Table 1A-1 shows two sets of numbers. One set gives the number of possible study hours; the other gives the corresponding number of leisure hours (given a total of 10 hours to allocate between leisure and study). The numbers are, in other words, inexorably tied to one another; each study-hour number is paired with a leisure-hour figure. It is this type of pairing process that a graph always illustrates. The leisure-study trade-off provides a perfect example. All the pairs in Table 1A-1 are characterized by one relationship: the sum of the hours spent studying and the hours spent relaxing must always equal 10.

All these points are captured somewhere along the line AG in Figure 1A-1 (assuming that negative numbers of hours are not allowed).

Figure 1A-1

To see how, notice that the vertical line at the left of Figure 1A-1 and the horizontal line at the bottom are the axes against which the pairwise linkage is to be charted. Each is divided off with a number scale, and the meaning of the numbers is indicated by the labels: "Hours of Study Time" (horizontally) and "Hours of Leisure Time" (vertically).

The slanting line carrying points labeled A through G has already been identified as the actual graph of the leisure-study relationship. Each point identified along that line corresponds to a pair in Table 1A-1. Take point B, for example. Point B in Table 1A-1 pairs 2 hours of study with 8 hours of leisure time. The dashed lines in Figure 1A-1 do the same thing. Passing down from point B to the study-time horizontal axis, note that 2 hours is associated with point B; moving left to the leisure-time vertical axis, similarly note that 8 hours is associated with point B. Table 1A-1 and Figure 1A-1 illustrate the same thing, for point B and every other point along the line.

1. In the horizontal or west-east dimension, a figure of 0 would be recorded on the line at the *(extreme left / extreme right / very bottom / exact center at the very top)*. In the vertical dimension, 0 would be recorded on the line at the *(extreme left / extreme right / very bottom / exact center at the very top)*.

2. The measuring line used to position numbers in the west-east dimension is called the _____ or the _____. The south-north measuring line is called the _____ or the _____.

3. In Figure 1A-1, point B stands for the combination of 2 hours of *(study / leisure)* and 8 hours of *(study / leisure)*. In Figure 1A-1, leisure hours are measured *(vertically / horizontally)* and study hours are measured *(vertically / horizontally)*. Point D stands for _____ hours of leisure and _____ hours of study; 9 study hours and 1 leisure hour would be a pair indicated by a point between points *(A and B / D and E / F and G)*.

4. The rate at which study hours can be turned into leisure time is _____ hour(s) for every 1 hour of study time sacrificed.

---

1. extreme left; very bottom **2.** horizontal axis; X axis; vertical axis; Y axis **3.** study; leisure; vertically; horizontally; 6; 4; F and G **4.** 1

Second Example: Money, Apples, and Oranges

Suppose that someone particularly interested in either apples or oranges decides that he will allocate $40 to the purchase of one or the other, or both. Let apples cost $2 per bushel, and let oranges cost $1 per dozen. Table 1A-2 records a few possible combinations of apples and oranges that this person might consider. Notice, for example, that devoting the entire $40 to apples would allow him to bring 20 bushels of apples home (point A in Table 1A-2). Devoting the entire $40 to oranges would allow him to bring 40 dozen oranges home (point G in Table 1A-2). Other intermediate combinations, designated elsewhere in Table 1A-2, would also be possible and should not be ignored. It is likely, in fact, that these intermediate points would be preferred to "specializing" exclusively in the consumption of one fruit or the other.

Table 1A-2

	A	B	C	D	E	F	G
Apples (bushels)	20	18	15	10	5	2	0
Oranges (dozens)	0	4	10	20	30	36	40

Figure 1A-2 is blank save for a series of vertical and horizontal "grid lines," used to help locate the point that matches up with any given pair of numbers. On Figure 1A-2, draw a graph that illustrates the points in Table 1A-2. First label your axis lines. Then pick a scale for each of the axes, i.e., choose how much distance you are going to use to represent 1 bushel of apples and 1 dozen oranges. With these scales in mind, plot the seven points of Table 1A-2 and label each with its letter identification. They should all lie along a straight line much like the one drawn in Figure 1A-1. After you have satisfied yourself that they do, draw the entire line by connecting the points. This "smoothing" allows the graph to reflect all the points that you could have marked off if you had had the time and patience—all combinations of oranges and apples (including fractions) that could be purchased with $40.

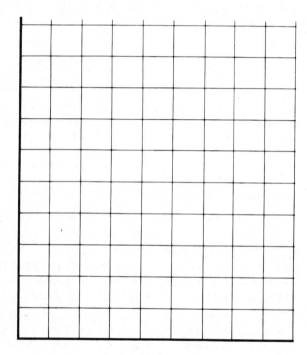

Figure 1A-2

This last idea bears repeating. You cannot, in Figure 1A-1, possibly find any combination of two positive numbers which add up to 10 that does not appear somewhere on line *AG*. Line *AG* includes every possible pair that satisfies this linking rule. Moreover, line *AG* can be trusted in another respect: it contains no point that does not meet the linking rule. In other words, line *AG* is an exact graphical representation of the "sum-to-10 rule" in the sense that (1) it includes *all* points that satisfy this rule, and (2) it includes *only* points that satisfy this rule. Similarly, the line that you drew in Figure 1A-2 includes all the combinations of apples and oranges which cost $40 and only those combinations which, indeed, cost $40.

5. In the apples-oranges example, our fruit lover would have loved to have purchased 20 dozen oranges and 20 bushels of apples. He *(could / could not)* do that, however, because he had *(more than enough money / insufficient funds)*. That combination would cost _____.

6. In the study-leisure example, the rate of exchange between study time and relaxation time was _____ hour devoted to studying for every 1 hour of forgone relaxation. In the apples-oranges example, the tradeoff was _____ dozen oranges for every bushel of forgone apples.

7. Take any point inside the triangle formed by the three lines of Figure 1A-1 (the line *AG* and the two axis lines). The pair of measurements for any such point (circle the correct completion of the sentence):

a. must together total more than 10.

b. must together total less than 10.

c. must together total 10.

d. may total more than 10 or less than 10.

8. Which alternative in question 7 correctly describes the pair of measurements belonging to any point outside line *AG* (above and to the right)? *(a / b / c / d)*

9. If we redid this example by assuming that there were a total of 11 hours rather than 10 to allocate, what would happen to line *AG* (as the line indicating all possible combinations)? (Again, circle the correct answer.)

a. It would move outward (i.e., upward and to the right), remaining parallel to the present line.

b. It would move inward (i.e., downward and to the left), remaining parallel to the present line.

c. Its position would not change.

d. It would pivot or rotate outward on point *A*.

---

5. could not; insufficient funds; $60 **6.** 1; 2 **7. b** (For example, take any point other than *B* on the vertical broken line running between *B* and the indication for 2 on the horizontal axis. This is a typical point inside the triangle. That point must stand for 2 study hours and, because it lies below point *B*, less than 8 hours of leisure time for a total of less than 10.) **8. a** **9. a** (The hour-for-hour tradeoff would persist, but the line would have to be drawn higher so that the total number of hours allocated between leisure and study would equal 11 > 10.)

Third Example: The Guns-or-Butter Diagram

One of the first graphical diagrams that you will encounter in the text is the guns-or-butter chart of Chapter 2. As Table 1A-3 shows (reproduced from Table 2-1 in the text), it involves pairs of figures once again.

Table 1A-3

	A	B	C	D	E	F
Butter (millions of pounds)	0	1	2	3	4	5
Guns (thousands)	15	14	12	9	5	0

The background of the guns-or-butter case is fundamentally one of scarcity. The economy has only a limited and fixed stock of machinery, labor, and all the other things needed to produce such items as guns or butter. Some of these resources can be used in the production of either commodity. Labor, for instance, can be transferred from the production of guns to the production of butter, or vice versa (with due allowance for the training time that might be required to make labor proficient in its new location). If labor were switched from, say, work on guns to work on butter, the result would be an increase in the output of butter and a corresponding reduction in the output of guns. If resources were fully employed, the inevitable cost of getting more of one commodity must, by extension of this example, always be a reduction in the supply of another.

The "guns-or-butter" metaphor first arose in Nazi Germany. By the end of the 1930s, Hitler's government had turned so much of German industry toward rearmament that there were shortages of some civilian goods, butter among them. The late and generally unlamented Hermann Goering made a famous speech in which he sought to appease the public's complaints by declaring, "We must choose between guns and butter!" Some choice.

As a further exercise in graph drawing, draw the guns-or-butter diagram for yourself in Figure 1A-3. Use the figures in Table 1A-3. As before, first label your two axes. Measure quantity of guns in the vertical dimension (as the text does) and quantity of butter horizontally. Ordinarily, you want to make use of all the space available on a graph. In Figure 1A-3, the maximum butter quantity to be recorded is 5 (million pounds); so put 5 at the bottom right-hand corner. There are 15 little squares sitting on the horizontal axis line; if 5 goes below the end of the fifteenth square, then 1 must go below the end of the third one, 2 below the end of the sixth, and so on. As to guns, your maximum is 15 (thousand); so put 15 at the top left, with the smaller numbers correspondingly below. Notice that (in the matter of graph distances) your two number scales can be different. Here, the same distance in inches which measures 5 million pounds of butter (horizontally) records 15,000 guns (vertically).

Having put labels and numbers on your axes, indicate on the graph the six points in the table. (This is known as plotting the points.) Identify them by let-

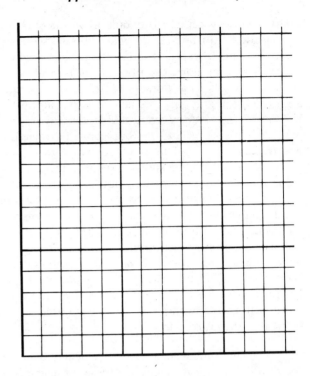

Figure 1A-3

ter and join them with a smooth curve. You have, at this point, completed a graph of the guns-butter production-possibility frontier *(PPF)*. What can you learn from it? Why was it worth the trouble? Four different observations spring to mind:

1. The area of the graph above and to the right of the frontier (the curved line *ABCDEF*) represents more desirable but unattainable territory. Points in that region represent larger guns-butter combinations than those represented by the frontier line, but they are unattainable unless or until the economy acquires more productive agents or develops better techniques for using what it has. The process of economic growth can be represented as a gradual outward shifting of the frontier.

2. The graph area below and to the left of the frontier is fully attainable. If the economy's actual guns-butter production were to be represented by a point in this area, it would signify (*a*) that the economy was not fully using all its available resources, or (*b*) that although it was employing them fully, it was somehow failing to use them to the best advantage. We assume that the economy can reach any point on the frontier without disrupting its social order and without undue strain on its productive agents and that its people will want production to reach this line. Both of the two commodities are scarce relative to the desire for them.

3. If both the unattainable area above the curve and the undesirable area below the curve were removed from consideration, then only the frontier would re-

main. The decision which people in this economy (or their leaders) must somehow make about what to produce can thus be represented as the problem of deciding which point along the frontier ABCDEF to choose. To describe this as a "guns-or-butter" decision can be a bit misleading; it suggests (all) guns or (all) butter. If both guns and butter were desirable, though, it is most likely that points A and F would both be rejected in lieu of some intermediate point such as C or D.

4. In actual life, decisions of what to produce have somehow been made for a long time; they are still being made. A decision of this nature is not something that need be made only once and can then be forgotten, for tastes change and so do productive conditions. It is a little more realistic, then, to think of an economy which is currently operating at some point such as D, and which might, for example, be disposed to spend its "peace dividend" and move toward having a little more butter. This would mean a movement away from point D and toward point E.

10. The figures in the guns-or-butter table represent *(maximum / minimum)* combinations of these two commodities which some imaginary community could produce per unit of time. The figures stand for *(money values / physical quantities)* of guns and butter.

11. If all available resources or inputs were devoted to butter production, butter output would be _____ million pounds and gun output would be _____ thousand guns. If the economy wished to have 9000 guns per period, butter output could not exceed _____ million pounds.

12. Suppose that the community is producing a total of 1 million pounds of butter. If it wants to increase this by a further 1 million pounds, then the required decrease in gun production would be _____ thousand. If the community were producing 4 million pounds of butter and wanted to increase this by 1 million (to a total of 5 million), then the required decrease in gun production would be _____ thousand.

13. Suppose that the community is producing 15,000 guns and is considering a reduction to 14,000. The change would make possible a butter increase of _____ million pounds. Alternatively, if the community currently produces 9000 guns and decides on a reduction to 5000, then a butter increase of _____ million pounds would be possible. If gun production were to be increased from 9000 to 10,000, this 1000 increase would call for a reduction in butter output of approximately _____ million pounds.

---

10. maximum; physical quantities   **11.** 5; 0; 3   **12.** 2; 5   **13.** 1; 1; 1/3

Notice that your two answers in question 12 were different, indicating that the cost of butter in terms of guns changed as more butter was produced. This notion will be important later.

One essential distinction that pervades economic thought is the difference between movement along a curve and shifts of a curve. It has already been noted in the context of the guns-or-butter example of Table 1A-3 that a society disposed toward having a little more butter could move from a point like D toward a point like E. Notice, however, that such a move clearly indicates that more butter means fewer guns. Point D represents 3 million pounds of butter and 9000 guns; point E represents 4 million pounds of butter but only 5000 guns. Without any increase in resources or advances in technology, this sort of movement along the PPF is, nonetheless, society's only option.

When the things which are normally held constant in the construction of a curve are allowed to change, however, the entire curve can actually shift. Suppose, for example, that the economy whose guns-vs.-butter tradeoff was represented in Table 1A-3 was to discover a better way to make butter—a way that would use fewer resources that are applicable to the production of guns. Table 1A-4 reflects such a change.

Table 1A-4

	A'	B'	C'	D'	E'	F'
Butter (millions of pounds)	0	2	4	6	8	10
Guns (thousands)	15	14	12	9	5	0

Compare Tables 1A-3 and 1A-4. The technological improvement reflected in Table 1A-4 shows that butter production doubles for any given level of gun production except the maximum.

Graph the production-possibility frontier defined in Table 1A-4 on Figure 1A-4. (You will need a different scale on the butter axis.) Label the points and smooth the curve. Now replicate your graph of the production-possibility frontier from Table 1A-3 on Figure 1A-4. The frontier should have shifted out in moving from Table 1A-3 to Table 1A-4 for every level of gun production but one—the one in which no butter at all is produced so that 15,000 guns can be manufactured. That makes sense, though, because the technological advances in the production of butter increase the opportunities of the economy except in the case where it ignores the new butter technology and specializes entirely in the production of guns. Movement from D to E is no longer necessary. Shifting from D to D' increases butter production to 4 million pounds even though gun production holds at 9000.

Figure 1A-4

Slope: Straight Lines One way to describe a straight-line relationship between some variable X and another variable Y is to assert that X and Y are linked so that any given change in X always generates exactly the same change in Y. That is, in reality, the way that many problems and relationships are often presented. Starting with X and Y occupying some initial positions, we often ask, "What would happen to Y if X were to change its position (i.e., its value)?" Put a more useful way, perhaps, we might ask, "What change in Y would be forthcoming if X were to increase or decrease by 1 unit?"

To get a picture of what is going on, think of starting somewhere on a straight-line graph and making little movements to the right in two stages. Think, in particular, first about making a strictly horizontal movement of sufficient length to indicate a 1-unit increase in the X value. Since the move was horizontal, the Y value will not have changed. Then think about a vertical movement up or down to signify a change in Y of a very special dimension: a vertical distance precisely equal to the amount of movement required to return to the straight line. For example, in either of the two little diagrams composing Figure 1A-5, the true path traced out is ABDE, but the movement from B to D can be considered in two parts. First, there is a probing movement from B to C (the 1-unit change in X which takes the point momentarily off its true path along the line). Then, there is a second, correcting movement from C to D (the matching change in Y required to get back on the line). If BC's length indicates a 1-unit increase in X, then CD's length must indicate the rate at which Y must change in response to X to stay on the straight line. On the graph, this vertical measure of the change is called the *slope* of the line ABDE.

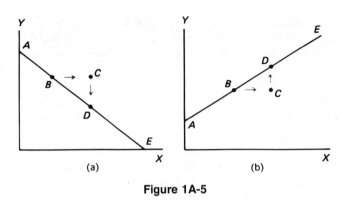

Figure 1A-5

Several points about the slope of a line should now be clear:

1. Slope is always a number that measures a rate of change. It is the amount by which some variable Y must change in response to a 1-unit change in X if we are to stay on the same straight line.

2. If the graph line is straight, one single number measures its slope at any and all points. This is just another way of saying that a straight line is one whose direction does not change.

3. The slope always assumes a negative value if the X-Y relation is an inverse one—one in which a positive increase in X requires a reduction in Y. Both the study-leisure and the apples-oranges examples qualify, and both straight lines drawn above to reflect them have negative slopes. In terms of what we draw, therefore, the slope is negative if the graph falls down to the right. The slope is, conversely, positive and the line climbs up toward the right if the X-Y relation is a direct one.

Now consider a little more fully the technique for measuring or illustrating graphically the slope of a straight line. We have said that the slope of the graph line ABDE in Figure 1A-5 is measured by the length of CD. This assumes that BC is of a length equal to 1 unit of X. We could equally well have said that slope is measured by the fraction CD/BC, with the lengths of CD and BC representing the numbers for which they stand. Since BC corresponds to the number 1, CD/BC reduces to CD anyway. The only objection to defining slope to be CD/BC is that at first it seems needlessly clumsy; but measuring slope as the more general fraction CD/BC is a reminder that the Y movement (CD) can be considered only relative to the amount of movement envisioned in the variable X (BC).

Some people find it helpful to think of slope as "the rise over the run." "The rise" is the vertical distance involved; in Figure 1A-5 terms, the rise is *CD*. "The run" is the horizontal distance; it is *BC* in Figure 1A-5 terms. So the "rise over run" rule would, in this instance, cause us to place *CD* over *BC*.

It is tempting to associate the measure of slope with the steepness with which the graph line rises or falls, so a steeply tilted line is taken as one with a high slope value, positive or negative. Sometimes this conclusion is valid, but don't overlook the fact that the steepness with which a graph line rises or falls depends in part on the scale chosen for the graph. Diagrams (a) and (b) in Figure 1A-6 both portray exactly the same relationship, and either is a perfectly respectable illustration. Notice, however, that the horizontal scale has been stretched in (b) in comparison with that used in (a). This stretching makes the line look flatter in (b) than in (a) even though the slope in both is +1/2.

The trick is that relative steepness accurately reflects relative slope only when the scales are the same. When you have two lines on the same graph, therefore, you can certainly say that the steeper line has the larger slope, in absolute value—more negative if the two lines are negatively sloped and downward-sloping or more positive if the two lines are positively sloped and upward-sloping. In Figure 1A-6(c), for example, line I has a slope of 4, line II has a slope of 2, 4 is greater than 2, and I is clearly steeper than II. In Figure 1A-6(d), line I has a slope of −4, line II has a slope of −2; the number 4 is still greater than 2, and −4 is more negative than −2, so line I is again steeper than line II.

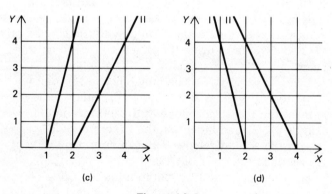

Figure 1A-6

Figure 1A-7 contains six different graphs. In each, the variable *X* signifies the magnitude being measured horizontally, and *Y* the magnitude being measured vertically. Circle the correct letter or letters below.

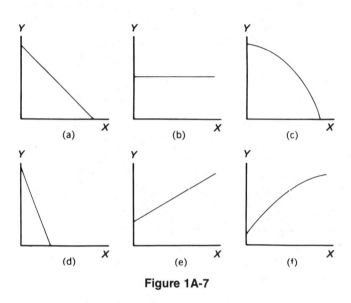

Figure 1A-7

14. Diagrams (*a / b / c / d / e / f*) illustrate an inverse relation between *X* and *Y*.

15. In diagram (*a / b / c / d / e / f*), *Y*'s response to a change in *X* is zero.

16. The *X-Y* relation is positive rather than inverse in diagram(s) (*a / b / c / d / e / f*).

17. Among the diagrams illustrating an inverse relation, the slope is constant in diagram(s) (*a / b / c / d / e / f*).

18. The diagram best suited to illustrate the relation between an adult's daily food intake in calories, measured along *X* axis, and his or her weight, measured along *Y* axis, would be (pick two which could be correct) (*a / b / c / d / e / f*).

19. The relationship between one's age (*X*) and one's height (*Y*) would probably be illustrated best by (*a / b / c / d / e / f*).

20. The most probable relation between the number of study hours you put in before a given examination (*X*) and the examination grade you can expect to earn (*Y*) is illustrated best by (or is supposed to be illustrated best by) diagram(s) (*a / b / c / d / e / f*).

21. Assume, in diagram (*d*), that the graph line meets the *Y* axis at 10 units and that it meets the *X* axis at 5 units. (You may want to write these figures on the diagram.) A 1-unit increase in *X* must therefore be accompanied by a (*0- / ½- / 1- / 2- / 4- / 10-*) unit (*increase / decrease*) in *Y*. This ratio is (*constant / variable*), depending upon the position on the line.

22. In diagram (*b*), let the graph line meet the *Y* axis at 4 units. When the value of *X* is 0, then the value of *Y* must be

(0 / 1 / 2 / 4 / *can't tell*). Similarly, when the value of *X* is 10, then the value of *Y* must be (0 / 1 / 2 / 4 / *can't tell*).

23. In diagram (e), let one point on the graph line represent the point where *X* = 0 and *Y* = 4. This point, on the diagram, would be (*at the extreme left / near the center / at the extreme right*). Let another point on the graph line represent the point where *X* = 3 and *Y* = 5. These two points indicate an underlying relation which holds that every single unit increase in the value of *X* must be accompanied by (*an increase / a decrease*) in the value of *Y* equal to (¼ / ⅓ / 1 / 3 / 4).

Note: If you find yourself stuck on any of these questions, or if you have answered incorrectly, do not be too concerned: the unfamiliar is seldom easy. Go back and review earlier material if necessary, until you are reasonably sure you understand why each answer is correct. **14.** a, c, d **15.** b **16.** e, f **17.** a, d **18.** e and/or f **19.** f **20.** f [Although (e) would be reasonably correct, presumably the payoff for continued investment in study hours tapers off, as indicated by the bend in (f)'s graph line. If you thought (a) was correct, you have some justification to provide in this semester's examinations!] **21.** 2-; decrease; constant [Start with the point at the *Y* axis, where *X* = 0 and *Y* = 10. From there, a 5-unit increase in *X* (from 0 to 5) would have to be matched by a 10-unit decrease in *Y* (from 10 to 0). This ratio is constant because the line is straight; and 5 for 10 is equivalent to 1 for 2.] **22.** 4; 4 (A horizontal line means that the value for *Y* stays the same, no matter what value is assumed by *X*.) **23.** at the extreme left; an increase; ⅓ (A 3-unit increase in *X*, from 0 to 3, is matched by a 1-unit increase in *Y*, from 4 to 5; 3 to 1 is equivalent to 1 to ⅓.)

---

24. Slope is a measure of the rate at which the value of *Y* changes for each change of (*0 units / 1 unit / the same number of units*) in the value of *X*.

25. A graph line has the same slope value throughout when that line is (*curved / rising / straight / falling*).

26. We can graphically illustrate or measure slope in terms of a right-angled triangle below the graph line. Slope is the fraction or ratio obtained by putting the length of the (*vertical / horizontal*) side of the triangle over the length of the (*vertical / horizontal*) side.

27. When an *X*-*Y* relation is inverse, then its graphical illustration can be considered the path of a point which (*falls / rises*) as it moves to the right. The slope value of such a relation is (*positive / zero / negative*).

28. In diagram (b) of Figure 1A-7, the slope of the line illustrated is (*positive / negative / zero / impossible to tell*).

29. Two positions of *X* on a straight graph line are 5 and 7. What is the value of slope if the corresponding values for *Y* are:

a. 5 and 7? . . . . (−3 / −2 / −1 / 0 / 1 / 2 / 3 / *infinity*)
b. 4 and 2? . . . . (−3 / −2 / −1 / 0 / 1 / 2 / 3 / *infinity*)
c. 2 and −2? . . . . . . (−3 / −2 / −1 / 0 / 1 / 2 / 3 / *infinity*)
d. 4 and 4? . . . . (−3 / −2 / −1 / 0 / 1 / 2 / 3 / *infinity*)
e. −2 and −8? . . . . (−3 / −2 / −1 / 0 / 1 / 2 / 3 / *infinity*)
f. −8 and −2? . . . . . (−3 / −2 / −1 / 0 / 1 / 2 / 3 / *infinity*)

---

24. 1 unit **25.** straight **26.** vertical; horizontal **27.** falls; negative **28.** zero **29. a.** 1 **b.** −1 **c.** −2 **d.** 0 **e.** −3 **f.** 3

Slope: Curved Lines A curved line is one whose slope continually changes; i.e., the amount of change in *Y* required to accommodate a 1-unit change in *X* varies according to the position from which this change begins. Consider the curved line *ABCDEF* in Figure 1A-8. Suppose we are at point *B*. If we know the exact *X* and *Y* values associated with every point on this line, then we should have no difficulty in learning what the changes in both *X* and *Y* would be as a result of moving from point *B* to point *E*. Moreover, we could put the usual right-angled triangle underneath the line, with corners at points *B* and *E*, and from it develop a value for the slope—a value called the *arc slope* from *B* to *E*.

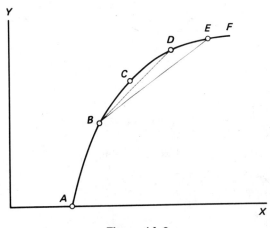

Figure 1A-8

The arc slope would not, however, be the slope of the curved line itself; it would really measure the slope of the straight line running between points *B* and *E*. We would get a different and somewhat higher slope figure if we dealt similarly with a change from point *B* to point *D*, and a still different value for a change between points *B* and *C*.

For some purposes, it is quite sufficient to know the arc slope from point *B* to *E*, or to *D*, or to *C*. For other problems, however, it can be essential to know the value of the slope of the curved line exactly at some point like point *B*.

Does it make sense to speak of the slope of a line precisely at a single point? Certainly point *B*, considered in isolation, has no slope and no direction. When point *B* is considered as part of the line *ABCDEF*, however, its slope is another matter. The slope of the line is a measure of the direction in which it runs, computed in terms of the scales on the two axes. Think for the moment of *ABCDEF* as the path traced by a moving automobile traveling around a curve. The direction of movement of that automobile changes continually, since it follows the curve, but we can say that the automobile is headed in a specific direction at any specific moment, like the exact moment when it passes over point *B*. We can certainly do so in the sense that a compass mounted on the car's dashboard at that exact moment would give an exact reading.

But how is this direction at *B* to be indicated on a piece of graph paper? The accepted answer is quite simple: by a tangent drawn to the curved line at point *B*. The tangent to a curved line is itself, by definition, a straight line; it does not cross the curved line, and it touches it at only one point. By inspection of Figure 1A-9(*a*), for example, it is easy to see how the slope of the tangent line *FJ* is to be considered as a measure of the slope of the curved line at point *B*; and line *GH* does the same for point *D*. We can, of course, apply the usual right-angle technique for computing slope to each such straight line.

What does this slope mean? Figure 1A-9(*b*) redraws the guns-or-butter production-possibility frontier from Table 1A-4. At point *B*, a tangent line is drawn, and its slope, −(*JN*/*MN*), represents the slope of the guns-or-butter schedule at point *B*. It is, intuitively, a reflection of how many guns need to be sacrificed to increase the production of butter not by 1 million pounds but by 1 pound—a much smaller number. In reality, the slope of the line at point *B* is the sacrifice in guns required to finance a minuscule increase in butter production; and after all, 1 pound is a small quantity when it is compared with 1 million pounds.

30. Figure 1A-10 consists of eight separate diagrams, each illustrating a small segment of a graph line. In each, the numbers indicate the length of the adjacent straight-line segment. What is the slope of each line *AB*? Where line *AB* is curved, it is the slope at point *C* that is desired. Circle the correct answer for each diagram.

Figure 1A-9(a)

Figure 1A-9(b)

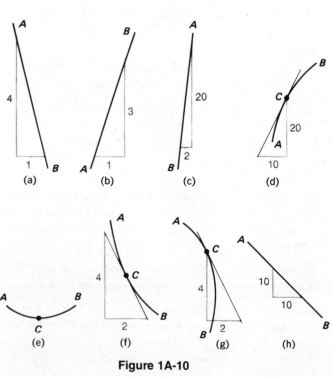

Figure 1A-10

a. (−4 / −3 / −2 / −1 / 0 / 1 / 2 / 3 / 4 / 10 / infinity)
b. (−4 / −3 / −2 / −1 / 0 / 1 / 2 / 3 / 4 / 10 / infinity)

c. (−4 / −3 / −2 / −1 / 0 / 1 / 2 / 3 / 4 / 10 / infinity)
d. (−4 / −3 / −2 / −1 / 0 / 1 / 2 / 3 / 4 / 10 / infinity)
e. (−4 / −3 / −2 / −1 / 0 / 1 / 2 / 3 / 4 / 10 / infinity)
f. (−4 / −3 / −2 / −1 / 0 / 1 / 2 / 3 / 4 / 10 / infinity)
g. (−4 / −3 / −2 / −1 / 0 / 1 / 2 / 3 / 4 / 10 / infinity)
h. (−4 / −3 / −2 / −1 / 0 / 1 / 2 / 3 / 4 / 10 / infinity)

a. −4 b. 3 c. 10 d. 2 e. 0 f. −2 g. −2 h. −1

Two or More Lines on a Graph So far our discussion has run in terms of the interpretation of a single line on a graph. But most text diagrams will include two or more lines, usually intersecting at one or more points on the graph. Some of your classmates (or certainly some upperclassmen) will even joke about the "fundamental theorem of economics": Whenever two lines intersect, it is more likely than not that the economics instructor will spend two class periods describing something "essential."

The supply-and-demand diagram of Chapter 4 is a good example. The demand line, or demand curve, is drawn as usual—from two sets of figures paired together. Table 1A-5 provides one example of a demand curve.

Table 1A-5

	Price of Wheat (per bu)	Quantity Demanded (million bu per month)
A	$5	9
B	4	10
C	3	12
D	2	15
E	1	20

It shows a relationship between the quantities of wheat that buyers in some market would demand (i.e., be prepared to buy) if the price were to stand at any one of five possible levels.

It does not matter whether this is a real market or an imaginary one. The precise figures in the table are not especially important, either. This schedule is intended simply to illustrate the reasonable (and important) notion that as the price of wheat falls, buyers probably will want to buy a larger total amount than they did before. In other words, quantity of wheat bought should be expected to be inversely related to the price of wheat.

It is also possible to prepare another schedule, indicating what sellers of wheat (the producers of wheat, the suppliers of wheat) are prepared to do. In this case, it seems reasonable to assume that if the price were to go up, then suppliers would try to supply a larger quantity because the higher price would generate a higher return on their efforts. Alternatively, if the price were to fall, then they would choose to supply less. Table 1A-6 represents this different relation, showing quite clearly that the quantity of wheat supplied is directly related to the price of wheat.

Table 1A-6

	Price of Wheat (per bu)	Quantity Demanded (million bu per month)
A	$5	18
B	4	16
C	3	12
D	2	7
E	1	0

At this stage, it is not particularly essential that you fully understand the ideas conveyed by the demand and/or supply schedules. What matters for the moment is that you recognize something familiar in the construction: the demand curve consists of two sets of inversely related figures, neatly paired one with the other; the supply curve consists of two sets of positively related figures, equally neatly paired with each other. This means that either can be depicted as a line on a graph—both can even be depicted together on the same graph.

Why? Despite their differences, there is a fundamental similarity between the two schedules. Although they represent the attitudes or the intentions of two entirely different groups of people, the two schedules match one another in that one column refers to price and the other to quantity. It is only because they match in this respect that both can be depicted on the same graph. If we are to make any sense out of two or more lines on the same graph, these lines must refer to the same kinds of things, measured in the same kinds of units.

In Figure 1A-11, draw the lines corresponding to these two schedules. (Plot the five points for each schedule and join them with a smooth curve.) Label your demand curve *DD* and your supply curve *SS*.

Your two lines should cross at one point, and one point only. That is the point signifying a price of $3 per bushel and a quantity of 12 million bushels. Its significance is that at this level of price, and no other, the intentions of buyers and the intentions of sellers match. In these circumstances, the price of $3 will be called an "equilibrium price," and the quantity of 12 million bushels an "equilibrium quantity." At a price of $3, buyers want to purchase exactly

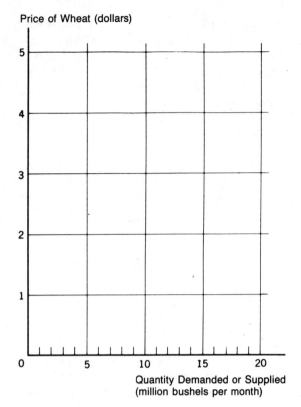

Figure 1A-11

the 12 million bushels that suppliers are willing to deliver.

Conclusion Graphs were made to help people grasp ideas with as little expenditure of time and effort as possible; but if you want to take advantage of this device, you must learn the rules and you must ask the right questions:

1. What does the graph measure on each axis? What are the labels on the axes? Each line on a graph indicates some kind of relation or linking rule between the two sets of numbers.

2. Which way does the line run? Does it fall to the right or rise to the right? If it falls, then the relation between the two sets of numbers is an inverse one—as one rises, the other falls. If it rises to the right, then the two sets of numbers move in the same direction and represent a direct relationship.

3. Is the line straight or curved? If it is straight, the ratio of the change in the value of Y to the change in the value of X is constant. If the line curves, this ratio varies.

4. If there are two or more lines on a graph, then there are two or more schedules in the background. What kind of relationship is involved in each schedule, and why is it important to bring the schedules together on the same graph? Usually the two lines cross one another at some point, and usually this intersection is important because at this point the two schedules match one another. Why is this matching important?

Review Complete as before.

31. One point on a graph indicates a value for X of 4 and a value for Y of 10. Another point indicates that $X = 5$ and $Y = 8$. If these two points are joined by a straight line, then the slope of that line is _____.

32. The slope of a straight line is -3. Movement from one point to another along that line results in an increase in Y from 10 to 16. What might have been the associated change in X? It must have *(risen / fallen)* by *(6 / 3 / 2 / 1 / 1/2)*.

33. A line on a graph appears as the upper half of a circle: it starts out at the origin of the graph, rises, and then falls, until finally it drops to the horizontal axis from which it started. Which of the following correctly describes the slope of this line as it moves from the origin to the right?

a. It will have a changing but positive slope value throughout.

b. It will first have a negative slope (toward the left-hand side), and its value will grow larger as the line proceeds to the right. Eventually, though, the slope will turn positive.

c. It will first have a positive slope, and its value will grow larger as the line proceeds to the right. Eventually, though, the slope will turn negative.

d. It will first have a positive slope, but its value will diminish as the line proceeds to the right. The slope will eventually reach a value of zero at the top of the semicircle, and then it will turn negative.

34. In Figure 1A-11, the DD curve has a *(negative / positive)* slope. Its value is *(constant / changing)* throughout the line. The SS curve in this figure has a *(negative / positive)* slope. Its value is *(constant / changing)* throughout the line.

31. -2 **32.** fallen; 2   **33.** d   **34.** negative; changing; positive; changing

SUGGESTED ANSWERS TO QUESTIONS IN THE TEXT:
Appendix to Chapter 1

1. The idea is that the sum of leisure time X and study time Y is 16 hours, so $X+Y = 16$, and you should graph $Y = 16 - X$.

2. It is a straight line with slope $= -1$.

3. Six hours of leisure leaves 10 hours of study; plot ($X = 6$, $Y = 10$).

4. Graph $X + Y = 18$, or $Y = 18 - X$. This new line is out further from the origin but is parallel to the original line.

5. Do not send the scatter graph home!

6. The slope of $Y = 10 + 0.5X$ is 0.5 *everywhere*. The slope of $Y = (X-2)^2$ *changes for each point* (according to $2X - 4$). Draw tangencies to the curve and note slopes of 0, -2, almost 3 (2.82), and slightly more than 6 (6.32) when Y equals 0, 1, 2, and 10, respectively (X equaling 2, 1, 3.41, and 5.16, respectively).

7. Plot money supply measured along one axis against GNP measured along the other. The scatter suggests correlation, but it cannot indicate causality.

CHAPTER 2

BASIC PROBLEMS OF ECONOMIC ORGANIZATION

Most of this chapter is organized around a series of fundamental ideas and concepts. They are all related, but they are all distinct. They are important as a group because they define the essence of the economic problem and the source of economic opportunity for an advanced economy. They are important individually because they introduce tools for and methods of thinking about the world that will be carried throughout the text. It is essential, therefore, that you grasp each of them before you proceed.

When you have finished, you should be able to meet the following objectives.

LEARNING OBJECTIVES

1. State (a) the three basic economic problems that confront *all* societies regardless of their political organization and (b) the single underlying fact that gives rise to these problems.

2. Distinguish between several alternative economic systems and understand how mixed economies display characteristics of the extreme alternatives.

3. Differentiate between inputs and outputs; list the three major factors of production.

4. Show how a production-possibility frontier (*PPF*) illustrates the three basic economic questions as well as the underlying truth from which they grow. Explain, as well, how the *PPF* illustrates (a) efficiency, (b) opportunity cost, and (c) the law of diminishing returns.

5. Explain (a) why it is impossible for an economy to move outside its given frontier, (b) how it is nonetheless possible for the frontier to shift out over time, and (c) the undesirable circumstances under which an economy might operate beneath its frontier.

6. Understand the importance of (a) specialization, (b) the division of labor, (c) money, (d) factors of production, and (e) capital and property rights in the functioning of a modern economy.

The real productive inputs for any economy are the items genuinely needed to satisfy life's material demands. Money plays a crucial part in the production process; it will be considered at length in due course. Money is not, however, one of the basic real inputs upon which an economy is built. It is something else—special, but different. It is the device with which the cooperative employment of real inputs can be effectively arranged. It is a kind of lubricating oil that allows the machinery of an economy to operate with a minimum of friction.

The basic inputs from which our material wants for goods and services are satisfied are labor, capital goods, and natural resources. These are the factors of production. The output that we produce comes from the labor effort of men and women, using tools and machinery mainly to process raw materials obtained from our natural resources. Every society has only a finite supply of productive inputs—the real sources of economic value. There is, as a result, a physically imposed limit on the total output of goods and services which any one society can produce. Goods of economic value are, in other words, scarce.

It is impossible to produce enough to satisfy everybody's desire for everything even in rich societies. Today, many poor economies are still hard-pressed to turn out enough in the way of elemental food and shelter for their populations. Richer societies are easily capable of covering life's basic necessities for all their members, but our interest here is not with necessities alone. It is with consumers' *total* demands. Once necessities have been met, consumer wants pass quickly to comforts and to luxuries. In this sense, even rich societies face the law of scarcity introduced in Chapter 1: total consumer demands outrun total productive capacity defined by the limited supplies of productive inputs.

1. a. Three basic social problems arise from the law of scarcity; they are _____, _____, and _____ goods are to be produced.

b. The total stock of inputs available to any economy is limited. If the proportion of stock devoted to the production of some good A were to increase, then there would remain fewer inputs for the production of other goods B, C, D, and so on. The output of (at least one / all / none) of these other goods would therefore have to (rise / fall). Questions of how much to produce of A (of B, of C, etc.) are all part and parcel of the (what / how / for whom) problem.

c. Output restricted by limited input availability must somehow be shared by any society's members. This is the (what / how / for whom) problem.

---

a. what; how; for whom **b.** at least one; fall; what **c.** for whom

---

The problem of *how* goods should be produced is a little trickier. It is the problem of the exact mix of resources to be used in the manufacture of any given commodity.

It may strengthen your grasp of both *what* and *how* problems to consider instances in which they would not arise at all. The *what* problem emerges because resources are versatile; i.e., because they have more than one possible use or occupation. To see why this is so, suppose, for the sake of argument, that resources are not versatile. Suppose, in particular, that the types of machines and labor and raw materials that are useful in the production of some good A are totally useless in the production of any other goods. Suppose, in fact, that all resources are specialized in this way so that they can be used in the production of only a single, specific good. Were that the case, there would be no opportunity to swap less of A for more of B (for example). There would be no problem of what to produce because there would be only one combination of goods that could be produced which would maximize welfare—the production of as much of every good as possible given the limitation of its requisite input.

The question of *how* similarly arises because there are usually many ways of producing any particular good. Were there only one "recipe" for producing A, though, there would be no way of substituting a little more of one input for a little less of another. And if this single-recipe condition held throughout the economy, then there would be no problem in determining how things should be produced. If they are to be produced at all (i.e., if they are to be included in the answer to the *what* question), then they must be produced according to the one and only formula.

The more general situation, of course, is one in which there is more than one known productive technique (e.g., workers can be substituted for machines, and vice versa). If so, then *how* exists as a social problem.

2. Several alternative economic systems are all capable of answering the three economic questions of *what, how,* and *for whom.* The most primitive relies on _____ to provide the decision-making apparatus. Answers to the fundamental questions come simply from the traditions that dictate how things have always been done.

An economy in which the government makes all the decisions about production and distribution is called a _____ economy. It (would have to be dictatorial / would have to be democratic / could be democratic, dictatorial, or anything in between) to qualify under the definition, but it would give enormous powers to the government.

A third approach, labeled the _____ economy, uses a system of prices, markets, profits and losses, incentives, and rewards to answer the questions almost automatically. What is produced? Goods that generate the _____. How are they produced? By the process that is _____. For whom are they produced? For the people with _____ earnings generated from their provision of labor services and/or their ownership of capital and resources.

Mixed economies are the (most / least) common across the world today. They include aspects of (market and command / command and custom / market, command, and custom) in the mechanisms that they have established to handle economic scarcity.

---

custom; command; could be democratic, dictatorial, or anything in between; market; largest profit; least costly; wealth (or money); most; market, command, and custom.

The nature of all three of the fundamental questions can be explored by using a **production-possibility frontier** (denoted *PPF*). Figure 2-1 here duplicates Figure 2-2 in the text and serves as an illustration. Recall that a *PPF* reflects all the combinations of goods that an economy can produce given its fixed supply of inputs. Where? On and under (downward and/or below) the curve. Point *D* in Figure 2-1, for example, makes it clear that the economy could afford to produce 9000 guns and 3 million pounds of butter. It could, just as well, produce 8000 guns and 3 million pounds of butter (point G) or 9000 guns and 2 million pounds of butter (point H). It could not, though, produce 10,000 guns and 3 million pounds of butter (point I). It does not have the input stock to be able to do that, and that combination lies outside (upward and/or to the right) of the frontier.

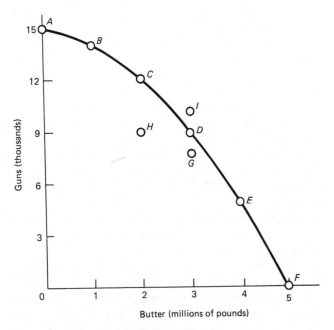

Figure 2-1

Because a graph has only two dimensions, the *what* problem must be described against a graphed *PPF* as a choice between only two goods—guns and butter in Figure 2-1. The principles would be the same if there were 20 or 20,000 goods, though. The problem of *what* is ultimately a choice between a little more of this and a little less of that. The slope of the *PPF* shows this most dramatically because it is always negative.

The *how* question is subsumed in the definition of the frontier itself. If new technology or clever insight were to bring forth a new production technique for butter, e.g., then the frontier itself would change because the economy could produce more butter using fewer inputs. Output of *both* guns and butter could then increase *simultaneously* from a point on the old frontier. It follows, then, that the existing frontier captures all the combinations of gun production and butter production that are the best the economy can do. If it could produce more of either with no cost, then it would. So *how* does the economy produce its goods? With the most efficient techniques available. **Efficiency** is, in fact, defined as the state of having achieved a point on the *PPF*, so

An economy is producing efficiently when it cannot produce more of one good without producing less of another.

Insight into how the *for whom* question is answered can also be gleaned from a production-possibility frontier, but only indirectly. The answer to the question of distribution does not show up in the construction of the schedule; it is, instead, picked up as an inference of the point that a society actually selects. If the economy picks a point that indicates a strong concentration in producing the type of good that only a particular group of people favors, for example, then we need not look very far to find out "for whom the bell tolls." It tolls for them.

3. a. Which of the following are measured along the axes of a *PPF* graph?

(1) Quantities of productive inputs or resources.

(2) Quantities of finished commodities.

(3) Values of finished commodities.

b. Each and every point on such a graph (whether on the curve or off it) stands for some combination of the two goods involved (e.g., so many guns produced and so much butter produced per unit of time). With a given input stock, some of these points would be attainable, others would not. Specifically, with respect to production, the economy could operate:

(1) anywhere on the curve and only on the curve.

(2) anywhere on the curve or anywhere inside it (below and to the left).

(3) anywhere on the curve, inside it, or outside it.

c. In order to operate outside the curve (above and to the right of it), the economy would have to (pick one or more):

(1) somehow increase its stock of inputs.

(2) discover some new production techniques enabling any given input stock to produce more output than before.

(3) remove some incompetent bureaucrats from their jobs.

(4) eliminate the sources of significant abuse of monopoly power.

d. If the economy did somehow add to its input stock, or if it did discover new production techniques, then the production-possibility curve would:

(1) remain unchanged.

(2) move appropriately inward and to the left.

(3) move appropriately outward and to the right.

e. If there is a law of scarcity, then the economy will want to make good use of its limited input supply; that is, it will want to operate on the production-possibility frontier and not inside it. Should the economy be operating inside the curve, this would be attributable to some inefficiency or breakdown in economic organization. Specifically (pick one or both):

(1) some part of the input supply must be unemployed.

(2) the input supply, if fully employed, is somehow being used improperly. The best available production techniques are not being used, or some inputs are in the wrong jobs.

a. (2) b. (2) c. (1) and (2) d. (3) e. both (1) and (2)

The production-possibility frontier drawn in Figure 2-1 is curved. It is, more specifically, concave (bowed away from the origin). Increasing the production of butter by million-pound increments results in increasingly larger reductions in the number of guns that can be simultaneously produced. To move from 1 million pounds of butter to 2 million pounds (from point B to point C) would, for example, require a 2000-unit reduction (14,000 − 12,000) in the production of guns. To move from 2 million pounds of butter to 3 million would require a 3000-unit reduction (12,000 − 9,000). And so on. A full accounting of the possible reasons behind this shape would be complicated and inappropriate at this early stage. Still, one background factor deserves some careful attention even now—the **law of diminishing returns.**

The nature of this law is most easily illustrated by assuming that only two inputs, say, A and B, are needed for production of some commodity X. Input A (which can be taken to be land) is available in some fixed and limited quantity only. Input B (labor, in the text example) can be varied in quantity employed. The question with which the diminishing-returns law deals is now at hand. We would like to have more of X. The supply of input A, which is essential for X production, is limited. To what extent can we get more X by adding more of input B to the fixed A quantity?

4. The diminishing-returns law gives the following answer: Up to a point, more B will yield more X, but the cost of getting additional X, in terms of the additional B quantity required, will steadily *(increase / decrease)*. To say the same thing differently, the "payoff" from each extra unit of B employed, in terms of the number of extra units of X resulting, will *(increase / decrease)*. In fact, a point may ultimately be reached at which, because of the restricted supply of A, the payoff from an extra unit of B employed would be *(zero / infinity)*.

Notice that this law is expressed in terms of physical quantities of A, B, and X; that is, it is expressed in *(money / "real")* terms.

For illustrative purposes, it is convenient to use an example involving two inputs only. Most actual productive processes involve more than two, of course (e.g., tools, equipment, and seed grain in addition to labor and land), but the essential insight gleaned from a two-factor example is extremely robust. For diminishing returns to apply when there are more than two inputs involved, *(all the inputs / at least one input, but not all inputs / one and only one input)* must be fixed in available supply.

increase; decrease; zero; "real"; at least one input, but not all inputs

5. This question uses a specific, illustrative example to develop more fully the relation between the production-possibility frontier, the shape of that frontier, and the diminishing-returns law.

A certain economy produces only two consumer goods, X and Y. For manufacture of these goods, it has three kinds of resources: (1) a fixed stock of resources useful only in the production of X; (2) a similarly fixed stock of different resources useful only in the production of Y; and (3) a fixed labor force of 100 workers capable of working in either occupation. Table 2-1 indicates the amounts of X and Y producible daily when various quantities of labor work with the specialized resources.

Since we are interested in looking at the production-possibility frontier, we must consider how much the economy can produce of both goods when it is operating efficiently. Table 2-1 defines efficiency in the production of either good; i.e., the table indicates the *maximum* amount of output that can be produced by various amounts of labor. To be efficient, the economy must make sure that the production of each good is proceeding at the pace indicated in Table 2-1. That is, however, not enough. To guarantee that the output of one good cannot be increased without reducing the output of the other, the economy also must make certain that the entire labor force is fully employed.

Table 2-1

No. of Workers	Daily X Production	No. of Workers	Daily Y Production	Corresponding X Production
0	0	0	0	600
10	40	10	5	_____
20	105	20	12	_____
30	200	30	20	_____
40	300	40	28	_____
50	390	50	36	_____
60	450	60	43	_____
70	500	70	49	_____
80	550	80	54	_____
90	580	90	58	_____
100	600	100	60	_____

There are 100 workers in the labor force. If all 100 are employed in the production of X, then the economy will produce 600 units of X and 0 units of Y. Why? Because Table 2-1 shows that while 100 workers can produce 600 units of X, devoting all the workers to the production of X leaves nobody to help in the production of Y; Table 2-1 also shows that 0 workers produce 0 units of Y. Suppose there are 40 workers employed in the production of X. In that case, _____ units of X would be produced, while _____ units of Y would be produced by _____ workers.

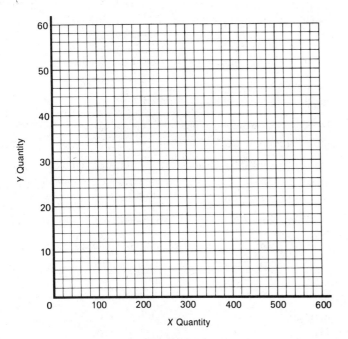

Figure 2-2

Fill in the blanks in the extreme right-hand column of Table 2-1 with the proper levels of maximum production of X. Draw the resulting *PPF* on the graph scales provided in Figure 2-2.

300; 43; 60; table column: 580, 550, 500, etc. [The order of the figures in the "Daily X Production" column is inverted; the *PPF* should be concave and anchored by points (X = 600; Y = 0) and (X = 0; Y = 60).]

---

6. a. According to Table 2-1, diminishing returns first appears in the production of X when the total of workers employed rises to (10 / 20 / 30 / 40 / 50 / 60 / 70 / 80 / 90 / 100).

b. The corresponding diminishing-returns point in Y production is (10 / 20 / 30 / 40 / 50 / 60 / 70 / 80 / 90 / 100).

c. This diminishing-returns phenomenon occurs because as output and employment are increased (select one answer):

(1) the competence or skill of the workers later employed is less than that of the workers first employed.

(2) each worker has proportionately less of the fixed or specialized resource to work with.

(3) the product must sell for a lower price.

---

a. 50   **b.** 60   **c.** (2)

One of the more fundamental concepts of economics that is most easily demonstrated in terms of a production-possibility frontier is the notion of **opportunity cost.** Most actions have a cost; everyone who has ever had to manage a personal budget knows that. The problem is that monetary costs do not necessarily reflect "true economic costs"—the value of the opportunity forgone. Opportunity costs are those true costs.

7. To get some practice in computing opportunity costs from production frontiers, return to the data of Table 2-1. Suppose that production is 600 X units daily and zero Y. If it were instead decided to produce 5 Y units daily, a sacrifice of (zero / 5 / 20 / 40 / 600) X units would be required. Each of the 5 Y units would cost (zero / 4 / 5 / 10 / 20) X units. Suppose now that X output is 500 units, so that Y output can be (zero / 4 / 5 / 10 / 20) units daily. To raise this Y quantity to 28 would require reduction of X output to (zero / 100 / 250 / 400 / 450)—a drop of (zero / 10 / 20 / 50 / 100) units. Each extra unit of Y would therefore cost (1 / 5½ / 6¼ / 8 / 10) units of X.

The greater the amount that total Y output happens to be, the (higher / lower) would be the cost of obtaining further Y output, measured in terms of X given up. Whenever a production-possibility frontier is concave, as it is (or should be if you drew it correctly) in Figure 2-2, each additional unit of either good costs slightly more (in terms of sacrifice of the other good) than its predecessor. Each 1-unit increase in Y means a small, vertical, upward movement on the graph. To stay on the curve, this movement requires a (leftward / rightward) movement to compensate—(a reduction / an increase) in X. If further increases in Y were desired, these compensating (leftward / rightward) movements (the required reductions in X) grow (larger / smaller).

20; 4; 20; 450; 50; 6¼; higher; leftward; a reduction; leftward; larger

---

8. In a model in which there exists only one discretionary input (i.e., one input that can be employed in the production of either X or Y), it is easy to get the idea that the law of diminishing returns is the only thing operating to produce the concave, outward bending of the production-possibility curve. This problem will present an example in which the *PPF* is a straight line despite the existence of diminishing returns in both X and Y for two distinct inputs.

22   2 Basic Problems of Economic Organization

Table 2-2 summarizes the production of either X or Y for various combinations of capital (K) and labor (L). It shows, for example, that 30 units of X (or Y) would be produced if 10 units of capital and 10 units of labor were employed. If 10 units of labor were combined with 30 units of capital, 48 units of X (or Y) would be produced, and so on.

Table 2-2
Production Schedule for Either Good X or Good Y

Labor Employment (units of X or Y)	Capital Employment			
	0	10	20	30
0	0	0	0	0
5	0	20	30	32
10	0	30	40	48
15	0	32	48	60

Table 2-3

	X Production			Y Production		
Case	Capital	Labor	Output	Capital	Labor	Output
A	0	0	0	30	15	60
B	___	___	___	0	0	0
C	10	___	___	___	10	___
D	10	10	___	___	___	30
E	20	___	40	___	___	___
F	20	___	___	___	___	30
G	___	___	___	10	15	___

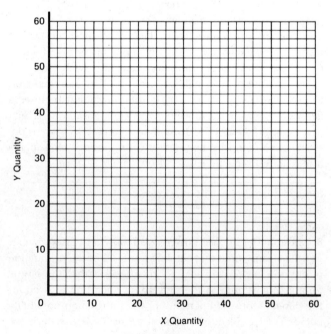

Figure 2-3

Suppose, throughout this exercise, that the economy is endowed with 30 units of capital and 15 units of labor. Both inputs can be employed in either industry according to the data recorded in Table 2-2. Fill in the blanks in Table 2-3 on the basis of Table 2-2 and the endowment constraints; assume full employment of both capital and labor. Plot points A through G on Figure 2-3 and draw the production-possibility frontier.

a. For any level of employment of labor, X and Y (do / do not) display diminishing returns. For 10 units of labor, for example, the output of X increases by _____ units as capital employment increases from 0 to 10 units, by _____ units as capital employment increases from 10 units to 20, and by _____ units as capital employment rises from 20 units to 30. Per unit of capital, the return to the employment of capital is therefore _____ , _____ , and _____ , respectively, for the three increments just noted.

b. For any level of employment of capital, X and Y (do / do not) display diminishing returns. For 30 units of capital, the per unit return to labor is _____ , _____ , and _____ as labor employment climbs from 0 units to 5 units, 5 to 10 units, and 10 to 15 units, respectively.

c. The production-possibility frontier drawn in Figure 2-3 is (concave / convex / a straight line) because _____
_____
_____.

d. Point G (is / is not) on the PPF because _____
_____
_____.

table rows: B—30, 15, 60; C—5, 20, 20, 40; D—30, 20, 5; E—10, 10, 5, 20; F—5, 30, 10, 10; G—20, 0, 0, 32   **a.** do; 30; 10; 8; 3; 1; 0.8   **b.** do; 6.4; 3.2; 2.4   **c.** a straight line; inputs are always used in the same proportion regardless of whether they are employed in the production of X or the production of Y (This is a difficult question to which we will return.)   **d.** is not; the 20 units of L devoted to X are, essentially, unemployed because they are totally unproductive when not paired with at least a little capital.

9. a. Suppose, given the data of Table 2-1, that the number of workers increases from 100 to 200 (the fixed amounts of X resources and Y resources remaining unchanged). The production-possibility curve would then move outward (circle the correct answer):

(1) until its end points indicated 1200 units of X and 120 units of Y.

(2) by some undetermined amount larger than suggested by the end points noted in alternative **(1)**.

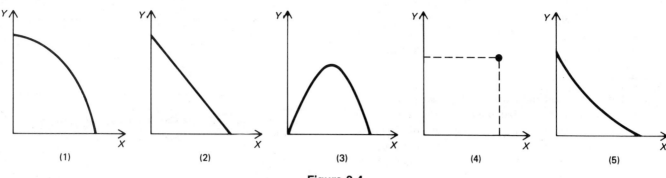

Figure 2-4

(3) by an undetermined amount much smaller than suggested by the end points noted in alternative (1).

(4) not at all.

b. Suppose that X is a necessity (say, food) and that Y is a luxury item. Assume, in particular, that every worker (or family) must have at least 3.5 units of X daily in order to live. The population still consists of only 100 workers, and they choose to produce 450 units of X and 28 units of Y. (Mark this point on Figure 2-2.) If output were equally distributed, this means each worker would receive 4.5 units of X per day and a little more than ¼ unit of Y.

Now let the number of workers rise from 100 to 200, and assume that an extended X-production table indicates that 200 workers could produce 700 units of X if they specialized. If all workers were allocated the subsistence level of X, what quantities of X and Y would be produced?

(1) 700 units of X plus about the same amount of Y per worker as before.

(2) 700 X and no Y at all.

(3) More than 700 units of X and about the same amount of Y per worker as before.

(4) Impossible to tell from information given.

---

a. (3) b. (2)

10. The following questions will investigate your understanding of "Pictures in an Exhibition."

a. Consider the production-possibility curves drawn in Figure 2-4 in answering the following questions:

(1) An economy produces only two goods and employs all inputs in exactly the same proportion. Which of the alternatives drawn in Figure 2-4 most accurately reflects this circumstance? _____

(2) An economy produces only two goods, and one of those goods displays increasing returns to scale. Which panel in Figure 2-4 most accurately reflects this circumstance? _____

(3) An economy produces only two goods. All the inputs are entirely specialized for the production of one good or the other; i.e., the X inputs would be useless in the production of Y, and the Y inputs would be useless in the production of X. Which alternative most accurately reflects this circumstance? _____

b. Consider the production-possibility curves drawn in Figure 2-5 in answering the following questions. (In each panel, the lighter schedule represents an original curve, while the darker schedule represents what happens to the frontier after something has changed the economy.)

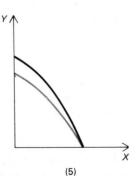

Figure 2-5

(1) Suppose that scientific invention increased the productivity of resources used only in the production of X. Which panel most accurately reflects this development? _____

(2) Many scientists believe that we are exhausting our natural resources. Assume that there are two inputs, labor and natural resources, used to produce one of two goods, X and Y, but assume that resources are employed only in the production of Y. Which of the alternatives in Figure 2-5 most accurately reflects what would happen if the scientists were correct and there were no improvement in the technology involved in producing Y? _____

(3) Now assume that technology improves the efficiency of resources in the production of Y for the economy described in (**2**). Which alternative might now be appropriate? _____

a. (1) 2 (2) 5 (3) 4 **b.** (1) 3 (2) 2 (3) 5

Section C of the chapter discusses the subject of *capital*. "Capital" is a word with too many meanings; you must understand the particular meaning applied in this discussion. Capital here does not mean money. It means productive inputs which have, themselves, been manufactured. The notion of capital includes durable items like blast furnaces, factory buildings, machine tools, electric drills, tack hammers, and so on. It also includes stocks of semifinished goods. These are goods which are on the way to becoming consumer goods but which are still manufactured inputs to be used in later stages of the production process.

Capital is important only because it "pushes back" the law of scarcity: it makes possible the production of more consumer goods. Every nation would like to become "capitalistic" in the sense of having a large stock of capital relative to its population. However, there is a cost involved in the production of capital goods. The same resources that can be devoted to the production of capital goods can also be employed to produce consumer goods, and so there is a choice to be made between capital and consumer goods. Recall the production-possibility frontiers drawn in Figure 2-5 of the text which displayed the tradeoff between consumption goods and investment goods. Countries which climbed farther on the frontier away from the consumption axis found themselves on a higher curve the next year but enjoyed less consumption in the current year.

11. As essential as capital is to the modern economy, heavy reliance on capital is but one characteristic of successful advanced economies in the world today. List two others in the spaces provided:

a. _____

b. _____

an elaborate use of specialization; an intricate division of labor; or an extensive use of money.

12. Specialization (or division of labor) is rampant in a modern economy because it increases the output obtainable from a given resource supply. The consequences of specialization include (circle as many as are correct):

a. the exchange of goods.

b. the use of money.

c. social interdependence.

d. an intensified law of scarcity.

e. possibly a sense of alienation on the part of members of the society involved.

a, b, c, and **e**

13. a. Circle all the following that qualify as capital:

(1) An oil refinery

(2) An issue of General Motors stock

(3) Cash in a business owner's safe

(4) A screwdriver

(5) Money borrowed by a business firm from a bank to expand its operations

(6) A steel-ingot inventory held by a steel company

(7) Unsold automobiles held by an auto manufacturer

(8) An inventory of groceries held by a supermarket

b. Money *(is / is not)* counted as part of capital because (circle one):

(1) it is essential to production.

(2) it has no part to play in production.

(3) it is not actually useful in production, although it is essential to have money in order to buy the real inputs that are needed for production.

c. To qualify as capital, the item in question *(must be / need not necessarily be)* an input that is useful or necessary at some stage of production, and the item must be *(of a type found only in highly developed economies / a primary factor of production / manufactured)*.

a. (**1**), (**4**), (**6**), (**7**), and (**8**) **b.** is not; (**3**) **c.** must be; manufactured

It is essential to remember two elementary characteristics of capital: First, capital goods have no merit in and of themselves. In the final reckoning, only consumer goods are important. Capital goods are produced and have value only because they are roundabout ways of producing consumer goods. Second, the resource employed in constructing a capital good—a good designed to contribute to increased production in the future—could have been used to satisfy current consumption demands. There is, therefore, an element of time which must be considered when investment in capital is contemplated.

14. a. Any developed nation possesses a large stock of capital; and much of each day's productive effort goes into maintenance and expansion of that stock. Consequently, today's productive effort is significantly devoted to satisfying *(yesterday's / today's / tomorrow's)* needs, while the consumer goods actually enjoyed today result from *(yesterday's / today's / tomorrow's)* effort.

b. Circle as many of the following as are correct:

(1) The larger the available stock of capital, the larger the output of consumer goods that is possible.

(2) In terms of a production-possibility frontier, additions to the stock of capital can push the frontier upward and outward.

(3) A decision to produce or not to produce more capital goods is not part of the decision of *what* goods to produce.

(4) In a fully employed economy, a decision to produce more capital goods is a decision to produce fewer consumer goods in the immediate future.

c. When reference is made to "a capitalist economy," the speaker is probably contemplating an economy (pick one or more):

(1) in which most capital goods are privately owned.

(2) in which the stock of capital is large relative to the population of that economy.

(3) that is not under communist or socialist direction, so property rights to the capital do not flow to the government.

---

a. tomorrow's; yesterday's **b.** (1), (2), and (4) **c.** (1), (2), and (3) [*Note:* There is room for dispute concerning properties (2) and (3), particularly in the face of sweeping economic reform in Eastern Europe and the Soviet Union. A dictionary definition of capitalism may not specify that the stock of capital must be large relative to the country's size or population; nevertheless, the "capitalist" countries are typically those in which the stock is large. However, even the few remaining communist countries may be "capitalist" in the sense of having relatively large capital stocks in terms of their population, and nearly every country in the world wants to have an even larger stock.]

---

15. This question is designed to demonstrate the gains from trade that might be available through specialization. Suppose that there are two countries, cleverly called Country A and Country B. Country A has 10 units of labor available for employment in the production of some good X, a second good Y, or some combination of the two; labor is the only factor of production required to produce either X or Y. Assume that Country A can produce up to 10 units of X by employing 1 unit of labor for each and every unit of X desired and that it can produce up to 10 units of Y by employing 1 unit of labor for each and every unit of Y. *(Neither good / Both goods)* display(s) diminishing returns in Country A. Graph the *PPF* for Country A in Figure 2-6(a).

Country B, meanwhile, has 24 units of labor available. Suppose that B can produce up to 6 units of X by employing 4 units of labor for each and every unit of X desired and that it can produce up to 12 units of Y by employing 2 units of labor for each and every unit of Y. *(Neither good / Both goods)* display(s) diminishing returns in Country B. Graph the *PPF* for Country B in Figure 2-6(b).

The *opportunity cost* of X, in terms of units of Y sacrificed to produce 1 unit of X, is _____ unit(s) of Y per unit of

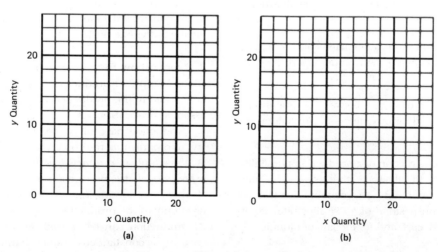

Figure 2-6

X in Country A and _____ unit(s) of Y per unit of X in Country B. If B were to offer to sell Country A any amount of good Y that A wanted to purchase at a "price" of 1.5 units of Y for each unit of X, then Country A *(would / would not)* accept; it *(could / could not)* use the offer to move its effective frontier out as far as possible by *(specializing in the production of X / specializing in the production of Y / evenly splitting its production of X and Y)*. Show this maximal trading frontier on Figure 2-6(a).

Country B *(would / would not)* be inclined to make such an offer. It *(could / could not)* use the offer to move its effective frontier out, and it would do best given the offer "price" by *(specializing in the production of X / specializing in the production of Y / evenly splitting its production of X and Y)*. Show this new frontier on Figure 2-6(b).

The gains from trade are, in this case, *(maximized / minimized)* by both countries when each specializes completely in the production of the good in which it has the

_____

These gains would be available for any "price" between _____ unit(s) of Y for each unit of X on the low side and _____ unit(s) of Y for each X on the high side. Country A would benefit most from trade if the price were on the *(high / low)* side.

_____

Neither good; the graph: a straight line from (X = 10, Y = 0) to (X = 0, Y = 10); Neither good; the graph: a straight line from (X = 6, Y = 0) to (X = 0, Y = 12); 1; 2; would; could; specializing in the production of X; the graph: a straight line from (X = 10, Y = 0) to (X = 0, Y = 15); would; could; specializing in the production of Y; the graph: a straight line from (X = 0, Y = 12) to (X = 8, Y = 0); maximized; comparative advantage; 1; 2; high.

REVIEW CONCEPTS

1. State a firm understanding of the three fundamental economic questions confronting all societies: *what* to produce, *how* to produce the desired products, and *for whom* to produce them; all reaffirm your understanding that the root of all three problems is *scarcity*.

2. Distinguish the differences between market and command economies, and describe how mixed economies display the characteristics of both.

3. Differentiate, again, the difference between output and input, on the one hand, and various factors of production, on the other.

4. Describe how the construction of a production-possibility frontier can be used to illustrate the *what, how,* and *for whom* questions confronting an economy. Explain, as well, how the shape and position of a *PPF* illustrates (a) efficiency, (b) opportunity cost, and (c) the law of diminishing returns.

5. Describe how locating an economy in relation to its innate *PPF* can reveal how well it is allocating resources and how fast it might grow, thereby pushing out its frontier.

6. Understand the role played in an advanced economy of (a) specialization and the division of labor, (b) money, (c) factors of production including the special nature of capital, and (d) the definition of property rights.

QUIZ: Multiple Choice

Quizzes are provided at the end of chapters in this *Guide* to test your understanding of the material. Answers are found, with brief explanations, at the end of the *Guide*.

1. When production is subject to the influence of the law of diminishing returns, steps to increase output by 1 unit will:
(1) require smaller and smaller amounts of the variable input as output expands.
(2) require less of the variable input, because more will do more harm than good and actually cause total output to fall.
(3) increase steadily the cost of hiring each additional unit of the variable input.
(4) require greater and greater amounts of the variable input as output expands.
(5) necessarily imply none of the above.

2. The three economic problems of *what, how,* and *for whom* goods shall be produced apply:
(1) mainly to totalitarian or centrally planned societies, in which the problem of planning arises directly.
(2) only or principally to free enterprise or capitalist societies, in which the problem of choice is most acute.
(3) only or almost entirely to the less developed societies, since development alone is largely a question of meeting these three problems.
(4) to all societies, regardless of stage of development or form of political organization.
(5) to none of the above necessarily, since they are problems for the individual business firm or family, not for society.

3. There cannot be a problem of *what* goods to produce if:
(1) the supply of productive resources is small, so it must be devoted to the production of goods selected from a set of essential necessities.
(2) production has not yet reached the stage at which the law of diminishing returns begins to operate.
(3) the supply of productive resources is sufficiently large to make possible the production of some luxury goods.
(4) every productive input is so specialized that it can be used only in the production of one good and no other.
(5) production can be carried on under conditions of decreasing or constant cost, rather than increasing cost.

4. If the law of diminishing returns is to apply strictly according to its definition, then the increase in output:
(1) must come from a proportionate increase in all inputs.
(2) comes from an increase in some inputs, but at least one input must remain fixed in quantity.
(3) must come from an increase in one input only, all others remaining fixed in quantity.
(4) must grow less because of a decline in the competence or skills of inputs later applied.
(5) may be proportionate in physical quantity to the increase in inputs, but the value of that extra output must decline.

5. The economic problem of *what* goods to produce:
(1) may be a problem for any individual firm seeking to make a profit, but is not in any sense a problem for society as a whole.
(2) can be illustrated as the problem of choosing a point on the production-possibility curve.
(3) is a problem whose root is found in the law of diminishing returns.
(4) arises only when the stock of productive resources is very small, so nearly every available factor of production must be devoted to the production of necessities.
(5) arises only when all productive inputs are so specialized that each can be used only in the production of one good and no other.

6. The economic problem of *how* to produce goods would not exist:
(1) if the required proportions of inputs were fixed for all commodities, so substitution of one input to replace, at least in part, another input in production would be impossible.
(2) only if production had not been carried to the point where the law of diminishing returns had begun to set in.
(3) if the economy's stock of capital were small relative to its labor force.
(4) in a technically advanced society, since proper technology would have established the best possible method of producing each good.
(5) in any circumstance, because the problem of how to produce goods is an engineering problem throughout and not an economic problem.

7. A production-possibility frontier illustrates the maximum amounts of finished goods that can be produced from the limited supply of available productive inputs or factors. On the axes of this diagram are measured:
(1) quantities of productive inputs.
(2) prices of productive inputs.
(3) the quantity of inputs on one axis and the value of finished goods on the other.
(4) the money value of finished goods.
(5) quantities of finished goods.

8. On the heavy production frontier drawn in Figure 2-7, which point corresponds to the economy's valuing food most heavily?

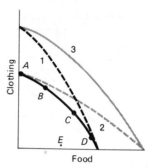

Figure 2-7

(1) A.
(2) B.
(3) C.
(4) D.
(5) E.

9. The heavy curved line in Figure 2-7 is drawn to illustrate a country's production-possibility curve. A shift in this curve to the position indicated by the line marked "1" would be appropriate to illustrate:
(1) a change in the tastes of the population whereby its members want more food produced and less clothing.
(2) the appearance of some new resources useful only in the clothing industry.
(3) an improvement in technology applicable to both industries.
(4) a change in the production mix involving an increase in clothing output and a decrease in food output.
(5) the development of a better technology in the food industry alone.

10. Which alternative in question 9 would have applied if the heavy curve in Figure 2-7 had shifted to position 2?
(1).
(2).
(3).
(4).
(5).

11. Which alternative in question 9 would have applied if the heavy curve in Figure 2-7 had shifted to position 3?
(1).
(2).
(3).
(4).
(5).

28   **2**   *Basic Problems of Economic Organization*

12. Figure 2-8 shows outputs of wheat obtainable on a fixed plot of land by varying the input of labor. The curve that correctly illustrates the law of diminishing returns is:

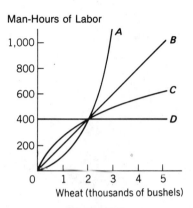

Figure 2-8

(1) *A*.
(2) *B*.
(3) *C*.
(4) *D*.
(5) either *A* or *C*.

13. A production-possibility frontier is intended to show:
(1) the exact amounts of two goods that an economy will decide to produce.
(2) the most valuable combination of two goods that an economy can produce.
(3) the alternative combinations of products available from a given quantity of resources.
(4) when the law of diminishing returns first begins to take effect.
(5) none of the above.

14. Suppose that actual output is marked by a point inside a guns-and-butter production-possibility frontier. This would signify that:
(1) it is impossible to produce more guns without the sacrifice of some butter output.
(2) either all available resources are not being fully employed or they are not being employed to the best advantage.
(3) the law of diminishing returns cannot be in operation.
(4) the diagram illustrates something which cannot possibly happen.
(5) the law of diminishing returns must be in operation.

15. Suppose that an economy can produce at most 200 units of some good X if it is producing 300 units of another good Y; i.e., let X = 200 and Y = 300 be one point on its production-possibility frontier. Assume that another point on this frontier would see 240 units of X associated with 290 units of Y. Which of the following points would also be on the frontier if it displayed the usual concave shape?
(1) 280 units of X and 270 units of Y.
(2) 160 units of X and 310 units of Y.
(3) 280 units of X and 280 units of Y.
(4) 160 units of X and 315 units of Y.
(5) 280 units of X and 285 units of Y.

16. Suppose that you are considering the relative financial merits of two opportunities for your summer vacation. In the first, you would live at home (for free but not necessarily with freedom) and work 40 hours per week at $5 per hour for 10 weeks. You will need a car, but assume that your neighbor will sell you a "junker" for $100. It will consume $100 in gas and $150 in oil over the 10 weeks if used only to get to and from work; after that, you know that it will fall totally and irreparably apart. The other opportunity is to work at a camp in the south of France. You will receive the equivalent of $500 in francs but will have to purchase round-trip airfare on your own. It will cost $450 on Fly-by-Night-Only Charter. Room and board will be provided by your French employer. The fun of going to the south of France has an opportunity cost of:
(1) $2000.
(2) $1750.
(3) $1700.
(4) $2050.
(5) $50.

SUGGESTED ANSWERS TO QUESTIONS IN THE TEXT: Chapter 2

1. Definitions.

2. The maximum number of haircuts possible is $1000/\frac{1}{2}$ = 2000. No shirts can be made with 2000 haircuts, so (0,2000) is on the frontier. To make one shirt always requires the release of 5 hours of time; i.e., the sacrifice of $5/\frac{1}{2}$ = 10 haircuts; the slope of the frontier is thus -10. So graph $H = 2000 - 10S$.

3. Plot the following points: A = (0 butter, 15 guns); B = (2,14); C = (4,12); D = (6,9); E = (8,5); F = (10,0). Connect the points. Notice that the butter intercept doubles but the guns intercept is unchanged.

4. Think of a few yourself—teaching economics?

5. There were arguments that slaves were property and, because they had to be housed and fed from birth and trained from adolescence, represented "human" capital—human elements of roundabout production. I am sure that you can find a lot to write about such a dehumanizing thought.

6. The voluntary army should bring its pay into line with the true opportunity cost; otherwise, nobody would join. The cost of the army would then more accurately reflect its social cost.

7. Depletion causes the frontier to contract gradually. Invention and technological change could slow the rate of that contraction, or perhaps even turn it around.

8. Diligent's frontier would be concave and shift outward as his time allotment increased from 10 to 15. If he makes no change in his inefficient study habits, however, his "grade output" will not change.

9. Draw the 1990 frontier higher than the 1982 frontier. Draw the 1990 point close to the 1990 frontier (and above the 1982 frontier), but then draw the 1982 point further in from the 1982 frontier to reflect the high unemployment of the early 1980s.

C H A P T E R 3

MARKETS AND GOVERNMENT IN A MODERN ECONOMY

The two sections of this chapter provide an introduction to the workings of a price system in an advanced mixed economy. In the first, the means by which markets solve the three fundamental problems of economics are presented in general terms. The specifics of their operation are the topics of Parts Two and Three of the text, so be patient. Section B develops a broad list of reasons why a government might choose to intervene in a functioning market system. It outlines how the innate efficiency of a market system might break down or lead to an undesirable outcome, and thereby identifies broad roles for government to play. At the same time, it highlights the need for government to devise some means with which to finance itself.

When you have covered the material in the text and this *Guide*, you should be able to satisfy the following objectives.

LEARNING OBJECTIVES

1. Describe what Adam Smith meant by the "invisible hand." Indicate the particular system of political and economic organization that Smith was advocating when he introduced this phrase.

2. State the requirement that must be satisfied if the invisible hand is really to function just as Smith said it would.

3. Describe briefly how a market system settles the three basic problems of *what*, *how*, and *for whom* goods are produced. Explain (recognizing that the approach here is an introductory one) what economists mean in saying that the resolution of these problems is an interdependent process and that the system being described is therefore titled "general equilibrium."

4. Outline what economists mean by a "mixed economy," indicating the major elements embodied by a free enterprise system.

5. Describe three roles that government might play in a mixed economy, and indicate how each might influence the economy's answers to the fundamental questions of *what*, *how*, and *for whom*. Indicate the market system failures that would suggest a need to play each role.

6. Define and explain briefly the significance of *(a)* monopoly (imperfect competitor), *(b)* externality, *(c)* public good, and *(d)* equity, particularly in the context of the potential role of government. Underscore the role and function of taxation.

A pure **market economy**, sometimes labeled "free enterprise" or "competitive capitalism," permits individual ownership of capital goods and land. Why? Because it is believed that this private ownership encourages initiative and productivity. A market system will tolerate inequality since the lure of higher income encourages the introduction of new and better commodities as well as new and better production techniques. The fundamental rationale behind this faith in the efficiency of the market system is perhaps best described in terms of Adam Smith's notion of the **invisible hand.** In his words, cited even before the text chapter begins, "Every individual endeavors to employ his capital [physical and human] so that its produce may be of greatest value...[attends to] only his own security, only his own gain...[being] led by an invisible hand to promote an end which was no part of his intention ...that of society more effectually than when he really intends to promote it [society's]." The present author added the bracketed words to, in part, emphasize that people contribute all their assets—their possessions

3 Markets and Government in a Modern Economy

and their skills—to a degree that they alone control in the pursuit of their own individual well-being. The market mechanism functions so that the interaction of all such people solves the three central problems of economies—*what, how,* and *for whom.*

A **command economy,** by way of extreme contrast, is one in which these questions of resource allocation are solved by the government and by individuals doing exactly what they are told to do. A command economy forbids, for the most part, the very private ownership that is the cornerstone of the market system. Why? Perhaps on the claim that private ownership leads to unfair distributions of income. Perhaps on the grounds that an individual's control over economic resources can never lead to the production of precisely the output mix that the government feels is best. For whatever reason, a pure command economy is the polar opposite of a market economy.

Neither of these extremes represents the reality of the American economic system. Most, if not all, advanced industrial economies of the world are **mixed economies,** in which both private and public institutions exercise control over economic resources. Private institutions exert their control through markets; public institutions do the same through regulations and fiscal incentives. It is, therefore, necessary to study both types of institution to understand how they can "coexist" in a mixed economy like the one we observe in the United States.

The market system is essentially one of exchange. Each person specializes (usually in cooperation with others) in producing some commodity or service. Each good or service produced is then sold for a money price. The money proceeds are shared among those who helped in the production. Each person's money share is his or her claim on the commodities and services that have been produced.

1. a. One vital part of the pricing system is *the market for consumer goods.* The text speaks of the *two* market fronts on which consuming families face business enterprises, however, so there is a second vital part of the pricing system. There is, in short, a second market with which families must deal. This is the market for _____

_____.

b. In the market for finished goods, the individual consumer (or family) is a *(buyer / seller).* In the market for productive inputs, the individual consumer is a *(buyer / seller).* By contrast, the business firm whose task it is to manufacture consumer goods or to ready them for sale is a *(buyer / seller)* in the consumer-goods market and a *(buyer / seller)* in the productive-input market.

The workings of the market system are best understood in the context of a *perfectly competitive, laissez-faire* economy. To that end, consider an economy for which the government exists only to provide an internal framework of law and order. Assume, in addition, that there are no monopolies. Assume, in other words, that no buyer or seller is sufficiently large to be able to affect the market price at which any good is being bought or sold. Prices are, nonetheless, extremely flexible in their response to *collective* changes on either the demand side (buying) or the supply side (selling) of the market.

2. This question will lead you through a description of how such an economy could solve the three fundamental economic questions.

a. Consumers use their "dollar votes" (the money incomes that they have available for purchasing commodities) to buy the goods that they want the most. If enough of them want some of these goods badly enough, then their collective bidding might push the prices of those goods up relative to the prices of others. It is important to note, however, that *(any / no)* single individual can influence a market price. To see why, suppose that you feel a sudden urge to purchase a small collection of compact discs—say, enough to play for an entire day without repeating a single song. Your going to the store and buying these discs will *(spur a large increase in / have no effect on)* the price that distributors and retailers charge for discs. Your increment in demand would simply *(be noticed and exploited / go unnoticed)* by the retailer. An increase in the demand for compact discs by all college students could, *(however, provide some pressure for prices to rise somewhat / in fact, cause an excessive and exaggerated price increase).*

So, prices can rise in response to widespread changes in the desirability of particular items. Suppliers observe market conditions and pay special attention to prices. They will move to produce commodities whose prices are high (relative to production costs) and to reduce or cut down entirely on production of goods whose prices are relatively low. In this way, the problem of *(what / how / for whom)* goods shall be produced is settled. Producers are consciously trying to *(earn profits / satisfy consumer preferences).* In so doing, though, they are also *(earning profits / satisfying consumer preferences).*

b. The same perfectly competitive market system can operate effectively to settle the question of *for whom* goods will be produced. Productive inputs such as labor (be it skilled or unskilled), land, and capital carry prices just like consumer goods and services. These prices *(are certainly / are not)* part of the pricing structure of a market system. Since individuals supply inputs for the system, the resulting money incomes of all individuals are governed by (circle one):

(1) the market prices of inputs and the input quantities that they own.

---

a. productive inputs (notably labor)   **b.** buyer; seller; seller; buyer

(2) only the prices of the inputs that they own.

(3) only the input quantities that they own.

The *for whom* problem is one of distributing (whether fairly or unfairly) the available consumer-goods supply among society's members. The relative size of an individual's money income settles this question in a laissez-faire market system. It all comes down to (1) "Who owns what?" and (2) "What is it worth?" There are, clearly, two questions relating to (1) the distribution of the ownership of productive inputs and (2) the relative prices of those inputs.

c. Now turn to the question of *how* goods are to be produced. Consider the following example. Suppose that a given quantity of some consumer good of some value can be made with either *(a)* 2 units of capital and 10 units of labor or *(b)* 10 units of capital and 2 units of labor. Suppose further, but only for simplicity, that *(a)* and *(b)* are the only two combinations that will produce this good.

The *how* problem is now easily illustrated as one of choosing between these two methods. To make the choice properly, producers must know *(the price of the finished good / which process is more efficient / the prices of labor and capital)*. "The maximally efficient method" is that method which costs *(less / more)* than any other method. The *how* question persists until *(input / finished-good)* prices are known, and it is settled by reference to these prices. For example, if capital were to cost $2 per unit and labor cost $3, then method *(a / b)* above would be preferable. If capital cost $3 and labor $2, then method *(a / b)* would be preferable.

---

a. no; have no effect on; go unnoticed; however, provide some pressure for prices to rise somewhat; what; earn profits; satisfying consumer preferences   **b.** are certainly;   **(1)**   **c.** the prices of labor and capital; less; input; *b*; *a*

Perfectly competitive market economies are sometimes conceptualized as mazes of interdependencies. You will, through Parts Two and Three of the text, build toward an understanding of how these interdependencies work. Many of their implications are, however, quite intuitive. Try to see if you can see through the *general-equilibrium* linkages to answer the following questions—not by reading more in the text or the *Guide* but by thinking about the structure that is described.

3. Consider five types of people, labeled A through E, whose relevant attributes are described below:

A: Owns a coal mine; likes ice cream; hates fancy dessert yogurt

B: Works in a coal mine; likes yogurt and ice cream

C: Owns fancy yogurt company; hates dessert

D: Works at a yogurt factory; hates dessert

E: Works at an ice cream plant; hates dessert

Assume that there are enough of each type of person so that changes in their economic condition could affect a market price.

a. If prolonged war in the Middle East were to interrupt oil supplies, raise oil prices, and thereby increase the demand for coal, would the following *increase, decrease,* or *stay the same?* (Write your answers in the blanks below. If you cannot tell from the information provided, write "can't tell.")

(1) A's earnings . . . . _____

(2) B's wage . . . . _____

(3) C's earnings . . . . _____

(4) D's wage . . . . _____

(5) E's wage . . . . _____

b. If a nationwide mine workers' settlement increased B's wage without extending A's market, would the following *increase, decrease,* or *stay the same?* (Again, indicate if you can't tell.)

(1) A's earnings . . . . _____

(2) C's earnings . . . . _____

(3) D's wage . . . . _____

(4) E's wage . . . . _____

a. All increase. [A higher demand for coal should increase the earnings of A—the coal-mine owner. He will increase his demand for ice cream and (perhaps eventually) pay his labor (B) a higher wage. Higher demand for ice cream and yogurt increases the earnings of the owner of the yogurt company (C), who will pay the people who work for him (E) more. The higher income for coal miners increases the demand for yogurt, so it eventually produces a higher wage for the people who work at the yogurt factory (D).]   **b. (1)** decrease [Paying labor more means less income for the owner (A).]   **(2)** increase   **(3)** increase [Richer coal miners mean more demand for both ice cream and yogurt, so the wages paid to people working at the yogurt company (D) and the earnings of the owner of the yogurt company (C) should increase.]   **(4)** can't tell [The demand for ice cream may fall or rise depending upon whether or not the reduced demand from the coal-mine owners is larger or smaller in magnitude than the increased demand from the coal miners. The wages paid to people working at the ice cream plants (E) may therefore fall or rise.]

Section B of the chapter introduces the various roles that government might play in very broad terms. These roles are catalogued according to the equity, efficiency, and stability difficulties that typically plague an economy left to its own devices. The existence of monopolies, or other forms of significant market imperfection, creates inefficiency that government might try to ameliorate. So do externalities, good or bad, and public goods that need societal support to be financially viable. Competitive laissez-faire solutions do not necessarily produce fair or just distributions of income, and governments sometimes try to use devices like progressive income taxation and social safety nets to diminish inequities. Fiscal and monetary policies have, since the 1930s, been used to try to shave off the peaks of economic boom and fill in the troughs of economic bust. The experience of the 1930s is, in fact, strong historical evidence that we cannot rely on laissez-faire policy to avoid dramatic turns in the long-term business cycle. It should be noted, however, that government intervention need not be the best solution. Many times, the medicine of government policy is worse than the economic disease that it was intended to cure. We should, in short, avoid the error of the monarch who awarded a medal for singing to the second of two contestants after hearing only the first contestant sing.

4. This question will explore the potential roles of government in a mixed economy.

a. If monopoly power allowed the owner of a firm to produce too little, to charge too high a price, to earn an extraordinary rate of profit, and to ignore competitive pressures of potential competitors, would it alter society's answers to the three fundamental questions?

(1) Would the answer to *what* change? *(yes / no / probably)*

Why? _____

(2) Would the answer to *how* change? _____

Why? _____

(3) Would the answer to *for whom* change? _____

Why? _____

b. If freedom to dump pollution into the air allowed a polluter to produce too much and charge too little regardless of competitive pressures, would answers to the questions change?

(1) Would the answer to *what* change? _____

Why? _____

(2) Would the answer to *how* change? _____

Why? _____

(3) Would the answer to *for whom* change? _____

Why? _____

c. If instability in the business cycle increased risk so that the price charged for a given good were higher than otherwise would have been appropriate and production were therefore smaller than otherwise appropriate, would answers to the questions change?

(1) Would the answer to *what* change? _____

Why? _____

(2) Would the answer to *how* change? _____

Why? _____

(3) Would the answer to *for whom* change? _____

Why? _____

d. If policy were enacted to redistribute income, would answers to the questions change?

(1) Would the answer to *what* change? _____

Why? _____

(2) Would the answer to *how* change? _____

Why? _____

(3) Would the answer to *for whom* change? _____

Why? _____

e. Listed below are three policy options that a government might consider:

1. Enact a minimum-wage law that prohibits the payment of any hourly wage rate below $3.75.
2. Construct a new toll-free highway.
3. Enact progressive taxes on incomes that reduce the spending power of rich citizens.

Item *(1 / 2 / 3)* illustrates an influence *directly* exerted on the decision as to *what* goods shall be produced. Item *(1 / 2 / 3)* illustrates a similar influence on *how,* and item(s) *(1 / 2 / 3)* on for whom.

a. (1) yes; Too little of one good also means too much of another. **(2)** probably; The most efficient process is probably not used, if not by the monopolist, then by the producers of other goods. **(3)** yes; The monopolist is earning relatively more than otherwise and therefore takes more dollar votes to the marketplace. **b. (1)** yes; Too much of one good also means too little of another. **(2)** yes; The process chosen makes more pollution than it would if the polluter had to pay to pollute. **(3)** probably; Never say never in general equilibrium. **c.** The answers of **a** apply except that the income distortion would probably not weigh heavily in **(3)**. **d. (1)** probably; The people receiving the income would probably want different things than the wealthier people, and giving them more dollar votes would cause the market system to accommodate. **(2)** probably; The scales of various industries might change and thereby change the most appropriate production process. **(3)** yes; This is the point of the policy. **e.** 2; 1; 1 and/or 3 (*Note:* Indirect effects on answers to all three questions can be expected from each alternative.)

5. Listed below are several examples of policies a government might implement in trying to modify the workings of an automatic price system. Write in the blanks which of the three motives for government action—*efficiency* concerns, *equity* concerns, and *stability* concerns—is closest to the rationale that might underlie each policy.

a. Pure food and drug laws . . . . _____

b. Minimum-wage laws . . . . _____

c. Pollution limitations . . . . _____

d. Free penicillin . . . . _____

e. Rent controls . . . . _____

f. Military draft . . . . _____

g. Unemployment compensation . _____

a. efficiency **b.** equity **c.** efficiency **d.** equity **e.** equity **f.** equity and/or efficiency **g.** equity (and stabilization—you will see why in Part Four)

6. When the invisible hand breaks down because it cannot bring a monopoly to produce the correct output, government might (*intervene in the market / subsidize a more worthwhile activity / redistribute income*) to try to correct the inefficiency created. In the face of an externality, government might (*intervene in the market / subsidize a more worthwhile activity / stabilize the macroeconomy*) to try to ameliorate the resulting inefficiency. When society notices that an unacceptably large proportion of its citizens are impoverished, its government might (*subsidize a worthwhile activity / redistribute income / stabilize the macroeconomy*) to try to reduce the inequities derived from the distribution of inputs and their relative prices. Faced with many people driven to poverty because they cannot find work, a government might (*intervene in the marketplace / subsidize a worthwhile activity / stabilize the macroeconomy*) to try to diminish the associated economic and social losses.

Indicate in the parentheses provided below whether the listed policies are designed to intervene in a market (I), subsidize a worthwhile activity (SU), redistribute income (R), or stabilize the macroeconomy (ST). Some policies may work in more than one area, so record two or three answers when necessary.

a. Antitrust laws . . . . ( )

b. The Clean Air Act . . . . ( )

c. An arranged increase in interest rates . . . . ( )

d. The food-stamp program . . . . ( )

e. Federal support of public education . . . . . ( )

f. Food and drug regulations . . . . ( )

g. More public-works projects during recession. ( )

intervene in the market; intervene in the market; redistribute income; stabilize the macroeconomy **a.** I (prohibiting certain types of behavior by suppliers of certain goods) **b.** I (limiting emissions by setting clean air standards that must be met by enforcing a set of regulations) **c.** ST (This is monetary policy.) **d.** R (tax revenue collected from society at large to underwrite the food purchases of needs-qualified individuals and families) **e.** SU and R (Education is a public good, but federal support directed at needy students and/or school districts is a form of redistribution.) **f.** I (prohibiting the marketing of drugs and foods that do not meet certain standards) **g.** SU and ST (Public-works projects are generally focused on providing public goods, and if they are increased during recession, it is stabilizing fiscal policy.)

REVIEW CONCEPTS

1. Describe how laissez-faire perfect competition allows Adam Smith's invisible hand to answer the *what, how,* and *for whom* questions.

2. Indicate how perfect competition allows the invisible hand to work.

3. Understand how market prices for inputs and outputs can lead a market system to select *what* to produce and *how* to produce it. Indicate further how prices determine money votes and thereby allocate output across the population.

4. Describe the range of organization of a mixed economy, noting command and free enterprise components.

5. Outline the potential efficiency, equity, and stabilization failures of market systems which produce roles for government, and link each to specific governmental activity.

6. Take special note of the inefficiencies associated with monopoly power, externalities, and the potential underprovision of public goods. Relate each to the need for taxation.

QUIZ: Multiple Choice

1. Capital (considered as a factor of production, or as one of the three major inputs of land, labor, and capital) means:
(1) manufactured productive inputs.
(2) undeveloped natural resources, such as iron ore not yet mined.

(3) the financial assets of producing businesses.
(4) the same thing as the nation's total money stock.
(5) none of these things.

2. One vital reason why indirect, or "capital-using," methods of production have not displaced direct methods in economically less developed nations is that:
(1) the governments of such nations have not issued enough money to finance indirect production methods.
(2) people do not realize that indirect methods would produce more consumption goods.
(3) there are no indirect methods that would actually produce more consumption goods.
(4) such areas lack a properly functioning price system.
(5) the introduction of such indirect methods would involve a sacrifice of present consumption that less developed societies cannot easily afford.

3. The economic problem of *how* goods are produced is solved in market economies:
(1) through the decisions of consumers in the marketplace as reflected by the prices of finished goods.
(2) by means of the profit motive, which prompts producers to try to keep their costs of production at a minimum.
(3) by means of the extensive use of capital goods.
(4) by means of extensive specialization, which may or may not involve large-scale use of capital goods.
(5) by none of the above ways, since *how* to produce goods is not a basic problem in market economies.

4. The economic problem of deciding *what* goods to produce includes, among other things:
(1) the necessity of deciding the degree to which specialization is to be employed in the manufacture of goods.
(2) a decision about the quantity of advertising that should be used to encourage the sale of whatever has been produced.
(3) the choice between the production of consumer goods and the production of capital goods.
(4) the need to establish a central government, since all decisions on *what* should be produced are ultimately made by such governments.
(5) the need to establish a system of pure (or perfect) competition.

5. We speak of land, labor, and capital as the basic grouping of the factors of production. Which of the following is correct with respect to whether or not money, stocks, and/or bonds should be counted as capital?
(1) All three (money, stocks, and bonds) count.
(2) Stocks and bonds count, but money does not.
(3) Money counts, but stocks and bonds do not.
(4) Money and stocks count, but bonds do not.
(5) None of the three counts.

6. A major social problem to which specialization and division of labor give rise is:
(1) the need to use paper money.
(2) the need to use capital.
(3) interdependence.
(4) the need to learn economics.
(5) none of these.

7. In economics, the term "imperfect competitor" is applied to a seller who:
(1) operates outside the system of specialization and money pricing.
(2) supplies a sufficiently large quantity of the good involved to be able to affect its price.
(3) seeks to distort the pattern of consumer tastes (through advertising campaigns and the like).
(4) knowingly or unknowingly uses inferior production methods.
(5) is not correctly described by any of these descriptions.

8. Figure 3-1 depicts a production-possibility frontier involving capital goods and consumer goods. What is the significance of points *A* and *B*?

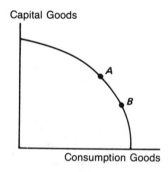

Figure 3-1

(1) They indicate possible demands for capital goods and consumer goods—*A* representing capital-good demand and *B* consumer-good demand.
(2) They represent possible and alternative combinations of maximum output which the economy in question could produce.
(3) They indicate the maximum possible quantities of capital goods and consumer goods which could be produced—*A* indicating maximum possible capital-good output and *B* maximum possible consumer-good output.
(4) Movement from *A* to *B* would indicate the growth of output resulting from the use of capital goods.
(5) There is no significance at all, since production-possibility diagrams refer to consumer goods only, not to capital goods.

9. In Figure 3-1, operation at a point such as *A* indicates production of some capital goods. Assuming this is more than

sufficient to replace capital goods currently being worn out, then continued operation at *A* should result in:
(1) an inward movement of the whole curve.
(2) no change in the curve, but a move from *A* to *B*.
(3) no change necessarily either in the position of the curve or in the operation of the economy at *A*.
(4) no change in the curve, but a move from *A* to a point inside the curve.
(5) an outward movement of the frontier.

10. Figure 3-2 depicts a production-possibility frontier with respect to consumer goods X and Y. The economy involved makes full use of a money pricing system. The significance of points like *A* and *B* is that:

Figure 3-2

(1) either is a possible operating point and, if selected, indicates a verdict on *what* combination of X and Y to produce that was reached because prices accurately reflected consumer preferences.
(2) either is a possible operating point that might be reached quite independently of the operation of the price system; the curve in question refers to production, not prices.
(3) either can be chosen as an operating point, therefore indicating the combination of X and Y having maximum money value but not necessarily the combination which maximally satisfies consumer preferences.
(4) either is simply a typical point on the curve, whose position (all points thereon) has been established by consumer preferences expressed through the price system.
(5) either is a possible operating point, but a money pricing system is bound to show that *A* is a point preferable to *B*.

11. In a money-using, capitalist society, the economic problem of *for whom* goods shall be produced is primarily settled because:
(1) each producer looks for the type of consumer or market most likely to be interested in the product offered and then tries to tailor that product so that it is particularly appealing to the consumer or market.
(2) consumers bid up the prices of those goods they most want to have and refuse to bid, or bid only a low price, for goods they find less attractive.
(3) business firms bid for the services of productive inputs according to their usefulness in production, thus giving each input supplier a money income that can be used to buy goods.
(4) competition operates so as to keep profits low and therefore keeps prices at a level which consumers can afford to pay.
(5) income is distributed in keeping with the needs of individual consumers.

12. Which alternative in question 11 best describes the process by which the problem of *what* goods shall be produced is primarily settled, in a society which relies on the mechanism of money and prices?
(1).
(2).
(3).
(4).
(5).

13. If it is true that most of the goods a certain society consumed today were produced in the past, and that most of its production today is intended for future consumption, then it must be true that this society makes extensive use of:
(1) specialization and division of labor.
(2) money.
(3) a money pricing system.
(4) advertising.
(5) capital.

14. In a decentralized, capitalist society, the reliance on a market pricing system is not expected to help settle which of the following economic problems?
(1) Distributing money incomes among the members of the society.
(2) Helping a consumer with given tastes and a limited income to decide how best to spend that income.
(3) Deciding how much of the available resource supply is to be devoted to manufacturing any given consumer good.
(4) Choosing the particular kinds of inputs (factors of production) that should be used for the manufacture of any given consumer good.
(5) Determining the particular output of goods and services which the society really needs, regardless of the tastes of any or all individual consumers therein.

15. The government role that significantly affects the question *for whom* is:
(1) promotion of equity.
(2) promotion of efficiency.
(3) promotion of stabilization.
(4) all the above.

SUGGESTED ANSWERS TO QUESTIONS IN THE TEXT: Chapter 3

1. Produce corn, using all productive labor and land for the farmers who own the land and the people who work on the farms. Figure TQ3-1 shows the circular flow.

Figure TQ3-1

2. *Pollution limitations:* improving efficiency (public "bad")
AIDS research: improving efficiency (public good)
Income supplements: equity
Water regulation: efficiency
Monetary policy: stability

3. Scarce goods have, almost by definition, low supply. With high demand, they also have high prices and thus the market allocates the scarce supply to those few who can afford the expenditure.

4. Money goes in the opposite direction, i.e., from businesses to the suppliers of inputs and from households to the suppliers of outputs.

5. Smith did not think highly of the ability of government to intervene successfully in a market. He believed that the invisible hand would supply everything worthwhile.

6. Yes, there are lots of potential government failures. Name one at your own peril—your failure may be someone else's necessity and success story.

7. *National defense:* efficiency in providing a public good
Social security: equity in providing income in times of need and/or retirement
Interest on debt: efficiency, in moderation, by paying the price of allocating spending over time; and stabilization in financing deficit fiscal policy
Unemployment insurance: equity
Justice: efficiency and equity
Pollution control: efficiency (controlling a public "bad")
Basic science: efficiency (public good)

CHAPTER 4

BASIC ELEMENTS OF SUPPLY AND DEMAND

There is a common expression among people who think about economic issues: "It's all a matter of supply and demand." This expression is, for the most part, exactly correct. Properly framed, the essence of almost any economic question can be approached from a supply-demand perspective; properly interpreted, the answer to almost any economic question can be explained in terms of supply-demand intuition. This chapter will provide you with your first systematic exposure to these tools—two of the most powerful tools of economic analysis. By the end of your work here, the following objectives should be within easy reach.

LEARNING OBJECTIVES

1. Define demand and supply; understand their graphical representations.

2. Describe the law of downward-sloping demand, and provide three economic forces that contribute to the resulting negative slope of a typical demand curve.

3. Explain why a supply curve is normally positively sloped.

4. Describe and define the market-clearing price. Explain how a competitive market operates to move toward that price.

5. Explain what is meant by "other things being equal" in the context of a demand curve. Discuss the significance of the five factors that are held constant in the construction of a demand curve.

6. Explain what is meant by "other things being equal" in the context of a supply curve. Discuss the significance of the four factors that are held constant in the construction of a supply curve.

7. Explain precisely how changes in the factors identified in objectives 5 and 6 work to change market equilibrium. Be clear about how to graph the effects of each. Be equally clear that the factors that influence demand are different from the factors that influence supply.

8. Understand and thereby avoid three sources of confusion in analyzing changes in markets: (a) the meaning of "other things equal," (b) the difference between shifting curves and movement along curves, and (c) the critical word "willingly" in the definition of supply and demand.

Many forces can operate to push the observed price of any given commodity higher or lower: changes in people's tastes, changes in their incomes, changes in the costs of production, changes in the prices of substitute products, etc. The list is nearly endless. If we are to explain the price that a commodity actually takes in the marketplace, therefore, we will need to have a firm grasp on several essential, fundamental points. First and foremost, the forces that can influence price can be divided into two distinct groups:

▶ One group of forces operates through its influence on the behavior of buyers of the commodity. We sum up what buyers want to do through the device of a demand schedule, or demand curve. The demand curve is concerned exclusively with buyer attitudes—not with sellers.

▶ The second group of forces operates through its influence on the behavior of sellers. This we represent by means of the supply schedule, or supply curve. The supply curve reflects solely seller (not buyer) attitudes.

The division between these two groups of people is nearly absolute. Its importance in correctly analyzing

4 Basic Elements of Supply and Demand

the workings of even the simplest of markets cannot be overstated. In all but a very few exceptional cases, economic forces *directly* influence either the demand side of a market or the supply side of a market, *but not both*.

1. This question will explore the forces that play on the demand side.

a. The text notes that the demand curve is, typically, downward-sloping. To explain why its slope is negative, list three reasons why the quantity demanded should increase as the price of some good falls:

(1) _____

(2) _____

(3) _____

b. The text also identifies five economic forces that determine precisely where a demand curve must be located; i.e., five factors other than price are identified as determinants of demand. Changes in these factors shift the entire demand curve. List them:

(1) _____

(2) _____

(3) _____

(4) _____

(5) _____

a. (1) New buyers enter. (2) More is purchased by existing consumers. (3) New uses might become economical. **b.** (1) income (2) size of the market (3) prices of substitute or complementary goods (4) tastes (5) particular commodity-specific factors

2. We will now explore the forces that play on the supply side.

a. The text notes that the supply curve is, typically, upward-sloping. To support this slope, give one important reason why suppliers must be paid a steadily increasing price to increase the quantity that they are willing to sell: _____

_____

Explain how it works: _____

_____

_____

b. The text also identifies four economic forces that determine precisely where a supply curve must be located; i.e., four factors other than price are identified as determinants

of supply. Changes in these factors shift the entire supply curve. List them:

(1) _____

(2) _____

(3) _____

(4) _____

a. law of diminishing returns; To increase output, more and more of some variable inputs will have to be added to work with relatively fixed supplies of other inputs; they become increasingly less productive. **b.** (1) costs of production (2) technology (3) taxes and/or subsidies (4) market structure

3. Each of the 10 prices (P) below is associated with a particular quantity (Q). In Figure 4-1, mark the 10 points corresponding to these (Q,P) pairs. Join them with a smooth curve.

P :	$10	$9	$8	$7	$6	$5	$4	$3	$2	$1
Q :	1	2	3	5	8	12	15	20	25	40

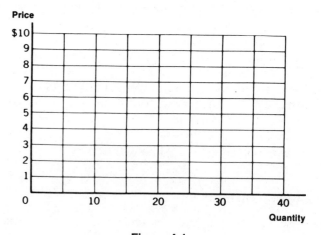

Figure 4-1

a. In this schedule, the lower the price, the *(lower / higher)* the quantity. These figures therefore suggest a *(supply / demand)* curve.

b. Also plot the following 10 (Q,P) pairs in Figure 4-1. Join them with a smooth curve.

P :	$10	$9	$8	$7	$6	$5	$4	$3	$2	$1
Q :	26	25	24	22	20	18	15	10	0	0

The shape of this second curve suggests that it represents a *(supply / demand)* curve.

a. higher; demand **b.** supply

4. a. Given the data of question 3, what would be the market-clearing price? . . . .
. . . . $(10 / 9 / 8 / 7 / 6 / 5 / 4 / 3 / 2 / 1)

b. Why would this be the market-clearing price? (Circle one.)

(1) It is about midway in the total schedule of prices.

(2) It is the price that sellers have decided should be charged for this commodity.

(3) It is the only price at which the quantity buyers want to purchase just equals the quantity sellers want to supply.

---

a. 4   **b.** (3)

---

5. a. If (still using the data provided in question 3) price stood temporarily at a level of $6, what would be the situation? (Circle one.)

(1) Quantity offered for sale would exceed quantity demanded. Competition among sellers would drive price higher.

(2) Quantity demanded would exceed quantity offered for sale. Competition among buyers plus seller awareness of shortages would drive price higher.

(3) Quantity demanded would exceed quantity offered for sale. Competition among sellers plus buyer awareness of shortages would drive price lower.

(4) Quantity demanded would be less than quantity offered for sale. Competition among sellers would drive price lower.

b. If price stood temporarily at a level of $3, which alternative in part **a** would apply? . . . . (1 / 2 / 3 / 4)

---

a. (4)   **b.** 2

---

6. When economists refer to the **law of downward-sloping demand**, they are speaking of a particular kind of behavior among buyers that is observed with so few exceptions that it can be designated a "law" of behavior. Circle as many of the following as correctly describe or illustrate this law:

a. If the price of X falls, at least some X buyers will increase the quantity they purchase by at least some small amount.

b. When people have more income to spend, they normally increase their purchases of any commodity.

c. Demand curves normally slope downward as they run to the right.

d. The quantity of any commodity bought ultimately tends to decline as it goes out of style or is superseded by something of better quality.

e. When the price of X rises significantly, people tend to reduce the quantity of X that they purchase.

f. If the price of butter falls considerably, the drop will tend to reduce purchases of oleomargarine.

---

a, c, e (The law of downward-sloping demand has to do with the influence of price on quantity demanded. Item **b** does not illustrate this law because it refers to an income change; changes in income shift the entire demand curve in or out for all prices. In item **d**, the change in purchases is not set off by a price change; tastes change, to be sure, but the entire curve shifts when they do, regardless of the price. Item **f** does refer to a price change, but it is a change in the price of another commodity. Like items **d** and **b**, this change generates a shift in the entire curve for each and every price.)

---

7. If the price of any good falls, then the quantity which buyers want to purchase will rise because **(a)** new buyers are attracted and/or **(b)** existing buyers increase their purchases. The text cites two background reasons for such increases: the **substitution effect** and the **income effect**.

a. First, if X's price were to fall, buyers may substitute X for Y. Even though the price of Y remains unchanged, Y would now be relatively more expensive. This would be (an income / a substitution) effect and would apply to (only old / only new / both old and new) buyers. Similarly, if X's price were to rise, (only old / only new / both old and new) buyers may substitute Y for X because Y would now be relatively (more / less) expensive.

b. A fall in X's price resembles an increase in income, because buyers can now purchase the same amount of X and have money left over. With this "increase in income," buyers may want to purchase more of various goods—including good X. This is (a substitution / an income) effect, and it applies (only to old / only to new / to both old and new) buyers.

c. These two effects apply (only for price reductions / only for price increases / for both price reductions and increases).

---

a. a substitution; both old and new; only old; less (Only current consumers can substitute away from a commodity.)   **b.** an income; only to old   **c.** for both price reductions and increases

---

8. Put (S) in the parentheses below if the description suggests the substitution effect; put (I) if the income effect is indicated; put (N) if neither is appropriate:

a. A family decides its guests cannot tell the difference between butter and margarine; consequently, it switches some of its purchases from butter to margarine. . . . . . . ( )

b. A sharp increase in rents forces the family to move to a smaller apartment. . . . . ( )

c. Butter prices go up, and the family switches more of its purchases from butter to margarine. . . . . ( )

d. The family receives a considerable increase in income and therefore buys, among other things, more butter and more apartment space. . . . . ( )

---

a. N **b.** I **c.** S **d.** N (These two "effects" are intended to apply to the consequences of a price change only. In cases **a** and **d**, the behavior change was not set off by a price change. There would also be an income effect in case **c**, but it would be very small, since the proportion of income devoted to purchasing either margarine or butter must be minuscule.)

It is essential to keep in mind that a demand curve is a conditional schedule; it answers an "if this, then that" type of question. It shows, in particular, that if the price of some good were to stand at some specified level, then consumers would be willing to purchase the indicated quantity. In Figure 4-2, the demand curve indicates that if the price were equal to A0, then consumers would want to buy a quantity AF (or 0C). Should the price fall to B0, then the quantity demanded (willingly) by consumers would rise to BG (or 0E).

Figure 4-2

When equilibrium in the marketplace has been worked out, there will be just one price for which the quantity *willingly* demanded will equal the quantity *willingly* supplied. The quantity read from the curve does not depend at all upon whether or not that quantity is feasible to supply at the given price. It reflects only the desires of consumers who worry only about their own preferences and what they can afford. The quantity read from the supply curve does not depend upon whether or not people want that much. It reflects only the ambitions of suppliers who worry only about their costs and their anticipated profits (given the quoted price).

Remember, too, that price is not the only factor that influences consumers' decisions to buy. The income that they receive, the prices of other goods, and their own tastes also have an effect. Rather than try to capture all these effects in one curve, economists have historically favored charting the price effect on the quantity demanded under the assumption that the other factors do not change. Buyer behavior for one good is thus insulated against disturbances arising from other sources, and we can indicate how this behavior changes solely in response to changes in the price of the good in question. This is the "other things equal" or "other things constant" assumption.

These other determinants of demand do, of course, change. These changes are recognized by a shift in the entire demand curve to an appropriate new position; *each price* is, in other words, *associated with a new quantity demanded.*

In Figure 4-3, for example, the *dd* demand curve is shown as shifting to an entirely new position, *d'd'*, because, say, buyer incomes have increased. Demand curves are always drawn on the basis of an *other things equal* assumption, and these "other things" include consumers' incomes; if incomes change, then the demand curve must change position accordingly. Referring to Figure 4-3, consumers would have been buying quantity 0C given price A0 if demand curve *dd* were applicable. With higher incomes, though, they want to increase their purchases to 0E. This doesn't mean they will succeed in buying quantity 0E at price A0. The supply curve will have an influence on that. Our concern for the moment is with demand, not supply, and it is with what buyers *want* to do. The point is that at each and any price, because of the income rise, consumers will *want* to buy a larger quantity than they would have demanded previously.

Figure 4-3

The same notions apply equally well to supply curves. A supply curve is also a conditional schedule; it shows that if the price of some good were to stand at some specified level, then suppliers would be *willing* and able to deliver the indicated quantity to market.

Figure 4-4 illustrates this point. If, for example, price were equal to A0, then quantity AF (or 0C) would be *willingly* supplied. If the price fell to 0B, then the quantity supplied would fall to BG (or 0E). These quantities depend only upon the parameters of the suppliers' decisions; they *do not* indicate, *in any way, shape,* or *form,* the willingness of consumers to purchase the indicated quantities at the indicated prices.

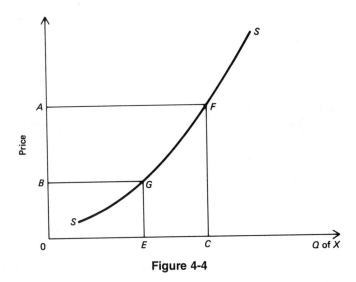

Figure 4-4

Price is, of course, not the only factor that influences the disposition of suppliers to sell. If the costs of production climb, then suppliers will want to produce and sell fewer units. If costs climb high enough, in fact, they may shut down entirely. Technological advances in the production process would, meanwhile, have the opposite effect. Taxes, market structure, production costs, etc., all influence the supply response to any specific price. A supply curve is, therefore, an *other things equal* curve just like a demand curve. It assumes that all the factors, other than the price of output, which influence suppliers' decisions are fixed. If any one of these "other things" changes, then the entire supply curve must shift to a new position to be appropriate.

The next set of questions will exercise your understanding of changes in demand and supply (i.e., shifts in demand and supply curves).

9. The four panels of Figure 4-5 illustrate these ideas. In each, one curve, either demand or supply, has shifted position because of a change in some influencing factor other than price. The solid lines indicate an initial position; the broken lines, a new position. In panel (a), for example, the notion is that demand has shifted from curve dd to d'd'.

a. Indicate in the table below whether the market-clearing price and quantity would *increase* or *decrease* in response to the changes portrayed in the indicated figures:

	Price	Quantity
Panel (a)		
Panel (b)		
Panel (c)		
Panel (d)		

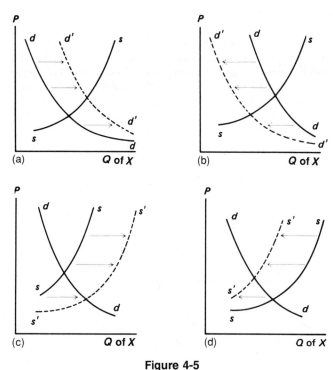

Figure 4-5

b. Each of the following events could reasonably be expected to change the position of a demand or supply curve for some commodity X. For each, indicate which panel in Figure 4-5 best illustrates its likely effect on a supply-demand representation of the market for X.

(1) The costs of manufacturing good X increase.( )

(2) Consumer tastes shift away from X in favor of some other good. . . . . ( )

(3) The demand for some good Y, another commodity that can readily be produced by the suppliers of X in the place of X, increases. . . . . ( )

(4) A recession reduces the incomes of the people who demand X. . . . . ( )

(5) The price of a substitute commodity increases.( )

(6) The government removes a heavy tariff on imports of X from abroad. . . . . ( )

(7) The price of an input essential in the production of X increases dramatically. . . . . ( )

(8) Emigration produces a sudden reduction in the number of people demanding X. . . . . ( )

44   4   Basic Elements of Supply and Demand

(9) The government increases the fines that must be paid by the producers of X for the pollution that they must emit. . . . . ( )

---

a. Panel (a): Price and quantity both increase as demand climbs. Panel (b): Price and quantity both fall as demand falls. Panel (c): Price falls and quantity climbs as supply increases. Panel (d): Price climbs and quantity falls as supply contracts.   **b.** **(1)** *b* (supply contracts)   **(2)** *b* (demand falls)   **(3)** *d* (supply of X contracts)   **(4)** *b* (demand falls)   **(5)** *a* (demand expands)   **(6)** *c* (supply expands)   **(7)** *b* (supply contracts)   **(8)** *b* (demand shrinks)   **(9)** *d* (supply contracts)

10. a. Fill in the blanks in Table 4-1 with:

(1) the most appropriate graphical representation from panels (a) through (d) in Figure 4-5.

(2) an explanation of your answer to part **(1)**.

(3) the direction that the equilibrium price would move (+ = up and − = down).

(4) the direction that the equilibrium quantity would move [same convention as in **(3)**].

The first row of the table is filled in to help elucidate the directions.

b. In general, an increase in supply will (lower / raise) the price and (lower / raise) the market-clearing quantity. A decrease in supply will (lower / raise) the price and (lower / raise) the quantity.

c. In general, an increase in demand will (lower / raise) the price and (lower / raise) the market-clearing quantity. A decrease in demand will (lower / raise) the price and (lower / raise) the quantity.

---

a. B: panel (d), production more expensive, +, −; C: panel (a), market size increased, +, +; D: panel (b), substitute out of X, −, −; E: panel (d), cost of production increased, +, −; F: panel (a), income increased, +, +; G: panel (c), cost of production diminished, −, +   **b.** lower; raise; raise; lower   **c.** raise; raise; lower; lower

11. When either the demand or the supply curve shifts in position, things are thrown "out of equilibrium," and a new market-clearing price and quantity must be established. It is easy to draw supply and demand curves upon a page or blackboard, but the market does not have such pretty little diagrams laid out for its inspection. The market has to fumble its way toward its new equilibrium. Without knowing the curves, how does it get there? Question 5 has already touched upon this matter; now it is examined in a little more detail.

a. Figure 4-6 reproduces panel (a) of Figure 4-5; i.e., it depicts one possible shift in one of the two curves. Specifically, note the arrow and the new broken-line position. It shows (an increase / a decrease) in (supply / demand).

Before this change, the market-clearing price was $A0$, and the quantity bought and sold was $0E$. Now demand has increased—again, let's say, because of an increase in consumer incomes. At the $A0$ price, buyers would now like to buy the larger quantity ($0E$ / $0F$ / $0G$). But this buyer wish does not match the supplier wish. To furnish this

Table 4-1

Change in Condition	(1) Figure	(2) Rationale	(3) Price	(4) Quantity
A. Good X is clothing that has gone out of style.	b	change in taste shifts *dd* in . . .	(−)	(−)
B. Pollution tax on supplier	___	_____	___	___
C. Opening of market to foreign buyers	___	_____	___	___
D. Price of substitute good falls	___	_____	___	___
E. Market structure requires more advertising	___	_____	___	___
F. A 10% across-the-board income-tax cut	___	_____	___	___
G. Robot makes production more efficient	___	_____	___	___

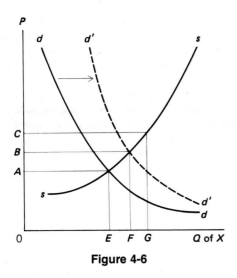

Figure 4-6

larger quantity in full, suppliers would require the price (C0 / B0 / A0). This in turn does not match consumer wishes. The new equilibrium must ultimately be a compromise in which price is (C0 / B0 / A0) and quantity bought and sold is (0E / 0F / 0G).

b. How is this new equilibrium reached? The market can discern, even without looking at supply and demand curves, that the quantity demanded *(exceeds / falls short of)* the quantity supplied at the old price A0. Buyers find it *(difficult / easy)* to buy all they want to buy; suppliers find it *(difficult / easy)* to sell what they want to sell at the A0 price. Thus, on both buying and selling sides, the pressure is toward a *(higher / lower)* price. This pressure persists as long as the price holds at any level at which quantity demanded exceeds quantity supplied. This disequilibrium pressure ends when—with the demand curve at its $d'd'$ position—price reaches the level of (C0 / B0 / A0).

In the opposite situation—a decrease in demand or an increase in supply—the mechanism just outlined works in reverse.

---

a. an increase; demand; 0G; C0; B0; 0F; **b.** exceeds; difficult; easy; higher; B0

---

12. The two panels of Figure 4-7 show special cases of possible demand or supply curves: a horizontal line in panel (a), and a vertical line in panel (b). As a demand or as a supply curve, what would such a line mean? (Never mind whether such a curve would be reasonable or not. The question is: What is the information which such a line would convey?)

a. A demand curve indicating desire to buy some fixed quantity at any price (at least within the range of prices indicated by the length of the line drawn), with no intention of ever buying any greater quantity, would be illustrated by panel (a / b).

b. A supply curve indicating that any quantity (at least up to the quantity indicated by the length of the line drawn) would be supplied at the indicated price, but no quantity at all at any lower price, would be illustrated by panel (a / b).

c. A demand curve indicating willingness to buy any quantity (at least up to the quantity indicated by the length of the line drawn) at the indicated price, but refusal to buy any quantity at any higher price, would be illustrated by panel (a / b).

d. A supply curve indicating willingness to supply some fixed quantity, regardless of price (even at zero price), but refusal to supply any greater quantity, no matter how high the price (at least within the range of prices indicated by the length of the line drawn), would be illustrated by panel (a / b).

---

a. *b* **b.** *a* **c.** *a* **d.** *b*

---

13. Identify whether each of the following involves a shift in the demand curve or a change in the quantity demanded:

a. Auto sales rise as consumer incomes rise. . . . . (shift / change)

b. Fish prices *fall* after the Pope allows Catholics to eat meat on Friday. . . . . (shift / change)

c. A gasoline tax lowers the consumption of gasoline. . . . . (shift / change)

d. A disastrous wheat blight causes bread sales to fall. . . . . (shift / change)

e. The wheat blight causes peanut butter and jelly sales to fall. . . . . (shift / change)

---

a. shift [The demand curve shifts out as income rises. This is panel (a) of Figure 4-5, with X measuring auto sales.] **b.** shift [(Demand falls and the curve shifts in as people substitute meat for fish on Friday.) This is panel (b) of Figure 4-5, with X measuring fish.] **c.** change [The quantity demanded falls as the after-tax price of gasoline climbs along a given demand curve. This is panel (d) of Figure 4-5, with X measuring the consumption of gasoline.] **d.** change [The quantity demanded falls as the blight shifts the supply curve in (up) and moves the price of bread up along a fixed demand curve. This is also panel (d) of Figure 4-5, with X measuring the consumption of bread.] **e.** shift [The demand curves for peanut butter and jelly shift in as the price of a complement good rises; the market-clearing quantity falls against a fixed supply curve. This is panel (b) of Figure 4-5, with X measuring either peanut butter or jelly sales.]

Figure 4-7

14. For parts **a, c, d,** and **e** of question 13, write in the spaces below whether the indicated changes in market-clearing quantity should be expected to be associated with a *higher* or *lower* market-clearing price:

Part **a** .... _____

Part **c** .... _____

Part **d** .... _____

Part **e** .... _____

---

a. higher [The upward shift in the demand curve portends a higher market-clearing price—again, panel (a) of Figure 4-5.]   **c.** higher [The upward shift in the supply curve portends a higher market-clearing price—panel (d).]   **d.** higher [The upward shift in the supply curve still portends a higher market-clearing price—panel (d).]   **e.** lower [The downward shift in the demand curve portends a lower market-clearing price—panel (b).]

15. Indicate whether the following statements are *true* or *false*, and explain why in terms of the four panels of Figure 4-5:

_____ **a.** Failure of Brazil's coffee crop will lower the prices of coffee, tea, lemon, and cream. _____

_____

_____

_____

_____ **b.** A fad for long skirts will lower the price of wool and raise the price of salt. _____

_____

_____

_____

_____ **c.** A new yen for meat will lower the prices of grain and raise the prices of hide and horn. _____

_____

_____

_____

_____ **d.** Development of the sugar beet raised the rents paid on tropical cane lands. _____

_____

_____

_____

---

a. false; Failure of the coffee crop means that coffee will be in short supply; panel (d) tells us to expect the price of coffee to climb. Demand for substitutes of coffee (like tea) will shift up [panel (a)], so their prices will rise. So, too, will the prices of the complements of tea (lemon). Only the price of cream might fall, but some people do take cream with their tea.   **b.** false; Longer skirts may mean higher demand for wool (more wool per skirt); panel (a) tells us to expect the price of wool to increase. There should be no effect on the price of salt unless an income effect contracts demand; then the price might fall as shown in panel (b).   **c.** false; Higher demand for meat will increase the demand for cows and what they eat. They eat grain, so panel (a) tells us to expect higher grain prices. The supply of hides should increase, meanwhile, so panel (c) suggests that their price should fall.   **d.** false; Sugar beets lowered the demand for cane, and thus the land it is grown on. Panel (b) tells us that the rent on that land should have fallen.

You will, by now, have noticed that you have been asked repeatedly to consult the four panels of Figure 4-5, and you might be wondering why. There are two answers. First, remember the dichotomy that was noted very early in this chapter. Things that affect demand affect demand; things that affect supply affect supply. It is the rare exception when some change in circumstance directly affects both demand and supply. The answer to "What happens to market equilibrium if…?" is thus found in one of the four panels of Figure 4-5. How do you know which one? Does the change you are considering affect demand? If so, then panels (a) and (b) apply. If not, then panels (c) and (d) apply. Does it make demand (supply) expand? Then panel (a) [panel (c)] applies. If not, then it is panel (b) [panel (d)] that shows what happens. That's it; you're done. And if most of economics is nothing but supply and demand, then you already know a lot!

Second, you will not always have Figure 4-5 handy. During an exam, for example, your instructor might not appreciate your referring to a picture from your *Study Guide*. Not to worry, though. If you have consulted Figure 4-5 with sufficient frequency and attention, then you can easily reproduce any of its four panels when you need to. The easiest way to answer "what if" sorts of questions is, in fact, to draw your own versions of Figure 4-5. How? Start with some initial supply and demand curves; show the usual slopes unless told otherwise. Then decide whether the effect that you are considering affects the demand side or the supply side. Demand side? Draw a higher or lower demand curve, depending upon whether demand expands or contracts in response to the change in circumstance that you are considering. There, you have your own version of panel (a) or panel (b). Compare market-clearing quantity-price pairs, and read the answer. Supply side? Draw a new supply curve above or below the original. Look at your own version of panel (c) or panel (d), compare the equilibria, and read the answer. Simple? Good!

The text identifies three pitfalls of incorrect logic that must be avoided when we conduct supply-and-demand analysis of various markets. The first two are closely related: (1) care must be taken to remember what is being assumed constant, and (2) care must be taken to determine whether the market adjustment to be studied shifts a demand or a supply curve, or does something else. If the adjustment occurs in one of the forces that is normally assumed to be held constant (income, tastes, other prices, etc., on the demand side and costs, technology, market structure, taxes, etc., on the supply side), then a shift in one schedule or the other is appropriate. The final pitfall warns us to remember that demand and supply curves reflect quantities that people are willing to purchase and supply, respectively, at any given price. Equilibrium will involve a single price, but demand and supply curves cover the entire domain of possible prices.

16. a. Consider the following statement: "A simultaneous increase of demand and decrease of supply is statistically and logically impossible. Demand and supply are identically the same thing." Into which pitfall has the speaker fallen?

_____

_____

What would happen to market-clearing price and quantity if demand rose and supply fell at the same time? _____

_____

b. Now consider Figure 4-8. What is the market-clearing price if *dd* and *ss* represent demand and supply schedules, respectively? _____
Now let supply move to *s's'*. This represents a *(contraction / expansion)* of supply. Suppose that the government was to impose a price ceiling at 0A so that the price could not climb. The market-clearing quantity would be _____, read from *(supply curve ss / supply curve s's' / demand curve dd)*. There would be a *(shortage / surplus)* equal to _____

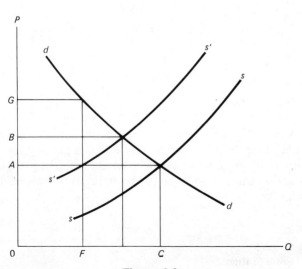

Figure 4-8

because the quantity demanded would be _____, read from *(supply curve ss / supply curve s's' / demand curve dd)*.

If a black market arose for X in which people who possessed some of the good could sell it at an illegally high price, what price would clear the market? _____ What price would clear the market if the government had not interfered? _____ What would be the effect of the government's action?_____

_____

_____

_____

a. all three (The speaker missed the interpretation that things normally held fixed must have changed, requiring shifts in the demand and supply curves. The speaker also presumed that equilibrium always exists when price questions are answered by quantities along supply and demand curves.) Higher demand and lower supply increase the price, but quantity can go either way. (To see why, experiment by drawing a few higher demand curves on Figure 4-8.) **b.** 0A; contraction; 0F; supply curve *ss*; shortage; *FC*; 0C; demand curve *dd*; 0G; 0B; a larger contraction in the quantity supplied than necessary, and a higher-than-necessary market-clearing price

REVIEW CONCEPTS

1. Understand that demand schedules reflect quantities of some specific good or service *willingly* demanded by households for various prices and that they are represented by downward (negatively) sloping demand curves. Similarly, understand that supply schedules reflect quantities of some specific good or service *willingly* supplied by firms for various prices and that they are represented by upward (positively) sloped supply curves.

2. Note that the law of downward-sloping demand applies because (1) buyers enter (leave) the market, (2) buyers extend (diminish) their purchases, and (3) product utilization expands (contracts) as the price falls (rises). These three sources of negative correlation can be summarized by income and substitution effects. (Read the sentence without the parenthetic terms; then reread it, substituting each parenthetic word for the word immediately preceding it.)

3. Note, as well, that the quantity supplied is usually thought to be positively correlated with price because of the law of diminishing returns.

4. Market-clearing equilibrium prices are achieved when the quantity willingly supplied matches the quantity willingly demanded. When the quantity demanded exceeds (falls short of) the quantity supplied, increased (decreased) relative scarcity pushes the price up (down) toward equilibrium (same convention as in concept 2).

5. Demand curves are constructed assuming that (1) income, (2) the size of the market, (3) the prices of other goods, (4) tastes, and (5) product-specific factors are *all* unchanged.

6. Supply curves are constructed assuming that (1) the costs of production, (2) technology, (3) taxes and/or subsidies, and (4) market structure are *all* unchanged.

7. Note that (1) higher (lower) incomes, (2) larger (smaller) markets, (3) increases (decreases) in the prices of substitutes, (4) reductions (increases) in the prices of complements, (5) heightened (diminished) desirability, and/or (6) improved (eroded) product quality causes demand to increase and the demand curve to shift up and out (down and in). Note as well that (1) higher (lower) costs, (2) diminished (improved) technology, (3) higher (lower) taxes on factors of production, and/or (4) lower (higher) subsidies favoring factors of production cause supply to decline and the supply curve to shift up and in (down and out). *None* of these factors directly influences *both* supply and demand simultaneously (same convention as in concept 2).

Tip on Technique One last reminder: Draw the appropriate picture when you are confronted with any kind of supply-demand problem. Even if you do it in your head, the discipline of envisioning the graph will help you keep track of what is changing and what is staying the same, first on the demand side and second on the supply side. You will find it easier to avoid errors caused by confusing changes in quantities demanded and supplied (movement along curves) with changes in demand and supply (shifts of curves).

QUIZ: Multiple Choice

1. A complete and correct definition of the demand curve for commodity X is "The demand curve for some good X shows:
(1) how much of X would be bought at the equilibrium price."
(2) how, as people's incomes rise and they have more money to spend, their purchases of X would increase and by how much."
(3) how the amount of money people spend to purchase X changes as the price they must pay for it changes."
(4) the amount of X that would be bought each period, at each and any price, assuming other factors influencing demand (income, tastes, etc.) remain constant."
(5) the amounts of X to be supplied in each period, at each and any price, assuming other factors influencing sale remain constant."

2. The law of downward-sloping demand holds that:
(1) an excess supply over demand will cause a reduction in price.
(2) people normally buy more of a commodity as their incomes rise.
(3) a demand schedule generally runs from northeast to southwest when it is illustrated graphically.
(4) the quantity willingly purchased normally increases when the price of a commodity falls.
(5) the quantity of any good purchased will ultimately decline as it goes out of style or is replaced by something of better quality.

3. One reason frequently given to explain, at least in part, the law of downward-sloping demand is:
(1) we are slightly better off when the price of something we buy falls; it is as if our incomes have risen slightly, and so we buy a little more.
(2) most commodities, over a sufficiently long period of time, tend to lose their markets in favor of newer and more attractive goods.
(3) the law of scarcity permits us to consume only so much of a commodity, no matter how much of it we may wish to have.
(4) a reduction in the price of many commodities cannot be expected to bring in very many new buyers.
(5) the producers of a given commodity are not likely to offer any quantity for sale if its price falls below some critical level.

4. The government declares that it is prepared to purchase any and all gold supplied to it by domestic gold mines at a price of $410 an ounce. Which, if any, of the four panels of Figure 4-9 would illustrate this demand situation? (The labels P and Q on the axis lines refer, respectively, to price and to quantity.)

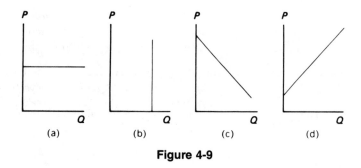

Figure 4-9

(1) *a.*
(2) *b.*
(3) *c.*
(4) *d.*
(5) None of them.

5. A patient must purchase some exact quantity of a particular drug (no more and no less) and will pay any price, if necessary, in order to obtain it. Which, if any, of the four panels of Figure 4-9 could be used to illustrate this situation?
(1) *a.*
(2) *b.*
(3) *c.*
(4) *d.*
(5) None of them.

6. I can buy sugar in a supermarket at a fixed price of 40 cents per pound. This price applies to any quantity—1 pound, 5 pounds, 100 pounds. The store is so obliging that it will even sell me fractions of a pound at the same price per pound—e.g., 20 cents for a half-pound. Which, if any, of the four panels of Figure 4-9 can be used to illustrate this supply situation?
(1) *a*.
(2) *b*.
(3) *c*.
(4) *d*.
(5) None of them.

7. An increase in consumers' money incomes prompts them to demand a greater quantity of consumer good X for *any* price. Which, if any, of the four panels of Figure 4-9 could be used to illustrate the demand side of this situation?
(1) *a*.
(2) *b*.
(3) *c*.
(4) *d*.
(5) None of them.

8. The producers of commodity X are willing to supply strictly positive quantities to a particular market. Any time they are asked to supply a larger quantity, however, they must be persuaded by the offer of a higher price. Which, if any, of the four panels of Figure 4-9 can be used as shown to illustrate this situation?
(1) *a*.
(2) *b*.
(3) *c*.
(4) *d*.
(5) None of them.

9. Which, if any, of the four panels of Figure 4-9 could illustrate the law of downward-sloping demand?
(1) *a*.
(2) *b*.
(3) *c*.
(4) *d*.
(5) None of them.

10. Suppose that the demand curve for commodity X shifts its entire position to the left (or downward). One reasonable explanation for this shift would be:
(1) the available supply of X has decreased for some reason.
(2) the price of X has increased, so people have decided to buy less of it than they did before.
(3) consumer tastes have shifted in favor of this commodity, and they want to buy more of it than they did before at any given price.
(4) the price of X has fallen, so people have decided to buy more of it than they did before.
(5) none of these events.

11. Four of the five events described below might reasonably explain why the demand curve for beef had shifted to a new position. One is not a suitable explanation. The single exception is the claim that the demand for beef had changed because of:
(1) a rise in the price of some good which consumers regard as a substitute for beef.
(2) a fall in the price of beef.
(3) an increase in the money incomes of beef consumers.
(4) a widespread advertising campaign undertaken by the producers of beef (starring Bruce Willis but not Cybil Sheppard).
(5) a change in people's tastes with respect to beef.

12. When applied to the demand for commodity X, the phrase "other things equal," or "others things constant," means that:
(1) the price of X is held constant.
(2) both buyer incomes and the price of X are held constant.
(3) buyer incomes, tastes, and the price of X are held constant.
(4) all factors that might influence the demand for X, including the price of X, are held constant.
(5) none of the above.

13. An increase in the cost of materials needed to produce commodity X causes:
(1) the demand curve to move upward (or to the right).
(2) the supply curve to move upward (or to the left).
(3) both the demand curve and the supply curve to move upward.
(4) the supply curve to move downward (or to the right).
(5) none of the above—there is no reason why this change need occasion a shift of either curve.

14. In prosperous times, the equilibrium price and quantity of some commodity X may go up simultaneously. Such a situation:
(1) is one of the few recognized exceptions to the law of downward-sloping demand.
(2) is precisely what the law of downward-sloping demand says is to be expected.
(3) is the consequence of a demand curve running from southwest to northeast.
(4) cannot be explained by means of ordinary supply-curve and demand-curve analysis.
(5) is not correctly described by any of the preceding.

15. Beef supplies are sharply reduced because of drought in the beef-raising states, and consumers turn to pork as a substitute for beef. In the beef market, these two phenomena would be described in terms of supply and demand as:
(1) a leftward (or downward) shift in the demand curve.
(2) a leftward (or upward) shift in the supply curve.
(3) a rightward (or upward) shift in the demand curve.

(4) a rightward (or downward) shift in the demand curve.
(5) both a leftward (or downward) shift in the supply curve and a leftward (or upward) shift in the demand curve.

16. Which alternative in question 15 would be correct with respect to the events described had that question referred to the pork market?
(1).
(2).
(3).
(4).
(5).

17. Let the price of a good be $5 (in a competitive market). If buyers wish to purchase 4000 units per week at that price while sellers wish to sell 5000 units per week, then:
(1) price will tend to fall below $5 and suppliers will tend to offer less than 5000 units.
(2) price will tend to rise above $5 and suppliers will tend to offer more than 5000 units.
(3) price will tend to fall below $5 and buyers will tend to buy less than 4000 units.
(4) price will tend to rise above $5 and suppliers will tend to offer less than 5000 units.
(5) something is wrong—this could not occur in a competitive market.

18. Supply curves are typically "positively sloped." The meaning conveyed by any such curve is that:
(1) any increase in costs of production will result in a higher price.
(2) the lower the price, the larger the supply that consumers are prepared to buy.
(3) the higher the price, the larger the quantity suppliers will wish to sell.
(4) the larger the quantity suppliers have to sell, the lower the price they will have to quote in order to dispose of it.
(5) none of the preceding.

SUGGESTED ANSWERS TO QUESTIONS IN THE TEXT: Chapter 4

1. Definitions.

2. Supply increasing means that the quantity supplied increases for any price. When drawn, this looks like a shift to the right (and down, since supply curves have positive slopes). Demand increasing means that the quantity demanded increases for any price. When drawn, this again looks like a shift to the right (but up, since demand curves have negative slopes).

3. Changes in prices of substitutes, income, etc., can change the demand for hamburgers. Reductions in labor costs, rent, farm products, etc., can increase the supply of hamburgers. Cheap hot dogs might reduce the demand for hamburgers. The price of hamburgers and the quantity of hamburgers should then fall as demand contracts, creating downward pressure on the wages paid to workers at McDonald's (subject to minimum-wage constraints).

4. Price too high means that the quantity supplied exceeds the quantity demanded. Inventories build, and the prices called out by suppliers fall. If the price is too low, the opposite happens.

5. **a.** The freeze should contract supply and raise the price [panel *(d)* in Figure 4-5].
b. High prices for oil lower the *quantity of oil demanded*—movement along the demand curve and not a shift in the demand curve.
c. Health concerns over meat should (1) increase demand for granola and push its price up [panel *(a)* in Figure 4-5]. It should also reduce the supply of leather, also driving that price up [panel *(d)* again].
d. To the extent that marijuana is a substitute for cocaine, its price should rise as demand expands [panel *(a)*]. The driving force is contracted supply of the substitute (?) cocaine, which should increase its price [panel *(d)*].

6. **a.** Moving *along* a supply curve [panel *(a)* in Figure 4-5]
b. Reduces price and reduces (equilibrium) quantity demanded (moving along a supply curve) [panel *(b)*]
c. Moving along a demand curve [panel *(c)*]
d. Increases price and lowers (equilibrium) quantity demanded (moving along a demand curve) [panel *(d)*]

7. **a.** Increased military spending increases the supply of boots—price change along demand curve [panel *(c)* in Figure 4-5].
b. Shift in demand as Catholics substitute for fish [panel *(b)*].
c. Price change along demand curve caused by supply curve shifting up [panel *(d)*].
d. Price change caused by some sort of supply contraction as in (3) [panel *(d)*].
e. Demand shifts *for soybeans* as the price of wheat climbs [panel *(a)*].
f. Price change (the wage is the price of labor) because supply contracted [panel *(d)*].

8. Demand stays the same. The quantity of shoes demanded falls as supply contracts [panel *(d)* in Figure 4-5]. The equilibrium price therefore climbs and quantity falls, moving along a fixed demand curve.

9. Consult Figure TQ4-1. Schedules *ss* and *dd* indicate initial supply and demand; the points listed on the table are represented explicitly on the graph. Equilibrium occurs at 20 units and a price of $6. A tripling of demand would create a new curve *d'd'* as drawn with a new equilibrium appearing at 30 units with a price of $8. Meanwhile, an initial price of $4 would create an original quantity demanded of 30 units and a new quantity demanded of 90 units. In either case, the quantity supplied would equal 10 units. There would be fights in the halls for scarce pizza, or there would be a black market for pizzas clearing at $8 (originally) and $9.33 after the demand shift.

Figure TQ4-1

CHAPTER 5

SUPPLY AND DEMAND IN INDIVIDUAL MARKETS

Before you concentrate on the new material to be presented in Chapter 5, you should make certain that you are in firm command of the material covered in Chapter 4. The foundation upon which almost all microeconomics is built was laid in that final chapter of the introduction. Unless you have mastered the basic ideas of supply and demand that were advanced there, you will have a great deal of trouble making any progress here. We begin, then, with a quick review of the Learning Objectives that were assigned in Chapter 4 of this *Guide*. Read through them carefully to determine if you have picked up enough baggage to be able to move on; they should all be more than familiar.

Paraphrased slightly, the Learning Objectives of Chapter 4 included:

1. Define supply and demand; represent each graphically.

2. Explain three forces that contribute to the usual negative slope of a demand curve; explain why the supply curve is usually positively sloped.

3. Define market-clearing price and quantity, and explain why competitive markets tend to move toward equilibrium.

4. Understand why the construction of a demand curve assumes "other things being equal": income, tastes, market size, prices of other goods, and commodity-specific factors.

5. Understand why the construction of a supply curve assumes a *different* set of "other things being equal": production costs and technology, taxes and/or subsidies, and market structure.

6. Explain how changes in these "other things" work to change market equilibrium by shifting demand *or* supply curves; show each graphically.

Should any of these notions appear foreign to you, return to Chapter 4 for some further review.

The study of microeconomics is the study of relative prices. Why are cars so expensive? Why is sand so cheap? Why is gasoline now so expensive when it used to be so cheap? Why do doctors earn so much money? Why are some athletes paid even more? Are there really 150 taxes buried in the price of a suit (as one presidential candidate claimed in 1980)? The answers to these and other questions will be found in pitting individual tastes against the scarcity of resources. They are interesting to economists in their own right, but they also contribute to our understanding of macroeconomics, our understanding of the distribution of income, our understanding of the sources of judgmental tradeoffs between, for example, equity and efficiency, and much more. These understandings are the goals of our study of microeconomics.

Chapter 5 begins that study by covering two major topics: (1) the effects of changes in supply and demand and (2) the price elasticities of supply and demand. Applications of both are presented through a set of examples ranging from simple supply shocks to the equity-efficiency tradeoff in designing a tax structure. When you have completed this chapter, you should have mastered the following new objectives.

54 5 Supply and Demand in Individual Markets

LEARNING OBJECTIVES

1. Define the price elasticity of demand, and indicate how to compute its numerical coefficient.

2. Relate differences in the value of the price elasticity of demand to (1) differences in the character of various goods (necessities vs. luxuries, e.g.) and (2) differences in the direction of change in total revenue as quantity increases along a demand curve.

3. Define elastic demand, inelastic demand, and unitary demand elasticity, and relate each to the sensitivity of total revenue to changes in quantity.

4. Define the price elasticity of supply. Relate the notions of momentary equilibrium, short-run equilibrium, and long-run equilibrium to the price elasticity of supply, noting in particular that supply becomes more elastic as the time period being considered expands.

5. Explain the difference between changes in demand and changes in the quantity demanded. Tell what causes each.

6. Delineate, with the help of graphs, the effect on market equilibrium of changes in supply, demand, and/or both. Understand how to apply this skill in analyzing changes in market conditions, changes in government policy, the effects of alternate policies, etc.

7. Relate the concept of time to both the price elasticity of demand and the price elasticity of supply.

The first major topic in this chapter is one that was introduced in Chapter 4: changes in demand or supply. Price is one important factor influencing the quantity of good X that will be bought, but it is by no means the only influencing factor. Other factors include the level of consumer incomes, consumer tastes or preferences, and the prices at which goods competing with X are selling. The demand curve for X does not ignore these other factors; it assumes that they are held constant. If any of these factors changes, then the demand curve must be redrawn in an appropriate new position. If consumer incomes rise, for example, it is likely that the demand curve for X will shift to the right (or upward), as in Figure 5-1. This is just a particular way of saying that consumers will want to buy more of good X at every price if they have more spendable income. And what happens? For the circumstance depicted in Figure 5-1, the market-clearing quantity bought and sold rises from 0A to 0B, and the price goes up.

Figure 5-2, drawn alongside Figure 5-1, shows a different circumstance. It displays a change in the equilibrium position, to be sure. Purchases have again risen from 0A to 0B, but price has fallen instead of rising. Why? Because this second change was initiated by a shift of the supply curve. In summary, then:

▶ Figure 5-1 illustrates an increase in demand—a shift of the entire demand curve to a new position—and shows equilibrium price and quantity rising simultaneously.

▶ Figure 5-2 illustrates an increase in the equilibrium quantity demanded—a movement along a demand curve from one point thereon to another—caused by an increase in supply. The position of the demand curve has not changed, and the equilibrium price has declined.

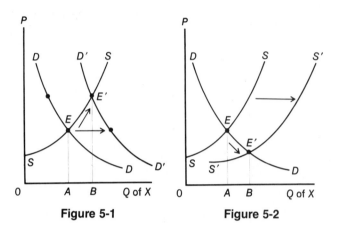

Figure 5-1   Figure 5-2

The phrases "increase in demand" and "increase in quantity demanded" have significantly different meanings. An increase in demand (Figure 5-1) occurs when some factor other than the price of good X changes, causing buyers to change their decisions; the entire demand curve shifts. An increase in quantity demanded (Figure 5-2) occurs when more of X is bought because its price fell. (The price fell because some background factor caused the supply curve to shift in position.)

1. a. A change in quantity demanded means precisely (circle one):

(1) a change in the schedule of quantities that producers will offer for sale at each and any possible price caused by some change in background conditions.

(2) a change in the particular quantity of some good which producers offer for sale caused by a change in the market price of that good.

(3) a change in the particular quantity of some good which consumers buy caused by a change in the market price of that good.

(4) a change in the schedule of quantities that consumers will buy at each and any possible market price caused by some change in background conditions.

b. Which alternative in part **a** properly describes a change in supply? .... (1 / 2 / 3 / 4)

c. Which alternative properly describes a change in demand? .... (1 / 2 / 3 / 4)

d. Which alternative properly describes a change in quantity supplied? .... (1 / 2 / 3 / 4)

---

a. (3)   **b.** 1   **c.** 4   **d.** 2

2. a. As already noted, Figure 5-1 illustrates an increase in demand. This figure also illustrates an *(increase in supply / increase in quantity supplied)*.

Barring the exceptional case of a perfectly flat supply curve, this increase in demand will *(always / sometimes / never)* set off a price increase. Notice that the increase in quantity supplied in Figure 5-1 does not bring about any price reduction. It is just the supplier response to a higher price. As long as there is some slope to the supply curve (i.e., as long as a higher price elicits a larger quantity supplied), the price increase set off by the increase in demand is smaller than it would otherwise have been.

b. By way of contrast, Figure 5-2 depicts an increase in quantity demanded. This increase came about only because of an *(increase in supply / increase in quantity supplied)*. Such an increase in quantity demanded *(will always / might / would never)* be the reason for a price increase. It is simply the buyer response to a lower price. This difference in the effect upon price in large part explains why all the tedious distinction between the two kinds of increases and decreases is necessary.

c. An example framed in terms of quantity reduction can cement this distinction. Suppose, for the sake of illustration, that the production of good X is disrupted by lengthy strikes. The supply quantity available is greatly reduced, and the price rises as a result. This would be an instance of *(a decrease / an increase)* in *(quantity supplied / supply)*, followed by *(a decrease / an increase)* in *(quantity demanded / demand)*. The price rise would have been set off by the decrease in *(demand / supply)*, and not by the decrease in quantity *(demanded / supplied)*.

---

a. increase in quantity supplied; always **b.** increase in supply; would never **c.** a decrease; supply; a decrease; quantity demanded; supply; demanded

---

The concept of **price elasticity** was devised to indicate the degree to which quantity demanded (or supplied) would respond to any price change. Compare the two demand curves D_1D_1 and D_2D_2 drawn *to the same scale* in Figure 5-3; they are drawn there to reflect two potential demand curves for the same good X. Both curves satisfy the ordinary "law of demand," which is that any price reduction should produce an increase in the quantity demanded and purchased. D_2D_2 is the more elastic of the two, though, because the quantity demanded is more responsive to any change in price. Why? Notice that if the price were to fall from p_a to p_b, for example, then the quantity demanded would grow by a larger amount along the D_2D_2 curve; if the price were to rise from p_a to p_c, on the other hand, the quantity would shrink further along D_2D_2. In either direction, therefore, quantity is more responsive to changes in price—more price-elastic—along D_2D_2.

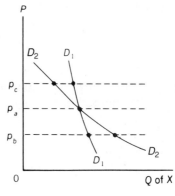

Figure 5-3

3. a. If we say that "demand in this situation is highly price-elastic," we mean that any price reduction would produce a relatively *(large / small) (decrease / increase)* in purchases and that a price rise would yield a relatively *(large / small) (decrease / increase)* in buying.

b. To describe supply as "decidedly price-inelastic" would mean that any price increase would call out a relatively *(large / small) (increase / decrease)* in quantity offered for sale and that any price reduction would produce a relatively *(large / small) (increase / decrease)* in the quantity supplied.

---

a. large; increase; large; decrease **b.** small; increase; small; decrease

---

Terms like "highly elastic" or "decidedly inelastic" are imprecise. The task now is to give a more exact meaning to elasticity. The text defines the price elasticity of demand as

$$E_D = \frac{\% \text{ change in quantity demanded}}{\% \text{ change in price}}$$

The sign of this expression is assumed to be positive by convention. Given this numerical expression, three different possibilities emerge:

$E_D > 1$, representing elastic demand

$E_D = 1$, representing unitary elasticity

$E_D < 1$, representing inelastic demand

The importance of the distinction between these three cases will become increasingly clear as you progress through your study of economics. Your first introduction to this importance comes in the linkage between the price elasticity of demand and the sensitivity of revenue to changes in the price. If the price of some good were to increase by 10 percent, for example, revenue generated by its sale could go up, remain the same, or go down depending upon whether demand were inelastic, displayed unitary elasticity, or were elastic (respectively). To see why, take each case one at a time:

1. If demand were price-elastic, then the 10 percent increase in the price would have to be associated with a reduction in the quantity demanded of more than 10 percent to get a number greater than 1 out of the elasticity formula. That would mean that quantity would be falling faster than price was rising, and revenue would fall (recall that revenue is simply price times quantity).

2. If demand displayed unitary price elasticity, then the 10 percent increase in the price would be matched by a 10 percent reduction in the quantity demanded to get 1 out of the elasticity formula. That would mean that revenue would remain exactly the same.

3. If demand were price-inelastic, then the 10 percent increase in the price would have to be associated with a reduction in the quantity demanded of less than 10 percent to get a number less than 1 out of the elasticity formula. That would mean that revenue would actually rise with the price.

The text defines the price elasticity of supply in a like manner:

$$E_S = \frac{\% \text{ change in quantity supplied}}{\% \text{ change in price}}$$

No adjustment in sign is required, in this case, because increases in prices are always matched with increases in quantities supplied along the usual upward-sloping supply curve. The same differentiation between elastic, unitary, and inelastic supply can be made, but the demand-side connection to revenue is not valid. The next set of questions will explore and illustrate these points.

4. Table 5-1 shows demand for some commodity at prices from $10 to $1. Use these figures to draw a demand curve in the upper part of Figure 5-4.

Table 5-1

Price	Quantity	Revenue	Price	Quantity	Revenue
$10	0	____	$5	20	____
9	4	____	4	24	____
8	8	____	3	28	____
7	12	____	2	32	____
6	16	____	1	36	____

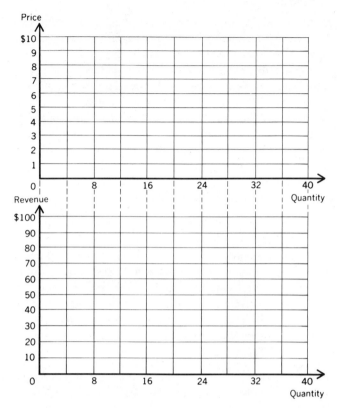

Figure 5-4

A certain amount of revenue received by suppliers (i.e., expenditure by buyers) will be associated with each possible quantity bought (and hence with each possible price). If price were $9 so that 4 units would be purchased, for example, then revenue would equal $36. Show the proper revenue amounts in the 10 blanks noted in Table 5-1. Then complete the lower part of Figure 5-4 to show the quantity-revenue relationship (e.g., with quantity 4, revenue is $36, etc.).

Table columns: $0, $36 (= $9 × 4), $64, $84, $96; $100, $96, $84, $64, $36 [The demand curve is a straight line from (Q = 0, P = 10) through (Q = 40, P = 0); the revenue curve is a parabola peaking at (Q = 20, Rev = 100) and equaling zero at both Q = 0 and Q = 40.]

5. a. Notice the interesting behavior of the revenue curve as you move down the length of the straight-line demand curve that you should have drawn on the top panel of Figure 5-4. As price falls, revenue (pick one):

(1) remains the same at all quantities.

(2) falls throughout the entire price range.

(3) rises first, reaches a peak, and then falls.

(4) falls first, reaches a minimum, and then climbs.

b. If the price fell from $7 to $6, then total revenue would (*rise / stay the same / fall*). How is this possible when the lower price meant that each unit that was purchased at $7 would now be purchased at $6? For the 12 units demanded at $7, in fact, lowering the price by $1 would result in $12 less revenue being collected. The key to the mystery is, of course, found in the observation that the lower price means that a larger quantity is demanded and thus sold. Only one question remains: Is the revenue collected from the sale of these extra units enough to overcome the initial loss just noted? Sixteen units would be demanded if the price were $6—an increase in the quantity demanded of _____ units, bringing in an additional $_____ in revenue. In this case, the increase in revenue generated by selling more units *(would be / would not be)* enough to offset the initial loss.

Now suppose that the price fell from $4 to $3. Selling the _____ units demanded at $4 for a dollar less would result in a revenue loss of $_____. The associated increase in the quantity demanded of _____ units would meanwhile bring a counterbalancing revenue gain of $_____. The loss would *(outweigh / exactly balance / fall short of)* the gain, and total revenue would *(fall / stay the same / increase)*.

a. (3) b. rise; 4; 24 (= 4 × $6); would be; 24; 24 (= 24 × $1); 4 (= 28 − 24); 12 (= 4 × $3); outweigh; fall

6. "Price elasticity" means the responsiveness, or "stretch," of quantity to any given price change. We can reach a more explicit statement of what demand elasticity means with respect to price just by using the phenomenon noted in question 4—that revenue may, for a given price change, go up, go down, or remain constant.

If there is enough "stretch" in quantity demanded when price goes down to cause revenue to go up, then we designate this section of the demand curve as *elastic* (or as priceelastic). If revenue stays constant, it displays *unitary elasticity*. If revenue falls, it is *inelastic*. This means the demand curve of question 4 is elastic for prices from $_____ to $_____ and inelastic for prices from $_____ to $_____ .

10; 5; 5; 0

7. Put (E) for price elastic, (U) for unitary elastic, or (I) for price inelastic in the parentheses below according to which term most accurately describes each demand situation:

a. Price falls from $6 to $5 and revenue falls from $60 to $55. . . . . ( )

b. Price falls from $6 to $5 and revenue stays the same. . . . . ( )

c. Price climbs from $5 to $6 and quantity purchased falls from 80 to 60. . . . . ( )

d. Price drops from $6 to $5 and there is no increase in quantity demanded. . . . . ( )

e. Price climbs from $300 to $301 and there is no reduction in quantity demanded. . . . . ( )

f. Price climbs and revenue climbs by $10. . . . . . . ( )

g. Price climbs from $5.00 to $5.01 and people stop buying the stuff completely. . . . . ( )

a. I (The price reduction does not create enough of a quantity increase to keep revenue from falling.) **b.** U (The price reduction creates just enough of a quantity increase to maintain revenue.) **c.** E (Revenue falls from $400 to $360; the quantity reduction must have been larger, in percentage terms, than the price increase.) **d.** I (This is perfectly inelastic demand.) **e.** I (same) **f.** I (Price increase, quantity reduction, but revenue still climbs.) **g.** E (This is perhaps perfectly elastic demand.)

8. Instructors in economics always illustrate inelastic demand on the blackboard by means of a steeply sloping (nearvertical) line. Question 6 shows that this method of illustration can be quite deceptive. No straight-line demand curve has a uniform elasticity, but the demand curve constructed in question 4 always reported the same "responsiveness" to each $1 price change: an increase (or decrease) of 4 in quantity demanded. In percentage terms, however, the drop in price from $10 to $9 was *(far more / much less)* drastic than the drop from $2 to $1; the latter reduction cut the price in half. That is why the elasticity of this demand curve is different in different regions. It is, in fact, different at every point.

To be more precise, note that any straight-line demand curve with some slope to it, no matter how steep, will always display a section in which the quantity demanded is elastic with respect to price (i.e., $E_D > 1$). All you need to do is move *(up / down)* the curve to a price that is sufficiently *(high / low)*. You can always find a region that is inelastic, too. Finally, there is always one point where the price elasticity of demand is unity. (Convince yourself that the point of unitary elasticity is always the midpoint of the line.)

much less; up; high

We can compute the **price elasticity coefficient** by (*a*) putting the quantity change in percentage terms, (*b*) putting the price change in percentage terms, and (*c*) forming the quotient of these two changes. When we do this between two points on a demand or supply curve, however, the denominator of the percentagechange calculations is ambiguous. The text suggests using averages as the basis of the computations of percentage changes. Suppose, for example, that you are interested in the price elasticity of demand between two points on a demand curve: (Q_1, P_1) and (Q_2, P_2). The price elasticity of demand could then be computed according to

$$E_D = \frac{\{(Q_2 - Q_1)/[(Q_2 + Q_1)/2]\} \times 100\%}{\{(P_2 - P_1)/[(P_2 + P_1)/2]\} \times 100\%}$$

The numerator here represents the change in quantity from Q_1 to Q_2 as a percentage of the *average* of Q_1 and Q_2. The denominator represents the change in price from P_1 to P_2 as the *average* of P_1 and P_2. And, of course, the 100 percent factors cancel.

9. a. Using question 4 data, compute price elasticity coefficients between the prices indicated below.

(1) Between price $8 and price $7 . . . . _____

(2) Between price $5 and price $4 . . . . _____

(3) Between price $3 and price $2 . . . . _____

b. This elasticity-coefficient idea is just an extension of the three-way system of division outlined in the section preceding question 4. For example, in the unit-elastic case, the two percentage changes cancel one another out—they must be equal. This makes the elasticity-coefficient figure *(1 / greater than 1 / less than 1)*. In the price-elastic case, the price elasticity coefficient must be *(1 / greater than 1 / less than 1)* so that the percentage change in quantity is *(greater than / equal to / less than)* the percentage change in price. In the inelastic case, the elasticity coefficient must be *(1 / greater than 1 / less than 1)* for the *(opposite / same)* reason.

a. (1) $\frac{(12-8)/[(12+8)/2]}{-(7-8)/[(7+8)/2]} = \frac{4/10}{1/7.5} = \frac{4 \times 7.5}{10} = 3$

(2) $\frac{4/18}{1/4.5} = \frac{4 \times 4.5}{18} = 1$

(3) $\frac{4/30}{1/2.5} = \frac{4 \times 2.5}{30} = 0.33$

b. 1; greater than 1; greater than; less than 1; opposite

10. a. A *perfectly elastic* demand curve is depicted as a horizontal line. Such a line illustrates the ultimate in elasticity (i.e., "infinite elasticity") because it means that (pick one):

(1) no matter what the change in price might be, within the range of prices indicated by the length of this line, there would be no response in quantity purchased.

(2) the slightest increase in price above the level at which this horizontal line runs would cause purchases to fall all the way to zero.

b. *Perfectly inelastic* demand signifies a vertical line, or zero elasticity. Which alternative above correctly indicates why such a demand curve would represent the ultimate in inelasticity? . . . . *(1 / 2 / neither)*

Notice that the two extreme cases of perfectly elastic and perfectly inelastic demand constitute exceptions to the point made in question 8. When a demand curve is illustrated as perfectly horizontal or perfectly vertical, the slope of that line does tell you what the elasticity of the demand curve is.

c. A demand curve with unitary elasticity everywhere along its length *(can / cannot)* be a straight line. It is characterized instead in terms of revenue, linking price and quantity numbers such that total revenue must be *(always rising as the price climbs / always constant regardless of price / always falling as the price climbs)*. It is shaped like a rectangular hyperbola (remember your geometry from high school?).

a. (2) **b.** 1 **c.** cannot; always constant regardless of price

The idea of responsiveness to a price change applies just as easily to supply as it does to demand. In dealing with supply, however, we cannot use the association of elasticity to revenue. Why? Because the revenue asked by suppliers moving along a supply curve almost never has the "either-direction" character of the revenue paid by consumers moving along a demand curve. Along a conventional supply schedule, a higher price always means a higher quantity and thus more revenue. Nevertheless, we can use the same elasticity-coefficient ("responsiveness") notion already developed for demand; recall that

$$E_S = \frac{\text{percentage change in quantity supplied}}{\text{percentage change in price}}$$

11. a. Perfectly inelastic supply would be represented by a *(vertical / horizontal)* line, and perfectly elastic supply by a *(vertical / horizontal)* line.

b. Perfectly elastic supply appears as a *(vertical / horizontal)* line because that indicates the "ultimate" in responsiveness. It indicates simply a particular price; it says that any desired quantity is available at that price; it says that if price were to drop even slightly below this level, quantity supplied would *(fall to zero / become infinitely large)*.

When you enter a supermarket and find you can buy as little or as much as you wish of any given item at its fixed price, in effect you are facing a perfectly elastic supply curve.

a. vertical; horizontal **b.** horizontal; fall to zero

If there should be an increase in demand, price will rise, and suppliers will want to increase their supply offers. The extent to which they can do so depends on the amount of time they are given in which to increase production.

12. a. If an increase in demand were sudden and suppliers had no reserve inventories on hand, then no greater quantity could be offered immediately, despite the price rise. If so, the supply curve would have to be shown as *(perfectly* *elastic / perfectly inelastic)*. This is what economists refer to as the new *(long-run / short-run / momentary)* equilibrium.

b. Given a little time, suppliers could adjust to a demand surge by working their plant and equipment harder (e.g., by adding an extra shift of workers). The result of this increase in supply quantity would be the new *(long-run / short-run / momentary)* equilibrium.

c. If the shift in demand were sustained, then existing and potential new suppliers would have even more time to build new plants and install new equipment. There would be a further increase in the quantity offered in supply. Finally, therefore, an equilibrium price that indicates *(long-run / momentary / short-run)* equilibrium may be reached.

d. Note carefully that all this is just a statement about price elasticity of supply. It says that the degree of responsiveness of supply to a price change will depend on the amount of adjustment time suppliers can have. The longer this time period, the *(higher / lower)* will be the price elasticity (the elasticity coefficient) of supply. The same kind of dependence of elasticity on time *(can / cannot)* be made for the demand side.

---

a. perfectly inelastic; momentary **b.** short-run **c.** long-run **d.** higher; can

---

The concept of market equilibrium was introduced in Chapter 4. A price-quantity pair represents an equilibrium situation if the quantity supplied at the specified price exactly matches the quantity demanded at that price. Markets tend to move toward these equilibria all by themselves. Excess supplies caused by excessively high prices tend to lead suppliers to cut their prices in an effort to liquidate their surpluses; this tendency constitutes automatic pressure on the prices to move down toward an equilibrium when they are too high. Shortages caused by bargain prices tend to lead suppliers to hike their prices to take advantage of the high levels of excess demand; this tendency constitutes the opposite pressure on prices to move up toward equilibrium when they are too low.

Comparisons of market equilibria are therefore appropriate analytical tools with which to trace the effects of various changes in any given market. If markets tend toward equilibrium all by themselves, then we can get a fair idea of the impact of some change in, say, the demand schedule by tracing what happens to market equilibrium. If, to continue the example, higher demand meant that the equilibrium price rose, then we could conclude that higher demand would begin to push the price upward as soon as demand conditions changed.

The methodology based on this type of reasoning is called **comparative statics**. It is the method through which many economic investigations are conducted; it is, in fact, the method employed in applications of supply-and-demand analysis that occupy the latter portion of Chapter 5.

When you are asked to trace the effect of some sort of demand or supply adjustment, you are being asked to do some comparative statics of your own. You should not, in this effort, hesitate to use the graphical tools that you know. First draw a typical supply-and-demand graph and identify the equilibrium intersection. Then ask yourself whether the adjustment to be studied affects the demand side or the supply side of the market. Few factors affect both sides simultaneously, so there should be one answer to this question. Decide whether the required adjustment is out (up) or in (down), and draw a new schedule in the appropriate position. Find the new equilibrium and you are finished. Comparing the new equilibrium with the old, you can read directly from the graph the direction of the effect you were asked to analyze. Playing around with the shapes of the supply and demand curves that you drew, you can even uncover the sensitivity of the result to supply-and-demand elasticities.

13. a. Plot the following supply schedule in the upper part of Figure 5-4 (question 4), using the Q_1 supply figures in Table 5-2. (The Q_2 fill-in blanks are for part *b* of this question.)

Table 5-2

P	$ 1	$ 2	$ 3	$ 4	$ 5
Q_1	0	12	20	24	26
Q_2	___	___	___	___	___
P	$ 6	$ 7	$ 8	$ 9	$10
Q_1	28	29	30	31	32
Q_2	___	___	___	___	___

With the demand curve previously drawn, the equilibrium price indicated is $*(3 / 4 / 5 / 6)*.

b. A tax of $1 per unit sold is now levied on the suppliers of this commodity. *Note:* Such a tax is an increase of $1 in the cost per unit, so the suppliers will now sell only at $5 the particular quantity they were formerly willing to sell at $4. Enter the new supply-schedule figures in the Q_2 rows of Table 5-2, then graph the new supply curve in Figure 5-4. Make it a broken or dotted line or draw it in a different color so that you can distinguish this after-tax supply schedule from the pre-tax schedule previously drawn.

c. The new equilibrium price will be approximately $*(3.00 / 3.10 / 3.60 / 4.00 / 4.50)*. The price received by suppliers is $*(2.00 / 3.10 / 3.50 / 4.50)*.

---

a. 4 **b.** table rows: 0, 0, 12, 20, 24; 26, 28, 29, 30, 31 **c.** 4.50; 3.50 (= price − tax = $4.50 − $1.00)

The question of the incidence of a tax, like the one posed in question 13, is interesting because it shows that the greater portion of a tax may be paid by either buyers or sellers. The first thing to recognize in your study of such taxes is that their imposition can be modeled as a simple change in supply. A sales or production tax can be seen as reducing the quantity that suppliers willingly offer at any given price (assuming some nonzero price elasticity of supply)—i.e., as a leftward shift in the supply curve like the one you just drew. [For the $1 tax of question 13, you produced the Q_2 values by picking a price (say, $3), noting that the supplier would receive $1 less than that price after the tax was paid (say, $2), recording the quantity that the supplier would deliver at that *after-tax* price (12 units for $2 = $3 − $1). The point (12,$3) is thus on the after-tax supply curve.

Alternatively, the tax may be viewed as increasing the price required to induce suppliers to produce the same quantity—an equivalent upward shift in the supply curve. [Before the tax, the supplier in question 13 facing a $2 price would willingly produce 12 units. To continue to produce 12 units after the $1 tax, the supplier must continue to receive $2 after the tax is paid. The price paid by consumers must, in other words, be $3 if the supplier is to maintain output. The point (12, $3) is still on the after-tax supply curve.] In either view, the intuition behind the shift in the supply schedule is simple: if suppliers don't get the full price that they require for their product, then they won't produce the full amount.

14. a. In the case of a per unit commodity tax of the sort imposed on the market in question 13, the degree to which the price paid by consumers increases in response to the tax depends upon the shapes of the supply and demand curves. Which of the following circumstances (circle one or more) would make it likely that the price paid by consumers would increase by a large proportion (> 50%) of the tax?

(1) Highly price-elastic demand.

(2) Highly price-inelastic demand.

(3) Highly price-elastic supply.

(4) Highly price-inelastic supply.

The price received by suppliers in this case would *(fall significantly / fall slightly / necessarily remain the same)*.

b. Which alternative(s) in part **a** (select one or more) would leave the after-tax price paid by consumers closer to the pre-tax price? _____ The price received by suppliers would *(fall by almost the full value of the tax / fall slightly / necessarily remain the same)*.

---

a. (2) and (3) ; fall slightly (Draw some graphs with, e.g., identical supply shifts measured against price-elastic demand, on the one hand, and price-inelastic demand, on the other. The market-clearing price will increase more with the inelastic demand. Repeat the process with price-elastic and -inelastic supply.)
b. (1) and (4); fall by almost the full value of the tax

---

15. The various panels of Figure 5-5 display some possible illustrations of comparative static exercises in the market for apartments. In each case, *DD* represents an initial demand curve, *SS* represents an initial supply curve, *E* represents an initial equilibrium, and *E'* represents a new equilibrium supported by either a new supply curve *S'S'* or a new demand curve *D'D'*. For each of the following, indicate in the parentheses provided which panel most accurately reflects the indicated change in the market for apartments:

a. A residence tax to be added to the rent ...... (   )

b. A fire that reduces the quantity of available apartment units .... (   )

c. A major transfer of residents to new jobs in another area .... (   )

d. Rent control that prevented rents from rising to their equilibrium levels .... (   )

e. An increase in the incomes of the residents ... (   )

---

a. *c* (See incidence coverage above.)   **b.** *c* (simple reduction in supply)   **c.** *b* (simple reduction in demand)   **d.** *d* (equilibrium read from supply curve)   **e.** *a* (simple reduction in demand)

---

16. Necessities tend to be the types of goods that are relatively price-inelastically demanded; they are needed regardless of the price (within reason), and so the quantity demanded *(is / is not)* terribly sensitive to changes in the price. The purchase of necessities also tends to exhaust a higher percentage of the income earned by families on the lower end of the income scale. Luxury goods tend to be the opposite; they can be forgone easily if the price climbs and are therefore usually *(elastically / inelastically)* demanded. Look at the two demand curves in Figure 5-6; the curve in panel *(a / b)* portrays a demand schedule that shows that good *(X / Y)* should be thought of as a necessity in the vicinity of a $10 price. Let supply be perfectly elastic at a price of $10. Draw the appropriate supply curve in both panels of Figure 5-6; it should be *(horizontal at P = $10 / sloped upward through point A / sloped downward through point A)*.

Now suppose that the government wants to raise as much money as possible by placing a $2 tax on one of the two

5 Supply and Demand in Individual Markets 61

Figure 5-5

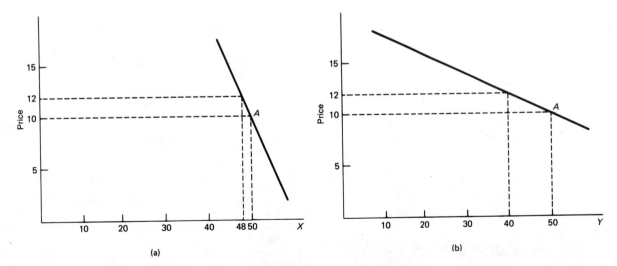

Figure 5-6

goods. The tax would raise $_____ in tax revenue if it were applied to good X and $_____ in revenue if it were applied to good Y. This is because (X / Y) is more inelastically demanded at $P = \$10$ and the $2 increase in the price causes a (smaller / larger) reduction in the quantity demanded. Were the government to pursue a program of taxing X instead of Y, would this be a more equitable policy? _____ Why or why not? _____

_____

_____

is not; elastically; a; X; horizontal at $P = \$10$; 96 (48 units of X still demanded with $2 tax means that tax revenue = 48 × $2 = $96.); 80 (40 units of Y demanded after the tax means that tax revenue = 40 × $2 = $80.); X; smaller; no; The efficiency of taxing necessities with low price elasticities causes low-income families to spend a higher proportion of their incomes paying the tax than high-income families would spend.

17. Consider Figure 5-7. The equilibrium price for X is $_____ and the equilibrium quantity is _____ units. Were the government to want to restrict consumption to 500 units, it could exercise a number of policy options. It could, first of all, impose a price (ceiling / floor) of $_____ ; the quantity demanded would then be _____ units, but the quantity supplied would be _____ units. A (shortage / surplus) of _____ units would result in the short run, but suppliers would quickly catch on that the production level was unsustainable. They would, therefore, lower their output to 500 units, where the price they received would exceed the price required to get them to supply 500 units by $_____ . Alternatively, the government could set a production quota at 500 units, and suppliers would receive a price of $_____ for every unit that they sold. Finally, the government could issue ration tickets and announce that one ticket and no more than $5 would be required to purchase 1 unit of X. If the tickets could be bought and sold, they would command a price of $_____ Why? _____

_____

_____

_____

7; 750; floor; 9; 500; 1000; surplus; 500; 4; 9; 4; They would assume a value equal to the difference between what people would be willing to pay for X and what they were allowed to pay.

18. Examine Figure 5-8. It shows demand and supply curves for wheat for different years. Fill in Table 5-3 with the required price and quantity data as well as the identification of the supporting supply and demand curves; row 1 is completed to illustrate the procedure.

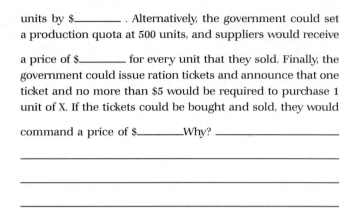

Figure 5-8

Table 5-3

Year	Price	Quantity	Demand Curve	Supply Curve
1980	$2	500	DD(1980)	SS(1980)
1985				
1990				
1995				
2000				

Figure 5-7

Plot the price and quantity data that you recorded in the table on Figure 5-9, label the points by year, and connect them. You have plotted a line that *(slopes upward / is horizontal / slopes downward)*. Is it a supply curve or a demand curve? _____ Why? _____
_____
_____
_____

Figure 5-9

Table rows: 1985—$2, 1000, *DD*(1985), *SS*(1985); 1990—$2, 1500, *DD*(1990), *SS*(1990); 1995—$2, 2000, *DD*(1995), *SS*(1995); 2000—$2, 2500, *DD*(2000), *SS*(2000); is horizontal; neither; It collects the intersections of many different supply and demand curves, not points along any one supply or demand curve. (Note your identification of demand and supply curves in the two rightmost columns of the table in Fig. 5-9.) The intersections would have represented a supply curve only if the supply schedule had remained fixed from 1980 through 2000; they would have represented a demand curve only if demand had been unchanged. They would have been one point if both had been constant

REVIEW CONCEPTS

1. The price elasticity of demand is defined as the ratio of a *percentage* change in the quantity demanded with respect to an underlying *percentage* change in the price. Notationally,

$$E_D = \frac{\Delta Q/Q}{\Delta P/P} = \frac{\Delta Q}{\Delta P} \cdot \frac{P}{Q}$$

Necessities tend to have low elasticities; luxuries, high elasticities.

2. Revenue is related to changes in price through the price elasticity of demand. A higher price will cause revenue to climb, fall, or stay the same if $E_D < 1, E_D > 1,$ or $E_D = 1$, respectively; i.e., if demand is inelastic, is elastic, or displays unitary elasticity.

3. The price elasticity of supply is the ratio of a *percentage* change in the quantity supplied with respect to an underlying *percentage* change in price. It rises with the length of time.

4. The quantity demanded of some good X changes with its price. Demand changes with tastes, prices of other goods, income, and the size of a market. The quantity supplied of some good X changes with its price. Supply changes with technology, input prices, and other production-specific factors.

5. Market equilibrium occurs at a price where the quantity willingly demanded exactly equals the quantity willingly supplied. Government action can change the equilibrium by changing demand and/or supply.

QUIZ: Multiple Choice

1. Consumers have budgeted a fixed money amount to buy a certain commodity. Within a certain range of prices, they will spend neither more nor less than this amount of money on this commodity. Their demand in this price range would properly be designated as:
(1) in equilibrium.
(2) perfectly elastic.
(3) perfectly inelastic.
(4) highly inelastic, but not perfectly so.
(5) unit-elastic.

2. The price elasticity of demand equals:
(1) amount of price decrease divided by amount of quantity increase.
(2) percentage change in revenue divided by percentage decrease in price.
(3) percentage change in revenue divided by percentage increase in quantity demanded.
(4) percentage change in quantity demanded divided by percentage change in price.
(5) none of the above.

3. When the words "total revenue" are used in any discussion of demand curves, their meaning is:
(1) the profit, after deduction of costs, which the suppliers of the commodity involved earn from selling it to consumers.
(2) the total amount of money consumers will spend on the commodity at any particular price.
(3) the income suppliers will receive from sales if they sell the quantity they hope to sell.
(4) the quantity of the commodity that is associated with any particular price.
(5) null; the words "total revenue" cannot have any meaning in relation to demand curves.

4. The concepts of "momentary," "short-run," and "long-run" supply curves were intended to bring out which fact?
(1) Over a long period of time, gradual increases in skill and/or improvements in the art of production tend to bring down the price of any commodity.
(2) Price increases as the cost of transport to any given market increases.
(3) The extent to which quantity supplied will respond to a given price or demand change depends on the amount of time given to producers to adjust their operations to this change.
(4) In order to make the supply-curve idea meaningful, it is necessary to speak of the quantity that will be supplied per period of time.
(5) Although demand may exert some short-run influence, ultimately the price of any commodity must always be determined by the cost of its production.

5. As the result of an increase in family income in a certain community, purchases of butter rise from 1000 pounds daily to 1500 pounds daily. As a further result, the price of butter per pound rises from $1.25 to $1.50. This behavior:
(1) cannot be explained by the demand-curve-and-supply-curve analysis of price determination.
(2) represents a movement by consumers upward along their demand curve to a point of higher price and greater quantity.
(3) must be explained as a shift in the supply curve.
(4) represents a movement of price and quantity to a position above the equilibrium level.
(5) must be represented by a shift in the demand curve to a different and higher position.

6. If a 10 percent reduction in a commodity's price brings a 5 percent increase in the amount of money people spend to buy that commodity, then in this region of the demand curve, demand is (with respect to price):
(1) elastic.
(2) unit-elastic.
(3) inelastic, although not perfectly so.
(4) perfectly inelastic.
(5) perhaps any of these—the information given is insufficient to determine elasticity.

7. Which alternative in question 6 would have been correct if the 10 percent reduction in price had caused a 5 percent increase in the quantity of the commodity that people buy?
(1).
(2).
(3).
(4).
(5).

8. If I can buy any quantity I please of a commodity at a fixed price, this means that the supply curve which confronts me is:
(1) perfectly inelastic.
(2) perfectly elastic.
(3) unit-elastic.
(4) elastic, but not necessarily perfectly elastic.
(5) none of these things, necessarily.

9. The government levies an excise tax of 5 cents per unit sold on the sellers in a competitive industry. Both supply and demand curves have some elasticity with respect to price. When this tax is represented on the supply-and-demand diagram:
(1) the entire supply curve shifts leftward by an amount indicating 5 cents, but (unless demand is perfectly elastic) price will not rise.
(2) the entire supply curve shifts upward by an amount indicating less than 5 cents, but (unless demand is highly elastic) price will rise by the full 5 cents.
(3) the entire supply curve shifts leftward by an amount indicating something less than 5 cents.
(4) the entire supply curve shifts upward by an amount indicating 5 cents, but (unless supply is perfectly elastic) any price rise will be less than 5 cents.
(5) the entire demand curve shifts upward by an amount indicating 5 cents, and price will rise by exactly 5 cents.

10. The change brought about by the tax levy described in question 9 could be described as:
(1) a decrease in supply followed by a decrease in quantity demanded.
(2) a decrease in quantity supplied followed by a decrease in quantity demanded.
(3) a decrease in supply followed by a decrease in demand.
(4) a decrease in quantity supplied followed by a decrease in demand.
(5) none of the above.

11. A perfectly inelastic supply curve would be shown in the ordinary supply-and-demand graph as:
(1) a vertical line.
(2) a horizontal line.
(3) a straight line, but neither horizontal nor vertical.
(4) a curved line.
(5) perhaps any of the above.

12. Which alternative in question 11 would be correct for the graphical portrayal of a perfectly inelastic demand curve?
(1).
(2).
(3).
(4).
(5).

13. A change in quantity demanded, as distinct from a change in demand, means:
(1) that buyers have decided to buy more (or less) than they did before, at every price including the existing price.

(2) that the elasticity of demand with respect to price has increased or decreased.
(3) simply that the quantity of purchases has changed, regardless of the factor which brought about this change in buying.
(4) that the market price has fallen or risen, and buyers have changed their total purchases accordingly.
(5) that there is an increase in total purchases, but not a decrease.

14. Which alternative in question 13 would be correct for a change in demand rather than a change in the quantity demanded?
(1).
(2).
(3).
(4).
(5).

15. Following the OPEC price rise, consumers of gasoline and oil products reduced their purchases, but by a much smaller percentage. This means that their demand curve for such products:
(1) was price-elastic.
(2) shifted slightly to the right.
(3) was price-inelastic.
(4) shifted slightly to the left.
(5) was unit-elastic with respect to price.

16. If a demand curve displays unitary price elasticity throughout its entire length, then:
(1) the demand curve is a straight line, and total expenditure by buyers is the same at all prices.
(2) the demand curve is not a straight line, and total expenditure by buyers falls as price falls.
(3) the demand curve is a straight line, and total expenditure by buyers first increases and later decreases as price falls.
(4) the demand curve is not a straight line, and total expenditure by buyers rises as price falls.
(5) none of the above is correct.

17. An increase in demand for a certain product occurs. A new short-run equilibrium is established, but it gradually gives way to a new long-run equilibrium price. In the normal case, these prices would be related to the original price as follows: Long-run equilibrium price would be:
(1) higher than both the short-run and the original prices.
(2) lower than the short-run price but could be higher than the original price.
(3) lower than both the short-run and the original prices.
(4) higher than the short-run price but lower than the original price.
(5) related to the short-run and original prices in a manner not indicated by any of the above.

18. Suppose that the demand curve for wheat is perfectly inelastic with respect to price. If a tax of 50 cents per bushel sold were imposed on suppliers, then:
(1) price would rise, but by less than 50 cents, and there would probably be some reduction in the quantity bought and sold.
(2) price would rise by the full 50 cents, but there would be no reduction in the quantity bought and sold.
(3) price would rise, but by less than 50 cents, and there would be no reduction in the quantity bought and sold.
(4) price would rise by the full 50 cents, and there would definitely be a reduction in the quantity bought and sold.
(5) none of the above is correct.

19. A crop failure reduces the amount of wheat available, and so the price rises. In precise terms, this is:
(1) a decrease in the quantity supplied followed by a decrease in demand.
(2) a decrease in supply followed by a decrease in demand.
(3) a decrease in the quantity supplied followed by a decrease in the quantity demanded.
(4) a decrease in supply followed by a decrease in the quantity demanded.
(5) none of these things.

20. Early in the 1970s, OPEC raised oil prices very sharply by forming a cartel. In elementary supply-and-demand-curve terms, OPEC's action of restricting world trade in oil could be described as:
(1) a leftward shift of the supply curve.
(2) a leftward shift of the demand curve.
(3) a rightward shift of the supply curve.
(4) a rightward shift of the demand curve.
(5) an increase in equilibrium price, but with no change in either demand curve or supply curve.

21. Which of the following observations would tend to make you expect that some good would display a price-inelastic demand curve even if you did not know exactly what good it was?
(1) The good in question is more of a necessity than a luxury for most people.
(2) There do not exist substitutes for the consumption of this good.
(3) The time period allowed to respond to a change in price is very small.
(4) All or any of the above.
(5) None of the above.

22. Which of the following describes a supply curve of unitary elasticity drawn in the usual price-quantity quadrant?
(1) A straight line drawn from the origin with a constant and positive slope.
(2) A rectangular hyperbola bowed out from the origin.

(3) A straight line drawn from any "price intercept" with a constant and positive slope.
(4) A horizontal line drawn at the market-clearing price.
(5) A vertical line drawn at the market-clearing quantity.

SUGGESTED ANSWERS TO QUESTIONS IN THE TEXT: Chapter 5

1. Good harvest shifts a fairly inelastic supply curve out. Equilibrium moves down along an inelastic demand curve to support a (much) lower price and lower revenue.

2. More price elastic: perfume and ice cream because they are closer to luxuries than necessities in the pairs; chocolate ice cream and automobiles because there are more substitutes for these goods than there are for ice cream and automobile tires, respectively.

3. Demand would be inelastic, with $E_D < 1$.

4. Assume that demand and supply both show some price elasticity.
   a. Output and price up along supply curve (demand-curve shift)
   b. Output down and price (paid by renters) up along demand curve (supply shift)
   c. $200/month greater than market-clearing rent: no change; $200/month less than market-clearing rent: output and quantity down along supply curve (horizontal effective demand with excess real demand)
   d. Output up and price down along demand curve (supply shift)
   e. Output down and price up along demand curve (supply shift)

5. Rent regulation breeds excess demand at the regulated rent.

6. Demand stayed constant. The expected contraction in supply (with price up and quantity down along demand curve) did not materialize because supplies from other sources made up for the loss of Iraqi oil.

7. Minimum wages can increase the quantity of labor offered (supplied) and decrease the quantity of labor demanded. A binding minimum wage therefore creates a surplus of labor. Ceiling can do the opposite.

8. The following table applies. Numbers in parentheses are calculated. The notes indicate the order in which the answers can be computed.

Q	$\Delta Q/Q_{avg}$	P	$\Delta P/P_{avg}$	E_D	Revenue
$(21,000)^b$	—	5	—	—	$(105,000)^c$
—	$(0.33)^a$	—	$(\frac{5}{7.5} = 0.67)$	0.5	—
15,000	—	10	—	—	$(150,000)^d$
—	$(0.22)^e$	—	$(\frac{2}{11} = 0.18)$	1.2	—
$(12,000)^f$	—	12	—	—	$(144,000)^g$
—	(na)	—	(na)	2.0	—
(na)	—	15	—	—	(na)

a. $0.33 = E_D \cdot (\Delta P/P_{avg}) = 0.5 \times 0.67$.
b. This quantity Q_b solves $\frac{Q_b - 15,000}{\frac{1}{2}(115,000 + Q_b)} = \frac{\Delta Q}{Q} = 0.33$.
c. $105,000 = 21,000 \times \$5$.
d. $150,000 = 15,000 \times \$10$.
e. $0.22 = E_D \cdot (\Delta P/P_{avg}) = 1.2 \times 0.18$.
f. This quantity Q_f solves $\frac{15,000 - Q_f}{\frac{1}{2}(15,000 + Q_f)} = \frac{\Delta Q}{Q} = 0.22$.
g. $144,000 = 12,000 \times \$12$.

This example verifies the elasticity/revenue relationship.

9. Consult Figure 5-10 in the text, reproduced here as Figure TQ5-1(a) to show where the $2000 tariff fits in. The demand for domestic cars thereby shifts up from DD to $D'D'$ in Figure TQ5-1(b) because the price of substitutes has increased. As a result, the price of domestic cars climbs as quantity expands along the supply curve of domestic production—curve SS. Domestic manufacturers and their employees are happy.

10. **a.** Supply down by 5 percent with elasticity of 0.05 means that price must increase by 100 percent.
   b. Elasticity is a ratio of percentages; it is thus unitless.
   c. Supply down by 50 percent means that price must increase by 500 percent to keep the price elasticity equal to 0.1. Crime should increase if addicts steal to feed their habits. A successful rehab program would shift demand in; quantity would fall by 50 percent and price would stay the same (the shifts would match).

11. Triangle $0ba$ is similar to triangle aPC. Therefore, $0P/Pa = Cb/Ca$. Note, as well, that $0P/Pa = P/(a - P)$.

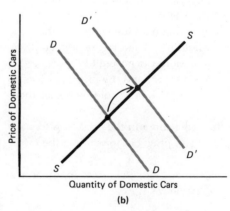

Figure TQ5-1

CHAPTER 6

DEMAND AND CONSUMER BEHAVIOR

Demand theory provides the framework within which we study the economic factors that produce and affect demand curves. The power of demand curves as tools for economic investigation has already been noted—showing that power was one of the fundamental points of Chapters 4 and 5. This chapter explores their sensitivity to changes in income, prices, and tastes by postulating and manipulating a model of consumer behavior. Having completed the chapter, you will have met the following objectives.

LEARNING OBJECTIVES

1. Define total utility and marginal utility; distinguish between the two.

2. Explain the law of diminishing marginal utility and its importance in economic analysis.

3. Explain why an individual's utility is maximized subject to an income constraint if the marginal utility derived from the last dollar spent is the same for all the goods purchased.

4. Express the utility-maximizing rule mathematically, and show how it combines with the law of diminishing marginal utility to produce downward-sloping demand curves.

5. Define substitution and income effects more precisely (terms first appearing in Chapter 4), and explain how they work to produce downward-sloping demand curves.

6. Explain how market demand curves are derived from the horizontal summation of individual demand curves.

7. Describe the paradox of value, and resolve it through application of the utility-maximizing rule.

8. Define consumer surplus and explain how it is used.

Consumers—like you, your classmates, your friends and their families—ordinarily have only a limited amount of money to spend in any given period of time on the things that they need or want. Each good has a market price which usually cannot be altered by bargaining or bickering. You must decide which goods to buy and how much of each good to buy, knowing from the quoted prices that each purchase will exhaust part of your limited income or budget.

If your budget were so large that you could buy all you wanted of all the goods that interested you, then there would be no problem of choice and the study of economics would not be a story about you and your life. Unless I miss my guess, though, that is not the case. You must choose. You might have to decide, for example, whether to buy 2 more units of one good (call it good A) at a price of $1 per unit or 1 more unit of a different good (good B) at a price of $2. Either purchase would entail the same $2 outlay, but your limited budget might easily tell you that you can't have both. You must, therefore, carry inside your head some personal measuring scale which says that buying the 1 unit of B would yield you more satisfaction than would purchasing the 2 units of A (or vice versa). Tastes differ, of course. The individual next to you, with the same income, might well make the opposite choice.

This small A-or-B choice illustrates the more general problem of how to make the best use of a limited income. There are literally thousands of different assortments of goods that any one individual might be able to afford, and each one is slightly different from the next. Which among them is the "best" choice? The answer lies in weighing personal tastes against price-income-determined budget constraints, but that is perhaps easier said than analyzed formally. Prices and in-

68 6 Demand and Consumer Behavior

comes are objective, easily understood concepts, but tastes are more difficult. We have to devise some analytic concept to represent what we mean by personal "tastes," "preferences," or "needs."

Economists have developed the notion of **utility** to accomplish this representation. Each consumer is thought to evaluate commodities on the basis of his or her personal quantitative standard of satisfaction or utility. A certain buyer may reckon, for example, that buying 1 unit of A would yield 70 utility units ("utils"), 2 units would yield a total of 120 utils, and a third A unit would raise the satisfaction meter to 150 utils.

In real life, nobody is conscious of putting exact numerical values on each quantity of each good consumed. The utility notion represents consumers as being a lot more precise than they actually are, but don't be too impatient with the idea of utility on this account. It says that consumers must do something at least approximating this, even if only intuitively, if they want to make the best possible use of a limited income. This quantitative utility idea is employed because it is a way of showing how a consumer will go about "maximizing satisfaction," i.e., making the best possible use of a limited income in the light of his or her own set of preferences.

The very first step is to distinguish carefully between **total utility** and **marginal utility**. In the example above, the buyer derived a total utility of 70 utils from consuming 1 unit of A, 120 utils from 2 units, and 150 utils from 3 units. Marginal utility is the extra utility contributed by the last unit consumed (the unit that is just at the edge or margin of consumption, so to speak). The marginal utility of the first unit of A must be 70 (because its consumption raised total utility from 0 to 70). The marginal utility of the second unit must be 50 (because total utils rose from 70 to 120); and that of the third unit must be 30 (moving the utility measure from 120 to 150).

The second step is to note the **principle of diminishing marginal utility**. This principle says that as consumption of any single good increases, the total utility derived from that consumption will increase at a decreasing rate; i.e., marginal utility gradually decreases. The third ice-cream cone (or the third beer) may add to your satisfaction, but not so much as the first one did; the fifth one may add still a little more satisfaction, but not so much as the third one did. In these circumstances, your total satisfaction is still rising, but the payoff from each additional (marginal) unit consumed is becoming less and less.

1. a. If the total utilities associated with the consumption of 1, 2, and 3 units of B were to be, respectively, 100, 160, and 200, then the corresponding marginal utilities would be _____, _____, and _____ .

b. Which of the following sets of total utility figures (designated for 1, 2, 3, and 4 units consumed) illustrates the idea of diminishing marginal utility?

(1) 200, 300, 400, 500.

(2) 200, 450, 750, 1100.

(3) 200, 400, 1600, 9600.

(4) 200, 250, 270, 280.

c. Which of the following sets of marginal utility figures (once again defined for 1, 2, 3, and 4 units consumed) would likewise illustrate the diminishing marginal utility principle?

(1) 200, 150, 100, 50.

(2) 200, 300, 400, 500.

(3) 200, 200, 200, 200.

(4) 200, 250, 270, 280.

a. 100; 60; 40 **b.** (4) **c.** (1)

Now we use the ideas of total and marginal utility to illustrate the idea of maximizing satisfaction, or making the best possible use of a given income. Suppose that your fixed weekly budget will allow consideration of only three goods: A, B, and C. Table 6-1 shows your personal schedule of total utility for these three goods.

You want to spend your fixed income so that the one specific A-B-C combination which you choose will yield the maximum number of utility units; i.e., you want to spend your money in a way which maximizes your level of satisfaction. In reading Table 6-1, it is safe to assume that the utility units for A are of the same kind as those for B and C. As a result, your total satisfaction would be 995 utility units (165 plus 700 plus 130) if you buy 2 units each of goods A, B, or C.

Table 6-1
Total Satisfaction, Measured in Utility Units, Derived from Consumption of:

	1 Unit	2 Units	3 Units	4 Units	5 Units	6 Units	7 Units	8 Units	9 Units	10 Units	11 Units	12 Units
A	95	165	210	240	258	268	275	280	285	289	293	296
B	400	700	900	1,000	1,020	1,030	1,038	1,044	1,048	1,050	1,051	1,052
C	70	130	180	225	265	300	328	348	360	366	370	373

Table 6-2
Marginal Satisfaction or Utility, Measured in Utility Units, When Consumption Is:

	1 Unit	2 Units	3 Units	4 Units	5 Units	6 Units	7 Units	8 Units	9 Units	10 Units	11 Units	12 Units
A	95	70	45	30	18							
B	400	300	200	100								
C	70	60	50									

In this table, the three sets of utility values are assumed to be independent of one another. That is, the amount of utility you get for any given quantity of A is not affected by the amount you happen to be consuming of B or of C. This is not necessarily true in real life; A and B might, for example, be close substitutes. The assumption of independence is made here only for the sake of simplicity and clarity.

2. Use the information in Table 6-1 to record, in Table 6-2, the marginal utilities of the indicated quantities of goods A, B, and C. To speed things up, a few of the marginal utility figures are already entered; check to see that they are correct.

table rows: A—10, 7, 5, 5, 4, 4, 3; B—20, 10, 8, 6, 4, 2, 1, 1; C—45, 40, 35, 28, 20, 12, 6, 4, 3

Suppose that you, as the consumer whose preferences are reflected by the utility function described in question 2, have $52 per week to spend on commodities A, B, and C. These are the only goods available, or at least the only goods in which you have any interest. Let the price of good A be $1, the price of B be $2, and the price of C be $4. How much of A, B, and C should you purchase for maximum satisfaction? There are plenty of combinations of A, B, and C that you could afford with $52, but which one buys the maximum total utility?

One possible combination is 12 units of A, 10 of B, and 5 of C; it would yield a total of 1611 utility units. Is this best? No. If you reduced your purchases of A by 4 units and used the surplus money to purchase an extra unit of C, your utility would increase by 19 utility units. The utility lost by reducing your consumption of A (16 utils) would be more than compensated by the utility gained from consuming 1 more unit of C (35 utils).

Marginal utility is the critical factor in measuring losses and gains, but it is not the only critical factor in evaluating utility-maximizing equilibrium. In the example above, the last units of A purchased were not, when compared with C, the utility bargains that they might have looked like if only price were considered, but looking at marginal utility numbers alone would have been equally misleading. To see if utility is maximized, what must be asked is really this: Are the three commodities offering equally good utility returns per dollar spent? In other words, is the marginal value of the dollar the same regardless of what good it is spent on? If it is—if the three goods are contributing equally to utility per dollar expended—then utility is maximized.

The method with which to check whether or not this is happening is simple. The ratios of marginal utility to price must be computed for each good. (An old physics trick can provide some insight here. The units of evaluation should be units of utility per dollar spent. If marginal utility is measured in units of utility per units of consumption and prices are measured in dollars per unit of consumption, then marginal utility divided by price must be in units of utility per dollar because the units of consumption cancel.) If the ratios of marginal utility to price are equal, then utility is maximized. If they are not, then there exists some adjustment in consumption that will increase utility—an increase in the consumption of the good with the high utility payoff per dollar and a reduction in the consumption of the good with the low utility payoff per dollar.

3. a. Use the data of Table 6-2 to compute the marginal utility–price ratios indicated in Table 6-3 given A's price of $1, B's of $2, and C's of $4.

Table 6-3
Marginal Utility Units per Dollar of Outlay (*MU* Divided by Price of the Commodity), When Consumption Is:

	1 Unit	2 Units	3 Units	4 Units	5 Units	6 Units	7 Units	8 Units	9 Units	10 Units	11 Units	12 Units
A	95	70	45	30	18							
B	200	150	100	50								
C	17.5	15	12.5									

b. Table 6-3 has several combinations of goods A, B, and C generating equal marginal utilities per dollar. Circle the *MU*-per-dollar figures in this table for three of them, namely:

(1) 6 of A, 5 of B, 5 of C (common *MU*/$ = 10)

(2) 8 of A, 6 of B, 8 of C (common *MU*/$ = 5)

(3) 12 of A, 8 of B, 9 of C (common *MU*/$ = 3)

Among these three potential utility-maximizing "shopping baskets," only one can be bought for $52, namely _____ .

c. Given your income constraint and the prices quoted by the market, the best possible expenditure of $52 is 8 of A, 6 of B, and 8 of C. Table 6-1 indicates that the total number of utility units attained from this A-B-C combination is *(1030 / 1658 / 3050)* units.

To check that this combination really maximizes utility, experiment with a change. Reduce your C purchases from 8 units to 7. This saves you $4, which you use to buy 2 extra units of good B. Combining the reduction in total utility from lower C purchases with the increase from higher B purchases, the net change in total utility would be *(an increase / a decrease)* of *(8 / 7 / 6 / 5 / 4)* units.

a. table rows: A—same as Table 6-2; B—10, 5, 4, 3, 2, 1, 0.5, 0.5; C—11.25, 10, 8.75, 7, 5, 3, 1.5, 1, 0.75   **b.** (2)   **c.** 1658; a decrease; 6

4. a. Referring still to Tables 6-1 through 6-3, suppose that your spendable income is reduced from $52 to $36 per week. Show the details of your new equilibrium (utility-maximizing) position in Table 6-4(a).

Table 6-4(a)

Quantity Purchased (units)	Price	Expenditure	Marginal Utility	MU/$
A ___	$1	___	___	___
B ___	2	___	___	___
C ___	4	___	___	___

b. To compensate you for the pain that you suffered in part **a**, suppose finally that your budget is back to $52 but that the price of commodity C has been reduced from $4 to $3. Show the details of your resulting equilibrium position in Table 6-4(b).

Table 6-4(b)

Quantity Purchased (units)	Price	Expenditure	Marginal Utility	MU/$
A ___	$1	___	___	___
B ___	2	___	___	___
C ___	3	___	___	___

a. table rows: A—6, $6, 10, 10; B—5, $10, 20, 10; C—5, $20, 40, 10   **b.** table rows: A—11, $11, 4, 4; B—7, $14, 8, 4; C—9, $27, 12, 4   (*Note:* in referring to marginal utility value, use the value of the last unit actually purchased and not the next unit that would be purchased.)

5. a. Both Chapters 4 and 5 stressed the distinction between an *increase (or decrease) in demand* and an *increase (or decrease) in quantity demanded*. Question 4**a** illustrates this: There was a leftward shift of the consumer demand curve caused by an income drop. You bought _____ units of A with $52 of income. After income fell to $36, however, your purchases were only _____ units even though A's price was unchanged. In Chapter 5 language, this is a decrease in *(demand / quantity demanded)*.

b. The reduction in C's price from $4 in question 3 to $3 in question 4**b** illustrates an increase in the *(demand for C / quantity of C demanded)*.

That is, out of the utility background, we can identify consumer demand curves. For example, with a budget of $52, and with A's and B's prices $1 and $2, respectively, you would buy _____ units of C if its price were $4 and _____ units if its price were $3. Other points on the C demand curve would be derived by considering other prices of C, *holding income at $52 and the prices of A and B at $1 and $2.*

a. 8; 6; demand   **b.** quantity of C demanded; 8; 9

In summary, then, the problem of consumer behavior is choosing the combination of goods one can afford (given income and prices) that maximizes total utility (given individual tastes and preferences). The rule for solving this problem sets the ratios of marginal utilities to prices equal for all goods; i.e., utility will be maximized for all goods I and J with prices P_I and P_J and marginal utility values represented by MU_I and MU_J if

$$\frac{MU_I}{P_I} = \frac{MU_J}{P_J} = \text{marginal utility per dollar of income}$$

Satisfying this condition guarantees that the utility derived from spending the last dollar of income (the marginal dollar) will be the same regardless of where it is spent. There exist, therefore, no affordable rearrangements of consumption that can increase utility.

To see why this last interpretation holds, suppose that your common marginal utility of a dollar is *K* units of utility; *K* can be any number. Now consider reducing your purchases of some good A by $1. Your utility would fall by *K* units. What to do with the extra dollar? What would happen if you devoted it to increasing the purchase of *any* other good B? That would generate an increase in utility of *K* units for a net change in total utility of zero. No change in your consumption pattern will increase your total utility.

6. Back in Chapter 4, the text spoke of the two "effects" which explain why more of a commodity is bought if its price falls, and why less is bought if its price rises. In this question and the one following, we use the idea of marginal utility to examine in more detail the nature of these two effects.

a. Specifically, these effects are (1) the *(substitution / institutional)* effect and (2) the *(envy / income)* effect.

b. Table 6-5 is similar in general construction to Tables 6-1 and 6-2. It shows the levels of marginal utility *(MU)* and total utility *(TU)* associated with different quantities of commodities X and Y, measured in satisfaction units. (Commodities X and Y are the only ones you can buy, or the only ones in which you are interested.)

Table 6-5

No. of Units Consumed	MU of X	TU of X	MU of Y	TU of Y
3	32	348	20	130
4	28	376	18	148
5	24	400	16	164
6	20	420	14	178
7	16	436	12	190
8	12	448	10	200
9	8	456	8	208
10	5	461	5	213
11	3	464	3	216

Suppose that the prices of X and of Y are $2.40 and $1.00, respectively, and that you have just $20 per period to spend. Given the data in Table 6-5, what will be your equilibrium or maximum-satisfaction X-Y combination? In this situation, you will buy _____ units of X and _____ units of Y. The total satisfaction units you obtain, from X and Y combined, will be _____ .

c. Now let the price of X drop from $2.40 to $1.00. The price of Y is still $1, and you still have $20 to spend. What will be your new equilibrium position? (Since the prices of X and Y are now equal, look for an X-Y combination with equal *MU*s, purchasable for just $20.) You will now buy _____ units of X, as compared with 5 previously, and will now buy _____ units of Y, as compared with 8 previously.

In the new situation, the quantity of X has *(increased / decreased)*. This is not surprising, since X's price has fallen. The quantity of Y has *(increased / decreased)*. Why this should happen is not immediately obvious. Y's price has not fallen; indeed, the price of Y has risen relative to the price of X.

d. What has happened is this: In part **b** you were spending considerably more than half your income on X. The reduction in X's price considered in part **c** had an effect similar to a substantial rise in your income; in fact, your total satisfaction level has climbed from the original total of 600 units to *(620 / 664 / 670 / 674)* units. How so? You have used the *practical equivalent of a larger income to buy more X* and *more Y*.

When X's price falls, there are two effects which operate on your desire to purchase X and Y. Insofar as X and Y are substitutes, you will be disposed to buy *(more / less)* Y and more X. But countering this is the income effect just discussed, which makes you inclined to buy *(more / less)* X and *(more / less)* Y. In this case, the income effect won out over the substitution effect. Had X and Y been "better" substitutes for one another, then the quantity of Y chosen might have fallen instead of rising.

---

a. substitution; income **b.** 5; 8; 600 (*Note*: At $X = 5$ and $Y = 8$, $MU_X/P_X = 24/\$2.40 = 10$, while $MU_Y/P_Y = 10/\$1 = 10$.) **c.** 10; 10; increased; increased **d.** 674; less; more; more

---

7. Question 6 was based upon the notion that X and Y were substitutes. We should therefore have expected that any reduction in the price of X would reduce purchases of Y. This substitution effect can, as in question 6, be blurred or concealed by an income effect—the effect of the increase in real income caused by the price reduction that inspires the typical consumer to buy more of everything, including Y. To get a measure of the "pure substitution effect," which is uncluttered by the income effect, some type of economic benchmark was needed to establish a constant basis of comparison. Economists have found such a benchmark—the level of utility or satisfaction. This question is designed to show you how this helps us isolate the substitution effect. It asks you to consider how you would respond to the lower price of X if your money income were simultaneously reduced just enough to permit you to achieve at best only your original level of satisfaction.

a. Let the price of X fall from $2.40 to $1.00 while your budget income simultaneously falls from $20 to $12. Assume that the price of Y is $1 throughout. The top and bottom rows in Table 6-6 summarize the two situations discussed in question 6. Fill in the details of the equilibrium situation required by the conditions just outlined in the blank spaces in the middle row.

Table 6-6

Budget	X Price	Y Price	X Quantity	Y Quantity	Satisfaction Units
$20	$2.40	$1.00	5	8	600
12	1.00	1.00	____	____	____
20	1.00	1.00	10	10	674

Compare the top row with the one you have just completed. X's price has fallen, but so has income, and you adjust your purchases as best you can. When you have done

72   6   Demand and Consumer Behavior

so, your satisfaction level *(has risen / is unchanged / has fallen)*. There is no income effect arising from the lower price for X, because your money income has been deliberately (if temporarily) squeezed by just enough to keep your satisfaction constant.

Compare purchases in these two situations. Purchases of X *(rise / fall)* from 5 to *(3 / 7 / 10)*. This is the pure substitution effect (of the reduction in X's price) upon X purchases. Purchases of Y *(rise / fall)* from 8 to *(5 / 7 / 10)*. This is the pure substitution effect on Y purchases. We get what we would expect if X and Y were substitutes and X's price fell: *(an increase / a reduction)* in Y purchases.

b. Now we return you to your $20 income (with the reduced price of X still in effect). This means we compare the middle row in the table with the third row. Purchases of X rise further from 7 to 10; those of Y, from 5 to 10. These are the income effects of the reduction in X's price. All we have done is to "break apart" the price reduction of question 6. We observe first the results of the pure substitution effect (comparing the top row with the middle one) and then the results of the income effect alone (comparing the middle row with the bottom one). In question 6, we went straight from the top to the bottom row (the two effects combined) without any intermediate pause.

To summarize, with matters still put in terms of a reduction in the price of X: Given such an X-price reduction, the substitution effect tends to *(increase / leave unchanged / decrease)* X purchases and to *(increase / leave unchanged / decrease)* Y purchases. The income effect of such a price reduction (with a small qualification noted below) tends to *(increase / leave unchanged / decrease)* X purchases and to *(increase / leave unchanged / decrease)* Y purchases.

a. table row: 7, 5, 600; is unchanged; rise; 7; fall; 5; a reduction   **b.** increase; decrease; increase; increase

8. A consumer has $50 per week to exhaust on either commodity X (price $5) or commodity Y (price $4).

For each of the four cases below, indicate, if you can, whether or not this consumer is "at equilibrium," i.e., deriving the maximum-attainable satisfaction. If you lack sufficient information to answer, explain why. If you know the consumer is not at equilibrium, indicate the required direction of movement (e.g., "buy more of X and less of Y," "buy less of X and more of Y," "buy more of both," etc.).

a. Purchases are now 2 of X and 10 of Y. Total utility of X at this level is considered to be 500 utility units; total utility of Y, 400 units. _____

b. Purchases are now 6 of X and 5 of Y. Total utility of X at this level is considered to be 400 utility units, and the marginal utility of X is 60 units. Total utility of Y is 800 units, and the MU of Y is 30 units. _____

c. Purchases are now 6 of X and 5 of Y. The MU of X at this level is considered to be 25 units; the MU of Y, 20 units. _____

d. Purchases are now 6 of X and 4 of Y. The MU of X at this level is considered to be 25 units; the MU of Y, 20 units. _____

a. impossible to tell—marginal utility values are not given   **b.** Buy more of X, less of Y. (Note: $MU_X/P_X = 60/\$5 = 12$; $MU_Y/P_Y = 30/\$4 = 7.5$.)   **c.** now at equilibrium (Note: $MU_X/P_X = 25/\$5 = 5 = MU_Y/P_Y = 20/\$4 = 5$.)   **d.** Buy more of both. Marginal utility values are balanced with prices, but not all income is spent.

The text notes that a market demand curve can be produced by the "horizontal" addition of individual demand curves—i.e., the summation, for every price, of the quantities demanded by all the individuals participating in the market.

9. a. Table 6-7 records the quantities of some good X that each of three people would demand for a variety of prices. Fill in the column indicated for the market demand schedule if these three people were the only people interested in X at any price.

Table 6-7

Price	Individual A	Individual B	Individual C	Market Demand
$8	2	0	0	___
7	3	0	1	___
6	4	0	3	___
5	5	0	5	___
4	6	1	7	___
3	7	3	10	___
2	8	5	14	___

b. If individual A's income were to increase, *(higher / identical / lower)* quantities would be entered in the Market Demand column for *(the equilibrium price only / all prices / all prices below $5)*. If X were considered a close substitute for Y by individual B only and the price of Y were to fall, then (higher / identical / lower) quantities would be entered in the Market Demand column for (the equilibrium price only / all prices / all prices below $5).

---

a. table column: 2, 4, 7, 10, 14, 20, 27   **b.** higher; all prices; lower; all prices below $5

---

10. The relation between the utilities of commodities B and C in Table 6-1 illustrates something of Adam Smith's **paradox of value**. Smith was puzzled by the fact that commodity prices often are poor indicators of the true relative usefulness of commodities. Water, which is essential for life, is cheap. Diamonds, which have no such necessity status, are expensive.

In the equilibrium of question 3, you were buying _____ units of B and _____ units of C. In this position, the total utility of B was _____ units, and the total utility of C was _____ units. Measured in terms of total utility furnished, B is the more useful or desirable of the two commodities. Yet the market sets a higher price per unit on C.

The explanation is that market prices are influenced by (marginal / total) utility. The (marginal / total) utility of extra units of a commodity such as B declines sharply after a certain total quantity is consumed. If the supply offered were sufficiently large, then consumers would bid a price for extra units of B reckoned only in terms of its low (marginal / total) utility, and this price would hold for the entire supply. If B's supply were sufficiently reduced, however, then its price (would rise very sharply / would rise a little but not much / would fall). The "utility bargain" consumers get from purchasing a commodity with high total utility at a low price is termed: _____

When the price of C fell from $4 per unit to $3, total utility (rose / fell / stayed the same). At the same time, consumer surplus (rose / fell / stayed the same). If Figure 6-1 were to illustrate the demand curve for C in the $2 to $5 price range, then the change in consumer surplus caused by the price reduction from $4 to $3 would be (area EDF / area KFIL / area EGIF / area FHI).

If the government were to stick a tax onto the $3 price of C so that $4 became the after-tax price, then the government would collect revenue equal to (area DGHF / area EGHF / area 0GIL), and consumer surplus would fall by (area EDF / area KFIL / area EGIF / area FHI). The amount of consumer surplus not extracted by the government in tax revenue—the deadweight loss of the tax—would be (area EDF / area ILM / area FHI).

6; 8; 1030; 348; marginal; marginal; marginal; would rise very sharply; consumer surplus; rose; rose; area *EGIF*; area *EGHF*; area *EGIF*; area *FHI*

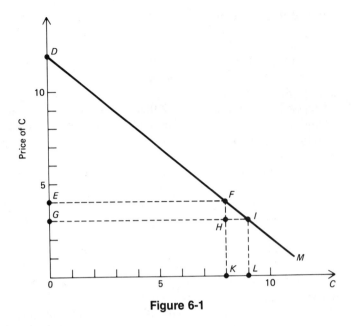

Figure 6-1

REVIEW CONCEPTS

1. Utility is a measure of satisfaction. Marginal utility is the rate at which that measure changes as the consumption of *one* good changes.

2. The law of diminishing marginal utility holds that the welfare value of successive units of any good declines. It generally supports downward-sloping demand curves.

3. Utility is maximized subject to a budget constraint if the ratios of marginal utility to price for all goods are equal, i.e., if the marginal utility of the last dollar spent is the same regardless of where it is spent.

4. Utility maximization requires that

$$\frac{MU_X}{P_X} = \frac{MU_Y}{P_Y}$$

for any goods X and Y. As the price of X climbs, the quantity of X consumed should fall (in most cases) so that MU_X rises with price; demand curves are, as a result, generally downward-sloping.

5. Substitution effects (compensated substitution) and income effects (responses to changes in "real" income) usually contribute to the negative correlation between price and the quantity demanded.

6. Market demand curves reflect, for any price, the total quantity demanded across many individuals. They are the "horizontal sum" of individual demand curves.

7. Consumer surplus represents the difference between what people would have been willing to pay for a given quantity of some good, one unit at a time, and how much they actually had to pay in a market quoting one price for all units.

6 Demand and Consumer Behavior

QUIZ: Multiple Choice

1. The marginal utility of a commodity is:
(1) an indication of the last use to which the commodity has been put or the use to which it would next be put if more were available.
(2) the same thing as the price of that commodity.
(3) the relationship that the total utility generated by consuming that commodity bears to the total utility of all other commodities that are consumed.
(4) the extra utility yielded by consuming each successive unit of that commodity.
(5) the same thing as the total utility derived from consuming that commodity.

2. The paradox of value refers to which of the following?
(1) Prices of commodities are not always proportional to the total satisfaction that they give us; witness the fact that some of the absolute necessities of life are inexpensive.
(2) It is impossible to explain the price of a commodity in terms of either demand factors alone or supply factors alone.
(3) It is impossible to explain why people's tastes are what they are or why they vary from one person to the next.
(4) Some consumers tend to value commodities according to their price, even to the point of buying more if price goes up.
(5) None of the above.

3. The income effect captures which of the following economic phenomena?
(1) If people's money incomes fall, then they will normally purchase less of any given commodity.
(2) Any fall in price of a major purchase has an effect similar to a small rise in people's incomes, and this may prompt them to buy even a little more of that good.
(3) The amount of certain goods purchased may actually decrease as people's incomes rise.
(4) As people's incomes rise, they save proportionately more out of income, so they actually spend a smaller fraction of their incomes.
(5) If the price of a good drops, it is as though the prices of all other goods have risen, in relative terms, so smaller quantities of those other goods will tend to be bought.

4. When a consumer is maximizing his or her utility subject to the constraint of income and given prices, then:
(1) the total satisfaction derived from each commodity must equal the total satisfaction derived from every other commodity.
(2) the ratio between the total satisfaction derived from any commodity and the price of that commodity must be equal for all commodities.
(3) the satisfaction derived from the last tiny unit of each commodity bought must be equal among all commodities.
(4) the ratio between the total satisfaction derived from any commodity and the total expenditure on that commodity must be equal for all commodities.
(5) none of the preceding descriptions is necessarily correct.

5. A consumer's demand curve for any given commodity is most likely to shift to the right (or upward) with:
(1) a rise in the price of substitutes or a fall in the price of complements.
(2) a rise in the price of either substitutes or complements.
(3) a fall in the price of substitutes or a rise in the price of complements.
(4) a fall in the price of either substitutes or complements.
(5) none of these cases.

6. You have $20 per week available to spend as you wish on commodities A and B. The prices of these commodities, the quantities you now buy, and your evaluation of the utility provided by these quantities are recorded in Table 6-8.

Table 6-8

	Price	Units Bought	Total Utility	Marginal Utility
A	70¢	20	500	30
B	50	12	1,000	20

For maximum satisfaction, you should:
(1) buy less of A and more of B.
(2) buy the same quantity of A, but more of B.
(3) buy more of A and less of B.
(4) buy more of A and the same quantity of B.
(5) remain in your present position, since that position is the best-attainable one.

7. You regard goods X and Y as substitutes. If the price of X rises and there is some income effect from this price rise, then this *income effect* should induce you to:
(1) purchase more of good Y only if the price of X falls short of the price of Y.
(2) purchase less of good Y.
(3) purchase the same amount of Y.
(4) purchase more Y only if the price of X now exceeds that of Y.
(5) do none of the above.

8. Which alternative in question 7 would have been correct if it had referred to the *substitution* effect rather than the income effect?
(1).
(2).
(3).
(4).
(5).

9. The price of good X is $1.50 and that of good Y is $1.00. If a consumer considers the marginal utility of Y to be 30 units, and is maximizing utility with respect to purchases of X and Y, then he or she must consider the marginal utility of X to be:
(1) 15 units.
(2) 20 units.
(3) 30 units.
(4) 45 units.
(5) none of the above necessarily, because the information given is insufficient to tell.

10. If, in question 9, the figure of 30 units had been the total (rather than marginal) utility of Y, which alternative would be correct with respect to the total utility of X?
(1).
(2).
(3).
(4).
(5).

11. The price of good X falls. The income effect (if any) of this price change:
(1) will normally cause X purchases to increase.
(2) will normally cause X purchases to decrease.
(3) may cause X purchases either to increase or to decrease, there being no "normal" consequence.
(4) by definition, neither increases nor decreases X purchases.
(5) will not apply, since income effects refer to changes in spendable income, not to price changes.

12. If the marginal utility of a commodity is zero, then:
(1) total utility for this commodity has reached a maximum.
(2) the commodity in question has no utility; i.e., it is not one that consumers want to use.
(3) the paradox of value must be involved.
(4) the consumer has reached his or her equilibrium position with respect to purchase of this commodity.
(5) total utility for this commodity must be zero also.

13. A consumer moves to a new equilibrium position as a result of some change either in market price or in income. In this new equilibrium situation, marginal utilities are all lower than they were in the old equilibrium situation. Tastes or preferences are unchanged. This consumer:
(1) is definitely worse off in the new situation.
(2) is definitely better off in the new situation.
(3) is worse off in the new situation if income has changed, but not otherwise.
(4) is better off in the new situation if price has changed, but not otherwise.
(5) may be better off or worse off in the new situation, since the information given does not necessarily indicate one or the other.

14. The idea of "consumer surplus" reflects the notion that:
(1) the gain consumers obtain in some purchases exceeds the gain suppliers obtain from selling.
(2) the purchase of many goods is an immense bargain to consumers, because they would have been willing to pay far more than they actually do in order to get them.
(3) the marginal utility of the first units of a product consumed may considerably exceed the total utility which this product supplies.
(4) total utility increases either when consumer incomes rise or when the prices they must pay for goods fall.
(5) when demand is price-inelastic, buyers can obtain a larger quantity for the expenditure of less money.

SUGGESTED ANSWERS TO QUESTIONS IN THE TEXT: Chapter 6

1. Definitions.

2. MU (hamburger)/$2.00 = MU$ (coke) / $0.50
$= MU$ (pizza) / $1.00
$\geq MU$ (hot dog) / $1.50

3. *Substitutes*: beef, lamb, and pork; gum and cigarettes (?); etc.

Complements: beef and ketchup (?); cigarettes and air travel (?); etc.

Independent: beef, etc., and paperbacks

4. This holds only if the prices of all goods are constant. It is the ratio of marginal utility to price that is constant over all goods in equilibrium.

5. Now that we have a VCR, we don't go to movies. How about you? My consumer surplus is zero.

6. Consult Table TQ6-1(a) for marginal utility numbers.

Table TQ6-1(a)

Days Skied	Marginal Utility
1st	30 − 0 = 30
2d	25
3d	18
4th	15
5th	10
6th	5
7th	0
8th	−3

The demand for skiing, given 1 million skiers with this utility function, is given in Table TQ6-1(b).

The reason that marginal utility gives the demand curve is that total utility is cardinal and given in dollar values. Slightly less than 3,000,000 ski days should be expected for a price of $20 per day.

76   6   Demand and Consumer Behavior

Table TQ6-1(b)

Price	Quantity Demanded
$30	1,000,000 × 1 = 1,000,000
25	2,000,000
18	3,000,000
15	4,000,000
10	5,000,000
5	6,000,000

7. Recall the definition of price elasticity and solve for the missing piece of information.

8. The market demand curve becomes flatter and flatter, but the percentage changes stay the same. To see why, consider the following simple example: Suppose that a 10 percent increase in price caused two people to reduce their consumption 10 percent from 10 units to 9 units. Together, they would reduce their total consumption from 20 units to 18 units—a 10 percent reduction.

9. Addictive substances typically show "necessity-like" low price elasticities. The 10-cent tax mentioned represents a 10 percent price increase for cigarettes. With an elasticity of 0.4, this would translate into a 4 percent reduction in the quantity demanded because perfectly elastic supply means that the equilibrium price would climb by the full 10 percent. Cigarette demand would fall by 0.04 × 10 billion = 0.4 billion, leaving the quantity demanded at 9.6 billion. Tax revenue would therefore equal $0.10 × 9.6 billion = $960 million. Draw your graph with a horizontal supply curve shifting up from $1.00 to $1.10.

10. Something like Figure TQ6-1 applies.

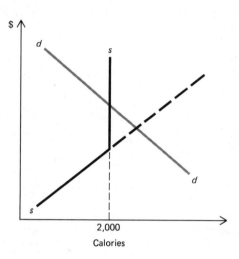

Figure TQ6-1

APPENDIX 6

GEOMETRIC ANALYSIS OF CONSUMER EQUILIBRIUM

The purpose of this appendix is the same as that of Chapter 6: to explain how consumers can use their fixed incomes to their own best advantage, given their own personal tastes, in the face of universal prices. It begins with the same stylized description of the consumer's dilemma, and it reaches the same results. In fact, only the method of description is different; the whole problem of maximizing satisfaction subject to a budget constraint is illustrated on a single graph.

So why bother? To be sure, the graph deals with a very simple case in which only two goods are involved, but the geometry will nonetheless reveal with increased clarity the general nature of making choices among many times that number of goods in the face of scarcity. The content of the analysis is not, in other words, confined to the two cases that can be drawn on a piece of graph paper.

More importantly, though, the geometric approach frees us from the assumption that consumers put numerical values onto the satisfaction derived from consuming each unit of a commodity—an assumption which many economists dislike. The geometry assumes, instead, that people can display their preferences simply by ranking possible combinations of goods. Constructing the geometry of consumer decision making requires only that consumers are able to express a preference between two or more alternative combinations of any number of goods, i.e., that they are able to say which combination of goods they want. An approach that features consumers' ranking of preferences as the driving force of demand theory is far easier to swallow than one that relies on consumers' ability to quantitatively evaluate consumption bundles.

Having worked through this appendix, you should accomplish the following learning objectives.

LEARNING OBJECTIVES

1. Define (a) an indifference curve and (b) an indifference map.

2. Explain why indifference curves may vary from one individual to the next.

3. Show that it would be impossible for an indifference curve representing normal preferences to run in the southwest-to-northeast direction.

4. Draw a line at any angle across an indifference-map graph, starting at the origin. Move northeast along that line, crossing indifference curves as you do so. Explain whether, in this movement, you are reaching lower levels of utility, are reaching higher levels, or are not changing the utility level at all.

5. Describe what is meant by a budget (or consumption-possibility) line.

6. Explain how the budget line shifts with a price increase (reduction) for one of the two goods involved. Explain how it would move for an income increase (decline).

1. a. Indifference curves are intended to depict a consumer's tastes. Any single indifference-curve line, such as the ones in Figure 6A-1, is made up of a series of points. Each point on such a line stands for a different (*amount of money / level of satisfaction / combination of two commodities*). What these points—all the points on any one indifference curve—have in common is that they all represent the same (*amount of money / level of satisfaction / combination of two commodities*) in the eyes of the consumer.

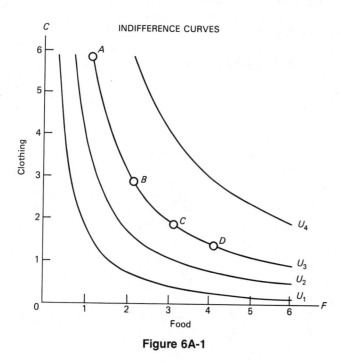

Figure 6A-1

b. We can represent a consumer's **indifference map** by drawing any one or two of (*several / an infinite number of*) indifference lines or curves. Given any two such indifference curves, the one lying farther from the graph's origin must stand for the (*higher / same / lower*) level of satisfaction. On Figure 6A-1, draw a 45° line from the origin of the graph. The four points at which this line crosses the four indifference curves indicate four different clothing-food combinations. The farther the indifference curve lies from the origin, the larger is the indicated level of consumption of both food and clothing and thus the higher the level of utility (recall that marginal utility is always positive, so supplements in the consumption of any good without some sacrifice of another must improve utility).

c. If two different clothing-food combinations lie on the same indifference curve, then the second must represent more food and less clothing (or vice versa) than the first. (You cannot be at the same level of satisfaction as before if you have more food *and* more clothing or if you have less food *and* less clothing.) This is indicated by the fact that any single indifference curve runs in a generally (*northeast-to-southwest / northwest-to-southeast*) direction.

---

a. combination of two commodities; level of satisfaction **b.** an infinite number of; higher **c.** northwest-to-southeast

---

2. a. Now set aside for a moment the indifference-curve idea. Turn, instead, to what you could buy (regardless of your tastes) if you were provided with a given income and faced with a particular set of prices.

In the simple two-good case discussed here, all the possible combinations purchasable can be represented by a straight line on a graph—the **budget line** or **consumption-possibility line** in Figure 6A-2.

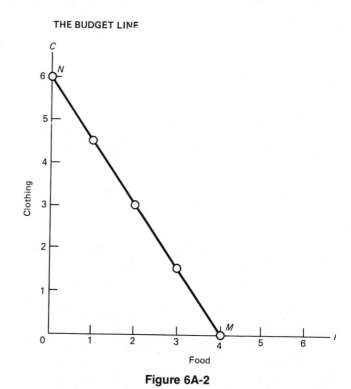

Figure 6A-2

Be sure you understand the information which this budget or consumption-possibility line is intended to convey. Each and every point on this line stands for a different (*amount of money income / level of satisfaction / combination of the two commodities*). The combinations are all different, but they all have one thing in common: given the prices specified, they (*can all be purchased for the same amount of money / all stand for the same level of satisfaction*).

b. You can move up or down this budget line as you wish; all the points located there are equivalent in the sense of costing the same amount of money. Which point should you choose? That is a matter of taste. The various food-clothing combinations on the budget line are not equivalent in the sense of generating the same level of satisfaction. You should pick the combinations which you like *most*—the combination which *maximizes your satisfaction*.

The mention of tastes pulls us back to indifference curves again. The task of moving back and forth along the budget line, seeking the maximum-satisfaction food-clothing combination, is just a matter of finding the point on this budget line which reaches the (*highest- / lowest-*) attainable indifference curve. This is illustrated in Figure 6A-3. The highest-attainable indifference curve is always the one which lies farthest *(from the origin / from the budget constraint)* on an ordinary graph.

---

a. combination of the two commodities; can all be purchased for the same amount of money **b.** highest-; from the origin

---

It is important to note that the division of tastes and budget concerns that is apparent in the organization of questions 1 and 2 is more than an accident. It is a division that is, in economic terms, equally clear and well defined. Factors that influence preferences are reflected only in indifference curves; factors that influence what you can afford are reflected only in the budget line.

3. a. Studying Figure 6A-3, you will see that point *B*, the equilibrium or maximum-satisfaction point, is one at which the indifference curve is just tangent to the budget or consumption-possibility line. That is, equilibrium is a situation where the slope of the indifference curve exactly matches the slope of the budget constraint.

It happens that the slope of the budget line is a matter of the prices of the two commodities involved. This question explores the matter more fully.

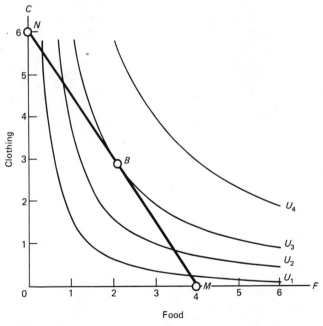

Figure 6A-3

The slope of the line in Figure 6A-3 (neglecting its negative sign) is $6/4$, or $1\frac{1}{2}$. At the two extreme positions, you could have either 6 of C and zero F (point *N*) or 4 of F and zero C (point *M*). If you move any distance down the line from point *N*, you find that this $6/4$ (or $3/2$) swapping ratio applies. If you move from *N* to the middle dot on *NM*, you must give up 3 units of C, but you gain 2 units of F.

The prices of F and C govern this swapping ratio. Giving up 3 units of C (price $1) recovers $3 of your budget. This you can use to buy 2 units of F (price $1.50). So, whether measured at $6/4$, $3/2$, or $1.50/$1.00, the slope measures market swapping terms, and those terms are determined by relative prices.

To exercise your understanding of this point, suppose that a budget limits combined expenditure on clothing (C) and food (F) to $40. With the prices for C and F as indicated in Table 6A-1, first compute the slope of the consumption-possibility line (the budget line) as a ratio of C/F (i.e., maximum affordable C over maximum affordable F), and then compare that slope to the ratio P_F/P_C. F is the commodity measured along the horizontal axis. Assume that all slope values are preceded by an unrecorded minus sign.

Table 6A-1

			Ratio C/F	Ratio P_F/P_C
A	$P_C = \$1$,	$P_F = \$4$	___ / ___	___ / ___
B	$P_C = \$5$,	$P_F = \$2$	___ / ___	___ / ___
C	$P_C = \$2$,	$P_F = \$10$	___ / ___	___ / ___

table rows: A—40, 10; $4, $1; B—8, 20; $2, $5; C—20, 4; $10, $2

4. We conclude with a brief survey of the effects of a change in income or in price upon the equilibrium position.

a. Consider income changes first. If your income is halved, then you must cut down on your purchases. The income cut means—look at Figure 6A-4—a shift of the budget line *(away from / toward)* the origin. The new half-the-income budget line *(is / is not)* parallel to the old one because the prices that define the slope *(have / have not)* changed (see question 3 again if you do not know what prices have to do with anything).

In this new and painful income situation, you will not necessarily buy food and clothing in the same proportions as before. You must cut your purchases, and while you may indeed cut each of them by 50 percent, you may choose not to. The point you pick on your new budget line will be governed, as before, by your tastes. You may wind up buying relatively more food and less clothing, or vice versa.

b. An increase in the price of food or of clothing works somewhat like an income reduction: it pulls you down to a lower satisfaction level. But compare Figure 6A-5 (illustrating an increase in food price) with Figure 6A-4 (income reduction). In both instances, the budget line shifts in position. In Figure 6A-5, the new budget line *(is / is not)* parallel with the old one. The point is that if you wanted to spend all your income on clothing, an increase in the price of food would not affect

EFFECT OF INCOME CHANGE ON EQUILIBRIUM

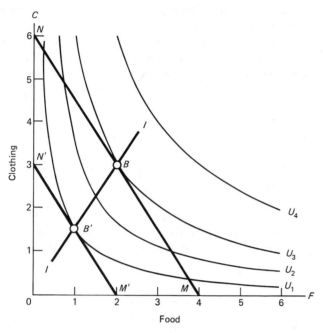

Figure 6A-4

you in the least. Point N (Figure 6A-5) would therefore still be attainable. At the other extreme, if you continue to spend all your income on food, despite the higher price of food, then a doubling of its price would *(leave you unaffected / require that you halve your purchases)*.

EFFECT OF PRICE CHANGE ON EQUILIBRIUM

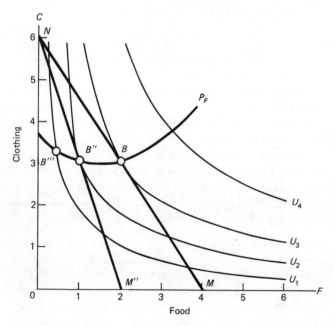

Figure 6A-5

That is why the budget line shifts as it does. As before, you pick the best-attainable position on your new budget line, as your personal tastes dictate. There is more to be said on these topics, but it must be left for more advanced texts.

a. towards; is; have not   **b.** is not; require that you halve your purchases

5. In the upper part of Figure 6A-6, the line AB_0 is a consumer's initial budget line, and E_0 is his or her equilibrium point thereon. The curved line is an indifference curve for this consumer, and it is tangent to the budget line at this E_0 point. (The two other curved lines are also indifference curves.) The price of good X is $4 along constraint AB_0.

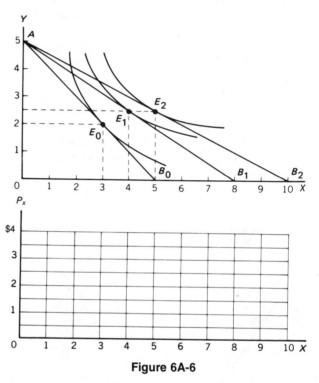

Figure 6A-6

a. The consumer's income or budget must be:

(1) $50.

(2) $20.

(3) $10.

(4) $5.

(5) $2.

(6) impossible to tell.

b. The price of good Y must be:

(1) $1.

(2) $2.

(3) $3.

(4) $4.

(5) $5.

(6) impossible to tell from diagram.

c. The budget or consumption-possibility line shifts from position AB_0 to position AB_1. Such a shift could be caused only by:

(1) a fall in the price of X.

(2) a rise in the price of X.

(3) a rise in the price of Y.

(4) a fall in the price of Y.

(5) an increase in income.

d. Quantitatively, what change is indicated by the shift from AB_0 to AB_1? That is, whether it is the price of X, the price of Y, or income that has changed, what is its new value?

(1) $50.

(2) $20.

(3) $10.

(4) $5.

(5) $2.50.

(6) $2.

(7) $1.

e. If a further shift in the AB line occurs, from AB_1 to AB_2, which alternative in part **c** explains it? . . . .
. . . . (1 / 2 / 3 / 4 / 5)

f. Which alternative in part **d** indicates the new value of the magnitude which has changed? . . . .
. . . . (1 / 2 / 3 / 4 / 5 / 6 / 7)

g. Use the lower part of Figure 6A-6 to show the demand curve of the consumer in the preceding questions for commodity X. This demand curve is to be drawn given the particular level of income and price of good Y indicated by the preceding questions. Plot three points on this curve, correctly indicating the consumer's demand for X in these circumstances. (*Hint:* What price or prices of X must go with the three consumption-possibility lines illustrated? What quantity or quantities of X will be bought? Join these three points with a smooth curve.)

---

a. (2) (*Note:* $20 = 5 \times $4, where 5 is the maximum X that can be purchased.) **b.** (4) (*Note:* income = $20 with 5 units of Y maximum, meaning that Y costs $4 per unit.) **c.** (1) **d.** (5) ($2.50 per unit of X exhausts $20 if, as indicated, a maximum of 8 X units can be purchased.) **e.** 1 (another fall in the price of X) **f.** 6 [$2 = P_X, so $20 can support a maximum of 10 units of X.] **g.** There are three combinations of price and quantity that can be gleaned from the top of Figure 6A-6: ($P_X = $4, X = 3$), ($P_X = $2.50, X = 4$), and ($P_X = $2, X = 5$), from budget lines AB_0, AB_1, and AB_2, respectively.

REVIEW CONCEPTS

1. An indifference curve plots combinations of goods which generate the same level of satisfaction or utility. Their position relative to each other is a matter of individual taste; they reflect individual preferences.

2. Indifference maps run from northwest to southeast because more of one good must always be associated with less of another if total satisfaction is to remain constant. Put a different way, more of two goods (without any sacrifice in a third) is usually thought to *always* increase utility; linear movement away from the origin must therefore be associated with increased satisfaction.

3. A budget line plots combinations of goods which cost the same. Their slopes reflect relative prices, so they rotate as the price of one good changes and shift in parallel as income changes.

4. Utility is maximized when the slope of an indifference curve equals the slope of a budget constraint at a point of tangency between the two.

QUIZ: Multiple Choice

1. The position and shape of any indifference curve for any particular consumer are governed:
(1) by his or her tastes and by the amount of income defining the budget constraint.
(2) solely by the prices of the goods purchased.
(3) by tastes, by the amount of income available, and by the prices of the goods purchased.
(4) by the prices of the goods purchased and by the amount of income available, but not by tastes.
(5) solely by his or her tastes.

2. Which alternative in question 1 correctly names the factor or factors governing the budget line?
(1) .
(2) .
(3) .
(4) .
(5) .

3. On an indifference-curve map, a consumer's approach to the equilibrium position is properly described as follows:
(1) The consumer moves to that point on the budget line representing the combination of goods having the highest money value.
(2) The consumer moves to that point on the budget line where the slope of the budget line equals the ratio of the two prices.
(3) The consumer moves along the budget line until the extra utility supplied by one good is just equal to the extra utility supplied by the other.

82   6   Demand and Consumer Behavior

(4) The consumer picks the highest-valued indifference curve which is attainable along the given budget line.
(5) The consumer picks the highest-valued budget line which intersects the given indifference curve.

4. One of the following five statements describing indifference-curve analysis is incorrect. Which one?
(1) Each point on an indifference curve stands for a different combination of two goods.
(2) Each point on a budget line stands for a different combination of two goods.
(3) All the points on an indifference curve stand for the same level of satisfaction.
(4) All the points on a budget line cost the same amount of money.
(5) All the points on an indifference curve cost the same amount of money.

5. You are told that an indifference curve involving goods X and Y runs from southwest to northeast. Your response to this statement is that this:
(1) must indicate an increase in the consumer's income.
(2) is impossible because it would indicate that the consumer gets no satisfaction from either good X or good Y.
(3) must indicate a change in the consumer's tastes.
(4) must indicate a change in the price of either X or Y.
(5) is impossible because larger quantities of both X and Y cannot indicate the same level of satisfaction unless the consumer wants no more of either of these two goods.

SUGGESTED ANSWERS TO QUESTIONS IN THE TEXT: Appendix to Chapter 6

1. Using ">" to denote "preferred to" and "≈" to denote "indifferent to," consider Figure TQ6A-1. There, indifference curves I and II cross at point A. Because moving from point B to C to D involves more of both X and Y, $D > C > B$. Because B and A are on the same indifference curve (curve II), $B \approx A$. Because D and A are on the same indifference curve (curve I), $D \approx A$. So it must be that $D \approx B$, but $D > B$. This contradiction was caused by the intersection of curves I and II.

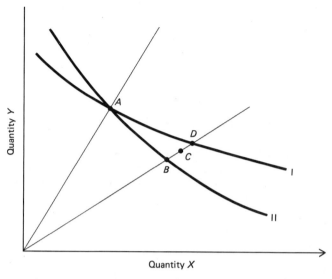

Figure TQ6A-1

2. Move along the budget constraint in the direction of the interior of the area that is (a) above the indifference curve *and* (b) below the budget constraint. These points are affordable *and* generate higher satisfaction.

3. As the price of food increases from $1.50 to $3.00 and finally to $6.00 per unit, the quantity demanded falls from 2 units to 1 unit and finally to 0.5 unit. Downward sloping for reasons of substitution and income effects.

4. As long as the number always increases as the curve gets further from the origin, the tangency of the curve indicating the highest utility is unaffected.

5. Consult Figure TQ6A-2.

Appendix 6 Geometric Analysis of Consumer Equilibrium

Figure TQ6A-2

CHAPTER 7

PRODUCTION AND BUSINESS ORGANIZATION

There are, early in the 1990s, more than 17 billion businesses in the United States. The majority are independent proprietorships, but such businesses are hardly ever very large. For average annual sales of less than $40,000, proprietors work long and hard (50 to 60 hours per week). They typically face chronic cash flow problems, but they find bankers reluctant to lend them money, especially in the wake of a rash of bank failures. Help in these matters is sometimes available from the Small Business Administration and/or small-business investment companies, but not always. Proprietors own their own businesses and are thus their own bosses, of course, but they face personal income taxation if they are unusually successful and unlimited liability if they are not.

The least popular form of business organization is the partnership. Partnerships are typically larger than individual proprietorships, with average annual sales in the neighborhood of $200,000, but the good news might stop there. Partners face the personal income tax, risk, and unlimited-liability difficulties, just like proprietors, and frequently experience very similar cash flow problems. In addition, partners share decision-making authority with other people. Partnerships may, therefore, appear to some to capture all the bad characteristics of proprietorships without garnering any of the advantages of incorporation.

Corporations represent the third and last major form of business organization. They tend to be large and powerful. Their average annual sales hover around $2 million, but over 250 corporations sell more than $1 billion in goods and services annually. Owners typically forfeit decision-making authority to professional managers, but they are rewarded for this sacrifice with personal liability that is limited to the amount of their investment. Corporations can last forever, too, so a voluntary or involuntary decision of one owner to leave the corporation is hardly ever noticed—his or her stock is simply sold in the market or bequested in a will to someone else. Corporate income is subject to the corporate income (profits) tax, and dividends are awarded out of the remaining after-tax income to individual stockholders. These dividends are, of course, subject themselves to the personal income tax. The system therefore effectively sets up a sort of double taxation that has made the corporate income tax one of this country's most controversial taxes.

Having worked through the story of the computer-software company in the text and the problems recorded here, you should have met the following objectives.

LEARNING OBJECTIVES

1. Explain the differences between the three major forms of business organization: proprietorship, partnership, and corporation.

2. Explain the three roles that firms play in a modern economy.

3. Explain the meaning of unlimited liability as it applies to each of the three forms.

4. Explain why any growing business is likely to find itself in potentially acute need of more capital financing.

5. Explain the propensity of large businesses to be incorporated.

6. List the advantages and/or disadvantages of investing money in each of the three business forms.

7. Outline what is meant by the "divorce of ownership and control" in large corporations. List social problems that this divorce might create.

This chapter also begins your exposure to the fundamental concepts with which economists investigate the purpose of forming a business in the first place—the production and subsequent supply of goods and/or services. Having worked through their presentation, you should also have accomplished the following additional objectives.

ADDITIONAL LEARNING OBJECTIVES

8. Define a production function and relate it to the notions of (a) total product, (b) marginal product, and (c) average product.

9. Explain the law of diminishing marginal returns. Define constant, increasing, and decreasing returns to scale, and relate each to the law of diminishing marginal returns.

10. Compare and contrast measures of total productivity and the productivity of a particular input. Relate both to technological change and the law of diminishing marginal returns.

11. Distinguish between momentary run, short run, and long run in the context of production.

12. State and explain the stylized facts that describe the growth of the aggregate U.S. economy since the turn of the century. Describe why it can be said that the experience of the United States over the past two decades has not been as profitable as its experience over the century taken as a whole.

The first part of this chapter concentrates on the form that a business takes. Be it proprietorship, partnership, or corporation, the form chosen is almost always dictated by the amount of money needed to operate in the chosen line of work and the "critical mass" required to achieve efficient production. In many industries, in fact, there is simply no room for choice, and only large corporations are found. If large quantities of money are required for successful and efficient operation in some line of work, then no individual proprietorship or small partnership will be found. In other areas of business, there are choices, and other forms can flourish (or at least hope to).

The need for money—*financial* capital—can be explained in terms of two distinct phenomena. First, firms typically find it necessary to buy expensive, long-lasting machinery, tools, equipment, buildings, etc.; i.e., firms usually find it impossible to operate without making substantial investments in procuring and maintaining physical capital. They have to pay for this physical capital before it earns enough return to pay for itself, so they need some money "up front." Second, there is an inevitable lag between the money expenditure (for labor, raw materials, transportation costs, etc.) and money receipts (from the sale of product). A growing and vital business therefore needs **working capital** even when it is not buying more physical capital. Both needs work constantly to make just about every business feel "cash poor."

Incorporation is, above all else, a device that makes it easier to raise large quantities of money. Ownership shares in a corporation can be sold to a small number of people or to a large number of people at a price which reflects the value of the ownership claims that they represent. People will buy these shares because they can be attractive financial assets. They can be bought in almost any quantity. They release the shareholder from any concern about running the business; professional managers are hired to do that. The limited liability that they carry guarantees that, even in the very worst of circumstances, shareholder losses will be no larger than the purchase price of the stock. They can be sold at any time without the corporation's consent (though perhaps not without a spousal consent or needle). And it is *incorporation* that opens the door to this form of money harvest.

The text illustrates these points by showing how the need for money might inspire a fictitious software company to grow from a small proprietorship into a successful corporation. The following questions emphasize the lessons of that story.

1. Five people own equal shares in a partnership. For any one of the five, **unlimited liability** holds that that person is responsible for *(20 percent of the partnership's debts, up to the amount he or she has invested in the business / 20 percent of the partnership debts, no matter how large the amount / 100 percent of the partnership debts, if necessary, in the event that other partners cannot pay their shares, no matter how large the amount).*

---
100 percent of the partnership debts, if necessary, in the event that other partners cannot pay their shares, no matter how large the amount

---

2. Note that in this chapter the word "capital" has a meaning quite different from that given it in Chapter 3. "Capital" in the physical sense of that earlier chapter means *(money used to finance a business / money loaned with a strong element of risk involved / manufactured productive inputs, not money).* "Capital" in this present chapter means *(money / machines / computers and other high-tech equipment).*

---
manufactured productive inputs, not money; money

3. a. A corporation *(must / may or may not)* have common stock. The law which created the corporate form says that a corporation must have owners—and the stockholders are its owners.

This stock *(must / may or may not)* be listed on an exchange, such as the New York Stock Exchange. (Actually, only a surprisingly small number of giant corporations have their stock so listed. Many corporations are "private," in the sense that their stock is not publicly listed for trading. Sometimes this stock is held entirely or almost entirely by members of a single family and only rarely changes hands.)

b. A corporation *(must / may or may not)* have bonds outstanding. The vital difference between stocks and bonds is that bonds are *(certificates of ownership / IOUs)*. The corporation is free to borrow (i.e., issue such IOUs) or not to borrow, as it sees fit.

---

a. must; may or may not **b.** may or may not; IOUs

We move now to the essence of most business production. Having been introduced to the workings of supply and demand in the product markets, it is now time to consider the various decisions that businesses must make in servicing those markets. Scarcity and need determine why it costs more to purchase some goods than others, but what determines wages and salaries? Why are some occupations more highly paid than others? If all inputs are employed to work together to produce a specific output, how are their respective contributions assessed in the computation of their appropriate rates of compensation? How is it that the return to capital has held steady over the past 90 years despite an increase in the size of the capital stock compared with the size of the labor force? After all, a lot has happened since Teddy Roosevelt was in the White House.

The answers to these and other questions will again be found in the workings of supply and demand—this time in the markets for inputs. In a product market, for example, you have seen that demand for any good arises from the utility that the good provides to the consumer. In an input market, demand arises from the productivity that the good can offer the employer in the production of some other good that people are willing to buy. The demand for an input is, therefore, a derived demand based not upon the immediate, innate value of that input to the firm but upon the ultimate value of the final good being produced. Still, we will see that the basic principles of supply and demand hold in this input arena just as they do in the output arena.

The first concept to grasp is the notion of a *production function*. Suppose that engineers and scientists defined a process through which certain types of inputs could be employed to produce a certain type of output. A production function representing that process would record the maximum output that could be produced from various (all possible) combinations of inputs, given the specific state of technology defined by the engineers. Conversely, the production function would also identify all the various combinations of inputs that could be combined to produce a particular level of output.

4. a. The total amount of output measured in physical units of production is called _____. Average product is the ratio of *(the change in total product / total product)* to *(the change in the employment of one input / the change in the employment of all inputs / the total employment of all inputs / the total employment of one input)*; it is *(an input-specific concept / defined for a production process as a whole)*. Marginal product is *(also input-specific / also defined for a process at large)*. Marginal product is the ratio of *(the change in total product / total product)* to *(the change in the employment of all inputs / the change in the employment of one input / the total employment of all inputs / the total employment of one input)*.

b. Consider a production function that relates the quantity of some good produced *(X)* with the quantities of capital *(K)*, labor *(L)*, and material *(M)* employed. Indicate in the blanks provided whether each stated formula applies to the total product, the marginal product, or the average product of capital, labor, or material. Use MP_K, for example, to indicate the marginal product of capital; AP_L, the average product of labor; etc. If the stated definition applies to none of the possible combinations, write "n/a."

(1) Change in K/change in X = ... _____

(2) Change in X/quantity of L = ... _____

(3) Quantity of X/quantity of K = ... _____

(4) Change in X/change in L = ... _____

(5) Quantity of X = ... _____

(6) Quantity of K/quantity of M = ... _____

(7) Change in X/change in K = ... _____

(8) Quantity of K/quantity of X = ... _____

---

a. total product; total product; the total employment of one input; an input-specific concept; also input-specific; the change in total product; the change in the employment of one input **b.** (1) n/a (2) n/a (3) AP_K (4) MP_L (5) $TP_K = TP_L = TP_M$ (6) n/a (7) MP_K (8) n/a

5. Table 7-1 provides the data for a production function that relates the employment of capital *(K)* and labor *(L)* to maximum output levels of some good Y. Fill in the blanks for the average and marginal products of labor given capital employment of 4 units and 8 units.

7 Production and Business Organization

Table 7-1

	4 Units of Capital Employed				8 Units of Capital Employed		
Labor	TP	MP_L	AP_L	Labor	TP	MP_L	AP_L
0	0		undefined	0	0		undefined
		22					
1	22		____	1	22.5		____
		20					
2	42		____	2	44		____
3	60		____	3	64.5		____
4	76		____	4	84		____
5	90		____	5	102.5		____
6	102		____	6	120		____
7	112		____	7	136.5		____
8	120		____	8	152		____
9	126		____	9	166.5		____
10	130		____	10	180		____

Graph the total product curves for both levels of capital employment in the top panel of Figure 7-1 (use different-colored pencils or pens to differentiate the two cases); graph the marginal and average product curves for both cases in the bottom panel of Figure 7-1 (use the same colors). [When drawing the marginal product curves, use the convention of plotting the value against the halfway points of labor employment. The marginal product of the second unit of labor with 4 units of capital is, for example, given as 20; plot the point (1.5, 20) on the marginal product curve.]

---

table columns for 4 units of capital: MP_L — 18, 16, 14, 12, 10, 8, 6, 4; AP_L: — 22, 21, 20, 19, 18, 17, 16, 15, 14, 13; columns for 8 units of capital: MP_L — 22.5, 21.5, 20.5, 19.5, 18.5, 17.5, 16.5, 15.5, 14.5, 13.5; AP_L — 22.5, 22, 21.5, 21, 20.5, 20, 19.5, 19, 18.5, 18

Notice from the table and perhaps more vividly from the graphs that doubling the capital stock from 4 units to 8 units increases (1) total product, (2) average product, and (3) marginal product for each level of labor employment. Working with more capital, labor is, quite simply, more *productive*.

6. Refer again to the data of Table 7-1. Suppose that 3 units of labor are employed and that the capital stock increases from 4 units to 8 units. Labor productivity, measured in terms of output per unit of labor, should increase from _____ to _____, an increase of _____ percent. If 8 units of labor were employed, then the growth in labor productivity would be from _____ to _____ for a _____ percent increase.

20; 21.5; 7.5; 15; 19; 26.67

The increase in productivity just investigated might have been the result of technological change instead of capital deepening. For example, some new invention might have made each piece of capital listed on the left-hand side of Table 7-1 work like two pieces. If that were so, then the matching of labor employment to total product recorded on the right-hand side would apply *even with 4 units of capital employed*. The productivity gains that you just noted would have been the result of new technology and not of an increase in the capital stock.

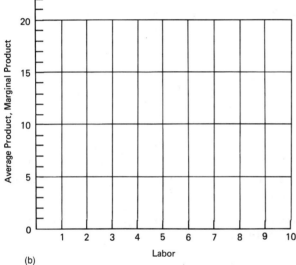

Figure 7-1

7. The law of diminishing returns is widely observed; it holds that the marginal product of any input should (eventually) decline as the employment of that input *(climbs / falls)*. In Table 7-1, *(both / only the right-hand / only the left-hand / neither)* total product schedule(s) generate(s) marginal product curves for labor that *(obey / contradict)* this law. Because the law of diminishing returns is defined in terms of the marginal product of some input, it applies when the *(employments of all inputs are being changed simultaneously / employments of all inputs are being changed simultaneously and proportionately / employment of only one input is being changed while all other levels are held fixed)*. The law also applies *(when technology is unaltered / even if the technology changes as employment changes)*. Why? Because marginal product is defined for a given production function and thus is defined only for a specific production technology.

---

climbs; both; obey; employment of only one input is being changed while all other levels are held fixed; when technology is unaltered

The notion of marginal product is input-specific; it measures the response in total product of a change in the employment of any input under the assumption that the employment of *all other inputs is constant*. Returns to scale are a measure of the response in total product when all inputs move together—not arbitrarily in a cacophony of simultaneous change, but proportionately. The term *constant returns to scale* refers to the circumstance in which multiplying the employment of *all* inputs by the same factor results in the multiplication of output by the *same* factor. Double all inputs and you get twice the output. Quadruple all inputs and you get 4 times the output. Multiply all inputs by some number k and you get k *times* the output. (The best visual image for constant returns to scale is replicating a production plant. Everything else being equal, you can always double the output of any plant by building its twin next door.)

A situation characterized by *decreasing returns to scale* is the poor cousin to constant returns to scale: double all inputs and get *less than* twice the output; multiply all inputs by k and get *less than* k times the output. The opposite occurs with *increasing returns to scale*: double all inputs and get more than twice the output. If decreasing returns are the scourge of size, then increasing returns are the blessing of size. Firms requiring the use of a specific natural resource sometimes display the former; industries having a "volume technology" to exploit, the latter.

8. The right-hand side of Table 7-1 shows one possible production response to increasing the capital stock from 4 units to 8 units; call it alternative A. Table 7-2 shows four alternative schedules for $K = 8$ units, labeled "B," "C," "D," and "E." On the basis of the inferences that you can make by comparing the left-hand side of Table 7-1 with these alternatives, indicate in the parentheses below which of these schedules conform to the specified characteristic when linked with the left-hand side of Table 7-1.

Table 7-2

Labor	Alt B	Alt C	Alt D	Alt E
0	0	0	0	0
1	24.5	20.5	18.5	25.5
2	48.0	40.0	36.0	50.0
3	70.5	58.5	52.5	73.5
4	92.0	76.0	68.0	96.0
5	112.5	92.5	82.5	117.5
6	132.0	108.0	96.0	138.0
7	150.5	122.5	108.5	157.5
8	168.0	136.0	120.0	176.0
9	184.5	148.5	130.5	193.5
10	200.0	160.0	140.0	210.0

a. Increasing returns to scale ...... ( )

b. Constant returns to scale ...... ( )

c. Decreasing returns to scale ..... ( )

d. Diminishing returns to labor ..... ( )

a. B and E (The five cases in which you can trace the effect of doubling both inputs all produce more than a doubling of output.) **b.** A (The five cases in which you can trace the effect of doubling both inputs all produce a doubling of output.) **c.** C and D (The five cases in which you can trace the effect of doubling inputs all produce less than a doubling of output.) **d.** A, B, C, D, and E (All show diminishing returns right from the start. To see this, compute the marginal products.)

The real point of question 8 is that the law of diminishing returns is compatible with increasing, decreasing, and constant returns to scale. Returns to scale and marginal productivity refer to two distinct things: returns to scale reflect what happens with a proportional change in *all* inputs; marginal productivity shows what happens with a change in only *one* input (all the others held fixed).

9. Indicate in the parentheses provided which of the following would be reactions that you would expect to see undertaken by a firm in the momentary run (MR), in the short run (SR), or in the long run (LR):

a. Adopting a new, computerized production technique that involves reworking the assembly line. .... ( )

b. Adopting a new, computerized production technique that improves inventory control. .... ( )

c. Having 50 percent of the employees work overtime, amounting to an extra 10 hours per week per worker. ( )

d. Reopening an existing assembly line located closer to a new and developing market. .... ( )

e. Recognizing a new market development that threatens half the firm's existing market share. .... ( )

f. Reworking the technology of the assembly technique to reduce material waste by 50 percent. .... ( )

g. Increasing the work force by 10 percent to increase capacity utilization by 5 percent. .... ( )

h. Doubling the work force to take advantage of increasing returns to scale. .... ( )

a. LR **b.** SR **c.** SR **d.** LR **e.** MR **f.** LR **g.** SR **h.** LR (because you need to double the capital stock to take advantage of IRS)

10. Which of the following empirical statements are true in regard to the experience of the aggregate U.S. economy?

a. Total productivity has risen in the United States by an average rate of 1.5 percent per year throughout the twentieth century. .... (T / F)

b. On average, labor productivity grew faster than the 1.5 percent annual rate of growth of total productivity throughout the twentieth century. .... (T / F)

c. The return to capital has held remarkably steady in the United States since the turn of the twentieth century. ... . (T / F)

d. There has, since 1970, been a decline in the rate of growth of the real wages that support the American standard of living. .... (T / F)

All the statements are true.

11. Since all the statements recorded in question 10 are true, there must be an economic justification for each that is consistent with the fundamentals of production. Match each of the following with the empirical statement that it helps explain:

a. The rate of technological progress nearly matched the rate at which diminishing returns affected capital. .... (a / b / c / d)

b. Sustained technological progress accounted for sustained growth in overall productivity. ...... (a / b / c / d)

c. The capital stock of the United States grew faster than the number of hours of labor supplied throughout most of the twentieth century. .... (a / b / c / d)

d. The rate of growth of total productivity has declined against historical trends. .... (a / b / c / d)

a. c **b.** a **c.** b **d.** d

12. Which of the following represent substitution of one factor of production for another with an unchanged technology (S), which represent technological change (T), and which represent neither (N)?

a. A firm replaces an oil-fired boiler with a regenerative heat-capture system. .... (S / T / N)

b. Following a successful unionization drive by clerical workers, a university buys personal computers for its faculty and thereby reduces its secretarial work force. .. (S / T / N)

c. A publishing firm reduces its employment of staff editors and increases its reliance on computer typesetting with a spelling/grammar check program. .... (S / T / N)

d. A manufacturing firm improves its quality guarantee by replacing human quality control with an optic surveillance system. .... (S / T / N)

e. A manufacturing firm improves its quality guarantee because it determines that it must assure its customers that it can match the quality of its foreign competition. . . . . (S / T / N)

a. T **b.** S **c.** S **d.** S or T (depending upon whether or not the optic system was an alternative all the while) **e.** N

13. Assume that the law of diminishing returns always holds. Which of the following statements is true?

a. If average product exceeds marginal product, then average product must be climbing. . . . . (T / F)

Why?_____

_____

_____

b. Average product is, in fact, always above marginal product. . . . . (T / F)

Why?_____

_____

_____

a. F; $AP > MP$ means that the incremental increase in total product is smaller than the average, so the average must fall. (Think about a .300 hitter going 1 for 10 in a doubleheader. What happens to his batting average with a "marginal" batting contribution of .100? It falls!) **b.** T (except perhaps for the first unit of employment); For the first unit of employment, MP and AP essentially match; for the second, with MP falling as dictated by the law of diminishing returns, AP falls only half as far; and so on. [For example, let $AP(1) = MP(1) = 20$ and $MP(2) = 10$; then $AP(2) = (20 + 10)/2 = 15 > 10$.] AP always falls slower from a higher point, so it must always exceed MP.

REVIEW CONCEPTS

1. Business establishments can be organized as individual proprietorships, as partnerships, or as corporations. Understand their differences even as they perform functions of management, resource accumulation, and exploitation of economies of mass production.

2. Corporations allow owners to limit their potential liability to the amount they have invested, but usually require their releasing the reigns of control to a management team.

3. A production function relates total production to the employment of inputs.

4. The average product of some input is total output divided by the level of employment of that input. Its marginal product reflects the rate at which total output changes as employment changes—all other inputs held constant. Marginal product declines in homage to the law of diminishing returns.

5. Returns to scale reflect the response of total output to *proportionate* changes in *all* inputs. Diminishing marginal productivity can be consistent with increasing, decreasing, or constant returns to scale.

6. Time period is critical in defining the sort of adjustments available to firms. Few adjustments can be undertaken instantaneously (in the momentary run). The short run allows the firm time to manipulate the employment of some inputs (e.g., labor). Anything can be altered in the long run, including capital stock and embodied technology.

QUIZ: Multiple Choice

1. The term "limited liability" is frequently used in enumerating the characteristics of a corporation. It means that:
(1) any officer of the corporation is strictly limited in his or her ability to speak for the corporation and commit it to any liability.
(2) once shareholders have paid for their stock, they have no further financial obligation, regardless of how much trouble the corporation gets into.
(3) the corporation's liability to pay dividends to its stockholders is a limited one, since it need pay them only if it has earned a profit.
(4) there are certain obligations which a corporation can legally refuse to pay.
(5) the corporation has only a limited obligation to meet claims made by any single person or firm against it (provided it has acted within the scope of its charter), so there is some protection for its assets and financial position.

2. A corporation's obligation to pay interest on bonds it has issued is properly described by which of the following statements?
(1) Interest *must* be paid regardless of whether a profit has been earned or not.
(2) Interest *must* be paid only when a profit has been earned.
(3) Interest need not be paid even if a profit has been earned, but it *must* be paid before any dividend is paid.
(4) Normally, interest ranks ahead of dividends, but there are some circumstances in which a dividend can be paid without payment of bond interest.
(5) Interest ranks behind dividends and is paid only after dividends have been paid in full.

3. In considering the order or ranking in which a corporation is obligated to pay out various sums of money, payment of dividends on common stock takes precedence over:
(1) corporation income taxes.
(2) local property taxes.
(3) the salaries of management.
(4) bond interest.
(5) none of these obligations.

4. A corporation that is considering debt financing (financing via a bond issue) must recognize that:
(1) bonds always involve a fixed annual charge to be paid to debt holders whether the corporation has earned profits or not.
(2) the issuance of debt gives the debt holders a voice in the management of the corporation's affairs, so they may usurp some part of management's authority.
(3) the new debt holders are not necessarily the same group as the original stockholders, so the ownership shares of those stockholders are diluted by debt financing.
(4) it does not actually bring in any additional cash to the corporation.
(5) this method of financing first requires an amendment to the corporation's charter.

5. Today's most common ownership and control arrangement for large American corporations is best described by which of the following statements?
(1) The professional managers are also the group owning a majority or near-majority of stock, so they can make all major decisions without real consideration of the wishes of minority stockholders.
(2) The professional managers make all the major decisions, and the board of directors does not usually intervene unless it is losing confidence in those managers.
(3) The professional managers control the company on all matters of importance except for basic decisions on such matters as production, new plants, and new products, these being left to the board of directors as stockholder representatives.
(4) The board of directors makes the decisions on all matters of real importance, the role of the professional managers being confined to routine matters.
(5) The stockholders rather than the board of directors are increasingly making major decisions, through voting-power control exercised at stockholder meetings.

6. The usual progression through business forms is:
(1) partnership, proprietorship, corporation.
(2) proprietorship, partnership, corporation.
(3) partnership, corporation, proprietorship.
(4) proprietorship, corporation, partnership.
(5) nonexistent because there does not exist a typical evolution.

7. Which of the following sources of investment capital comes from internal sources?
(1) Stock sales.
(2) Bank loans.
(3) Depreciation.
(4) Bond sales.
(5) None of the above.

8. The personal income tax of the United States is, through the personal returns of stockholders, applied:
(1) in full to any corporation's entire income regardless of whether or not it is distributed in the form of dividends.
(2) only to that part of profits that is actually distributed as dividends.
(3) only to that part of income not paid out as dividends but held instead as retained earnings.
(4) neither to dividends nor to retained earnings.
(5) both to dividends and to retained earnings, but with dividends getting preferential treatment.

9. If question 8 had referred to the U.S. corporate income tax, then the correct answer would have been:
(1) .
(2) .
(3) .
(4) .
(5) .

10. The law of diminishing returns holds that:
(1) the total product of any input must eventually reach a maximum and turn downward as the employment of that input increases.
(2) the average product of any input must eventually reach a minimum and turn upward as the employment of all inputs increases proportionately.
(3) the marginal product of any input should eventually begin to decline as the employment of that input increases.
(4) the marginal product of any input should eventually begin to decline as the employment of all inputs increases proportionately.
(5) the average product of any input should rise before it falls as the employment of that input increases.

11. If a production process displays diminishing returns for all inputs, then:
(1) it cannot display constant returns to scale.
(2) it must display decreasing returns to scale.
(3) it cannot display increasing returns to scale.
(4) all the above are true.
(5) none of the above is true.

12. If the average product of some input is observed running higher than its marginal product, then:
(1) the marginal product must be increasing with the employment of that input.
(2) the marginal product must be converging toward the average product.
(3) the average product must be increasing with the employment of that input.
(4) the average product must be falling with the employment of that input.
(5) the total product must be falling with the employment of that input.

13. Let production be defined by the function described in Table 7-3. With 3 units of capital on site, the average product

of the fourth unit of labor is:
(1) 13.
(2) 11.
(3) 10.
(4) 18.
(5) 16.

Table 7-3
Total Product

Labor	Capital Stock		
	$K = 2$	$K = 3$	$K = 4$
0	0	0	0
1	10	16	20
2	19	29	38
3	27	41	54
4	34	52	68
5	40	62	80
6	45	71	90

14. Let production be defined by the function described in Table 7-3. With 5 units of labor employed, the marginal product of the third unit of capital is:
(1) 12.4.
(2) 10.
(3) 9.
(4) 22.
(5) 18.

15. Let production be defined by the function described in Table 7-3. Which of the following statements is true?
(1) Production conforms to the law of diminishing returns with respect to K only when L is greater than 3 units.
(2) Production conforms to the law of diminishing returns with respect to L only when K is equal to 4.
(3) Production conforms to the law of diminishing returns with respect to L only.
(4) Production conforms to the law of diminishing returns with respect to K only.
(5) None of the above is true.

16. Let production be defined by the function described in Table 7-3. Given the information provided, it would appear that production displays:
(1) decreasing returns to scale.
(2) constant returns to scale.
(3) increasing returns to scale.
(4) tendencies to exploit labor.
(5) tendencies to exploit capital.

17. Let production be defined by the function described in Table 7-3. If the function were to display constant returns to scale given the total products recorded there for $K = 2$, then the output associated with $K = 4$ and $L = 6$ would have to equal:
(1) 20 units.
(2) 27 units.
(3) 38 units.
(4) 54 units.
(5) 90 units.

18. Which of the following adjustments to economic circumstance might a firm be able to accomplish in the long run?
(1) Adoption of a new computer-based production technology that replaces 50 percent of the labor working the assembly lines.
(2) Increased capacity utilization accomplished by hiring a third shift of workers.
(3) Reduction of the work force by 30 percent in the face of stiff foreign competition.
(4) Adoption of cost-cutting measures throughout middle management.
(5) All the above are possible in the long run.

19. As a matter of historical record, it is widely agreed that:
(1) total productivity in the United States has risen, on average, by nearly 0.5 percent per year since the turn of the twentieth century.
(2) labor productivity has increased in the United States faster than total productivity over the past nine decades even though the ratio of capital stock to labor force has remained remarkably constant.
(3) the rate of growth of total productivity in the United States over the past 20 years has averaged almost 1 percentage point less than the average over the past 90 years.
(4) the return to capital has increased dramatically in the United States since the turn of the twentieth century—an increase due in large part to a deepening of the U.S. capital stock relative to that of the rest of the world.
(5) none of the above statements is true.

20. A total product curve has been drawn on a piece of graph paper. If a second curve is drawn to reflect technological progress which makes labor more productive, then this second curve will:
(1) appear everywhere below the original curve and be flatter.
(2) appear everywhere above the original curve and be flatter.
(3) appear everywhere below the original curve and be steeper.
(4) appear everywhere above the original curve and be steeper.
(5) appear above the original curve until diminishing returns set in.

SUGGESTED ANSWERS TO QUESTIONS IN THE TEXT: Chapter 7

1. Definition.
2. Reading down the MP column: $2.8 (= 114K - 86K)/(20K - 10,000) = 28/10)$, 2, 1.6, 1.4.

Reading down the *AP* column: $86K/10K = 8.6, 5.7, 4.47, 3.75, 3.28$.

3. Graph the points with output on the vertical axis and horsepower on the horizontal axis.

4. Each point should be 20 percent higher against the vertical axis.

5. Apply definition across the table. For horsepower = $10K$, for example, the marginal product per inch diameter in pipe is $(141 - 43)/(24 - 12) = 98/12 = 8.17$.

6. Plug in the numbers to show that the formula applies. Marginal products are given by

$$MP_H = 1.72(H/10,000)^{-0.6}(P/12)^{1.7}$$

and

$$MP_P = 6092(H/10,000)^{0.4}(P/12)^{0.7}$$

7. K = your stand, grill, frig, etc.
L = you and your employees.
M = dogs, chips, condiments, etc.

You could, in the short run, reduce your orders of materials, lay off some people, and shorten your hours (e.g., open at halftime, etc....). In the long run, you could get a smaller stand and/or otherwise adjust your capital stock.

8. Hiring more people would move you along a production function for a given capital stock. Buying or renting a microwave instead of a grill would change technologies and thus the production function.

9. (a) substitution; (b) new technology; (c) substitution; (d) new technology.

10. Diminishing returns can coexist with any returns-to-scale parameter. (See question 5.)

11. Marginal product decreasing means that the increase in output is always smaller for successive increments of employment. Thus, the next increase in output is always smaller than the last, which was smaller than all of the previous; the next increase is thus always smaller than the average of the previous increases. Including this smaller number in the average must, as a result, reduce the average.

CHAPTER 8

ANALYSIS OF COSTS

This chapter explores the nature of costs. *Minimum production costs* of a firm are represented along a total cost schedule that depends on the level of output. Inputs used in their least-cost combination are the link between output and cost, and it is the ability to adjust (or not to adjust) their employment that provides the distinction between the two components of total cost: variable cost and fixed cost. The major objective here is for you to obtain a solid understanding of an economist's perspective of cost accounting so that subsequent descriptions of market structure will make sense. By the end of the chapter, you should have mastered the following objectives.

LEARNING OBJECTIVES

1. Define and describe total cost, fixed cost, variable cost, marginal cost, and average cost. Understand what these measures of cost are designed to reflect, and understand how they are related to one another. Derive, in particular, the associated average and marginal cost statistics from total, fixed, and variable cost.

2. Explain the link between productivity and cost. When the law of diminishing returns applies, marginal costs increase with output; when it does not apply, marginal costs can either fall with output or remain constant.

3. Demonstrate why constant input prices and constant returns to scale imply a horizontal marginal cost curve in the long run.

4. Demonstrate precisely why marginal cost *always* intersects average cost at the minimum of any U-shaped average cost curve.

5. Demonstrate why production costs are minimized when inputs are hired in combinations such that the ratios of their marginal products to their prices are all equal. Explain what this "least-cost rule" implies about substitution within production processes as the prices of inputs change.

6. Understand opportunity cost, and apply it to management decisions of firms and individuals.

7. Explain carefully the information which a balance sheet is intended to convey. List the major categories appearing on the two sides of a balance sheet, and indicate the meaning (or definition) of each of those categories.

8. List the major items appearing on an income statement. Indicate the information which an income statement is intended to convey.

9. Explain the role of (a) depreciation and (b) opportunity cost in the correct and accurate construction of an income statement.

Total costs include all the costs incurred in producing and selling a product. In the markets of our everyday experience, every firm incurs production costs; production costs are like death and taxes—unavoidable (if you want to make anything). Selling costs are, however, different. They may or may not be important components of a given firm's cost picture, depending upon the nature of its product and the structure of its market. Wheat farmers, for example, do not advertise their product; they take the price as given and sell as much as they can. For them, selling costs are exclusively delivery costs. Automobile manufacturers, by way of contrast, spend millions of dollars every week on advertising of all types—everything from television commercials on national networks to small-print ads in narrowly distributed weekly newspapers. Be they foreign or domestic manufacturers, their selling operations include trying to manipulate buyers by changing tastes and adjusting prices. Why the difference? The market faced by the auto giants is entirely different from the market faced by the wheat farmer.

To avoid confusing these two sources of cost, this chapter concentrates exclusively on production costs. Selling costs depend so critically upon market structure that discussion of their contribution to total cost is postponed until later. Total cost has two parts and one important derivative:

1. **Variable costs** are those costs whose total amount varies with the amount of output produced. For example, direct labor cost is a cost whose total should rise as the amount of output rises because it usually takes more labor to produce more stuff; it is thus one component of variable cost.

2. **Fixed costs** are those costs which are fixed in amount regardless of the level of output and which would accordingly have to be paid by the firm even if its output were zero. Interest on a bond issue is a cost the firm must pay whether it is operating at zero output or at maximum capacity, for example; it is thus a component of fixed cost.

3. **Marginal cost** is a measure of the increase in total cost resulting from a 1-unit increase in output. Since it depends only on costs that change with output, marginal cost can also be defined in terms of the increase in variable cost resulting from a 1-unit expansion in output.

The distinction between fixed and variable costs turns out to be important and interesting. Sometimes you cannot understand a firm's situation and the problems that it faces until you have grasped the distinction between these two kinds of costs. Marginal cost, though, depends only upon variable costs. Why? Because fixed costs do not, by their very definition, change as output is increased or reduced.

1. In the parentheses below, put (V) if you think the item would contribute to variable cost and (F) if you think that it would be part of fixed cost:

a. The cost of purchasing raw materials .... ( )

b. Depreciation on machinery when the rate of production is considered to be the primary source of depreciation. .... ( )

c. The annual fire-insurance premium on plant buildings. .... ( )

d. A tax levied on the firm for each hour of labor employed. .... ( )

e. Depreciation on machinery when time rather than quantity of output produced is considered to be the factor principally responsible for the depreciation .... ( )

f. Salaries paid to supervisors on an annual basis .. ( )

g. Local property taxes on buildings .... ( )

h. The cost of purchasing electric power to run the machines .... ( )

i. The cost of maintaining an active research and development department .... ( )

j. A royalty paid for the use of certain machines according to number of units produced .... ( )

k. Extra pay for overtime work by labor .... ( )

---

a. V b. V c. F d. V e. F f. F g. F h. V i. F j. V k. V

2. The figures in columns (1) and (2) of Table 8-1 indicate the estimated total cost incurred in producing quantities of output from 0 to 20 units weekly for a particular firm.

a. In column (3), complete the missing figures for *average cost*—the cost per unit of output, or total cost divided by number of units produced.

Table 8-1

(1) Output	(2) Total Cost	(3) Average Cost	(4) Average Variable Cost	(5) Increase in Total Cost	(6) Marginal Cost
0	$50.00	undefined	undefined		
				$14.00	$7.00
2	64.00	$ ____	$7.00		
				7.00	3.50
4	71.00	17.75	____		
				9.00	4.50
6	80.00	13.33	5.00		
				____	____
8	90.00	____	____		
				10.50	5.25
10	100.50	10.05	5.05		
				11.00	____
12	111.50	____	____		
				13.00	6.50
14	124.50	8.89	5.32		
				____	____
16	140.50	8.78	5.66		
				____	11.00
18	162.50	____	6.25		
				40.00	____
20	202.50	10.13	7.63		

b. Table 8-1 indicates that, for this firm and this product, average cost reaches its minimum level at an output in the vicinity of (10 / 12 / 14 / 16 / 18 / 20) units.

c. In column (5), complete the missing figures for increases in total cost; i.e., indicate the rise in cost resulting from an increase from 0 to 2 units, from 2 to 4, etc. Notice that these figures are not lined up opposite 0, 2, 4 units, etc. Instead, they are set between 0 and 2, between 2 and 4, etc., to indicate that each figure marks the cost of moving from one output figure to the next one. If output is increased from 2 units to 4, for example, total cost rises by $7; if it is reduced from 4 units to 2, total cost falls by $7.

d. To obtain marginal cost, the figures in column (4) must be divided by 2. Marginal cost is, more precisely, the ratio of a change in total cost divided by a change in output. If that output change equals 1, then the change in total cost is marginal cost. If it is some number other than 1, however, then the change in total cost must be adjusted to a "per unit" level by dividing by the change in output. Complete the missing marginal cost figures in column (6).

Note carefully that marginal cost, even though it is also a per unit cost measure, is not the same thing at all as average cost. Marginal cost measures *only* the change in total cost resulting from the *last* unit produced. Because this table deals with 2-unit output changes, column (6) is not precisely accurate as a measure of the marginal cost of each individual unit. If the table were enlarged to show unit-by-unit (rather than 2-unit-by-2-unit) changes, then, for example, the marginal cost figure for the 9th unit produced would be a little below the $5.25 recorded in column (6) for the 8-to-10-unit region. The marginal cost figure for the 10th unit would, meanwhile, be a little higher than $5.25. This complication notwithstanding, $5.25 is a reasonably close estimate of the average marginal cost of increasing output from 8 units to 10 units.

a. table column (3): 37.00, 11.25, 9.29, 9.03 **b.** 16 **c.** table column (5): 10.00, 16.00, 22.00 **d.** table column (6): 5.00, 5.50, 8.00, 20.00

3. a. Plot the total cost curve described in Table 8-1 on Figure 8-1 (i.e., plot the several points indicated by these columns; then join them with a smooth curve).

b. Use columns (1) and (3) of Table 8-1 to plot the average cost *(AC)* curve on Figure 8-2. Also in Figure 8-2, use columns (1) and (6) to plot the marginal cost *(MC)* curve. (Because the MC values are in-between points, record them opposite odd-numbered quantities of output—1, 3, 5, 7, etc.) Mark your two curves on Figure 8-2 as *AC* and *MC*, respectively.

c. Figure 8-2 indicates that (pick one or more):

(1) the *AC* curve cuts through the bottom point of the *MC* curve as it moves to the right through higher output levels.

(2) the *MC* curve cuts through the bottom point of the *AC* curve as it moves to the right through higher output levels.

(3) the *MC* curve eventually begins to climb as it continues to move to the right through higher output levels.

Figure 8-1

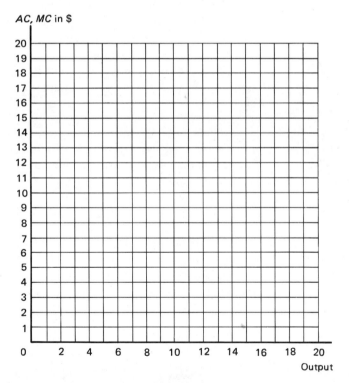

Figure 8-2

(4) the *MC* curve eventually begins to fall as it continues to move to the right through higher output levels.

c. (2) and (3)

It is important to note that the ultimate climbing of the marginal cost curve just noted and displayed in your version of Figure 8-2 can be attributed directly to the law of diminishing returns. How can this linkage be seen in Table 8-1? Notice that the increase in total cost required to increase output by 2 units falls through 6 units of total production but then begins to climb. Since this increase in cost is driven entirely by the costs of purchasing productive inputs, it must be the case that increasing quantities of inputs are required for each successive increment in output beyond 6 units. The law of diminishing returns must therefore be ravaging the marginal productivity of the inputs whose purchase defines variable cost.

For the purists who remember that the law of diminishing returns is defined in terms of marginal products that are in turn defined in terms of increases in the employment of one input with all other employment levels held fixed, there is one more wrinkle to add. It may not be the case that only one input is involved in defining variable cost in Table 8-1; there is not enough information to tell. There is, however, enough information to tell that the employment of at least one input is being held fixed, and that is enough. Where is that information? It is buried under the positive fixed cost defined by the total cost of producing nothing. Positive fixed costs tell us that a fixed quantity of at least one factor of production is required to get under way, and its employment is held constant throughout Table 8-1. The law of diminishing returns therefore applies to all other inputs which must get by with a limited quantity of this initial factor.

4. Recall once again that the total cost of production can be separated into two parts: fixed cost and variable cost. Fixed cost is the cost that would be incurred even at zero output. If you divide each of these three cost measures (total, fixed, and variable) by the quantity of output being produced, then you get three corresponding per unit figures: *average cost* (AC), *average fixed cost* (AFC), and *average variable cost* (AVC). Because total cost is made up of fixed cost and variable cost, though, it must be true that (AC = AFC − AVC / AC = AFC + AVC / AFC = AC + AVC).

AC = AFC + AVC

5. a. Now compute a few average fixed cost values for Table 8-1. When output is 4, AFC would be $_____; when output is 8, AFC would be $_____; when output is 12, AFC would be $_____.

Notice that the mathematical computation involved is not overwhelmingly complicated. As we move to higher outputs, we are just dividing $50 by successively larger figures. On a graph which shows what happens to per unit costs as output is increased, AFC would *(rise / stay the same / fall)* continuously. AFC, in fact, falls along a rectangular hyperbola as a fixed money cost is spread out over more and more output.

b. To compute average variable cost for any output, you must first compute variable cost by subtracting *(marginal / fixed / variable)* cost from total cost. In the case of Table 8-1, for example, you must subtract $_____ from total cost. Complete column (4) of Table 8-1 by writing in the three missing AVC figures—those for outputs of 4, 8, and 12 units. Using the AFC and AVC figures that you have already computed, check to make certain that AFC + AVC = AC. Graph both AFC and AVC on Figure 8-2.

---

a. 12.50; 6.25; 4.17; fall **b.** fixed; 50; table column (4): 5.25, 5.00, 5.12

6. a. Suppose that we had used a case in which AVC initially fell in constructing Table 8-1. Note that AVC is nothing more than the average of all the previous marginal costs. Why? Because the marginal cost (MC) schedule traces the increase in cost caused by producing each unit of output in sequence (first, second, etc.), and AVC is simply the average of these cost increments. So if AVC fell as output moved from (e.g.) 2 units to 3 units, from 3 to 4 units, and from 4 to 5 units, then MC for the third, fourth, and fifth units of output would have to be *(greater than / equal to / smaller than)* the corresponding AVC figures. Only then could the inclusion of each extra MC figure pull the average down as specified. In sum, therefore, if AVC is falling as output climbs, then MC must be *(less than / equal to / greater than)* AVC.

What if AVC were rising with output? In that case, each increment in cost would have to be *(greater than / equal to / smaller than)* the previous average to push the average higher. Marginal cost would, in other words, have to be *(greater than / equal to / smaller than)* AVC. Finally, if AVC and MC were equal, then adding the cost of 1 more unit of output would *(increase / have no effect on / decrease)* the average. If the average of 116 numbers is 10.73342 and you add a 117th number that happens to equal 10.73342, then the average remains 10.73342.

b. This point can be illustrated by an example involving classroom grades. In a given class of students, the average examination grade is always 70. Now we add a few new students (some extra, or "marginal," students) to this class. They are weaker students; they always score between 50 and 55 on examinations. So, when added to the class, they *(increase / pull down)* the class average from 70 to, say, 65. (When the marginal value is below the average, then the marginal value pulls down the average.)

We add a few more students. They are a little better; they score from 60 to 63, but they will still score below the new class average of 65. As a result, then, the average grade is *(pulled down / increased)* just a little—say, from 65 to something like *(64 / 66)*.

Now add one more student who always scores 64. This addition does not change the class average. (When marginal equals average, average does not change.)

Finally, add a few students who always score above 64. Their addition will *(increase / decrease)* the class average from its new low. (When the marginal value exceeds the average, then the marginal value pushes up the average.)

---

a. smaller than; less than; greater than; greater than; have no effect on **b.** pull down; pulled down; 64; increase

---

It follows from question 6 that marginal cost always intersects average variable cost at the minimum of the average variable cost curve. How so? Question 6 tells us that MC must be running below AVC if AVC is falling. If, on the other hand, AVC is climbing, then question 6 tells us that MC must be running above AVC. As average variable costs stop falling and start to climb (i.e., as the AVC curve reaches its lowest point), therefore, the MC curve must somehow pass from being underneath AVC to being on top of AVC. The MC curve must, in other words, cut through AVC precisely where AVC stops falling and starts to climb—its minimum point.

7. The implications of question 6 go beyond average variable costs. To grasp them fully, consult Figure 8-3. Notice that it shows a U-shaped AVC curve intersecting the MC curve at the minimum of the AVC curve. Notice, too, that the average cost (AC) curve is also U-shaped. As output gradually expands from the zero level, it shows that AC will initially *(rise / fall)*, because fixed cost is being spread over increasingly *(larger / smaller)* outputs. However, as plant capacity is approached, AC must ultimately *(rise / fall)* because of the influence of *(fixed cost / the law of diminishing returns)*.

In these circumstances, the MC curve must also cut through the exact minimum of the AC curve. Why? For exactly the same reasons as those developed in question 6. If the marginal increment to cost were less than, equal to, or greater than the previous average, then average cost must fall, stay the same, or rise, respectively. Notice, finally, that the intersection of MC with AC will *(always occur at a higher level of output / usually occur at a higher level of output / always occur at a lower level of output)* than its intersection with AVC.

---

fall; larger; rise; the law of diminishing returns; usually occur at a higher level of output (as long as fixed costs are greater than zero)

Figure 8-3 therefore illustrates the general relationship that must exist between the three most important per unit cost measures. Given the law of diminishing returns, the average cost curve should be U-shaped, and the marginal cost schedule must cut through its bottom point. An average variable cost curve may or may not be U-shaped, but it most certainly will rise as plant capacity is approached. If AVC is U-shaped, though, and if it has a *unique* bottom point, then marginal cost will cut through the AVC point.

Short-run cost curves of the type illustrated in Figure 8-3 can be used to answer one set of questions: Given the plant that the new firm now operates and assuming fixed input prices, what would it cost, on average, to produce a particular level of output, and how much extra would it cost to produce 1 more unit? The firm could, however, ask a different set of questions if it broadened its time perspective. It could, for example, contemplate how to achieve the smallest average production cost if it had enough time to exercise complete freedom over the size of its plant. Put another way, the firm might try to determine what size plant would produce some (any) given output at the lowest possible cost given the current state of technology and the current level of input prices.

When a firm considers this second type of question, it is moving beyond the short-run limitation of its present fixed plant size. It is thinking in terms of discretion over the size of its plant, and it is beginning to look for the output that would yield maximum profit over the long run. For this purpose, it needs some notion of long-run average costs. These are not the same as the costs represented for a plant of one specific size, as in Figure 8-3. Long-run costs are, instead, computed on the basis of the optimal plant size for each and every output—the one consistent with the lowest attainable average cost for that output.

The construction of a long-run average cost schedule must therefore be based firmly upon the assumption that the firm has complete and reliable average cost data for each and every size of plant that it might choose to consider.

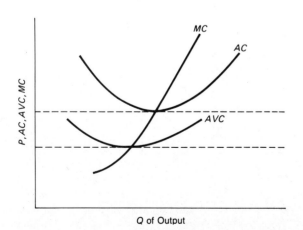

Figure 8-3

8 Analysis of Costs

8. This question investigates the link between the production function developed in Chapter 7 and the cost curves developed in the present chapter in the context of short- and long-run production decisions. To that end, consider the production function recorded in Table 8-2; it indicates the level of output associated with various levels of labor employment (L) for 1, 2, and 3 units of capital (K). In the long run, the firm in question will have discretion over its employment decisions concerning both capital and labor. In the short run, however, the chosen capital stock is fixed, and only the quantity of labor employed can be adjusted. Assume throughout the problem that the unit price of capital is $5 and that the unit price of labor is $10.

a. Record the short-run total cost and average cost values for all three possible levels of capital employment in Table 8-3. Graph all three short-run AC curves in Figure 8-4.

Table 8-2

L	K = 1	K = 2	K = 3
0	0	0	0
2	15.0	17.0	17.5
3	21.5	25.0	24.5
4	27.0	32.5	31.5
5	32.0	38.5	38.5
6	36.0	44.5	45.0
7	39.5	51.0	51.5
8	42.0	56.0	58.0
9	44.0	62.0	64.5
10	45.0	66.0	70.0

Table 8-3

(a) K = 1			(b) K = 2			(c) K = 3		
Output	Total Cost	Average Cost	Output	Total Cost	Average Cost	Output	Total Cost	Average Cost
0	____	undefined	0	____	undefined	0	____	undefined
15.0	____	____	17.0	____	____	17.5	____	____
21.5	____	____	25.0	____	____	24.5	____	____
27.0	____	____	32.5	____	____	31.5	____	____
32.0	____	____	38.5	____	____	38.5	____	____
36.0	____	____	44.5	____	____	45.0	____	____
39.5	____	____	51.0	____	____	51.5	____	____
42.0	____	____	56.0	____	____	58.0	____	____
44.0	____	____	62.0	____	____	64.5	____	____
45.0	____	____	66.0	____	____	70.0	____	____

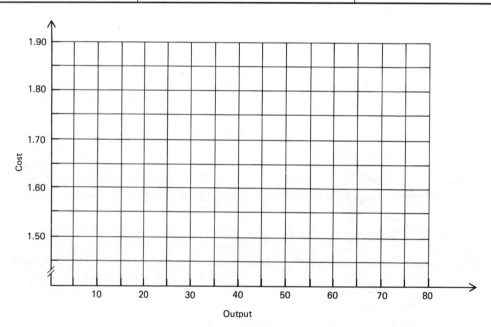

Figure 8-4

b. Movement from 1 unit of capital to 2 units of capital captures a region of *(increasing / constant / decreasing)* returns to scale. We know this for two reasons. First, doubling inputs causes output to increase by *(more than / exactly / less than)* 100 percent. Second, the minimum of the short-run AC curve for K = 2 is *(higher than / exactly equal to / lower than)* the minimum for K = 1. For K = 1, the minimum short-run average cost is $_____; for K = 2, it is $_____.

c. Movement from 2 units of capital to 3 units of capital reflects a region of *(increasing / constant / decreasing)* returns to scale. The minimum of the short-run AC curve for K = 3 is $_____, which is *(higher than / exactly equal to / less than)* the corresponding minimum for K = 2.

d. Were the firm to consider moving from K = 1 to K = 3, then it would review two sets of production data whose production numbers indicate *(increasing / constant / decreasing)* returns to scale. Multiplying both inputs by a factor of 3 causes output to *(less than / exactly / more than)* triple. The corresponding minima of the short-run AC curves are identical.

e. Suppose that you are working for the firm and are asked how much labor and capital should be employed to produce output at the smallest possible average cost. You would recommend that _____ units of capital be operated by _____ units of labor to produce _____ units of output.

---

a. table columns for K = 1: total cost—$5, 25, 35, etc., in increments of $10; average cost—$1.67, 1.63, 1.67, 1.72, 1.81, 1.90, 2.02, 2.16, 2.33; columns for K = 2: total cost—$10, 30, 40, etc., in increments of $10; average cost—$1.76, 1.60, 1.54, 1.56, 1.57, 1.57, 1.61, 1.61, 1.67; columns for K = 3: total cost—$15, 35, 45, etc., in increments of $10; average cost—$2.00, 1.83, 1.75, 1.69, 1.67, 1.65, 1.64, 1.63, 1.64 **b.** increasing; more than; lower than; 1.63; 1.54 **c.** decreasing; 1.63; higher than **d.** constant; exactly **e.** 2; 4; 32.5

Consideration of long-run costs provides a wealth of information. Most importantly, it identifies the smallest average expenditure on inputs that can support any given level of output. Since it is constructed assuming discretion over the employment of *all* factors, the input combination that produces this smallest average cost *must* satisfy the least-cost rule. That is to say, the combination of inputs associated with any output-cost pair defined by minimum average costs over the long term is characterized by the equality of the ratios of the marginal products to prices of *all* inputs.

9. a. Suppose that 200 units of some good X are being produced using inputs A, B, and C. The quantities employed, prices, and MPs of inputs A, B, and C are shown in Table 8-4.

The total cost of producing 200 units of output is $*(90 / 100 / 110 / 120 / 130)*. The least-cost rule *(is / is not)* being satisfied.

Table 8-4

	A	B	C
Quantity employed	10	30	20
Price	$2	$1	$3
MP	2	3	1

Leave input A to one side in order to compare B and C. The last unit of B employed added *(1 / 2 / 3 / 4)* unit(s) of X to output. Since B's price is $1, each of these units costs approximately *(10 / 25 / 33 / 39 / 75)* cents. By way of contrast, the last unit of C employed added *(1 / 2 / 3 / 4)* unit(s) of X. Since C's price is $3, that unit cost $*(1 / 2 / 3 / 4)*.

b. The conditions of part **a** mean that total cost could be reduced by increasing the employment of *(B / C)* and decreasing that of *(B / C)*. What would output be if the employment of C were reduced by 3 units and the employment of B were increased by 1 unit? Assuming that C's MP remains constant over the 3-unit change, it would be *(196 / 197 / 200 / 201 / 203)* units of X. Total cost would, as a result of this change, *(rise / fall)* from $110 to $*(100 / 102 / 106 / 108 / 112)*.

c. As the employment of B rose, we should expect B's MP to *(rise / fall)*; as the employment of C fell, we would expect C's MP to *(rise / fall)*. Thus, as the changes indicated are made, we would be *(approaching / moving away from)* the least-cost position.

d. Now reverse the MP numbers for B and C given at the beginning of this question; make them 1 and 3, respectively. This revised situation *(would / would not)* then be a least-cost position, assuming that A's employment did not change. Suppose, for one final example in this question, that the MPs of A, B, and C are 4, 2, and 6, respectively. Let their prices remain as before. This *(would / would not)* be a least-cost position.

---

a. 110; is not; 3; 33; 1; 3 **b.** B; C; 200 (Adding 1 unit of B would increase output by 3 units, offsetting the 3-unit decline caused by reducing the employment of C.); fall; 102 **c.** fall; rise; approaching **d.** would; would

10. Consider the data recorded in Table 8-5. Assume that land is the input whose employment can be adjusted only in the long run.

a. Plot the short-run MC and AC curves in Figure 8-5.

b. Now assume that the price of labor doubles. Plot the resulting revised MC and AC curves in Figure 8-5 using a different color this time. Which of the following statements accurately describes the result of this price increase?

(1) Both marginal cost and average cost shift down.

(2) Both marginal cost and average cost shift up.

102 8 Analysis of Costs

Table 8-5

(1) Output (tons of wheat)	(2) Land Inputs (acres)	(3) Labor Inputs (workers)	(4) Land Rent ($ per acre)	(5) Labor Wage ($ per worker)
0	15	0	12	5
1	15	6	12	5
2	15	11	12	5
3	15	15	12	5
4	15	21	12	5
5	15	31	12	5
6	15	45	12	5
7	15	63	12	5

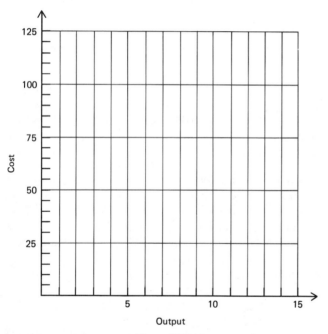

Figure 8-5

(3) Marginal cost shifts up, but average cost is left where it is.

(4) Average cost shifts up, but marginal cost is left where it is.

(5) Average cost shifts up or down depending upon the elasticity of demand, but marginal cost definitely shifts up.

c. Suppose that part **b** had referred to a doubling of the cost of land. Which of the statements there would then have been correct? _____

d. Finally, assume that overall productivity doubles. Which of the statements listed in part **b** would now apply? _____

a. the graph: For *AC*, plot (1,$210.00), (2,$117.50), (3,$85.00), (4,$71.25), (5,$67.00), (6,$67.50), and (7,$70.78); for *MC*, plot (1.5,$25.00), (2.5,$20.00), (3.5,$30.00), (4.5,$50.00), (5.5,$70.00), and (6.5,$90.00). **b.** the graph: for *AC*, plot (1,$240.00), (2,$145.00), (3,$110.00), (4,$97.50), (5,$98.00), (6,$105.00), and (7,$115.78); for *MC*, plot (1.5,$50.00), (2.5,$40.00), (3.5,$60.00), (4.5,$100.00), (5.5,$140.00), and (6.5,$180.00). **(2)** **c.** **(4)** (Changes in fixed cost do not affect marginal cost; they affect average cost, though, through average fixed cost.) **d.** **(1)**

11. Which of the following statements are true (T) or false (F)?

a. Average costs are minimized when marginal costs are at their lowest point. (T / F)

b. Because fixed costs never change, average fixed cost is a constant for each level of output. . . . . (T / F)

c. Average cost is rising whenever marginal cost is rising. . . . . (T / F)

d. The opportunity cost of spilling oil in the Atlantic Ocean is zero because no one pays to sail or swim there. (T / F)

e. A firm minimizes costs when it spends the same amount on each input. . . . . (T / F)

All are false.

Accounting concepts are among the realities of life in the economic age. The second section of this chapter provides an introduction to two of the basics: the balance sheet and the income statement. The **balance sheet** is a snapshot of financial health—it reflects the economic condition of an economic entity at some prescribed point in time. The **income statement** is, by way of contrast, a motion picture—it reflects growth or problems over a given period of time; it clarifies the blur between two different snapshots. The principal lesson to be mastered here concerns the kinds of information that these two accounting forms are intended to convey. The balance sheet is a point-in-time statement. Its primary function is to record what the company is "worth," as closely as can be estimated, at some point in time. The balance sheet begins by listing the firm's assets: everything it owns—cash, buildings, equipment, inventory, and so on. Each item is given a money value, the best possible estimate of its money worth at that point in time. Sometimes the estimating job isn't easy. There is no problem in figuring the worth of a given amount of cash, but reckoning the true present worth of a factory building or of an elderly machine may be a tough job. Among these assets, the company can and should include legitimate money claims on others (e.g., money owed by its customers); and, sometimes, "intangible" assets are included.

The firm's "worth" is not likely to be the same figure as the total dollar value of its assets, though. Any debts owed to others—its liabilities—must be deducted to get an accurate portrait of financial health. The resulting figure is **net worth**. It must be true, therefore, that

Total assets = total liabilities + net worth

because net worth is, by the definition just suggested, simply the arithmetic difference between the total value of assets and the total value of liabilities.

Balance sheets are ordinarily drawn up to reflect this definition precisely. Assets are typically listed in one column, while liabilities are listed in a second adjoining column and net worth is recorded below liabilities. To say that "the balance sheet always balances" is just to say that the Assets column total must be the same as the Liabilities plus Net Worth column total.

Turn now to the income statement. The income statement is a period-of-time statement. Its primary function is to record how much profit the company earned from its sales during that period (e.g., 1 year). It begins by listing the total of goods sold during the period in question, at their sale price. All the expenses that ought properly to be charged as part of the cost of making and selling the goods in question are then deducted from this total sales figure, but only the expenses that ought to be so charged. What's left after deduction of these expenses is the company's profit for the period in question.

Care must always be taken to avoid the most common of income-statement mistakes. It need not be the case, for example, that income statements record only cash transactions. It is true that the sales total is likely to be matched by a cash inflow of approximately the same amount; but some of the "expenses" listed on an income statement need not entail any disbursement of cash during the period involved. Meanwhile, some cash disbursements made during the period will not show up on the income statement at all.

If some items shown on an income statement do not stand for cash transactions, and if some cash transactions during the period are not shown on that statement, then net profit (at the bottom of the income statement) is certainly not going to be an accurate record of the change in the company's cash position, but it was never intended to be. Every item on an income statement, or on a balance sheet, has a money figure appended. But in almost all instances, this is using "money" in its abstract, "estimate-of-value" sense, not its "cash-on-hand" sense. If you want to know how much cash a company has, its balance sheet is a very good place to look, but don't look for it under esoteric categories like net worth or retained earnings. Just look under cash on hand.

12. In December 1990, the Utter Confusion Manufacturing Company was formed, with the sale for cash of 5000 shares of common stock at $10 apiece.

Show this firm's balance sheet as of December 31, 1990, in Table 8-6. Assume that the proceeds from the entire $50,000 stock sale were still held in cash and that no other transactions had yet taken place. Note that Table 8-6 is set up in the conventional way: a column headed "Assets" at the left and a column headed "Liabilities and Net Worth" on the right.

Table 8-6

Assets		Liabilities and Net Worth	
Cash..........	$____	Liabilities.......	$____
		Net worth:	
		Capital.......	$____

Now suppose that the firm's operations during 1991 can be described as follows:

1. Money received (all in cash):
   A. Sales of merchandise manufactured .. $115,000
   B. Bonds sold (100 bonds @ $1000) 100,000
2. Money paid out (all in cash):
   A. Machinery purchased $170,000
   B. Raw materials purchased for use 50,000
   C. Wages paid to labor 24,000
   D. Interest paid on bond issue 10,000

All raw materials purchased were fully used up in manufacturing before the end of the year (i.e., the closing inventory of raw materials was zero). All goods manufactured during 1991 were sold during 1991 (i.e., zero finished goods remained in the closing inventory). Depreciation on machinery was estimated at 10 percent, or $17,000 (the machinery that was worth $170,000 when bought—say, on January 1—was estimated as being worth only $153,000 on December 31; it was partly "used up" or worn out by use during the year, but that does not mean a cash outlay of $17,000). The interest rate paid on the bonds is 10 percent. Note that item 2D shows interest paid as $10,000, so it must be true that the bonds were floated (i.e., that the $100,000 was borrowed) on January 1, 1991.

a. How much cash did Utter Confusion have on December 31, 1991? (Start with the $50,000 raised from the sale of stock. Add the money received from sales of merchandise and bonds, listed above; then deduct the various cash outlays also listed.)

$_____

b. Draw up the firm's balance sheet for December 31 in Table 8-7. There are three steps involved:

(1) Run through the information above for assets held at the end of the year; they will have to be listed at their

proper value on that date. (*Hint:* You have already dealt with cash; you should find only one other asset.)

(2) Do the same for liabilities. (*Hint:* You should find only one.)

Table 8-7

Assets (thousands)		Liabilities and Net Worth (thousands)	
Current: Cash....	$ ____	Current Liabilities.......	$ ____
Fixed:		Long-term liabilities:	
Machinery $ ____		Bonds.........	$ ____
Less: dep'n allowance		Net worth: Capital $ ____	
$ ____	$ ____	Retained Earnings $ ____	$ ____
	$ ____		$ ____

(3) Repeat the process one more time for net worth. Remember that net worth must be whatever figure is needed to prop the balance sheet into balance. Follow the convention of dividing net worth between capital and retained earnings. Leave financial capital at $50,000 (because no more stock was sold during the year). Let retained earnings be the line within net worth to perform the balancing act.

---

balance sheet: assets (cash)—50,000, liabilities—0, net worth—50,000 **a.** 11,000 (= $50,000 + $115,000 + $100,000 − $170,000 − $50,000 − $24,000 − $10,000 = $265,000 − $254,000) **b. (1)** Under assets, note cash at $11,000 and machinery at $170,000. After depreciation of $17,000, total assets amount to $164,000. **(2)** Bonds, at $100,000, are the only liability. **(3)** Net worth equals $64,000—$50,000 in financial capital and $14,000 in retained earnings.

---

13. In this and the three questions which follow, you will develop the firm's income statement for 1991 using the information already furnished in question 12.

Remember that this income statement should (a) record revenue earned from sales in 1991, (b) deduct the costs of making and selling the goods in question from this revenue, and (c) show the income (or profit) remaining after that deduction. It should also indicate the disposition of that profit (paid out as a dividend, or retained within the business). The sales figure is obviously $115,000. Raw materials purchases and wages are clearly expense items to be subtracted from sales revenue. Are there other items? Should the machinery expenditure of $170,000 be included as a cost to be deducted on the income statement? .... (Yes / No)

---

no (Only costs that should be applied against the goods sold in 1991 should be deducted. The $170,000 did not go into the making of those goods; the firm still has something worth $153,000 left out of its initial $170,000 outlay on December 31.)

---

14. a. Is there any "machinery cost" associated with 1991 production? _____ If yes, what is it and how much did it amount to? _____

b. This depreciation (*was* / *was not*) a cash outlay. It (*should* / *should not*) be recorded as an expense on the 1991 income statement (*despite* / *because of*) this fact.

---

a. yes; depreciation, $17,000 (This is an estimate, in money terms, of the extent to which the machinery was "used up" or worn out as a result of its work in 1980.) **b.** was not; should; despite

---

15. The 1991 bond sale of $100,000 (*should* / *should not*) appear on the income statement. Interest paid on that debt (*should* / *should not*) appear. Explain why. _____

---

should not; should; The fact that the company borrowed $100,000 to buy machinery and the like has nothing to do with the income statement, but the interest it must pay on borrowed money is a cost of doing business. It must, therefore, be recorded as an expense.)

---

16. Draw up the income statement for 1991 in Table 8-8.

Table 8-8

Sales...		$ ____
Less manufacturing cost of goods sold:		
Raw materials bought..................	$ ____	
Labor cost (wages).....................	$ ____	
Dep'n. on machinery...................	$ ____	$ ____
Gross profit......................................		$ ____
Deduct bond interest		$ ____
Net profit and addition to retained earnings		$ ____

Sales amount to $115,000. Manufacturing costs include $50,000 for raw materials, $24,000 for labor, and $17,000 in depreciation. Gross profit must therefore equal $24,000 (= $115,000 − $50,000 − $24,000 − $17,000). Net profit of $14,000 therefore remains after paying $10,000 in bond interest.

---

17. The addition to retained earnings figure on this income statement is (*the same as* / *different from*) the retained earnings figure on the year-end balance sheet. This (*is* / *is not*) a coincidence. The earnings retained in the business figure on the balance sheet is the total of all the income (profit) earned since incorporation minus all the dividends paid out throughout that period. Utter Confusion has reigned for only 1 year, so the figures match. If Utter Confusion's income statement for the following year ended with an addition to retained earnings of $18,000, then the retained earnings on the balance sheet for December 31, 1991, would be $(14,000 / 18,000 / 28,000 / 32,000)$.

---

the same as; is not; 32,000

---

18. Elements of opportunity cost should always be included in a firm's cost calculations. Suppose, for example, that you run your own firm. You should, therefore, include the cost of your own labor—at, say, $5 per hour—in reckoning costs. Suddenly, you learn that you could get a job down the street at $10 per hour. This new opportunity means that your cost computations factor your labor into the total at *(zero / $5 / $7.50 / $10)* per hour. (Of course, you may prefer to run your own business. If so, you may be happy to continue to run it, even though conceivably it might seem to be running at a loss when this full accounting of opportunity cost of your labor is made.

$10

REVIEW CONCEPTS

1. Note the definitions of total cost *[TC(Q)]*, variable cost *[VC(Q)]*, and fixed cost *(FC)*. Understand that

$$TC(Q) = FC + VC(Q)$$

Notice that the Q notation explicitly identifies the components of costs which vary with quantity.

2. Recognize that average cost *[AC(Q)]*, average variable cost *[AVC(Q)]* and average fixed cost *[AFC(Q)]* are all simple quotients of expenditure and output:

$$AC(Q) = [TC(Q)]/Q$$
$$AVC(Q) = [VC(Q)]/Q$$
$$AFC(Q) = FC/Q$$
$$\text{and } AC(Q) = AVC(Q) + AFC(Q)$$

3. Understand that marginal cost *[MC(Q)]* represents a rate of change in cost as output adjusts, so

$$MC(Q) = \Delta TC/\Delta Q = \Delta VC/\Delta Q$$

Marginal cost increases with output because of diminishing marginal productivity.

4. Relate the intuition behind the correlation between average cost and marginal cost:

    a. $AC(Q)$ increases with Q if $MC(Q) > AC(Q)$.
    b. $AC(Q)$ declines as Q increases if $MC(Q) < AC(Q)$.
    c. $AC(Q)$ is unchanged as Q increases if $MC(Q) = AC(Q)$.

5. Given constant input prices and constant returns to scale, marginal cost is constant in the long run. Explain why.

6. Argue why costs are minimized when the ratios of marginal product to price are equal for all inputs (by showing how costs could be reduced if the ratios are *not* equal).

7. Show why cost minimization implies that

$$P_I/MP_I = MC$$

for all inputs *I*.

8. Explain the difference between balance sheets and income statements, and describe how they are related.

QUIZ: Multiple Choice

1. Fixed costs facing any firm in the short run include:
(1) any cost whose total is established at the time the input is purchased.
(2) the minimum cost of producing any given quantity of output under the most favorable operating conditions.
(3) any cost whose per unit charge has been settled for some considerably future period, such as a long-term wage contract with a labor union.
(4) total expenses which must be covered even if nothing is produced.
(5) none of these things.

2. Marginal costs facing any firm considering a change in output represent:
(1) extraordinary overtime charges that must sometimes be paid to increase output.
(2) the cost incurred even if the firm produces zero output.
(3) the difference between the total cost actually incurred to produce any given output and the smallest possible total cost of producing that output.
(4) the increase in total cost that accrues from a 1-unit increase in quantity produced.
(5) the increase in total cost that accrues from any increase in quantity produced, whether 1 unit or more.

3. Suppose that the property taxes paid by a firm on its plant are increased; i.e., suppose that its fixed costs climb. As a result, the marginal cost curve for this firm would:
(1) move to the right.
(2) move to the left.
(3) move upward.
(4) move downward.
(5) not move at all.

4. Total cost in a certain plant, at an output level of 1000 units daily, is $4900. If production were to be reduced by 1 unit (to a total of 999 units), total cost would become $4890. Within this output range:
(1) average cost *(AC)* exceeds marginal cost *(MC)*.
(2) *AC* and *MC* are approximately equal.
(3) *MC* exceeds *AC*.
(4) no comparison between *MC* and *AC* is possible, since the information given is not sufficient to determine *MC*.
(5) no comparison between *MC* and *AC* is possible, since the information given is not sufficient to determine *AC*.

5. Let average costs be minimized at output X_o. Which of the following statements is also true at X_o?
(1) Average variable cost will be equal to total fixed cost at X_o.
(2) Profit for the firm must be at its maximum level at X_o.
(3) Marginal cost will be equal to average variable cost at X_o.
(4) Marginal cost will be equal to average cost at X_o.
(5) None of the above is necessarily true at X_o.

6. If marginal cost exceeds average cost within a certain range of plant output, then any increase in output within that range should cause average cost:
(1) to rise.
(2) to fall.
(3) to rise or fall, depending upon the change in variable cost.
(4) to remain constant.
(5) to rise, fall, or remain constant, depending upon market conditions.

7. In a certain plant, marginal cost is $2.00 at 400 units of output weekly, and it is $2.50 at 500 units of output. If output climbs within this 400-to-500 range, then average cost:
(1) must rise.
(2) must fall.
(3) must remain constant.
(4) may rise, may fall, or both, but cannot remain constant throughout this output range.
(5) must fall and then rise.

8. If a firm has employed all its inputs so that the ratios of marginal product to price are the same for all inputs, then:
(1) the marginal product of each input is equal to its price.
(2) the firm is producing the maximum-profit output at minimum cost.
(3) the firm is producing the maximum-profit output, but it may or may not be producing that output at minimum cost.
(4) the firm may or may not be producing the maximum-profit output, but it is producing its present output at minimum cost.
(5) the firm may or may not be producing the maximum-profit output, and it may not even be producing its present output at minimum cost.

9. The production function alone will tell a firm:
(1) what it will cost to produce any given quantity of output.
(2) the maximum-profit level of output.
(3) the various combinations of inputs that should be used in order to produce any given quantity of output most efficiently, i.e., at the least money cost.
(4) the various combinations of inputs that could be used in order to produce any given quantity of output.
(5) none of these.

10. A, B, and C are inputs employed to produce good X. If the quantity of A used were increased, then we would ordinarily expect A's marginal product to:
(1) increase, in all circumstances.
(2) increase if the quantities of B and C were left unchanged, but not necessarily to increase if the quantities of B and C were increased in the same proportion.
(3) decrease, in all circumstances.
(4) decrease if the quantities of B and C were left unchanged, but not necessarily to decrease if the quantities of B and C were increased in the same proportion.
(5) decrease if the quantities of B and C were increased in the same proportion, but increase if the quantities of B and C were left unchanged.

11. A firm employs inputs A and B so that the marginal product of A is 60 and the marginal product of B is 40. The prices of A and B are $4 and $2, respectively. Assuming that A and B are the only inputs involved, this firm is:
(1) producing its present output at minimum cost, but definitely is not earning maximum possible profit.
(2) not producing its present output at minimum cost, and is not earning maximum possible profit.
(3) producing its present output at minimum cost, but may or may not be earning maximum possible profit.
(4) not producing its present output at minimum cost, but nevertheless is earning maximum possible profit.
(5) possibly in any of the positions just described—the information furnished is insufficient to tell.

12. In question 11, change the price of input A from $4 to $3. If all the other information still applies, which alternative in question 11 is now correct?
(1).
(2).
(3).
(4).
(5).

13. A manufacturing corporation sells an issue of long-term bonds. Its income statement for the period in which the bonds were sold should record:
(1) both the bond sale and any interest paid during the period.
(2) the bond sale but not any interest paid.
(3) any interest paid but not the sale of bonds.
(4) neither the bond sale nor any interest paid.
(5) only that fraction of the bond sale chargeable to that period.

14. An income statement records no depreciation expense for particular machinery, even though that machinery was used for production during the year. This accounting procedure could be justified:
(1) if the company did not find it necessary to spend money on the maintenance or repair of the machines during the year.
(2) if depreciation entries totaling to the original cost of the machines had already been made on earlier income statements.
(3) if sales for the year were below normal, so the company decided not to charge any depreciation cost for the year.

(4) if the company responded to an increase in market prices by estimating that the money worth of the machinery was unchanged even though it underwent some physical depreciation through use during the year.
(5) by simply stating that depreciation entries are properly made on the balance sheet, not the income statement.

15. "A balance sheet must always balance" because:
(1) total assets, properly specified, must equal total liabilities, properly specified.
(2) net profit is defined as total revenue earned minus total expenses.
(3) the definition of net worth is total assets minus total liabilities.
(4) current assets plus fixed assets must equal current liabilities plus long-term liabilities.
(5) the definition of net worth is capital stock plus retained earnings.

16. A company's total assets at the end of 1990 were $100,000, and its total liabilities were $70,000. At the end of 1991, its total assets were $115,000, and its liabilities totaled $75,000. It paid dividends totaling $15,000 in 1991. Assuming no change in its capital stock, its net profit after taxes for 1991 must have been:
(1) $10,000.
(2) $15,000.
(3) $20,000.
(4) $25,000.
(5) $30,000.

17. A company's 1990 income statement shows a net profit earned (after taxes) of $200,000. This means that on its end-of-1990 balance sheet, as compared with its end-of-1989 balance sheet:
(1) the total of assets should be up by $200,000, and so should the total of liabilities plus net worth.
(2) retained earnings should be up by $200,000 minus the total of dividends paid.
(3) current assets minus current liabilities should be up by $200,000.
(4) cash on hand minus expenditures for new fixed assets should be up by $200,000.
(5) net worth should be up by $200,000 minus the total of any bond interest paid.

18. A company's total assets were $600,000 and its total liabilities were $400,000 at the end of 1989. At the end of 1990, its total assets were $550,000 and its total liabilities were $200,000. During 1990, it (a) paid a dividend of $50,000 and (b) sold additional shares of its own stock for $100,000. With these figures, its net profit after taxes for 1990 must have been:
(1) zero.
(2) $50,000.
(3) $100,000.
(4) $150,000.
(5) $200,000.

8 Analysis of Costs 107

SUGGESTED ANSWERS TO QUESTIONS IN THE TEXT: Chapter 8

1. Remember that the categorization should depend upon the time frame; in the long run, everything is a variable cost.

2. Definitions. Recall that MC, since it reflects how costs change as output is altered, depends only upon variable cost.

3. MC and AVC do not change; TC, AC, and AFC shift up. Minimum occurs where $MC = AC = \$60$ at 5 units.

4. AC above (below) MC means that the next increment lowers (increases) the average; i.e., AC is falling (climbing). Only when $MC = AC$ is AC neither rising nor falling; i.e., it is at its minimum.

5. Diminishing returns mean that successive increases in employment (costing the same, say, $c) generate smaller and smaller increases in output. MC, as the change in cost divided by the change in output, must therefore climb because the denominator climbs against a constant numerator ($= \$c$). The falling part relates the "eventually" clause in the definition of diminishing returns.

6. **a.** Fixed cost equals $15 \times \$12 = \$180$. MC is the cost of the labor required for each unit increase in output: $30, $25, $20, $30, $50, $70, $90. Variable cost is total labor times the wage: $30, $55, $65, $105, $155, $225, $315.
b. Doubling the wage increases AC and MC (doubles, in fact, MC but not AC).
c. Doubling productivity cuts MC and AC in half. (Factor prices and productivity both influence cost curves.)

7. **a.** Average costs are minimized when marginal cost equals average cost; AC is falling where MC is minimized.
b. $AFC = FC/$output; FC may be fixed, but output changes with output.
c. AC is rising whenever $MC > AC$, but AC falls with MC rising where $MC < AC$.
d. The absence of a market does not imply the absence of value.
e. The least-cost rule collapses to this only in very special circumstances.

8. **a.** Airplane costs $\$100 + (1 \times \$40) = \$140$, including the opportunity cost of the travel time; the bus costs $\$50 + (6 \times \$40) = \$290$.
b. Airplane: $\$100 + (1 \times \$4) = \$104$; bus: $\$50 + (6 \times \$4) = \$74$.
c. How much is your time worth? More than $10 per hour? Then take the plane!

9. The income statement would look something like:

Net sales	$10 million
Less: Costs	$ 9 million
Net income	$ 1 million
Less: dividends	0
Addition to retained earnings	$ 1 million

APPENDIX 8

PRODUCTION, COST THEORY, AND DECISIONS OF THE FIRM

This appendix deals with one of the topics that the chapter discusses: how to choose among input combinations so as to obtain that particular alternative which costs the least. If we limit the number of inputs to two (e.g., labor and capital), the idea of the "production function" can be illustrated by a series of *equal-product lines*. On the same diagram, we may easily draw any number of *equal-cost lines*. Taken in combination, equal-product and equal-cost lines readily outline the whole business of cost minimization.

Having worked through the appendix in this simplified two-input case, you should be able to meet the following objectives.

LEARNING OBJECTIVES

1. Define (in terms of the graphical illustration of the production function) *(a)* an equal-cost line and *(b)* an equal-product line.

2. Explain why the minimum-cost point for any given output is found at the point of tangency between an equal-cost line and the equal-product line for that particular output.

3. Show how it is possible to develop a firm's total cost curve by referring to a series of these tangency points.

1. From Table 8A-1, show in Figure 8A-1 the various capital-labor combinations that will produce an output of 346 units. Join these points with a smooth curve. Repeat the process for outputs of 490 and 282. For identification, label the three curves $q = 282$, $q = 346$, and $q = 490$.

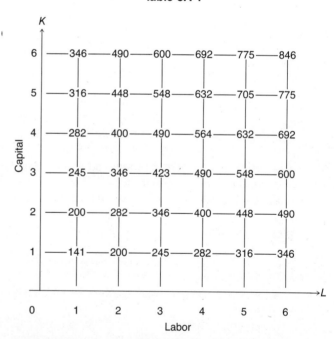

Table 8A-1

A tabular picture of a production function relating amount of output to varying combinations of labor and capital inputs

When you have 3 capital units and 2 labor units available, the engineer tells you your maximum attainable output is 346 units. Note the different ways to produce 346. Do the same for 490. (The production function shown in the table is a special case of the "Cobb-Douglas production function," one given by the formula $Q = 100\sqrt{2LK}$.)

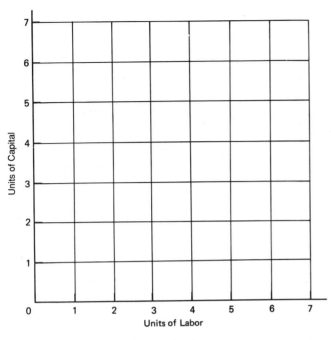

Figure 8A-1

Each of the three resulting curves in Figure 8A-1 is an equal-product line. It is correctly described as follows (circle one):

a. Each and every point on the curve stands for a different combination of labor and capital, all of which can be purchased at the same total expense.

b. Each and every point on the curve stands for a different quantity of output, all of which cost the same to produce.

c. Each and every point on the curve stands for a different combination of labor and capital, all of which can be employed to produce the same level of output.

c

2. a. Equal-cost lines may also be drawn in Figure 8A-1. Suppose that labor costs $2 per unit and that the rental cost of capital is $3. Pick, at random, any dollar amount that would be sufficient to buy a few units of land and capital at these prices—say, $12. Now draw a line which shows all the possible combinations of capital and labor which (given these prices) $12 can finance exactly. If, for example, the entire $12 were spent on capital, then you could rent *(1 / 2 / 3 / 4 / 5 / 6)* units. So one point on the $12 equal-cost line would, in Figure 8A-1, fall on the *(vertical / horizontal)* axis—the one measuring capital.

Another possibility would be to spend the entire $12 on labor units. If so, $12 could employ *(1 / 2 / 3 / 4 / 5 / 6)* units; and another point on the $12 equal-cost line would be on the opposing *(vertical / horizontal)* axis.

The full $12 equal-cost line is a straight line joining these two end points. (Draw this line in Figure 8A-1.) Take any combination of capital and labor costing exactly $12 (given the two prices specified)—for example, 2 land units and 3 labor units. The point on the diagram corresponding to these two values falls on the line just drawn. That is, this line sums up all the possible capital-labor combinations which $12 will buy.

b. Which of the equal-product curves drawn earlier does this $12 equal-cost line barely touch at a point of tangency? *(the 282 line / the 346 line / the 490 line / none of them)*

a. 4; vertical; 6; horizontal   **b.** the 346 line

3. One point on this equal-cost line is 1.5 units of labor and 3 units of capital. The output which this combination would produce, according to Figure 8A-1, would be *(less than 282—probably about 250 / between 282 and 346—probably about 300 / between 346 and 490—probably about 420 / more than 490—probably about 530)*. In the given circumstances and the goal of minimizing cost, it *(would / would not)* be sensible to spend $12 to buy this particular combination of inputs.

between 282 and 346—probably about 300; would not

4. a. Which alternative in question 1 correctly describes the equal-cost line you have drawn? . . . . *(a / b / c)*

b. Remember that the cost figure of $12 was picked at random. There is nothing to indicate that it is the amount of cost the firm would actually incur, or should incur; it is just some figure convenient for illustration. (There are plenty of other cost figures that could be used, and plenty of other equal-cost lines that could be drawn; we'll come to this in a moment.) Suppose, in the meantime, that we assume arbitrarily that the firm did have just $12 to spend and wanted to spend it to the best advantage. Expressing this $12 as an equal-cost line, what would the firm seek to do? (Circle one.)

(1) Move up or down that line seeking the highest-attainable equal-product curve.

(2) Find the point on the equal-cost line which represents the lowest dollar outlay for the labor and capital inputs.

(3) Move up or down that line seeking the lowest-attainable equal-product curve.

c. Still assuming capital and labor prices of $3 and $2, respectively, draw in Figure 8A-1 the equal-cost line signifying total expenditure of $6—another cost figure picked at random. Now note the properties of the two equal-cost lines. They are *(parallel / not parallel)*. The line for $12 cost lies *(below and to the left / above and to the right)* of the $6 cost line.

Thus, given a fixed pair of input prices, the higher the cost figure selected, the *(higher and farther to the right / lower and farther to the left)* the corresponding equal-cost line will be. If the input prices are the same for any two or more such lines, then they will be parallel; i.e., they will have the same slope. Given such fixed input prices, the terms of exchange between capital and labor (the rate at which you could exchange a little less of one for a little more of the other) are fixed, regardless of the amount available to be spent.

a. *a* **b.** (1) **c.** parallel; above and to the right; higher and farther to the right

---

5. Draw a third equal-cost line parallel to the previous two, but this time draw it so that it just touches your 282 equal-product curve at one point. Drawing this line parallel to the other two implies that (pick one):

a. the dollar expenditure on each of the inputs is the same.

b. it touches the same equal-product curve as did the other two.

c. the prices of land and labor are again $3 and $2.

The equal-cost line you have just drawn stands for a dollar outlay of approximately $(5 / 10 / 12 / 15 / 18). (*Hint:* Use the same device employed in question **2a**. Go to either one of the line's two endpoints, where all the money is spent on one of the two inputs. How much does it cost to buy that particular quantity?)

---

c; 10

---

6. a. As you study these equal-product and equal-cost curves, it becomes evident that the points of tangency between them—the points where an equal-cost curve just touches an equal-product curve—are important. Why is that so? (More than one of the alternatives may be correct.)

(1) Because it indicates, for any given level of output, the lowest possible equal-cost line that can be reached—i.e., it indicates minimum cost for that output.

(2) Because it indicates, for any given level of outlay on factors, the highest possible equal-product line that can be reached—i.e., it indicates the maximum output that can be obtained for that dollar outlay.

(3) Because it indicates maximum-profit output level.

(4) Because it indicates the minimum possible level of output that can be attained for any given dollar outlay.

b. You now have drawn three equal-cost curves, and two of them are tangent to equal-product curves. (An equal-product curve indicating somewhere around 140 units of output, had you drawn it, would be tangent to the third equal-cost curve, which was identified with cost $6.)

Studying carefully these tangency points, you will notice that each such point defines a pair of numbers. For the two tangency points involved here, therefore, there are two pairs of numbers corresponding to cost and output. Which of the following accurately describes these pairs?

(1) Output 282, cost $12; output 346, cost about $10.

(2) Output 282, cost about $10; output 346, cost $12.

(3) Output 346, cost $12; output 490, cost $15.

(4) Output 282, cost $12; output 490, cost $15.

c. Now think through the significance of these pairs of figures. Given the specified prices of capital and labor, an output of 282 units cannot be produced for less than $(6 / 10 / 12 / 15 / 20), and an output of 346 units cannot be produced for less than $(6 / 10 / 12 / 15 / 20). The significance of these two pairs of figures, then, is that (pick one):

(1) one of them is maximum-profit output.

(2) they are two points on the total cost curve.

(3) they discourage anyone from studying economics.

d. Given the production function and input prices, the firm can develop its total cost curve, that is, the minimum cost of production, in the given circumstances of technology and input prices, for each and any level of output. (We have here developed the minimum cost for two levels of output. The cost for the many other possible levels would be obtained by consulting other tangency points between equal-cost and equal-product curves.)

Students often make the mistake of assuming that the firm first settles on its maximum-profit output level and then finds the cost of producing that output. Not so. Cost is one of the elements in profit computation, and you can't pick your maximum-profit output until you know the total cost of each and all possible outputs. So the sequence is (circle one):

(1) first pick maximum-profit output; then find the minimum cost of producing that output.

(2) first establish the minimum cost of producing any and all outputs; then combine cost and revenue data to pick maximum-profit output.

---

a. (1) and (2) **b.** (2) **c.** 10; 12; (2) **d.** (2)

---

7. Any point where equal-cost and equal-product lines are tangent to one another is a minimum-cost point. At this point, they have the same slope. Using *K* and *L* as symbols for capital and labor, respectively, the slope of the equal-(*cost / product*) line is always $-P_L/P_K$. The slope of the equal-(*cost / product*) line is always $-MP_L/MP_K$. A point at which the two slope values are equal is always a minimum-cost point.

---

cost; product

Do not be too disturbed if these matters of slope cause you difficulty. The essential point, which is not too hard to grasp, is that a least-cost point must be one where an equal-product line is just tangent to an equal-cost line. When we go on to express this tangency point in terms of the slopes of these two lines, we are just trying to state the nature of this least-cost position in a more precise (and mathematical) form.

In particular, you may have trouble understanding why the slope of any equal-product line must be $-MP_L/MP_K$. Here is a rough explanation: Slope is always the ratio of the two changes needed to move from one point on the line to another point very close by. Suppose that capital is reduced by 1 tiny unit and that labor must be increased by 2 tiny units to compensate (stay on the equal-product line). That would make the slope of the equal-product line $-\frac{1}{2}$.

When capital was reduced, output fell—by an amount dictated by MP_K. The amount of labor needed to make up that output loss was dictated by MP_L. Since it took the addition of 2 L units to compensate for the removal of 1 unit of K, labor's MP must be only one-half that of capital. The slope of an equal-product line can therefore be measured by the ratio of MPs as well as by the ratio of input quantity changes.

8. a. If the conditions of production are such that for any given output level there is only one possible input combination, then (circle one):

(1) there is no production function.

(2) there are no equal-product curves.

(3) this is a case of fixed proportions.

Figure 8A-2 contrasts this case, the "fixed-coefficients case," with that assumed up to this point. Both curved and right-angled lines illustrate equal-product curves for some given output quantity. (You can, of course, draw as many of these equal-product curves as you wish, one for each possible output level. Figure 8A-2 shows only one illustrative curve for each situation.) A curved line implies that (*different input combinations are* / *only one input combination is*) possible for the output in question. A right-angled line implies that substitution of one input for another (thus producing a different input combination) (*is* / *is not*) possible.

b. In Figure 8A-2, the inputs are A and B and the required "mix" has (arbitrarily) been made 3 to 2. If B inputs were to be increased from 2 to 3 (with A inputs at 3), this would mean (*a rightward* / *an upward*) movement away from the "corner" on the right-angled equal-product line. With B inputs increased to 3, total output would be (*increased* / *unchanged* / *decreased*), for we would still be on the same equal-product line.

This means that in the fixed-proportions case, the marginal product (*MP*) of each input must be (*positive* / *zero* / *negative*). The least-cost marginal product rule set out in the chapter cannot be applied in this case, but then there is no need for it, either; there is no longer any problem of choice. Given any set of positive input prices, there is only one possible cost figure associated with each possible output level, assuming the inputs are used to the best advantage.

There is considerable dispute over the extent to which the fixed-proportions case is found in reality. In part, it may be a question of what you mean by "input" or "factor." If you speak in general terms of "labor" or "capital," substitution is certainly possible. The more specific you become about the type of labor or capital, though, the more likely fixed proportions seem to become.

---

a. (3); different input combinations are; is not **b.** an upward; unchanged; zero

9. Figure 8A-3 illustrates a production function involving the employment of inputs X and Y. The two curved lines are

Figure 8A-2

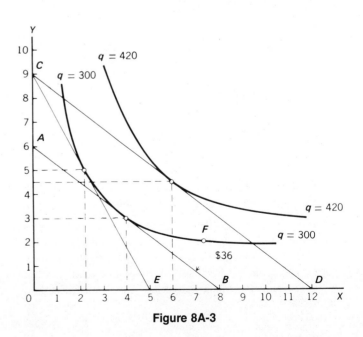

Figure 8A-3

equal-product lines for outputs of 300 and 420 units. *AB* and *CD* are equal-cost lines. *AB* marks a cost outlay of $36.

a. From examination of *AB*, the price of X must be $(2.50 / 4.50 / 5.50 / 6.00 / 8.00), and the price of Y must be $(2.50 / 4.50 / 5.50 / 6.00 / 8.00). The minimum total cost of producing 300 units of output is $(36 / 45 / 54 / 100 / 160). Average cost is (5 / 10 / 12 / 15 / 60) cents per unit. The quantities of X and Y used to produce 300 units of output at minimum cost could be (2.25 of X and 5 of Y / 4 of X and 3 of Y / 5 of X and 9 of Y / 8 of X and 6 of Y). Given the above prices of X and Y, equal-cost line *CD* must indicate a total outlay of $(36 / 45 / 54 / 100 / 160).

b. Suppose that the firm is operating at point *F*. This (would be / would not be) a minimum-cost point. Operating at *F*, the quantity of output produced would be (100 / 300 / 360 / 400 / 420) units. Total cost of that output would be (approximately) $(36 / 45 / 54 / 100 / 160). Average cost would be (approximately) (5 / 10 / 12 / 15 / 60) cents. For this expenditure amount, the maximum output quantity that could be produced would be (approximately) (100 / 300 / 360 / 420 / 500) units.

c. Suppose that equal-cost line *CD* (still signifying the same total cost amount as before) shifts to position *CE*. This would indicate (a decrease / an increase) in the (price of X / price of Y / quantity of output produced). Specifically, the price of (X / Y) would have (risen / fallen) to $(3.50 / 4.00 / 6.00 / 7.80 / 10.80). This shift in *CD* (would / would not) require a comparable shift in line *AB*.

d. Given part **c**'s price change, the minimum cost of producing 300 units of output would become $(36 / 45 / 54 / 100 / 160). The X and Y quantities needed to produce that 300-unit output would be (2.25 of X and 5 of Y / 4 of X and 3 of Y / 5 of X and 9 of Y / 8 of X and 6 of Y). The total (minimum) cost of producing 420 units would then be (approximately) $(36 / 45 / 54 / 86 / 150).

---

a. 4.50 (= $36/8); 6.00 (= $36/6); 36 (tangency); 12 (= $36/300); 4 of X and 3 of Y (tangency); 36   **b.** would not be; 300 (equal-product curve); 45(≈ 7.5 × $4.50 + 2 × $6.00); 15; 360 (must be < 420 and > 300)   **c.** an increase; price of X (Y intercept fixed means the price of Y unchanged); X; risen; 10.80; would   **d.** 54; 2.25 of X and 5 of Y (tangency); 86

REVIEW CONCEPTS

1. Equal-product lines (isoquants) display combinations of inputs which produce the same level of output; they are typically convex-bowed away from the origin. Higher equal-product lines indicate higher levels of output.

2. Equal-cost lines display combinations of inputs whose employment involves the same total expenditure (total cost); they are straight lines whose slopes equal the ratio of input prices. Higher equal-cost lines indicate higher total cost, but they are parallel because they reflect the same prices and slopes.

3. The minimum cost of producing any level of output is read from the lowest equal-cost line which intersects the corresponding equal-product line—an intersection of one point characterized by a tangency between equal-cost and equal-product lines.

4. The minimum-cost tangency guarantees that the least-cost rule is satisfied, i.e., that

$$\frac{MP_I}{P_I} = \frac{MP_J}{P_J}$$

for all inputs I and J. A series of tangencies for various output levels therefore fully describes the foundation of a total cost curve for a given firm with a given technology (reflected by the equal-product lines) and a given set of input prices (reflected by the slope of the equal-cost lines).

QUIZ: Multiple Choice

1. Any equal-cost line drawn on an equal-product-curve diagram involving product X and inputs A and B indicates:
(1) different quantities of X, showing the increase in X that would result from an equal increase in cost.
(2) the various quantities of A and B that would cost the same for various prices of either A or B.
(3) all the various combinations of A and B (in physical quantities of each) that could be purchased for a given level of expenditure.
(4) different combinations of A and B (in physical quantities of each) that could be employed to produce some given quantity of X.
(5) none of the above, because no such line can be drawn on an equal-product-curve diagram.

2. Which alternative in question 1 correctly describes any equal-product line?
(1) .
(2) .
(3) .
(4) .
(5) .

3. A diagram showing a collection of equal-product curves illustrates:
(1) the total cost curve.
(2) the separate marginal products of the inputs involved.
(3) the point of maximum profit.
(4) the production function.
(5) different quantities of the product involved that would be equally profitable to produce.

4. The slope of an equal-cost line is a measure of:
(1) the ratio of the price of the factor on the vertical axis to the price of the factor on the horizontal axis.

(2) the ratio of the price of the factor on the horizontal axis to the price of the factor on the vertical axis.
(3) the various outputs which may be produced at a given cost.
(4) the total cost of producing a given output.
(5) the marginal productivity of one of the factors.

5. If factor or input proportions are fixed, then:
(1) all marginal products must be zero.
(2) all marginal products will be higher than they would be if proportions were not fixed.
(3) all marginal products will be the same as they would be if proportions were not fixed.
(4) all marginal products of all inputs must be equal, but they will not be zero.
(5) none of the above is correct.

6. In Figure 8A-4, the line GH is an equal-cost line for inputs A and B. A shift of GH to a position such as GJ could be caused by:
(1) a fall in the price of input A with no change in the price of B.
(2) a rise in the price of both inputs.
(3) a fall in the price of input B with no change in the price of A.
(4) a rise in the price of input B with no change in the price of A.
(5) a proportionate reduction in the price of both inputs.

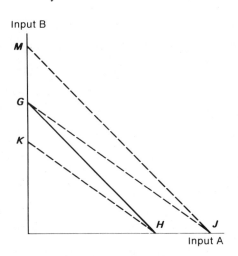

Figure 8A-4

7. Suppose, in Figure 8A-4, that the equal-cost line GH had instead shifted to position MJ (there being no change in the total cost figure assumed). Which alternative in question 6 would correctly explain this shift?
(1).
(2).
(3).
(4).
(5).

8. Suppose, in Figure 8A-4, that the equal-cost line GH had instead shifted to position KH. Which alternative in question 6 would correctly explain this shift?
(1).
(2).
(3).
(4).
(5).

9. It is assumed that one of the following is given or held constant when an equal-cost line such as GH in Figure 8A-4 is drawn. Which one?
(1) Total expenditure on input A.
(2) Total expenditure on input B.
(3) Quantity of the product produced.
(4) Total expenditure on either A or B, but not both.
(5) Total expenditure on the two inputs combined.

10. Had question 9 referred to an equal-product rather than an equal-cost line, which alternative in that question would then have been correct?
(1).
(2).
(3).
(4).
(5).

11. Equal-product lines and equal-cost lines have one property in common: any point on either of these two lines is intended to mark some:
(1) quantity of finished total output.
(2) figure of total cost expressed in dollars.
(3) combination of physical quantities of inputs.
(4) pair of input prices.
(5) figure of total sales revenue in dollars.

12. When the difference between the fixed-proportions (FP) and variable-proportions (VP) cases (with respect to the use of inputs in production) is illustrated by means of equal-product curves or lines, it shows up as follows: The equal-product curve:
(1) is a straight line in the FP case, but it is a right angle in the VP case.
(2) is a right angle in the FP case, but it is a curved line in the VP case.
(3) is a curved line in the FP case, but it is a right angle in the VP case.
(4) is a right angle in the FP case, but it is a straight line in the VP case.
(5) is a curved line in the FP case, but it is a straight line in the VP case.

SUGGESTED ANSWERS TO QUESTIONS IN THE TEXT: Appendix to Chapter 8

1. Given a wage (w) paid to labor (L) and rent (r) paid to land (A), equal-cost lines have the formula

$$\$C = rA + wL$$

In terms of slope and intercept with land measured up the vertical axis, that formula translates into

$$A = (\$C/r) - (w/r)L$$

As the wage w climbs, therefore, the line gets steeper, so tangencies must occur further up the equal-product curves, showing more land employed per unit of labor.

2. Land = 3 and labor = 2. Output doubling is accomplished by doubling all inputs if input prices are fixed; land = 6 and labor = 4 thus conforms with $q = 692$.

Let L^* and A^* minimize the cost of producing q^* for any q^*; designate that cost $C^*(q^*)$. Now suppose that you are considering producing kq^*, where k is any number; let $C_k(kq^*)$ represent the minimum cost of producing kq^*. Constant returns to scale imply that

$$C_k(kq^*) = kC(q^*)$$

because you can produce kq^* by employing k times each input. As a result, though, $C_k(kq^*)$ can be smallest only if $C(q^*)$ is the lowest cost involved in producing q^*; i.e., $C(q^*)$ must equal $C^*(q^*)$. Since this can be accomplished only by employing L^* and A^*, kq^* can be produced at minimum cost only if kL^* and kA^* are employed. Since factor intensity was A^*/L^*, it remains $kA^*/kL^* = A^*/L^*$.

CHAPTER 9

SUPPLY AND PRICING IN COMPETITIVE MARKETS

Chapter 8 presented the litany of cost concepts that occupy every economist's mind (at least some of the time). We are now ready to apply those concepts to an analysis of how a competitive firm decides how much it wants to produce when confronted by a market which "calls out" some arbitrary price over which it has no control. The link between cost and the output decision will be based upon an assumption that firms are motivated primarily by a desire to maximize their profits. It will, in particular, be assumed that every firm chooses its desired level of output for any price by maximizing the difference between the revenue that it can earn by selling the targeted output *at the given price* and the *minimum* cost required to produce that output. Our study will provide insight into not only the firms' individual and market supply curves but also the structural and efficiency properties of competitive markets.

Having completed your work in this chapter, you should have accomplished the following objectives.

LEARNING OBJECTIVES

1. Describe the notion of perfect competition in terms of structure and in terms of how it limits the sphere of economic variables over which a competitive firm has influence.

2. Identify the profit-maximizing goal of each firm, and indicate decision rules through which each firm can achieve that goal.

3. Review clearly the notions of total cost, fixed cost, variable cost, average cost, and marginal cost.

4. Develop the supply curve of a competitive firm in terms of marginal cost.

5. Explain break-even (p = minimum AC) and shutdown ($p <$ minimum AVC) conditions and their relevance to the competitive marketplace.

6. Explain the long-run and short-run equilibrium conditions for the competitive firm and the competitive market.

7. Explain the efficiency of perfect competition in terms of (a) marginal cost and marginal utility and (b) consumer surplus and net social welfare.

This is, to be sure, an elaborate and complicated list of objectives, but this is a chapter of unusual importance. There are not very many purely competitive markets in the world, but an understanding of their implications and workings is essential in understanding the significance of the imperfections that we find throughout most of reality. Perfect competition is, in short, another one of those benchmark notions against which a wide variety of other concepts can be cast and thereby more easily understood.

Perfect competition can be characterized in terms of three simple conditions. In a perfectly competitive market, the firm (1) is faced with a market price for its output over which it has no control (it is too small relative to the market to be able to affect the price), (2) can act under the (accurate) presumption that it can sell as much or as little as it wants to at the given price without incurring selling costs of any kind, and (3) selects its desired level of output and sales for any given price so that its profits are maximized.

1. a. Economists refer to both "the firm" and "the industry"; the difference between these terms is important. The individual unit producing and selling output in the hope of making a profit is the *(firm / industry)*, and its supply curve shows what it alone would offer for sale at each possible price. The total of all individual units operating together is the *(firm / industry)*, and the supply curve of this aggregate shows total quantity that will be offered for sale by *all these units* at each possible price.

b. A *competitive firm* is one operating under the special conditions of perfect competition. Remember carefully what was said above: *Under these conditions, the firm can choose the quantity of output it is going to produce and sell, and it is assumed to choose the quantity which (given the market price offered) generates the highest-attainable profit.* "Profit" here means (pick one):

(1) total cost incurred in producing output minus total revenue or income from selling that output.

(2) total revenue or income from selling output, without regard to costs incurred.

(3) total revenue or income from selling output minus total cost incurred in producing that output.

c. Under conditions of perfect competition, the short-run industry supply curve can be derived from the supply curves of the individual firms *(by adding the price received by each firm for a given quantity to determine total costs / by adding the quantity produced by each firm for a given price to determine market quantity supplied / only by a trained statistician)*. The short-run market supply curve therefore depends critically upon *(the number of firms in the market / the output of each firm at each price / the number of consumers in the market)*.

---

a. firm; industry **b.** (3) **c.** by adding the quantity produced by each firm for a given price to determine market quantity supplied; the number of firms in the market *and* the output of each firm at each price

---

The terms "revenue" and "cost" are used extensively in the next few chapters. They need careful review. *Revenue*, or *total revenue*, is equal to the total number of units sold multiplied by the market price at which they sold. *Total cost* captures all costs incurred in producing and selling that output. This chapter deals with the special situation of pure (or perfect) competition, however, so there are no selling costs; there are only production costs. Recall, as well, that total cost can be divided into two distinct parts:

1. *Variable costs*, which reflect those costs whose value varies with the amount of output produced

2. *Fixed costs*, which are constant, due, and payable regardless of the level of output (even if output collapses to zero)

In addition, two other derivative cost notions are important:

3. *Marginal costs*, which measure the extra cost that would be incurred if the firm were to produce 1 more unit of output

4. *Average cost*, which equals the ratio of total cost to total output

Recall, finally, that each of the statistics is based upon the *minimum* cost of producing various levels of output.

2. Table 9-1 records a wide variety of cost and revenue information for various levels of output and two possible price specifications. It shows the total revenue obtained at each price for various quantities of output from 10 to 20 as well as the profit to be earned from each of these outputs. Complete the blanks in this table.

Table 9-1

Quantity	Cost Data			Revenue Data			
				Price = $11.20		Price = $8.80	
	Total Cost	Average Cost	Marginal Cost	Revenue	Profit	Revenue	Profit
10	$100.50	$____		$____	$11.50	$____	$____
12	111.50	____	$____	134.40	____	____	____
14	124.50	____	____	156.80	32.30	____	____
16	140.50	____	____	179.20	____	____	____
18	162.50	____	____			____	____
20	202.50	____	____			____	____

a. From Table 9-1, it is clear that the profit-maximizing output for a price of $11.20 would be *(12 / 14 / 16 / 18 / 20)* units. At this output, average cost would be $_____ and marginal cost would approximate $_____ .

b. At a price of $8.80, profit-maximizing output would be *(12 / 14 / 16 / 18 / 20)*, with average cost equaling $_____ and marginal cost approximating $_____ .

---

table columns: average cost—10.05, 9.29, 8.89, 8.78, 9.02, 10.13; marginal cost—5.50, 6.50, 8.00, 11.00, 20.00; columns for price = $11.20: revenue—112.00, 201.60, 224.00; profit—22.90, 38.70, 39.10, 21.50; columns for price = $8.80: revenue—88.00, 105.60, 123.20, 140.80, 158.40, 176.00; profit— −12.50, −5.90, −1.30, 0.30, −4.10, −26.50 **a.** 18; 9.02; 11 **b.** 16; 8.78; 8

---

3. a. Price *(P)* and *(average / marginal)* cost are equal at the output which maximizes profit. To see why, think of a firm expanding weekly output from 1 unit to 2, from 2 to 3, and so on. As output changes, average costs change, and so do marginal costs. For maximum profit, the firm should halt output expansion when *(MC has fallen / AC has fallen / MC has risen / AC has risen)* to a level exactly equal to price. To go further would be to produce goods whose incremental (marginal) cost exceeded the price that would be received, and profit *would fall.*

b. Refer once again to Table 9-1. Notice that it does not pay to produce and sell the 17th and 18th units at a price of $8.80 even though they could be sold profitably if the price were $11.20. This is so because the firm has a plant of fixed size, and per unit costs begin to rise when its capacity output is approached. Specifically, total cost will rise by $(6.50 / 8 / 11 / 20) for each of the 17th and 18th units. The simple but basic point involved is this: In profit terms, it pays to produce and sell an extra unit of output only if the extra revenue that an extra unit earns (here, the price of that unit) exceeds the extra cost (marginal cost, the rise in total cost) which must be incurred in producing that extra output unit.

a. marginal; MC has risen   **b.** 11

4. The relation between revenue, costs, and profit can be directly illustrated by a diagram. In Figure 9-1, draw the total revenue line for a price of $11.20. (Just show the points that would indicate revenue from 2 units sold at $11.20 each, from 4 units so sold, etc. Then join your points.) Now plot total cost.

Figure 9-1

Total profit for any output is the distance measured vertically down from the total revenue (TR) line to the total cost (TC) line. The search for maximum profit is thus the search for the output level at which this distance is greatest.

Draw a similar TR line for price $8.80 in a different color. Note that at most outputs, TC is higher than TR; at any such output, a loss would be incurred. For identification, mark your first line "$11.20" and your second "$8.80."

Finally, draw two more lines for prices of $7 and $4 in still different colors if possible. Completing the missing figures in Table 9-2 will help with this last bit of graphing.

Table 9-2

Quantity	Price = $7			Price = $4		
	Revenue	Total Cost	Profit	Revenue	Total Cost	Profit
10	$ 70.00	$110.50	−$30.50	$40.00	$100.50	−$ 60.50
12	84.00	111.50	_____	48.00	111.50	_____
14	98.00	124.50	−26.50	56.00	124.50	−68.50
16	112.00	140.50	_____	64.00	140.50	_____
18	126.00	162.50	−36.50	72.00	162.50	−90.50
20	140.00	202.50	−62.50	80.00	202.50	−122.50

the graph: Your four TR lines should be four straight lines radiating out from the origin, with a price of $11.20 supporting the highest and a price of $4 associated with the lowest; neither the $7 nor the $4 line should intersect TC.
table columns: profit for $7— −27.50, −28.50; profit for $4— −63.50, −76.50

There will clearly be no level of production for which the firm of Tables 9-1 and 9-2 could break even if the price fell much below $8.80. Were that to happen, the firm would have to decide if it should continue to operate at a loss or shut down completely (supplying 0 units of output even while incurring fixed costs). To make that decision correctly, one point must be stressed: No firm can totally escape loss just by shutting down. The firm of Tables 9-1 and 9-2 faces fixed costs of $50 that must be paid regardless of its chosen level of output (e.g., interest on some debt, taxes on some property), and it is stuck with these costs unless it declares bankruptcy. Given this constraint, it must simply do the best it can even in difficult times. It must pick the output that maximizes profit; and if the price is so low that no output yields a positive profit, then this decision rule translates directly into one of minimizing its losses. In the worst of all situations, it can limit its losses to its fixed cost by shutting down. Short of that, it may be able to produce an output for which there is economic loss that is smaller than fixed cost; but it must find a way to cover its variable cost to be able to do so.

5. a. To continue with our specific example, suppose that the market price facing the firm of Tables 9-1 and 9-2 is $7. Application of this rule would mean that the firm should (pick one):

(1) shut down.

(2) produce 10 units of output, since a loss of $30.50 is preferable to a loss of $50.00.

(3) produce 14 units of output, since the loss at that output ($26.50) is lowest among the figures listed in Table 9-1 and is preferable to a $50.00 loss.

b. If market price were to be $4, then the firm should *(operate at output 10 / operate at output 14 / shut down).*

c. The general rule which emerges out of these considerations is (pick one):

(1) if there is some output at which loss would be less than the amount of fixed cost, produce and sell that output; shut down operations if loss exceeds fixed cost at all (nonzero) outputs.

(2) shut down whenever there is no output at which it is possible to earn a profit or at least to break even.

(3) if there is some output at which loss would be greater than the amount of fixed cost, produce and sell that output; shut down operations if loss is less than fixed cost at all (nonzero) outputs.

---

a. (3)   b. shut down (because $4 per unit does not cover even minimum variable cost, and so $50 is less than any operating loss)   c. (1)

In summary, the preceding questions have illustrated a two-part rule for profit-maximizing output decisions. First, pick the output at which $MC = P$; this is the best possible (nonzero) operating point because profits are maximized if this best possible (nonzero) output yields a loss. Second, compare this loss with fixed cost. If the loss is less than fixed cost, then operate at that output. If the loss exceeds fixed cost, then disregard the $MC = P$ rule, and shut down. *Warning:* The first of the two rules stated above applies only in the special case of pure (or perfect) competition treated in this chapter. It is a special instance of a more general rule. When we turn to imperfect competition, in Chapters 10 and 11, the same general reasoning will apply, but the profit-maximizing rule will be restated in a different and more general form.

6. An example may illustrate more fully the nature of the *shutdown rule*—the second of the two rules just noted. Figure 9-2 depicts two different situations. The height of each block indicates the dollar value of revenue or of cost when the firm is at its best possible operating position. The two situations are exactly alike with respect to total revenue, total cost, and operating loss incurred. They differ only in the distribution of costs between fixed and variable. Fixed costs are larger and variable costs are smaller in situation *(1 / 2).*

The shutdown rule says the firm should cease production in situation *(1 / 2)* and should continue to operate despite

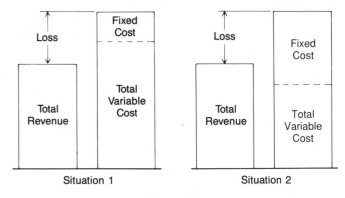

Figure 9-2

loss in situation *(1 / 2).* The reasoning behind this rule was explored in question 5. The firm analyzed in Figure 9-2 is stuck with a loss no matter what it does. It can, however, make sure that its loss is never larger than its fixed cost. If it can find an operating level at which the revenue earned from sales more than covers its variable cost, then some part of that revenue can be applied against fixed cost to reduce its loss. The $P = MC$ rule is then *(still / not)* useful, because it *(will / will not)* indicate the minimum-loss operating level. Figure 9-2 therefore suggests an alternative statement of the shutdown rule: A firm should shut down when total revenue (at the best possible operating position) is *(less / greater)* than total *variable* cost.

More specifically, notice that the blocks in Figure 9-2 stand for TR and TC at some particular level of output (the one indicated by the $P = MC$ rule). Divide TR by that quantity and the quoted market price emerges (since TR = price × quantity). Divide total variable cost by that quantity and average variable cost, or variable cost per unit of output, emerges. It is possible, therefore, to frame the shutdown rule in terms of price and average variable cost: A firm should shut down when the quoted market price *(exceeds / is less than)* average variable cost.

The special significance of this alternative is that it is framed in terms of market price. It indicates the threshold price below which the firm should decide to stop supplying anything to the market. A price which is just equal to average variable cost is the razor's edge, so the firm's supply curve "breaks" at this price. Below it, the firm shuts down; above it, the competitive firm picks its profit-maximizing output from its *marginal cost schedule*.

2; 1; 2; still; will; less; is less than

---

7. Now consider Figure 9-3. The three horizontal lines shown there indicate the demand curves facing a competitive firm which correspond to three possible market prices. [*Remember:* the firm in pure (or perfect) competition has no selling problems. It can sell as much or as little as it pleases at the prevailing market price, without advertising or other sales cost. It therefore faces a perfectly elastic demand curve.]

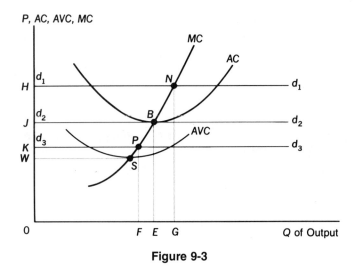

Figure 9-3

a. For example, if price were $H0$, then the firm could move anywhere along d_1d_1. The point at which MC has risen to equality with that market price is N; i.e., if $H0$ were the market price, then the firm would produce and sell quantity (0F / 0E / 0G). Note carefully that in this position, price is above AC so that the firm would be (earning a positive economic profit / just breaking even / incurring a loss).

b. If price happened to be $J0$, then the firm's demand curve would be (d_1d_1 / d_2d_2 / d_3d_3), and its maximum-profit output would be (0F / 0E / 0G). It would then be (earning a positive economic profit / just breaking even / incurring a loss).

c. If price were $K0$, the firm's best possible position would be to produce (nothing / output 0F / output 0E). In this position, its loss would be (less than / equal to / greater than) the amount of its fixed cost.

d. If price fell so low that it did not even cover average variable cost, then the firm would do better to cease operations entirely. On Figure 9-3, the boundary of this shutdown price zone is marked by price ($H0$ / $J0$ / $K0$ / $W0$). This price is (greater than / just equal to / less than) the minimum level of (average variable / average fixed) cost.

---

a. 0G; earning a positive economic profit b. d_2d_2; 0E; just breaking even c. output 0F; less than d. $W0$; just equal to; average variable

---

All the preceding work has concentrated on the short-run notion of equilibrium from the competitive, profit-maximizing firms' perspective. We now turn to consider the long run.

8. We have portrayed perfect competitors as price takers, but where does that price come from? The answer is simple—from a market equilibrium. At any moment of time, it could, for example, be any of the prices highlighted in Figure 9-3: $H0$, $J0$, $K0$, or even $W0$. However, it is argued that there is a long-run tendency for price to gravitate toward level $J0$, the (break-even / shutdown) price.

The reasoning behind this argument is not difficult to grasp. Suppose that the market price is below $J0$. This would mean that all supplying firms would be losing money. (For convenience, suppose that every firm operates along the cost curves shown in Figure 9-3—all producing the same product with the same technology and paying the same input prices.) If the price were to persist below $J0$ for a long period of time, then some firms would eventually leave the market. Either they would go voluntarily when some of their fixed-cost obligations came up for renewal and offered them an opportunity to exit or they would be forced out by the bankruptcy courts. In any case, when they left the market, the market supply curve would (shift in / stay in the same place / shift out) and the market price would (rise / stay the same / fall).

If, on the other hand, the market price were higher than $J0$, then existing firms would be making extraordinary profits. These surplus profits would attract other firms to the industry because the typical firm is earning a "normal" return on its invested capital even at the break-even price. As these new firms enter, though, the market supply curve will (shift in / stay in the same place / shift out) and cause the market price to (rise / stay the same / fall).

Notice that a firm bent on profit maximization has no special incentive to try to produce the output defined by the minimum of its average cost curve. With the technology that supports Figure 9-3, the lowest average cost that could be attained is BE. It is consistent only with output (0F / 0E / 0G), but the firm will produce that output only if the market price happens to be ($H0$ / $J0$ / $K0$ / $W0$). For prices higher than that, output should be (higher than / exactly equal to / smaller than) 0E and average cost would be (higher than / exactly equal to / smaller than) BE. For prices smaller than $J0$, output should be (higher than / exactly equal to / smaller than) 0E and average costs would be (higher than / exactly equal to / smaller than) BE.

---

break-even; shift in; rise; shift out; fall; 0E; $J0$; higher than; higher than; smaller than; higher than

---

In sum, then, there is a tendency for the market price to fall if it is higher than the break-even price and to rise if it is below the break-even price. In the long run, therefore, we can expect equilibrium to be characterized by the equality of price and the minimum of the average cost curve. Combining this expectation with the short-run profit-maximizing condition that price equals marginal cost (anything possible in the short run is also possible in the long run), it is clear that the complete description of long-run equilibrium is

$$P = MC = \text{minimum } AC = \text{break-even price}$$

9. It follows from this long-run tendency of price to converge to the minimum of the average cost curve that we *(must / need not)* know the market demand curve to determine the market-clearing long-run equilibrium price. That equilibrium price is, always, given by *(the minimum of the average cost curve of the typical firm / the intersection of demand and short-run supply / the intersection of the marginal cost curve of the typical firm and its average variable cost)*.

need not; the minimum of the average cost curve of the typical firm (Equilibrium always occurs at the break-even point because of adjustments in the number of firms of the type just noted.)

10. To see why the individual firm has no power over the price of its output, consider the following mental exercise. Suppose that one firm tries to increase its price above an established equilibrium. The result would be *(a collapse / an explosion)* of its market share and the *(entry / exit)* of a competitor to take its place. Raising the price is a bad idea! Now suppose that the wary firm tries the opposite strategy—a lower price. The result would be *(an increase / a decrease)* in the number of consumers wanting to buy its output, *(an increase / a decrease)* in its desired level of output, and *(a reduction / an increase)* in its pure economic profit below zero (meaning subpar return on its investment). Another bad idea!

The analytical implication of this exercise is that even though market demand curves for competitive markets are usually *(upward-sloping / horizontal / downward-sloping)*, the effective demand curve facing an individual competitive firm is *(upward-sloping / horizontal / downward-sloping)* through the established price. Any attempt to move from that curve would be disastrous.

a collapse; entry; an increase; a decrease (because the lower price would move the firm down and in along its positively sloped MC curve); a reduction; downward-sloping; horizontal

11. We are now ready for a more thorough exploration of the long run. Recall that the long run allows enough time for firms to exit or enter a market or industry at will. It allows firms to adjust their plant size if economical. It allows, in the broadest of terms, the maximum possible supply adjustment to any change in market or industry demand. The question is: What will happen to prices?

a. Let us start with a competitive industry consisting of identical firms that finds itself initially in full long-run equilibrium. For each and every firm, therefore, price (P) must equal minimum long-run average cost (LAC), which in turn must equal long-run marginal cost (LMC). Panel (a) of Figure 9-4 shows this for the typical firm with equilibrium price equal to J0; the typical firm produces output _____ . There must be enough of these firms to support an industry supply curve SS that intersects market demand at price J0; i.e., the total quantity supplied must equal the total quantity demanded at price J0. This is shown in panel (b) of Figure 9-4. Since 0A is this market-clearing quantity and each firm produces 0a given price J0, there must be enough firms (say, n firms) so that n(0a) = 0A.

Now suppose that there is a sudden increase in demand to something like $D'D'$—the broken-line demand curve in panel

(a): Typical Firm

(b): Market or Industry

Figure 9-4

(b). The fundamentals of supply and demand tell us that price must increase from J0 to _____ in the short run. Why? Because the SS curve drawn in panel (b) is a short-run curve for a fixed number of firms, all of whom respond to the higher price by increasing their own outputs from 0a to _____ in panel (a). They will all be employing their given plant and equipment more intensively in this short-run response to the higher output price.

Because the output price has risen, though, each firm now makes profit above and beyond the normal return that was expected on its investment in physical capital. These excess profits attract new firms, and the SS curve begins to shift to the (right / left). Industry output will have risen for two reasons. First, each of the firms already operating in the market before the influx of higher demand would be producing more (movement along the old SS curve); second, new firms would have entered the market (creating a shift in the SS curve). Both reasons (or either one) will call for greater employment of *all* inputs, and their prices may or may not climb as a result.

b. Assume, only for the moment, that input prices do not climb. (Maybe this is a small industry relative to the supply of inputs, so a pulse in demand generated from this industry is inconsequential, or maybe there are lots of unemployed inputs sitting around waiting to be hired at the going price—it doesn't matter why.) In this case, the long-run supply curve must be a (positively sloped / horizontal / negatively sloped) line through point E in panel (b) of Figure 9-4. Why? Because the long-run cost curves depicted in panel (a) are not affected. Price (J0 / K0) must always be the long-run equilibrium price because it continues to represent the minimum average cost possible. The long-run supply curve is supported, then, by an increase in the number of firms until their combined $S'S'$ curve intersects the $D'D'$ curve in panel (b) at a point like (E_1'' / E_2'' / E_3''). Total output will ultimately increase because there are now more firms, (each producing more output than before / each producing the same output as before / each producing less output than before).

c. Now suppose, by way of contrast, that input prices *are* affected as the demand for input increases. We should expect to see input prices (rise / fall), and we should also expect to see this change reflected in the final price of output.

Two effects would now be working on the price of this finished good. Entry of new firms, by increasing industry supply, pushes price (down / up) from its new short-run level K0. But higher input cost tends to push price (down / up). Referring again to panel (b) of Figure 9-4, notice that the long-run outcome should be one in which the price has (fallen / risen) somewhat from the K0 level, but has (fallen / risen) somewhat from its original J0 level.

---

a. 0a; K0; 0b; right   **b.** horizontal; J0; E_2''; each producing the same output as before   **c.** rise; down; up; fallen; risen

12. Figure 9-5 shows marginal cost, average cost, and average revenue (per unit of revenue) for a particular firm operating in a perfectly competitive market. The firm wishes to operate so as to maximize its profit.

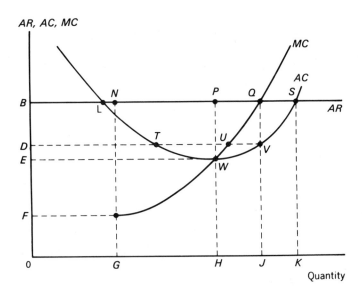

Figure 9-5

a. At what level of output will the firm operate?

(1) 0G.

(2) 0H.

(3) 0J.

(4) 0K.

(5) B0.

b. Which of the following correctly indicates the price at which it would sell its product?

(1) 0G.

(2) D0.

(3) BF.

(4) 0K.

(5) B0.

c. Which correctly indicates the level of average cost at this maximum-profit output?

(1) PH.

(2) VJ.

(3) SK.

(4) DV.

(5) EW.

d. Which correctly indicates the level of marginal cost at the maximum-profit output?

(1) 0G.
(2) D0.
(3) BF.
(4) 0K.
(5) B0.

e. Which rectangle correctly indicates the total cost of producing the maximum-profit output?

(1) DVJ0.
(2) BQJ0.
(3) BPH0.
(4) BSK0.
(5) EWH0.

f. Which rectangle correctly indicates the firm's total revenue at the maximum-profit output?

(1) DVJ0.
(2) BQJ0.
(3) BPH0.
(4) BSK0.

(5) EWH0.

g. Which rectangle correctly indicates total profit earned at this output?

(1) BQJ0.
(2) DVJ0.
(3) BQVD.
(4) BPH0.
(5) None of the preceding four.

---

a. (3) b. (5) c. (2) d. (5) e. (1) f. (2) g. (3)

13. This is a more difficult problem. You have been employed as a consultant in profit maximization. Each row of Table 9-3 provides you with some information about the operation of a different competitive firm. You are to sort through the information provided in each to make a recommendation of what the firm should do given its own particular circumstance. Answer in each case by recording *one* of the numbers 1 through 7 in the last column according to the following code:

1. Firm is now at correct position.
2. Firm should increase price.
3. Firm should decrease price.

Table 9-3

Case	Price	Q of Output	Total Revenue	Total Cost	Total Fixed Cost	Total Variable Cost	Average Cost	Average Variable Cost	Marginal Cost	With Increase in Output, MC Would	Answer
a.	$2.00	10,000		$16,000			At minimum level			rise	
b.			$10,000		$2,000		$4.00	$3.00	$6.00	rise	
c.	2.00	2,000			2,000	$5,000			2.00	fall	
d.			6,000	6,000		4,500	At minimum level	0.75		rise	
e.	5.00	2,000						5.25	5.00	rise	
f.			20,000	18,000			3.60		4.00	rise	
g.		4,000	16,000	16,000			At minimum level	5.00	3.00	fall	
h.	4.50				9,000	12,000	5.25	At minimum level		rise	
i.		3,000	9,000					3.25	3.00	rise	
j.		2,000	16,000		3,000			7.00	8.00	rise	

4. Firm should increase quantity of output and sales.
5. Firm should decrease quantity of output and sales.
6. Firm should shut down operations.
7. A nonsense case—figures supplied are inconsistent and could not all be correct.

The same number may, of course, be used more than once. Enough information is provided in each case despite the blanks. Notice, though, that there is at least one "nonsense" case, in which the numbers provided are inconsistent and could not possibly be correct; in such cases, tell your clients to come back later!

Note: These problems are not easy. They require that you know the profit-maximizing rules for the firm in pure (or perfect) competition (price to equal marginal cost; marginal cost to be rising with any increase in output; production to be shut down in the event of a loss exceeding fixed costs). They also require firm understanding of the relationships among the various cost curves.

Listed here are lines of reasoning that produce answers to the 10 cases of Table 9-3:

a. (1) Get AC from Q and TC; $AC = \$1.60$.
(2) Get MC from fact that AC is at minimum: $MC = \$1.60$.
(3) $P > MC$, therefore increase output.
Answer: 4

b. (1) Get AFC from AC and AVC; $AFC = \$1$.
(2) Get Q from AFC and TFC; $Q = 2000$.
(3) Get P from Q and TR; $P = \$5$.
(4) $P < MC$; therefore decrease output.
Answer: 5

c. $P = MC$, but MC is falling. Therefore output should be increased.
Answer: 4

d. (1) Get Q from TVC and AVC; $Q = 6000$.
(2) Get P from Q and TR; $P = \$1$.
(3) Get AC from Q and TC; $AC = \$1$.
(4) Get MC from the fact that AC is at minimum; $MC = \$1$.
(5) $P = MC$, and there is no loss; therefore the current position is okay.
Answer: 1

e. (1) $P = MC$, but check for possible loss.
(2) $P < AVC$, and therefore loss exceeds TFC; shut down.
Answer: 6

f. (1) Get Q from TC and AC; $Q = 5000$.
(2) Get P from Q and TR; $P = \$4$.
(3) $P = MC$, and there is no loss; therefore the current position is okay.
Answer: 1

g. MC is said to be falling; therefore output should be increased. But AC is said to be at its minimum level through which MC should be rising. This alone indicates an impossible case. Moreover, at that minimum AC level, $AC = MC$. This must mean that $AC = \$3$. But AVC alone is specified as $\$5$, which further makes this an impossible case.
Answer: 7

h. (1) Get TC from TFC and TVC; $TC = \$21,000$.
(2) Get Q from TC and AC; $Q = 4000$.
(3) Get AVC from Q and TVC; $AVC = \$3$.
(4) Get MC from fact that AVC is at minimum; $MC = \$3$.
(5) $P > MC$; therefore increase output.
Answer: 4

i. (1) Get P from Q and TR; $P = \$3$.
(2) $P = MC$, and MC is rising, but check for possible loss.
(3) Compare P and AVC. The fact that $P < AVC$ indicates not only that there is a loss, but one of such magnitude that the firm should shut down.
Answer: 6

j. (1) Get P from Q and TR; $P = \$8$.
(2) $P = MC$, and MC is rising, but check for possible loss.
(3) Get TVC from Q and AVC; $TVC = \$14,000$.
(4) Get TC from TVC and TFC; $TC = \$17,000$.
(5) Since TR is $\$16,000$, the loss is $\$1000$. This is less than TFC of $\$3000$, so firm should continue to operate.
Answer: 1

14. Perfect competition breaks down under circumstances of decreasing costs. When marginal cost is falling as output climbs, average cost must be (*rising / falling / constant*), and higher outputs must be associated with (*higher / lower / identical*) profits for any price. The first few firms to achieve this type of decreasing-cost situation will therefore be able to (*increase / decrease*) output and (*raise / cut*) prices at the same time to (*drive out / complement minimally / compete with*) slower firms with higher costs. The result of this process can be (*monopoly / a few sellers of the same good / price warfare among large suppliers*).

falling; higher; increase; cut; drive out; Any of the choices is a possible outcome.

15. Figure 9-6 depicts demand/marginal utility curves for some good X for two different people (A and B) on the left side and supply/marginal cost curves for X for two different firms (I and II) on the right. Assume that these two people and two firms represent the entire market for X and that the market is competitive. Carefully draw the market supply and demand curves for X on the middle graph, and fill in the blanks in Table 9-4 for the resulting equilibrium.

a. Notice in Table 9-4 that the efficiency condition that $MU = MC = P$ (*is / is not*) satisfied for both firms and both individuals. Total consumer surplus at equilibrium is $ _____ .

Table 9-4

	Price	Quantity Demanded (units)	Quantity Supplied (units)	Marginal Utility/ Marginal Cost
Market	$ ____	____	____	$MU = MC = $ $ ____
Individual A		____		$MU = $ ____
Individual B		____		$MU = $ ____
Firm I			____	$MC = $ ____
Firm II			____	$MC = $ ____

124 9 *Supply and Pricing in Competitive Markets*

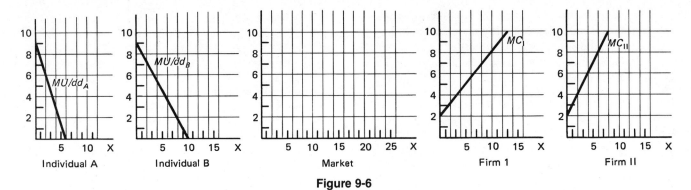

Figure 9-6

b. Suppose that an economic planner wants to call out a single price for X that would generate an allocation of consumption and work effort that would maximize total consumer surplus in the X market. What price would be specified? $_____

in off-peak times when dd_1 represents the market demand curve? $_____ What price should be charged during the peak period when dd_2 is the demand curve? $_____ Is the old generator ever used during an off-peak time? _____ What price should be charged during the peak time if dd_3 were the demand curve? $_____

---

the graph: The demand curve should be a straight line connecting (X = 0, price = $9) and (X = 16, price = $0); the supply curve should be a straight line from (X = 0, price = $2) and continuing through (X = 8, price = $5). table rows: market—$5, 8, 8, $5; individual A—3, $5; individual B—5, $5; firm I—5, $5; firm II—3, $5 **a.** is; $16 [The consumer-surplus triangle is given by its corners: (0,$9), (0,$5), and (8,$5); its area is ½ × ($9 − $5) × (8 − 0).] **b.** $5 (The key here is that the planner would mimic the market.)

the graph: Your combined curve should be their horizontal sum: flat at $2 from 0 to 100,000 units of output; vertical at 100 from $2 to $4; flat at $4 from 100,000 to 150,000 units of output; vertical at 150,000 above $4.
2; 5; no; 6

REVIEW CONCEPTS

16. Consult Figure 9-7. Panel (a) shows the marginal cost schedule for a power generator; marginal cost is constant at $2 up to 100,000 units, but 100,000 units is an absolute capacity constraint. Panel (b) shows a similar schedule for an older generator. Draw, in panel (c), the marginal cost schedule for the firm owning these two generators.

What price should, from a social perspective, be charged

1. Firms operating in perfectly competitive markets take price as given and choose the output which maximizes profit. That output is X^*, defined by

$$P = MC(X^*) \text{ if } P \geq \min AVC$$

but $X^* = 0$ if $P < \min AVC$.

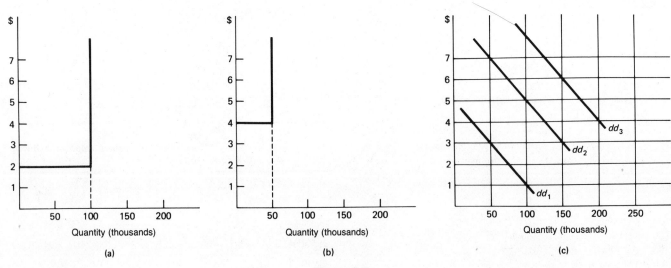

Figure 9-7

2. The supply curve for an individual competitive firm is its marginal cost curve above the shutdown point where $MC = \min AVC$; it is zero below that point.

3. The break-even point is defined by the minimum of AC. Price equal to that minimum supports maximum economic profits of zero at X^* where $P = MC(X^*) = AC(X^*)$.

4. The break-even point defines long-run competitive equilibrium because firms enter the market when prices are higher (attracted by positive economic profit, shifting the short-run industry supply curve out and lowering the price along the market demand curve) *and* because firms (eventually) leave in response to lower prices (repelled by negative economic profit, shifting the short-run industry supply curve in and raising the price along the market demand curve).

5. Perfectly competitive markets lead to $P = MC = MU$, and thereby maximize net social welfare (measured by consumer surplus).

QUIZ: Multiple Choice

1. The profit-maximizing rule for a firm in perfect competition is "price equal to marginal cost." This rule means that a firm should:
(1) keep increasing output quantity (Q) until price (P) has risen to match marginal cost (MC).
(2) keep increasing Q until P has fallen to match MC.
(3) keep increasing Q until MC has fallen to match P.
(4) keep increasing Q until MC has risen to match P.
(5) keep decreasing P until P matches MC.

2. The supply curve of a firm in perfect competition is the same thing as:
(1) its entire marginal cost curve.
(2) a part of its marginal cost curve.
(3) its average cost curve.
(4) the region of its average cost curve over which AC rises or remains constant as output increases.
(5) none of these.

3. A firm operating in circumstances of perfect competition faces a market price of $10. It is producing 2000 units of output daily, at a total cost of $19,000. This firm:
(1) should increase the amount of its output to improve its profit position.
(2) should reduce the amount of its output to improve its profit position.
(3) should shut down to minimize its loss.
(4) may or may not be at the output level yielding maximum profit—the information furnished is not sufficient to cover this point.
(5) is apparently now at its maximum-profit position.

4. Suppose that the firm described in question 3 sees its total cost climb to $19,010 as it increases its output to 2001 units. Would this additional information change your answer to that question? The correct alternative would now (or still) be:
(1).
(2).
(3).
(4).
(5).

5. A firm operating in a perfectly competitive industry finds that its total revenue does not cover its total cost at its best possible operating position (for any nonzero output). This revenue is, nonetheless, more than sufficient to cover fixed cost. This firm:
(1) is incurring a loss, and would improve its position by shutting down.
(2) is incurring a loss, but minimizes that loss by continuing to operate at its present position.
(3) is incurring a loss, but could reduce or perhaps remove it by increasing its production and sales.
(4) is incurring a loss, but the information given is not sufficient to indicate whether it would minimize that loss by continuing to operate or by shutting down.
(5) may be incurring a loss or earning a profit—the information furnished is insufficient to tell.

6. Which alternative in question 5 would have been correct had that question specified that the firm's total revenue (although still insufficient to cover total cost) was more than sufficient to cover its total variable cost?
(1).
(2).
(3).
(4).
(5).

7. A firm which tries to maximize profits under short-run conditions of perfect competition will:
(1) try to set average cost equal to price.
(2) try to produce the output for which its average cost is at the lowest-attainable level.
(3) try to produce the output for which average cost is just equal to market price.
(4) try to make its total revenue just equal to its fixed cost.
(5) take none of these actions, necessarily.

8. The long-run equilibrium condition, "price equal to minimum per unit (average) cost," used in the theory of perfect competition:
(1) is a rule which the firm need not consider in the short run, but must obey in the long run if it wants to choose the output level that will maximize its profit.

(2) is a rule which the firm must obey in the short run only if it wants to choose the output level that will maximize its profit.
(3) is not a rule which any profit-maximizing firm need consider in either the short or the long run. The condition simply indicates a situation toward which it is said all firms will be pushed in the long run.
(4) is a rule which any profit-maximizing firm must respect in both the short run and the long run.
(5) has no status either as a profit-maximizing rule or as a situation toward which firms will tend to be pushed, whether in the short or the long run.

9. A firm is operating in circumstances of perfect competition. It is producing that quantity of output at which average cost is at its minimum level. This firm:
(1) must be at its maximum-profit output level, but may or may not be charging the best price it could get for that output.
(2) must be at its maximum-profit output level and need not reconsider its price, since this is a market price over which it has no control.
(3) is not at its maximum-profit position and should increase its output.
(4) is not at its maximum-profit position and should decrease output.
(5) may or may not be at its maximum-profit position—the information furnished is insufficient to tell.

10. Given the usual downward-sloping shape of a market demand curve, what should be the effect of a tax that affects only the fixed cost of every firm in a competitive market on the price received by and the quantity supplied by each competitive firm?
(1) Price up and quantity up.
(2) Price up and quantity down.
(3) Price down and quantity up.
(4) Price down and quantity down.
(5) None of the above will *necessarily* happen.

11. A firm operates under conditions of perfect competition. At its present level of output, all the following have a value of $1: the price it is charging, its marginal cost, and its average cost. Marginal cost would rise with any increase in output. This firm:
(1) is definitely at its maximum-profit position.
(2) is definitely not at its maximum-profit position.
(3) may or may not be at its maximum-profit position; average variable cost would have to be known before answering.
(4) may or may not be at its maximum-profit position; total cost and total revenue would have to be known before answering.
(5) may or may not be at its maximum-profit position; total fixed cost would have to be known before answering.

12. A firm operating in a perfectly competitive industry is producing a daily output which supports total revenue equal to $5000. That output is its profit-maximizing output. The firm's average cost is $8, its marginal cost is $10, and its average variable cost is $5. Its daily output is:
(1) 200 units.
(2) 500 units.
(3) 625 units.
(4) 1000 units.
(5) impossible to tell from the information furnished.

13. The fixed cost for the firm described in question 12 is:
(1) $10.
(2) $100.
(3) $500.
(4) $1500.
(5) impossible to tell from the information furnished.

14. The daily profit earned or loss incurred by the firm in question 12 must be:
(1) a loss of $500.
(2) neither profit nor loss, for the firm just breaks even.
(3) a profit of $500.
(4) a profit of $1000.
(5) impossible to tell from the information furnished.

15. Economists refer to the "break-even point" for a competitive firm. This break-even point occurs at the output level where:
(1) marginal cost (*MC*) equals average cost (*AC*).
(2) average variable cost (*AVC*) equals average fixed cost (*AFC*).
(3) *MC* equals *AVC*.
(4) *AC* equals *AVC*.
(5) *MC* equals *AFC*.

16. A firm operating in a perfectly competitive market produces and sells 200 units of output daily at a price of $7. Its average cost is $4.99. If it were to increase output and sales to 201 units daily, average cost would rise to $5. To maximize its profit, and from the information supplied, this firm should:
(1) increase its output, since marginal cost (*MC*) is approximately $6.
(2) reduce its output, since *MC* is approximately $6.
(3) remain at its present output, since *MC* is approximately $7.
(4) certainly not reduce its output, and probably increase it, since average cost is less than the price.
(5) increase its output, since *MC* is approximately $5.01.

17. A firm must sell its product at a market price of $1.90. Its present operating figures are as follows: average cost, $2.00; marginal cost, $1.50; average variable cost, $1.50; total fixed cost, $500 per period. By the rules of maximum profit (or

minimum loss) for a competitive firm, this firm would:
(1) definitely increase its present output level.
(2) definitely reduce its present output level.
(3) remain at its present output position.
(4) shut down.
(5) perhaps increase or perhaps decrease its output—the one critical figure needed to make this decision is lacking.

18. If the short-run marginal cost curve of a typical firm in a competitive industry should fall continuously over a substantial range of increasing outputs, then you should expect that:
(1) new firms would enter that industry.
(2) the profit earned by this typical firm could be expected to rise.
(3) the marginal cost of this firm should exceed its average cost through the output range in question.
(4) the total amount of fixed cost which this firm must pay should fall.
(5) perfect competition is likely to give way to imperfect competition.

19. Because of a city tax reduction, the total fixed cost a firm must pay is reduced by $500 monthly. The firm operates in conditions of perfect competition. If the firm seeks to maximize its profit, this cost reduction should (at least in the short run) result in:
(1) a reduction in price.
(2) an increase in output.
(3) an increase in price.
(4) a reduction in output.
(5) no change in output or in price.

20. Given the usual downward-sloping shape of a market demand curve, what should be the effect of a tax on inputs that increases the marginal cost schedule (at every output) of each firm in a competitive industry on the market price and total output?
(1) Price up and quantity up.
(2) Price up and quantity down.
(3) Price down and quantity up.
(4) Price down and quantity down.
(5) Cannot tell from the information given.

21. A firm operates in a perfectly competitive market. The market price at which it can sell its product is $5. At its present level of output and sales, average cost (total cost per unit of output) is $4. This firm:
(1) could increase its profit by increasing its output.
(2) could increase its profit by reducing its output.
(3) is making a profit, but the information furnished is insufficient to indicate whether that profit would be increased by any increase or decrease in output.
(4) is not making any profit and should shut down operations.
(5) is not making any profit but is nevertheless doing better than it would do if it were to shut down.

22. Which alternative in question 21 would have been correct had the figure of $4 referred to marginal cost, not average cost?
(1).
(2).
(3).
(4).
(5).

23. Given the situation of question 21, if both AC and MC were $4, then we would expect (in the long run with the usual downward-sloping demand assumption):
(1) the market price to fall and the quantity to fall.
(2) the market price to rise and the quantity to fall.
(3) the market price to fall and the quantity to rise.
(4) the market price to rise and the quantity to rise.
(5) nothing, because we haven't sufficient information.

SUGGESTED ANSWERS TO QUESTIONS IN THE TEXT: Chapter 9

1. a. "A competitive firm will produce output up to the point where price equals *marginal cost*," if it is to maximize profits.
b. "A firm's shutdown point comes where price is less than *the minimum of average variable* cost."
c. "A competitive firm's supply curve depends only on its *MC above the shutdown price where MC = AVC*."
d. The rule does *not* hold for downward-sloping *MC*. Given diminishing returns, *MC* eventually turns up; $P = MC$ on downward slope is a profit minimum, not maximum. To see why, consider increasing output by 1 unit from downward intersection; profits climb!
e. "A competitive firm *chooses output to set marginal cost equal to price*." It has no power over price.

2. If a firm is covering *VC*, then it is covering at least some fraction of *FC*. This is fine for a while, but only for a while.

3. The profit maximization output is 4000 units for each fixed cost listed. Note that maximum profits are positive for $FC = \$0, \$55,000$, and $\$30,000$ and negative for $FC = \$100,000$ and $\$1,000,000$. What you paid for the house is irrelevant.

4. Price = 21: $Q^* = 3000$; profits = $\$63,000 - \$130,000 < \$0$; firms should exit.
Price = 40: $Q^* = 4000$; profits = $\$160,000 - \$160,000 = \$0$; stable long-run equilibrium.
Price = 60: $Q^* = 5000$; profits = $\$300,000 - \$210,000 > \$0$; firms should enter.

5. $E_s = [(4001-4000)/4000]/[(40.02-40.00)/40.00] = 0.5$. For the industry supply, multiply the single-firm quantity by 2000 for each price. The supply elasticity does not change. Both the numerator and the denominator of the "percentage change in quantity" part of the elasticity ratio are multiplied by 2000; the 2000s therefore cancel and do not change the elasticity estimate.

6. At competitive equilibrium, the price that people are willing to pay for output is less than the smallest MC for firm C. If C produced 1 unit more and B 1 unit less, total industry cost would increase by $[M_cC(1) - MC_B(\text{last})]$. Economies of scale drive "Mom and Pop" stores out of business, except for locational advantages (convenience, etc.). The legislation would increase food prices because equal shares would not achieve total cost minimization, which only occurs when MCs are equal across firms.

7. Short-run demand is more inelastic than long-run demand. Consult Figure TQ9-1. At some initial price and quantity P_0 and Q_0, short-run demand DD is drawn steeper than long-run demand dd to reflect relatively less elastic demand at (Q_0, P_0). A decline in supply from s_0s_0 to s_1s_1 produces a dramatic price spike in the short run with little contraction in quantity (movement from E to E_D). Over time, however, conservation and substitution possibilities are exploited; greater quantity reduction relieves some price pressure, and equilibrium moves toward E_d along s_1s_1.

8. The definition of pure economic profit includes the opportunity cost of owners' labor and capital investment. It is driven to zero in perfect competition, so there is no excess.

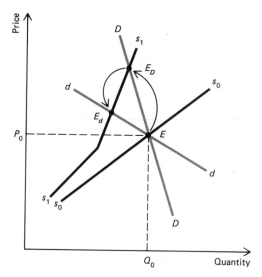

Figure TQ9-1

9. The combined supply curve is MC for the first plant up to the lowest MC for the second; then it is the horizontal sum of the two. If low demand intersects the combined curve at a price below value where plant number 2 cuts in, then the off-peak price should be that intersection, and the second plant should lie idle. If peak demand intersects the combined curve above the second plant's minimum MC, then the price should still be defined by that intersection; only this time, both plants operate where the price equals their respective marginal costs.

APPENDIX 9

SPECIAL CASES OF COMPETITIVE MARKETS: SUPPLY AND DEMAND AT WORK

Chapters 5 through 8 have led you through the development of applying the fundamental notions of supply-and-demand analysis to competitive markets. Before you go on to the study of imperfect competition, though, it is useful to note that much of that analysis can be summarized in terms of two general propositions. There are exceptions to each, but applying a few usual results to specific problems will make these exceptions less unexpected. They are not the economic equivalent of irregular verbs, which must be memorized; they are, instead, special cases of a conventional world, and are perhaps more easily understood in that context. By the time you have finished your work in this brief appendix, then, you should not only understand why the propositions are valid representations of the norm but also recognize the potential for exception when it occurs. Completing this appendix should enable you to meet the following objectives.

LEARNING OBJECTIVES

1. Explain why, in general, an increase (a reduction) in the demand for a commodity tends to increase (reduce) the price of that commodity if supply does not change. At the same time, the quantity demanded usually increases (declines).

2. Explain why, in general, an increase (a reduction) in the supply of a commodity tends to lower (raise) the price of that commodity if demand does not change. At the same time, the quantity bought and sold usually increases (declines).

Proposition 1(a) in this appendix states that an increase in demand—supply being constant—will generally raise price. Be very clear on this: this is a proposition about movement along fixed supply curves. An "increase in demand" means a shift of the whole demand curve to the right, as in Figure 9A-1. If the supply curve does not shift (i.e., "supply being constant"), and if the outcome is that price is raised (e.g., from $C0$ to $F0$ in Figure 9A-1), then there is a strong likelihood that the supply curve must slope upward as illustrated by SS in Figure 9A-1.

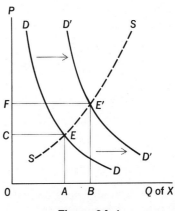

Figure 9A-1

Of course, price would also increase if SS were vertical or perhaps even backward-bending. So what happens to the quantity bought and sold in equilibrium?

Note that part (b) of Proposition 1 reads, "For most commodities, an increase in demand will increase the quantity demanded." If quantity is to increase with price, though (as it does in Figure 9A-1, going from 0A to 0B), then the SS supply curve must be upward-sloping. Proposition 1 could therefore be reworded to say, "In general, supply curves are positively sloped." The way to discover the nature of the supply curve in a competitive market is to change the position of demand and see where the new equilibrium quantity-price pair lies.

1. a. The significance of a supply curve which is positively sloped is that, in the event of an increase in demand, we would expect quantity bought and sold to *(increase / remain unchanged / decrease)* and price to *(increase / remain unchanged / decrease)*.

b. There are numerous exceptions to this general rule. Supply curves can be flat or vertical, for example. There can also be backward-bending, or falling, supply curves (i.e., the supply line points downward rather than upward if you run your eye along it from left to right). Most of this appendix is taken up with the reasons behind the general rule for supply curves and the reasons for the exceptions.

Figure 9A-2 shows three different supply-curve situations: i, ii, and iii. Its parts illustrate different cases discussed in the text. Panel (i) shows Case 2, panel (ii) shows Case 1, and panel (iii) shows Case 3.

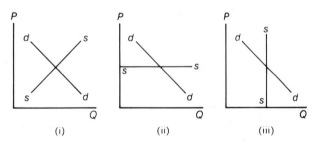

Figure 9A-2

(1) The constant-cost case is illustrated by *(i / ii / iii)*.

(2) The perfectly inelastic supply case is *(i / ii / iii)*.

(3) The increasing-cost case is *(i / ii / iii)*.

(4) The perfectly elastic supply case is *(i / ii / iii)*.

(5) The economic-rent case is *(i / ii / iii)*.

(6) The case in which quantity supplied would respond neither to a price rise by increasing nor to a price fall by decreasing is *(i / ii / iii)*.

(7) The case in which suppliers are ready to sell, at the prevailing price, a greater quantity or a smaller quantity than they now sell is *(i / ii / iii)*.

c. Suppose an increase in buyer incomes pushed each of the demand curves of Figure 9A-2 to the right. The result would be a change in price and/or quantity bought and sold. For each alternative presented below, circle one or more answers, as appropriate. ("N" signifies that the outcome described fits none of the three panels of Figure 9A-2.) Given this increase in demand:

(1) price will rise in the case(s) illustrated in panels *(i / ii / iii / N)*.

(2) quantity bought and sold will increase in panel(s) *(i / ii / iii / N)*.

(3) Both price and quantity will increase in panel(s) *(i / ii / iii / N)*.

(4) price will not rise in panel(s) *(i / ii / iii / N)*.

(5) quantity will not increase in panel(s) *(i / ii / iii / N)*.

(6) neither price nor quantity will increase in panel(s) *(i / ii / iii / N)*.

(7) price will rise and quantity will fall in panel(s) *(i / ii / iii / N)*.

a. increase; increase **b. (1)** ii **(2)** iii **(3)** i **(4)** ii **(5)** iii **(6)** iii **(7)** ii **c. (1)** i and iii **(2)** i and ii **(3)** i **(4)** ii **(5)** iii **(6)** N **(7)** N (The backward-bending case is not illustrated in Figure 9A-2.)

2. The term "economic rent" of Case 3 in the text was first used because it was thought the rental of undeveloped land illustrated the case involved. The owners of such land might receive a high rent if the demand were sufficiently high, but they would be willing to lease the same amount of land for a low rent if necessary. The supply curve to illustrate this situation would be *(perfectly elastic / perfectly inelastic / neither perfectly elastic nor perfectly inelastic / backward-bending)*.

perfectly inelastic

3. a. In one case, Case 4 in the text, an increase in price might decrease the amount suppliers offer for sale. This is the *(backward-bending supply / economic-rent / increasing-cost / inelastic-supply)* case. The commodity or service most commonly associated with this case is *(farm goods / labor service / manufactured goods / monopoly supply)*.

b. The explanation for the backward-bending case is that with a higher price (circle one):

(1) it will be impossible for the supplier to furnish the same amount of service as before.

(2) fewer people want to supply this service.

(3) the supplier can enjoy the same or more income and more leisure time.

(4) the supplier wants to reduce the amount of income obtained from supplying this service.

(Note that there is normally a limit on the degree of backward bend. Supply is unlikely to be cut back to such an extent that the supplier's money receipts are actually reduced.)

a. backward-bending supply; labor service **b.** (3)

4. Economists blithely recognize rising supply curves, horizontal supply curves, vertical supply curves, and even some special backward-bending curves (as in the case of labor supply). They suddenly become cautious, however, if falling supply curves are suggested—i.e., any supply curve which goes beyond the perfectly horizontal into the northwest-to-southeast region.

Given such a supply curve, an increase in demand would lower price, not raise it. Economists caution against accepting this case without explanation because it seems to run contrary to the law of scarcity. If resources are scarce, then any increased demand pressure on any part of those resources should, if anything, raise price, not lower it.

The thought that springs to mind to justify a falling supply curve involves "economies of scale" or mass-production opportunities. Opportunities for lower per unit costs at larger outputs arise from time to time, and firms will try to exploit them for as long as they exist. The firm that fails to seize such an opportunity could easily be driven out of business. Henry Ford, the founder of mass-production techniques, drove many small carriage builders into the ground when they did not follow his lead. To expand beyond the point where economies of scale disappear could, however, be equally disastrous. Occasionally, though, expansion that exploits lower per unit costs can continue until one large firm covers the total quantity demanded in its market at almost any price. Such a firm is called a _____.
Putting this story into the supply-and-demand context, many cases of economies of scale which look to the untrained eye like falling-supply-curve cases are really cases of _____

monopoly; shifts of short-run supply curves to the right

Proposition 2 in this appendix reads, "An increase in supply of a commodity, the demand curve being constant, will almost certainly lower price and increase the quantity bought and sold." This is an assertion about demand curves (just as Proposition 1 was an assertion about supply curves). It is illustrated by Figure 9A-3: an increase in supply (a shift of SS to position $S'S'$) produces a lower price and a larger quantity bought and sold because the demand curve is negatively sloped. Notice that Proposition 2 is much firmer about the probable consequences than is Proposition 1; the appendix therefore spends little time discussing exceptions to this general characteristic of demand.

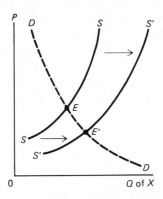

Figure 9A-3

5. a. Proposition 2 is just a restatement of (circle one):

(1) the law of supply and demand.

(2) the law of downward-sloping demand.

(3) the principle of demand elasticity.

b. The text does pause for a moment to note that the extent to which price will fall with any given supply increase (or rise with any given supply decrease) will be governed by demand elasticity with respect to price.

Figure 9A-4 illustrates this point. It shows two different demand curves: D_2D_2 is more elastic than D_1D_1. If supply were to increase in the manner indicated by the shift of SS to position $S'S'$, then the price reduction would be greater if the demand curve were $(D_1D_1 \,/\, D_2D_2)$ than if it were $(D_1D_1 \,/\, D_2D_2)$. (*Remember:* It is dangerous to associate price elasticity with the slope of the demand curve. It is, however, safe to consider slope to be an indicator of elasticity if two demand curves

Figure 9A-4

are drawn on the same diagram. At the point where they intersect, the flatter curve is the more elastic of the two.)

The price rise associated with a reduction in supply will be greater the more (*elastic / inelastic*) demand is with respect to price.

---

a. (2) **b.** D_1D_1; D_2D_2; inelastic

---

6. Throughout most of your work in microeconomics thus far, it has been taken for granted that market forces will automatically push a competitive price to its equilibrium level at the intersection of demand and supply curves. A change in demand or supply will, of course, produce a period of disequilibrium during which the market seeks out its new equilibrium, but that period is presumed to be short.

The dynamic-cobweb theory argues that these conclusions oversimplify matters. The consequences of a disturbance in supply or demand may, in fact, be a series of oscillations, with price swinging first above and then below the equilibrium level. The cobweb theory really involves two supply curves. First, there is the "true" supply curve—the schedule of quantities producers would want to supply, given various possible prices. It is a conventional supply curve, running approximately from southwest to northeast; i.e., the higher the market price, the more producers will wish to sell. In elasticity terms, this curve (*is perfectly price-elastic / has some price elasticity / is perfectly price-inelastic*).

Complications arise when producers are assumed to have to make their decision on the quantity to be shipped to market before that market opens, and consequently before they know what the market price is going to be. In the cobweb case, their forecasts generally prove to be wrong. In the text's example, it is assumed that all suppliers estimate that the coming period's price will be the same as last period's price, so they produce the quantity they would like to sell at last period's price (according to their "true" supply curve) and ship that quantity to the market.

The assumption is that there is no holding back on any part of this supply quantity, once shipped. It must sell—all of it—for whatever price the market establishes. This means we have a second supply curve, one different from the "true" curve. This supply curve (*is perfectly price-elastic / has some price elasticity / is perfectly price-inelastic*). When this supply reaches the market, things work out just as they are supposed to, in competitive conditions. Given a certain demand, an equilibrium price is quickly reached. But if demand conditions happen to have changed since the previous period, it will not be the same price as that earlier-period one, and consequently not the price that suppliers had anticipated. This is when they learn that their forecasts were wrong.

For illustrative purposes, suppose this most recent price is (due to a decrease in demand) lower than the earlier-period price. Next time around, suppliers must again guess what the price is going to be. Again (in the simplest version of the cobweb) they assume it will be what it was in the most recent period—the lower price. So (consulting their "true" supply curve) they ship a smaller quantity. Again the market works out an equilibrium: this time, smaller quantity, higher price. Another wrong forecast!

If suppliers stick rigidly to their belief that the next-period price will be the same as the previous-period price, the result could easily be a series of prices that swing from high to low to high. In extreme cases, these oscillations might even grow wider and wider. Of course, suppliers are unlikely to be so stupid as to cling to a forecasting method that proves to be consistently incorrect. Nevertheless, the cobweb theory does help to explain cyclical price swings in markets for some farm products.

---

has some price elasticity; is perfectly price-inelastic

REVIEW CONCEPTS

1. An increase in demand (reduction in demand) cast against a constant supply *usually* causes the equilibrium price to climb (fall) and the equilibrium quantity to climb (fall).

2. An increase in supply (contraction in supply) cast against a constant demand *usually* causes the equilibrium price to fall (climb) and the equilibrium quantity to climb (fall).

3. Dynamic theories like the cobweb suggest that convergence to the new equilibrium might generate a series of price and quantity adjustments which cycle around that equilibrium; they sometimes refuse even to converge.

QUIZ: Multiple Choice

1. An increase in supply will lower price unless:
(1) supply is perfectly inelastic.
(2) demand is perfectly elastic.
(3) it is followed by an increase in quantity demanded.
(4) demand is highly inelastic.
(5) both demand and supply are highly inelastic.

2. An increase in demand will not raise price if:
(1) the case is that of pure economic rent.
(2) demand is highly elastic.
(3) supply is perfectly elastic.
(4) it is followed by an increase in quantity supplied.
(5) demand is perfectly inelastic.

3. Which panel in Figure 9A-5, if any, depicts the pure-economic-rent case?
(1) *a*.
(2) *b*.
(3) *c*.
(4) *d*.
(5) None of them.

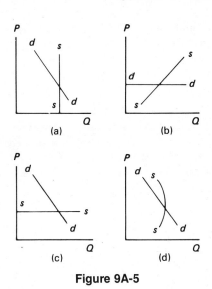

Figure 9A-5

4. Which panel in Figure 9A-5, if any, depicts the perfectly inelastic supply case?
(1) *a.*
(2) *b.*
(3) *c.*
(4) *d.*
(5) None of them.

5. Which panel in Figure 9A-5, if any, depicts the constant-cost case?
(1) *a.*
(2) *b.*
(3) *c.*
(4) *d.*
(5) None of them.

6. If a good is produced under constant-cost conditions, the effect of a $1 tax on each unit sold would normally be:
(1) to raise price to consumers by $1.
(2) to raise price to consumers by less than $1 if demand is elastic.
(3) to require that the entire tax be paid by producers unless demand is perfectly elastic.
(4) to raise price to consumers by less than $1 if demand is inelastic.
(5) none of these.

7. The dynamic-cobweb supply-and-demand case refers to which of the following?
(1) A situation in which there is an interaction between supply and demand curves, so a shift in one curve may set off a shift in the other, thus making it difficult for a stable equilibrium price to develop.
(2) The tendency of price to be pulled toward the critical point at which supply and demand curves diverge.
(3) A situation in which any disturbance of equilibrium price may set off a series of price oscillations, possibly with the swings growing wider as they continue.
(4) The case in which consideration is given to the quantity that will be demanded and the supply offered per period of time, instead of one in which the time factor is disregarded, as it is in ordinary supply-and-demand analysis.
(5) A situation in which both the demand curve and the supply curve are highly elastic, so any price fluctuations caused by a movement of either curve tend to be extremely wide.

8. The results observed in the dynamic-cobweb supply-and-demand case depend in large part on the assumption that:
(1) the supply curve for the commodity is inelastic.
(2) the commodity involved can be stored and kept in inventory, so sellers can withdraw part of their supply from the market if they do not like the price that prevails.
(3) the demand and supply curves intersect at a price that is satisfactory neither to suppliers nor to buyers.
(4) suppliers decide on the quantity they will send to market in the coming period on the basis of an earlier-period price.
(5) both the demand curve and the supply curve are highly inelastic, so any shift in either curve results in a large change in price.

9. "Increasing costs" means:
(1) the same thing as perfectly inelastic supply.
(2) that at any higher price a larger quantity will be supplied.
(3) any upward shift in a supply curve due to an increase in input prices.
(4) any leftward shift of the supply curve following an increase in demand.
(5) none of the above, necessarily.

10. If the revenue received by a factor of production is classed as a pure economic rent, and if the demand for this factor declines, then:
(1) the price of this factor will fall, but the quantity bought and sold will remain unchanged.
(2) the price of this factor will fall, and the quantity bought and sold will decline.
(3) the price of this factor will remain unchanged, but the quantity bought and sold will decline.
(4) both the price of this factor and the quantity bought and sold will remain unchanged.
(5) none of these is true.

11. Perfectly elastic supply indicates:
(1) constant cost.
(2) increasing cost.
(3) decreasing cost.
(4) that revenue received by suppliers is designated as economic rent.
(5) that a certain fixed supply will be offered no matter what the price may be.

12. If a commodity's return is in the nature of a pure economic rent and a tax is imposed on the commodity, then:

(1) the incidence of the tax is borne wholly by the suppliers, and price to the buyers will not change.
(2) the incidence is borne wholly by the buyers.
(3) the incidence will be shared between the suppliers and the buyers.
(4) the output of the commodity will fall and its price will rise.
(5) the output of the commodity will not fall but its price will rise.

13. If the land suited for growing wheat is fixed in quantity, the supply curve for wheat:
(1) should still have some price elasticity to indicate that as price rises, supply quantity offered will increase.
(2) must rise vertically, i.e., be perfectly inelastic.
(3) may in consequence be backward-bending.
(4) might be perfectly horizontal, since the supply of wheat and the supply of wheat-growing land are two different things.
(5) will not be influenced by the price offered for wheat.

SUGGESTED ANSWERS TO QUESTIONS IN THE TEXT: Appendix to Chapter 9

1. **a.** Vertical supply curve for labor.
  b. Upward shift in demand curve; price climbs as equilibrium moves along supply curve.
  c. Backward-bending supply for labor.

2. *Case 1:* SS shifts up by amount of tax; equilibrium up by amount of tax.
  Case 2: up by amount of tax; equilibrium price up by less than 100 percent of tax, with part paid by suppliers.
  Case 3: No change in equilibrium; suppliers pay all the tax.
  Case 4: Supply shifts up by amount of the tax, with an indeterminant effect; equilibrium quantity could rise or fall. Draw it to see.

3. Consult Figure TQ9A-1. Starting at Q_1, price P_1 emerges. In the next period, firms respond by producing Q_2, but that quantity commands only P_2 in the marketplace. The steepness of DD suggests that this price is so much lower than the expected P_1 that the subsequent quantity response produces $Q_2 < Q_1$. When the cycle starts over, therefore, it starts further from equilibrium than before—a cycle which, when repeated, can only diverge.

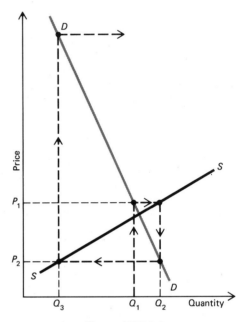

Figure TQ9A-1

CHAPTER 10

MARGINAL REVENUE AND MONOPOLY

Perfect competition was defined in Chapter 9 to reflect a market structure which incorporates many small firms selling identical products. It has been studied extensively, as was noted there, not because of its wide application to reality but because of its analytical properties. Perfect competition, for example, was seen to support allocational efficiency characterized by the inability to make one person better off without hurting someone else. Perfect competition is, as a result, a standard against which the inefficiencies of other market forms can be measured. Additionally, the workings of perfect competition are easy to understand and easy to work with; there is a certain methodological convenience in examining certain economic issues first in the context of competitive markets. The list of reasons for concentrating on perfect competition can, of course, be extended, but that is not the point of Chapter 10. It is, instead, to turn to different types of market organization spawned by the failures of the competitive model—the rampant forms of imperfect competition.

This chapter presents the sources and patterns of imperfect competition as well as a theoretical discussion of monopoly (the exact opposite of perfect competition) based upon the notions of marginal cost and marginal revenue (a concept defined here). The germ of the content of the entire chapter is found in the quotation from Adam Smith's *Wealth of Nations* that precedes the text chapter: "The monopolists, by keeping the market constantly understocked, ... sell their commodities much above the natural price, and raise their emoluments, whether they consist of wages or profit. ..." Having worked through the chapter, you will have achieved an understanding of not only precisely where the truth in that statement lies but also the following objectives.

LEARNING OBJECTIVES

1. Prepare a general overview of the patterns of imperfect competition and the sources of that imperfection (cost conditions and barriers to competition).

2. Understand the functional and definitional distinctions among the various forms of imperfect competition.

3. Develop insight into the notion of marginal revenue and its role in determining the profit-maximizing level of output (output such that marginal cost equals marginal revenue).

4. Recognize that the profit-maximizing rule for perfect competition, price equals marginal cost, is simply a special case of the more general rule that marginal revenue equals marginal cost.

The intuition behind the sources of imperfect competition is easy to understand. Imperfect competition can arise whenever firms face a demand curve with some measure of negative slope; that slope gives firms some degree of power over not only the quantity that they choose to produce but also the price at which they will sell that output.

1. Figure 10-1 starts on the left-hand side with monopoly and proceeds to the right along two branches. Along the top branch, the number of firms selling the same product increases from 1 (the monopoly box) to a few (in box A) to an arbitrarily large number (in box B). Along the bottom branch, the number of firms producing differentiated but nearly identical products increases from 1 to a few (in box C) to an arbitrarily large number (in box D). Label each box by the market structure suggested by the process just noted (box C is already labeled "differentiated oligopoly"), and record an example of each type of structure from your knowledge of the American economy (consult Table 10-1 in the text).

10 Marginal Revenue and Monopoly

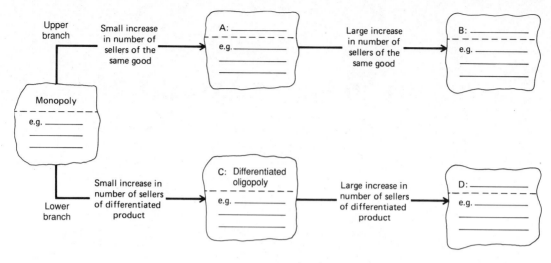

Figure 10-1

Along which branch would you expect advertising total expenditure to grow with the number of firms? _____ Provide a list of industries that display monopoly structures. _____

_____

_____

the figure: A—oligopoly; steel, chemical, etc.; B—perfect competition; farm products (wheat, corn, etc.); C—differentiated oligopoly; autos, computers, etc.; D–monopolistic competition; retail trade (gasoline, food products, etc.) lower; local telephone, electricity, gas utilities, cable TV, etc.

2. a. There are two major sources of market imperfection. One, listed under the general rubric of "cost conditions," can be represented graphically. Which of the panels of Figure 10-2 illustrate relative cost circumstances that might lead to imperfectly competitive market structures? _____ The existence of "natural monopoly" *(does / does not)* fall under this classification; if it does, which panel illustrates natural monopoly? _____ What name should be attached to the structure suggested by panel *(b)*? _____

b. The second rubric is entitled "barriers to entry" and incorporates a variety of situations. Indicate with (B) in the parentheses provided those items in the following list that can reasonably be included in this second category:

(1) 17-year patents for new products . . . . ( )

(2) Regulated entry into an industry . . . . ( )

(3) Tariff protection from foreign competitors . . ( )

(4) Artificial product differentiation . . . . ( )

(5) Deliberate overinvestment in capacity to threaten new entrants with impossibly low price competition . . ( )

Figure 10-2

c. In the case of product differentiation, the distinction between products (whether real or perceived) generates market power by moving the demand curve that the firm faces (in / nowhere / out) relative to the market demand curve for the general class of product. The result is that panel (a / b / c) of Figure 10-2 can become an appropriate representation of the firm's individual market situation.

---

a. panels (a) and (b); does; panel (a); oligopoly **b.** All items qualify as a "barrier." **c.** in; a and/or b

---

3. One measure of the control (or potential control) over price is the **concentration ratio**. The four-firm ratio is, for example, the percentage of the total industry output produced by the largest four firms in an industry. In perfectly competitive markets, we should expect that this ratio would be nearly equal to (0 / 25 / 50 / 75) percent. From 1947 through 1972, this ratio (rose dramatically / rose slightly / remained constant / fell slightly / fell significantly) within the United States from 37 percent to (45 / 38 / 37 / 36 / 25) percent. It is likely that this trend (overestimates / accurately estimates / underestimates) the change in concentration because_____

0; rose slightly; 38; overestimates; it ignores the recent influx of foreign competition

---

Turn now to an examination of the profit-maximizing behavior of a monopoly firm. Analytically, this monopoly case is decidedly easier than the so-called intermediate cases—those not perfectly competitive, yet not completely monopolistic. It would be unwise to tackle these more intricate cases before having mastered the elementary ideas of monopoly pricing.

The terms and diagrams involved in a description of monopoly pricing may seem complicated at first, but the basic idea involved is simple. The monopoly firm is assumed to be motivated by profit in exactly the same way that the perfect competitor was motivated in Chapter 9. The results will be different only because the monopolist has power over price as well as quantity.

To review the basic ideas of profit maximization, make certain that you are comfortable with each of the following thoughts and observations:

1. "Maximizing profit" means earning as much revenue net of costs as market and production conditions will permit.

2. To be able to maximize profit, there must be something the firm can do that will influence its profit. There must be some variable which the firm can control and which changes profit.

3. This chapter assumes that the monopoly firm can control the quantity it sells, just like the perfectly competitive firm. It looks, quite simply, for the particular quantity that will maximize its profit. In this respect, the monopoly firm is exactly like the perfectly competitive firm.

4. The monopoly firm is also assumed to know the price which that profit-maximizing quantity will fetch. More generally, it knows the demand schedule for its product, so it knows the price which goes with each possible quantity sold.

5. From this demand schedule, it is easy to develop a revenue schedule (total revenue being quantity sold multiplied by price per unit)—a schedule showing revenue associated with each possible quantity sold.

6. The firm must also know the total cost of each and every level of output. By bringing together the revenue and cost schedules, it can identify that output at which the excess of revenue over cost (profit) is greatest. It can determine, as well, the price to charge for this maximum-profit output just by going back to its demand schedule. Again, this is just what the competitive firm does. The only difference is that competitive firms face different demand conditions. The perfect competitor faced a perfectly elastic demand curve, so the price was taken as given. The monopoly firm we are now considering faces a "tilted" demand curve, so it can exercise some influence over the price it charges for its product.

The next seven questions will lead you through an illustrative example of precisely how this process works for a pure monopolist.

4. Columns (1) and (2) in Table 10-1 represent a demand schedule. Assume that a firm has done its market research homework accurately so that it knows all about this schedule and can thereby identify the quantities that it can sell at various prices. This firm must operate under conditions of (perfect / imperfect) competition, since as the output to be sold increases, price (remains constant / must be reduced). Subsequent questions will assume, in fact, that this firm has monopoly power over the market represented by the demand schedule in Table 10-1.

---

imperfect; must be reduced

---

5. Now turn to the determination of profit-maximizing output and price.

a. Column (3) of Table 10-1 shows total revenue—price times quantity. As a small exercise, complete the four blanks in this column. Use the figures in columns (2) and (3) to illustrate total revenue in the upper panel of Figure 10-3; i.e., show the total revenue associated with various output quantities. Join the points with a smooth curve.

10 Marginal Revenue and Monopoly

Table 10-1

(1) Price	(2) Quantity	(3) Total Revenue	(4) Extra: Quantity	(5) Extra: Revenue	(6) Marginal Revenue
$14.00	10	$140			
			7	$64	$9.14
12.00	17	204	8	46	5.75
10.00	25	___			
				29	___
9.00	31	279	8	33	4.13
8.00	39	312			
			11	___	3.45
7.00	50	___			
				14	___
6.50	56	364	7	14	2.00
6.00	63	378	8	13	1.63
5.50	71	391			
5.00	80	___			
			10	5	0.50
4.50	90	405	11	___	−0.09
4.00	101	___			
			___	−5	−0.38
3.50	114	399			

b. Notice, incidentally, that this demand schedule becomes price-inelastic when price is sufficiently low—specifically, when price falls below $(8 / 7 / 6 / 5 / 4)$.

a. table column (3): 250, 350, 400, 404 **b.** 4 (Marginal revenue turns negative.)

6. a. Table 10-2 shows the firm's total cost and marginal cost for production of the commodity whose demand curve is detailed in Table 10-1. Table 10-2 is similar in construction to the tables presented in previous chapters, but just to refresh your memory on the process of computing extra cost, complete the four blanks in columns (3) and (4) of the table with the proper figures.

The graph of columns (1) and (2) of Table 10-2 has already been drawn in the top panel of Figure 10-3 as a total cost curve (TC). Mark the curve that you drew earlier with "TR" to distinguish it from the cost curve. Now plot the marginal cost curve (denote it "MC") in the bottom panel of Figure 10-3.

Table 10-2

(1) Output	(2) Total Cost	(3) Extra Cost	(4) MC per Unit
0	$ 90		
5	150	$60	$12.00
10	185	35	7.00
15	215	30	6.00
20	235	___	___
25	250	15	3.00
30	262	12	2.40
35	272	10	2.00
40	280	8	1.60
45	286	6	1.20
50	291	5	1.00
55	295	4	0.80
60	300	5	1.00
65	308	___	___
70	318	10	2.00
75	330	12	2.40
80	345	15	3.00
85	365	20	4.00
90	400	35	7.00

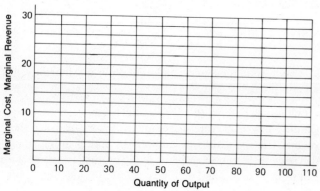

Figure 10-3

b. It is now possible to see at once why the profit-maximizing process outlined here is a simple one. The firm is doing nothing more than searching for the output at which the vertical distance between TR and TC is greatest. This distance, for any output, is (fixed cost / price / profit or loss). (If TR is above TC, it is profit; if TC is above, it is loss. It is thus preferable to look for "greatest vertical distance" with TR above TC. The greatest distance with TC on top marks the maximum possible loss—somewhat less desirable as an operating position.)

a. table columns: (3)—20, 4; (4)—8, 1.60 **b.** profit or loss

7. a. Figure 10-3 is too small to indicate quickly the precise maximum-profit position, but even a glance is sufficient to indicate that this best possible position is approximately (45 / 65 / 85) units of output.

Suppose that the firm searches for the profit-maximizing output by gradually increasing its output and sales, pausing at each increase to see if its profit position has improved. Each extra unit of output brings in a little more revenue (unless demand had reached its price-inelastic range); each extra unit incurs a little more cost. The profit position will be improved if the small amount of extra revenue (exceeds / is equal to / is less than) the small amount of extra cost.

b. In more precise terms, the extra revenue brought in from the sale of 1 extra unit of output is **marginal revenue(MR)**. It is the increase in total revenue resulting from the sale of that 1 further unit. For maximum profit, the firm should increase its output and sales as long as MR exceeds marginal cost (MC)— the increase in total cost occasioned by that 1 extra unit. Total profit increases, with each unit increase in output, by an amount equal to the difference between MR and MC.

If the firm were to find itself operating where MR falls short of MC, then it should (increase / decrease) its level of production and sales. The position where MR is (less than / equal to / greater than) MC represents a balance of marginal increments; it characterizes maximum profitability.

c. Column (4) in Table 10-1 shows the extra number of units sold if price were reduced. Column (5) shows the extra revenue (positive or negative) that would result from that price reduction. Complete the blanks in these two columns.

a. 65; exceeds **b.** decrease; equal to **c.** table columns: (4)—6, 6, 9, 13; (5)—38, 9, −1

8. Although column (5) in Table 10-1 carries "extra-revenue" figures, these are not *marginal* revenue figures, since MR is a per unit concept. The top figure in column (5), for example, is $64, but it came from an increase of 7 units sold. The $64 must be divided by 7 to get the MR figure of $9.14 in column (6). [For a reason to be discussed in a moment, even the column (6) figures are not precisely accurate MR figures; they are, however, reasonable approximations.] Complete the missing MR figures in column (6). Plot the marginal revenue curve (denote it "MR") in the lower panel of Figure 10-3.

table column (5): 4.83, 2.33, 1.00

Marginal revenue is a concept of sufficient importance that you should pause for a moment to make sure you have it straight. Note, in particular, three specific points:

1. Marginal revenue is precisely analogous to marginal cost. Marginal cost is the extra cost resulting from the last unit of output produced. Similarly, marginal revenue is the extra revenue yielded by the last unit of output produced and sold.

2. Marginal revenue falls as the quantity of sales increases. It can even turn negative (and will, if demand becomes price-inelastic so that revenue falls as sales increase).

3. The marginal revenue figures recorded in column (6) in Table 10-1 are not precisely accurate, since that table records only price changes of $1 or 50 cents. A more precise marginal revenue table would show extra revenue from each separate extra unit, not from an average across anywhere from 6 to 11 extra units.

9. The general profit-maximizing rule holds that firms expand their output until they reach the level where marginal cost matches marginal revenue—and that they should stop there.

Chapter 8 gives a profit-maximizing rule for the firm in perfect competition: P equals MC. This is nothing but a particular instance of the MR equals MC rule. Why? Because perfect competition is based on the assumption that the demand curve facing the individual firm is perfectly horizontal, or perfectly price-(elastic / inelastic). That is, if market price were $2, then the firm would receive (less than $2 / exactly $2 / more than $2) for each extra unit that it sold. In this special case, then, marginal revenue is (greater than / exactly equal to / less than) price per unit (which could be called average revenue, or revenue per unit). In cases of perfect competition, therefore, P equals MC and MR equals MC are two ways of saying the same thing.

elastic; exactly $2; exactly equal to

10. a. In imperfect competition, the firm's demand curve is (tilted / flat). From inspection of the figures in Table 10-1 [compare columns (1) and (6)], it is evident that with such a demand curve, marginal revenue at any particular output is (greater than / the same thing as / less than) price.

b. Why is this so? Suppose that you can sell 4 units at a price of $7 or 5 units at a price of $6. Revenues associated with these two prices are $28 and $30, respectively. Marginal revenue from selling the fifth unit is equal to $(2 / 5 / 6 / 7 / 28 / 30). It is the difference in revenue that can be obtained as a result of selling the 1 extra unit. Why only $2 when the price at which that fifth unit can be sold is $6? Because to sell that fifth unit, price has to be reduced, and this lowers the price which applies to all 5 units. The first 4, which could have been sold at $7, now bring only $6 each, so revenue takes a beating of $4. You must subtract this $4 from the $6 which the fifth unit brings in to compute the net change in total revenue. In this case, the net gain in revenue is $2—marginal revenue.

c. Notice also that MR and price elasticity are related. Recall that demand is price-inelastic if, when price is reduced, revenue goes (down / up). This means that MR is (negative / zero / positive) when demand is inelastic with respect to price. MR is (negative / zero / positive) when demand displays unitary price elasticity. When demand is price-elastic, MR is (negative / zero / positive). Check to make sure that the MR and TR curves that you drew in Figure 10-3 conform to the results of this question.

a. tilted; less than b. 2 c. down; negative; zero; positive

11. Now return to the fortunes of the monopoly firm represented in Tables 10-1 and 10-2. The tables do not provide sufficient unit-by-unit detail to show the exact maximum-profit output level, but Table 10-1 does indicate that MR is $1.63 between sales totaling 63 and 71. The MR figures fall as sales are expanded, so the $1.63 would apply near the midpoint of this range, say, at an output of 67. MR would be somewhat higher between 63 and 66 and somewhat lower between 68 and 71.

Similarly, MC (Table 10-2) would be about $1.65 at an output of 67 units, so the maximum-profit position would fall very close to 67 units produced and sold per period. Check to make sure that the MR and MC curves that you drew in the bottom panel of Figure 10-3 intersect at roughly 67 units.

To sell this output, the firm would charge a price (see Table 10-1) of about $(7.00 / 5.75 / 4.00 / 1.60). Its total revenue [look for nearby figures in column (3)] would be roughly $(380 / 580 / 780). Total cost (Table 10-2) would be roughly $(310 / 510 / 710), leaving profit per period of about $70.

5.75; 380; 310

12. In the section of the text headed "Let Bygones Be Bygones," it is emphasized that a firm, in setting output and price according to MR = MC, will disregard fixed cost. This does not mean that fixed cost can be ignored completely; maximum profits could be negative, for example, if fixed costs were too large. Nonetheless, in the determination of the profit-maximizing production/sales point, marginal revenue and marginal cost are the critical parameters.

a. Suppose that a monopolist's fixed costs increase, perhaps because a flat tax is levied against the firm's property. Would this tax raise the firm's AC curve? . . . . (yes / no)

b. Would the tax affect the monopolist's variable cost, or the AVC curve? . . . . (yes / no)

c. Would the tax affect the monopolist's marginal cost curve? . . . . (yes / no)

d. If the MC curve were unaffected, would such a flat tax change the maximum-profit output? (Presumably the tax would not affect output demand, so it would have no effect on marginal revenue.) . . . . (yes / no)

e. If the tax did not affect MC, MR, or maximum-profit output, would the price be changed? . . . . (yes / no)

a. yes b. no (because the tax affects only fixed cost and the AFC curve) c. no (MC depends only on variable cost.) d. no (unless it drove profits below zero) e. no (again, not unless profits turned negative and production ceased)

13. Figure 10-4 shows the per unit cost and revenue measures confronting a monopolist. The DD line is the market demand curve. MR is the corresponding market marginal revenue curve. AC is the firm's average cost curve, and MC represents the corresponding marginal cost schedule.

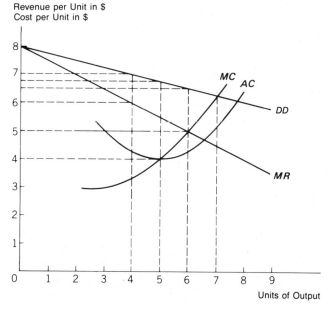

Figure 10-4

a. Which line indicates the demand curve facing the monopolist firm? . . . . _____

b. If output were 4, what must price be? . . . . _____

c. What is marginal revenue at 4 units of output? _____

d. At what level of output does average cost fall to its minimum level? . . . . _____

e. What price would clear the market if output were set at this minimum AC level? . . . . _____

f. What would total cost be at this level? . . . _____

g. What would total revenue be? . . . . _____

h. What would profit be? .... _____

i. At what output would profit be maximized? .. _____

j. What is marginal revenue at this output? .. _____

k. What is marginal cost at this output? ...... _____

l. What is average cost at this output? (Assume it is 20 cents above minimum level.) .... _____

m. What is price at this output? .... _____

n. What is total profit at this output? ...... _____

a. DD **b.** $7 **c.** $6 **d.** 5 **e.** $6.75 **f.** $20 **g.** $33.75 **h.** $13.75 **i.** 6
j. $5 **k.** $5 **l.** $4.20 (roughly) **m.** $6.50 **n.** $13.80

14. This is another one of those profit-maximizing-consultant problems. It is more difficult than the straightforward computational questions that preceded it, but it is designed to test whether or not you have a thorough understanding of the concepts. What would you recommend in each of the seven cases listed in Table 10-3? In each case, the firm in question is a monopoly and wants to maximize its profits (or minimize its losses). Enough information is supplied in each case, though you may have to fill in some of the blank spaces in the table to do your job; that is, presumably, why you were hired. Note that there is at least one "nonsense case," in which the figures are inconsistent and cannot be correct. Ferreting out such a circumstance could lead you to tell your client to do a better job in picturing either his or her market or cost structure.

Answer for each case by putting one of the numbers 1 through 5 from the code below into the extreme right-hand column of the table. (The same number may of course be used for more than one question.)

1. Firm is now at correct position.
2. Firm should increase price and reduce quantity produced and sold.
3. Firm should reduce price and increase quantity produced and sold.
4. Firm should shut down operations because loss at best possible operating position exceeds fixed cost.
5. A nonsense case—the figures supplied are inconsistent and could not all be correct.

a. 3 ($MR > MC$ means output should be increased; price will have to be reduced.) **b.** 1 (AC at the minimum means that $AC = MC$; in this case, $AC = \$4000/1000 = \$4$, and that matches MR.) **c.** 2 (Price $= TR/Q = \$8000/4000 = \$2$. Since $MR < P$, so $MR < \$2 = MC$, output should be reduced to bring MR up to equality with MC.) **d.** 2 ($MC > MR$, so output should be reduced. This firm is now maximizing revenue, not profit.) **e.** 5 (MR cannot exceed price.) **f.** 2 ($AC = TC/Q = \$6000/2000 = \$3$. Since $\$3 = P > MR$, it must be that $MR < MC$.) **g.** 4 ($MR = MC$, so profit is highest, but it is negative. $TR = \$2.50 \times 10,000 = \$25,000 < TC = AC \times Q = \$3 \times 10,000 = \$30,000$.)

REVIEW CONCEPTS

1. Imperfect competition takes many forms: monopoly—a single seller; oligopoly—a few sellers of the same product; monopolistic competition—many sellers of close substitutes. They take their market power from downward-sloping demand curves which allow them to choose *both* price *and* quantity.

2. Decreasing costs and various barriers to market entry create and maintain imperfectly competitive market structures.

3. Profits are maximized at output X^* where $MC(X^*) = MR(X^*)$. For firms in a competitive market, $P = MR$, so $P = MC(X^*)$ defines the profit-maximizing position. For an imperfect competitor facing a sloped demand curve, $P^* > MR(X^*) = MC(X^*)$.

Table 10-3

Case	Price	Marginal Revenue	Quantity of Output	Total Revenue	Total Cost	Fixed Cost	Average Cost	Marginal Cost	Answer
a.	$8.00	$4.00	2,000			$2,000	$4.00	$3.00	
b.	5.00	4.00	1,000		$4,000	1,000	At minimum level		
c.			4,000	$ 8,000			1.80	2.00	
d.	8.00	zero		32,000		5,000		4.00	
e.	1.00	2.00	10,000			2,000	2.00	2.00	
f.	3.00		2,000		6,000		At minimum level		
g.	2.50	2.00	10,000			4,000	3.00	2.00	

QUIZ: Multiple Choice

1. Which of the following are possible sources of imperfectly competitive markets?
(1) Declining average costs over the range of possible quantities demanded.
(2) Legal barriers to entry.
(3) Perceived product differentiation.
(4) Tariff protection from foreign competition.
(5) All of the above.

2. The average percentage of domestic manufacturing output contributed by the largest four firms across all industries in the United States is:
(1) about 50 percent.
(2) about 12 percent.
(3) about 38 percent.
(4) about 5 percent.
(5) over 60 percent.

3. If a firm's marginal revenue exceeds its marginal cost, maximum-profit rules require that the firm:
(1) increase its output in both perfect and imperfect competition.
(2) increase its output in perfect but not necessarily in imperfect competition.
(3) increase its output in imperfect but not necessarily in perfect competition.
(4) decrease its output in both perfect and imperfect competition.
(5) increase price, not output, in both perfect and imperfect competition.

4. Whenever the demand curve facing a given firm is perfectly elastic:
(1) the firm cannot be operating under conditions of perfect competition.
(2) the profit-maximizing rule which sets marginal cost equal to marginal revenue does not apply.
(3) price and marginal revenue must be one and the same for every quantity.
(4) price and marginal cost must be one and the same for every quantity.
(5) none of these conclusions is necessarily correct.

5. A firm operating in a perfectly competitive market is different from a monopolist because, among other reasons:
(1) a competitive firm can sell as much as it wishes at some given price, whereas a monopoly must lower its price if it wishes to increase the volume of its sales by any significant amount.
(2) a monopoly can always charge a price yielding a significant profit, whereas a competitive firm can never earn such a profit.
(3) the price elasticity of supply offered by a monopolist is higher than that offered by a competitive firm.
(4) a monopolist seeks to maximize profit, whereas a competitive firm's output decision rule equates price and average cost.
(5) a monopolist deliberately seeks to operate at the minimum level of average cost, but a competitive firm does not.

6. The term "oligopoly":
(1) is the general rubric for imperfect competition.
(2) refers to a situation in which the number of competing firms is large but the products differ slightly.
(3) refers to a situation in which the number of competing firms is small but greater than 1.
(4) refers to the form of imperfect competition which sees firms as acting like a monopoly, regardless of the number of firms or type of product.
(5) none of these.

7. If a profit-maximizing monopoly has reached its equilibrium position, then:
(1) price must be less than marginal cost.
(2) price must be equal to marginal cost.
(3) price must be greater than marginal cost.
(4) price may be equal to or below marginal cost, but not above it.
(5) none of the above is necessarily correct, since equilibrium does not require any particular relation between price and marginal cost.

8. The term "marginal revenue" refers to:
(1) the price that can be obtained for the very last unit sold.
(2) total revenue divided by the total number of units sold.
(3) total revenue minus the price received for the very last unit sold.
(4) the difference between the increase in total revenue generated by the sale of the last unit and the increase in total cost generated by the production of that unit.
(5) the difference between the increase in total revenue generated by the sale of the last unit sold and the reduction in total revenue caused by selling all the other units at a (usually) lower price.

9. Monopoly exists:
(1) whenever there is only one seller of a particular product.
(2) whenever the seller has at least some degree of control over the price she or he can charge.
(3) whenever the profit earned by the seller exceeds the amount that should properly be earned as interest on money invested, plus an allowance for the risk undertaken.
(4) whenever a seller manages to maintain his or her position through successful advertising.
(5) in none of these situations, necessarily.

10. Marginal revenue could exceed price:
(1) in circumstances of oligopoly.
(2) and does, in all genuine monopoly situations.
(3) if, somehow, increased sales were associated with higher prices.
(4) in the circumstances of "differentiated" products.
(5) in no conceivable circumstances whatsoever.

11. A firm operating in a situation of imperfect competition has determined that marginal revenue is $2.00 and average cost is $1.75. It has also observed that $1.75 is the lowest sustainable average cost given current technology and input prices. To maximize profit, this firm should:
(1) increase price.
(2) decrease price.
(3) decrease output and sales.
(4) leave price and output unchanged.
(5) perhaps do any of these things; the information given is insufficient to tell.

12. Which alternative in question 11 would be correct had it specified that price rather than marginal revenue is $2?
(1).
(2).
(3).
(4).
(5).

13. The essential characteristic of imperfect competition is that the single firm's:
(1) demand curve has a downward tilt.
(2) marginal revenue exceeds the price it charges.
(3) average cost curve falls over a substantial or large range of outputs.
(4) product is differentiated from one firm to the next.
(5) average cost curve rises over a substantial or large range of outputs.

14. If the price a firm obtains for its output were higher than the marginal cost associated with that particular output, then maximum-profit rules would require that the firm:
(1) increase its output in both perfect and imperfect competition.
(2) increase its output in perfect but not necessarily in imperfect competition.
(3) increase its output in imperfect but not necessarily in perfect competition.
(4) decrease its output in both perfect and imperfect competition.
(5) increase price, not output, in both perfect and imperfect competition.

15. Which alternative in question 14 would have been correct if that question had stated that the price is smaller than the marginal cost?
(1).
(2).
(3).
(4).
(5).

16. To explain why imperfect competition is far more prevalent than perfect competition, economists lay considerable emphasis upon the fact that:
(1) advertising has now become more powerful than price as a sales weapon in many markets.
(2) marginal revenue tends to equal or even to exceed price in many markets.
(3) average cost continues to fall until a large output has been reached in many industries.
(4) a high price charged to consumers has become the most effective method of maximizing profits.
(5) marginal revenue tends to fall significantly below price in many markets.

17. A correct statement of the relationship between marginal revenue (MR) and price elasticity of demand holds that MR is:
(1) negative when demand is inelastic.
(2) zero when demand is inelastic.
(3) positive when demand is inelastic.
(4) negative when demand displays unitary elasticity.
(5) positive when demand is perfectly elastic.

SUGGESTED ANSWERS TO QUESTIONS IN THE TEXT: Chapter 10

1. Consult the definitions.
General Motors: oligopoly in the United States, monopolistic competitor worldwide (?)
Local telephone company: local monopoly
Sears: monopolistic competitor
Farmer Jones: perfect competitor
Your college: (?)

2. Profit maximization means that firms maximize sales (total revenue) *net of costs*. Sales are maximized where marginal revenue is zero (at the peak of the total revenue "hill"). Since marginal costs are usually positive, this occurs at a higher output than the profit-maximizing level, so price is lower and quantity is higher. The competitive output can, however, be higher still (with an even lower price) because competitors can operate in the inelastic region of demand where $MR < 0$. If "sales" is interpreted as quantity, though, production would increase to the maximum quantity demanded at the lowest relevant price—a situation of negative profit not even covering the minimum average cost associated with competitive equilibrium.

3. Constant TR means MR equals 0.

4. The slopes of TC and TR are equal at $q = 4$; i.e., MR equals MC.

5. The four-firm index equals 55 ($17 + 14 + 12 + 12$); the eight-firm index equals 81 ($55 + 9 + 8 + 7 + 2$). If Delta and United merged, the four-firm index would include Northwest; it would climb to 64. The eight-firm index would add another 2 percent carrier and climb to 83.

6. Consult Figure TQ10-1. A horizontal demand curve means that price is fixed at, e.g., P. Total revenue is $TR(q) = Pq$ and $MR = P$. Profits are maximized where $MR = MC$, but $MR = P$ means that $MC = P$, as well [to be a long-term equilibrium, $P = \min(AC)$, too]. Panel (a) shows all this. Panel (b) shows $TR(q)$ linear with slope P and $TC(q)$ parallel (and tangent, so profits are zero) at the same output q^*. Note that MC stops declining at $q_1 < q^*$, so $C(q)$ starts to grow progressively steeper for $q > q_1$.

7. MC equals $1000 (= $600 + $400). On the demand side, price equals $3000 - 0.01Q$, so MR equals $3000 - 0.02Q$. MR equals MC at 100,000 units of output.

8. $0 < MC = MR$ for the profit-maximizing monopolist. As a result, $MR > 0$, so demand must be price-elastic.

9. Use calculus and algebra. Even if you do not know calculus, take the MR and MC curves as given and do the algebra.

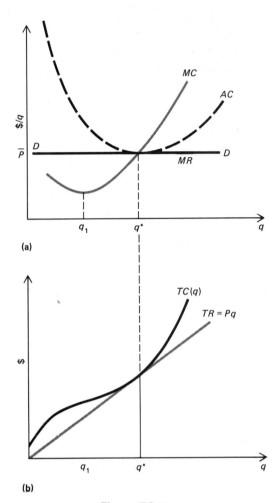

Figure TQ10-1

CHAPTER 11

OLIGOPOLY AND MONOPOLISTIC COMPETITION

Chapter 10 explored the various sources of monopoly power. Based upon the results of the survey presented there, it is perhaps surprising that the profitability of supplying a market in the United States appears to increase only slightly as the concentration of market power in the hands of a few suppliers climbs. Perhaps even more surprising are the observed high advertising budgets for firms servicing concentrated American industries. If these firms were exploiting a truly strong market position of the type considered in the previous chapter, one might expect just the opposite—high profits and little advertising. If you have that kind of power, why not use it? And why advertise if you have no competition? In addition, empirical studies have found that concentrated industries have typically produced large research and development budgets. This is perhaps reassuring (suggesting that large firms are not necessarily lazy firms), but it is a third observation that is not explained very well by our models of monopoly behavior. Concentrated industries have, finally, displayed little in the way of flexibility in the pricing of their products. This is a troublesome reminder that size itself can breed potential for laziness—concentrated industries might be the homes of firms too big to bother constructing procedures with which to maintain efficient prices.

The theoretical basis for understanding these observations cannot, quite clearly, rest entirely on the pure-monopoly modeling of Chapter 10. It will rest, instead, on modelings of intermediate forms of imperfect competition—market structures that lie somewhere between the efficiencies of perfect competition and the potential perversities of monopoly. Chapter 11 provides an overview of a few of these models. Upon completion of your work in this area, you will have accomplished the following objectives.

LEARNING OBJECTIVES

1. Review the determinants of market power, and understand how cost structure, barriers to entry, and the potential for collusion influence the translation of that market power into a particular market structure of imperfect competition. Be comfortable with the spectrum of imperfect competition, stretching from perfect competition at one extreme to monopoly at the other. Identify examples of industries which appear at various spots along the length of this spectrum.

2. Understand the potential risks and gains involved in collusion between a few firms on price and/or quantity.

3. Reproduce and manipulate a few simple models of noncollusive behavior in imperfectly competitive markets and monopolistic competition.

4. Conceptualize how the profit-maximizing behavior that is hypothesized by economists can be perceived even within the constraints of bounded rationality that corporate management usually displays. Understand, for example, the profit motivations behind rule-of-thumb pricing behaviors like markup pricing.

5. Evaluate to your own satisfaction the Schumpeterian hypothesis that significant market power leads to extensive and socially desirable programs of research and development that would otherwise not be forthcoming. Do you think the hypothesis correct? How do you think it should affect policy reaction to firms' exploiting market power?

6. Understand how imperfect competition leads to prices which exceed marginal cost, and use deadweight loss to evaluate the associated welfare cost.

Oligopoly, the circumstance in which there exist only a few sellers of the same good, is conceptually the simplest intermediate case of imperfect competition. It can emerge as the prevailing market structure for many reasons. Oligopoly can, first of all, appear whenever average costs decline through levels of output equaling 20 to 40 percent of market demand. These situations are, to some degree, "natural oligopolies" in the same sense that "natural monopolies" display declining costs across the demand of the entire market. They reflect economies of scale that should be exploited. Other, more artificial and sometimes less desirable conditions can, however, also produce oligopolistic markets. These include both legal and illegal barriers to entry; tariffs, patents, and tacit or explicit price collusion to threaten potential entrants are all examples which fall under the general rubric of artificial constraints on competition. The first few questions will examine your understanding of oligopoly models.

1. Empirical research has uncovered patterns of correlation between the degree of concentration displayed by various industries and nonproduction activities such as research and development, advertising, and price administration. Indicate in the parentheses whether the following descriptions most likely apply to a high-concentration industry (H) like motor vehicles, a moderate-concentration industry (M) like chemicals, a low-concentration industry (L) like printing, or a perfectly competitive industry (P).

a. Industry A shows negligible expenditure on research and development (measured as a percentage of total sales), negligible expenditure on advertising, and no price administration. . . . . ( )

b. Industry B shows a normal rate of profit, small expenditure on research and development as well as advertising (each less than 1 percent of total sales), but the highest level of price administration. . . . . ( )

c. Industry C shows a normal rate of profit, high expenditure on research and development as well as advertising (each around 1.7 percent of total sales), and a moderate level of price administration. . . . . ( )

d. Industry D shows a normal profit rate, the highest expenditure on research and development, expenditure on advertising that is nearly comparable, and a high degree of price administration. . . . . ( )

from Table 11-1 in the text: **a.** P **b.** L **c.** H **d.** M

2. The case of **pure oligopoly** illustrates with special clarity the problems confronting the firm in imperfect competition. In this situation, the number of firms engaged in close competition is (large / small, or comparatively small), while the products they sell are (uniform / differentiated).

The important consequence of this uniformity, or "homogeneity," of product is that all firms must charge the same price. If any one company tries to raise its price and the others do not follow suit, that company will most probably (gain / lose some of its / lose all or practically all of its) customers. On the other hand, if this company reduces price, it is most likely that all rivals will be forced to follow suit. Each firm therefore has some influence over the price buyers must pay, particularly because of its ability to reduce price.

small, or comparatively small; uniform; lose all or practically all of its

The knowledge that "we're all in the same boat" may produce a tacit agreement among the firms to abide by some given price. (Economic theory still has a long way to go in describing how oligopoly members reach pricing agreements that they can live with.) With price established by agreement, the participants then use competitive weapons other than price (notably advertising or, more generally, selling effort) to secure business. There is rivalry among the member firms; there is a struggle for business; there is competition; but there is rarely any price competition. In the event of a serious downturn in business, though, even an explicit and illegal agreement to forgo using price as a competitive weapon may weaken.

One interesting consequence of this method of competition is that each supplier may try hard in its advertising to persuade the buying public that its product is "different" as part of the attempt to retain and expand its share of the market even though the competing products can be essentially uniform (i.e., no one firm's product is really worth much more than any other firm's product). On the surface, then, the competing products may seem to be "differentiated." If you examine the advertised differences carefully, however, you may find that they are trivial and that, for analytic purposes, the products are really homogeneous (think of toothpaste).

To review, then, oligopolistic firms in the same industry must recognize that they are mutually interdependent. The actions of one firm always affect the circumstances facing the others. This point is most clearly illustrated in a careful consideration of the profitability of collusion and the temptation to cheat. Cheating, it can be shown, can pay dividends, but it can also produce significant losses.

3. To see why all this is true, consider Figure 11-1. On that graph, dd represents the effective demand curve facing some oligopolist who abides by a colluding agreement with a few competitors. It could, for example, be the result of a consistent 30 percent share of total sales for any price along a market demand curve. Notice that every reduction of $1 in the price produces, for the firm when all other firms conform, an increase in sales of 10 units. Marginal revenue is given by mr. Average cost and marginal cost are assumed, for simplicity only, to be constant at $4 per unit regardless of output level.

On the basis of the assumption of perfect collusion, the firm will maximize profits along dd by agreeing to a price

Figure 11-1

cheating firm's profits would fall to $_____ as sales declined to _____ units.

It is clear, therefore, that successful cheating is better for a single firm than successful collusion, but it entails the risk of reducing profitability if all the firms catch on and follow to protect themselves. Were the process to continue, in fact, the firms would, collectively, end up producing the *(competitive / monopoly / duopoly)* output and selling it at the *(competitive / monopoly / duopoly)* price. In terms of Figure 11-1, price would converge to $_____ , output would converge to _____ units, and pure economic profit would converge to $_____ .

7; 30; 90; reducing: 6.50; 40; 100; 87.50; 35 (A price of $6.50 translates into sales of 35 units along *dd* and a profit of $2.50 per unit sold.); competitive; competitive; 4; 60; 0

of $_____ , therefore selling _____ units and earning excess profits of $_____ .

Now suppose that the firm could, by lowering its price relative to that of its colluding partners (i.e., by cheating on its colluding agreement), pick up an extra 20 units of sales for every $1 reduction in price. It could, in other words, increase its market share at the expense of other firms by lowering its price alone. The resulting demand and marginal revenue curves are represented in Figure 11-1 by $d'd'$ and mr', respectively. The firm could, in this case, move to a new profit-maximizing position by *(reducing / maintaining / increasing)* its price to $_____ and selling _____ units. The result would be $_____ in excess profits.

It is, of course, highly unlikely that the other firms would not catch on. Suppose, in response to the cheating of the first firm, that all the other firms changed their prices to the cheater's new price. *dd* would again be relevant, and the

4. Now consult Figure 11-2. Panel *(a)* represents the *MC* schedule of one of two oligopolistic firms facing the market demand curve *DD* of panel *(b)*. Remember the text's argument that colluding firms tend to share the monopoly output between themselves. Draw the combined *MC* curve of the two firms in panel *(b)*.

Acting as a monopolist, profit-maximizing colluders equipped with knowledge of this joint *MC* curve could agree to charge a price of $_____ for an expected _____ units of sales. Each firm would, under the agreement, expect to sell _____ units.

---

the graph: The joint *MC* curve is a straight line from $(Q = 10, P = \$2)$ with half the slope of the *MC* curve of panel *(a)*.

7; 30; 15

(a)

(b)

Figure 11-2

11 Oligopoly and Monopolistic Competition

Another distinct form of imperfect competition has been identified by the economics literature—one in which many manufacturers market nearly identical products that are somehow differentiated from one another. It is a situation which gives each firm some degree of *monopoly* power over its own version of the product in question (i.e., some power to set its own price), but which does not remove the firm effectively from the pervasive *competition* offered by the many other producers of many slightly different items—items which are, in reality, all very close substitutes. Thus, this form of market structure has been dubbed **monopolistic competition.**

5. The fact that there are many sellers of similar goods suggests that it is fairly easy for new firms to enter a monopolistically competitive industry and for old firms to leave. New firms will be tempted to enter, in fact, whenever existing firms are making excess pure economic profit; and existing firms will leave when pure economic profits are persistently negative. This potential for entry and exit is, clearly, a second (long-run) parallel between monopolistic competition and the perfectly competitive market structure studied in Chapter 9.

a. Insofar as new firms *do* enter, they take over some part of the market of already-operating firms. This means that the demand curve facing any one of these existing firms tends to be pushed *(to the right or upward / to the left or downward)*, and thereby *(reduces / increases)* the profit of existing firms. If the entry tendency persists, every firm's demand curve will wind up just touching, or tangent to, the average cost curve. Such a tangency situation means that the firm in question can *(still earn a profit / just break even / operate only at a loss)*. When this tangency point is reached for the typical firm, the profit feature which attracted new entrants *(still / no longer)* exists.

b. In this differentiated-seller model, each firm's demand curve is assumed to be *(tilted / flat)* because product differentiation supposedly *(gives some / does not give any)* degree of monopoly power to the firm. If the demand curve is tilted, though, and if things wind up with this demand curve just touching the average cost curve, then the tangency point *(must / cannot)* occur at the very bottom of the AC curve. (A tangency point is one at which the two curves involved have the same slope. If the demand curve is tilted at the point in question, then the AC curve must be negatively sloped, as well.)

c. The hypothetical monopolistically competitive firm therefore winds up earning no profit, yet operating at an output level which is *(less than / equal to / greater than)* its minimum-AC output. In the sense that a larger output would reduce its AC, this firm has "excess capacity." Economists were much taken with these ideas when Edward H. Chamberlin introduced them. They suggested that "differentiated competition" might not work quite as perfect-competition theory had suggested it would. In squeezing out profits, it might not, in particular, achieve minimum average cost. Recall that perfect competition supports long-run equilibrium with minimum average cost of production and zero profits sustained by a price set equal to average *and* marginal cost.

Chamberlin would have insisted that any comparison between the supposed "long-run" results of perfect and monopolistic competition must not be used to condemn monopolistic competition. He was convinced that monopolistic competition was the near-universal and inevitable situation. Perfect-competition theory might point to an "ideal" situation, but he was certain that this ideal was unattainable in real-life circumstances.

---

a. to the left or downward; reduces; just break even; no longer **b.** tilted; gives some; cannot **c.** less than

6. For an industry structure that satisfies the characterization of monopolistic competition, long-run equilibrium is represented by a tangency between a firm's average cost curve and the effective demand curve for its differentiated product. It is, as a result, necessary that *(P > MC / P = MC / P < MC)* in equilibrium because the effective demand curve is *(negatively sloped / positively sloped / horizontal)*. Furthermore, the properties of cost curves require that *(MC > AC / MC = AC / MC < AC)* at the equilibrium level of output. Compared with the perfectly competitive equilibrium, therefore, the monopolistic competitor produces *(too much / too little / just the correct amount)*.

Now consider the plight of a monopolistic competitor in an industry whose production costs have suddenly increased. In the short run, economic profits for this firm would be *(less than zero / equal to zero / still slightly positive)*. In the long run, firms would *(enter / exit / proceed as before)*, so the effective demand curve facing our firm would *(shift in for every price / shift out for every price / do nothing)*. The result, ultimately, would be *(lower / higher / identical)* prices and *(negative / zero / positive)* economic profits.

It was observed in Chapter 10 that a lump-sum tax would affect neither the price decision nor the output decision of a profit-maximizing monopolist. We can now see that this conclusion *(applies equally well / does not apply at all)* to the monopolistic competitor; even a change in AC with no change in MC can affect the output of a monopolistic competitor.

$P > MC$; negatively sloped; $MC < AC$; too little; less than zero; exit; shift out for every price; higher; zero; does not apply at all (Refer to Fig. 11-3 in answering these questions. In fact, drawing pictures is usually a good idea when confronted with unfamiliar comparative-statics questions.)

7. Compared with perfect competitors, imperfect competitors probably pay, in practice, *(more / the same / less)* attention to maximizing profits. This should be expected, in part, because most earn *(positive / zero / negative)* economic profits and *(are / are not)* on the same knife-edge of economic viability as their perfect-competitor colleagues.

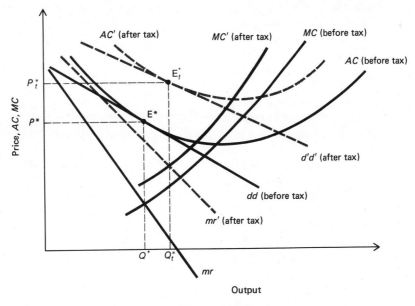

Figure 11-3

"Bounded rationality" is given as one reason for this behavior; it is a notion that focuses attention on the expense and difficulty involved in collecting and processing the information required to set marginal cost precisely equal to marginal revenue. Instead of making the effort to accomplish that task, it is argued, "rules of thumb" emerge in boardrooms all across the country to help guide executives in making their pricing and output decisions without detailed knowledge of the underlying marginal schedules.

Markup pricing is the most popular of these rules, but the dimension of that markup is not a number that executives agree upon without some market analysis. It is, of course, this analysis that, in the long run, can make the search for a pricing rule look like a procedure that implicitly tries to maximize profits. Executives may not compute marginal cost and marginal revenue schedules, but they might still behave as if they do. This question is designed to illustrate how this "deception" might be achieved.

For a monopoly firm facing demand curve DD in Figure 11-4, profits would be maximized by setting a price equal to $_____ and expecting to sell _____ units. Relative to average cost, that price amounts to a _____ percent markup over cost. Now complete Table 11-1 to convince yourself that a sequence of trial markup percentages could lead a careful manager to the profit-maximizing intersection of MR and MC without computing either schedule.

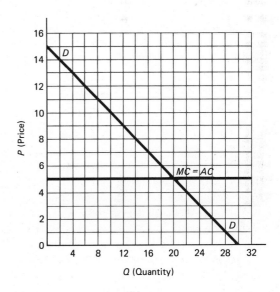

Figure 11-4

Table 11-1

Percentage Markup over Price	Price	Output (units)	Profit
60	$_____	_____	$_____
80	_____	_____	_____
100	_____	_____	_____
120	_____	_____	_____
110	_____	_____	_____
105	_____	_____	_____

less; positive; are not; 10; 10; 100 (*Remember*: Marginal revenue for a linear demand curve has the same intercept and twice the slope.); table rows: 60—8, 14, 42; 80—9, 12, 48; 100—10, 10, 50; 120—12, 8, 48; 110—10.50, 9, 49.50; 105—10.25, 9.5; 49.88 (The manager might, after noting that markup increases generated higher profits until 120 percent, begin to back up until the peak at 100 percent was discovered.)

8. The Schumpeterian hypothesis about the large firms which dominate imperfectly competitive markets postulates that "big business may have had more to do with creating our (high) standard of life than (with) keeping it down." This hypothesis is based, at least in part, upon the notion that (research and development expenditure / purchasing power / real competition) seems to be concentrated most heavily in the largest firms on the American scene. Since Edwin Mansfield has argued that the social return to invention is (3 / 0.5 / 5) times the private gain, it can certainly be argued that research and development is (overfunded / properly funded / underfunded). Moreover, the private gain to invention is (larger / smaller) for large firms than it is for small firms. The case can be made, therefore, that we should tolerate big business if big business conducts a large proportion of this country's research into new products and new production processes. The effect on our total expenditure on research and development of any policy or circumstance that reduces industrial concentration, like the breakup of AT&T, may thus be a source of major concern. Nonetheless, small success stories, like Apple Computers, sometimes turn into big success stories. Policy designed to foster research should therefore be the product of a balanced approach; it should not, in particular, concentrate its efforts exclusively on fostering big-business research at the expense of other sources of ingenuity and invention.

---

research and development expenditure; 3; underfunded; larger

---

9. As has been shown throughout Chapters 10 and 11, $P > MR$ along a sloping demand curve and $MR = MC$ at the profit-maximizing output. As a result, the price which a monopolist charges is (too high / too low / just right) relative to the competitive price. Since monopoly firms face downward-sloping demand curves (otherwise they would have no monopoly power, right?), the monopolist must therefore produce (less output than / more output than / the same output as) the competitive firm. On the basis of the efficiency properties of the perfectly competitive market, it is thus clear that the marginal utility derived from consuming the monopolist's product is (greater than / less than / equal to) the marginal cost of producing the good in question.

Consult Figure 11-5. The long-run equilibrium output and price must equal _____ units and $_____, respectively, if the illustrated cost structure were representative of a competitive market. A profit-maximizing monopolist would, meanwhile, sell _____ units at a price of $_____. The result would be a reduction in consumer surplus from $_____ to $_____. Of that reduction, $_____ would go to the monopolist in the form of excess economic profit, and $_____ would represent lost welfare that would disappear (deadweight loss).

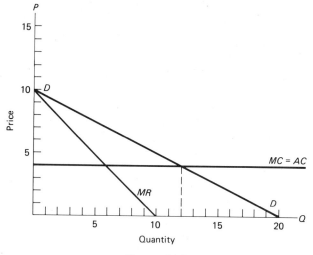

Figure 11-5

The dimension of actual deadweight loss caused by imperfect competition across the United States appears to be (less than / about equal to / more than) what might be expected. The loss has been estimated by Arnold Harberger to be in the neighborhood of (0.1 / 5.0 / over 10.0) percent of GNP. To conclude, in light of these numbers, that monopoly power should not be a major concern would, however, be to ignore the distortion in the distribution of income that excessive monopoly profits can create. More study is required to conclude that imperfect competition is a "nonproblem."

---

too high; less output than; greater than; 12; 4; 6; 7; 36; 9; 18; 9; less than; 0.1

---

10. Suppose that the monopolist depicted in Figure 11-5 faces an $18 lump-sum tax on profits. The profit-maximizing monopolist would then (increase / decrease / maintain) the quoted price to support a (larger / smaller / constant) level of production and sales.

Suppose, instead, that government taxes the monopolist's implicit return to capital and that the effective (constant) marginal cost of production therefore increases from $4 to $6 per unit. Output would (fall to / rise to / continue to remain fixed at) _____ units; price would (climb to / fall to / stay put at) $_____, representing an increase in price (equal to / less than / greater than) the $_____ increase in unit costs.

---

maintain; constant; fall to; 6; climb to; 8; less than; 2 (Neither option worked very well, did it?)

REVIEW CONCEPTS

1. Declining costs and artificial or collusive barriers to entry can give firms operating in a particular market some degree of market power and thus some discretion of *both* quantity

and price. Monopoly is one possible result—a single seller of a particular commodity. Oligopoly is another—a few sellers of the same product; oligopolists need to be aware of the actions and reactions of other firms when they contemplate changes in their behavior. Monopolistic competition is a third possible structure—many sellers of close substitutes; long-run equilibrium here presents zero pure economic profit but inefficient cost allocations.

2. Oligopolists can try to collude in a way that mimics a monopoly supplier, but there are risks. Collusion is illegal. Collusion presents circumstances in which it is profitable to cheat; but if all partners cheat, then every firm can end up worse off.

3. Colluding oligopolists maximize their joint profits by producing where the marginal cost of each firm is set equal to the marginal revenue of market demand.

4. Monopolistic competitors maximize profits where marginal cost equals the marginal revenue of the demand for their specific variant of product. Free entry and exit drive long-run equilibrium profits to zero, but the slope of the monopolistic competitors' demand curves precludes production at minimum average cost.

5. Bounded rationality in firm behavior notes the difficulty in correctly assessing market demand; it leads to markup pricing rules (e.g.), which can be adjusted with experience to converge toward profit-maximizing pricing behavior.

6. The Schumpeterian hypothesis suggests that large firms support valuable research and development that would not otherwise be forthcoming.

7. Imperfect competitors generally produce too little and charge prices in excess of marginal cost. The welfare cost of their approach can be measured in terms of diminished consumer surplus—the deadweight loss that results from their exploiting whatever market power is available.

QUIZ: Multiple Choice

1. Which of the following characteristics tends to prevail in highly concentrated markets?
(1) Slightly higher than normal profits.
(2) Above-average advertising expenditure.
(3) Above-average research and development expenditure.
(4) Below-average price flexibility.
(5) All the above.

2. Which of the following represents an artificial but nonetheless legal barrier to entry that might support an oligopolistic market structure?
(1) Price setting below the lowest price which a potential new entrant could afford to charge.
(2) A tariff that kept all but a trickle of foreign products off the domestic market.
(3) Product differentiation among a few producers.
(4) Average cost curves that reach their minima at roughly 30 percent of market demand.
(5) All the above.

3. Which alternative to question 2 would have been correct if the barrier to entry were a cost barrier?
(1).
(2).
(3).
(4).
(5).

4. Which alternative to question 2 represents an illegal barrier to entry that might support an oligopolistic structure?
(1).
(2).
(3).
(4).
(5).

5. OPEC presents to the world a market structure most accurately represented by:
(1) the bounded-rationality model.
(2) a collusive oligopoly model with incomplete market coverage.
(3) the monopolistic competition model.
(4) the "collusive oligopoly acting like a monopolist" model.
(5) perfect competition.

6. Which alternative to question 5 would have been correct if the market in question had been the breakfast cereal market in the United States?
(1).
(2).
(3).
(4).
(5).

7. Which alternative to question 5 would have been correct if the market in question had been the market for soybeans?
(1).
(2).
(3).
(4).
(5).

8. If we consider an industry of many sellers of differentiated products, and if entry into this industry is free, then we should expect the long-run equilibrium position of the typical firm in this industry to have which of the following properties?
(1) Average cost (AC) would be at its minimum possible level, and the price charged (P) would be equal to that AC.
(2) AC would be at its minimum level, and P would be above that AC.

(3) AC would be above its minimum level, and P would be above that AC.
(4) AC would be above its minimum level, and P would be equal to that AC.
(5) AC would be above its minimum level, but P would equal that minimum.

9. One reason why a firm operating under conditions of imperfect competition is likely to want to use an administered or markup price is:
(1) a lack of sufficient knowledge of marginal revenue at various levels of output.
(2) a lack of sufficient knowledge of marginal cost at various levels of output.
(3) the desire to have a break-even point occurring at a high level of output.
(4) the fear that charging a higher price would attract new competition into the field.
(5) the notion that this price corresponds to the most efficient plant output level.

10. The Schumpeter hypothesis is:
(1) big business is not necessarily bad business.
(2) firms never really have the power over price and output that economists attribute to them.
(3) research and development is more than sufficiently supported by a consortium of government, small business, and big business.
(4) innovation would be accelerated if managers of large firms were required to be owners of large firms.
(5) all the above.

11. In light of the pros and cons of imperfect competition, policy should probably be directed at:
(1) keeping the barriers to competition low.
(2) attacking anticompetitive business conduct.
(3) tolerating bigness if it is founded in technology.
(4) encouraging the research and development efforts of large and small firms.
(5) all the above.

12. Consider Figure 11-6. A profit-maximizing monopolist facing demand curve DD would maximize profits by:
(1) selling 4 units at a price of $2.
(2) selling 4 units at a price of $6.
(3) selling 8 units at a price of $2.
(4) selling 10 units at a price of $2.
(5) selling 5 units at a price of $5.

13. Which answer to question 12 would have been the correct description of the competitive equilibrium?
(1).
(2).
(3).
(4).
(5).

Figure 11-6

14. Which answer to question 12 would have been correct if the monopolist were trying to maximize revenue?
(1).
(2).
(3).
(4).
(5).

15. The monopolist of question 12 creates distortions whose welfare cost, measured in terms of consumer surplus, equals:
(1) $2.
(2) $4.
(3) $6.
(4) $8.
(5) $10.

SUGGESTED ANSWERS TO QUESTIONS IN THE TEXT: Chapter 11

1. Consult Table TQ11-1.

2. Equilibrium in monopolistically competitive markets occurs to the left of the minimum of the average cost curve, so output is too small; price is too high and does not match marginal cost. The resulting deadweight loss is the cost of diversity. Is it worth it? That depends upon the quality of the diversification.

3. Decreasing costs may or may not cover the scope of the market. A few competitors may be enough, but only if watched carefully to prevent explicit and implicit collusion. What about R&D? One competitor, or a couple, could find real advantage in bringing a new product to market if a large fraction of its value could be appropriated. Some of that incentive may be lost when there is only one producer.

4. The basic structure of the figures would remain essentially unchanged. Average cost could, for example, easily

Table TQ11-1

	Perfect Competition	Monopoly	Colluding Oligopoly	Monopolistic Competition
Number of firms	Many	1	Few	Many
Collusion	None	None	Yes	None
Price vs. MC	$P = MC$	$P \gg MC$	$P \gg MC$	$P > MC$
Price vs. LAC	$P = LAC$	$P \gg LAC$	$P \gg LAC$	$P \geq LAC$
Efficiency	Efficient	Large loss	Large loss	Moderate to small loss

maintain its U-shape if adopting initial improvements in quality made a few later improvements easier to accommodate. Eventually, though, "diminishing productivity" should set in. Demand, meanwhile, should be downward-sloping because the willingness to pay for incremental increases in quality can be expected to decline. People might, for example, be willing to pay more for the option of choosing the first Model T color besides black than they would for the options of a second or third. Cast in this way, the geometry seems to suggest a correlation between low quality (and fewer colors for Model T's) and high concentration of market power.

5. Refer to Figure TQ11-1. A unit tax adds $\$x$ per unit, increasing "effective" marginal cost and reducing output from Q_m to Q'_m along the marginal revenue curve MR. A higher price, P'_m, would result. Note that P'_m and Q'_m are both further from the ideal $P^* = MC(Q^*)$ and Q^*.

higher than $AC = MC = \$100$. This offer truncates the demand curve open to the monopolist at P_w, and results in an effective marginal revenue curve MR_E indicated by the heavy line drawn horizontal at P_w up to quantity Q_w read from demand curve DD (the monopolist would lose the entire market changing anything above P_w) and then falling abruptly to the original MR for quantities larger than Q_w. The monopolist would therefore see MC equal to effective marginal revenue at Q_w and would charge P_w.

b. A prohibitive tariff, (greater than $\$150 - P_w$) would cause things to revert back to the text's Figure 11-4. A small tariff T would move the world's offer price to $P_w + T$ for domestic consumers, distorting Figure TQ11-2 slightly, and thereby raising domestic prices above P_w and reducing domestic consumption below Q_w.

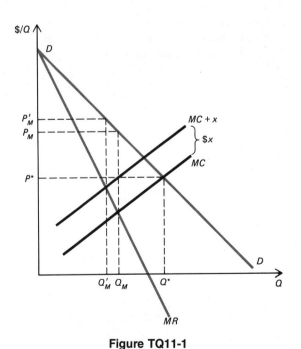

Figure TQ11-1

6. **a.** Consult Figure TQ11-2; it duplicates the text's Figure 11-4, but adds the foreign offer to sell Q at P_w slightly

Figure TQ11-2

7. Consult Figure TQ11-3. The typical portrait of long-run equilibrium for a monopolistic competitor is drawn there. The small slope assigned to demand curve dd puts the zero maximum-profit quantity Q_m [where $P_M =$

$AC(Q_M)$ and $MR(Q_M) = MC(Q_M)$] lower than the Q^* associated with minimum average cost [also, min $AC = AC(Q^*) = MC(Q^*)$]. The monopolistic competitor therefore produces too little, relative to the perfect-competition solution, and incurs an average cost of production which is too high. Meanwhile, $P_M = AC(Q_M) > MC(Q_M)$, so consumers who weigh marginal utility against P_M set $MU > MC$. Welfare would improve on the margin if output rose so that MU might fall toward a climbing MC.

Figure TQ11-3

8. The portion of the market demand curve above P_L would disappear, and the effective demand curve would be horizontal at P_L over to DD. Marginal revenue would then match the horizontal section until Q_L, and then it would jump down to the market MR curve. $P_L = MC$ would characterize the profit-maximizing price, or perhaps just below P_L so that potential entrants would turn aside. The limit price is P_L. See Figure TQ11-4. The heavy line is effective demand; the heavy dotted line is corresponding marginal revenue.

Figure TQ11-4

9. a. The price elasticity of demand is not infinity for the monopolistic competitor; it is for the perfect competitor.
b. $P = MC$ for the perfect competitor; $P > MC$ for the monopolistic competitor to an extent determined by the slope of demand.
c. Profits are zero for both.
d. Part **b** shows inefficiency for monopolistic competition as demand becomes more inelastic.

CHAPTER 12

UNCERTAINTY AND GAMES IN ECONOMIC BEHAVIOR

Firms and households have, in our discussions up until now, been allowed to approach their decisions armed with complete and perfect information; actors in the economic play, in short, have been blessed with a clear picture of their economic circumstance and an equally clear portrait of the ramifications of their decisions. It is, however, never that easy. In real life, imprecise and fuzzy perceptions of economic circumstance complicate every decision, and economists have begun to consider seriously the effects of these complications. Chapter 12 introduces you to two major avenues of analysis.

Section A looks into decisions made under circumstances of uncertainty from two sources. The first is derived from the fact that the future is unknown. The best information available is frequently no better than a collection of possible futures with no prospect of resolution before a decision must be made. The second is derived from the potential that sudden and unforeseen events might dramatically alter even the basic components of an actor's economic condition. Hedging, speculation, and insurance all come into play in this arena.

The second section of Chapter 12 takes explicit note of the interdependence of decisions taken by more than one actor. The range of outcomes that one person must consider as he or she makes a specific decision can easily depend not only upon prior decisions by other people, but also upon their response to the very decision being considered. Economists have long applied game-theoretic constructions to analyze the strategic interaction among decisions, and those applications are now being assimilated into mainstream economic theory even as they grow significantly in number.

As you work through this material, you will develop some additional analytical skill in dealing with more realistic models of economic life. By the end of the chapter, you should have accomplished the following learning objectives.

LEARNING OBJECTIVES

1. Speculators look to buy low and sell high across geographically defined markets, across time, and across states of nature. In so doing, they improve economic welfare by smoothing consumption instability *and* price instability.

2. Speculative markets allow people to hedge against unwelcome risk. Risk-averse individuals will, for example, buy insurance so that they can increase their expected utility by stabilizing consumption over different states of nature.

3. Efficient insurance markets can operate (a) when there exist many independent events or states of nature and (b) when there is little chance of moral hazard and/or adverse selection. Governments sometimes intervene by providing social insurance when private markets fail to operate.

4. Game theory has been applied by economists to analyze the strategic interactions of firms, households, and governments. The basic structure involves (a) identifying the players, (b) specifying the various actions or strategies available to each player, and (c) completing a payoff table which records the outcomes of each combination of players' strategies.

5. Underlying this structure is the notion that all players (a) identify their individual goals, (b) recognize the goals of the other player(s), and (c) think through all the possible outcomes for each and every possible strategy. Players then pick the strategy with the highest payoff relative to their goals, assuming that the other player(s) does (do) likewise.

6. There sometimes exists a dominant strategy for a given player—a strategy which provides the best outcome regardless of what the other player(s) does (do). If all players have a dominant strategy, then the game is solved by a dominant equilibrium.

7. Equilibria are more frequently Nash in character—a situation in which no player can make himself or herself better off by switching strategies, given the action(s) of the other player(s). Cooperative and noncooperative equilibria can then exist.

8. Perfect competition in the absence of externalities supports a noncooperative Nash equilibrium which is efficient. In many other situations, however, a cooperative equilibrium which must be supported by some sort of intervention can be socially superior to the noncooperative Nash equilibrium.

The self-motivated actions of speculators and arbitragers tend to moderate price and consumption instability in a wide variety of markets. Acting in their own individual best interest, these people generate an improvement in social welfare above and beyond the level of their individual gains. The source of this gain can be found in the principle of diminishing marginal utility, because it is diminishing marginal utility that leads to the conclusion that stable consumption is economically beneficial. The underlying point is simply put: Starting at some average level of consumption, *diminishing marginal utility* means that any increase in utility generated by some increase in consumption is smaller than the reduction in utility that would be generated by an equal reduction in consumption. Speculators simply shave off the high-price peaks with their corresponding low levels of consumption and fill in the low-price valleys with their corresponding high levels of consumption. Insurance offers the same sort of stable consumption, but also at a cost—people can reduce fluctuation in their own consumption by purchasing protection against various losses for a specified premium.

1. Assume that the demand curve for some good Q drawn in Figure 12-1 applies equally well to two different regions of the country—region A and region B. Suppose, additionally, that 10 units of Q are available initially in region A while only 6 units are available in region B.

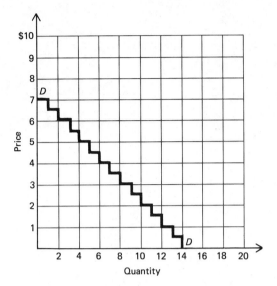

Figure 12-1

a. Any demand curve can, under some usual conditions, be considered (*a total cardinal utility curve* / *a cardinal marginal utility curve* / *a production schedule*). In that case, the marginal utility of the last unit supplied in A would equal

$_____, while the marginal utility of the next unit which could be supplied in B would equal $_____. Without any transportation cost, the transfer of 1 unit from A to B would cause utility in A to (*rise* / *fall*) by $_____ and utility in B to (*rise* / *fall*) by $_____ for a net gain in welfare of

$_____. The transfer of a second unit of Q from A to B would similarly (*increase* / *decrease*) total welfare, this time by $_____. The transfer of a third unit from A to B would, finally, (*increase* / *reduce*) total welfare by $_____. Total welfare across the two regions would, in fact, be maximized when the supply available in A equaled _____ units and the supply available in B equaled _____ units. In that circumstance, the marginal utility of the last unit supplied to A would be $_____ and the last unit supplied to B would be

$_____. The total transfer of _____ units from A to B would, in fact, maximally (*increase* / *reduce*) total welfare by

$_____. In general, total welfare is maximized where (*the marginal utilities of the last unit supplied were equal across regions* / *the total utilities of consumption were equal across regions* / *the quantities supplied across regions were equal*).

b. Now suppose that it costs $0.75 per unit to transport Q from one region to the other. The first unit transferred (*from A to B* / *from B to A*) would again improve total welfare, this time by $_____. The next unit transferred would, however, see (another increase / a reduction) in total welfare of $_____. The advent of transportation costs would, as a result, (increase / reduce) the gain in total welfare by _____ percent, from $_____ to $_____. There would exist no beneficial transfers of supply if, in fact, transportation costs were greater than $_____ per unit.

---

a. a cardinal marginal utility curve; 2.50; 4.00; fall; 2.50; rise; 4.00; 1.50; increase; 0.50 [= $3.50 − $3.00]; reduce; 0.50 [= $3.00 − $3.50]; 8; 8; 3.50; 3.50; 2; increase; 2.00; the marginal utilities of the last unit supplied were equal across regions
b. from A to B; 0.75 [= $1.50 − $0.75]; a reduction; 0.25 [= $0.50 − $0.75]; reduce; 37.5 [= ($0.75/$2.00) × 100%]; 2.00; 0.75; 1.50 (the welfare gain associated with the transfer of the first unit)

---

2. Consider Figure 12-2. It shows the demand for some good X in every period of a three-period supply cycle. Assume that 30 units of X are supplied in the first period of the cycle and that nothing is supplied in either period 2 or period 3.

Figure 12-2

a. If every unit of X were consumed in the first period, then consumption in periods 2 and 3 would be _____ units, and total welfare over the entire cycle would equal $_____ — the (area under the demand curve to the left of 30 units on the horizontal axis / value assumed by the demand curve above 30 units on the horizontal axis / total area under the demand curve).

b. Now assume that consumption is smoothed over the three periods so that consumption is 10 units in each. Without any carry costs, the price in each period would equal $_____.

Total utility in each period would equal $_____, for a total over the three periods of $_____. Total welfare (would / would not) be maximized in this case because (the marginal utility of consumption in each period would be equalized / the total utility of consumption in each period would be equalized). This is true despite the fact that the price of X would be _____ percent higher in period 1 than it was before.

c. Assume, as an additional complication, that it costs $5 in interest and storage fees to hold 1 unit of X for one period and $10 to hold 1 unit for two periods. As a result, the price of X would be $_____ (higher / lower) in period 2 than in period 1 and $_____ (higher / lower) in period 3 than in period 1. The only distribution of consumption over the three periods which would (1) support this price pattern and (2) exhaust total supply over the three-period cycle would have consumption equal _____ units, _____ units, and _____ units in periods 1, 2, and 3, respectively. The price of X would therefore be $_____ in period 1, $_____ in period 2, and $_____ in period 3. Welfare in period 1 would then amount to $_____; in period 2, $_____; and in period 3, $_____. Total welfare over the cycle would then be $_____ — (higher / lower) than the lumpy consumption pattern of part **a** and (higher / lower) than the costless storage case of part **b**. In comparing the costless storage case with the costly storage case of part **c**, however, welfare falls by $_____, an amount which is (greater than / less than) the total storage fees of $_____.

d. Draw the price pattern for several cycles in Figure 12-3, and confirm that it corresponds to the pattern suggested in Figure 12-1 in the text.

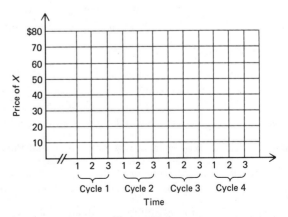

Figure 12-3

a. 0; 1050 [= 0.5(30)($50 + $20); the area under the demand curve to the left of 30 units on the horizontal axis   **b.** 40; 450; 1350; would; the *marginal utility of consumption in each period would be equalized*; 100 ($40 instead of $20)   **c.** 5; higher; 10; higher; 15 [*Note:* The holding fees suggest that $P_2 = P_1 + \$5$ and $P_3 = P_1 + \$10$. The slope of the demand curve is -1, so $X_2 = X_1 - \$5$ and $X_3 = X_1 - \$10$. The solution must therefore satisfy the condition that $[X_1 + (X_1 - 5) + (X_1 - 10)] = 30$, or that $3X_1 - 15 = 30$. It follows that $X_1 = 15, X_2 = 10$, and $X_3 = 5$.]; 10; 5; 35; 40; 45; 637.50 [= area of the trapezoid under the demand curve to the left of 15 units]; 450.00; 237.50; 1325; higher; lower; 25; less than; 100 [= $5(10) + $10(5)]   **d.** the graph: Plot prices of $35, $40, and $45 in succession; connect the points and see that the sawtooth pattern of text Figure 12-1 emerges.

3. Consult Figure 12-4. A cardinal utility schedule dependent upon the level of income is drawn there; it displays a (*diminishing / constant / increasing*) marginal utility of income.

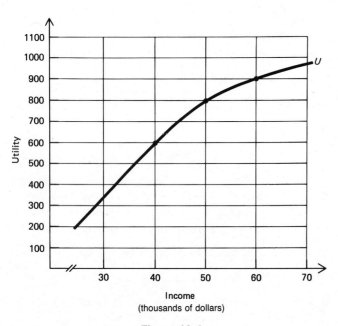

Figure 12-4

a. Suppose that income is $50,000 per year; in terms of utility measured on the vertical axis in utils, this $50,000 would produce utility equal to _____ utils.

b. Now suppose that we consider a "lottery" which has an expected payoff of $0 but which will return a gain of $10,000 with a probability of 50 percent or a loss of $10,000 with a probability of 50 percent. Would taking this lottery improve welfare? _____ To see why or why not, notice that $60,000 would produce _____ utils of utility—a gain of _____ utils over $50,000. An income of $40,000 would, meanwhile, produce _____ utils of utility—a reduction of _____ utils from $50,000. Losing $10,000 therefore produces a (*larger / equal / smaller*) change in utility than gaining an extra $10,000 because marginal utility is (*increasing / constant / decreasing*).

c. To put this another way, the average level of utility that could be expected if the lottery were taken would be _____. This level could be achieved with a fixed income of $_____. The risk involved in the lottery therefore costs, in terms of constant-income alternatives, $_____—the difference between $50,000 without the lottery and the $_____ value of taking the lottery.

d. Finally, assume that the lottery is not optional. Assume, instead, that it necessarily faces an individual with the utility schedule graphed in Figure 12-4. How much would this person pay to get out of the uncertainty of receiving $40,000 with a 50 percent probability or $60,000 with a 50 percent probability? The lottery yields the same average utility as a constant income of $_____. The person would, therefore, pay $_____ for an insurance policy that would remove the risk of the lottery—thereby guaranteeing an income of $_____ even though the lottery produces an average income of $_____.

---

diminishing   **a.** 800   **b.** no; 900; 100; 600; 200; larger; decreasing   **c.** 750; 46,500 (roughly; subsequent answers based on this estimate); 3500; 46,500   **d.** 46,500; 3500; 46,500; 50,000

4. Now suppose that the utility schedule is given by the straight line drawn in Figure 12-5. To avoid any lottery (e.g.,

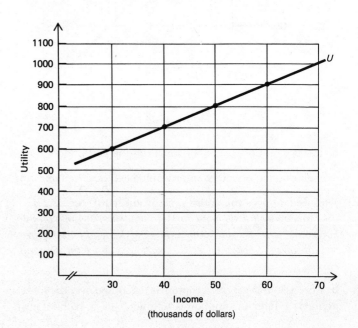

Figure 12-5

the case in question 4 with $10,000 on either side of $50,000) with an expected return of $0, an individual with this schedule would be willing to pay $_____. Why? _____

_____

_____

_____

$0; Fig. 12-5 shows constant marginal utility, so the individual displays no aversion to risk and maximizing the expected payoff of the lottery is the same as maximizing utility.

5. Let utility for some individual be given by $U = \sqrt{y}$, where y represents income. Suppose that this individual holds a lottery ticket which will pay $144 half of the time and $56 half of the time. The expected payoff from the lottery would be $_____. Utility in the good state of nature, when the lottery pays $144, would be _____ utils, while utility in the bad state of nature, when the lottery pays $56, would be _____ utils, so the expected utility offered by the lottery would equal _____ utils. This individual would be willing to sell the ticket for any price greater than $_____, because *(the marginal utility of the constant income offered by the sale of the ticket for such a price would be greater than the marginal utility of payoff offered by even the good state of nature / the total utility of the constant income offered by the sale of the ticket for such a price would exceed the expected utility of holding the lottery ticket)*. For any individual averse to risk, the minimum acceptable price for any lottery ticket is *(greater than / equal to / less than)* its expected payoff.

100; 12; 7.48; 9.74; 94.90; the total utility of the constant income offered by the sale of the ticket for such a price would exceed the expected utility of holding the lottery ticket; less than

6. a. Efficient insurance markets can exist if there are *(many / only a few)* independent events and if there is little chance of _____ or _____.

b. Indicate whether each of the following circumstances illustrates a problem of *(a)* moral hazard, *(b)* adverse selection, or *(c)* too few independent events.

(1) The existence of some global occurrence can cause damage simultaneously in many places. _____

(2) The existence of some cataclysmic event can cause enormous damage in a small but populated area. _____

(3) The purchase of insurance against automobile theft makes owners less cautious about where they park their cars. _____

(4) High premium charges drive careful car owners to forgo theft insurance in lieu of "self-insurance." _____

c. Failure of private insurance markets frequently leads to government-financed programs of _____. List a few examples:

(1) _____

(2) _____

(3) _____

a. many; adverse selection; moral hazard **b. (1)** too few independent events **(2)** too few independent events **(3)** moral hazard **(4)** adverse selection **c.** social insurance; Examples include social security, the Price-Anderson insurance program against damage from nuclear power plant accidents, Medicaid health insurance, the Canadian national health system, etc.—there are many.

Economic life is full of circumstances in which competition among a few individuals, firms, or even nations degenerates into a process of jockeying for positions of strategic dominance. **Game theory** has been applied by economists to provide the structure for systematic analysis of these sorts of situations. Many of the questions which follow are generic game-theoretic questions, but their wide applicability is demonstrated by the variety of issues considered in the text: oligopoly behavior, arms negotiations, international trade policies, pollution-control decisions, and so on.

7. Consult Figure 12-6. It is constructed just like the payoff matrices discussed in the text, with two firms (A and B) and four strategies (I and II for firm A and III and IV for firm B). The numbers in the boxes indicate outcomes: the

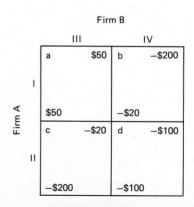

Figure 12-6

the number in the upper right corner applies to firm B, while the number in the lower left corner applies to A. Cell c, for example, corresponds with firm A playing strategy II and firm B playing strategy III; note, in this case, that firm A would lose $200 while firm B would lose only $20.

The payoff matrix in Figure 12-6 shows that strategy I *(is / is not)* a dominant strategy for firm A. If A were to choose strategy I over II when B chooses III, then A would *(earn $50 / lose $200 / lose $20 / lose $100)* instead of *(earning $50 / losing $200 / losing $20 / losing $100)*; on the other hand, if A were to choose strategy I over II when B chooses IV, then A would *(earn $50 / lose $200 / lose $20 / lose $100)* instead of *(earning $50 / losing $200 / losing $20 / losing $100)*.

Strategy III *(is / is not)* a dominant strategy for firm B, as well, so cell *(a / b / c / d)* is a dominant equilibrium. It *(is / is not)* a Nash equilibrium, as well, because _____

_____

_____

is; earn $50; losing $200; lose $20; losing $100; is; a; is; any dominant equilibrium is a Nash equilibrium because neither firm (no player, in general) would see an incentive to switch strategies, given what the other firm (player) is doing

8. Figure 12-7 displays a different payoff matrix for two firms, A and B. *(Firm A has / Firm B has / Both firms have / Neither firm has)* a dominant strategy; it is strategy _____ for firm A and strategy _____ for B. The Nash equilibrium is indicated by cell *(a / b / c / d)* because firm B _____

_____

and firm A will certainly choose strategy _____ as soon as it realizes that B will play strategy _____ .

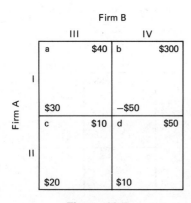

Figure 12-7

Firm B has; neither I nor II; IV ; d; will always choose strategy IV; II; IV

9. Figures 12-8 through 12-11 display four more payoff matrices for firms A and B. Complete Table 12-1 by identifying A's dominant strategy, B's dominant strategy, the cell indicating a dominant equilibrium, the cell indicating a Nash equilibrium, and the cell indicating a cooperative equilibrium. If one of these categories is not exhibited by any figure, write "n/a" in the corresponding blank.

Figure 12-8

Figure 12-9

Figure 12-10

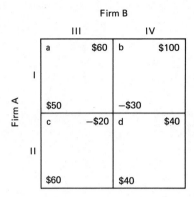

Figure 12-11

Table 12-1

	Fig. 12-8	Fig. 12-9	Fig. 12-10	Fig. 12-11
A's dominant strategy	____	____	____	____
B's dominant strategy	____	____	____	____
Dominant equilibrium	____	____	____	____
Nash equilibrium	____	____	____	____
Cooperative equilibrium	____	____	____	____

table columns: Figure 12-8—strategy I, n/a, n/a, cell a, cell a; Figure 12-9—n/a, strategy III, n/a, cell c, cell c; Figure 12-10—n/a, n/a, n/a, cell d, cell a; Figure 12-11—strategy II, strategy IV, cell d, cell d, cell d

10. Pollution abatement can cost any firm money, raising its products' prices and damaging its market share (if it acts alone). The key to effective abatement regulation is therefore frequently seen to be one of getting all the polluting firms to act together to reduce pollution from all sources simultaneously. Figure 12-12 displays a payoff matrix which illustrates this point.

The two firms can choose to control their emissions or not. If they both choose to control their emissions, they each make $_____; this is the situation of cell (a / b / c / d). This (is / is not), however, a Nash equilibrium. Each firm has an incentive (not to control emissions / to control emissions) if it knows that the other will be acting to control emissions; it would then earn $_____ at the expense of the other firm, whose profits fall to $_____. The Nash equilibrium, therefore, is indicated by cell (a / b / c / d) where each firm earns $_____. Only a (noncooperative / cooperative) equilibrium supports the socially desirable control-control outcome of cell a.

100; a; is not; not to control emissions; 170; 20; d; 150; cooperative

REVIEW CONCEPTS

1. Speculators can improve welfare by buying low and selling high, and thereby smoothing consumption and price instability across space, time, and states of uncertain nature. Speculative markets allow people to hedge against unwelcome risk.

2. Purchasing insurance is one means of hedging; risk-averse individuals are willing to pay premiums, at least to some degree, to avoid the risk of an uncertain future. Private insurance markets can exist when there are many independent events and when there is little chance of moral hazard and/or adverse selection. Social insurance is sometimes provided in situations which cannot support private insurance markets.

3. Game theory has been applied by economists to analyze the strategic interactions of firms, households, and governments. It is based upon a structure which identifies players, specifies available strategies, and enumerates the outcomes of all the combinations of available strategies. Players act in their own best interest, assuming that the other players are doing the same thing.

4. The most common solution to a game is a Nash equilibrium from which no player has the incentive to move, given the observed actions of the other players. In some cases, a player can identify a dominant strategy—an action which produces the highest payoff regardless of what the other players do. If all players have a dominant strategy, then the solution to the game is a dominant equilibrium.

5. Cooperative and noncooperative equilibria are possible. Noncooperative Nash equilibria can be efficient under conditions of perfect competition in the absence of externalities. In other cases, the cooperative alternative can be socially superior.

QUIZ: Multiple Choice

1. The welfare gain associated with smoothing consumption is derived from:
(1) diminishing income effects.
(2) increasing returns to scale.
(3) the law of comparative advantage.
(4) diminishing marginal utility.
(5) increasing marginal productivity.

Figure 12-12

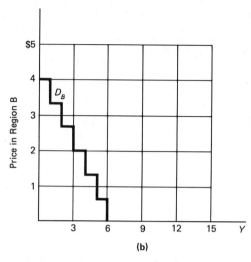

Figure 12-13

2. Panels (a) and (b) of Figure 12-13 show the demand for some good Y in two separate regions of the country—regions A and B. There are 4 units of Y supplied initially to region A and 5 units supplied to region B. The welfare-maximizing transfer of Y would, in this case, without any transportation cost, involve:
(1) moving 2 units of Y from A to B.
(2) moving 2 units of Y from B to A.
(3) moving 1 unit of Y from B to A.
(4) moving 1 unit of Y from A to B.
(5) moving all the Y units to region A.

3. The increase in total welfare generated by the maximally efficient transfer of Y identified in question 2 is equal to:
(1) $1.
(2) $2.
(3) $3.
(4) $4.
(5) $5.

4. Referring again to Figure 12-13, the transfer of no units of Y would be welfare-maximizing if the cost of transporting each unit from one region to the other were greater than:
(1) $0.67.
(2) $1.00.
(3) $1.33.
(4) $1.67.
(5) $2.00.

5. In general, total welfare is maximized across space, time, or states of nature in the absence of transfer costs when:
(1) the marginal utilities of consumption are equal everywhere.
(2) the level of consumption is equal everywhere.
(3) the total utility derived from consumption is equal everywhere.
(4) the total value added in production is equal everywhere.
(5) the slopes of the demand curves are equal everywhere.

6. An individual, starting with an income of $1000 and possessing the utility schedule drawn in Figure 12-14, faces a 50 percent chance of losing $100. Her expected utility would equal:
(1) 50 utils.
(2) 45 utils.
(3) 40 utils.
(4) 35 utils.
(5) 30 utils.

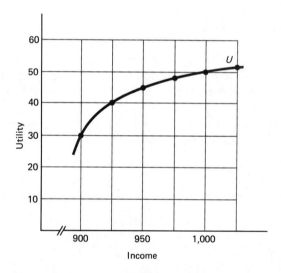

Figure 12-14

7. Which answer to question 6 correctly identifies her level of income if she could arrange to receive her expected level of income with certainty?
(1).
(2).
(3).
(4).
(5).

8. How much would the individual described in question 6 be willing to pay as an insurance premium to guarantee an invariant income (prior to paying the premium) of $950 — her expected income?
(1) $100.
(2) $75.
(3) $50.
(4) $25.
(5) It is impossible to tell from the information provided.

9. Figure 12-15 shows a payoff table for two firms, A and B. Which strategy is a dominant strategy for firm A?
(1) Strategy I.
(2) Strategy II.
(3) Strategy III.
(4) Strategy IV.
(5) None of the strategies available to firm A is a dominant strategy.

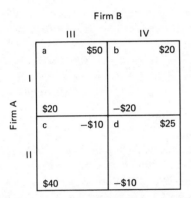

Figure 12-15

10. In Figure 12-15, which strategy is a dominant strategy for firm B?
(1) Strategy I.
(2) Strategy II.
(3) Strategy III.
(4) Strategy IV.
(5) None of the strategies available to firm B is a dominant strategy.

11. Again referring to Figure 12-15, which cell is a dominant equilibrium?
(1) Cell a.
(2) Cell b.
(3) Cell c.
(4) Cell d.
(5) None of the cells is a dominant equilibrium.

12. Which cell in Figure 12-15 is a Nash equilibrium?
(1) Cell a.
(2) Cell b.
(3) Cell c.
(4) Cell d.
(5) None of the cells is a Nash equilibrium.

SUGGESTED ANSWERS TO QUESTIONS IN THE TEXT: Chapter 12

1. Speculators try to buy low and sell high. When they see a downturn (an upturn) in prices, therefore, they are tempted to buy (to sell); if they do, they stabilize prices. Their actions tend to reduce the amplitude of price swings.

2. Taking $1 from the rich and giving it to the less well-off increases total welfare because the marginal utility of the $1 for the rich (marginal utility measuring the resulting welfare loss of a $1 transfer) is smaller than the marginal utility of the $1 for the less well-off (marginal utility measuring the resulting welfare gain of a $1 transfer). If all people are the same, then the marginal utilities of income are different only because income is different, and this sort of transfer improves welfare unless and until incomes are equilibrated.

3. Private insurance can appear when there are many independent events and when the chances of either adverse selection or moral hazard are small. The insurers tend to be actuarily fair in the premiums which they charge, and they survive because they (1) can spread risk across a multitude of independent events (thereby seldom facing a circumstance in which claim payments greatly exceed premium collections) and (2) can accurately compute reasonable likelihoods regarding the occurrence of various claim events (taking changes in behavior into account). Social insurance programs are required when one or more of these conditions are violated, but risk spreading still improves social welfare. Public moneys may then make up any shortfalls between premium collections and claim payments.

4. Expect large variations supported by higher transportation prices because there was little geographical area over which to average fluctuations in demand or supply.

5. Each person owns a small share of the risk in the computer company and has a variety of other sources of income over which to average. As long as the income generated by those sources is independent of the risk in the computer company, then the individual "self-insures" by spreading investment money around.

6. Stabilizing prices and consumption over time and across states of nature improves expected welfare. Arbitrage accomplishes this sort of stabilization, so making it illegal would cost society a source of welfare gain.

7. Table TQ12-1 shows the sequence, starting with A having M_0 missiles. The number held grows exponentially unless the country is subjected to a limit of (e.g.) 1000. Figure TQ12-1 shows the unregulated trajectories of both countries; bounded from above at 1000, the lines would turn horizontal at 1000, with Country A hitting the constraint 1 year earlier than Country R. Country A would hit the constraint in $\ln[1000/(1.1)M_0]$ years' time.

8. Without externalities, the noncooperative Nash equilibrium is efficient under conditions of perfect competition. The cooperative equilibrium, in such a case, might see firms exercising some market power (perhaps artificially maintained

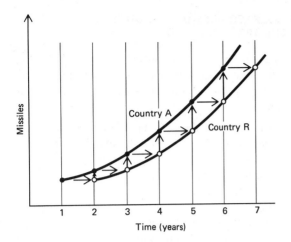

Figure TQ12-1

Table TQ12-1

	Year					
	1	2	3	...	T	(T + 1)
Country A	M_0	$(1.21)M_0$	$(1.33)M_0$		$(1.1)^T M_0$	$(1.1)^{T+1} M_0$
Country R		$(1.1)M_0$	$(1.21)M_0$		$(1.1)^{T-1} M_0$	$(1.1)^T M_0$

power, but power nonetheless) to lower output, increase prices, and generate deadweight loss. The opposite effect comes into play when negative externalities exist, because they are expensive to handle. No single firm, acting in its own individual interest, will suffer that expense, so the Nash equilibrium in these cases supports little or no effort to control the externality.

9. Cell D is not a Nash equilibrium because both have a motive to confess, if they think that their colleague will *not* confess. Cell B is not a Nash equilibrium because Scarface has an incentive to confess. Cell C is not a Nash equilibrium because Knuckles has an incentive to confess. Only in Cell A do the two players see no benefit to changing their behavior.

10. This is the point of section A of the chapter, set out against the colloquial view of the world which holds that people who do not make anything contribute nothing to the social good.

11. a. *Cell A:* U.S. free trade; Japan free trade; U.S. income at $6000; Japan income at $3000; total value of trade at $9000.

Cell B: U.S. protects; Japan free trade; U.S. income at $6100; Japan income at $1900; total value of trade at $8000.

Cell C: U.S. free trade; Japan protects; U.S. income at $4800; Japan income at $3200; total value of trade at $8000.

Cell D: U.S. protects; Japan protects; U.S. income at $5000; Japan income at $2000; total value of trade at $7000.

b. The Nash equilibrium is captured in cell D, with combined GNP $2000 lower than necessary.

c. The cooperative equilibrium is reflected in cell A, with combined GNP maximized.

d. There certainly is a small incentive for either country to deviate from the cooperative equilibrium, but moving to the Nash equilibrium would be expensive.

12. Utility with no fire $= 7 + 6 + 5 + 4 + 3 + 2 = 27$
Utility with fire $= 7$
Expected utility $= 0.8$ (utility with no fire) $+ 0.2$ (utility with fire)
$$= 0.8(27) + 0.2(7) = 21.6 + 1.4$$
$$= 23$$

Expected loss $= 0.2$ (5 units of housing) $= 1$ unit Given that as a premium, utility in either state with insurance $= 7 + 6 + 5 + 4 + 3 = 25$.

13. Var(kX) equals k^2var(X), so var$(X/4)$ equals $(1/16)$var(X). Applying this to the problem, the standard deviation of the shared risk is

$$[(1/16)\text{var}(X) + (1/16)\text{var}(X) + (1/16)\text{var}(X) + (1/16)\text{var}(X)]^{1/2} = SD/2$$

a. Straight application of the equation recorded immediately above.

b. Let the probability of peak demand be p for both systems. The likelihood that both will be in peak is then p^2. The likelihood that one will be in peak and the other will not is meanwhile $2p(1-p)$. Planning against those odds should make the utilities cut back on their maintained excess capacity.

c. Let the cost of holding inventory against demand per unit of time D be given by $C_H Q/2$, where C_H is the unit cost and Q is the quantity in any given order. Total cost $C_H Q$ is then divided by 2 because demand is assumed to be continuous, and half of any given order is sold by the midpoint of the order period. Let the cost of ordering during the period defining D be $C_O(D/Q)$, where C_O is the unit cost of an order and (D/Q) is the number of orders made in each period. The total cost of sales is thus

$$C_O(D/Q) + C_H Q/2$$

Differentiating with respect to Q to determine the optimal order and inventory which minimizes costs shows that

$$Q^* = (2DC_O/C_H)^{1/2}$$

Increasing D by a factor of 4 therefore doubles Q^*.

CHAPTER 13

INCOMES AND THE PRICING OF FACTORS OF PRODUCTION

Chapter 13 is the first in a series of chapters which focus on the distribution of income. Together, these chapters will bring the fundamentals of supply-and-demand analysis to bear on questions of how individual incomes are determined. Critical in this determination must be, of course, the ownership of the factors of production and the prices that they command. Chapter 13 begins, therefore, with a brief introduction into what economists mean when they speak of income and wealth and where they look to find the sources of income and wealth in a modern economy. There is, however, more to the distribution of income than simply cataloguing who owns what. There is, more specifically, the question of what determines how much everything is worth. The remainder of this chapter will combine with several subsequent chapters to tackle this more complicated question. Together, they work (1) to develop a consistent theory of income distribution based upon market determination of relative value and (2) to apply that theory to create an understanding of the employment of land, labor, natural resources, and capital.

Now that you have studied how pricing and production decisions are made in product markets, it is certainly timely to consider how pricing and employment decisions are made in input markets. You will recall that relative scarcity and need were seen to determine why it costs more to buy some goods than it does to buy others; but what accounts for the large differences that one observes in the wages and salaries offered to people engaged in various occupations? Scarcity? Need? Or something else? In addition, even casual consideration of any productive enterprise reveals that all inputs work interdependently to produce a given product or service. Given this complex interdependence, how can one compute levels of compensation that reflect accurately the importance of their respective contributions? How, more specifically, are wage rates determined? And interest rates? And land rents? And so on?

The answers to all these questions can be found by searching in the familiar surroundings of supply-and-demand analysis. The only fundamental difference between product markets and input markets lies in the sources of their supply and demand components. In a goods market, for example, demand materializes because the good being produced and sold generates some utility for the consumer; the consumer is willing to pay some positive price for the privilege of owning the good in question. In an input market, by way of contrast, factors of production are demanded only because they can be employed to produce such an item of value. The demand for inputs is therefore a *derived demand* based not upon the immediate, innate value of the input to a firm but upon the *value of some other good that it can be employed to produce*.

Examination of these issues begins with the demand side of an input market. Because a producing firm must hire labor, buy raw materials, and invest in machinery, it is the demander of productive inputs. Its demand is not, however, unlimited. It makes its employment decisions on the basis of least-cost combinations of inputs defined by its production function and the prices of those inputs. The derived demand for any input will therefore be seen to result from (1) the cost-minimizing behavior of profit-maximizing firms and (2) a marginal-productivity theory of income distribution.

The final section of Chapter 13 will show how this notion of derived demand can be used in a market context. It will, in particular, play derived demand against an arbitrary input supply schedule. Land is frequently used to illustrate the structure, but the application of the general methodology of supply-and-demand analysis is the fundamental insight. It is an insight which will be exploited repeatedly over the next three chapters.

Having completed your work in this chapter, you should have accomplished the following objectives.

LEARNING OBJECTIVES

1. Become familiar with the questions that are posed by the economists who work to understand the distribution of income. They ask questions about the determination of income (the *flow* of money to an individual during a given period of time) and wealth (the net value of the *stock* of accumulated economic assets).

2. Recognize the major sources of income and the major reservoirs of wealth in the United States.

3. Understand that the theory of the distribution of income is concerned with the determination of different people's incomes as well as with the allocation of the value of total product among the various factors that are employed interdependently to produce that product.

4. Explain how the distribution of income is the result of the workings of supply and demand in an economy's input markets.

5. Define the notion of derived demand for a factor of production, and explain why it is algebraically represented by its marginal revenue product, i.e., explain why the derived demand for any input can be represented by a schedule derived by multiplying the marginal product of that input by the marginal revenue of output.

6. Show precisely why, in cases of perfect competition, the marginal revenue product of any input, and thus its derived demand schedule, is equal to the competitive price of output multiplied by its marginal product.

7. Demonstrate why a firm that hires all inputs up to the point at which their prices equal their marginal revenue products will guarantee that (1) it is producing the profit-maximizing output and (2) it is incurring the least cost; i.e., (1) the marginal revenue of its sales will equal the marginal cost of its production, and (2) the least-cost rule will be satisfied.

8. Show how the market derived demand curve for any input is simply equal to the horizontal sum of the marginal revenue product curves of all the firms which employ that input.

9. Explain the Clark marginal-productivity theory of income distribution. In light of that theory, define the "exhaustion of product" property for constant-returns-to-scale production.

A significant schism developed in the wake of the Industrial Revolution between the people who owned the machinery and the people who worked the machinery, i.e., between the capitalists and the workers. Cities became both foci of industrialization and pockets of enormous poverty. The distribution of income evolved quickly into a question of dividing the riches earned by the machines between owner and laborer; and people making decisions about where to hold their wealth had to include a tangible asset other than land in their considerations. Economics became more difficult to understand, but not impossibly so.

1. a. Income is defined as the amount of money received from all sources during a given period of time (a year, a month, etc.). In the spaces provided below, list the major sources of income in the United States (labor income, rent, dividends, interest, and transfer payments) in the order of their importance:

(1) _____

(2) _____

(3) _____

(4) _____

(5) _____

b. Wealth consists of the net dollar value of assets owned at any particular time. In the spaces provided below, list the four major tangible assets and the four major financial assets that comprise wealth in the United States in the order of their importance:

Tangible assets:

(1) _____

(2) _____

(3) _____

(4) _____

Financial assets:

(1) _____

(2) _____

(3) _____

(4) _____

a. (1) labor income (70% of income in 1988) [income wages and supplements (56%), other labor income like pension contributions (6%), and proprietors' income (8%)] **(2)** transfer payments (15%) **(3)** interest income (13%) **(4)** dividends (2%) **(5)** rent (less than 1%) **b.** tangible assets: **(1)** own home (41% of wealth in 1984) **(2)** rental property (9%) **(3)** motor vehicle (6%) **(4)** other real estate (4%); financial assets: **(1)** interest-earning accounts (17%) **(2)** equity in business (10%) **(3)** stocks and mutual funds (7%) **(4)** checking accounts (1%)

The key to factor pricing is the marginal-productivity theory of a firm. To recall the fundamentals of this theory (see Chapter 7 for a thorough review), let some product X be produced from various combinations of inputs A, B, C, etc. Remember that any of the various production processes embodied in these combinations can be reflected by a mathematical production function—a systematic record of the maximum output of good X that can be produced from all possible combinations of inputs given a specific state of technology. For the purposes of derived demand, though, it is the derivative concept of marginal product that is most important. The **marginal product** (**MP**) of any input is the ratio of the change in total product to the change in the employment of that input, holding the employment of *all* other factors constant. The *MP* of factor A can, therefore, be thought of as the change in the output of X caused by a 1-unit change in the employment of *only* factor A.

2. Suppose that X is produced from three inputs, A, B, and C; a very small portion of the production function is recorded in Table 13-1.

Table 13-1

Output	Employment levels		
	A	B	C
200	10	30	20
203	10	31	20

a. Infer from Table 13-1 that *(the MP of X is 3 / the MP of A is 3 / the MP of B is 3 / the MP of C is 3)*.

b. If the employment of some input such as B were gradually to increase, then we should expect that the marginal product of B would gradually *(increase / decline)* because of the *(law of diminishing returns / relative scarcity of B that would result in the production process)*. Similarly, if the quantity of B employed were to decline, then we should expect that the marginal product of B would *(increase/decline)* because of the *(law of diminishing returns / relative scarcity of B that would result in the production process)*.

c. If the employment of some input such as B were gradually to increase, with the employment of inputs A and C held constant, then we should expect to see the marginal products of A and C *(increase / decrease)* because of the *(law of diminishing returns / relative scarcity of A and C that would result in the production process)*.

---

a. the *MP* of B is 3 **b.** decline; law of diminishing returns; increase; law of diminishing returns **c.** increase; relative scarcity of A and C that would result in the production process

---

The point of question 2 is that the value of the marginal product of any input depends upon the level of employment of all inputs even though it is defined in terms of changes in the employment of only itself. The more of input A (e.g.) that is employed, all other things equal, the higher should be the marginal products of inputs B and C—and any other inputs.

3. If a firm wants to maximize profits, it will attempt to produce the output that sets marginal costs equal to marginal revenue; and in defining marginal cost, it will be employing inputs at levels that satisfy the least-cost rule:

$$MP_A/P_A = MP_B/P_B = MP_C/P_C = \cdots$$

Steps in achieving that goal are listed below, but they do not appear there in the correct chronological order. Indicate their proper order by writing the corresponding numbers in the correct sequence in the space provided.

1. Pick the output where marginal cost equals marginal revenue.
2. Compute the least-cost combination of inputs for output levels in the anticipated range.
3. Compute marginal revenue for various levels of sales in the anticipated range from information about the demand side of the market.
4. Compute marginal cost for various levels of sales in the anticipated range from the least-cost data.
5. Collect information about input prices and the technology that defines how inputs can be utilized to produce various levels of output.

Order: _____

---

3 (*Note:* Step 3 can be accomplished at any time before the final comparison of marginal cost and marginal revenue—step 1), 5, 2, 4, 1

---

4. With the link between the least-cost rule, total cost, and profit maximization established, the link between profit maximization and derived demand can be explored more fully.

a. Let A be an input employed in the production of some good X. If the marginal product of A were measured at 2, then the 2 refers to *(units of A / units of X / dollars)*. Marginal product is, so to speak, the "payoff" in X output resulting from the employment of the last unit of A. Payoff is, however, more commonly thought of in money terms. To know what this *MP* payoff is worth in dollars, we must know how much money the sale of the additional units of X would bring in—i.e., we need to know the *(price of A / marginal revenue accruing from the sale of X)*.

b. If the marginal revenue accruing from the sale of 1 additional X unit were $3 (the *MP* of input A still equal to 2), then the dollar payoff resulting from hiring the last unit of A would be equal to $(*2 / 3 / 5 / 6 / 10 / 12*). (Disregard the slight drop in marginal revenue that might come from selling the second unit of X.)

168   **13**   *Incomes and the Pricing of Factors of Production*

c. The technical name for this dollar payoff is the **marginal revenue product** (**MRP**). That is, the *MRP* of, for example, input A is specifically equal to (circle one):

(1) the *MP* of A multiplied by marginal revenue accruing from sale of X.

(2) the *MP* of A multiplied by price of A.

(3) the *MP* of A alone.

d. In the special case of perfect competition—but only in that case—the *MRP* of A could be defined as the *MP* of A multiplied by the price of X, but employing the "marginal revenue of X" is more general. It applies equally well to all cases, perfect competition included. Barring the special case of perfect competition, the marginal revenue from the sale of X will *(rise / remain constant / fall)* as the firm increases its output and sales. As a result, as employment increases, the marginal revenue product of each and every input will *(rise / remain constant / fall)* for two reasons; they are:

(1) _____

_____

(2) _____

_____

a. units of X; marginal revenue accruing from the sale of X   **b.** 6   **c.** (1)   **d.** fall; fall **(1)** diminishing marginal revenue **(2)** diminishing marginal product

5. Suppose that a firm is satisfying the least-cost rule with respect to inputs A, B, and C and that it wants to find out if it is at its maximum-profit output level. To do this, it can look at any one of its inputs—say, input A. A's price might be $4 per unit, for example, and its *MP* might be 3. Assume that the firm knows that the marginal revenue from the sale of X is $1.

a. Under these conditions, A's *MRP* is $(1 / 2 / 3 / 4 / 7 / 12). Since it cost $(1 / 2 / 3 / 4 / 7 / 12) to buy that last unit of A, its employment *(added $1 to / subtracted $1 from / did not change)* total profit. The firm, remember, is satisfying the least-cost rule in making its employment decisions. It follows, therefore, that the same conclusion would have been reached had we looked at input B or input C. Hence, in the given circumstances, the firm *(definitely is / definitely is not / may or may not be)* earning maximum possible profit. In order for it to move toward higher profit, in fact, it should *(reduce / increase)* its output by *(reducing / increasing)* its employment of all inputs.

b. Now try a different example to illustrate the point more fully. Suppose that the *MP*s of A, B, and C are, respectively, 12, 8, and 2. Let their prices be, respectively, $6, $4, and $1. The firm *(is / is not)*, therefore, producing its current output at minimum cost.

Continue this second illustration by assuming that the marginal revenue from the sale of X is equal to $1. Input A's *MRP* would therefore equal $(12 / 10 / 8 / 6 / 4 / 2). Input B's *MRP* would meanwhile equal $(12 / 10 / 8 / 6 / 4 / 2). The *MRP* for input C would be $(12 / 10 / 8 / 6 / 4 / 2). This firm *(is / is not)* producing the profit-maximizing output. To achieve this maximum, it should *(increase / decrease)* its output by *(increasing / decreasing)* its employment of *(input A only / input B only / input C only / all inputs simultaneously)*.

c. As the firm makes these adjustments in employment, the marginal revenue products of all inputs *(fall / rise)*. The increase in the employment of each input should be halted when each *MRP* has *(fallen below / reached equality with / risen above)* the price of the *(input / finished product)*.

a. 3; 4; subtracted $1 from; definitely is not; reduce; reducing   **b.** is (The ratios of marginal product to price are 12/6 = 8/4 = 2/1 = 2.); 12; 8; 2; is not; increase; increasing; all inputs simultaneously (*MRP* > P for all inputs.)   **c.** fall; reached equality with; input

The process just described is nothing more than an elaboration of the *MR* = *MC* profit-maximizing rule set out in earlier chapters. Think of the firm (as we did in those earlier chapters) as gradually approaching this *MR* = *MC* output level, starting from an output at which *MR* exceeds *MC*. As output expands, *MR* gradually falls (unless the situation is one of perfect competition) and *MC* gradually rises. The higher output needed to achieve equality between marginal revenue and marginal cost is obtained by increasing the employment of all inputs. This increased employment must, however, be undertaken in a way which constantly satisfies the least-cost rule. If not, then each output along the way could be produced at lower cost, and the firm would be moving "above" its true total cost curve rather than "along" it.

With cost minimization maintained, expanding output moves toward the *MR* = *MC* maximum-profit position in the most efficient manner. Notice, though, that that final position can be described in terms of *MRP* as well as in terms of *MR* = *MC*. Marginal revenue products fall as employment increases. When they have fallen to the level of their respective input prices, for all inputs employed, then (*a*) the least-cost rule is automatically satisfied, so (*b*) the *MR* = *MC* maximum-profit rule is also satisfied. Question 6 illustrates this point explicitly.

6. a. Let the *MP*s for inputs A, B, and C be 12, 8, and 2, respectively. If you knew that the prices of A, B, and C were $6, $4, and $1, respectively, and that the firm had reached its maximum-profit output, then you would know that the *MR* from the sale of the last units of X must have been $(8.00 / 6.00 / 2.00 / 1.50 / 0.50).

b. Change now to a different set of figures. Let *MR* equal $2, the prices of A, B, and C equal $8, $4, and $10, and assume that the firm is operating at the profit-maximizing output. The marginal product of input A must be equal to (1 / 2 / 3 / 4 / 5); MP_B must be (1 / 2 / 3 / 4 / 5); and MP_C must be (1 / 2 / 3 / 4 / 5).

c. Use only a few steps of algebra to show that a firm which hires each and every input up to the point where its marginal revenue product exactly matches its quoted price automatically satisfies the more traditional least-cost rule expressed in terms of ratios of marginal products and prices. _____

_____

_____

_____

_____

_____

a. $0.50 (To check, notice that $0.50 × 12 = $6; $0.50 × 8 = $4; and $0.50 × 2 = $1.) b. 4 (To check, notice that $2 × 4 = $8); 2 ($2 × 2 = $4); 5 ($2 × 5 = $10) c. Start with $MRP_A = MP_A \times MR = P_A$ for any input A. Rearranging, notice immediately that $MR = MP_A/P_A$. Since this must be true for any and all inputs, it must also be true that $MP_A/P_A = MP_B/P_B = \cdots = MR$; and this is the traditional least-cost rule.

7. Consult Table 13-2. The outputs of identical fields of corn are recorded there for a variety of levels of employment of labor. Let there be 10 workers in an economy defined by the two cornfields, and let the world determine the price of corn at $2. Fill in the Marginal Product and Marginal Revenue Product columns of the table. The numbers that you record there will be used to demonstrate that paying labor (the only input here) its marginal revenue product will result in a level of output that maximizes the value of the corn crop in terms of the world price.

Table 13-2

Labor Employed	Corn Output (bu)	Marginal Product of Labor	Marginal Revenue Product of Labor
0	0	n/a	n/a
1	10	_____	$ _____
2	19	_____	_____
3	27	_____	_____
4	34	_____	_____
5	40	_____	_____
6	45	_____	_____
7	49	_____	_____
8	52	_____	_____
9	54	_____	_____
10	55	_____	_____

a. Suppose, initially, that seven workers toil in one field (field A) and three toil in the other (field B). The output of field A would be _____ bushels worth $_____ ; each worker, if paid his or her marginal revenue product, would receive $_____ . The output of field B would meanwhile be _____ bushels worth $_____ ; each worker there would receive $_____ . In response to the wages that you computed, you should expect that workers would want to move (from A to B / from B to A).

b. Suppose that the workers do indeed move so that four workers remain to work field A while six work field B. Output of field A would fall to _____ bushels with a value of $_____ , and output of field B would climb to _____ units worth $_____ on the world market. The total value of output would, in fact, climb from $_____ to $_____ .

c. To equalize the wages paid to workers in both fields so that there will be no incentive for workers to want to switch from one to the other, _____ workers would have to work each field. Were that the case, total output would climb to _____ bushels worth $_____ and each worker would earn $_____ . There (exists another / does not exist any other) distribution of workers that would increase the output of corn and thus increase the value of the economy's production on the world market.

table columns: marginal product—10, 9, 8, 7, 6, 5, 4, 3, 2, 1; marginal revenue product—20, 18, 16, 14, 12, 10, 8, 6, 4, 2 a. 49; 98; 8 (= $2 × MP = $2 × 4); 27; 54; 16 (= $2 × MP = $2 × 8); from A to B b. 34; 68; 45; 90; 152; 158 c. 5; 80; 160; 12; does not exist any other

8. You are once again a consultant on profit maximization. What would you recommend in each of the five cases listed in Table 13-3?

Table 13-3

Case	MR from X Sale	P of A	P of B	At Maximum Profit?	Answer
a.	$1	$ 2	$10	_____	_____
b.	2	6	18	_____	_____
c.	3	12	18	_____	_____
d.	4	9	18	_____	_____
e.	5	21	54	_____	_____

In each case, the production of some good X depends only upon the employment of inputs A and B. Assume for each case that the marginal product of input A is constant and equal to 3 and that the marginal product of B is constant and equal to 9. The heading "*MR* from X Sale" in Table 13-3 refers to marginal revenue at the current level of output and sales. Similarly, the expressions "*P* of A" and "*P* of B" denote the prices which the firm must pay for inputs A and B.

Indicate, for each case, whether or not the firm has achieved a position of maximum profit. Write "yes" or "no" in the column provided. Use the following numerical code to indicate, in the last column, what is wrong with the firm's present position.

1. Present position is the correct one.
2. For present output, employment of A is too high, employment of B too low.
3. For present output, employment of A is too low, employment of B too high.
4. Reduce output by employing less of both A and B.
5. Increase output by employing more of both A and B.

a. no; 3 (The *MRP*s are not equal to prices, so profits are not maximized; note, in particular, that $MRP_A = \$1 \times 3 > P_A = \$2$, but $MRP_B = \$9 < P_B = \$10$. As a result, you do not know if output is too high or too low. You do know that $MP_A/P_A = 3/2 > MP_B/P_B = 10/9$; the firm therefore needs to hire more A and less B to increase MP_A and reduce MP_B.) **b.** yes; 1 (The *MRP*s are equal to prices, so profits are maximized; note that $\$2 \times 3 = \$6$ for input A and $\$2 \times 9 = \$18$ for input B.) **c.** no; 2 (The *MRP*s are not equal to prices, so profits are not maximized; note that $MRP_A = \$3 \times 3 < P_A = \$12$, but $MRP_B = \$27 > P_B = \$18$. As a result, you again do not know if output is too high or too low. It is clear, however, that $MP_A/P_A = 3/12 < MP_B/P_B = 9/18$, so the firm needs to hire more B and less A to increase MP_B and reduce MP_A.) **d.** no; 5 (The *MRP*s are greater than prices for inputs, so the firm should increase employment of both to bring both *MRP*s down.) **e.** no; 4 (The *MRP*s are less than prices for both inputs, so the firm should reduce employment of both to increase both *MRP*s.)

The preceding questions have tried to indicate the considerations that are most important to a firm in deciding how much of any input it will want to employ, given some set of prices. If A's price were to rise or to fall, for example, then the calculations would have to be redone. In sum, the entire exercise is designed to isolate the considerations that lie behind a firm's demand for any input across a wide array of possible prices. In every case, however, the demand for any input is a *derived* demand. People want a finished good, such as X, for the satisfaction it provides them. Nobody wants an input such as A for that reason. Nevertheless, A is in demand because it is useful in the production of X. It is in this sense that the demand for A is "derived from" the demand for X.

We now turn briefly to the puzzling and difficult question with which the chapter began: the question of determining the forces which shape the distribution of income. What shapes the ultimate division of a cooperatively produced output? How much can any one contributing input expect to receive? Clearly, the demand for the input is important in settling this question. Demand (together with available supply) determines the price per unit of input services; and if you know something about relative input prices, then you know something about how those inputs are likely to share in the total value of goods produced.

The marginal-productivity analysis outlined in this chapter first began to emerge late in the nineteenth century. Economist John B. Clark, who did much to develop it, felt that this analysis pointed strongly toward the underlying laws which governed the distribution of real income (goods and services) among the inputs which had cooperated in the production of those goods and services. Clark pointed out (with one important caveat) that there would be just enough to pay off all the inputs of an interdependent production process, with no deficit and nothing left over, if each input were paid a price just equal to the market value of its marginal product.

9. Suppose that a total of 200 units of X are produced with a 10-30-20 combination of three inputs A, B, and C. Suppose further that the marginal products of A, B, and C are 9, 3, and 1, respectively. Finally, let X be a product to be sold in a competitive market at a price of $1. Complete Table 13-4 in light of this information.

Table 13-4

Input	Quantity of Input	MRP of Input	Total Payment of Input
A	_____ units	× $ _____	= $ _____
B	_____ units	× $ _____	= $ _____
C	_____ units	× $ _____	= $ _____
		Total payment	= $ _____

Assume now that A, B, and C are the only inputs required in the production of X. If each were paid according to its marginal revenue product, then total payments *(would be less than / would be just equal to / would exceed)* the total market value of the total amount of X produced; i.e., total payments to factors of production *(fall short of / exactly equal / more than exhaust)* $1 per unit × 200 units = $200.

table rows: A—10, 9, 90; B—30, 3, 90; C—20, 1, 20; total—200
would be just equal to; exactly equal

The Clark approach to income distribution has two attractive features. First of all, payment according to marginal revenue product just "exhausts the product" (under conditions of constant returns to scale, at least); i.e., there is just enough to go around. Moreover, payment according to (marginal) productivities carries with it some suggestion that the distribution is "fair" or "just." These qualities are not, however, enough to carry the day. It is generally conceded today that the distribution of income is too complicated to be handled in such simple terms. Opinions differ sharply as to the meaningful content of the marginal-productivity approach in a world of economic distortions and historical inequities. In addition, Clark's treatment works as outlined above only when production exhibits constant returns to scale, i.e., only when doubling or tripling all input quantities exactly doubles or triples output and when halving all input quantities exactly halves output. There is no necessary reason why production functions should display this property; many clearly do not. And if they do not, payment by marginal productivities will not "just exhaust the product." It will run short in some circumstances (decreasing returns to scale) and provide surpluses in others (increasing returns to scale).

10. The market demand for any input is the *(vertical / geometric / horizontal)* sum of the individual demand schedules of all the firms interested in employing that input; i.e., the sum of their *(marginal product / marginal revenue product / marginal utility)* schedules. More specifically, suppose that there are only three firms interested in employing some input X, and let them demand 3, 4, and 5 units, respectively, given a price of $3 per unit. Market demand at the $3 price would,

in this case, be ———— units. At a price of $4, though, we would expect, in general, that the quantity demanded by the market would *(increase / fall)* because the individual demands of the three firms would probably *(rise / fall)*.

---

horizontal; marginal revenue product; 12; fall; fall

---

11. a. Consider Figures 13-1 and 13-2. The one which illustrates the perfectly price-inelastic situation is *(13-1 / 13-2)*. A supply curve such as the one drawn in Figure 13-1 implies that if price should drop, say, from p_1 to p_0, then the quantity offered for sale would *(increase / decrease / remain the same as before)*. Sketch a demand curve in Figure 13-1 passing through the point on SS corresponding to p_1. Now sketch another to indicate a leftward shift of demand reducing the equilibrium price to p_0.

Figure 13-1

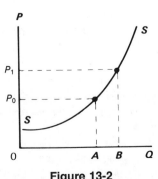

Figure 13-2

b. The significance of the special case drawn in Figure 13-1 is best understood by considering an input supply curve having the more customary shape drawn in Figure 13-2. If price were to fall from p_1 to p_0 in that arena, then the quantity offered for sale would *(increase / decrease / remain the same as before)*. Sketch two corresponding demand curves in Figure 13-2.

c. Implicit in Figure 13-2 is an essential question: Why does a drop in demand cause part (or all, if the drop is large enough) of supply to be withdrawn? What happens to the quantity of input services denoted by AB if they disappear from supply offered?

To answer this question, we need to spell out more carefully the nature of the supply curve. Suppose it was drawn specifically to reflect the supply of land offered for rental to farmers who want it for growing corn. A reduction in price from p_1 to p_0 could easily persuade the landowners to rent part (or all) of their land to other types of farmers (for example, farmers who want to rent land for barley growing). This could easily explain why a reduction in the quantity supplied equal to distance AB in Figure 13-2 might occur. If the demand of corn growers for land were to decrease, thereby reducing the land-rental price from p_1 to p_0, then the quantity AB would be transferred to farmers who want more land for barley production.

Note carefully that this story assumes that the land in question has at least one alternative use: it can be used for barley production as well as for corn production. If, however, the land had no alternative use—i.e., if it were literally useful only in the production of corn—then any contraction in the demand for land by corn growers would reduce only its price. The quantity of land supplied would *(increase / decrease / remain the same as before)*, and Figure 13-1 would apply. The landowners would not be happy about the price reduction, but they could do nothing about it.

---

a. 13-1; remain the same as before **b.** decrease **c.** remain the same as before

---

REVIEW CONCEPTS

1. Income is a flow of money; wealth is a stock of accumulated economic assets. The theory of the distribution of income is concerned with (1) the determination of income and (2) the allocation of total product among factors of production.

2. The demand for any factor of production is a derived demand which stems from the demand for the final product. It can be conceptually represented as a marginal revenue product—the increase in revenue which can be expected if the employment of the *one* factor in question were increased by 1 unit. It can be algebraically represented by the (multiplicative) product of marginal revenue and marginal product.

3. The derived demand for any factor in a perfectly competitive industry is the (multiplicative) product of the price of output and its marginal product; this is simply a consequence of the horizontal demand curves faced by perfect competitors which guarantee that price equals marginal revenue.

4. A firm hiring all inputs up to the point where their marginal revenue products all equal their prices will automatically (1) be producing the profit-maximizing output and (2) be operating at least cost. That is to say, (1) marginal revenue will equal marginal cost for the output chosen, and (2) the least-cost rule will be satisfied.

5. The market demand curve for any input is the horizontal sum of the derived demand curves of all firms employing that input.

6. The Clark theory of income distribution holds that all factors should be paid according to their marginal revenue products. Under conditions of constant returns to scale, this payment scheme exactly exhausts the total value of total output.

QUIZ: Multiple Choice

1. Karl Marx and Friedrich Engels expected that capitalism would make the rich richer and the poor poorer. That did not happen—at least not everywhere, as predicted. Which of the following is an accurate statement regarding the actual historical experience?
(1) Average working hours in the United States have declined steadily since the turn of the century.
(2) Per capita real incomes have risen steadily since the turn of the century.
(3) The distributions of wealth in the United Kingdom and the United States are less equitable than the corresponding distributions of income.
(4) The top 1 percent of the population in the United States currently holds title to 19 percent of the wealth.
(5) All the above.

2. The average income of American families in 1988 was approximately:
(1) $32,000.
(2) $46,300.
(3) $72,300.
(4) $54,600.
(5) $22,800.

3. If inputs A, B, and C together produce product X, then the marginal product of input A is:
(1) the extra output of X resulting from the employment of 1 extra unit of A, inputs B and C being increased proportionately.
(2) the amount of input A required to produce 1 extra unit of X, the amounts of inputs B and C being held constant.
(3) the extra output of X resulting from the employment of 1 extra unit of A, the amounts of inputs B and C being held constant.

(4) the amount of input A required to produce 1 extra unit of X, the amounts of inputs B and C being increased proportionately.
(5) none of the above.

4. According to John B. Clark's theory of income distribution, if 10 units of a particular input were employed, then the price paid to each of those units should be equal to the value of:
(1) the average of the marginal products of each of the 10 units.
(2) its own marginal product.
(3) the marginal product of the tenth unit.
(4) the average product of the 10 units.
(5) none of the above.

5. The marginal revenue product of input A used to produce product X is:
(1) the marginal product of A multiplied by the price of A.
(2) the average product of A multiplied by the price of X.
(3) the marginal product of A multiplied by the quantity of X produced.
(4) the average product of A multiplied by the marginal revenue of X.
(5) none of the above.

6. A firm operates in conditions of imperfect competition. The price of one of the factors of production, input A, is $10; its marginal product is 5. If this firm were operating at its profit-maximizing output, then the marginal revenue from the sale of X must be equal to:
(1) $1.00.
(2) $1.50.
(3) $2.00.
(4) $5.00.
(5) $10.00.

7. Given the information provided in question 6, the marginal revenue product of input A must have been:
(1) $1.00.
(2) $1.50.
(3) $2.00.
(4) $5.00.
(5) $10.00.

8. Consider a monopoly. The price of one of its inputs, input A, is $10, and the marginal product of A is 5. The price of its output is $2. The firm has satisfied the least-cost rule for input employment. This firm:
(1) is not producing its maximum-profit output and should contract production.
(2) is not producing its maximum-profit output and should expand.
(3) is producing its profit-maximizing output at least cost.
(4) is producing its maximum-profit output but could reduce its costs by employing less of input A and more of its other inputs.

(5) is producing its maximum-profit output but could reduce its costs by employing more of input A and less of its other inputs.

9. Return to the data provided in question 8. If you were told that marginal revenue must be one of the five following dollar amounts, then you would know that marginal revenue must be equal to:
(1) $1.00.
(2) $2.00.
(3) $3.00.
(4) $4.00.
(5) $5.00.

10. Now alter the information provided in question 8 in one respect only: assume that the firm operates in a perfectly competitive industry. Which alternative in question 8 would now be correct?
(1) .
(2) .
(3) .
(4) .
(5) .

11. The demand curve for labor in a simple, one-good economy is really:
(1) labor's total revenue curve.
(2) the residual left after rent has been paid.
(3) labor's total product curve.
(4) labor's marginal product curve.
(5) labor's average product curve.

12. Consider a simple, one-good economy with two factors of production—one of fixed supply and one of variable supply. If production in this economy were to display constant returns to scale, then:
(1) each factor should earn a return based on average productivity.
(2) the returns to both factors sum to a total which exceeds total output.
(3) the sum of the factor shares equals total product.
(4) the area under the total product curve is total output.
(5) both factors should receive the same return.

SUGGESTED ANSWER TO QUESTIONS IN THE TEXT: Chapter 13

1. Marginal product [in units of corn per (e.g.) hour of labor on the farm] is the increased yield that was generated by the last hour worked; marginal revenue product is the dollar value of that last increment. Marginal revenue product should be set equal to price because profits could be increased by adjusting employment if it is not. To see how, note that if $MRP > P$, then increasing employment by 1 unit would raise more extra revenue than it would cost. If $MRP < P$, on the other hand, then decreasing employment by 1 unit would save more expense than it would sacrifice in revenue. In either case, when MRP is not exactly equal to price, profits can be improved.

2. Grain, transportation, etc.

3. Consult Figure TQ13-1. Land is drawn there with perfectly inelastic supply at L^*. Price P^* sets $MP(L^*) = P^*$, so the L^*P^* rectangle reflects total payment for land. The residual is total payment to labor.

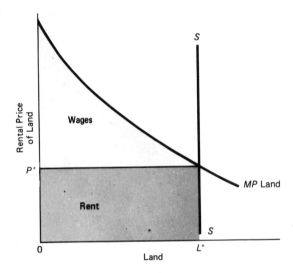

Figure TQ13-1

4. a. Average product is output per worker; marginal product is defined above.
b. Input contributions to production are interdependent, so it is impossible to determine what factor produced how much.
c. If all factors are paid according to their marginal products, then the total share paid to labor could be total product less the cost of raw material (but only if that exhausts the lists of inputs). This rule does not, however, provide any information about how to distribute labor's total share among the individuals who participated. That might be accomplished according to individual marginal productivity, but it might not.
d. Only in perfect competition is $P = MR$ so that $MRP = P \times MP$; more generally, $MRP = MR \times MP$.

5. Average real wages equal TP/L. If TP increases at a rate g_{TP} and labor supply increases at a rate g_L, then average real wages increase at a rate defined algebraically by $(g_{TP} - g_L) > 0$.

6. Pay marginal (revenue) products—that is the point. Given constant returns to scale, total product is exhausted. You cannot allocate the same dollar of total revenue to more than one person or factor.

CHAPTER 14

WAGES AND THE LABOR MARKET

Wages are, perhaps, the most important prices determined by the operation of a mixed economy. Total payments for wages and salaries account for over 75 percent of the national income of the United States, and that percentage is typical of developed, Western economies. Despite their importance, though, wages are just prices—prices determined by the interaction of supply and demand schedules in very special markets, to be sure, but simple prices nonetheless. It is the variation in economic structure across these markets that piques an economist's interest.

Chapter 14 introduces you to the scope of this variability. Why? To explain why real wages are so much higher in the United States and Western Europe than they are elsewhere around the world. To explain why wages and salaries differ so much across the populations of individual countries, and to explain the contribution of discrimination to that intracountry variation.

Completing your work on this chapter, therefore, you will have not only gained some insight into these fundamental issues of wage determination but also achieved the following more specific objectives.

LEARNING OBJECTIVES

1. Use a simple homogeneous model of a labor market to explain why wages can differ so dramatically from one country to another.

2. Explain the determinants of both the supply of labor and the demand for labor, noting in particular the reasons why the supply curve for labor might actually bend backward toward lower quantities as the real wage climbs above some critical value.

3. Understand the various economic reasons why wages can differ so dramatically from one type of occupation to another: compensating wage differentials, quality differences, elements of economic rent, the existence of noncompeting groups, and discrimination.

4. Present and evaluate critically the "iron law of wages" advanced by both Malthus and Marx (for different reasons), as well as the "lump-of-labor" fallacy embraced by some labor unions in time of trouble.

5. Relate the scope of discrimination in the United States to the empirical evidence of its manifestation in wage differentials. Provide a brief overview of the implications of the Equal Pay Act of 1963 and the Civil Rights Act of 1964.

6. Construct a model of discrimination based on noncompeting markets, and trace the effect of eliminating the discrimination on real wages and total income (GNP).

7. Understand the notion of comparable worth, and explain how imposing a system of mandatory comparable worth might affect the efficient operation of labor markets.

Although wages vary across the populations of most countries, the general wage level in the United States has risen markedly over the past century. This growth in real purchasing power has been supported by increases in the real wages paid to virtually every category of labor. Question 1 refreshes your memory about the meaning of the difference between the real wage and the nominal wage.

1. a. Real wages are (circle one):

(1) the same thing as nominal wages.

(2) nominal wages after allowing for tax and other withholdings deducted from such wages.

(3) nominal wages adjusted to reflect real purchasing power.

b. Between 1965 and 1985 in a certain country, (1) money wages tripled and (2) the consumer-goods price index rose from 400 to 600. It follows that real wages *(did not rise at all / rose by a factor of 1.5 / doubled / tripled / more than tripled)*.

c. It is often argued that, other things equal, an increase in population should lower wage rates because of the law of diminishing returns. That is to say, an increase in the labor force should lower wage rates (pick one):

(1) even if there were a corresponding increase in the available supply of other inputs such as raw materials and capital goods.

(2) with the supply of other inputs and technology held constant.

---

a. (3) **b.** doubled **c.** (2)

2. a. Figure 14-1 provides some insight into why real wages in North America are so much higher than they are in South America. From the units on the graph, in fact, it would appear that the real wage in North America is *(2 / 2.5 / 3)* times larger. One key to this difference is that *(the supply-of-labor curve is so much higher in the South America panel / the demand-for-labor curve is so much higher in the North America panel / the demand-for-labor curve is so much higher in the South America panel)*. Inasmuch as the demand-for-labor curve is a *(potential / derived / product)* demand curve, there are at least three reasons why it should be so positioned in panel (a) relative to panel (b). List them below:

(1) _____
(2) _____
(3) _____

b. Each of these has the effect of raising the productivity of North American labor and thus the wage that employers are willing to pay. The demand curve is, nonetheless, downward-sloping because *(the marginal product of labor declines as employment increases / the price of output declines as output and thus employment increases)*.

---

a. 2.5; the demand-for-labor curve is so much higher in the North America panel; derived (1) more resources in North America (2) more advanced technology in North America (3) more skilled labor force in North America
b. Both of the answers given contribute to the downward slope of the derived demand curve.

3. a. The supply of labor has at least three major determinants. List them below:

(1) _____
(2) _____
(3) _____

b. On the basis of the supply and demand curves depicted in Figure 14-2, indicate in the parentheses provided the likely effect on the real wage of each of the following economic adjustments. Denote an increase by (+), a reduction by (−), and no change by (0).

(1) An increase in the working population . . . . ( )

(2) A move toward shorter workweeks . . . . . . ( )

(3) An increase in labor-force participation by women . . . . ( )

(4) Passage of stronger child labor laws . . . . . . ( )

(5) Restriction of certain types of people from employment . . . . ( )

(6) A large wave of immigrants who all want to work . . . . ( )

COMPARATIVE WAGE RATES

Figure 14-1

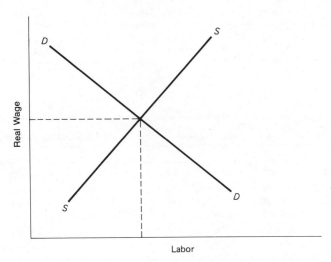

Figure 14-2

Buried in your answers to these wage questions are the answers to questions like: *(a)* Why do labor unions push for shorter workweeks? *(b)* Why does labor fear opening U.S. borders to anyone who wants to come? *(c)* Why do some drag their feet in the fight against discrimination on personal economic grounds?

a. (1) population (2) labor-force participation (c) hours worked per week
b. (1) − (because the supply curve would shift right) (2) + (because the supply curve would shift left) (3) − (because the supply curve would shift right) (4) + (because the supply curve would shift left) (5) + (because the supply curve would shift left) (6) − (because the supply curve would shift right)

4. a. Suppose that the hourly wage offered to you were to rise. Assume that you have some freedom over the number of hours you choose to work per day or per week. In these circumstances, you could, if you wished, work (circle one or more):

(1) the same number of hours and earn more daily or weekly income.

(2) more hours and earn more income.

(3) fewer hours and earn the same income.

(4) fewer hours and earn more income.

b. The fact that you might choose any one of the four alternatives of part **a** indicates the opposite and conflicting pulls of the *substitution effect* and the *income effect.*

When you are offered a higher wage for each hour worked, you are then sacrificing more money income than before for each hour you do not work; i.e., the opportunity cost of leisure is climbing. The higher hourly wage is thus an inducement to work *(more / fewer)* hours per day or week because "leisure (not working) has become more expensive." This by itself is the substitution effect. It encourages a worker to give up some *(working hours in favor of leisure / leisure hours in favor of work).*

c. Leisure time is (for most people) a desirable thing, however; as real incomes rise, most folks want more of it. The offer of a higher hourly wage makes more leisure possible *(with / without)* the sacrifice of any income. The pull of the income effect is toward *(fewer / more)* working hours and correspondingly *(fewer / more)* hours of leisure.

d. For example, suppose that you have decided to work 40 hours weekly given a $6 hourly wage, for a weekly income of $240. Were the wage offered to rise to $10, though, you could choose to earn $350 per week by working *(35 / 40 / 45)* hours. Were that the case, the *(substitution / income)* effect would have dominated.

---

a. All four are possible. **b.** more; leisure hours in favor of work **c.** without; fewer; more **d.** 35; income

The opposing pulls of income and substitution effects on labor supply give rise to the possibility of a backward-bending supply curve (of the sort illustrated later in Figure 14-6). As wages climb, the supply curve will display its usual positive slope (and positive wage elasticity) only if the substitution effect (which pushes people toward working more) dominates the income effect (which tempts people to work less). If the income effect dominates, as it may for high wages, then an increase in wages might actually inspire a reduction in the quantity of labor supplied.

This possibility raises the obvious empirical question: "Well, which is it? Is the slope positive or negative?" As usual, the answer is, "It depends." The evidence for adult males in the United States suggests a wage elasticity in the range of −0.1 to −0.2; i.e., a 10 percent increase in the real wage should be expected to cause a 1 to 2 percent reduction in the quantity of labor supplied. For adult females and teenagers in the United States, though, widely varied estimates suggest a positive correlation between wages and labor supply. Taking an average of these disparate values over the entire U.S. economy, most economists expect a wage elasticity for the over-16-year-old working population to lie somewhere between 0.0 (a vertical supply curve) and +0.2.

5. The term "economic rent" is not usually applied to labor. But in instances like Babe Ruth in the good old days of baseball and Michael Jordan in the good new days of the Chicago Bulls, it applies. Babe Ruth was paid the fantastic sum (for the 1920s) of $80,000 annually for playing baseball. Had diminished competition among baseball club owners forced him to do so, he would probably have played for $10,000 annually. His unique skill seems to have been in baseball alone, so it is unlikely that any alternative employment open to him would have paid anything like $80,000. (If the Babe played today, he could earn not only millions of dollars from his team's owner but also substantial supplementary income by extolling the benefits of (e.g.) certain types of footwear and cola in commercials, but that fact does not alter the reasoning. He would be paid for his endorsement because of his status as a baseball player earning a king's ransom every year.)

This means that Babe Ruth's labor supply curve to baseball clubs would be perfectly inelastic with respect to wage or salary prices (circle one):

a. from $80,000 annually to zero annually.

b. from $80,000 annually to some figure such as $8000 annually.

c. only at $80,000 annually; it would be less than perfectly elastic at *any* lower figure.

b. (It would cut to the vertical axes at the opportunity cost of not doing something else and playing amateur ball only in the evenings and on the weekends.)

6. There are four panels in Figure 14-3, one for each of the four parts to this question. For each part listed below, draw a new supply and/or demand curve in the corresponding panel to represent the effect of the change indicated, and predict the direction that the change will push the real wage and employment. For example, if one of the parts stated that there is an increase in the supply of labor, then you would draw a new supply curve to the right of the existing one and predict that wages would fall (−) and employment would climb (+). Record your predictions in Table 14-1.

a. The job becomes more onerous than usual, and people demand compensation for its additional burdens.

b. The job becomes extremely specialized, and only 10 people can accomplish the task that it requires.

c. Education and training improve the quality of the labor employed.

d. The job market is suddenly cut in half because of noncompeting discrimination.

Table 14-1

Part	Effect on Employment	Effect on Wages
a.	_____	_____
b.	_____	_____
c.	_____	_____
d.	_____	_____

a. The graph: draw the new supply curve above and to the left of *SS* because people are demanding more money to provide this type of labor service. Table row: quantity of labor falls (−) and wages increase (+)—an example of compensating differential in the making. b. The graph: draw the new supply curve vertical at 10. Table row: quantity of labor falls to 10 (−) and wages increase (+)—an example of collecting rent. c. The graph: draw the new demand curve above and to the right of *DD* because education and training have increased the marginal (revenue) product of labor and thus its derived demand. Table row: quantity of labor and wages both increase (+ and +). d. Same answer as for part **a**, but exaggerated—now an example of discrimination's creating noncompeting groups.

7. The idea of the iron law of wages evolved in the arguments of both Thomas Robert Malthus and Karl Marx (although for quite different reasons). The essence of the iron-law idea is that wages tend to be pushed to the (*competitive / minimum-subsistence / marginal product*) level. (Malthus' argument rested on the belief that population would increase until this level was reached; Marx's, on the belief that this outcome was part of capitalist exploitation of the labor force.)

Both theory and experience have led most economists to (*agreement / qualified agreement / disagreement*) with the idea. Figure 14-4 shows why. With the wage set at w^*, unemployment (*would / would not*) exist, and the operation of the labor market might eventually push the wage (*up / down*) to equilibrium at (w^* / w_E / w_M). There would, however, be no way for the market to push the wage down to the subsistence level because, while employers would love to see that happen, there would be (*excess supply / excess demand*) for labor at w_M that would push the wage back up.

(a)

(b)

(c)

(d)

Figure 14-3

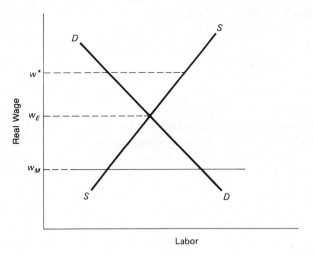

Figure 14-4

minimum-subsistence; disagreement; would; down; w_E; excess demand

8. a. Consult Figure 14-5. It shows two labor markets separated by discrimination. Demand curves in both are indicated with *DD* notation; both have the same slopes. The supply curves are vertical at 10 and 5, respectively. If that discrimination were to lapse, then the demand curve in panel *(a)* would apply to everyone. The result would be *(an increase / a reduction)* in the wage paid to those initially alone in market A from $_____ to $_____. This change would be caused by *(diminishing marginal productivity / diminishing labor utility / increasing productivity)*. At the same time, those who were initially confined to market B would see their wage *(climb / fall)* from $_____ to $_____, a change that can be attributed to *(diminishing marginal productivity / increased productivity / increased labor utility)*. The net effect would be an increase in the dollar value of output (GNP, if this were a macro model) of $*(10 / 15 / 20)*.

b. If the derived demand curve in market A were extremely inelastic, how would your answers to the qualitative parts of the above paragraph change?_____

_____

_____

_____

a. a reduction; 10; 8; diminishing marginal productivity; climb; 5; 8; increased productivity; 15 [Superimpose the trapezoid under $D_L D_L$ in panel *(b)* over the $D_H D_H$ trapezoid from $L = 10$ to $L = 15$; there remains a rectangle 5 units of labor wide and $3 high that reflects GNP gain.] **b.** If the curve $D_H D_H$ were sufficiently inelastic [sufficiently vertical through (10,$10)], then the addition of five workers from market B could lower the wage below $5. All five would not move, if that were the case, and the equilibrium wage in both markets would still exceed $5 (but not because of discrimination).

Notice, in passing, that the analysis of question 8 applies to all types of discrimination—discrimination caused by geography (wage differentials across countries), discrimination caused by sex or race, discrimination caused by noncompeting groupings within the larger labor market.

9. The notion of **comparable worth**—that people with similar value to a company should receive equal pay despite the conditions of their respective labor markets—has been advanced by some as a solution to the sorts of discrimination that are not covered well by either the Equal Pay Act

(a)

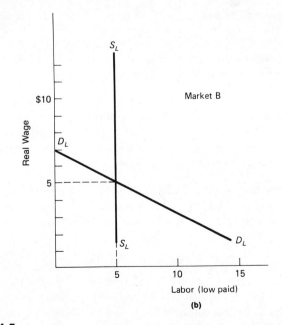

(b)

Figure 14-5

of 1963 (stipulating that men and women doing the same job should get the same pay) or the Civil Rights Act of 1964 (outlawing discrimination in hiring, firing, and employment). Comparable worth is fine in theory, but it runs into some problems even on theoretical grounds when placed in the context of operating labor markets.

To see this, suppose that company XYZ employs two different types of labor, A and B, who perform services of comparable worth for XYZ. Suppose further that the going weekly wage in the local labor market for type A labor is $250 while the going wage for type B labor is $350. Why might that be the case? Compensating differentials, noncompeting groups, discrimination, historical precedent, etc., are some reasons.

If XYZ wanted to pay A and B the same wage, then it would have to make a choice. If it were to choose $250, then it would see no change in its (*A-type* / *B-type*) labor market but it would experience (*excess supply* / *excess demand*) in its other labor market; it would (*not be able to hire as many type A workers as* / *not be able to hire as many type B workers as* / *be able to hire more type A workers than* / *be able to hire more type B workers than*) it wanted. Were it to choose $350, though, then its (*A-type* / *B-type*) labor market would remain in equilibrium and it would experience (*excess supply* / *excess demand*) in the other. It would (*not be able to hire as many type A workers as* / *not be able to hire as many type B workers as* / *be able to hire more type A workers than* / *be able to hire more type B workers than*) it wanted. Anywhere in between, a combination of both circumstances would occur.

A-type; excess demand; not be able to hire as many type B workers as; B-type; excess supply; be able to hire more type A workers than

REVIEW CONCEPTS

1. A simple supply-demand model of labor markets can explain differential wages in terms of different supply conditions, different demand conditions, or both.

2. The offered wage is the opportunity cost of leisure time. As the wage climbs, this cost explains a substitution effect — a substitution out of leisure. Higher wages mean higher incomes, though, and thus a counteracting income effect which increases the desirability of leisure time.

3. Compensating differentials, quality differences, economic rent, noncompeting groups, and discrimination can all be explored by applying supply-demand analysis to one or more labor markets.

4. Application of supply-demand analysis can also explore (a) conditions under which the "non law of wages" might apply, (b) the fallacy embedded in the lump-of-labor theory, (c) the effect on wages and output of eliminating discrimination, and (d) the efficiency implications of comparable worth.

QUIZ: Multiple Choice

1. The concept of noncompeting groups in the labor market is considered useful in explaining:
(1) structural unemployment.
(2) wage differentials among different categories of labor.
(3) the lack of mobility among older workers.
(4) the impact on nonunionized sectors of wage increases in unionized sectors of the economy.
(5) why wage rates in certain industries have risen faster than the average.

2. Imperfect competition in a labor market could be indicated by a situation in which:
(1) one firm makes wage determinations for an entire industry.
(2) different wages are paid for different jobs in order to compensate for differences in risk.
(3) different wages are paid for different jobs because the jobs have different requirements.
(4) the wages paid for certain jobs are really payments of economic rent.
(5) the excess of one wage rate over another is a compensating differential.

3. Determinants of the supply of labor for a given economy include:
(1) the size of its population.
(2) the rate of participation of its population in the labor force.
(3) the standard or legislated length of the workweek.
(4) the quality and level of skill embodied in the work force.
(5) all the above.

4. If everyone in the labor force were exactly alike (i.e., no difference in skills or competence), and if the labor market were perfectly competitive, then:
(1) any wage-rate differences would have to be explained as qualitative differentials.
(2) there would still be a considerable range of different wage rates explained only in terms of perceived differences in skill.
(3) any wage-rate differences could nonetheless be explained as compensating differentials.
(4) any wage-rate differences would have to be explained in terms of the differing wage policies adopted by different firms.
(5) there would necessarily be only one wage rate.

5. According to Malthus' analysis of wage determination:
(1) it is impossible for either employers or unions to fix wage rates at anything but the competitive level.
(2) employers will be able to force wages down to the equilibrium level by maintaining a high degree of unemployment.
(3) the long-run supply-of-labor curve is a horizontal line at the wage level at which workers will just be able to maintain and reproduce themselves.

(4) the money wage received by workers must always equal the real wage.
(5) employers will be able to force wages down to the subsistence level by maintaining a high degree of unemployment.

6. A trade union which wants simultaneously to raise wages for its members and to maintain as much employment as possible for them will be helped most by:
(1) an elastic derived demand for labor.
(2) an elastic supply of labor.
(3) an inelastic demand for the finished product.
(4) a perfectly competitive labor market.
(5) a perfectly competitive product market.

7. The substitution effect, applied to a worker's decision to change the number of hours worked daily when offered a different hourly wage, refers specifically to which of the following statements?
(1) If the wage offered to labor rises, then a worker's disposition is to buy better and more costly goods, so the worker must work longer hours.
(2) A general increase in wages tends to produce a general rise in consumer prices, which cancels out the worker's real-income gain.
(3) Leisure (nonwork) time is desirable, so a worker's normal inclination is to choose more leisure in response to any rise in real income.
(4) The cost of working is leisure (nonwork) time sacrificed; hence, if the wage offered labor fell, then leisure would become relatively less expensive.
(5) Any labor cost increase prompts employers to try to substitute capital for labor in production.

8. Which alternative in question 7 would have been correct had that question referred to the income effect rather than the substitution effect?
(1).
(2).
(3).
(4).
(5).

9. The "lump-of-labor" viewpoint is essentially a belief that:
(1) the quality of a handcrafted product is inherently superior to that of a machine-made product.
(2) the supply of labor will not vary significantly with the wage that is offered for it; i.e., the labor supply curve is almost perfectly inelastic.
(3) labor effort is the ultimate measure of value, and the prices of goods should reflect the amount of labor effort that went into making those goods.
(4) any commodity embodies a fixed quantity of labor (direct or indirect) in its manufacture, regardless of the production technique used.
(5) there is only a finite and fixed amount of useful work to be done.

10. The viewpoint referred to in question 9 arose principally out of:
(1) the experience of workers in the depression periods.
(2) the clash between income effects and substitution effects.
(3) the experience of workers in inflationary periods.
(4) the fact that the total labor supply curve is highly inelastic with respect to wages.
(5) the belief that the total fund of money out of which wages must be paid is essentially fixed in amount even in a growing economy.

11. Figure 14-6 illustrates a backward-bending labor supply curve and four possible demand curves. If the demand curve were to change from position 1 to position 2, then:
(1) the substitution effect would dominate over the income effect.
(2) the substitution effect and income effect would cancel one another out.
(3) the income effect would dominate over the substitution effect.
(4) the income effect and the substitution effect would work in the same direction.
(5) none of these statements would be correct.

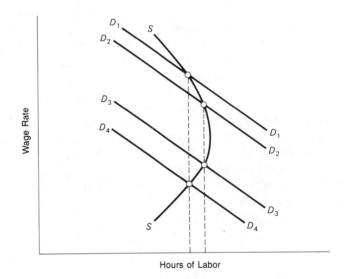

Figure 14-6

12. Referring to the same figure, if the demand curve were to move from position 2 to position 3, which alternative in question 11 would be correct?
(1).
(2).
(3).
(4).
(5).

13. Again referring to Figure 14-6, if the demand curve were to move from position 3 to position 4, which alternative in question 11 would be correct?

(1).
(2).
(3).
(4).
(5).

14. Still referring to Figure 14-6, if the demand curve were to move from position 4 to position 3, which alternative in question 11 would be correct?
(1).
(2).
(3).
(4).
(5).

15. To say that there is an economic-rent element in a person's income means that:
(1) this income comes at least in part from property ownership rather than from the labor supply.
(2) this income exceeds what it would be were the labor market perfectly competitive.
(3) if the price offered for this person's labor were increased, then he or she would want to reduce the number of daily hours worked.
(4) this income is much above average, but is the result of some relatively unique natural talent.
(5) this person's labor supply curve is perfectly inelastic with respect to price, at least within some range of prices, because he or she is somewhat unique.

16. Between two periods, the index of money wages fell from 600 to 540. The index of consumer prices fell from 400 to 300. This means that, between the two periods, real wages:
(1) rose by 50 percent.
(2) rose by 20 percent.
(3) rose by 10 percent.
(4) did not change.
(5) fell by 20 percent.

SUGGESTED ANSWERS TO QUESTIONS IN THE TEXT: Chapter 14

1. Review the definitions. Examples:
Compensating differentials: High-altitude steel welders make more than "on-the-ground" welders.
Economic rent (applied to labor): Rickey Henderson and Wayne Gretzky.
Noncompeting groups: College professors and auto mechanics; etc.

2. The relative size of supply; the relative size of markets; the relative productivity of labor. India should try to invest in technology that would improve labor productivity in the production of items that the world wants and allows, perhaps, for the exploitation of economies of scale.

3. a. Less imperfect competition should mean smaller differentials.
b. So should mobility that breaks down the geographical barriers to entry into high-paying labor markets.
c. More equal opportunity for education should make the distribution of productivity more equal and thus diminish wage differentials.
d. Less demand for "star products" should lower their rent.

4. Increased supply means wage should fall and the quantity supplied should climb along a sloping derived demand curve. The number of hours worked is a determinant of labor supply, just like population size.

5. They all serve as barriers either to the markets or to the places and connections of business transactions (clubs).

6. A number of examples can be listed, such as education paths by which women can secure the entry qualifications needed for high-paying jobs. There are lots of possible answers here; one is probably discussed in today's newspaper.

7. The lump-of-labor fallacy. Reducing the workweek would lower real wage measured by the week.

8. Fairness versus the efficiency of markets. Fairness would probably work through comparable worth to bring the high-paying male compensations down as the lower-paying compensations rose. Thus, the potential division in support.

9. Tax liability equals tW, so the after-tax wage W^P equals $W - tW = W(1 - t)$. The required table is presented as Table TQ14-1. Figure TQ14-1 depicts the data which support the Equilibrium Labor and Tax Revenue columns. Figure TQ14-2 plots tax revenue against the tax rate.

Table TQ14-1

Tax Rate (%)	W^P	Equilibrium Labor	Tax Revenue
0	$10.00	8	$ 0
15	8.50	10	15
25	7.50	10	25
33	6.67	6	20

14 Wages and the Labor Market   183

Figure TQ14-1

Figure TQ14-2

CHAPTER 15

LABOR UNIONS AND COLLECTIVE BARGAINING

Labor is not owned; it is "rented." This was one of the implications of the Civil War in the United States, and it is an implication that has had far-reaching effects on the labor markets of this country. Because labor is rented, there must exist, between management and labor, some sort of contract outlining compensation schedules, work rules, procedures, and avenues for voicing grievances in both directions. The first section of Chapter 15 conducts a review of the role of labor unions in the process of forming such contracts. Their history is briefly chronicled, as is the role of government in shaping that history. So, too, is their overall organization. The result is a reasonably thorough introduction into the issues surrounding unions before a cursory analysis of how unions try to increase wages is conducted in section B.

Having completed your work in this chapter, you will have accomplished the following objectives.

LEARNING OBJECTIVES

1. Review briefly the history of the labor movement in the United States. Understand the roles played by industrial unions and craft unions in that history. Describe the extent of union power in the 1990s in terms of both the size of membership and its influence beyond that membership.

2. List the three layers of structure that mark contemporary unionism, and discuss the evolution of each.

3. Outline the changing mood of the federal government in its treatment of unions. Cite the major pieces of legislation that were either applied to unions or written for unions [Sherman Antitrust Act (1890), Clayton Antitrust Act (1914), Railway Labor Act (1926), Norris-LaGuardia Act (1932), Wagner Act (NLRA, 1935), Fair Labor Standards Act (1938), Taft-Hartley Act (1947), etc.]. Characterize the current governmental view of unions.

4. Understand why collective bargaining (including negotiation about the economic package, work rules, union security, etc.), strikes, deregulation, foreign competition, and productivity restraint are issues of enormous concern among both scholars of the labor movement and members of the labor movement.

5. Explain how wage stickiness can be attributed to the actions of both sides of contemporary labor markets.

6. Explain how unions might try to increase wages by (1) restricting supply, (2) increasing demand, (3) negotiating higher wages explicitly, and (4) fighting monopsony power.

7. Summarize the aggregate effect of 60 years of union activity on (1) the relative wage of union members, (2) the share of GNP paid to labor, and (3) unemployment.

Nineteen million Americans belong to unions—about one-sixth of the adult labor force. The employment arrangements of many millions more nonunion members are dictated by union agreements about wages, hours, and work conditions. Even though the union share of the labor force has been in decline for nearly four decades (from more than 25 percent in 1950 to the current 16 percent), these data clearly show that union power is still a major economic force in the United States—it is a force that must be recognized.

1. If all or most workers within a large plant belong to the same union, this would most probably be classified as *(a craft / an industrial)* union. If all or most union members have the same occupation, or closely allied occupations, this would most probably be classed as *(a craft / an industrial)* union.

an industrial; a craft

15 Labor Unions and Collective Bargaining

2. Note in the parentheses provided whether the indicated efforts should cause union power (reflected specifically in the ability to maintain or increase high wages) to increase (I), decrease (D), or remain unchanged (U). When a particular industry is identified, presume that the question pertains to the union employed in that industry.

a. Deregulation in the airline industry .... ( )

b. Imposition of quotas to limit the importing of Japanese automobiles .... ( )

c. Increase in auto sales .... ( )

d. Elimination of import quotas .... ( )

e. Increase in unemployment as part of the business cycle .... ( )

f. Election of conservatives to the National Labor Relations Board .... ( )

g. Repeal of the National Labor Relations Act ..... ( )

h. Doubling of OPEC oil prices .... ( )

i. Eradication of the air-traffic controllers' union by the President .... ( )

j. Widespread adoption of robot technology ..... ( )

---

a. D (More competition in the product market tends to reduce prices and thus the derived demand for labor; it is therefore harder for a union to maintain high wages and wage increases.) **b.** I (The opposite of **a**: unions can exploit the market power of the employer even if it is artificially created by government intervention.) **c.** I (success in a unionized industry) **d.** D (the opposite of **b**) **e.** D (Excess supply of labor means that the threat of the layoffs that could accompany high wage settlements would be more severe and make higher settlements less attractive to union members.) **f.** D (Conservatives tend to want to diminish union power.) **g.** D (The National Labor Relations Act helped solidify union power; repeal would, presumably, do the opposite.) **h.** D (Doubling oil prices would weaken the economy, create recession, and make **e** apply.) **i.** D (Successful threats by government to the existence of unions weaken the power of others simply by changing the bargaining climate.) **j.** D (Weakened demand for labor undermines the ability of unions to demand high compensation.)

Several points can be made in light of the answers to question 2. First, much of recent history has worked against the power of unions, at least at the source of its traditional power. From the intervention of the President of the United States in the PATCO strike to the composition of the NLRB, the lot of the traditional labor union has declined. Second, general-equilibrium effects are rampant in the labor market, so "unchanged" was the answer to none of the parts of question 2. You are hereby challenged to come up with one significant change in economic circumstances that would not influence the power of some labor union to some degree. Let me know care of Wesleyan University, Middletown, Connecticut.

3. In 1890, the Sherman Antitrust Act was passed. For the next 20 years, its content was used as a weapon against union formation and activity even though the framers of this legislation never envisioned its application to labor markets. In 1914, another bill was passed specifically excluding labor unions from application of the Sherman Act; it was the _____ Act.

Clayton (Its ability to help unions achieve their objectives was perhaps delayed until the passage of the Norris-LaGuardia Act of 1932, given court interpretation.)

4. Are the following statements concerning the National Labor Relations Board true or false?

a. On petition from a union claiming to represent a majority of workers, the NLRB can take a secret ballot of the workers to determine if this claim is valid. .... (T / F)

b. If a majority vote upholds the union claim in part **a**, then the NLRB can require that the employer recognize the union as a collective bargaining agent and deal with it. .. (T / F)

c. The NLRB can enter a union-management dispute and seek to mediate the differences. .... (T / F)

d. If the dispute persists, the NLRB can, on petition to the courts, act as an arbitrator to settle it. .... (T / F)

e. The NLRB can designate an "unfair labor practice" and, if necessary, take the employer to court to enforce a cease-and-desist order against such practice. .... (T / F)

---

a. T **b.** T **c.** F **d.** F **e.** T

5. For each statement below, insert in the parentheses the number of the federal act which contains the provision or prohibition described. (The same number may be used more than once.)

1. Clayton Antitrust Act (1914).
2. Fair Labor Standards Act (1938).
3. Railway Labor Act (1926).
4. Norris-LaGuardia Act (1932).
5. Taft-Hartley Act (1947).
6. Wagner (National Labor Relations) Act (1935).
7. No federal act contains this provision.

a. Explicitly stated that workers have the right to form unions, to bargain collectively, and to engage in concerted activities for purposes of collective bargaining; also set up machinery to protect exercise of these rights by workers .. .. ( )

b. Explicitly accepted the premise of collective bargaining . ... ( )

c. Prohibited major unions from hiring salaried managers to administer their operations .... ( )

d. Prohibited individuals from being members of more than one union at one time .... ( )

e. Provided that the attorney general of the United States may secure a court injunction to suspend strikes during a dispute which "imperil(s) the national health or safety" ... . ( )

f. Established the National Labor Relations Board to act as watchdog against "unfair labor practices" on the part of employers .... ( )

g. Vastly reduced the employer's power to obtain federal court injunctions to break strikes or harass unions .. ( )

h. Sharply restricted the closed shop .... ( )

i. Established an hourly minimum wage for most workers in occupations involving interstate commerce ...... ( )

j. Defined "unfair labor practices" on the part of unions .. .. ( )

a. 7 b. 3 c. 8 d. 8 e. 6 f. 7 g. 4 h. 6 i. 2 j. 6

---

6. Deregulation and foreign competition can diminish the ability of unions to maintain high wages because both *(increase / decrease)* the market power of employers. As long as employers have market power, they can price their products *(above / at / below)* average cost, i.e., *(above / at / below)* the competitive price. Since the wage offered to labor by an employer operating in a competitive market is modeled to equal the multiplicative product of *(the price or marginal revenue of output and the marginal utility of labor / the price of output and the marginal product of labor / the price of capital and the marginal product of labor)*, labor working for an employer with market power can receive a wage that is *(higher than / equal to / lower than)* the competitive wage. If deregulation and foreign competition work to make the output market more competitive, therefore, they *(increase / reduce)* the ability of labor to derive a higher wage.

decrease; above; above; the price or marginal revenue of output and the marginal product of labor; higher than; reduce

---

7. There are four methods trade unions try to employ to raise the wages of their members. One is a simple and direct attempt to increase the wage rate by any means available. If a union were to make such an attempt, then it would have the greatest success at minimizing any associated increase in unemployment if the derived demand for labor were wage-*(elastic / inelastic)* and/or the supply of labor were wage-*(elastic / inelastic)*.

inelastic; inelastic

---

8. Which of the following union practices operate primarily by shifting the labor supply curve to the left, and which by moving the derived demand curve for labor to the right? In the parentheses after each, put (S) for supply curve or (D) for demand curve:

a. Writing featherbedding rules into local building codes .. .. ( )

b. Requiring long apprenticeship periods before allowing entry into an occupation or a profession .... ( )

c. Asking consumers to purchase only union-made goods . ... ( )

d. Imposing high initiation fees for entry into an occupation or a profession .... ( )

e. Limiting the use of labor-saving tools and equipment .. .. ( )

f. Agitating successfully for tariff protection .... ( )

g. Agitating successfully for limitations on immigration ... . ( )

a. D b. S c. D d. S e. D f. D g. S

---

9. The four panels of Figure 15-1 illustrate the four methods with which unions can try to increase the wage paid to their members. List the four methods in the spaces below, and identify which of the four panels is the most appropriate representation of each. The original demand and supply curves in each panel are designated DD and SS; the modified curves created by the union activity are designated D'D' and S'S' where appropriate.

(1) _____; panel ( )
(2) _____; panel ( )
(3) _____; panel ( )
(4) _____; panel ( )

b. Notice that employment falls in two of the cases and that employment increases in the other two cases. Circle the two serendipitous cases in which both the wage and employment increase.

a. (1) restrict supply; d (2) raise the standard wage; a (3) increase productivity; c (4) remove exploitation; c b. (3) and (4)

---

10. a. Two of the means by which unions can try to increase wages also tend to increase employment. They are:

(1) _____
(2) _____

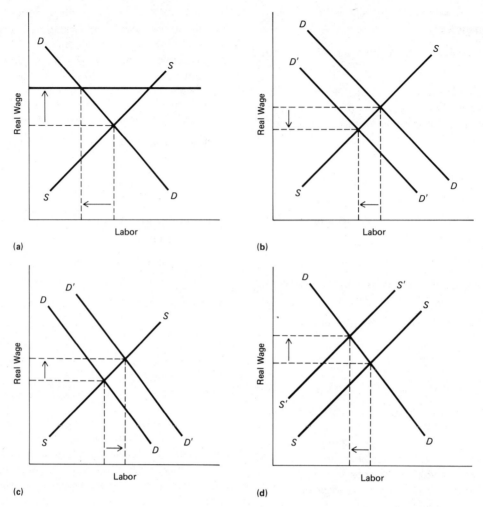

Figure 15-1

b. For a given increase in the quantity of labor demanded *at every wage*, the effect on wages is larger when the supply of labor is relatively more *(elastic / inelastic)*. The effect on wages is also larger when the derived demand for labor is relatively more *(elastic / inelastic)*.

c. There are two other ways that unions have tried to increase wages, but it turns out that they can cause employment to fall. They are:

(3) _____

(4) _____

d. The employment effect of either of these second two possible tools is larger when the derived demand for labor is relatively more *(elastic / inelastic)*. The wage elasticity of supply affects only the reduced-employment effect of one of these two choices; which one? _____.
The elasticity of supply affects only the level of *unemployment* in the other case.

a. (1) and (2) in either order: increase productivity; remove (reduce) exploitation   **b.** inelastic; inelastic   **c.** (3) and (4) in either order: restrict supply; increase the standard wage   **d.** elastic; restrict supply

REVIEW CONCEPTS

1. Labor unions still play an important, if diminished, role in the United States economy; their present structure is comprised of three layers: local unions, national unions, and a federation of unions (AFL-CIO).

2. The pattern of American unionism has evolved over the past century—out of a patchwork of craft unions and into a federation of industrial unions.

3. A union, once recognized by an NLRB election, negotiates contract language which defines direct compensation, fringe benefits, work rules, etc. The swing toward a political climate which allowed this structure to become standard began in the 1930s with the passage of the Wagner Act.

4. Business conditions which influence the profitability of any particular firm also influence the power of unions represented within that firm.

5. Unions try to affect wages by (1) restricting the supply of labor; (2) bargaining over the standard rate of compensation; (3) adopting policies which shift the productivity of labor; and (4) reducing exploitation by monopsony employers.

6. Unions seem to have raised the wages of their members, relative to those of comparable nonunion workers; but these relative gains seem to have been eroded recently by a period of high unemployment, increased competition from nonunion labor, and a conservative political climate.

QUIZ: Multiple Choice

1. Which of the following statements is accurate?
(1) The membership roles of unions totaled across the United States include approximately 19 million names.
(2) Less than 5 percent of the people employed in each and every manufacturing industry in the United States work under an arrangement negotiated by a union, whether or not they are union members.
(3) Union membership has leveled off recently, after growing for over 50 years.
(4) Union wages tend to be about 50 percent higher than nonunion wages, but the share of GNP devoted to labor has remained remarkably constant over the past 60 years.
(5) All the statements recorded above are accurate.

2. The term "industrial union" refers to:
(1) anything which can be characterized as a trade union.
(2) a trade union in manufacturing, but not one in service trades or agriculture.
(3) a union whose membership is drawn from individuals with the same craft skill.
(4) a union whose membership is drawn from the same given industry.
(5) an organization of employers in a given industry.

3. Collective bargaining agreements are usually negotiated by:
(1) the federation of national unions.
(2) the local union, but increasingly with the assistance of a national federation.
(3) the local union, but increasingly with the assistance of a national union.
(4) the national union, but increasingly with the assistance of a national federation.
(5) the national union, but increasingly with the assistance of the local union.

4. "Exclusive bargaining agent" refers to:
(1) the craft-union principle early adopted by the AFL in which each union had complete jurisdiction over workers in its class and two unions could not conflict in attempting to organize the same workers.
(2) the union recognized by the National Labor Relations Board as exclusively entitled to represent all workers within the group concerned in bargaining with management.
(3) a provision in the Taft-Hartley Act which restrains the union from attempting to bargain on behalf of nonmembers.
(4) the official who is designated by the union to negotiate with management on behalf of its members.
(5) none of the above.

5. One of the important principles by which Samuel Gompers ran the AFL was that:
(1) labor must learn to live within a capitalistic system and to realize that it was unrealistic to expect "more, more, and still more."
(2) wherever possible, member national unions should be organized by industry rather than by craft.
(3) although greater emphasis should be placed on business unionism, pro-union government intervention in collective bargaining was to be sought through political action.
(4) the autonomy of each member union with respect to its craft specialty must be clearly recognized.
(5) although labor must learn to live with capitalism, in the long run, effective business unionism would lay the basis for a philosophy of political action.

6. The act generally considered the most important piece of legislation in American labor history, in the sense of marking a real turning point in that history, is:
(1) the Landrum-Griffin Act (1959).
(2) the Wagner Act (1935).
(3) the Gramm-Rudmann Act (1988).
(4) the Fair Labor Standards Act (1938).
(5) the Walsh-Healy Act (1935).

7. According to the legislation from which it was created, the National Labor Relations Board must, among other things:
(1) issue injunctions where needed to prevent strikes in "essential" industries.
(2) exclude unions from legal complaints about "unfair union labor practices."
(3) see to it that the provision of the Taft-Hartley Act prohibiting the union shop is enforced.
(4) enforce the federal minimum-wage law with respect to interstate commerce.
(5) hold elections to see which union is entitled to act as collective bargaining agent for workers in a plant.

8. If the President wants to suspend a strike that seems to endanger the nation's welfare, he or she:
(1) may apply the "essential industry" provision of the Wagner Act.
(2) may apply the "restraint of trade" provision of the Clayton Act.

(3) may apply the "court injunction" provision of the Taft-Hartley Act.
(4) may apply the "national emergency" provision of the Landrum-Griffin Act.
(5) must simply use the prestige of his or her office to prevent it, since there is no provision in any federal act which gives the President any explicit power regarding suspension.

9. Over the past 60 years, the share of GNP devoted to paying labor has:
(1) grown slightly, thanks in large part to union power.
(2) more than doubled, thanks in large part to foreign competition.
(3) fallen, despite the best efforts of national unions.
(4) been halved, due in large measure to foreign competition.
(5) remained roughly constant, even through boom and recession.

10. The Taft-Hartley Act (1947), among other things:
(1) prohibited nonwage payments to union representatives by employers.
(2) made the "closed shop" illegal.
(3) provided the courts with legal justification to curb union formation and activity.
(4) removed labor unions from the possible charge of being a "conspiracy in restraint of trade."
(5) charged the National Labor Relations Board with the duty of making sure that employers did not engage in "unfair labor practices."

11. Had question 10 referred to the Clayton Act (1914), which alternative would have been correct?
(1).
(2).
(3).
(4).
(5).

12. Had question 10 referred to the Wagner Act (1935), which alternative would have been correct?
(1).
(2).
(3).
(4).
(5).

13. Which of the following could be evidence of imperfection in the general labor market?
(1) Protracted periods of wage stickiness.
(2) Rigid wage policies in major corporations and small businesses alike.
(3) Frequent periods of prolonged unemployment.
(4) A survey indicating rising wages and rising unemployment.
(5) All the above.

14. Given the initial conditions in a labor market characterized by the demand and supply curves shown in Figure 15-2, which of the following is the likely effect of union action that restricts the supply of qualified labor?

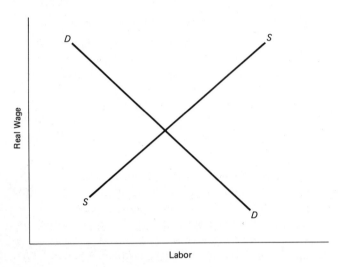

Figure 15-2

(1) Wages up and employment down.
(2) Wages down and employment up.
(3) Wages down and employment down.
(4) Wages up and employment up.
(5) Cannot tell from the information provided.

15. Which answer to question 14 would have been correct if the question had referred to an action that would increase the productivity of labor?
(1).
(2).
(3).
(4).
(5).

16. Which answer to question 14 would have been correct if the question had referred to an action that would increase the standard wage paid by management?
(1).
(2).
(3).
(4).
(5).

SUGGESTED ANSWERS TO QUESTIONS IN THE TEXT: Chapter 15

1. The structure is depicted in Figure TQ15-1. Note that collections of local unions are organized into national unions which are assembled into a federation of national unions.

15 Labor Unions and Collective Bargaining

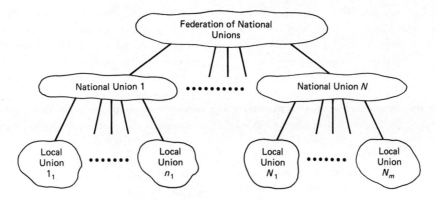

Figure TQ15-1

Monopoly power can be obtained by organizing all the people who can offer specific labor skills to employers into a national union of "workers."

2. What is your opinion here? Remember to support it on the basis of a tradeoff between individual well-being and societal well-being. If you argue against striking, what instrument should be allowed in its stead? If you argue for striking, how are vital services to be provided to the population during the strike?

3. Consider Figure TQ15-2. Panel (a) represents the union labor market; DD and SS are initial derived demand and supply curves, respectively. Panel (b) represents the unskilled, nonunion labor market; dd and ss are initial derived demand and supply curves, respectively. Assume initial equilibria at E^* and e^*.

Now let a minimum-wage law be passed at w_{min}. Employment in the unskilled market falls to l^+. Since l^- people want to work at w_{min}, the corresponding level of unemployment must equal $l^- - l^+$. A contraction in the demand for unskilled workers could easily increase the derived demand for skilled labor from DD to $D'D'$. Wages and employment in the union market could therefore increase at the expense of increased unemployment among the unskilled.

4. Cooperative elements come from mutually consistent goals—increased productivity, increased product demand, etc. Antagonistic elements come from objectives that run counter to one another—keeping costs down versus attaining high wage settlements, flexibility in hiring versus job security, etc. A good arbitrator should be able to recognize cooperative elements and exploit them in overcoming antagonistic ones.

5. a. Decreased productivity means lower derived demand, especially if nonunion bricklayers are available; lower wages and fewer union bricklayers should be expected. See panel (a) of Figure TQ15-3. Increased demand for nonunion bricklayers should increase their wage and their number; see panel (b) of Figure TQ15-3.

b. Decreased derived demand from lower marginal revenue produces lower wages and fewer union pilots; the opposite occurs for nonunion pilots. Panels (a) and (b) of Figure TQ15-3 apply, respectively, once again.

c. Increased supply for certain services reduces wages for doctors; panel (c) of Figure TQ15-3 applies this time.

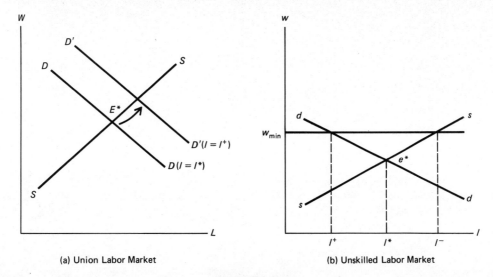

(a) Union Labor Market   (b) Unskilled Labor Market

Figure TQ15-2

The productivity of nurses increases, though, so their wages and number should increase; see panel (b).

d. Increased derived demand (higher marginal revenue) from greater power in the product market shifts the demand out. Panel (b) applies, showing higher wages and more workers.

e. Excess supply in the steelworker market reduces employment even as wages climb; panel (b) of Figure TQ15-2 applies. The ability of a minimum wage to create unemployment extends from unskilled labor all the way to highly skilled steelworkers; the binding minimum might be higher in the labor market for steelworkers, but the effect would be the same.

6. You should prefer to bargain with the regulated monopolist. There is more room for increasing the standard wage and derived demand (MR and MP components) without costing jobs because demand displays some imperfect elasticity and can therefore accommodate some increase in prices. In the other case, you would have to deal with an entire competitive industry (to do otherwise would be to drive union shops out of business and make room for nonunion shops). Restricting the supply of labor doesn't seem to apply here.

7. Restrict supply on a supply-and-demand graph. Incomes of the professions increase if demand is wage-inelastic in the relevant region.

(a)

(b)

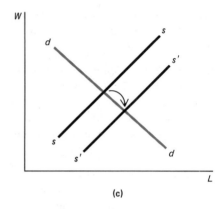
(c)

Figure TQ15-3

CHAPTER 16

LAND, NATURAL RESOURCES, AND CAPITAL

Preceding chapters have outlined how input prices are determined, with special emphasis on the wages paid to labor. It is now time to extend the analysis to include the determination of the economic rents and the return to capital.

Economic rent, strictly interpreted, is the return paid to an input which is available in fixed supply and which has only one possible occupation. Economic rent is, as a result, perhaps the simplest input price to analyze because it emerges immediately from markets characterized by perfectly inelastic supply. Rents are, nonetheless, critical in the accurate calculation of the economic and social costs of production. They also provide a convenient benchmark against which to measure the relative (in)efficiency of various taxation schemes.

Market determination of the return to capital is, by way of contrast, an extremely complicated process. The return to capital depends upon many factors, economic and psychological, that lie well beyond the straightforward intersection of a derived demand curve and a simple supply curve. It depends upon the willingness of people to forgo present consumption to finance increased consumption in the future. It depends upon the uncertainties inherent in forecasting the future, and the aversion of people to the risks that those uncertainties create. It even depends upon policies enacted on a macroeconomic and sometimes international level. For present purposes, however, only the simplest of theories will be explored. Brief mention of the many possible complications will be made, but the focus of the chapter will be a simple, but appropriate, description of the workings of the capital market.

This rather extreme caveat notwithstanding, your work in Chapter 16 will produce substantial insight into one of the most critical topics of contemporary research. Having completed the chapter, in fact, you will have accomplished the following objectives.

LEARNING OBJECTIVES

1. Explain the notion of economic rent, the circumstances under which it applies, and the inferences which can be drawn from those circumstances regarding the theory of efficient taxation (i.e., Ramsey taxes).

2. Explain how economic rent can be considered a legitimate production cost that does not carry with it a matching social cost; explore the role of opportunity cost in this context.

3. Understand the role of economic rent in developing a theory of externalities. Explain why appropriate rents might not be charged for certain of our natural resources.

4. Define precisely what economists mean when they speak of physical capital (structure, equipment, inventories, etc.), and understand why capital is not a primary factor of production.

5. Define the rate of return on capital, and relate it to the notion of an interest rate.

6. Explain the notion of present value and its importance in evaluating the potential profitability of a capital project. Record a formula for the present value of a perpetual asset which generates a constant return and of a more general asset which generates an arbitrary stream of returns into the future. Trace the sensitivity of the present value in either circumstance to changes in the interest rate.

7. Explain the major factors that determine (a) the derived demand for capital and (b) the supply of capital in the classical theory. Relate the theory to some of its major qualifications: (a) technological change, (b) uncertainty and risk,

(c) present and future inflation, and (d) macroeconomic shocks and policies.

8. State the relationship between the real rate of interest, the nominal rate of interest, and the rate of inflation. Explain why the classical theory of capital investment uses the real rate of interest as its price variable.

9. Define profit in a statistical sense, and explain the roles of (a) implicit rents, interest payments, and wages; (b) rewards for risk taking; and (c) monopoly rents in determining profit.

10. Explain the three types of risk involved in profit (default, pure, and innovation). Differentiate between natural scarcities, contrived scarcities, and innovation rents as parts of monopoly profit.

It is most convenient to begin with a precise definition of economic rent. Economic rent, recall, is the return paid to an input which is available in fixed supply and which has only one occupation; rent is paid, in other words, to an input that is useful only in the production of one single commodity. And because the input's employment is so limited, its supply curve with respect to that occupation is perfectly price-inelastic.

The problem here is, of course, understanding the precise meaning of "one single occupation." Land suited for corn production could, for example, almost certainly be used for other grain crops. The idea of economic rent was developed by nineteenth-century British economists like David Ricardo. When these economists spoke of "corn production," they really meant "grain production" or "food production"; i.e., they interpreted the words "occupation" and "commodity" rather broadly. It is now possible to speak of Iowa farmland in the same broad sense: if it were claimed that that land had only one occupation, then it would follow that its effective usefulness was pretty much limited to grain or food production. The only demand of any significance for that land would therefore come from the farmers who would want to use it for growing grain.

1. a. When an input has only a single employment, the supply curve facing demanders who want to use it in that employment will be perfectly inelastic with respect to price because the suppliers have no alternative to which to turn should price be low. They must supply the same quantity, if necessary, even at a very low price. If the market for this input is competitive, will the price necessarily be low? (Circle one.)

(1) Yes, if competitive forces are operating.

(2) It is impossible to tell. The price will be set where the demand curve crosses this perfectly inelastic supply curve; if demand for this limited supply were sufficiently large, the equilibrium price could easily be very high.

b. The single-occupation case illustrates how fallacious a "cost of production" theory of price can be. Suppose that the input in question is cows and that cows are useful only for giving milk. Now suppose, as well, that the demand for milk has driven its price to an extremely high level. The resulting derived demand for cows would certainly support a correspondingly high price for cows. It would, in such a situation, be *incorrect* to assert that (circle one):

(1) the price of cows is high because the price of milk is high.

(2) the price of milk is high because the price of cows is high.

In short, you (could / could not), in this case, give a meaningful explanation of the price of milk in terms of the costs involved in producing milk.

c. The cows-and-milk example illustrates the more general issue which produced the term "economic rent." It arose from David Ricardo's exploration of changes in the prices of food and land in early nineteenth-century England. As in the cows-and-milk example, a higher demand for food had driven up the rental price of land. Analytically, the proper conclusion was simple: the increased price of food could not be blamed on the higher rental price of land; land's price had risen because the demand for food had increased.

Remember, though, that this conclusion holds only for a single-occupation input available along a perfectly inelastic supply curve. To see why, suppose that land has many uses other than food production. Let the demand in some of those other uses drive up the rental price of land. Food producers of all sorts would then have to pay a higher price for that part of the total land supply which they employed, even though its higher price had nothing to do with the demand for food. In this case, the higher price of food (could / could not) legitimately be blamed on the higher cost of inputs required to produce food.

---

a. (2) **b.** (2); could not **c.** could

2. Economists' interest in the case of the single-occupation input with perfectly inelastic supply led them to ask another question: Does the payment made to such an input constitute a cost of production? At first, this may seem to be a dumb question. Each separate user of that input must pay the price, high or low, for the quantity of that input which he or she employs, and that outlay certainly is a cost of production.

On the other hand, production costs are supposed to reflect social cost, and Chapter 2 pointed out that the notion of opportunity cost is really the appropriate conceptualization of real social cost. The way to get more of some good A is to transfer some of the inputs used in the production of some other good B into the production of A, i.e., to sacrifice some consumption of B for the potential of increasing the production of A. This sort of substitution is possible, of course, only for inputs which can be used to produce either A or B.

Economic rents are, by definition, paid only to inputs which have just one possible occupation; they apply, therefore, only to inputs whose employment cannot be transferred from the production of one good to the production of another. In terms of opportunity cost, then, their employment *(still entails / does not entail)* a cost to society. When these inputs are put to work, their employment does not impose any sacrifice of any other commodity.

---

does not entail

---

3. From the perspective of a single farmer, one among many such farmers, the supply curve of single-occupation land will not be perfectly inelastic. If the rental market for land is a competitive one, then each farmer sees only the market price of land, at which price he or she can rent as much or as little as he or she wishes. To the farmer, land supply appears to be *(perfectly elastic / somewhat elastic / perfectly inelastic)* with respect to price.

Consider now the case of an input which happens to have several widely differing possible occupations, and whose total supply curve (the supply quantity offered to all buyers taken together) is perfectly price-inelastic. To any one class of buyers, the supply curve of this input will not be perfectly inelastic. To illustrate this point, suppose that the input in question can be used for making any of three goods (X, Y, and Z), so there are three types of potential buyers. Assume, for the sake of illustration, that the demand for this input on the part of those who use it for making X declines sharply. This demand is part of total demand, so the input's price should *(fall / rise)*. As a result, the producers who use it for making Y and Z should want to employ *(more / less)*. That is, the input's total fixed supply will be redistributed: more going to Y and Z, and less to X. To the producers of X, therefore, supply *(will / will not)* be perfectly inelastic; when their demand decreases (and the input's price consequently falls), the quantity supplied to them declines, as well.

---

perfectly elastic; fall; more; will not

---

4. Henry George's single-tax movement grew from the idea of perfectly inelastic supply. In his book, *Progress and Poverty*, George argued that the primary explanation for continuing poverty in the midst of economic progress was high land rent. Landlords were exacting large incomes from land which they (or their ancestors) had been shrewd (or lucky) enough to acquire before the present need for such land had evolved. Land's price was high *(a)* because the demand for it was exceedingly high and *(b)* because its supply, being fixed, had not expanded to match the increase in demand. Hence the *single-tax movement*—the single tax proposed being, of course, a tax on land.

Regardless of the merits or demerits of Henry George's single-tax movement, instances of perfectly inelastic input supply—if they can be found—have interesting implications for taxation policy. As an illustration, consider the case in which supply is not perfectly price-inelastic. Figure 16-1 might, for example, illustrate the fact that labor will work longer hours only if it is offered a higher price (wage for all hours supplied). If an increased demand for labor were to push the price up from p_0 to p_1, then that higher price would accomplish two things: *(a)* it would coax out the additional quantity supplied AB, which would not have been forthcoming at price p_0; and *(b)* it would ration out the total available supply 0B to those willing to pay the higher price.

Figure 16-1

Suppose now, with price at p_1, that a tax is levied on the sale of this input. Its effect would be to reduce the after-tax return received by labor to, say, p_0. As a result, the market quantity supplied would be reduced from 0B to 0A. The tax would have the unfortunate effect of "distorting production incentives"; i.e., people would decide to supply somewhat less labor in order to escape paying part of the tax.

By contrast, consider the case of perfectly inelastic supply shown in Figure 16-2. There, a price rise from p_0 to p_1 (brought about by an increase in demand) would accomplish *neither / only one / both)* of the results in the case of Figure 16-1. It *(would / would not)* coax out an additional supply quantity. It *(would / would not)* ration that available supply. Moreover, if a tax were to be levied on the employment of this input, results would be different in the inelastic-supply case.

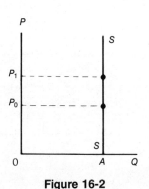

Figure 16-2

If such a tax were to reduce the after-tax return of suppliers from p_1 to p_0, for example, then (a large / a small / no) reduction in the equilibrium quantity would be forthcoming. Imposition of the tax in this second case (would / would not) cause any reduction in total real output, because there would be no reduction in quantity of work hours supplied.

only one; would not; would; no; would not

5. Modern tax theory has generalized the notion of taxing inputs whose supply is perfectly inelastic into what are called "Ramsey taxes." The observation which supports this generalization notes simply that taxes are more efficient in (a) raising revenue and (b) minimizing the loss in consumer surplus if they are imposed on goods with either (relatively) inelastic demand or inelastic supply. Figure 16-3 will help you explore the rationale behind this result.

In panel (a), a demand curve DD is drawn though point E to indicate, given supply curve SS, an equilibrium price and quantity pair of (price = $5, quantity = 9). Demand curve D'D' has also been drawn to reflect the effect of a $2-per-unit tax on the sale of good X. Since $5 is required by suppliers to produce X, the new, after-tax equilibrium quantity must be _____ units, for which people would spend $_____ per unit and suppliers would receive $_____ per unit. Before the tax, consumer surplus was $_____; after the tax it will have (risen / fallen) to $_____, a reduction of _____ percent. Tax revenue would, moreover, equal $_____.

Panel (b) repeats the process for a demand curve DD that, through the (price = $5, quantity = 9) equilibrium,

is relatively (more elastic / more inelastic). D'D' again represents effective demand after a $2-per-unit tax has been imposed. The after-tax equilibrium would, in this second case, be _____ units selling at a price of $_____, of which $_____ per unit would show up in the hands of the supplier. Consumer surplus would, in this case, (rise / fall) from $_____ before the tax to $_____ after the tax—a reduction of _____ percent; total revenue generated by the tax would, meanwhile, equal $_____. Note that the relative inelasticity of demand in panel (b) has allowed more revenue to be generated by the same per unit tax with a smaller loss in consumer surplus.

3; 7; 5; 13.50 (= area of triangle aEb = 0.5 × 3 × 9); fallen; 1.50 (= area of triangle aE'b'); 89; 6 (= $2 × 3 units); more inelastic; 7; 7; 5; fall; 40.50 (= area of triangle aEb = 0.5 × 9 × 9); 24.50 (= area of triangle aE'b'); 40; 14 (= $2 × 7 units)

6. a. The inability of an economy to charge economic rent for resources of fixed supply can generate an (over- / under-) utilization of those resources. Three reasons have been advanced to explain this inability. They are:

(1) _____

(2) _____

(3) _____

b. Now give an example from reality that illustrates each reason:

(1) _____

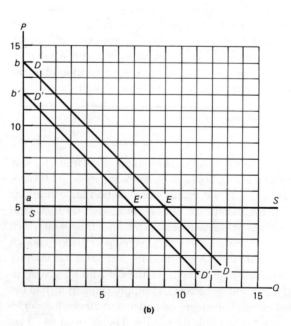

Figure 16-3

(2) _____

(3) _____

a. over (1) no ownership (2) no charge for use (3) excessive monitoring costs b. (1) grazing on common land (no ownership) (2) carbon emissions, which may cause global climate change (no charge) (3) illegal dumping of hazardous waste (excessive monitoring costs)

7. Consult Figure 16-4; *DD* there represents a demand curve for rental housing, while *SS* represents a short-run supply curve. The equilibrium rent for housing would, in this case, be $_____ .

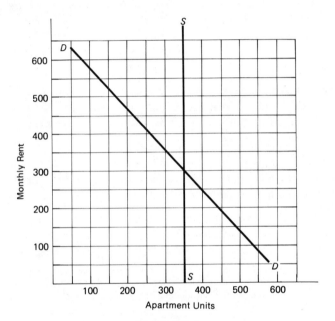

Figure 16-4

Suppose, first of all, that the rent control authorities have determined that rents should be lowered and have imposed a ceiling equal to 80 percent of the equilibrium price. The quantity of rental housing provided would, in the short run illustrated in Figure 16-4, *(increase / remain the same / decline)*, while the quantity demanded would *(increase / remain the same / decline)*. Additionally, the ceiling would *(provide incentives for / remove all incentives for)* landlords to increase the supply.

Now consider a 20 percent tax on rents collected by landlords. This policy would produce *(the same / a different)* equilibrium in the rental market in terms of quantity supplied in the short run. The rent paid would, meanwhile, *(climb / remain the same / fall)*, and a shortage of rental housing *(would / would not)* materialize. In the long run, though, the quantity supplied could fall along a sloped supply curve, and a shortage could thereby materialize.

300; remain the same; increase; remove all incentives for; the same; remain the same; would not

Economists make an explicit distinction between *financial assets* (money saved through some financial vehicle) and *physical assets* (real capital embodied in a stock of structures, equipment, inventories, and so forth). Grasping this distinction is essential to a sound understanding of how capital markets work to determine the rate of interest, otherwise known as the price of capital. Chapter 16 continues, therefore, by reviewing the definitions and economic roles of these two distinct assets.

The simplest view of financial capital is a picture of money—money which can be borrowed or lent. When you lend a quantity of money for a length of time, though, you usually expect to receive more than that quantity in return; i.e., you expect, and in fact have probably so contracted, to be paid something above and beyond the loan principal sometime in the future. Suppose, for example, that you were to agree today to lend somebody $1000 for a period of 1 year. You would do so only with the clear understanding that he or she would pay you more than $1000, say, $1100, in exactly one year's time. The extra $100 tacked onto the $1000 principal repayment is interest, and it translates in this simple case directly into an interest rate of 10 percent. To borrow money at this 10 percent interest rate means that it costs 10 cents per year for every dollar borrowed.

Clearly then, an **interest rate** is, in a very real sense, simply the price that must be paid by someone who wants to use somebody else's money for a specified period of time. It is, moreover, a price that is determined at least in part by the operation of a market for loanable funds. There are demanders in this market (those wanting to borrow money and willing to pay for that privilege), and there are suppliers (those with funds available for lending at a price). Whether lenders receive 5 percent per year, or 10 percent, or 15 percent depends upon the relative strengths of these two sets of economic actors.

The interest rate actually observed can, of course, depend on a large number of factors that are not easily captured in a simple supply-and-demand framework. The quoted rate might, for example, depend upon the degree of risk associated with a loan—the likelihood, as viewed by the lender, that the borrower might default on his or her obligation to repay. In general, the higher the risk, the higher the price—the higher the interest rate. If, in addition, inflation were rampant, then the purchasing power of the money to be returned at a later date would be diminished, and that should affect the price at which people would be willing to make loans. The higher the anticipated rate of inflation, the higher the price—again, the higher the interest rate.

Supply and demand are, nonetheless, at work in the determination of the rate of interest. We have seen that (potential) lenders work to generate the supply side—

the source of financial capital. But what of the demand side? The answer lies with those who want to invest in physical capital. Why? Because time is also a critical element in such investment.

If investors could somehow press a "dump" button on a piece of physical capital and make it instantaneously yield its entire flow of productive services in one enormous heap, then it would no longer be a capital good. It would, instead, be a consumption good. Investors could then pay for the "consumption capital," press the "dump" button, and sell its total product all in the same time period. They would not have to borrow any money to finance the operation (unless their product market turned out to be weaker than they had expected), and the complications of risk and inflation would be greatly diminished.

By way of contrast, the essence of physical capital is that it does not come equipped with a "dump" button; physical capital "pays off" very slowly. Despite this inherent delayed return, investors have to pay relatively quickly for any physical investment that they might want to undertake. In considering their investment options, therefore, they are forced to consider borrowing money to finance their plans, and so they are forced to consider the price of that money. In short, they become part of the demand side of a financial market simply by contemplating the investment opportunities offered to them by ownership of specific pieces of physical capital.

8. Consider an asset that will cost you $100, right now, to construct. If you construct it, there will be no payoff for 2 years, but this asset will pay you $121 2 years from now—nothing before that, and nothing after. This $121 is free of any incidental costs or expenses; it is the net return on your $100 outlay. The $121 return is safe; there is no uncertainty about its arrival. Notice that this capital asset has an annual rate of return of 10 percent. Ten percent is the annual interest rate at which a loan of $100 will "grow," with annual compounding of interest, into $121 in 2 years. The principal amount of $100 would earn $10 interest over the course of the first year. Left in the account as "extra principal," this interest would also earn interest so that $11 in total interest would be earned in the second year. The total value of the initial $100, measured at the end of year 2, would therefore be $121—$100 principal plus $21(= $10 + $11) in interest.

a. It should be clear that two dollar figures are involved: in the example, a cost figure of $100 today and a revenue figure of $121 just 2 years from today. An interest rate (10 percent annually in the example) "matches up" the two differing dollar figures, so the rate of return of a capital asset is best expressed as (*a dollar figure* / *an interest rate*).

b. If you had to borrow $100 to construct the asset of part **a** and could borrow this money at a cost of 5 percent annually, would you do so? (*yes* / *no*)

c. Would you borrow the money at 9 percent annually? (*yes* / *no*). At 11 percent annually? (*yes* / *no*)

---

a. an interest rate   **b.** yes (for you would be ahead of the game financially even after paying interest at 5 percent)   **c.** yes (for the same reason at 9 percent (*Remember:* There is no uncertainty about your $121 return.)); no (You would be out of pocket after paying interest at 11 percent.)

---

9. Suppose that you have money available to lend or to use in the purchase of some revenue-yielding asset. The market interest rate is 10 percent annually, but the borrowers in this market are of such good credit standing that the risk of any borrower's defaulting on his or her loan is virtually nonexistent. The owner of an asset such as the one described in question 8 (i.e., one guaranteeing a single return of $121 at the end of 2 years) offers to sell it to you.

a. If this asset were available for $90, would you buy it? (*yes* / *no*). If you did, then the interest rate that you would be earning on your outlay would be (*less than* / *more than*) 10 percent.

b. If the asset were available for $100, then it would be (*an unusually good buy* / *an unusually poor buy* / *as good as, but no better than, other available alternatives*).

c. Would you pay $102 for this asset? (*yes* / *no*). If you did, then the interest rate that you would be earning on your outlay would be (*less than* / *equal to* / *more than*) 10 percent.

---

a. yes; more than (actually 16 percent per year on the $90 that returns $121 in 2 years)   **b.** as good as, but no better than, other available alternatives   **c.** no; less than

---

10. a. Suppose that the market rate of interest is 4 percent annually instead of 10 percent. Would you now buy the asset of question 8 for $102, if you had the opportunity? (*yes* / *no*). If you did buy it, then the rate of return that you would be earning would be (*less than* / *equal to* / *greater than*) 4 percent.

b. Actually, with a market interest rate of 4 percent annually (i.e., if the return generally available for "investing" money capital were 4 percent per year), then the market price of this asset would stand at about $112 (more precisely, $111.85). Why? (Circle one.)

(1) Because $111.85 is the amount which, if lent out for 2 years at 4 percent annually, would "grow" to $121.

(2) Because the interest return or net productivity of this asset is 10 percent regardless of the amount of money laid out to build or buy it.

---

a. yes; more than   **b.** (1) (This asset's rate of return is 10 percent only if it can be bought or built for $100.)

To summarize, an asset's rate of return is an interest rate—a rate of return which can be computed from two pieces of information:

1. The amount it would cost to build or buy this asset
2. The net revenue which can be expected, along with the expected date(s) of its arrival (The term "net revenue" refers to revenue still remaining after any costs incurred in using the asset or collecting the revenue have been covered.)

Given this information, there is always one interest rate which indicates the rate of return.

Question 10 looked at a different, but related, question: What is the maximum amount that any potential investor should pay for a given asset? What is its present value? To reply, two pieces of information are again required:

1. As before, an accurate portrait of the stream of future *net* revenue which can be expected from the asset
2. The market interest rate

In question 10, therefore, the $100 asset yielding $121 just 2 years from now would have a present value of $100 if the market interest rate were 10 percent, but its present value would equal $111.85 if the market rate were 4 percent.

11. Suppose that you find that an asset's present value is different from its actual construction cost. What then? Suppose, in particular, that its actual cost is less than its present value. It *(would / would not)* then be profitable to borrow money to construct it. Why? Because this asset's rate of return would be *(less than / equal to / greater than)* the rate of interest.

If, on the other hand, its present value were less than its construction cost, then the asset *(would / would not)* be worth building. The market value of such an asset would be *(less than / equal to / greater than)* its construction cost, and its rate of return would be *(less than / equal to / greater than)* the rate of interest.

would; greater than; would not; less than; less than

12. a. Suppose that you own a piece of land which brings you net rental income (after allowing for maintenance cost, etc.) of $5000 yearly and that you expect this annual rental to continue well into the future. The present value of this land would be (circle one):

(1) $5000.

(2) the sum of all expected future receipts of $5000.

(3) the sum of all expected future annual receipts, each "discounted" to a present-value figure by means of the market interest rate.

b. Suppose the asset in part **a** is expected to yield $5000 each year into the indefinite future and thus represents a "perpetual-income stream." Each $5000 could then be thought of as the interest yield on a loan which has no maturity date (date for repayment of principal). What principal would have to be involved if its interest yield were $5000 annually and the interest rate were 4 percent annually?

$_____

c. There is a simple formula for computing the capitalized value of such perpetual-income assets. Write it down, and make sure the formula works for the case of part **b**. _____

_____

d. Is this formula consistent with the rule which holds that capitalized values are computed as the sum of the discounted values of all expected future revenues? (Circle one.)

(1) No—the perpetuity case has to be handled by means of a different formula because of the infinite number of expected future revenue items.

(2) Yes—this is a special case involving a constant net return into the indefinite future.

_____

a. (3)   b. 125,000   c. $V = \$N/i$, or $\$125,500 = \$5000/0.04$ d. (2)

13. a. You must decide whether asset A or asset B has the higher market value. Asset A promises to make four income payments of $1225 each at the end of years 1, 2, 3, and 4. Asset B promises to make five payments of $1000 each at the end of years 1, 2, 3, 4, and 5. The confidence with which payments can be expected is the same for both. The valuation rule to follow is to choose the asset which (circle one):

(1) has higher total income payments, regardless of the date on which these accrue.

(2) pays income for the longer period of time.

(3) pays off more quickly.

(4) yields the higher capitalized value, determined by discounting all income items by the market interest rate and then summing all these discounted values.

b. Do not try to value assets by what they would cost or did cost. Value them instead in terms of the future net revenues they are expected to generate in return, net of their cost, and discount these net revenues. The basic discounting formula is simple. Take any one item of expected future revenue, $\$N_t$. It is due to arrive t years from now. The market interest rate, expressed as a fraction (e.g., 5 percent = 5/100) is i. The present value of that expected future revenue item is $\$N_t/(1-i)^t$. The present values of assets A and B accordingly depend on the market interest rate. The higher this rate, the sharper the discounting knife. The further away in time any revenue item is, the more deeply it cuts. So the higher the interest rate, the more probable that asset (A / B) will have the higher discounted value.

---

a. (4) b. A (A and B have equal capitalized values when the interest rate is approximately 4.5 percent annually. At any lower rate, B has the higher value; at any higher rate, A has.)

---

14. Classical capital and interest theory suggests that interest rates will gradually fall over the long run as an economy grows and matures. As they do, the economy will gradually take up more "roundabout" methods of production (if you are hungry, you want things in a hurry; if you are rich, you can afford to wait). One example of a roundabout method would be a process involving a capital good which costs a lot to build and lasts for 50 to 100 years. Investors would have to wait a long time before they received the full payoff from such an investment.

Now consider a primitive example of roundaboutness. Assume that two alternative methods of producing 1 unit of some finished product exist. Both require the input of some labor now, but investors must wait until the finished product arrives or matures. Specifically, assume that method A requires 7 units of labor now and a delay of 2 years while method B requires only 5 units of labor now but a delay of 3 years. In this case, method B is the more roundabout because the waiting period is longer. Which method would be more attractive to investors, and thus producers? The answer to this question depends on the interest rate. Start with the case in which the market interest rate is 40 percent per year, and let the finished product be worth $10. Since this product accrues in the future (either 2 years or 3 years away), you must discount this $10 to get its present value. Discounted from 2 years ahead at the 40 percent rate, $10 is reduced to $5.11; discounted for 3 years, to $3.65. Suppose that labor costs 73 cents per unit. It makes no difference whether you use method A (hire 7 units of labor now at 73 cents each for a total cost of $5.11 and then wait 2 years) or method B (hire 5 units of labor now for a total cost of $3.65 and then wait 3 years). Either way, your payoff will be $10, and the return of your investment will be 40 percent—just the market rate.

Now suppose that the market rate is only 20 percent annually. Given the same input and output prices as before, both method A and method B would now be highly attractive. In both instances, their net productivity would still be 40 percent—twice the new market rate of return. But now raise the cost of the investment, which in our example means increasing the price of labor. Method A, which requires more labor than method B, will cease to be profitable (cease to earn the market rate of return), while method B is still profitable. At 20 percent interest, $10 discounts down to $6.95 for 2 years and $5.79 for 3 years.

If labor's price were $1 rather than 73 cents, however, it (would still / would not) pay to spend $7 (method A) to get a return with a present value of $6.95. It (would still / would not) pay to spend $5 (method B) to get a return with a present value of $5.79.

This illustrates the classical argument: A gradual fall in interest rates will prompt society to move from the less roundabout method (A) to the more roundabout one (B).

---

would not; would still

---

15. To summarize, suppose that market interest rates rise. The present value of any sum expected at some date in the future (would therefore rise / would nonetheless remain unchanged / would therefore fall). If, on the other hand, the interest rate should fall, then the present value of any asset would (rise / remain unchanged / fall). In both cases, of course, the future stream of income must be fixed to provide a suitable benchmark for comparison; if the powers which alter the interest rate also alter the income generated by an asset, then all bets are off.

---

would therefore fall; rise

This entire discussion of present value leads directly to the problem of determining the interest rate. Interest is the income received by people who supply financial capital (money) to borrowers, of course, but it is more instructive at this point to begin thinking of the interest rate as a price determined by the demand for loanable money and the supply of such money. What are the factors lying behind the demand curve and the supply curve for money? It has already been suggested that business firms considering various investment projects (the building of capital goods) are the demanders of financial capital. Their decisions to borrow will be influenced by the interest rate because some projects will be worth undertaking at low interest rates and not worth undertaking at high ones. Why? Because the rate of return of such projects (and remember that this return is expressed as an interest rate) will lie below a high market interest rate and above a low market interest rate. Computation of the rates of return of various possible investment projects must therefore lie behind the demand curve for loanable money.

The suppliers of lendable funds are, by way of contrast, people who save. They offer money to banks and other financial intermediaries for the promise of interest earnings on their saving, and so it is these folks who offer investors the opportunity of investment financing.

Having characterized both sides of the market for funds, a simplified classical version of capital and interest theory is now accessible. The three panels of Figure 16-5 illustrate its content. Note that it is the *real* interest rate (a percentage figure per annum) that is measured vertically on all three panels.

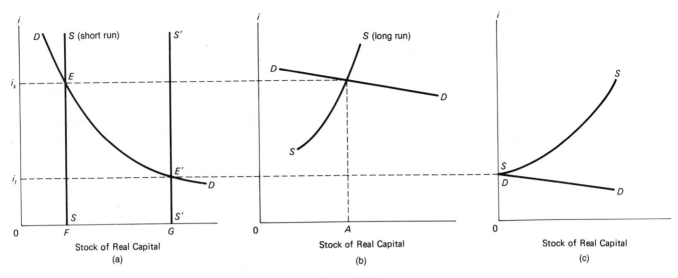

Figure 16-5

Panel (a) corresponds to Figure 16-5 in the text. It is assumed in both that all capital goods are identical so that their sum is a meaningful total denominated in physical units. The SS line in panel (a) indicates the economy's total stock of capital at some particular point in time. It stands for some figure such as 400 units of capital. The supply schedule SS is drawn vertically because the present capital stock is fixed at 400 units regardless of the real interest rate. Panel (a) depicts, quite simply, a situation in which there is not enough time to adjust the size of the existing capital stock; it is fixed at 400 units and will remain 400 units whether the interest rate is 2 percent, 10 percent, or any other figure.

The DD curve in panel (a) is the "demand" of business firms for capital goods. It intersects SS at point E, indicating an interest rate of i_s. To grasp the meaning of the DD curve, suppose that i_s indicates an interest rate of 8 percent. That being the case, then panel (a) shows that DD intersects SS at the 8 percent level. Why? Because firms estimate that the last (or marginal) units of that 400-unit capital stock have a rate of return of 8 percent. This is an estimate which is based on the cost of producing more capital goods *and* on the present value of the estimated net revenues that capital goods are expected to generate.

16. Suppose, now, that the situation is a little different. Suppose, in particular, that business firms are more optimistic about the stream of future returns that capital would likely generate with the capital stock at 400. Let them, in fact, believe that the last units of a 400-unit stock have a net productivity of 10 percent. With a market interest rate of 8 percent, these businesses would want to employ *(more than / just / less than)* 400 units of capital. Why? Because the rate of return of the next unit of capital would be greater than the 8 percent cost of borrowing. The interest rate would have to rise to 10 percent before their disposition to use more capital would disappear. That is to say, if business firms were more optimistic about the net productivity of capital, then the DD curve in panel (a) would lie (circle one):

(1) farther to the right than originally indicated.

(2) just where it is now.

(3) farther to the left than originally indicated.

It would intersect the SS curve at a point indicating an equilibrium interest rate of *(less than / exactly / more than)* 8 percent.

---
more than; (1); more than

17. Given the stock of capital indicated in panel (a) of Figure 16-5, the equilibrium, *short-run* interest rate in this economy is i_s. People in this economy are, however, still saving money, and they are willing to have this money be lent to business investors. The SS curve in panel (b) illustrates this situation. Its southwest-to-northeast direction emphatically depicts an underlying assumption that people would save and therefore offer more to borrowers if the interest rate were increased.

There is, of course, also a demand for this money. Business firms are willing to pay 8 percent on borrowed money because there are still some projects in which new capital goods (additions to the present total stock) would have a rate of return equal to 8 percent. Of course, large additions to the capital stock would lower its rate of return because of diminishing returns, but that comes later. For the time being, business firms are willing to borrow (in each period of time) the amount of money indicated by 0A in panel (b) at 8 percent because they think there is still useful employment for this amount of money at this rate.

Stop for a moment to consider the implications of the shape of curve DD in panel (b). It is drawn almost flat at rates even a little above 8 percent; the slope suggests that there are few potential borrowers who see projects with a payoff in excess of 8 percent. If the rate were to drop a bit below 8 percent, however, a substantial increase in the quantity of money capital demanded would be displayed; there must be plenty of unexploited projects with rates of return just slightly below 8 percent.

a. Distance 0A in panel (b) indicates, per period of time (circle one):

(1) the number of units of capital to be added to the capital stock.

(2) nothing whatsoever with respect to the capital stock.

(3) money that will be spent on construction of new units to be added to the capital stock.

b. As time goes by, then, the stock of capital goods will (fall / remain constant / increase). In terms of panel (a), the vertical SS curve will (move to the left from F toward 0 / remain in the same spot / move to the right from F toward G), and the interest rate will (fall / remain constant / increase).

This rightward movement of SS means that more and more homogeneous capital units are being built. The law of diminishing returns therefore applies (as long as there are no technological changes or large population influxes), and it causes the rate of return to capital to fall. Business firms will no longer pay 8 percent for money because there are no capital projects left that return 8 percent. In terms of panel (b), the DD curve should (fall / rise).

This shift in DD lowers the equilibrium interest rate and thereby depresses the public's disposition to save. At rates below i_s, in particular, the amount saved (and loaned) falls so much that, at a sufficiently low rate, saving collapses to zero. This point of all consumption is shown in panel (c) because SS cuts the vertical axis at i_l.

c. The classical theory of capital holds that the process of accumulation can come to an end after a sufficiently long period of time and a sufficient increase in the capital stock. In terms of panel (a) of Figure 16-5, the economy's capital stock must increase to the level indicated by _____ with an interest rate equal to _____ for this to be achieved.

In terms of panel (c), the DD curve would then begin at interest rate i_l because (circle one):

(1) there are no more projects worth undertaking at i_l.

(2) people will supply money only at rates below i_l.

---

a. (3) **b.** increase; move to the right from F toward G; fall; fall **c.** 0G; i_l; (1)

18. A number of qualifications must be attached to the classical theory of capital and interest to bring its structure and results into accord with contemporary reality.

a. For example, it is doubtful that people's consumption-saving decisions are greatly influenced by the level of the interest rate. At least, those decisions do not seem to be altered by moderate changes in the interest that they earn by saving.

Suppose that the decision to save out of income is unresponsive to any change in the interest rate. This would affect the (DD / SS) curve in panel (b) of Figure 16-5; it would, in fact, become a (vertical / horizontal / diagonal) line.

b. If real and money incomes were to rise gradually over time, then people could and in fact would save more money out of their incomes. This would affect the (DD / SS) curve in panel (b), shifting that curve to the (right / left).

c. Any potential investor trying to compute the income accruing to any proposed capital project must look into the future, and the future is always uncertain. Investors must, nonetheless, make their own best guesses about the future when thinking about borrowing money to finance a project. In the process of deciding whether or not to undertake the project, therefore, all investors must recognize that their best guesses might turn out to be overly optimistic. As a result, the estimated rate of return used in their decisions should be (reduced below / hiked above) their best guesses to reflect a hedge against the uncertainty. It is conservative to (cut down / increase) revenue estimates to allow for uncertainty, making it (more / less) likely that any specific project might be undertaken.

d. Estimates of likely rates of return are influenced also by a quite different factor: the climate of optimism or pessimism. If business firms, looking into the uncertain future with respect to projected capital plans, suddenly become more pessimistic, then their increased pessimism should shift the (DD / SS) curve in panel (b) to the (right / left).

Similarly, if lenders suddenly become more pessimistic about the likelihood that borrowers will be able to make good on their borrowing obligations, then the (DD / SS) curve in panel (b) would shift to the (right / left).

e. The rate of return to capital may be altered by technological change. Improved technology should (increase / decrease) capital's return. In panel (b) of Figure 16-5, this sort of technological change would shift the (DD / SS) curve to the (right / left).

Referring now to Figure 16-6, let S_1S_1 represent the initial short-run supply of capital, S_LS_L represent the long-run supply of capital, and DD represent the initial demand for capital; suppose, as well, that the short-run equilibrium is initially at point E_1. Now assume, for the sake of argument, that every increase in the supply of capital over time is accompanied by a technological advance that preserves the rate of interest. The long-run equilibrium rate of interest would now be _____ percent instead of _____ percent, and the long-run equilibrium stock of capital would be (higher / lower) than it would have been otherwise. Point (E_1 / E^* / E^{**}) would represent this long-run equilibrium. Draw a demand curve in Figure 16-6 that supports this equilibrium. With technological change, then, capital (deepening / widening) would continue further despite the higher long-run rate of interest.

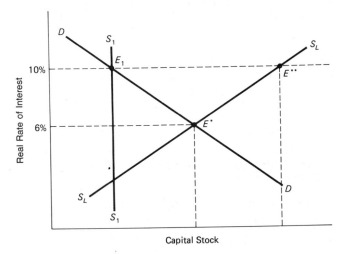

Figure 16-6

It is interesting to note that this is apparently what has been happening in the United States. Despite the tendency illustrated in panel (b) of Figure 16-5 for interest rates to (rise / remain constant / fall) over time, real interest rates in the United States have tended to (rise / remain constant / fall) over much of our recent history.

f. Inflation plays an important role in the determination of interest rates. Investment and lending decisions depend, in particular, upon the (natural / real / nominal) rate of interest. The equation that relates nominal and real rates is:

Nominal rate = real rate + _____

This equation explains why, in the face of 18 percent nominal interest rates and 16 percent inflation, investors can behave as if the real interest rate were really 2 percent.

g. Lenders also face uncertainties when they lend money. As a result, they require risk premiums in the interest rates that they charge; these premiums are derived from:

(1) _____

(2) _____

a. SS; vertical **b.** SS; right **c.** reduced below; cut down; less **d.** DD; left; SS; left. **e.** increase; DD; right; 10; 6; higher; E^{**} (Draw a downward-sloping demand curve through E^{**}.) ; deepening; fall; remain constant **f.** real; rate of inflation **g. (1)** the risk of default **(2)** their own aversion to risk

Focusing now on the concept of profit, classical economic theory identified three general types of inputs: land (resources), labor, and capital. If that were all there is to it, then where would profit fit into the picture? The remainder of this chapter will focus on this question.

19. Suppose that you run a roadside fruit and vegetable stand, situated on your own land. You would, typically, describe your net income as "profit." Part of that income should, however, properly be considered (rent / interest) earned by your land, while another part should be listed as (wages / profit) for the labor which you have supplied.

Similarly, it is possible to think of at least part of a corporation's earnings as interest on money which the shareholders put up. If you were self-employed, the parts of your income which you might call "profit" but which could fit into one of the other three categories might also be called ("implicit" / "unearned" / "surplus") wages, interest, or (income / rent / surplus).

rent; wages; "implicit"; rent

If there are some parts of profit which cannot be converted into implicit wages, implicit rent, or implicit interest in situations other than perfect competition, then it is necessary to answer another question: What useful function is performed or undertaken by the individual who receives a profit? Profit is the reward for doing what? There are, in response to this rather fundamental question, many different viewpoints.

20. a. One, associated at its inception with economist Frank Knight, views profit as the return for dealing with unavoidable (scarcity / competition among self-employed factors / entrepreneurship / uncertainty). Profit, or at least part of profit, is the reward society gives to those who shoulder the burden of uncertainty successfully. The only circumstances in which the profit-or-loss uncertainty would not exist would be those of perfect competition, but the conditions of perfect competition are (a goal toward which we should strive / unlikely to be attained / quite unattainable).

Three types of risk caused by this uncertainty were identified by Knight. List them in the following blanks:

(1) _____

(2) _____

(3) _____

b. The positive side to the risk of trying to exploit a new technology or other innovation is the monopoly power that success can bring. The power to control the price and the size of the market might be fleeting, but it is nonetheless real. In his work, Joseph Schumpeter argued that innovation lay at the very heart of productive capitalism and that it was the real justification for a "profits system." He felt that most of the gains in real income that have accrued under capitalism have come not from more careful allocation of a given stock of resources but from the creation of new goods and new productive techniques.

Innovation, in the Schumpeterian view, is a risky and uncertain business, and the majority of would-be innovators (fail / succeed). In this Schumpeterian view, situations of monopoly and of innovation are (inextricably linked / completely separate). A firm may be in a monopolistic position, but that position may have resulted entirely from successful innovation. Schumpeter thought that policymakers should be cautious in their opposition to monopoly; he was afraid that policies which are too harsh might destroy the very incentive to innovate upon which truly significant gains in real income depend. Schumpeter thought that most monopoly situations acquired through innovation are, in due course, toppled by other successful innovations originating elsewhere—producing what he called "the process of creative destruction."

---

a. uncertainty; quite unattainable **(1)** pure risk **(2)** the risk of bankruptcy or default **(3)** the risk of innovation and/or enterprise **b.** fail; inextricably linked

---

21. The monopoly view of profits is complicated by the fact that a genuine "monopoly return" may at the same time be a legitimate rent or interest return. Suppose that the original monopolist in a particular situation has an asset which, for some reason, is protected against competitive inroads. Such a monopolist would be earning a large monopoly return. Now suppose that this monopolist sells this asset at its full capitalized value (i.e., the value established by its total discounted future earnings). The purchaser must charge (the same price as / a higher price than / a lower price than) the original monopolist in order to receive (the normal competitive return / a monopoly return) on his or her money.

---

the same price as; the normal competitive return

To summarize, then, many sources of profits have been identified. One source embraces the implicit rents, wages, and interest payments collected by an entrepreneur or a major corporation in the course of doing business. The second source identifies profits as the reward for bearing risk—risk associated with the possibility of falling flat on your face (default), risk associated with the business cycle as you see it, and risk associated with undertaking an innovative project. Finally, profit can be the return to monopoly power, derived from natural scarcities, temporary scarcities produced by innovation, or contrived scarcities. Some of these sources are laudable, but others are the cause for some concern.

REVIEW CONCEPTS

1. Economic rent is the return paid to a specialized factor available in fixed supply. Payment of this rent is a cost of production, but it does not carry a corresponding social (opportunity) cost because the factor has no alternative and competing use. Efficient taxation capitalizes on (perfectly) inelastic supply because it causes no distortion in either the quantity supplied or the price paid *by the employer;* only the supplier bears the burden. Ramsey taxes generalize this notion to focus attention on factors displaying relatively inelastic supply schedules; they thereby minimize their inefficiency.

2. Common property resources are generally scarce, but rents are frequently uncollected. The "tragedy of the commons" analysis then applies.

3. Physical capital is the result of deferred consumption which yields a positive return by adding to future production potential. The rate of return to capital is a percentage computed from the ratio of net annual receipts and the dollar value of capital.

4. Present value is the value today of a stream of future returns. If these (net) returns are indexed by N_t and i represents an interest rate, then

$$V = \frac{N_1}{1+i} + \frac{N_2}{(1+i)^2} + \cdots + \frac{N_t}{(1+i)^t} + \cdots$$

If the asset has perpetual life, and if $N_t = N$, then

$$V = N/i$$

The higher the interest rate i, the lower the present value V in either case.

5. The derived demand for capital comes from its marginal product reflected by present value. High interest rates reduce the number of capital investment projects with positive present values and thus the demand for (new) capital. Low interest rates do the opposite, thereby encouraging capital-intensive investment.

6. The supply of funds necessary to finance investment in physical capital is generated by deferred-consumption saving.

7. Acceptance of the supply-and-demand structure of classical capital theory is subject to qualifications which relate to technological change, uncertainty and risk, inflation, and macroeconomic fluctuation.

8. The real rate of interest is equal to the nominal rate reduced by the rate of inflation.

9. Profits are revenues less costs, and they accrue to many owned, non-labor factors of production in the form of implicit rents. They can also represent rewards for risk taking and monopoly rents derived from continued scarcity.

QUIZ: Multiple Choice

1. Suppose that land is fixed in total supply but has many alternative uses (one of which is tobacco production). A 50 percent tax on the rental price of any land used for tobacco production would result in:
(1) a 50 percent increase in the rent which tobacco producers must pay.
(2) a 50 percent decrease in the rent paid by users of tobacco land.
(3) a 50 percent decrease in the rent received (net) by owners of such land.
(4) no change in the amount of rent paid or received.
(5) none of these consequences.

2. If supply were perfectly inelastic with respect to price, and if total demand were to decline, then:
(1) the quantity supplied would not fall, and price would fall more than it otherwise would.
(2) the quantity supplied would not fall, and price would fall less than it otherwise would.
(3) the quantity supplied would fall, and price would fall more than it otherwise would.
(4) the quantity supplied would fall, and price would fall less than it otherwise would.
(5) none of these results would necessarily occur.

3. If a productive input had only one opportunity for employment (i.e., if there were only one commodity it could help to produce), then the price paid to it:
(1) would tend to fall below the normal competitive level, because of the absence of competitive bidding.
(2) would be a cost to each of its separate users, but not a cost to the whole community or society.
(3) should not be counted as a cost by each of its separate users, although it would still be a cost to the whole community or society.
(4) would be a cost both to its separate users and to the whole community or society.
(5) would not be a cost either to its separate users or to the whole community.

4. It would be correct to say that economic rent is not a cost of production because:
(1) it is not a payment to a factor of production that actually makes a contribution to the output of finished goods.
(2) the suppliers of the input in question can receive the same price for employment in one occupation as they can in another.
(3) the rent payment in question is really a payment for buildings or improvements to the land, not for the use of the land itself.
(4) when this factor is used for the production of good A (e.g.), its employment does not entail any sacrifice of any other good B.
(5) competition among the suppliers will continually tend to push the price of this factor toward zero.

5. Economic analysis suggests that:
(1) society's resources cannot be allocated properly into employment unless competitive rent payments are made.
(2) rental payments to factors with relatively price-elastic supply should be taxed more heavily.
(3) economic rent does not enter into the cost of production.
(4) the allocation of resources can be distorted if certain input supplies are inelastic with respect to price.
(5) rental payments to factors with relatively price-inelastic supply should be taxed more heavily.

6. Ramsey taxes are:
(1) higher for relatively inelastically demanded goods.
(2) frequently criticized on equity grounds because necessities tend to be inelastically demanded.
(3) lower for relatively elastically supplied goods.
(4) computed to simultaneously minimize the loss in consumer surplus and maximize tax revenue.
(5) all the above.

7. The "tragedy of the commons" is, among the following list of examples, best illustrated by:
(1) the proliferation of fast-food hamburger joints.
(2) the overfishing of the Georges Bank.
(3) the development of a shopping center on the town commons.
(4) the poisoning of Harvard students on the "Commons."
(5) the overpricing of sweatshirts at the Yale "Co-op."

8. An asset's present value is:
(1) its original cost plus an estimate of maintenance expense throughout its lifetime.
(2) the same thing as its original cost.
(3) the sum of all its discounted net earnings.
(4) the sum of all its net earnings, without discounting.
(5) the rate of interest at which the asset would just become worth buying or building.

9. If the rate of return of any capital asset were to be computed, several items of information would be needed. Which among the following would not be required?
(1) The original cost of purchasing or constructing the asset.
(2) The means of financing the original purchase.
(3) The estimated maintenance or operating cost that must be paid in order to keep the asset in satisfactory operating (revenue-earning) condition throughout its life.
(4) The estimated revenue that the asset will produce throughout its lifetime.
(5) The degree of "riskiness" surrounding estimated revenue, i.e., the degree of uncertainty about future revenues.

10. According to the classical theory, which of the following accurately describes the role played by the law of diminishing returns in the determination of interest rates?
(1) As capital goods accumulate relative to the supplies of land and labor, the rate of return of new additions to the capital stock must fall.
(2) The cost of producing additional capital goods must necessarily increase (in the absence of innovation).
(3) A steady increase in output must lower the price of a consumer good and thus lower the return to capital.
(4) The classical theory explains why innovation cannot continually check the long-run tendency of the interest rate to fall.
(5) The classical theory must be used if the rate of return of any capital good is to be computed.

11. In classical investment theory, the rate of interest is determined by:
(1) the estimated rate of return to various capital projects.
(2) the extent to which the public wishes to use the income it receives for consumption.
(3) both the estimated rate of return to various capital projects and the extent to which the public wishes to use the income it receives for consumption.
(4) the estimated rate of return to various capital projects and the size of the capital stock.
(5) the estimated rate of return to various capital projects and the rate of technological development.

12. Classical investment theory holds that there should be:
(1) a tendency toward a long-run equilibrium in which the market interest rate would be zero.
(2) a tendency toward a long-run equilibrium in which gross investment would be constantly falling.
(3) a tendency toward a long-run equilibrium in which net investment would be maintained at a steady and nonzero rate.
(4) a tendency toward a long-run equilibrium in which saving out of income would be zero.
(5) no tendency toward any sort of long-run equilibrium.

13. The classical theory described in question 12 neglected the fact that:
(1) the amount saved out of income might be influenced by the interest rate.
(2) it is necessary to discount future items of income in order to establish their present value.
(3) while the interest rate may approach zero, it cannot actually reach zero.
(4) technological change might continually increase the rate of return to capital.
(5) people are typically impatient to consume now, rather than accumulate for future consumption.

14. A certain asset is expected to yield a steady net income (i.e., after allowing for all costs or expenses) of $100 annually from now until eternity. If the market rate of interest were 8 percent per year, then the market value of this asset should be:
(1) $800.
(2) $1250.
(3) $8000.
(4) $10,000.
(5) infinity.

15. If the market rate of interest rises, other things equal, then the present value of any given capital asset should:
(1) rise; and the more the asset's expected revenues extend far into the future, the more it will rise.
(2) rise; and the more the asset's expected revenues accrue in the immediate rather than the remote future, the more it will rise.
(3) fall; and the more the asset's expected revenues extend far into the future, the more it will fall.
(4) fall; and the more the asset's expected revenues accrue in the immediate rather than the remote future, the more it will fall.
(5) not be changed at all.

16. The present discounted value of $500 payable 1 year from now, at a market interest rate of 9 percent annually, is:
(1) $545.
(2) $500.
(3) a little more than $455 but less than $500.
(4) $455.
(5) a little less than $455.

17. Implicit in any discussion of capital and interest is a rule for the proper method of determining the worth, or value, of any asset. This rule instructs us to:
(1) value assets according to the original cost of construction or purchase, deducting from this cost figure an appropriate depreciation figure to arrive at present value.
(2) value assets according to the net revenue they are expected to yield in the future.
(3) value assets according to the discounted sum of the net revenue that they are expected to yield in the future.
(4) determine the dollar figure which represents the net productivity of the asset and then discount that net productivity figure by means of the interest rate.
(5) do none of the preceding.

18. If market interest rates generally fall, then the present value of any capital asset should:
(1) fall, since lower interest rates indicate that revenue amounts accruing at any future date are now given a higher present value.

(2) fall, since lower interest rates indicate that revenue amounts accruing at any future date are now given a lower present value.
(3) remain unchanged, unless relevant cost or revenue factors thereby changed.
(4) rise, because lower interest rates indicate that revenue amounts accruing at any future date are now given a lower present value.
(5) rise, because lower interest rates indicate that revenue amounts accruing at any future date are now given a higher present value.

19. Which alternative in question 17 would be correct had the question referred to the asset's rate of return instead of its present value?
(1) .
(2) .
(3) .
(4) .
(5) .

20. In a period of deflation (i.e., of generally falling prices), the "real" rate of interest obtained by any lender:
(1) will exceed the nominal rate.
(2) will become a negative figure.
(3) will fall below the stated rate, although not to the extent of becoming a negative figure.
(4) will become a meaningless, incalculable figure.
(5) will exceed the rate of unemployment.

21. The rate of return to any capital good could reasonably be described as:
(1) the rate of interest at which the capital good would just be worth buying or building, i.e., the rate of interest for which the present value of anticipated revenues would exactly match the present value of anticipated costs.
(2) the dollar amount of profit that would accrue if that capital good were bought or built.
(3) the same thing as the market rate of interest.
(4) the physical increase in output (as distinct from the money value) that would accrue if that capital good were bought or built.
(5) the percentage figure obtained by adding up all net revenues that would accrue from the capital good and dividing this total by its cost.

22. If business firms generally became more optimistic regarding the revenues that would accrue from the investment projects that they are planning, then the computed rate of return to that capital:
(1) would increase, since revenues enter into the computation of the rate of return.
(2) would decrease, since the rate of return is an interest rate, and the interest rate goes inversely to the value of the investment project.
(3) would not change, since the rate of return is governed by technical considerations, not by expected revenues.
(4) would probably fall, although there is a special case in which it would rise.
(5) may do any of the above, since the effect of a change in expected revenues upon the rate of return is unpredictable.

23. In the view of Frank H. Knight, profit should be regarded primarily as:
(1) the return received by an entrepreneur who faces a downward-sloping demand curve for the product in question and who seeks maximum profit in pricing that product.
(2) essentially a random distribution of profit among business firms—i.e., a distribution settled by chance, over which no firm has any control.
(3) the return received for activity in which some element of uncertainty is involved.
(4) only the return received by someone who engages in innovation.
(5) none of the preceding descriptions.

SUGGESTED ANSWERS TO QUESTIONS IN THE TEXT: Chapter 16

1. Inelastic supply means that the price is determined where demand matches that supply. If the price of some product (X) employing a factor (A) of fixed supply is high (because of high demand for X), then the derived demand for A is high; its price is thus high, determined by the price of X. Should the supply of A increase, though, its price should fall along the given derived demand curve, reducing the cost of employing A in the production of X, and thereby allowing the price of X to fall.

2. They would pay it—after swearing at the referees.

3. Think of any production process that proceeds in steps; there are, e.g., a lot of intermediate products in an automobile.

4. Consider a piece of capital. Its net dollar return per year per dollar invested is its rate of return. Its rental price would be the price charged by an owner to someone who wanted to use it for a period of time, say, a year. The rate of interest is the price of using money for a period of time, say, a year. If capital markets work perfectly, these are all the same in equilibrium.

5. a. The interest rate would climb because the derived demand curve would shift up; move along the supply curve.
b. The interest rate would climb because the supply curve would shift in; move along the demand curve.
c. The interest rate received by lenders would fall, but the rate of return to capital (before taxes are paid) would climb. See Figure TQ16-1.

Figure TQ16-1

6. **a.** Zero pure economic profit here, so it must be normal return paid to capital.
   b. Reward for risk (default during downturns; also pure risk because the cycles are unavoidable).
   c. Reward for risk (innovation; also some monopoly rent for a short time).
   d. Implicit rent paid for the land.

7. Innovation might increase the interest rate in the short run, but it would decline as the supply shifted out—new capital embodying the new technology. High government debt brings the long-run SS curve in, making the long-run interest rate higher and reducing the rate of capital accumulation even in the short run.

8. Play with the $PV = N/i$ formula. It comes from an infinite geometric series.

9. Consult Figure TQ16-2. Distance CB represents overuse—traffic jams, excessive automobile emissions, etc. There is a social cost to this congestion. The appropriate toll during the congested period is $0.10 per vehicle-mile (distance CE). The cost of using the highway during the peak period would then reflect its scarcity. People who have to use the highway during the peak time for reasons worth, on the margin, more than $0.10 per vehicle-mile would be helped; others would be hurt—overpaying to use the highway or adjusting the timing of their travel.

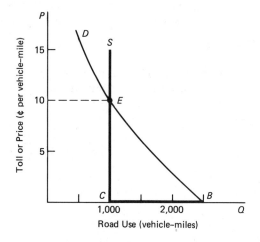

Figure TQ16-2

10. The general present-value equation, with $1/(1 + i) = K$, reads

$$V = \$NK + \$NK^2 + \cdots$$
$$= \$NK\{1 + K + K^2 + \cdots\}$$
$$= \$NK/(1 - K)$$
$$= \$N[1/(1 + i)]/[(1 + i - 1)/(1 + i)]$$
$$= \$N/i$$

For the lottery payoff, then,

$$V = \frac{\$5000}{0.06} = \$83{,}333.33$$

CHAPTER 17

MARKETS AND ECONOMIC EFFICIENCY

Part Four of the text will lead you through some of the thorniest topics of economic analysis. It begins in Chapter 17 with a discussion of the efficiency properties of an economic system that determines all prices and wages simultaneously. Previous chapters have shown that individual competitive markets lead to efficient solutions of the production question when they are allowed to operate without interference and without any influence from beyond their boundaries, i.e., under the partial-equilibrium assumption that all other prices and quantities in the surrounding economy are fixed and unchanging. But what about a general-equilibrium system in which the effects of production decisions in one market on the pricing and production decisions in another market are explicitly considered and allowed to feed back into the original decision? Can anything be said about efficiency, or lack thereof, in such a general-equilibrium setting?

In addition to gleaning some understanding of the qualifications that must be placed upon an economy to ensure that the answer to the last question is "Yes, efficiency is achieved," your work in this chapter will enable you to accomplish the following objectives.

LEARNING OBJECTIVES

1. Review the seven microeconomic steps, covered in previous chapters, with which competitive markets solve the simultaneous questions of *what*, *how*, and *for whom*.

2. Describe the circular pattern of interdependence between product and input markets, showing clearly the role played by households and businesses.

3. Describe in detail how the myopic actions of individuals and firms in a perfectly competitive economy would lead to the equality of marginal (social) cost, marginal utility, and price for every good at every firm and for every individual; i.e., illustrate the origins of the "first theorem of welfare economics" (which states that competitive economies achieve allocative efficiency).

4. List the conditions which must be satisfied before the existence of a competitive general equilibrium can be demonstrated, and illustrate the resulting efficiency in terms of a utility-possibility frontier.

5. Show how each of the qualifications listed in objective 4 leads to concern about the ability of the invisible hand to promote efficiency under a laissez-faire economic policy.

6. Describe the distributional-equity potential of perfectly competitive market economies.

Microeconomic analysis is, in its simplest form, conducted in partial equilibrium. Individuals maximize utility given limited income, product prices, and a pattern of tastes. Firms maximize profits given technology, some type of demand structure, and input prices. The next step toward generalization is to allow all individuals and firms to interact and thereby jointly determine an entire set of prices and quantities which clear a multitude of markets simultaneously. It is a step toward understanding the interdependence of interacting markets of all sorts (input markets interacting with other input markets, product markets interacting with other product markets, and input markets interacting with product markets), but it is also more than that. It is an analysis which speaks to the conditions which guarantee a Pareto notion of efficiency—that nobody can be made better off without hurting somebody else. It is an analysis which thereby identifies economic circumstances that undermine efficiency, and so it is an analysis which need not forget its heart; it can worry about equity as it does about efficiency, and it can fully explore the inherent tradeoff between the two.

1. a. In the spaces provided, list the seven steps with which an economy solves its *what, how,* and *for whom* questions. Indicate, as well, what is held constant in the usual partial-equilibrium analysis of each step.

(1) _____

_____

(2) _____

_____

(3) _____

_____

(4) _____

_____

(5) _____

_____

(6) _____

_____

(7) _____

_____

These issues, all involving the behavior of single markets, households, or firms, have all been subjected to partial-equilibrium analysis. They have, thus far, been explored under the assumption that *(all people are equal / all other things are equal / all government policies are equal)*.

b. It is not possible simply to build a general-equilibrium model of an entire economy by "tacking" partial-equilibrium models of individual sectors or markets together. If, for example, there were only three goods in an economy, X, Y, and Z, you could not lump supply-demand analyses of the three goods together and expect to produce an accurate picture of the entire economy. Why not? The reason lies in the "other things being equal" approach of partial-equilibrium models.

The demand curve for good X, for example, would be drawn as a function of the price of X given the assumption that all the other factors that might influence the demand for X (e.g., incomes, the price of Y, etc.) were held constant. But that need not be the case. If the price of Y were to change, or the level of consumers' incomes were to change, then the demand curve for X might shift to a new position.

Consider a specific illustration with two commodities: butter and margarine. Suppose that the markets for both are initially in equilibrium. Now let a technical development sharply reduce the cost of producing margarine. What would happen? In terms of supply and demand, we would expect to see the supply curve for margarine shift *(down / up)*, thereby establishing a new and *(higher / lower)* equilibrium price for margarine. The demand curve for butter, unaffected up to this point, was drawn *given the initial price of margarine*. Since the two goods are substitutes, though, the adjustment in the price of margarine just noted should make the demand curve for butter shift *(to the left / to the right)*, thereby producing a new and *(higher / lower)* price for butter. The demand curve for margarine, unaffected up to this point, was drawn *given the initial price of butter*, so it would now have to shift. This process would continue until some final, mutually compatible pair of prices was achieved.

The point of all this is simply that using ordinary supply-and-demand models to examine the economic consequence of some change in economic circumstance deliberately ignores the impact which that change might have on the equilibrium prices and quantities of other goods. Moreover, it deliberately ignores the feedback effects that changes in those equilibria might have on the original market. Sometimes the omissions make no difference, but sometimes they do.

a. (1) Competitive supply and demand schedules determine equilibrium in individual markets given other prices and incomes. **(2)** Marginal utility analysis determines individual demand curves given other prices and incomes. **(3)** Marginal cost curves determine competitive supply curves given technology reflected by production functions and the prices of inputs. **(4)** Firms operate to maximize profits given marginal revenue product curves (revenue side) and marginal cost curves (cost side). **(5)** Marginal revenue products determine derived curves for inputs given other input employment levels and output prices. **(6)** Supply schedules for inputs interact with derived demand curves to determine input prices, holding everything else fixed. **(7)** Factor prices are major determinants of the distribution of income, holding resource endowments fixed. all other things are equal **b.** down; lower; to the left; lower

2. a. General-equilibrium theory is cast within the special case of perfect competition because (more than one may be correct):

(1) it has special significance with respect to the "best" use of a given but limited stock of resources or inputs.

(2) with only a few monopoly exceptions, the structure of the real-life American economy corresponds reasonably well to the requirements of perfect competition.

(3) the American economy is highly "competitive" in many senses even though it does not completely satisfy the structural requirements of pure competition. This prompts some economists to think that analysis built as though perfect competition applied can still give useful results (in some cases) when applied to the American economy.

b. Perfect competition has special significance from a "welfare" standpoint. If we take as given the stock of resources, the conditions of their ownership, and the state of technology, then the set of prices which would emerge under perfect competition would yield (pick one):

(1) the most efficient allocation of all such resources among their various possible allocations.

(2) the most desirable distribution of income among the people who make up the population in question.

c. Table 17-1 is intended to illustrate the meaning of "efficient resource allocation." It assumes that the economy produces only three goods, X, Y, and Z. A general equilibrium has been reached with the quantities recorded on line 1 being supported in that equilibrium by the prices recorded on line 3.

Table 17-1

	X	Y	Z
1. Total quantities of goods produced and bought	3,000	4,000	5,000
2. Marginal utilities of goods for a typical consumer	100	50	200
3. Price of good	$2	$1	$4
4. Marginal cost of good	$2	$1	$4

Given the X, Y, and Z prices on line 3, the "typical consumer" (has / has not / may or may not have) reached his or her maximum-satisfaction position. Why? Because the ratios of marginal utility to price are all equal to _____ (a numerical answer is possible). If supplying firms operate under conditions of perfect competition, then, with prices as on line 3 and marginal costs as on line 4, they (have / have not) reached maximum-profit positions. Why? Because the prices of all three goods equal their _____.

Note the general-equilibrium quality of this situation. Consumers reach maximum-satisfaction positions by juggling their X, Y, and Z purchases. Producers adjust the level of their marginal costs by varying the quantity of X, Y, and Z that they produce and sell. The quantities on line 1 and the prices on line 3 must be such that they simultaneously satisfy both consumers and producers. The situation must be one in which neither consumers nor producers can see any advantage in any change of position.

The significant property of this situation is indicated by comparing line 2 with line 4. Here, prices are an accurate indication of marginal costs, and marginal cost is a money indicator of the real cost of getting another unit of X, Y, or Z.

(1) Complete your understanding of this equilibrium by computing the marginal rate of substitution (MRS) and marginal rate of transformation (MRT) for each of the three possible pairings of X, Y, and Z. Remember that MRS is a ratio of appropriate marginal utilities and MRT is a ratio of appropriate marginal costs. Record your answers in Table 17-2.

(2) For X and Y taken together, MRS equals _____, MRT equals _____, and the corresponding ratio of prices equals _____. Note the similar equality for X and Z taken together and Y and Z taken together.

d. Now suppose that all the figures—save one—in Table 17-1 are unchanged. Good X in this new case is produced under conditions of imperfect competition. This means that each producer of X will equate marginal cost with (the price of X / the marginal revenue from the sale of X). In imperfect competition, marginal revenue is (the same as / greater than / less than) price. The price of X is still $2; but its marginal revenue to producers is, say, $1. The MC figure for X on line 4 in the table must then be $1. All other figures are unchanged, and general equilibrium prevails. Note that the producers of X, by equating MR and MC, produce and sell a quantity of X which is (the same as / less than / more than) the quantity they would have produced by equating MC with price.

In this new case, consumers are still at equilibrium, but the prices they must pay are no longer a true indicator of real underlying marginal cost. Why? Because X's MC is $1, not $2. There is a contrived scarcity of X which buyers must accept as though it were a real scarcity, i.e., as though it really cost $2 in real resources to produce 1 more unit of X. It is evident that if the price of X were to fall to $1, a new general equilibrium would have to be worked out, with new X, Y, and Z prices and quantities. And it can be shown—although it is not easy to show—that the new X, Y, and Z quantities would represent a slight gain in the community's welfare.

To see the potential for this gain, note that the MRS between X and Y is still _____ and the MRS between X and Z is still _____. Nonetheless, the true MRT between X and

Table 17-2

	MU_X	MU_Y	MU_Z	MRS	MC_X	MC_Y	MC_Z	MRT
1. X and Y	100	50		2	$2	$1		2
2. Y and Z		50	200			$1	$4	
3. X and Z	100		200		$2		$4	

Y is now _____, and between X and Z it is _____. If $1 of resources were released from the production of Y and devoted to the production of X, then the production of Y would fall by 1 unit while the production of X could rise by _____ units. Utility would (rise / fall) by _____ units as a direct result of the change in Y, but it would (rise / fall) by _____ units with the associated change in X. The net effect would be (an increase / a reduction) in total welfare (utility) of _____ units.

---

a. (**1**) and (**3**) **b.** (**1**) **c.** has; 2; have; marginal costs (**1**) table rows: 1—$MU_Z = 200$, $MC_Z = \$4$; 2—$MU_x = 100$, $MRS = 50/200 = 0.25$, $MC_X = \$2$, $MRT = \$1/\$4 = 0.25$; 3—$MU_Y = 50$, $MRS = 100/200 = 0.5$, $MC_Y = \$1$, $MRT = \$2/\$4 = 0.5$ (**2**) 2; 2; \$4/\$2 = 2 **d.** the marginal revenue from the sale of X; less than; less than; 2; 0.5; $MC_X/MC_Y = \$1/\$1 = 1$; $MC_X/MC_Z = \$1/\$4 = 0.25$; 1 (1 over its MC); fall; $MU_Y = 50$; rise; $MU_X = 100$; an increase; 50 (*Hint*: Remember that *MRS* equals a ratio of marginal utilities and *MRT* equals a ratio of marginal costs.)

3. Kenneth Arrow and Gerard Debreu, both of whom have won Nobel Prizes, were among the first to prove the existence of competitive general equilibrium. Their proof depended upon a long list of qualifications. List at least five in the spaces provided; after each qualification, state *in parentheses* which competitive condition would have been violated if the qualification had been ignored.

a. _____

b. _____

c. _____

d. _____

e. _____

a. no increasing returns to scale (Otherwise, positive profits and prices in excess of marginal cost would emerge.) **b.** no externalities (Otherwise, the prices of some goods would not match their true social costs.) **c.** flexible wages and prices (Otherwise, unemployed resources would be possible.) **d.** no uninsurable risk (Otherwise, inefficient losses might occur.) **e.** no monopolies or other types of imperfect competition (Otherwise, prices in excess of marginal cost would be forthcoming.) (See the footnote to the section entitled "Detailed Analysis of General Equilibrium.")

4. The previous question began a list of qualifications that undermine the application of the efficiency virtues of the competitive general equilibrium to support a laissez-faire policy recommendation. This question will build on that list. Indicate in the spaces provided below the inefficiencies caused by each of the following circumstances:

a. Monopoly or monopolistic competition _____

b. Unrestrained water and/or air pollution _____

c. Discrimination against blacks in labor markets _____

d. Settlements that prevent wage responses to slack demand _____

e. Monopoly power in a labor union _____

f. Government regulation that prevents competition _____

a. Prices are too high and output too low, with wages and input prices distorted. **b.** Output is too high because marginal cost is too low; the price is too low, and input prices are distorted. **c.** Unequal pay for equal work produces distorted prices and a distorted income distribution. **d.** Unemployed resources appear during recession, while prices stay too high. **e.** Wages are too high, so prices are too high, output is too low, and other input prices are distorted. **f.** Government-created monopolies can lead to the problems in answer **a**.

5. Figure 17-1 displays several points relative to a utility-possibility frontier for a simple, two-person economy. Record in the spaces below which point(s) illustrate the effects of the following circumstances relative to a Pareto-efficient allocation indicated by point *E*:

a. An unethical distribution of income . . . . ( )

b. Unemployed resources . . . . ( )

c. Wage discrimination against individual I . . . . . . ( )

d. Unrestrained pollution in the production of a good consumed exclusively by II that hurts only I . . . . . . ( )

Figure 17-1

a. *J, K* (though some may object to *H* and *I*, as well) **b.** *D, F, G* **c.** *G* **d.** *G*
(The answers to the last two are not *H* or *J* because both involve inefficiencies that allow the possibility of improving the utilities of both *I* and *II*; the answers cannot, therefore, be on the frontier.)

Welfare economics has nothing necessarily to do with improving the status of the poor. It refers only to that branch of economics in which the words "better" and "worse" are used, i.e., in which it is said that some situation A is more desirable than some alternative situation B.

The statement "A is preferable to B" requires that its author apply some sort of evaluative metric or scale. Since individual preferences differ, this makes welfare economics a difficult and dangerous area. Nonetheless, the following statement seems fair: "Situation A is preferable to B if, in the course of a change from B to A, some people would be made better off while nobody would be made worse off." In the vernacular of economics, A would then be a Pareto improvement over B.

Very few of these convenient "nobody-worse-off changes" exist in reality, however, so the next step in welfare economics is to find situations in which the predicted gain of the gainers exceeds the predicted loss of the losers. In such a circumstance, the gainers could "bribe" the losers to make the change, or the gainers could be taxed by a sufficient amount to compensate the losers fully and still have some part of their gains left. A Pareto improvement is therefore possible even if it requires some extraordinary administration.

6. It is in this general Pareto sense that the equilibrium of perfect competition is declared to be "efficient." Once competitive equilibrium has been reached, it is impossible to find any alternative attainable combination of goods and services in which those whose welfare would be improved by the change could still be better off after they *(fully / less than fully)* compensated those whose welfare would suffer.

Note particularly that this is ultimately a matter of the "efficient" allocation of a given and limited resource stock– limited in the particular sense that it cannot yield enough output to satisfy everybody's demands for everything. Perfect competition allocates the stock of resources so that the combination of goods and services produced meets the requirement set out in the preceding paragraph; i.e., there are *no Pareto* improvements from a competitive equilibrium.

This "efficiency" definition is acceptable only insofar as the assumptions underlying perfect-competition theory are acceptable. The theory assumes that there *(are / are no)* significant economies of large-scale operations. There *(are / are no)* external diseconomies. (There is an external diseconomy if a plant pollutes the air or water and is not required to bear the cost which this pollution imposes.) The distribution of income, equal or unequal, is *(declared to be the most appropriate / accepted without comment on its desirability)*. The stock of resources is assumed to be *(fixed / increased)*, and the state of technology is assumed to be *(given / improving)*.

fully; are no; are no; accepted without comment on its desirability; fixed; given

REVIEW CONCEPTS

1. Competitive markets work despite the myopic actions of individuals. Utility maximizing produces demand curves in product markets. Marginal cost schedules serve as the corresponding supply curves for individual profit-maximizing firms. Corresponding marginal revenue product schedules support the demand side of input markets. They work against supply schedules for inputs to determine input prices and, given input ownership, the distribution of income.

2. More generally, firms supply goods and services demanded by households; households supply inputs demanded by firms.

3. Competitive equilibria are efficient because they lead firms to set marginal cost equal to price and they allow individuals to consume where ratios of marginal utilities also match ratios of prices. As a result, equilibrium is characterized by the equality of ratios of marginal (social) costs and ratios of marginal benefits (utility).

4. The efficiency result breaks down in the presence of (1) increasing returns to scale (prices > marginal cost), (2) externalities (price ≠ marginal social cost), (3) wage and/or price rigidity (quantity willingly demanded may not match quantity willingly supplied), (4) uninsurable risk (inefficient hedging), and/or (5) market power (price > marginal cost).

5. The distribution of income associated with an efficient competitive equilibrium may (or may not) produce a satisfactory distribution of income.

6. General equilibrium can be characterized by three sets of conditions:

$$MRS_{X,Y} = \frac{MU_X}{MU_Y} = \frac{P_X}{P_Y}$$

for any individual and any goods X and Y (1)

$$\frac{MC_X}{MC_Y} = \frac{P_X}{P_Y} \quad \text{for any goods X and Y} \quad (2)$$

$$\frac{MP_I}{MP_J} = \frac{P_I}{P_J} \quad \text{for any inputs I and J} \quad (3)$$

QUIZ: Multiple Choice

1. Any characterization of the general-equilibrium properties of perfect competition must include statements which imply that:
(1) the ratio of the marginal utilities of any two goods must, for all individuals, equal the corresponding ratio of their marginal costs.
(2) the marginal utilities of all goods consumed must be proportional but not equal to the marginal costs of those goods for each consumer.
(3) the marginal physical product of each input is equal to the price of that input.
(4) the marginal revenue product of each input is equal to the price of the finished good it produces.
(5) the ratio of total expenditure on any good to its price equals marginal utility.

2. The profit-maximizing motive in perfect competition differs from the profit-maximizing motive in imperfect competition in which of the following respects?
(1) The perfect competitor tries to equate price and average cost, which does *not* lead to maximum profit.
(2) The perfect competitor tries to equate price and marginal cost, which does *not* lead to maximum profit.
(3) The perfect competitor tries to equate marginal revenue and marginal cost, which does *not* lead to maximum profit.
(4) The imperfect competitor tries to equate price and marginal cost, which leads to a larger profit than the equating of marginal revenue and marginal cost.
(5) They differ in none of these ways, because the firms in both situations are equally interested in earning as much profit as possible.

3. The theory of perfect competition, according to most economists:
(1) gives a reasonably accurate description of real performance, even though it cannot be used to evaluate the efficiency of that performance.

(2) describes real performance in rough outline despite competitive imperfections, and is most important for appraising the efficiency of that performance.
(3) is most important for appraising the efficiency of real performance, even though it is not even approximately correct in describing that performance.
(4) bears almost no resemblance to real performance, and cannot be used to evaluate its efficiency, but is most important because its material is a lead into the theory of imperfect competition.
(5) with relatively minor monopoly exceptions, gives a closely accurate outline of real performance, and can be used to identify the monopoly exceptions.

4. Four of the following five alternatives state conditions which must be satisfied if the equilibrium conditions of perfect competition are to be satisfied. One alternative states a condition that is not required; i.e., one would not necessarily be the result of perfect competition. Which one?
(1) Price is equal to average cost.
(2) For each individual, and for each good he or she consumes, the ratio between marginal utility and price is the same for all such goods.
(3) Price is equal to marginal cost.
(4) There is no significant inequality in the distribution of income among individuals.
(5) Price is equal to minimum average cost.

5. Four of the following five alternatives state conditions which indicate that the conditions of all-around perfect competition are not satisfied. One alternative states a condition which must be satisfied to meet the requirements of perfect competition. Which one?
(1) Market prices are steady in the sense of being unresponsive to short-run changes in demand or in supply.
(2) Price is equal to average cost but not to marginal cost.
(3) Different wage rates are paid in different geographical locations for work whose requirements are exactly the same in both locations.
(4) Product differentiation yields a price that equals average cost but not minimum-attainable average cost.
(5) Marginal cost is equal to average cost.

6. The theory of perfect competition begins by recognizing two facts: Resources are scarce, and the price system is a mechanism for allocating the use or employment of those resources. From here, the theory gradually develops a set of rules which, if satisfied, indicate that scarce resources are being utilized efficiently. These rules are stated with special regard for a collection of influences which might drive results away from the perfectly competitive equilibrium. One such disrupting influence is:
(1) laissez-faire pricing activity in product and input markets.
(2) economic activity measured over time.

(3) interdependence among the inputs employed in many production processes.
(4) the presence of monopoly or of monopoly elements.
(5) spacial and/or geographical differences.

7. The theory of general equilibrium under perfect competition sets out rules for an efficient allocation of scarce resources. Even with these rules fully satisfied, however, equilibrium may not be "optimal" to the extent that:
(1) price is equal to marginal cost.
(2) external economies or diseconomies are present.
(3) the economy is led to specialize in the production of only a few goods.
(4) price is equal to average cost.
(5) it is possible to substitute one input or resource in place of another.

SUGGESTED ANSWERS TO QUESTIONS IN THE TEXT: Chapter 17

1. Couch your answer in terms of a circular diagram. Refer to the appropriate chapters if you have trouble with any of the seven steps.

2. No increasing returns to scale (natural monopolies like utilities, etc.); no externalities (like pollution or bees, etc.); flexible wages and prices (no long-term fixed contracts, etc.); no uninsurable risks [nuclear power plants (?)]; no imperfect competition (from whatever source).

3. a. Ratios of marginal utilities between any two goods for any individual (marginal rates of substitution) must equal the corresponding ratio of prices. (Otherwise, welfare can be improved by adjusting someone's consumption bundle.)
b. Ratios of marginal costs between any two goods must equal the corresponding ratio of prices. (Otherwise, the output mix can be adjusted to more closely match consumers' willingness to trade off one good for another; recall that MRS's are equal to the price ratios.)
c. Ratios of marginal products between any two inputs must equal the corresponding ratio of input prices. (Otherwise, costs are not being minimized and the output of at least one good can increase with no reduction elsewhere; i.e., the economy is *not* on its *PPF*.)

Monopoly power and/or externalities distort **b**.

4. *First theorem:* General equilibrium in a perfectly competitive market system achieves allocative efficiency.

Second theorem: Given any situation of allocative efficiency, there exists a distribution of resources for which that system is in a competitive equilibrium.

a. Allocative efficiency can be supported by any distribution of resources and thus income.
b. Allocative efficiency will not correct unequal distributions of resources.
c. Refers to the first theorem.
d. This is the first theorem.
e. Apply the second theorem.

5. Imperfect competition may put the economy below the *PPF* (i.e., it may not achieve allocative efficiency). The economy may grow faster given the Schumpeterian hypothesis, which holds that monopoly power generates the profit required for innovation. If this is true, then the economy may become better off over the long run. Consult Figure TQ17-1. There, a competitive economy grows from PPF_1 to PPF_2 over a period of time; specifically, it moves from E_1 on PPF_1 to E_2 on PPF_2. By comparison, an economy with a growth-amplifying monopolist moves from ppf^1 to ppf^2. Operating below both, such an economy could move from e^1 to e^2 with e^2 dominating E_2 (consumption of both goods is higher at e^2 than at E_2).

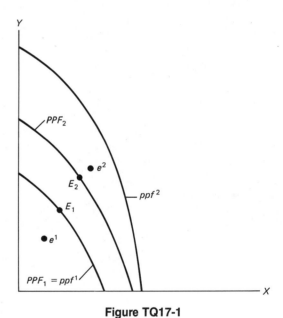

Figure TQ17-1

6. Any point on a *PPF* achieved by a socialistic economy is a point of allocative efficiency, and it can (by the second theorem) be supported as a competitive equilibrium with the appropriate redistribution of resources (income). Ponder how to do that. What might be the incentive effects? Can socialism, with all its administrative needs, get to the frontier? Does the theorem hold for points below the frontier?

CHAPTER 18

GOVERNMENT AND THE ECONOMY

Government has, in most advanced industrial countries, been growing in dramatic fashion over the past several decades. Government spending has climbed, both in absolute terms and in terms of a proportion of GNP. Taxation has been growing, as well. So have income-support programs and regulatory intervention into all levels of society. The size of government was, in fact, one of the hottest political issues of the 1980s in the United States, the United Kingdom, and elsewhere around the democratic world; and the controversy has certainly not subsided in the 1990s.

Chapter 18 begins a two-chapter discussion of the economic issues that surround this growth in government activity. Section A provides, to begin the process, a brief chronicle of its recent trends. The second section introduces you to an avenue of theoretical analysis, bearing the suggestive name of "public choice," that brings the old study of "political economy" up to date. Finally, the analysis developed in this second section is applied to the problem of economic externality in section C. The general notion of public goods (and bads) is reviewed there before a specific pollution example crystallizes the role of government in that type of market failure.

It must be emphasized from the beginning that "government failure" is as much of a possibility in many instances as "market failure." There can, and do, exist governmental policies that do more harm than good; and care needs to be taken that this potential is fully recognized so that specific cases of "the cure being worse than the disease" are more easily identified.

Proceeding through this first of two chapters, then, you will be able to accomplish the following objectives on the route to a preliminary understanding of how contemporary economic analysis deals with government activity.

LEARNING OBJECTIVES

1. Chronicle the changes in government spending, taxation, and regulatory activity over the past few decades, particularly in the United States. Contrast the growth in spending and taxation with the decline of regulation initiated by the Reagan administration.

2. List, explain, and provide examples of the four major functions that government must consider: provide and maintain a legal system, work to allocate resources with maximum efficiency, conduct programs of income redistribution, and conduct stabilizing macroeconomic policy.

3. Understand the genesis of "public choice": the need to determine whether government is organized in a way that allows it to achieve its objectives.

4. Identify various voting rules (unanimity, majority rule, supermajority rule) and the difficulties that might arise in their implementation. Explore their differences and similarities with the aid of a utility-possibility frontier.

5. Note the possibility that majority voting can cycle with no *un*ambiguous outcome; explain why this potential places enormous power in the hands of those who control the decision rules and the public agenda.

6. State Arrow's impossibility theorem (which holds that no majority voting scheme exists which will guarantee efficiency, respect individual preferences, and generate outcomes that are not dependent upon the ordering of the voting agenda). Construct an example showing how this theorem works.

7. Define the notion of externality. Relate it to the notion of a public good (bad). Analyze the inefficiency of, e.g., a pollution externality, and describe how various control mechanisms might work to ameliorate its social damage.

18 Government and the Economy

You are already familiar with a wide range of decisions through which government influences the everyday lives of people, businesses, and other economic agents across the nation and around the world. Earlier chapters in the text have reviewed the myriad of roles that government can play on a micro level. Regulation and antitrust action are but two items of a long list of micro-based roles that government has assumed. You will see in subsequent chapters how stabilization policies can be constructed to cope with macroeconomic variables like unemployment and inflation; you probably already know that they can make it more or less difficult to buy a house, sell a car, or pay for college. The point of the next two chapters is neither to reiterate previous work nor to "jump the gun" on future material; it is, instead, to investigate the norms against which these activities are measured and the way decisions about their directions are made in a democratic society.

1. a. Since World War I, the size of government, measured in terms of expenditures, taxation, and/or regulation has *(remained remarkably stable / fallen slightly since World War II after growing rapidly between wars / grown dramatically)*. Compared with spending amounting to slightly more than 10 percent of GNP prior to World War I, the sum of budgets across all levels of government in the United States had, by the 1980s, *(fallen back to 10 percent of GNP after peaking during the Carter administration at 21 percent / grown steadily to nearly 25 percent of GNP / stabilized at approximately 35 percent of GNP)*.

Over the same period of time, tax revenues collected by all levels of government have *(kept pace with / grown at a slightly slower pace than / grown at a slightly faster pace than)* expenditures, with enormous shortfalls coming during *(the Great Depression / World War II / the Reagan years)*. Nonetheless, tax revenues are still perhaps *(5 / 50 / 500)* percent larger now than they were at the turn of the century.

b. Regulatory activity, started perhaps in *(1913 / 1887 / 1778)* with the formation of the *(Federal Reserve System / Department of Agriculture / Interstate Commerce Commission)*, reached its high point during the *(Nixon / Carter / Reagan)* administration. The ability of the U.S. government to regulate some of the activities of some of its citizens is justified by reference to the U.S. Constitution. Specifically, interpretation of a phrase about *(avoiding taxation with representation / equal protection under the law / securing the public interest)* has led to social and economic regulation of all kinds. In the spaces below, list at least four industries which have faced significant regulation over the past half-century:

(1) _____
(2) _____
(3) _____
(4) _____

a. grown dramatically; stabilized at approximately 35 percent of GNP; grown at a slightly slower pace than; all three; 500   **b.** 1887; Interstate Commerce Commission; Carter; securing the public interest (**1**) through (**4**) any of the following: airlines; trucking; water traffic; utilities of all sorts; banking; pipelines; oil and gas

2. It is extremely interesting to note that the size of the government in a nation's economy seems to depend upon the size of that economy; measured as a proportion of GNP, poor, less developed countries show a tendency to tax and spend *(less than / more than / about the same as)* advanced countries. Circle the country in each of the following pairs whose government spends more as a fraction of GNP:

a. United States / Paraguay
b. United States / United Kingdom
c. United States / France
d. United States / Japan
e. United States / Germany
f. United States / Sweden
g. India / Switzerland
h. Sri Lanka / Netherlands

Notice that the United States, despite all the political furor about the size of the American government, ranks far from the top among developed countries in this ordering. In absolute terms, the size of the American government is enormous, of course; but relative to GNP, its size is considerably more modest.

less than **a.** United States   **b.** United Kingdom   **c.** France   **d.** United States   **e.** Germany   **f.** Sweden   **g.** Switzerland   **h.** Netherlands (Consult Fig. 18-2 in the text to confirm these answers.)

3. a. Government can serve four distinct functions in a mixed economy. List them in the spaces provided:

(1) _____
(2) _____
(3) _____
(4) _____

b. Each of the following activities falls into at least one of the four categories that you just identified; indicate which in the spaces provided:

(1) Cutting taxes to reduce unemployment _____

(2) Specifying that the manufacturer is liable for any harm caused by his or her product _____

(3) Placing a tax on a steel producer's pollution _____

(4) Legislating that it is illegal to discriminate on the basis of sex _____

(5) Enacting an income policy that penalizes larger-than-specified wage increases _____

(6) Enacting a program of aid to families with dependent children _____

(7) Enacting day-care help to allow women to work _____

(8) Writing laws that allow triple damages to be awarded in cases of gross and wanton negligence _____

a. (1) Prescribe legal framework **(2)** work toward macroeconomic stability **(3)** allocate resources efficiently **(4)** allocate resources equitably **b. (1)** macro stabilization **(2)** legal framework **(3)** promote efficiency **(4)** legal, efficiency, and equity objectives **(5)** macro stabilization **(6)** promote equity **(7)** promote equity and efficiency **(8)** legal framework

Much of the material that has been presented in previous chapters has indicated what governments that want to do certain things "ought to do" to accomplish their goals. Public choice analyzes whether in fact they do what they claim. Do they work to promote efficiency and equity, for example, or do they do the opposite even when their truly espoused goals are efficiency and equity? Are there barriers built into the way governments operate—the rules of their games—that prevent them from achieving their goals? If so, are there any general principles to be discovered to help break down those barriers?

Voting procedures define the rules of the decision-making game in the United States. We elect representatives who make decisions on our behalf and who want to continue to do so. These representatives therefore have an incentive to behave in a manner that will maximize their chances of (re)election. This behavior generates a supply of government activity, if you will, that is matched in the political arena against a demand for government activity generated by the voters. Two of the primary purposes of public-choice theory applied to the United States are therefore (1) to analyze the workings of this "political marketplace" and (2) to evaluate the properties of its likely set of outcomes. The next few questions will review your brief introduction to that endeavor.

4. Figure 18-1 provides three reproductions of the same utility-possibility frontier. Movement from point E in a specific direction can be used to illustrate the result of a Pareto-improving government activity; shade in the area that captures all possible Pareto-improving points relative to point E in panel (a). A second area captures all points that would signify a redistribution of resources from individual A to individual B; shade in the area capturing all such points in panel (b). A third area signifies government failure in which government activity would leave both A and B worse off. Shade in the area that captures all these points in panel (c).

(a)

(b)

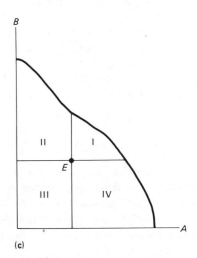
(c)

Figure 18-1

Of the three panels that you now have before you, panel (a / b / c) indicates with its shaded area all the possible outcomes that might arise from a unanimous voting rule. Why? Because both A and B would have to approve the activity, and that would happen only if the utilities of both A and B were increased. To illustrate the area of potential outcomes under majority rule (under the additional assumption that there are more type B people than there are type A people), you would need to combine the shaded areas of panels _____ and _____ .

Unanimity, as a voting rule, has its drawbacks. For one thing, any one individual can block a decision that can enhance the welfare of everyone else. This means that unanimity can produce only (a Pareto-improving / an income-transferring / a contractionary) government policy. In addition to being enormously cumbersome, therefore, unanimity would lead to the potential extortion of most of the gains of any policy by a clever skeptic from the population at large. Because anyone could play that game, unanimity would, more probably, lead to (a flurry of small actions / no action / the abandonment of government of any kind)—a (maintenance / shattering) of the status quo.

Majority rule, on the other hand, is not necessarily more efficient, but it is certainly more manageable. To avoid the potential tyranny of the majority, though, some important issues require majorities of (greater than 50 percent / less than 50 percent) to pass. Although it is subject to the pressures of special-interest groups in its most pragmatic form, majority rule seems to work fairly well in most circumstances.

---

figure panels: (a)—area I, (b)—area II, (c)—area III

a; a; b; a Pareto-improving; no action; maintenance; greater than 50 percent

---

Public-choice theory has extensively investigated the workings of majority rule, and its conclusions are not as reassuring as those gained from casual observation. For one thing, the result of a process involving majority rule need not be efficient. For another, there exists the possibility that a sequence of majority-rule referenda will cycle endlessly. That is the implication of the Arrow impossibility theorem: There exists no majority-rule scheme that guarantees (1) efficient outcomes which (2) respect individual preferences and (3) are independent of the order of the agenda. The possibility of cycling means, in particular, that control of the agenda can translate into control of the outcome. The next question explores this theorem.

5. a. Consider, first of all, the preferences of three people indicated in Table 18-1. Assume that, in voting between two options, each person votes for the option that ranks higher in his or her preference ordering. Record, in the blanks, the outcomes of majority-rule decisions in the following contests:

(1) Option I against option II _____

(2) Option II against option III _____

(3) Option I against option III _____

Table 18-1
Individual Rankings of Three Options

Individual	Options		
	I	II	III
A	First	Second	Third
B	Second	Third	First
C	Third	First	Second

b. Now suppose that the Rules Committee of the Process decides that option II will run off against the winner of an initial vote between I and III. The eventual winner will be option (I / II / III). If option I had been chosen to run off against the winner of a vote-off between II and III, however, then the winner would have been option (I / II / III). And finally, allowing option III to run off against the winner of a I-to-II contest would produce option (I / II / III) as a winner. There would, in fact, be (no / a single) unambiguous winner until the Rules Committee decided on the agenda—the order of the voting decisions. This is an example of the impossibility theorem that contributed to Arrow's winning a Nobel Prize in economics.

c. Suppose, now, that individual preferences have been formed on the basis of the net benefits indicated in Table 18-2. Let each individual vote "yes" for any program whose net benefit is positive for himself or herself, and "no" otherwise. Regardless of the order of the vote, (RR / FP / EI / SQ) would win in pairwise contests of any single project against the status quo despite the fact that social welfare would be increased by passage of (any of the three programs / only FP and EI / only FP and RR / only RR and EI / only EI / only RR / only FP).

Table 18-2
Net Benefits to Individuals

Individual	Railroad (RR)	Farm Program (FP)	Earthquake Insurance (EI)	Status Quo (SQ)
A	100	−15	−10	0
B	−20	100	−25	0
C	−20	−10	40	0

d. Consider the possibility of combining programs to accommodate the intensity of the preferences reflected in Table 18-2. Record, in Table 18-3, the net benefits of the indicated combined programs. Record, in columns (1) through (3) of Table 18-4, the preferred combined program based on the net benefits of Table 18-3 for the three indicated pairwise elections. Note, in column (4), the winner and, in column (5), the combined net benefit of the winning package. Any of these packages (would / would not) beat the status quo

Table 18-3
Combined Benefits to Individuals

	RR & FP	RR & EI	FP & EI	All Three
A	_____	_____	_____	_____
B	_____	_____	_____	_____
C	_____	_____	_____	_____

in a majority-wins election and *(would / would not)* beat a combination of all three.

On the basis of your entries in Table 18-4, it is clear that *(there exists / there does not exist)* an unambiguous winner to a sequence of pairwise elections. This is true despite the fact that *(the status quo / passage of all three proposals / passage of any two of the three proposals)* maximizes the increase in net welfare. In fact, among the three two-project combinations, *(FP & EI / RR & FP / RR & EI)* generate the largest increase in net welfare.

a. (1) I wins (A and B vote for I, while C votes for II.) **(2)** II wins (A and C vote for II, while B votes for III.) **(3)** III wins (B and C vote for III, while A votes for I.) **b.** II (Running I vs. III first means that III wins the first round and then runs against II in the second round and loses.); I (Running II vs. III first means that II wins the first round and then runs against I in the second round and loses.); III (Running I against II first means that I wins the first round and then runs against III in the second round and loses.); no **c.** SQ; any of the three programs **d.** Tables 18-3 and 18-4 should look like Tables 18-5 and 18-6, respectively:

Table 18-5

RR & FP	RR & EI	FP & EI	All Three
85	90	−25	75
80	−45	75	55
−30	20	30	10

Table 18-6

A	B	C	Winner	Net Benefit
RR & EI	RR & FP	RR & EI	RR & EI	65
RR & FP	RR & FP	FP & EI	RR & FP	135
RR & EI	FP & EI	FP & EI	FP & EI	80

would; would not; there does not exist (Cycling occurs just as above in part **a.**); passage of all three proposals; RR & FP

6. A variety of problems that inhibit the workings of the pure majority-rule system envisioned by the public-choice theorists can be found within the political system of the United States. For one thing, while there is a one-person, one-vote rule, money *(does / does not)* matter. It can cost well over $1 million to run for Congress, and that money can come from across the country if the district is targeted by a large Political Action Committee (PAC) or a special-interest group or two. Jesse Helms spent over $20 million to run for reelection to the Senate in 1990—over $400 per registered voter. For another, the lobbying activities of special-interest groups can produce unrepresentative government. Government "by the people and for the people" or the "best government that money can buy"?—that is the question. The U.S. government tends, in addition, to be *(shortsighted / longsighted)* because the longest term is *(2 / 4 / 6)* years for a *(a member of Congress / the President / a senator)*. This time limitation has a tendency to produce a *(high- / medium- / low-)* consumption economy aimed at making sure that the *(short / medium / long)* term is prosperous.

does; shortsighted; 6; senator; high-; short

7. Turn, now, to the notion of an **externality.** An externality is present when the benefits (in the case of a positive externality) and/or costs (in the case of a negative externality) of an activity spill over into the lives of other people without their paying or being compensated. Public goods represent the extreme case of externality on the positive side; pollution, on the negative side.

Consider the economic consequences of a negative externality—the emission of heavy, toxic smoke from a factory chimney. No matter how disagreeable it might be to those who work or live nearby, the factory's owners might feel no obligation to clean up their act until public pressure, usually in the form of legislation, forces them to do so. A more recent example is acid rain. Many utilities and manufacturers, especially those involved in metal processing, emit sulfur dioxide and nitrogen oxide from their smokestacks. These chemicals combine with moisture in the atmosphere to form sulfuric and nitric acid. The acidity of falling rain and snow is thereby increased, creating more acidic lakes and rivers in which fish cannot reproduce. Moreover, there may be long-term impacts on human health from these and other chemical emissions.

Table 18-4
Pairwise Preferences

Election	(1) Individual A	(2) Individual B	(3) Individual C	(4) Winner	(5) Net Benefit
RR & FP vs. RR & EI	_____	_____	_____	_____	_____
RR & FP vs. FP & EI	_____	_____	_____	_____	_____
RR & EI vs. FP & EI	_____	_____	_____	_____	_____

Presence of these sorts of externalities *(weakens / strengthens)* the case for laissez-faire. That case has assumed that the private market system, if fully competitive, would yield (in the form of market prices) an exact balance of costs and benefits. Insofar as externalities exist (and insofar as they are growing more widespread), the market system *(will still / cannot)* furnish an accurate or adequate measure of costs.

---

weakens; cannot

---

8. a. Figure 18-2 represents a simplification of Figure 18-6 in the text; the marginal social and private damages of pollution are assumed to be constant. The numbers recorded in Figure 18-2 can be used to explore four mechanisms with which a pollution externality of the type illustrated can be handled. Two involve indirect influence by the government; they are:

(1) _____

(2) _____

Two more would result from direct collective action; they are:

(3) _____

(4) _____

Figure 18-2

Given the curves defined in Figure 18-2, one of these actions is required because the privately determined level of pollution would be _____ tons, at which the marginal cost of abatement equals *(the marginal social damage caused by the pollution / zero / the marginal private damage caused by the pollution)*. That quantity *(exceeds / equals / is smaller than)* the efficient level of pollution—_____ tons, defined by the equality of the marginal cost of abatement and *(the marginal social damage caused by the pollution / zero / the marginal private damage caused by the pollution)*.

b. Suppose, first of all, that those hurt by the pollution offer to pay the polluter $4 for every unit of pollution not emitted. In this case, the marginal private damage caused by the pollution would *(climb by $4 / remain the same / fall by $4)* because each unit emitted would mean a loss of $4 in potential compensation. The result would be, on the basis of the private decision of the polluter, _____ tons of pollution. It would cost those paying the "bribe" $_____, but that would *(exceed / fall short of)* the reduction in extra social cost of $_____ that they otherwise would suffer. The end result *(would / would not)* be optimal, but it *(would / would not)* represent an improvement.

Second, the possibility exists that government would hold the polluter liable for the full extent of the social damage that his or her pollution produced. If it were 100 percent certain that these damages would be imposed, then the marginal social damage curve *(would / would not)* become the marginal private damage curve, and the optimal level of pollution *(would / would not)* be achieved. If the probability of assessing damages were not 100 percent, however, then there *(would / would not)* be some improvement as long as the chances of the polluter's being held liable were not 0 percent. (This last point is tricky until you think about it. Think about it.)

Direct control is, of course, also an option. Were the government interested in setting a standard above which the polluter could not stray, then it would set a maximum level of pollution at _____ tons. Alternatively, a tax of $_____ per ton could achieve the same result. The polluter would prefer the *(standard / tax)*, because that would allow the free emission of _____ tons of pollution.

---

a. (1) promoting negotiation given property rights **(2)** setting liability rules **(3)** setting standards **(4)** setting pollution taxes; 300; the marginal private damage caused by the pollution; exceeds; 100; the marginal social damage caused by the pollution **b.** climb by $4; 200; 400 ($4 × 100 tons of pollution not emitted); fall short of; 1000 = [$20 − $10] × 100 tons of pollution no longer emitted]; would not; would; would; would; would; 100; 10; standard; 100

---

9. Recalling that public goods are enjoyed by everyone, consider the two demand curves for some public good G represented in the two panels of Figure 18-3. If 10 units of G were offered, then the two people represented here would together be willing to pay $_____, $_____ from individual A and $_____ from individual B. This suggests that each person should *(necessarily pay an equal proportion / pay according to the marginal benefit that he or she would receive as indicated by the individual demand curves / pay according to* *how much he or she earns in income and how much property he or she owns).*

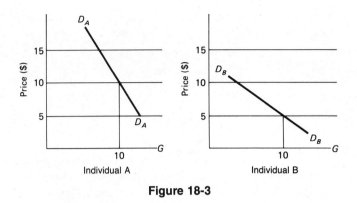

Figure 18-3

15; 10; 5; pay according to the marginal benefit that he or she would receive as indicated by the individual demand curves

REVIEW CONCEPTS

1. The economic roll of government has grown dramatically at all levels over the last half-century. There are four primary functions: *(a)* providing and maintaining a legal framework, *(b)* improving the efficiency of resource allocation, *(c)* conducting redistributive programs, and *(d)* conducting macroeconomic stabilization.

2. Public-choice theory investigates how well governments' rules allow their actions to perform these functions.

3. Various voting rules (unanimity, supermajority voting, simple-majority voting) have all been employed in various contexts, but each has its own sets of difficulties. Utility-possibility frontiers can be used to illustrate their outcomes and thereby illuminate their character.

4. Majority voting schemes can cycle (with no single program commanding an unambiguous majority), can lead to "tyranny by the majority," and can lead to inefficient outcomes. Arrow's impossibility theorem underscores the potential problems by showing that there exists no majority voting scheme which simultaneously guarantees efficiency, respects individual preferences, and generates outcomes independent of the voting agenda.

5. Externalities occur when costs or benefits extend beyond a specific market and thus price does not accurately reflect true marginal social cost and/or marginal social benefits. The resulting inefficiency can be redressed (1) by direct quantity intervention, (2) by price specification, (3) by the complete identification of property rights, or (4) by the definition of clear liability rules. While these tools are equivalent in theory (subject to rigid conditions), different circumstances are, in practice, best accommodated by different tools.

QUIZ: Multiple Choice

1. Which of the following statements is an accurate description of the history of government spending in the United States?
(1) The cost of government at all levels climbed from nearly 10 percent of GNP in 1913 to slightly less than 25 percent in the late 1980s.
(2) The cost of government at all levels climbed from 25 percent of GNP in 1913 to 35 percent in the early 1990s.
(3) The cost of government at all levels climbed from approximately 10 percent of GNP in 1913 to nearly 35 percent in the early 1990s.
(4) The cost of the federal government in the United States climbed from 10 percent of GNP in 1913 to more than 30 percent of GNP in the late 1980s.
(5) None of the above.

2. Taxation in the United States:
(1) has grown during the twentieth century at a rate that far exceeds the rate of growth of government spending.
(2) has grown at a rate that, until 1981, roughly matched the rate of growth of government spending.
(3) has fallen in size in terms of fraction of GNP since 1939, but has climbed in absolute terms.
(4) rose dramatically in the 1980s in an effort to balance the federal budget.
(5) none of the above.

3. The initial source of regulatory activity in the United States was a clause in the Constitution that made a point of:
(1) no taxation without representation.
(2) securing the public interest.
(3) guaranteeing equal pay for equal work.
(4) guaranteeing freedom of speech against inferior products.
(5) anticipating the Equal Rights Amendment.

4. Regulatory activity in the United States:
(1) began with the formation of the Interstate Commerce Commission in 1913 and reached a peak during the Reagan administration.
(2) began with the formation of the Interstate Commerce Commission in 1887 and reached a peak during the Carter administration.
(3) began with the advent of the Federal Reserve System to regulate banks and peaked with the deregulation of trucking and space travel during the Reagan administration.
(4) began with the formation of the Interstate Commerce Commission in 1887 and died with the deregulation of airlines during the Reagan administration.
(5) none of the above.

5. Regulation grew in the United States as it became clear that a laissez-faire policy was vulnerable to:

(1) pockets of poverty that are exploited by the more fortunate.
(2) the business cycle, which buffets the economic lives of nearly every citizen.
(3) inefficient and unfair discrimination on the basis of sex, race, and other factors.
(4) the flagrant abuse of the environment.
(5) all the above.

6. Government can play a number of roles in a mixed economy. These potential roles include:
(1) prescribing a legal framework that defines "the rules of the game."
(2) reallocating resources to accomplish greater efficiency in the face of, say, monopoly or pollution.
(3) effecting macrostabilization by prudent exercise of fiscal, monetary, and other policies.
(4) reallocating resources to accomplish greater equity.
(5) all the above.

7. Referring to the utility-possibility frontier depicted in Figure 18-4, a move that would illustrate a government failure might shift an economy from a point like A to:
(1) a point like B.
(2) a point like C.
(3) a point like D.
(4) a point like E.
(5) none of the above.

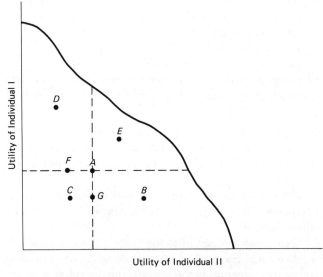

Figure 18-4

8. Referring again to Figure 18-4, a transfer of resources from individual I to II might move an economy from a point like A to:
(1) a point like B.
(2) a point like C.
(3) a point like D.
(4) a point like E.
(5) none of the above.

9. In Figure 18-4, a move that would have been approved by a unanimous voting rule would shift an economy from a point like A to:
(1) a point like B.
(2) a point like C.
(3) a point like D.
(4) a point like F.
(5) none of the above.

10. One last time on Figure 18-4, a move that would have been approved by a majority voting rule, given more people of type I than type II, might shift an economy from a point like A to:
(1) a point like B.
(2) a point like C.
(3) a point like D.
(4) a point like F.
(5) a point like G.

11. The Arrow impossibility theorem states that:
(1) it is impossible for people to agree, so a unanimous voting rule is necessarily a prescription for paralysis.
(2) it is impossible for a majority-rule system to last because of the tyranny that would necessarily be imposed by the majority.
(3) It is impossible for any voting rule to be analyzed because of the imponderables of the human mind.
(4) it is impossible for public-choice theorists to glean any insight from voting behavior because majority voting rules always produce ambiguous results.
(5) none of the above.

12. Whenever majority rule produces a potential for cycling:
(1) the power falls to those who set the agenda.
(2) the possibility of logrolling to accommodate the intensity of preferences might help reduce that potential.
(3) there exists no other voting rule that would preserve efficiency, respect individual preferences, and guarantee that cycling would not occur.
(4) the need for rules beyond those that prescribe voting procedures is paramount.
(5) all the above.

13. In the United States:
(1) there is a one-person, one-vote rule, but money and special interests are nonetheless powerful.
(2) the inherent democracy of one person, one vote overpowers all other factors in determining the outcome of any decision.
(3) the bureaucratic imperative is diminished by the watchdog arm of the U.S. Congress.

(4) the long time horizon of most politicians causes problems in maintaining short-term prosperity.
(5) all the above.

14. A public good is one in which:
(1) the cost of exclusion is low and the marginal cost of one more consumer is low.
(2) the cost of exclusion is high and the marginal cost of one more consumer is low.
(3) the cost of exclusion is low and the marginal cost of one more consumer is high.
(4) the cost of exclusion is high and the marginal cost of one more consumer is high.
(5) the cost of exclusion and the marginal cost of consumption are irrelevant.

15. Public goods and public bads:
(1) are just mirror images of themselves, with the effect of their provision extending beyond the producer.
(2) can both be analyzed as externalities—one positive and one negative.
(3) are subject to the same types of governmental intervention because markets for neither typically exist.
(4) are hard to evaluate because their utility or harm extends beyond the confines of one individual.
(5) are all of the above.

16. Referring now to Figure 18-5, the efficient level of emissions is indicated by:
(1) point A.
(2) point B.
(3) point C.
(4) point D.
(5) none of the above.

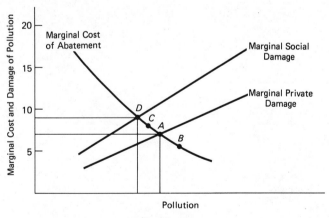

Figure 18-5

17. Referring a second time to Figure 18-5, the level of emissions that would emerge in response to a $2-per-unit emissions tax is indicated by:
(1) point A.
(2) point B.

(3) point C.
(4) point D.
(5) none of the above.

18. If half of the population of 10,000 were willing to pay $10 for the provision of a park and the rest were not willing to contribute a dime, then an expenditure of:
(1) $50,000 would match the town's collective demand price for parkland.
(2) a price less that $25,000 would reflect the town's collective demand for parkland.
(3) some amount of money for parkland would be appropriate only if one more person wanted to contribute to guarantee a majority of more than 50 percent.
(4) a price in excess of $50,000 would certainly reflect the town's true demand for parkland.
(5) none of the above.

19. The Coase result states that:
(1) negotiation would always solve an externality problem if only government would get out of the way.
(2) the potential exists for negotiation to diminish the magnitude of an externality if property rights are well defined and negotiation costs are not too severe.
(3) negotiation must be forgone in lieu of direct governmental intervention whenever an externality problem becomes too severe.
(4) negotiation will always generate an efficient solution as long as negotiation costs are not too high and property rights are clearly defined.
(5) none of the above.

SUGGESTED ANSWERS TO QUESTIONS IN THE TEXT: Chapter 18

1. Think about your experiences with all levels of government. The Reagan administration focused on cutting back the size of government, so there are a lot of examples in those 8 years of things that government no longer does; look at the budgets for those years for clues. Regulation peaked in the middle of the 1970s, so there are more examples during that period. What are state and local governments now doing in response to federal cutbacks? In response to taxpayer revolts?

2. Recall that the marginal cost of one more person enjoying a public good is small and that the cost of providing a public good is large relative to the marginal benefit that any one person (or small group of people) might receive. A public good therefore needs to be financed by the combined expenditure of money collected from many people, none of whom would find it individually worthwhile to provide the good alone. This is fine as long as utilization involves low marginal cost. Think of these insights as you consider the examples in your list.

3. His statement relates to government's role in providing public goods and handling externalities, i.e., the role of government in promoting efficiency. It does not speak to some of the other roles of government: promoting appropriate redistribution of resources, conducting appropriate stabilization measures, and creating appropriate legal frameworks. Believers in all sizes of government could adopt it, though, by defining their own views of what individuals are capable of doing "for themselves."

4. People with different preferences can sort themselves out by deciding where to live on the basis of the menu of public goods offered by various towns at various cost. Towns then try to meet the expectations of their citizens, which they find easier to accomplish when most citizens are of like mind. Think about public education as you ponder this question. Is it appropriate to have local provision with federal (minimum) quality standards? Or should all schools simply compete for students from any town?

5. **a.** Direct controls are possible, because the mills are clearly identified and located. Taxes might work, as well. Negotiation is not likely because property rights are not well defined; even if they were, the townsfolk might be difficult to organize into a cohesive negotiating unit. Liability rules could also work, but they would be expensive to enforce given the uncertainties of identifying the specific sources of environmental damage.

b. Direct control, as in answer **a.**

c. Probably not serious enough to warrant action, since smoke dissipates quickly outdoors in the fall.

d. Liability rules can work well because the source of "damage" is easily attributed. Perhaps control could be extended to revoking the licenses of repeated DWI drivers and sentencing DWI drivers involved in fatalities to jail terms.

e. Same as answer **d.** Should the licenses be suspended to recognize the recklessness of youth?

6. Market allocations are supported by specific prices and the distribution of income. Everyone has as much as he or she can afford, decided on the basis of unanimous agreement of each individual with himself or herself. There is always debate over how much national defense should be "purchased," because everyone gets the same amount. All moves made under unanimity are Pareto-improving.

7. Proceed with caution. Make your cases on the basis of cost, benefit, and likelihood of success; avoid government failure; and consider the secondary incentives that your ideas might create.

8. Defining property rights which allow region- or state-specific conditions to come into play would avoid interregional inefficiencies. So, too, would settling liability rules contingent upon regional or state-specific costs of attribution which were well defined. Uniform standards would not if potential damages were (e.g.) higher in California and lower elsewhere; different standards would have to be set for each region or state. Uniform charges would avoid the inefficiencies if regional behavior contributed to social costs felt throughout the country but not if they were asymmetrically distributed. The key is the extent of the externality.

To see this more clearly, consider panels (a) and (b) of Figure TQ18-1. In panel (a), the pollution of States I and II contribute to a collective (national) marginal social cost, and a single tax t^* would do the trick. Notice that there are no private costs drawn, for simplicity. Notice, as well, that the corresponding standards, Q_I^* and Q_{II}^*, need not be the same. Panel (b) shows the same marginal abatement cost curves but adds state-specific marginal social costs. In this case, two separate taxes ($t_I^* > t_{II}^*$) are required.

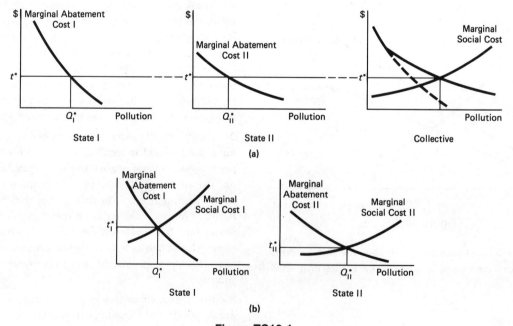

Figure TQ18-1

9. Consider Figure TQ18-2. Marginal private damage equals the marginal cost of abatement at point P; it therefore defines the laissez-faire level of emissions. Point E is the efficient outcome because marginal social damage equals the marginal cost of abatement.

   a. A direct control limiting emissions to 100 tons would achieve point E.

   b. A tax of approximately $15 per ton would bring the marginal private damage of emission, including the pecuniary cost of the tax, into intersection with the marginal cost of abatement at point E, so it would work, too.

   c. A liability law with 100 percent enforcement that held the polluter accountable for the damage above and beyond private damage would make the marginal private damage curve match the marginal social damage curve; the private point of emission would thus become E.

   d. The public should be willing to subsidize the difference between marginal social damages and marginal private damages. That potential subsidy would therefore become an opportunity cost of emission, so the effective marginal private damage curve would again move up to match the marginal social damage curve.

SUPPLY AND DEMAND WITH EXTERNALITIES

Figure TQ18-2

CHAPTER 19

GOVERNMENT TAXATION AND EXPENDITURE

Chapter 18 provided some insight into the theory behind any analysis of the role of government in a mixed economy; Chapter 19 now turns your attention to the actual roles assumed by governments at all levels in the American economy. The first section reviews the major expenditure patterns of federal, state, and local governments that define the American system of fiscal federalism. It is a system based primarily on the degree of spillover, or externality, in government programs: local governments tend to take care of local public goods with limited spillover beyond their boundaries; the federal government tends to take care of national public goods whose external effects span the country; and state governments handle programs in between.

The second section provides similar coverage for taxation in the context of a general discussion of the principles upon which our tax policies are constructed and evaluated. Toward the end of the chapter, additional theory is provided to introduce you to the notion of incidence—the economist's attempt to answer the complicated question: "Who pays this here tax, anyway?" This theory leads naturally to consideration of the distribution of the overall net burden (imputed tax liability net of returned benefit) of our tax, transfer, and public expenditure system. Of particular interest here is the legacy of the conservative fiscal revolution of the Reagan administration.

Having completed your work on this chapter, then, you will have accomplished the following objectives.

LEARNING OBJECTIVES

1. Describe the nature of the patterns of expenditure by local, state, and federal governments in the United States, and outline the recent evolution of those patterns into what we see today.

2. Relate, on the basis of these patterns, the construction of an efficient system of "fiscal federalism" and the blurring that necessarily occurs along the boundaries of the different levels of government.

3. Describe the conflicting principles of taxation—the benefit approach and the ability-to-pay approach—and the compromise between the two that has been accomplished in the United States.

4. Note specifically the difference between progressive and regressive taxation, and apply this distinction to differentiate the characters of various taxes employed in the United States.

5. Describe the character and importance of (a) individual income taxes, (b) sales taxes, (c) excise taxes, (d) payroll taxes, (e) corporate income taxes, and (f) property taxes in the United States.

6. List briefly the sources of erosion in the base of the federal income tax.

7. Outline the four pillars of the Reagan (conservative) fiscal revolution: (a) a retreat from Keynesian demand management in favor of reliance on private enterprise; (b) a budgetary emphasis on defense at the expense of civilian programs, with little concern for the potential damage of large deficits; (c) a reduction in the regulatory burden facing American business; and (d) a general reduction in the tax burden facing many American citizens.

8. Discuss efficiency as an issue in the design of a tax system, and relate it to (a) the Laffer curve, (b) the integration of the corporate income tax into the individual income tax, and (c) the flat-tax proposal.

9. Define the term "tax incidence," and explain why and how a tax might not fall on the economic agent identified in the tax codes.

10. Describe the procedure and the results of the Brookings study that concluded that the pattern of expenditure in the United States turns a mildly progressive tax structure into a fairly progressive fiscal structure.

The United States has, over the years, adopted a pattern of fiscal federalism that assigns various expenditure programs to the levels of government whose jurisdictions most closely match the geographical boundaries of their spillover effects. As a result, we see the federal government providing and managing programs like national defense, space exploration, and foreign affairs. We see local governments taking care of things like police protection, fire protection, public education, and other "local public goods." Finally, we see state governments administering highway, port, and welfare programs. Frequently the money required to support the programs at state and local levels flows down from the federal government, but the administration of the programs is conducted at the lowest possible level.

It should, of course, be noted that this structure is in a constant state of flux. The boundaries between governments and the spillover effects of programs are typically hard to define, and programs are forever being transferred from one level of government to another. Moreover, the growth in federal support for state and local administration of various programs was brought to an abrupt halt in the first years of the Reagan administration. What happens next is anybody's guess; but it will certainly affect almost everybody's life. The early years of the 1990s have been marked by serious budget problems in many states across the country and by the contraction of many state and locally funded public programs.

1. For the fiscal year 1992, annual expenditure by the U.S. federal government was estimated to be $(600 / 735 / 925 / 1094) billion. This is a total that exceeded the 1980 level of expenditure by nearly $575 billion. The largest single item within this total for 1992 was (interest on the public debt / national defense, veterans, and international affairs / education, labor, and development / income security including social security). The expenditure for this item amounted to $(537 / 437 / 337) billion. It should be noted that income security was, in 1980, the largest component; a change in federal priorities toward defense expenditure (is / is not) therefore suggested by even a cursory glance at expenditure patterns. Is another change coming with the "peace dividend"? We'll see.

1094; national defense, veterans, and international affairs; 337; is

---

Some idea of the enormous increase in the size and importance of the federal government within the past few generations can be gleaned by noting that in 1939, just before World War II, (1) total expenditure for national security was around $1 billion annually; (2) the federal social security program did not exist at all; and (3) other federal expenditures for health and welfare were of trivial importance. In sum, the federal government and its operations meant almost nothing in the everyday life of most people prior to the Second World War.

World War II changed all that. Ordinary citizens were then required to pay income taxes, to complete income-tax forms (a privilege previously reserved for the rich), and to meet a host of federal restrictions. Wartime rationing was temporary, but widespread federal taxation was not.

2. Development of the social security system has proven to be the most important factor accounting for growth in federal government outlays and collections since World War II. The demand for wider coverage has grown. Social security benefits, and deductions from wages and salaries to cover those benefits, have increased steadily. Social security is not only the second biggest item in the federal budget today; it is also but one item in a collection of "welfare security" programs that increased most spectacularly during the 1960s and 1970s. In 1970, total expenditure for "health, labor, welfare, and education" (i.e., expenditure for income security plus outlays for some of the other items listed in Table 19-1 of the text) came to $62.9 billion; in 1973, $99.1 billion; in 1976, $161.4 billion. For income security alone, the fiscal 1992 figure was $135 billion. That is down from 1980, but expenditure for income security has nonetheless (almost doubled / doubled / just about tripled) since 1970.

This postwar rise in welfare expenditures might have been offset (at least in part) by a decline in spending on national security after World War II, but this spending category did not fall as most people expected and hoped it would. Instead, "the cold war" began, and it was fought through the preparation of newly developed and horrendously expensive nuclear weapons. Beginning in the 1950s, and continuing thereafter, the total of spending on national defense persisted at levels that would have been literally incredible by the standards of 1939.

In recent years, this national-defense spending has, in comparison with items like income security and health, accelerated again after being relatively stable during the 1970s. The Vietnam war pushed it upward (although not by any spectacular amount). The expenditure total has risen since then, but the increases through 1981 probably reflected as much the impact of inflation as they did a larger fraction of real national product being directed toward weapons of war. Since 1981, though, the growth has been explosive, both in real terms and as a fraction of GNP.

---

doubled

Turning now to the revenue side of governments' ledger sheets, we will quickly see that two questions dominate any discussion of taxation: *"Who should pay?"* and *"How do we know if the person who should pay is, in fact, actually paying?"* Much of the remainder of this chapter deals with these two fundamental queries.

Suppose, for example, that the benefits to be derived from some public project will accrue entirely to an identifiable group of people from within the population. It might then be reasonable to assert that the tax revenues required to finance that project should be collected from the people who benefit; e.g., taxes for the construction of roads might be collected solely from the people who use the roads.

The welfare gains resulting from most public projects are, however, too diffuse to allow simple application of this "benefit principle." In most cases of public finance, therefore, policymakers must wrestle with the question of fairness and equity: How can society define a fair and equitable basis for distributing the burden of taxation? More specifically, how should the burden of financing government through taxes be distributed among the rich and the poor? What about the middle class? The debate on these issues is a never-ending one. One side argues that the rich should carry most or all of the burden simply because they are rich and can afford it, while the poor cannot. The opposition insists that "making money" is at least one of the incentives for personal initiative and effort. They argue that accepting the "soak-the-rich" philosophy may create a tax system that undermines incentive and encourages the most talented and inventive members of the population to move someplace where the tax laws are less severe.

In purely technical terms, the issues are summed up in the terms **progressive taxes** and **regressive taxes**. A progressive tax thrusts most of its burden on people of above-average income. A regressive tax bears more heavily on poorer people. A tax is not, however, progressive simply because it collects more money from a rich individual than from a poor one. To establish whether a tax is regressive or progressive, you must (1) find the amount of tax typically paid at various income levels within the population and (2) express this tax paid as a percentage of income. If these percentage figures rise as income rises—that is, if the percentage of income paid in tax rises as income rises—then the tax is progressive. If the percentage figures go down as you move to higher income levels, on the other hand, then the tax is regressive. If the percentage figure is pretty much the same at all income levels, then the tax is neither progressive nor regressive; it is **proportional.**

3. In order to know whether a tax is progressive or regressive, it is *(essential / not strictly essential)* to know how much money it typically collects from individuals at different levels of income.

One existing U.S. tax is easily classified within this progressive-regressive distinction; namely, the _____ tax. This tax is *(progressive / regressive)*, even after the Tax Reform Act of 1986.

essential; personal income; progressive

4. a. A tax levied as 1 percent on the first $5000 of income, 2 percent on the next $5000, 3 percent on the next $5000, and so on, would be *(progressive / proportional / regressive)*.

b. A tax of 10 percent on all income except the first $1000—that $1000 being exempt from tax—would be *(progressive / proportional / regressive)*.

c. If it is true that (among cigarette smokers) people with a yearly income of $8000 typically buy four packs of cigarettes per week, whereas those with an income of $16,000 typically buy six packs per week, then an excise tax of 10 cents per pack would be a *(progressive / proportional / regressive)* tax.

a. progressive **b.** progressive (This one is sneaky. The tax is almost proportional; but the tax, expressed as a percentage of income, goes up as income goes up.) **c.** regressive (The tax of, e.g., 40 cents weekly is a higher fraction of $8000 than 60 cents is of $16,000.)

5. a. The *benefit* approach to taxation argues that the distribution of tax levied between citizen A and citizen B should be proportional to the benefit each receives from the expenditures of government—a "pay for what you get" principle. Which of the following (one or both) may be considered a valid criticism of this principle?

(1) It assumes the particular tax in question can be linked to a particular type of expenditure. If a government's expenditures are large and varied, this is often difficult to determine.

(2) Even if a particular tax can somehow be linked to a particular type of spending (e.g., federal government spending on national defense), it is difficult to decide, in quantity terms, how much benefit rich citizen A derives from it in comparison with poor citizen B.

b. An alternative principle is that tax payments constitute a sacrifice by citizens and that the distribution of sacrifices should match people's *ability to pay*. It isn't altogether easy to establish what "ability to pay" really means, but one interpretation is that (pick one):

(1) every citizen should pay an equal amount of money in taxes, thus equalizing sacrifices.

(2) taxes should be levied and collected in strict proportion to the amount of income received by citizens.

(3) the tax system should be constructed so that the government collects its revenue from those who have the money.

a. both (1) and (2)   b. (3)

6. The ability-to-pay approach raises two distinct issues of equity. The first, simply put, asserts that equals should pay equal taxes. This is identified by economists as (horizontal / vertical / reasonable) equity. As simple as that assertion appears, it buries the fundamental question of how to determine when two people are equal. Are, for example, two people earning $30,000 per year equal if one of them has incurred $8000 in medical expenses? The tax codes say no. Medical expenses above 3 percent of adjusted gross income were deductible in 1991 (unless the taxpayer took the standard deduction), so the person who faced the medical problem could be taxed on the basis of an income of $22,900 (computed by subtracting $8000 less 3 percent of $30,000, or $7100, from $30,000) rather than $30,000.

The second equity issue involves the taxation of unequals; it is captured under the general rubric of (horizontal / vertical / redistributive) equity. This is the more controversial issue because of the (dis)incentive effects of income taxation.

horizontal; vertical

7. A tax imposed directly on an individual—i.e., a tax whose amount payable is calculated by some factor such as size of income or value of certain of that person's assets—is designated as (a direct / an indirect) tax. A tax levied on a transaction, most commonly on the purchase and sale of a commodity, is (a direct / an indirect) tax. Some taxes, such as the corporate income tax, do not fall neatly into either the direct or the indirect category. Problems of determining real incidence are usually more difficult with (direct / indirect) taxes.

a direct; an indirect; indirect

8. a. Disregarding social security taxes, the two taxes which yield the most revenue for the federal government, ranked in order of their revenue importance, are:

(1) _____

(2) _____

b. The most important tax at the level of state government is the _____ tax; the most important tax at the level of local government is the _____ tax.

c. The single most important expenditure item at the state and local government level is _____ .

a. (1) personal income tax   (2) corporation income tax   b. sales; property
c. education

9. The difference between a **sales tax** and an **excise tax** is this: if the tax applies to all items sold, omitting only items specifically named in the law as exempt, it is (a sales / an excise) tax. If, on the other hand, the tax applies only to commodities or services named in the law (e.g., liquor, cigarettes), it is (a sales / an excise) tax.

a sales; an excise

10. A **value-added tax** is computed on the basis of the value added to goods by various firms at various stages of production. If a textile firm were to pay $4000 for the yarn, material, and labor required to weave cloth which it sells for $10,000, then the value which it would add to these materials would equal $(4000 / 6000 / 10,000 / 14,000); a value-added tax would be levied on this amount.

Suppose another firm—a garment manufacturing firm—bought all this cloth and paid the full $10,000 for it. Suppose, as well, that it paid another $2000 for all its other raw materials, such as thread, and sold the resulting output of garments for $20,000. The value added by this firm would be $(2000 / 4000 / 6000 / 8000 / 10,000 / 20,000).

6000; 8000

11. The **marginal** tax rate applied to income is the fraction or percent (of the last dollar of income that must be paid in tax / obtained by comparing total tax against total income). Put another way, the marginal rate is the extra amount of tax individuals would be required to pay if their incomes were to climb by $1. The corresponding average tax rate is the percent (of the last dollar of income that must be paid in tax / obtained by comparing total tax against total income).

of the last dollar of income that must be paid in tax; obtained by comparing total tax against total income

12. It is frequently not an easy matter to determine whether a tax is progressive or regressive. The corporation income tax is a case in point; it takes a little thought to evaluate how this tax distributes its burden. The marginal tax rates applied to corporate profits by the Tax Reform Act of 1986 are given in Table 19-1. The bulge between $100,000 and $335,000 represents a technical correction for a tax break offered to small firms. It is therefore fair to represent the tax for large firms as very nearly proportional. In assessing its nature, then, you might be tempted by say that the tax is very mildly progressive.

Table 19-1

Level of Profit	Marginal Tax Rate (%)
Under $50,000	15
$50,000–$75,000	25
$75,000–$100,000	34
$100,000–$335,000	39
Above $335,000	34

Focusing only on the rate schedule is, however, the wrong way to think about the character of the corporation income tax. An accurate assessment of the burden of a tax can be accomplished only if one accurately gauges who actually pays it. Do corporations pay the corporate profits tax? No. Their owners, the *(bondholders / stockholders)*, pay the tax because it is levied against earnings which would otherwise belong to these owners.

Disregarding the different percentages applicable below $335,000, the 1986 corporate tax was proportional in the sense that its marginal rate applied to profit attributed to any stockholder was 34 percent regardless of whether he or she owned 1 share or 10,000 shares. Remember that in taxation the term "proportional" is intended to mean a tax which takes the same percent of income at every income level, right across the entire population; and the critical point here is that only a fraction of the population owns corporation stock, so the tax is a tax on a particular segment of the population.

Suppose, for the sake of argument, that all corporation stock is owned by poor people. (Never mind the fact that if they owned all that stock, they wouldn't be poor!) As a tax on the incomes of the poor, the corporation tax would then be a *(progressive / regressive)* one. Alternatively, suppose that all the stock is owned by rich people. That would make the tax *(progressive / regressive)*. The facts are that some people in the lower income brackets own a little stock; many in the middle brackets own a little more; but the great bulk of corporate stock is owned by people with above-average incomes. The corporation tax can (subject to the one vital qualification discussed in question 17) therefore be judged to be *(progressive / regressive)*.

stockholders; regressive; progressive; progressive

13. Some people complain that the corporation income tax imposes a burden of double taxation on stockholders. They mean that the dividends paid to stockholders out of after-tax corporate income *(are / are not)* subject to the personal income tax. Insofar as this specific double-taxation argument is valid, it applies *(to all corporate profit / only to that part of corporate profit which is paid out as dividends / only to that part of profit which is retained and undistributed)*.

are; only to that part of corporate profit which is paid out as dividends

14. The base of the individual income tax is eroded by a number of factors. First of all, the Tax Reform Act of 1986 allows (after 1991) personal exemptions of $ *(500 / 1050 / 2050)* for each person claimed on a tax return. In addition, many sources of income receive preferential treatment through what are known as *tax expenditures*. List at least five of these tax expenditures in the spaces provided below:

a. _____

b. _____

c. _____

d. _____

e. _____

The net effect of these tax expenditures is to *(increase / leave unaffected / decrease)* the effective progressivity of the U.S. personal income tax.

2050 **a. through e.** mortgage interest deductions (on primary residences), social security benefits (up to a point), implicit homeowner rents, retirement-account contributions made by employers and (to some degree) by employees, employer contributions for medical insurance, state and local tax payments (excluding sales taxes), capital-gains carryovers at death (There are others, as well; see Table 19-5 in the text.); decrease

15. The conservative fiscal revolution initiated during the Reagan administration worked to change the role of government in nearly every arena of its activity. Indicate, in the parentheses provided, whether the indicated role or variable increased (I), decreased (D), or stayed roughly the same (S) during the Reagan years in comparison with the previous two decades:

a. Regulatory activity .... ( )

b. Highest personal-income-tax rate .... ( )

c. Highest corporation-income-tax rate .... ( )

d. Federal deficits as a percentage of GNP ..... ( )

e. Defense spending .... ( )

f. Spending on civilian social programs .... ( )

g. Keynesian-style management of aggregate demand ( )

h. Unemployment rate (average) .... ( )

i. Total federal tax liability for wealthiest 10 percent of the population .... ( )

j. Total federal tax liability of poorest 10 percent of the population .... ( )

a. D **b.** D [reduced from 50 percent to 33 percent (28 percent for highest incomes)] **c.** D [reduced from 46 percent to 39 percent (34 percent for highest incomes)] **d.** I (increased from 1.1 percent to 4.2 percent) **e.** I **f.** S (for middle-class income-support programs) and I (for lower-class welfare-support programs) **g.** D (reliance on private enterprise) **h.** I (from 5.6 percent to 7.7 percent) **i.** I (grew by 3 percent) **j.** D (fell by 15 percent)

16. The Laffer curve, as a theoretical construction, simply notes the potential for high income-tax rates to eventually (encourage people to work more / encourage people to invest less / encourage people to work less). Figure 19-1 provides an illustration of such a curve. The 25 percent tax cut instituted by the Reagan administration in 1981 was based on the belief that the economy was being taxed to a point like (A / B / C) and that revenues would therefore actually climb with the reduction. That theory (did / did not) seem to work. On the basis of empirical work by Don Fullerton, in fact, it is most likely that the economy is being taxed to a point like (A / B / C).

Figure 19-1

A second type of reform of the individual income tax, known as the flat-tax proposal, has been advanced in both liberal and conservative quarters. It is estimated that the entire system as it now stands could be replaced by a proportional tax that takes (10 / 20 / 30) cents of every dollar earned by every American worker. Concern has been raised, however, that this amounts to (an even larger transfer of the burden of the tax from the poor to the rich / a transfer of the burden from the rich to the poor / no transfer of the burden at all). Since a strict flat tax would allow no deductions, in its purest form, there might also be an enormous (increase / decrease) in the value of property in the United States because mortgage interest payments would no longer be deductible.

---

encourage people to work less; C ; did not; A ; 20; a transfer of the burden from the rich to the poor; decrease

17. Suppose that the maximum corporation tax rate is raised from 34 to, say, 55 percent; but let corporations respond to this tax by raising their prices just enough to keep their after-tax profit unchanged. This would be a classic example of **tax shifting,** and the *incidence* of the extra tax would fall entirely on the (corporations / stockholders / corporations' customers). The possibility of significant tax shifting raises the interesting potential that most of the corporate tax, possibly even all of it, is not paid out of shareholders' incomes at all; it might be passed on to other people via higher prices. If a corporation's customers happened to consist almost entirely of people in the lower half of the income range, and if it did manage to shift the tax via higher prices, then the tax (with respect to this particular corporation, anyhow) would be (progressive / regressive). There is a fair amount of evidence to suggest that at least part of the corporate tax is shifted via higher prices for the goods corporations sell, but the evidence is not all in. The issue is still being debated and explored.

The words "shifting" and "incidence" are important with respect to taxes; study their meaning. The government may require that you pay a certain tax; but you do not really pay it if, through the device of charging a higher price or paying a lower price, you make the tax come out of someone else's pocket. You have shifted the tax, and the true incidence of the tax is on the person out of whose pocket the money really comes.

Problems of tax incidence can become extremely complicated; it may be difficult to establish what the facts really are. Business firm or individual A may manage to shift part or all of a tax onto B; B in turn may shift some part of it to C—and so on. The one tax which has almost no incidence problem is the _____ tax.

---

corporations' customers; regressive; personal income

18. Suppose that there are 100 people in an economy, and suppose that they can be ordered according to their incomes so that each earns $1000 more per year than the next lowest person. That is to say, suppose that person 1 earns $1000, person 2 earns $2000, and so on, up to person 100, who earns $100,000 per year. Let each pay 10 percent of his or her income in taxes, and let the revenue generated by the tax be divided equally among the first 50 people.

Figure 19-2 illustrates this structure. Line _____ illustrates the tax program, line _____ illustrates the transfer program, and line _____ illustrates the overall program in the same way that the curves on Figure 19-6 of the text portray the actual distribution of the net burden of the present U.S. structure. Is the overall program progressive? _____ Is the tax structure progressive? _____ Is the transfer program progressive? _____

Now let the 10 percent tax rate apply only to income above $10,000, so persons 1 through 10 pay no taxes but share in the

Figure 19-2

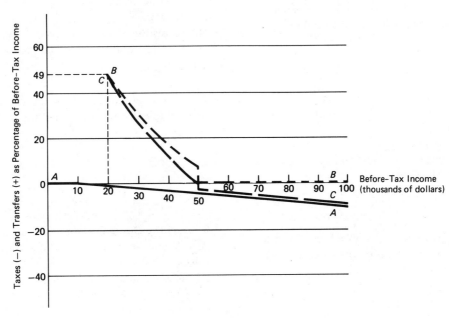

Figure 19-3

transfer program. New lines are required to portray this new structure; they are recorded in Figure 19-3. Line _____ now portrays the tax structure, line _____ portrays the new transfer schedule, and line _____ portrays the overall program. Is the transfer program now more progressive? _____ Is the tax system now more progressive? _____ Is the overall program now more progressive? _____

AA; BB; CC; yes; no (It is proportional.); yes; AA; BB; CC; no (It is unchanged.); yes; yes

REVIEW CONCEPTS

1. The United States has adopted a system of fiscal federalism with issues handled at the lowest possible level: national issues (like defense) at the federal level, local issues (like education) at the local level, and intermediate issues (like welfare) at the state level.

2. Government taxation and spending at all levels accounts for roughly one-third of GNP, with 70 percent of that total spent by the federal level.

3. Tax policy is informed by two opposing points of view—the benefits approach and the ability-to-pay approach. Taxes are progressive (regressive) if they take larger (smaller) proportions of higher incomes. Income taxes tend to be progressive by design; sales and excise taxes tend to be regressive by conduct.

4. The federal government raises most of its revenue from individual and corporate income taxes (with some raised through payroll and consumption taxes). Local governments employ property taxes most heavily. States rely on sales taxes and, in some cases, income taxes.

5. The fastest-growing federal tax is the payroll tax; its revenue is earmarked for social security.

6. The conservative fiscal revolution was based upon (1) macro policies emphasizing efficiency and not business-cycle management, (2) budgetary emphasis on defense and de-emphasis on civilian programs, (3) little concern about deficits, (4) reduced regulation, and (5) lower tax rates.

7. Questions of incidence are questions of who pays. They are related to questions about the degree to which various taxes create disincentives for people to work harder and/or save more. The benefit or transfer portrait of expenditure programs tends to offset regressive treatment of low-income taxpayers.

QUIZ: Multiple Choice

1. The largest single money item in the U.S. federal government budget is currently:
(1) energy, science, and environment.
(2) national defense and international affairs.
(3) interest on the public debt.
(4) general government (including justice).
(5) income security.

2. Any highway that is built by the government and made available toll-free to the public represents an example of:
(1) private consumption.
(2) a transfer expenditure.
(3) a welfare expenditure.
(4) monetary policy.
(5) none of the above.

3. A government might reasonably introduce a widespread program of transfer payments in order to:
(1) create a surplus in its budget.
(2) effect some change in the social decision on the question of *for whom* goods are to be produced.
(3) provide more social consumption.
(4) move the economy's production-possibility curve outward and to the right.
(5) reduce inflation.

4. The corporation income (profits) tax is defined as a tax levied on:
(1) only the dividends paid to stockholders.
(2) the value added to production by each corporation.
(3) the corporation's total net sales.
(4) additions to corporate retained earnings.
(5) dividends paid plus undistributed profits.

5. One type of income not subject to taxation at all under U.S. income-tax law is:
(1) income in the form of dividends from stock owned.
(2) income in the form of interest on corporation bonds owned.
(3) real income in the form of housing services from a house occupied by its owner.
(4) real income adjusted for the most recent year's inflation.
(5) income in the form of capital gains.

6. An argument made in favor of the corporation income tax is that:
(1) it taxes only earnings above the normal return on invested capital.
(2) without it, some fraction of corporation income may not be currently taxed at all.
(3) on balance, it is a regressive tax.
(4) it taxes the income received by bondholders.
(5) it means double taxation (at least in part) of corporation earnings.

7. Which alternative in question 6 would be correct had it referred to an argument against the corporation income tax?
(1).
(2).
(3).
(4).
(5).

8. The tax yielding the largest annual revenue for the federal government (disregarding social security withholdings from wages and salaries) is the:
(1) personal income tax.
(2) corporation income tax.
(3) value-added tax.
(4) excise tax on liquor and tobacco.
(5) property tax.

9. Suppose that the tax on an income of $20,000 is equal to $4000. Assume, as well, that the tax would rise to $4800 if this income were to rise to $22,000. The marginal rate of tax implicit in these figures is:
(1) 20 percent.
(2) about (but not more than) 21 percent.
(3) more than 21 percent, but just under 22 percent.
(4) 40 percent.
(5) none of the preceding.

10. A general sales tax, without any exempted commodities, is considered to be:

(1) a progressive tax because it applies to luxuries as well as necessities.
(2) a regressive tax because wealthy people spend a smaller percentage of their total incomes on taxed commodities, and hence the proportion of tax payments to income is greater for poor people.
(3) a progressive tax because wealthy people spend more than poor people.
(4) a regressive tax because more money is collected from a poor person than from a rich one.
(5) a proportional tax because everybody pays the same tax percentage on each purchase.

11. A proportional tax is correctly defined as one in which (taking the taxpaying population overall, or in terms of the typical taxpayer):
(1) the ratio of tax collected to income received is the same at all income levels.
(2) about the same amount of tax is collected per taxpayer, regardless of taxpayer incomes.
(3) the percentage of income taken in tax falls as income climbs.
(4) the amount of money taken in tax rises as income falls.
(5) the preceding descriptions do not apply (because none of them is correct).

12. Which alternative in question 11 would be correct had that question referred to the correct definition of a progressive tax?
(1).
(2).
(3).
(4).
(5).

13. Which alternative in question 11 would be correct had that question referred to the correct definition of a regressive tax?
(1).
(2).
(3).
(4).
(5).

14. The incidence of a tax is:
(1) its tendency to fluctuate in total amount collected, as the economy moves from boom to recession and back.
(2) its relative importance in the budget of the government involved.
(3) the extent to which payment can be avoided through one or more "loopholes."
(4) its burden, in the sense of identifying the people whose real incomes are actually reduced by that tax.
(5) the effect to which its imposition is likely to induce those who must pay it to work less, in an effort to avoid part of such payment.

15. How do the tax systems of state and local governments in the United States compare with the federal system?
(1) They are both more progressive.
(2) They are both more regressive.
(3) The state system is more progressive than the federal; the local system, less so.
(4) The local system is more progressive than the federal; the state system, less so.
(5) None of the preceding statements is correct.

16. The largest single tax expenditure in the existing federal personal-income-tax law concerns:
(1) the exclusion of pension contributions.
(2) illegal tax evasion by the self-employed.
(3) depletion allowances for crude-oil holdings.
(4) nontaxation of income in the form of services from owner-occupied homes.
(5) income from securities that by law are tax-exempt.

17. The Tax Reform Act of 1986 increased the total federal payments of
(1) the wealthiest 10 percent of U.S. households.
(2) the wealthiest 20 percent of U.S. households.
(3) the wealthiest 30 percent of U.S. households.
(4) the wealthiest 40 percent of U.S. households.
(5) the wealthiest 50 percent of U.S. households.

SUGGESTED ANSWERS TO QUESTIONS IN THE TEXT: Chapter 19

1. *Progressive federal taxes:* personal income tax, death and estate taxes, corporation income tax

Roughly proportional (though mildly regressive due to maximum liabilities): payroll (social security) tax

Regressive: excise taxes, highway tolls, customs duties

Trading the income tax for a consumption tax would likely be a move toward regressive taxation, since poorer people spend larger percentages of their incomes; in response to this observation, some argue that the consumption tax rate could be progressive. A universal sales tax could not incorporate such rate flexibility, though, and *would* be more regressive.

2. Economic equivalence may exist, but smoking is worse for people than eating bread. Taxes can be used as financial disincentives aimed at discouraging people from doing certain things, but their effect can be regressive unless accompanied by lump-sum rebates of the income forgone in paying the taxes. This would preserve the substitution effect of increasing the price of (e.g.) cigarettes, but it would eliminate the income effect.

For example, consider a $2-per-pack tax on cigarettes accompanied by a pledge to reimburse the money as a lump-sum credit against the personal income tax. The substitution effect would still discourage smoking, but the credit would dramatically reduce the loss in real income.

3. Progressive rates would eliminate the question of regressivity. The effect on saving should be positive because money saved would not be taxed and interest earned on saving would not be taxed *until the money was used to purchase something*. For most, then, this would be a tax-delaying ploy, much like the old individual retirement accounts. Those accounts did not stimulate as much saving as originally forecast, but their stimulus may have been overwhelmed by other changes in economic circumstances.

This is a good question for indifference-curve analysis, with utility depending upon consumption over two periods and the potential to consume in excess of income in the second period by saving in the first period.

4. Correlation does not imply causality. To analyze the experience correctly, you need a model that captures causality, a complete description of the tax cuts and how they were distributed, and some historical context to evaluate the impacts of changes in other economic variables.

5. Think of taxes that are the sticks of disincentive designed to discourage certain sorts of behavior. Pollution taxes are fine examples. Strong lobby groups generally oppose these taxes because they would not be required if the targeted behaviors were not privately profitable. Even when the advocates of social welfare carry the day, lobbyists oppose taxes and favor direct controls. That way their clients get to do some of what they want for free.

Consider, for example, the sulfur polluter. Let 100 tons per week be the targeted level of emission. With a standard, the polluter gets the first 100 tons free. With a tax designed to elicit 100 tons (say, $10 per ton), the polluter must pay $1000.

6. *Average tax rates based on AGI:* 0, 1.5, 6, 9, 15, and 19 percent

Marginal tax rates based on the indicated jumps in AGI: 3, 11, 11, 20, 21 percent (The tax is progressive on the basis of the adjusted gross income.)

Average tax rates based on TI: 0, 15, 15, 15, 21, and 24 percent

Marginal tax rates based on the indicated jumps in TI: 15, 15, 15, 25, and 25 percent

7. *Post-tax wages:* $10, $9, $8, and so on, down to $0
Pre-tax earnings: $10 times the number of hours worked
Tax revenues: $0, $200, $3900, $5700, $7400, $9000, $10,200, $11,200, $10,400, $5400, and $0

The Laffer curve plots tax revenue against tax rate; it seems to peak at 70 percent. The table is crafted so that the economy contracts as the tax rate climbs because people work fewer hours.

8. This is a thought question for which there are many answers. Some initial thoughts follow:

a. *An AIDS vaccine:* Global—subsidize its production and distribution.

b. *Pollution controls designed to reduce acid rain:* National/global—levy effluent charges or impose standards [with compensation (?)].

c. *Coastal defenses against ocean storms:* Local or national—make provision.

d. *A program directed at reducing factory noise in New Britain:* Local—engage in regulation [based on national or international standards to maintain competitive position (?)].

e. *CFC emissions reductions to prevent ozone depletion in the stratosphere:* Global—impose absolute standards or ban them [substitutes exist (?)].

CHAPTER 20

CURBING MARKET POWER: REGULATION AND ANTITRUST POLICIES

Government has three major roles to play in supporting a modern economy: maintain efficiency, promote macroeconomic stability and growth, and establish a fair distribution of income. This chapter concentrates on one of government's primary challenges in exercising its efficiency role—performing a watchdog function to prevent excessive abuse of market power. And it focuses your attention on the two major tools employed by the U. S. government to put some "teeth" behind its careful monitoring of business activity: regulation and antitrust activity.

Having completed your work in this area, therefore, you will have accomplished the following objectives.

LEARNING OBJECTIVES

1. Understand the inefficiencies of monopoly markets that produce too little and charge too much, and recall how to demonstrate the cost of those inefficiencies in terms of lost consumer surplus (i.e., deadweight loss).

2. Be familiar with the various tools available to curb the inefficiencies of monopoly distortions of price and output.

3. Understand thoroughly the economic regulation of imperfect competitors, paying particular attention to the circumstances under which regulation can improve or reduce general welfare.

4. Trace the evolution of antitrust activity to its modern formulation: Focus on improving efficiency and not just on preventing bigness itself.

Regulation is, in the United States, the most popular mechanism with which governments at all levels protect their citizens from potential abuses of market power, particularly when a natural monopoly is under scrutiny. Regulation, in its broadest context, includes all rules and laws designed to change or control the operation of an economic enterprise. There are, in fact, two major categories within that context: social and economic.

1. Place (E) or (S) in the parentheses provided to indicate whether each of the following regulatory activities is an example of an economic regulation or a social regulation:

a. Restraints on price-setting practices among firms. ( )

b. Clean air policy . . . . ( )

c. Limits on the rates of return earned by utilities . . ( )

d. Drug testing by the FDA . . . . ( )

e. Requirement to provide electricity to everyone who asks for it . . . . ( )

f. Constraints on entry into and exit from given markets . . . . ( )

a. E **b.** S **c.** E **d.** S **e.** E or S **f.** E

2. Price controls are frequently mentioned as a possible means of controlling the potential abuses of monopoly power. Pervasive use of price controls to control the occasional monopolist can, however, cause a plethora of economic problems. In the parentheses provided, note with (Y) those effects which might be expected to appear in a list of possible difficulties:

a. Alienation of business and government . . . . . . ( )

b. International trade problems . . . . ( )

c. Shortages and surpluses . . . . ( )

d. Absence of necessary flexibility in relative prices . . . .
. . . . ( )

e. Increased unemployment . . . . ( )

all Y (Enforced price specifications are likely to cause problems in every economic sphere where adjustment to unpredictable events is required.)

3. Consult Figure 20-1. For the indicated demand and cost curves, it is clear that the unregulated monopolist would produce _____ units of output for sale at a price of $_____. Excess pure economic profits of $_____ would then be earned.

Figure 20-1

Regulation to the point of zero profits would meanwhile require a price specification of $_____, at which _____ units of output would be expected. Consumer surplus would, in that case, increase from the unregulated monopoly level of $18 to $_____.

Ideal price regulation to the point where efficiency conditions were satisfied would, meanwhile, require a price specification of $_____, with _____ units of output expected only if the monopolist's losses in the amount of $_____ were covered. Consumer surplus would rise further to $_____, but would actually equal $_____ if the subsidy to cover the losses just noted were deducted. This (would nonetheless / would not) represent an improvement over the average cost pricing alternative.

———

6; 9; 6 (= $1 per unit × 6 units); 7; 8; 32 [= 0.5($15 − $7)(8 − 0)]; 5; 10; 10 (= $1 per unit × 10 units); 50 [= 0.5($15 − $5)(10 − 0)]; 40; would nonetheless

4. a. Imperfect competition (of which, remember, monopoly is but an extreme example) is undesirable from an economic standpoint mainly because of the (excess profits generated by the exploitation of price and quantity / distortions that it produces in the allocation of resources).

Chapter 9 noted that all perfectly competitive, profit-maximizing firms operate so that marginal cost is (lower than / equal to / higher than) the going market price. Since ratios of price reflect ratios of marginal utility, competitive equilibria thereby achieve maximum efficiency because the marginal cost of producing any good by any competitive firm is necessarily maintained at a level that is (lower than / equal to / greater than) the marginal benefit that its consumption produces. Total welfare (cannot / can) be made higher by rearranging resources even though each firm acts only to maximize its own profits.

For a monopolist, though, the equality of marginal benefit and marginal cost is not the result of self-motivated profit maximization. Since price is always (greater than / equal to / less than) marginal revenue along a sloped market demand curve, profit maximization requires that marginal cost be maintained at a level that is (higher than / equal to / lower than) the going price. Why? Because profits are maximized where marginal cost equals marginal revenue, and marginal revenue is less than price. Price ratios still reflect ratios of marginal utility, though, so monopoly power brings marginal cost in (higher than / equal to / lower than) marginal benefit. Total welfare (cannot / can) then be improved by rearranging resources. How? In a way which (brings resources into / moves resources out of) the monopolists' markets to (increase / decrease) their output.

b. Suppose, for example, that a monopoly firm sets its price equal to $2, with marginal revenue at $1. This would mean (by the profit-maximizing rule) that marginal cost must be $(1 / 2). The consumer would pay $2 for each unit bought, including the last unit, but that last unit would add only $1 to the total production cost. It would cost only another $1 (or just over $1 if marginal costs were increasing and very sensitive to output) to produce 1 further unit. Why shouldn't consumers be able to buy that unit for what it would cost to produce it? A resource is not being used to its best advantage if consumers, making decisions in terms of the prices which they must pay for additional units of various goods, halt their purchases at points where the extra cost of using resources to produce additional units are significantly lower than their prices. Overall, resources are not being allocated properly if $P \neq MC$.

---

a. distortions that it produces in the allocation of resources; equal to; equal to; cannot; greater than; lower than; lower than; can; brings resources into; increase   **b.** 1

---

5. As was just noted, the price which an unregulated monopolist charges is *(too high / too low / just right)* relative to the competitive price because price always exceeds marginal revenue along a downward-sloping demand curve and because profits are always maximized where marginal revenue is set equal to marginal cost. Since monopoly firms face downward-sloping demand curves (otherwise they would have no monopoly power, right?), a monopolist must therefore produce *(less output than / more output than / the same output as)* the competitive firm. On the basis of the efficiency properties of the perfectly competitive market, it is thus clear that the marginal utility derived from consuming the monopolist's product is *(greater than / less than / equal to)* the marginal cost of producing the good in question.

Consult Figure 20-2. The long-run competitive output and price for a market with the indicated cost structure must equal _____ units and $_____, respectively. An unregulated, profit-maximizing monopolist would, meanwhile, sell _____ units at a price of $_____. The result would be a reduction in consumer surplus from $_____ to $_____. Of that reduction, $_____ would go to the monopolist in the form of excess economic profit and $_____ would represent lost welfare that would disappear (deadweight loss).

Figure 20-2

The dimension of actual deadweight loss caused by imperfect competition across the United States has been estimated by Arnold Harberger to be in the neighborhood of *(0.1 / 5.0 / over 10.0)* percent of GNP. To conclude, in light of these numbers, that monopoly power should not be a major concern would, however, be to ignore the distortion in the distribution of income that excessive monopoly profits can create. More study is required to conclude that imperfect competition is a "nonproblem."

---

too high; less output than; greater than; 8; 6; 4; 8; 16; 4; 8; 4; 0.1

---

6. Suppose that the monopolist depicted in Figure 20-2 faces a lump-sum tax on profits of $8. The unregulated, profit-maximizing monopolist would then *(increase the price above $8 / decrease the price below $8 / maintain the price at $8)* to support a *(larger / smaller / constant)* level of production and sales.

Suppose, instead, that government taxes the monopolist's implicit return to capital and that the effective (constant) marginal cost of production thereby increases from $6 to $8 per unit. Output would *(fall to / rise to / continue to remain fixed at)* _____ units; price would *(climb to / fall to / stay put at)* $_____ , representing an increase in price *(equal to / less than / greater than)* the $_____ increase in unit costs.

---

maintain the price at $8; constant; fall to; 2; climb to; 9; less than; 2

---

7. The text notes three important pieces of antitrust legislation which laid the groundwork for subsequent antitrust activity:

1. The Sherman Antitrust Act (1890) (SA)
2. The Clayton Antitrust Act (1914) (CA)
3. The Federal Trade Commission Act (1914) (FTCA)

Match each of the following provisions to its landmark legislation by recording (SA), (CA), or (FTCA) in parentheses provided; if none applies, write "none":

a. Price discrimination that is not based upon cost differentials and is, instead, designed to lessen competition is declared illegal. . . . . ( )

b. Unfair and deceptive business activities and practices are declared illegal. . . . . ( )

c. No corporation can acquire another if such an acquisition would substantially reduce competition. . . . . ( )

d. Forming a monopoly is declared a felony. . . ( )

e. Lobbying for tariff protection against foreign competition is declared illegal. . . . . ( )

f. Restraint of trade or commerce among states is declared illegal. . . . . ( )

g. Restraint of trade or commerce with foreign nations is declared illegal. . . . . ( )

h. Imposing a contract which prohibits the purchase of a competitor's product is illegal. . . . . ( )

a. CA **b.** FTCA **c.** CA **d.** SA **e.** none **f.** SA **g.** SA **h.** CA

Antitrust policy is, of course, written with full knowledge that imperfect competition has both a good and a bad side. Unbridled exploitation of market power can, on the one hand, depress output and generate excessive prices and profits. On the other hand, however, there *do* exist economies of scale that should not be sacrificed simply for the sake of having many firms instead of few. There is, moreover, a demonstrable correlation between market concentration and research into discovery and development of new products and new processes. In light of this dichotomy of properties, it is the primary lesson of this chapter that antitrust activity should (1) keep the barriers to competition low, (2) tolerate bigness when size is determined by technology, and (3) be vigilant against anticompetitive practices whenever they occur.

8. a. One significant change in the way that the legal system of the United States deals with the potential problems of imperfect competition is found in the judicial attention paid to how business is actually conducted. It is, according to this new view of how the law should be enforced, more important to attack types of behavior that signify the abuse of market power than it is to concentrate simply on markets that display offensive types of industrial organization. These abusive methods of conducting business, including *(a)* price fixing, *(b)* output restraint, *(c)* market division, *(d)* predatory pricing, *(e)* resale agreements, and *(f)* price discrimination, *(are / are not)* necessarily confined to the concentrated industries with extreme and potentially profitable market power. Some of them can appear in competitive markets just as easily.

The following list of behaviors contains examples of the six types of conduct just noted. Identify each with the conduct that it represents, and record your answer in the space provided:

(1) An agreement between retailers and the manufacturer not to sell a certain doll for less than $25 _____

(2) The pricing of computers below production costs to prevent entry by potential competitors _____

(3) An agreement among suppliers of oil not to sell more than 1 million barrels per day _____

(4) A policy in which one firm sells hammers to hardware stores for $8.99 and to the Defense Department for $410.22 _____

(5) An agreement among sugar retailers to sell only in specified geographical regions of the United States _____

(6) An agreement among airlines to increase fares 20 percent over the weekend _____

(7) The destruction of thousands of pounds of coffee beans before they get to market _____

b. The recent judicial focus upon the conduct of business rather than the structure of business reflects the understanding that research and development into new products and into new cost-reducing technologies will continue in any market with any structure as long as collusion (tacit or overt) does not undermine competitive pressures (actual or potential). On the basis of this notion, concern about mergers should proceed on a case-by-case basis. General prescriptions should therefore be difficult to come by, but one is apparent: of the three types of merger activity— _____ , _____ , and _____ —the one most likely to be troublesome is the _____ type, which may lower competitive pressures by increasing the market concentration of the largest firms.

are not **a.** (1) resale agreements (2) predatory pricing (3) output restraint (4) price discrimination (5) market division (6) price fixing (7) output restraint **b.** vertical; horizontal; conglomerate; horizontal

---

Recent antitrust activity has, in fact, focused on promoting efficiency in business practices and not on attacking "bigness" per se. The notion underlying this concentration on conduct rather than structure in an economy which is facing increasing competition from around the world is that collusive agreements which try to fix prices are the most troublesome source of inefficiency. Large firms which can exploit decreasing costs as they compete internationally can be a source of economic strength as long as they do indeed compete.

REVIEW CONCEPTS

1. Regulation offers government one tool with which to influence how business is conducted. Economic regulation can be accomplished by controlling prices, production, standards, and exit and entry conditions. Social regulation is directed at correcting (negative) externalities.

2. Unregulated monopoly power allows firms to operate at socially inefficient levels, charging too much for too little product. Average cost price regulation eliminates excess profit, but it is not necessarily efficient. Ideal pricing, where price equals marginal cost, does not cover average production costs (for a natural monopoly with declining average cost and thus $AC > MC$).

3. Modern antitrust policies try to prohibit anticompetitive activities (like price fixing, price discrimination, tie-in agreements, etc.). They have evolved from earlier policies designed primarily to break up monopoly structures.

4. Antitrust policies also limit corporate mergers which would lessen competition; horizontal mergers are the most troublesome in this regard.

5. Efficiency improvement is the fundamental objective of current antitrust activity, with particular emphasis placed upon curbing collusive, price-fixing agreements in an unregulated, international business arena.

QUIZ: Multiple Choice

1. Which of the following would be considered a form of economic regulation?
(1) OSHA regulations designed to ensure safety in the workplace.
(2) EPA regulations designed to improve air quality.
(3) Public utility–control regulations designed to promote efficient and equitable pricing of electricity.
(4) FDA regulations designed to ensure the safety of new drugs.
(5) All the above.

2. Which of the following would be considered a form of social regulation?
(1) Product quality standards designed to protect consumers.
(2) Public utility–control regulations designed to promote efficient and equitable pricing of cable television.
(3) NRC regulations designed to ensure the safe operation of nuclear power plants.
(4) Insurance regulations designed to promote premiums which are fair and economically justifiable.
(5) All the above.

3. Which of the following represents a reason for suspecting that a natural monopoly might best serve a particular market?
(1) A tariff structure which allows domestic pricing above the world price.
(2) The presence of increasing returns to scale throughout a range of output which covers the entire market.
(3) The invention of a new product which is covered by a 17-year patent.
(4) The creation of monopoly power by an act of government which restricts market entry.
(5) All the above.

4. Consult Figure 20-3. An unregulated monopolist would operate by producing an amount which would clear the market at what price?

Figure 20-3

(1) $1.
(2) $2.
(3) $3.
(4) $4.
(5) $5.

5. Which price listed in question 4 would be the ideal, regulated price for the monopolist represented in Figure 20-3?
(1) $1.
(2) $2.
(3) $3.
(4) $4.
(5) $5.

6. How much would the monopolist in Figure 20-3 produce if regulated by average cost pricing?
(1) 9 units.
(2) 7 units.
(3) 5 units.
(4) 4 units.
(5) 1 unit.

7. If the monopolist in Figure 20-3 were to face an ideal price regulation, how much of a subsidy would be required, per unit, to sustain his or her activity?
(1) Exactly $5 per unit.
(2) Exactly $4 per unit.
(3) More than $2 per unit but less than $4 per unit.
(4) More than $1 per unit but less than $2 per unit.
(5) Exactly $1 per unit.

8. Net of the subsidy (judged to be $1.25 per unit), how much consumer surplus would be gained over the unregulated case if the monopolist in Figure 20-3 were to face ideal price regulation?
(1) $16.50.
(2) $10.00.
(3) $7.75.
(4) $4.50.
(5) Zero, since the subsidy exhausts the entire gain.

9. Which answer to question 8 would have been correct if that question had referred to average cost price regulation?
(1).
(2).
(3).
(4).
(5).

10. Which of the following made price discrimination not based on cost differentials illegal?
(1) The Sherman Antitrust Act.
(2) The Humphrey-Hawkins Act.
(3) The Clayton Antitrust Act.
(4) The Gramm-Rudman Act.
(5) The Federal Trade Commission Act.

11. Which answer to question 10 would have been correct if that question had referred to making the formation of a monopoly a felony?
(1).
(2).
(3).
(4).
(5).

12. Which answer to question 10 would have been correct if that question had referred to making unfair and deceptive business practices unlawful?
(1).
(2).
(3).
(4).
(5).

13. Current thinking about the application of antitrust legislation looks most critically upon:
(1) horizontal mergers.
(2) multinational mergers.
(3) vertical mergers.
(4) conglomerate mergers.
(5) mergers of any kind.

14. Firms which exercise market power charge prices above marginal cost because:
(1) profits are maximized where marginal revenue equals marginal cost, and downward-sloping demand places marginal revenue below price.
(2) such firms never operate in the elastic region of demand where marginal revenue is negative.
(3) the effective demand curve which they face is horizontal, indicating an ability to charge prices which exceed the market-clearing level.
(4) profits are maximized where price equals marginal cost, and downward-sloping demand places marginal revenue above price.
(5) increasing returns to scale and their associated declining average costs mean that marginal cost and price always exceed average cost.

SUGGESTED ANSWERS TO QUESTIONS IN THE TEXT: Chapter 20

1. Consider economic regulation and antitrust policies. Some components of each are more direct and allow less flexibility. Others are more indirect and allow correspondingly more flexibility. As you consider strengths and weaknesses, state the objectives of "restraint" explicitly.

2. Consult Figure TQ20-1; it duplicates Figure 20-3 in the text. Note $P_M > P_R > P_I$ and $Q_M < Q_R < Q_I$. Deadweight loss falls as P_M converges to P_I, but profits turn negative after P_R. Beyond P_R, therefore, tax revenue from elsewhere is required and brings with it the effects of its own distortions. If P_M is not very much different from P_I, this tax distortion might cause a larger welfare reduction. Also, different people lose and gain, so different people prefer different approaches.

3. Economic interests create a demand for regulation; legislators and government officials offer the supply. The usual circular-flow portrait of a market is fuzzy, but the "I'll scratch your back if you scratch mine" analogy holds reasonably well.

4. Review the case now that you have completed the chapter. In answering, pay special attention to the "conduct" of trade.

5. Consult Figure TQ20-2. Note that $MR = MC$ at $Q^*/2$; the corresponding price would be in the neighborhood of $400. Meanwhile, the ideal regulated price is about $100, supporting output Q^* where $MC = DD$ (and $DD = MB$, remember). Note that $AC(Q^*) \approx \$175 > \$100 =$ price, so some subsidy would be required.

Figure TQ20-1

6. **a.** Excerpts from the major antitrust laws are presented in Table TQ20-1. Section 1 of the Sherman Act is slightly targeted at conduct; Section 2 reveals its major focus to be structure. Sections 2 and 3 of the Clayton Act speak most directly to conduct; Section 7 returns to structure. The Federal Trade Commission Act is addressed primarily at conduct.

Table TQ20-1
The Antitrust Laws

Sherman Antitrust Act (1890, as amended)

§1. Every contract, combination in the form of trust or otherwise, or conspiracy, in restraint of trade or commerce among the several States, or with foreign nations, is declared to be illegal.

§2. Every person who shall monopolize, or attempt to monopolize, or combine or conspire with any other person or persons, to monopolize any part of the trade or commerce among the several States, or with foreign nations, shall be deemed guilty of a felony....

Clayton Antitrust Act (1914, as amended)

§2. It shall be unlawful...to discriminate in price between different purchasers of commodities of like grade and quality...where the effect of such discrimination may be substantially to lessen competition or tend to create a monopoly in any line of commerce....*Provided*, That nothing herein contained shall prevent differentials which make only due allowance for differences in the cost....

§3. That it shall be unlawful for any person...to lease or make a sale or contract...on the condition, agreement, or understanding that the lessee or purchaser thereof shall not use or deal in the...commodities of a competitor...where the effect...may be to substantially lessen competition or tend to create a monopoly in any line of commerce.

§7. No [corporation]...shall acquire...the whole or any part...of another [corporation]...where...the effect of such an acquisition may be substantially to lessen competition, or to tend to create a monopoly.

Federal Trade Commission Act (1914, as amended)

§5. Unfair methods of competition...and unfair or deceptive acts or practices...are declared unlawful.

b. Structure is easier to monitor, but there are increasing returns to scale in some industries which can be captured only by one (or a few) firms. Conduct is harder to monitor, but it can allow these sorts of efficiencies to be exploited.

7. Consider your experiences, here. Consult Figure TQ20-3 for some ideas, but add your own.

8. Start with $MC > 0$. Since profits are maximized where $MR = MC$, $MR > 0$ and demand is price-elastic. All that notwithstanding, MC and/or AC could cut demand in its in-

Figure TQ20-2

*Industries where prices are significantly affected by government regulation.

Figure TQ20-3

elastic region. A higher price should produce high profits in all cases (if the regulation is binding, then the monopolist wants a higher price). Revenue will, meanwhile, climb with price through the inelastic region of demand; but it will fall as price rises into the elastic region.

9. The key here is to see if the index *climbs* by more than 100 points. A merger between American and United would, e.g., take a $20^2 + 10^2 = 400 + 100 = 500$-point total into a $30^2 = 900$ total; an increase of 400 points. Table TQ20-2 summarizes the six possible mergers. Each entry records a "paired-but-separate" total to the left of the slash and a merger total to the right. If the number to the left of the slash exceeds the number to the right by more than 100, then the guideline of 100 points would suggest that the Justice Department would bring a challenge. American would have trouble merging with anybody. United could merge only with Piddly. US West could also merge with Piddly.

Table TQ20-2

	American	United	US West	Piddly
American	400	—	—	—
United	500/900	100	—	—
US West	436/676	136/256	36	—
Piddly	416/576	116/196	52/100	—

CHAPTER 21

INCOME DISTRIBUTION AND THE STRUGGLE AGAINST POVERTY

Americans seem to be driven by two distinct motives as they work to shape their society. Americans want, on the one hand, to have a chance to live the "American dream"—to work hard, to work honest, perhaps to be lucky, but somehow to wind up a success in life. They want the opportunity to become wealthy, or at least to get ahead, and they do not think it fair or appropriate for economic or social policy to get in the way.

Americans also want to provide some measure of equity across the land. They are bound by the very wording of the Constitution to try to provide equal opportunity for all people. They have not always been very successful in that effort, though, and they have tried to compensate. The social fabric of the United States is filled with programs that try to help those individuals and families who have not been fortunate enough to ride opportunity to a position of economic security.

As noble as these two goals are, it is one of the major lessons of economics that they frequently get in each other's way. The very programs that provide some measure of protection for the disadvantaged cost money to run; they therefore require tax revenues to operate, and taxation makes achieving the American dream more difficult. The programs, themselves, are often accused of generating disincentives among the disadvantaged against attempting to get ahead. The whole business is summarized in what Arthur Okun called "the big tradeoff." It is the classic tradeoff between equity and efficiency.

Having completed your work in this chapter, you will have accomplished the objectives listed below. The major lesson of the chapter is not, however, recorded explicitly in the Learning Objectives; it is, instead, implicit in the debate over the effectiveness of antipoverty programs. The objectives make it clear that the debate hinges on the theoretical tradeoff between equity and efficiency, but the fundamental lesson of the chapter is that the debate must be conducted in the context of the practical, political world of interdependent government decision making.

The trend in government during the Reagan administration was, for example, toward a reduction in the size of antipoverty programs. The purported rationale for these reductions was couched in terms of a tightening of qualifying requirements to make certain that only the truly needy were receiving benefits; but was that really what was going on? The reductions were also consistent with the objectives of the supply-side tax cuts and the increased reliance on the private sector that were the cornerstones of the Reagan presidency. A more honest rationale for cutting welfare programs might have been couched in terms of a belief that the government had strayed too far toward promoting equity at the expense of economic efficiency.

LEARNING OBJECTIVES

1. Become familiar with the questions that are posed by the economists who work to understand the distribution of income—questions about the determination of income (the *flow* of money to an individual during a given period of time) and wealth (the net value of the *stock* of accumulated economic assets).

2. Recognize the major sources of income and the major reservoirs of wealth in the United States.

3. Recognize the Lorenz curve as a tool used to investigate relative (in)equality in the distribution of income and/or wealth. Outline *(a)* the information that these curves are intended to convey, *(b)* the link between that intention and their construction, and *(c)* the interpretation of the bulges that they usually portray.

4. Come to grips with the distributions of income and wealth within the United States—their relative (in)equality in historical and international contexts.

5. Explain the observed differences between typical distributions of ability and their corresponding distributions of income. Outline and explain potential sources of inequality in the distribution of income both across the United States and elsewhere around the globe.

6. Define poverty in the United States, and discuss its various sources (differences in property wealth, ability, education, and training; discrimination; and inequality of opportunity).

7. Contrast three notions of equity (equality of political rights, opportunity, and outcome), and use Arthur Okun's notion of a leaky bucket to delineate the costs of providing increased equality.

8. Record a list of the major welfare programs still in place in the early 1990s (food stamps and child nutrition; AFDC; aid to the needy aged, blind, and disabled; Medicaid; housing assistance; etc.). Note the comparative expense of running each. Understand how qualifying standards might impose very high effective marginal tax rates on the working poor.

9. Define two views of poverty (poverty resulting from social and economic circumstances over which the poor have no control and poverty resulting from maladaptive behavior), and trace the implications of both for government activity.

10. Critically analyze the notion of substituting a negative income tax for the plethora of welfare programs currently in place.

Income is defined as the amount of money received from all sources during a given period of time. The major sources of income in the United States are labor income, rental earnings, dividends, interest earnings, and transfer payments. *Wealth*, meanwhile, consists of the *net* dollar value of tangible assets (homes, rental properties, other real estate, motor vehicles, etc.) and financial assets (interest-earning accounts, business equity, stocks and bonds, etc.). The distribution of either across the population can be illustrated by a *Lorenz curve*—a schedule which plots the percentage of total income or wealth received or owned by the poorest x percent of the population. Questions 1 through 4 will explore your understanding of these curves.

1. a. Consider a group consisting of 10 individuals. The first receives a weekly income of $1, the second $2, and so on, with the tenth receiving $10. The first individual is low man on the income totem pole, representing the bottom 10 percent (ranked in terms of income) of this particular population. The $1 received by this poverty-stricken person is about 2 percent of the total weekly income received by all, which totals $55. Complete Table 21-1 by computing the requisite percentages. For example, the lowest 20 percent of the population consists of the $1 individual plus the $2 individual. Their combined income total of $3 is about 5½ percent of the combined incomes of all 10; i.e., $3 is about 5½ percent of $55. So 5½ should go in the first blank box of Table 21-1.

Table 21-1
Percent of Income Received by Lowest:

10%	20%	30%	40%	50%	60%	70%	80%	90%	100%
2									100

b. Draw the Lorenz curve illustrating this distribution of income in Figure 21-1.

c. If the distribution of income were more unequal than that indicated at the beginning of this question, then the Lorenz curve would *(bulge closer to the lower right-hand corner / be drawn nearer to the 45° diagonal)*; if it were less unequal, the curve *(would bulge closer to the lower right-hand corner / be drawn nearer to the 45° diagonal)*.

---

a. table row: 5½, 11, 18, 27¼, 38, 51, 65½, 81¾   **c.** bulge closer to the lower right-hand corner; be drawn nearer to the 45° diagonal

2. Suppose, using the data provided in question 1, that a 20 percent income tax is imposed by the government. Such a tax would collect, assuming no disincentive effects, $11 in revenue. Assume further that it costs $1 to administer the

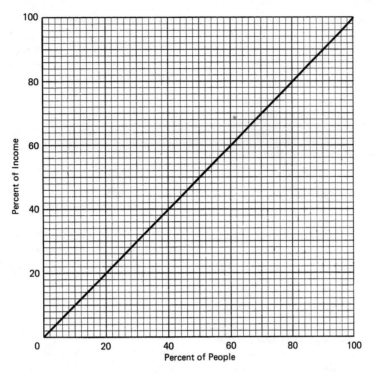

Figure 21-1

tax and that the remaining $10 is distributed to everyone as equal $1 "social" payments. Fill in the blanks in Table 21-2, and draw a new Lorenz curve in Figure 21-1 to illustrate the resulting after-tax and -payment distribution of income; use a different color pencil or pen for clarity.

---

table rows: taxes paid—$0.40, $0.60, $0.80, $1.00, $1.20, $1.40, $1.60, $1.80, $2.00; income after taxes—$1.60, $2.40, $3.20, $4.00, $4.80, $5.60, $6.40, $7.20, $8.00; income after taxes and payment—$2.60, $3.40, $4.20, $5.00, $5.80, $6.60, $7.40, $8.20, $9.00; percent of total income—8.1, 14.4, 22.2, 31.5, 42.2, 54.4, 68.1, 83.3 the graph: The Lorenz curve should be closer to the 45° line—a more equal distribution of income achieved by a redistributive tax-subsidy scheme.

3. The following list records changes in a Lorenz curve that might be expected in response to some change in economic circumstance:

1. Movement up toward the 45 line
2. Movement away from the 45 line
3. No movement at all

Using the numbers from the list above, indicate in the parentheses provided the likely effect of the following changes in economic condition on a Lorenz curve illustrating a distribution of income:

Table 21-2

Person	10%	20%	30%	40%	50%	60%	70%	80%	90%	100%
Income	$1.00	$2.00	$3.00	$4.00	$5.00	$6.00	$7.00	$8.00	$9.00	$10.00
Taxes paid	$0.20	___	___	___	___	___	___	___	___	___
Income after taxes	$0.80	___	___	___	___	___	___	___	___	___
Income after taxes and payment	$1.80	___	___	___	___	___	___	___	___	___
Percent of total income after the program received by the lowest indicated %	3.3%	___	___	___	___	___	___	___	___	100%

a. A 5 percent proportional income tax whose revenues are not redistributed .... ( )

b. A 5 percent proportional income tax whose revenues are redistributed equally to everyone .... ( )

c. A progressive income tax (which taxes higher incomes at a higher rate) whose revenues are not redistributed ..( )

d. A progressive income tax (which taxes higher incomes at a higher rate) whose revenues are redistributed equally to everyone .... ( )

e. A 5 percent sales tax whose revenues are not redistributed .... ( )

f. A deep recession that reduces employment for the working-class poor .... ( )

---

a. 3 (Everyone loses 5 percent, so the total loses 5 percent and the percentage of disposable income received by any one person is therefore unchanged.) **b.** 1 (See, e.g., question 2; people with the higher incomes pay more in tax than they receive in reimbursement.) **c.** 1 (Taking a larger tax bite from those with the higher incomes reduces their share of the total pie.) **d.** 1 (even more strongly, for the same reason as in part **b**) **e.** 2 (Lower-income classes spend a higher proportion of their incomes and thus would sacrifice a higher proportion of their incomes to a sales tax on those expenditures.) **f.** 2 (Prolonged unemployment certainly lowers income, especially at the lower end of the income distribution.)

4. Table 21-3 records data that describe the distribution of income in the United States in 1984. Plot the corresponding Lorenz curve in Figure 21-2.

Table 21-3

Cumulative Percentage of People	Cumulative Percentage of Income
20	4.7
40	15.7
60	32.7
80	57.1
100	100.0

For each of the following, record in the parentheses provided whether the corresponding Lorenz curve would be much further away from the 45° line (MA), slightly further away from the 45° line (SA), slightly closer to the 45° line (SC), or much closer to the 45° line (MC) than the curve you just drew:

a. A Lorenz curve depicting the distribution of income in the United States in 1972 .... ( )

b. A Lorenz curve depicting the distribution of income in the United States in 1929 .... ( )

c. A Lorenz curve depicting the distribution of income in an "industrializing" nation in 1984 .... ( )

d. A Lorenz curve depicting the distribution of wealth in the United States in 1984 .... ( )

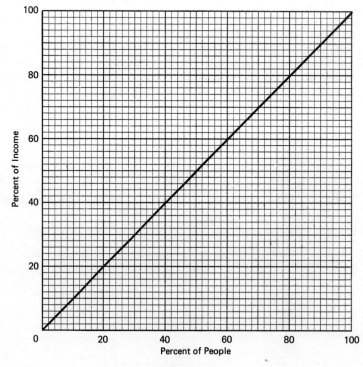

Figure 21-2

e. A Lorenz curve depicting the distribution of income in the United Kingdom in 1988 . . . . ( )

---

a. SC **b.** SA **c.** MA **d.** MA (*Remember:* The top 0.5 percent holds 14 percent of the nation's wealth.) **e.** SC (or MC depending upon your perspective)

The data show, as reflected in the answers to question 4, that the distribution of income in the United States has grown slightly more equal over the past 60 years. The lowest 20 percent of the population received roughly 3.8 percent of the income in the late 1920s and 4.6 percent in 1989. The trend has not, however, proceeded entirely in one direction. The distribution was slightly more equal in the middle of the 1970s, with the lowest 20 percent of the population then receiving their highest percentage ever—roughly 4.7 percent of total income.

The notion that industrialization would help only the rich has not been borne out by experience. Enormous inequality is displayed by the industrializing countries (where Dickens might still apply), and the distribution of wealth throughout most of the world is extremely concentrated at the top. Nonetheless, most of the economies in the industrialized world display distributions of income without a large, thoroughly impoverished underclass.

5. The very concept of equality is at best a slippery and controversial issue. Most people would agree that equal opportunity, equal access to adequate education, and equal access to the electoral process are essential elements of the American experiment in democracy. But what about a (more) equal distribution of income? Should, more specifically, a progressive-income-tax system be used to redistribute income? There is no definitive response to this question with which everyone would agree. There are simply too many potential sources of inequity in the distribution of income that would exist regardless of the economic policy of the U.S. government. List at least seven in the spaces provided below:

a. _____
b. _____
c. _____
d. _____
e. _____
f. _____
g. _____

---

a. through **g.** ability, occupation, education, work effort, property, risk taking, inheritance, discrimination, experience and role models, etc.

6. Figure 21-3 plots the distributions of ability and income in the United States. Label the two curves correctly. The importance of the discrepancy between the two distributions is that differences in ability cannot entirely explain observed differences in earnings across the American population.

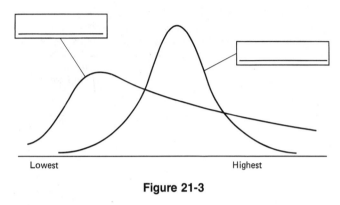

Figure 21-3

The curve that peaks first is income (the left box).

Classical economists believed that the distribution of income was determined by economic law and that nothing could change it. Wages, rents, and profits were all determined in the marketplace, they thought, and any attempt to alter the distribution that emerged from that determination would be futile. A majority of Americans in the 1960s, however, would have nothing to do with that conclusion. Before he died, President John Kennedy announced a "war on poverty" as part of the New Frontier; his dreams were embodied in the Great Society programs of the Johnson presidency. To what end? The percentage of American families living below the poverty line fell from 22 percent in 1960 to 11 percent in 1970. The percentage was still roughly 11 percent in 1980, but it climbed to something in excess of 15 percent by 1982. The percentage stood at 14 percent in 1988 and 13 percent in 1989. Poverty is still a problem in the United States; and it is, at least in absolute terms, still growing.

7. The poverty line is determined by computing (*a maximum poverty index* / *a minimum-subsistence income* / *an average American's food budget*). Social workers provide some information for the computation, and their numbers are corroborated by multiplying a subsistence food budget by (2 / 3 / 4). Why? Because families at the lower end of the income scale typically spend (*one-quarter* / *one-third* / *one-half*) of their incomes on food. In 1962, the poverty-line income for a family of four was $3100; in 1989, the same benchmark income was $(7800 / 9675 / 10,625 / 12,675).

---

a minimum-subsistence income; 3; one-third; 12,675

8. Table 21-4 records the incidence of poverty in some of the major demographic groups of the United States in 1982 and 1985. The percentages all (rise / stay the same / **fall**) during that 3-year period, but this is more reflective of recovering from deep recession than it is of winning the war on poverty. The number of people in or close to poverty, in fact, (**rose** / stayed the same / fell) from 1982 to 1985.

Table 21-4
Incidence of Poverty in Different Groups, 1982 and 1985

Population Group	Percent of Group in Poverty	
	1982	1985
White	12.0	11.4
Black	35.6	31.3
Hispanic	29.9	29.0
Children under 6	23.8	21.5
Elderly	14.6	12.6
Married couples	7.6	6.7
Families headed by women	40.6	34.0
Total	15.0	14.0

Families headed by women ranked (**first** / second / third) on the list, with _____ percent of their numbers falling below the poverty line. Blacks ranked (second / **first** / fourth), with _____ percent. Perhaps most tragically, children under the age of 6 rank (**above** / the same as / below) the overall average, with _____ percent—more than 1 child in every 5 in the richest country in the world.

Referring now to Figure 21-4, note that the average income of the bottom one-fifth of the population (ranked by income) has climbed _____ percent since 1930, from $_____ (real 1984 dollars) to $_____. As a percentage of national income, however, the income earned by the lowest 20 percent of the population (fell / **remained roughly the same** / rose), to stand at (2 / **5** / 10) percent in 1984. Through the lowest 20 percent, therefore, 60 years of history has (shifted the Lorenz curve in toward the 45° line / **done little to the Lorenz curve** / shifted the Lorenz curve away from the 45° line), indicating (a trend toward greater equality / **no significant trend toward greater equality** / a trend toward less equality) in the lower incomes. Put another way, the average income of the lowest 20 percent of the population has climbed only because (total income has fallen / total income has remained the same / **total income has risen**).

---

fall; rose; first; 34 (in 1985, down from 40.6 percent in 1982); second; 31.3 (again down from the recession's 35.6 percent, but less significantly); above; 21.5 (down slightly from 23.8 percent); 130; 3000; 8000; remained roughly the same; 5; done little to the Lorenz curve; no significant trend toward greater equality; total income has risen

---

9. Figure 21-5 can be used to illustrate the **disincentive** or **leaky-bucket** consequence of income redistribution. The horizontal and vertical axes measure, respectively (to the same scale), the incomes of the upper half and the lower half of the population.

This diagram has a 45° line emerging from the origin. If there were complete equality in income distribution (if each individual received exactly the same income as every other individual), then the words "upper half" and "lower half" would be meaningless. Alternatively, the so-called upper half (any half) of the population would receive exactly the same total income as the so-called lower half. The distribution between them would have to be represented by some point (such as E) on this 45° line. (Remember: The scales on the two axes are the same.)

Figure 21-4

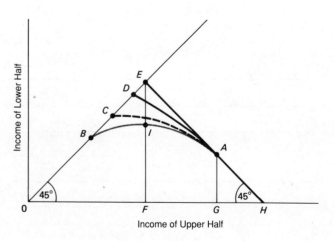

Figure 21-5

a. In fact, incomes are not equally distributed. On this diagram, then, the point indicating the distribution between the two halves must lie *(to the right of and below / to the left of and above)* the 45° line. (Somehow, it always seems to work out that the upper half gets more income than the lower half.)

Suppose that total income received by both halves is 0H, divided between an upper-half total of 0G and a lower-half total of GH. Let us (temporarily) record this total and its division on the horizontal axis. This axis is reserved, however, for upper-half income receivers, and they will probably object to this trespass by those lower-half people on their territory. So draw a 45° line from point H extending up to the other 45° line. Point E is where the two lines meet. On EH, pick point A such that AG is equal to GH.

Now we have things sorted out as they should be. 0G (measured horizontally) is the upper-half income total; AG (measured vertically) is the lower-half total. Point A indicates the distribution of income between the two halves. Any movement toward greater equality of income distribution would mean a move away from A *(toward / and also away from)* E. Suppose there is such a movement, with absolutely no disincentive, or leaky-bucket, effect. That is, suppose that the population's entire income total is *(reduced / not reduced at all)*. On the diagram, this redistribution movement will follow the straight line EH, from A toward E.

b. It is usually argued that any movement directed toward greater equality of income distribution would have at least some disincentive consequences; i.e., there would be at least a small leak in the bucket. Suppose this redistribution is tackled by means of heavier progressive income taxation. The extra taxes thus collected from higher-income people would be passed on to lower-income groups via a **negative income tax** or some other such transfer-payment device. Insofar as people try to avoid heavier taxation by working shorter hours, or in other ways earning less money income, the total of real GNP would *(fall / rise)*. The path of redistribution will no longer run along the straight line EH. Starting at A, it will drift *(above / below)* EH. The total of real income will become *(less / more)* than it was at point A. The more sweeping the intended income redistribution (i.e., the farther the planned movement from A toward E) the *(less / more)* pronounced this disincentive effect is likely to be.

c. The three curved lines in Figure 21-5, DA, CA, and BA, show three possible sets of disincentive consequences. Among them, the smallest disincentive effect is indicated by *(DA / CA / BA)*.

Notice that line CA is approximately flat in the region close to point C. This means that if redistribution toward complete equality were pressed hard enough, the resulting drop in total GNP would be sufficient for the real income of the lower half, in absolute terms, to *(increase only slightly / not increase at all / decrease)*. In relative terms, though, the share of the lower half would *(still increase / remain constant / decrease)*.

d. The most drastic disincentive effect is illustrated by line BA. If redistribution effects were such that total income follows this path, then the lower-income half of the population would at first (as the movement from A toward B commences) experience a moderate *(increase / decrease)* in real income. Soon, however, the real income of even this lower half of the population would *(increase / decline)* in absolute terms.

If the likely redistribution path were DA, then society might well decide that some movement from A toward D is worthwhile: the sacrifice of total real income could be justified by the resulting greater equality. But if the probable path of redistribution were indicated by BA, or even by CA, then the cost in terms of total real income sacrificed would be greater, and society would be forced to put a higher priority on income equality if either of these two paths were to be followed for even a short distance away from A.

---

a. to the right of and below; toward; not reduced at all   **b.** fall; below; less; more   **c.** DA; not increase at all; still increase (The upper half's getting less means that total income is falling even though the income received by the lower half is constant. The fractional share of the lower half must therefore rise as the denominator—total income—falls.)   **d.** increase; decline

---

How big are the leaks? What are their sources? First, there are the administrative costs of running welfare and tax-redistribution programs. Although these costs might be enormous in absolute terms in an economy as large as America's, they do not mount up very quickly relative to the magnitudes of the programs actually administered.

Second, there is the potential for welfare programs to create disincentives to work. Jerry Hausman of MIT has determined that these effects are potentially significant, but his work is disputed by many others who find that, for example, the elasticity of the supply of labor to changes in the wage rate is quite small.

Third, there is the potential for progressive taxation to retard saving and investment and thus growth. Okun, himself, discounted this worry by noting that saving and investment accounted for 16 percent of GNP in 1929 and 16 percent of GNP in 1973; 1929 was before the imposition of the full force of the progressive income tax, and 1973 was at the height of the American welfare state. In response to the tax incentives with which the Reagan program tried to stimulate investment and saving, incidently, the combined total of saving and investment actually fell to 13 percent of GNP.

Finally, there are potentially harmful changes in attitude and behavior that might be fostered by a progressive tax and welfare state. More people might cheat on their taxes, or lay around and not work, and so on. These costs are hard to measure, and their jury is still out.

The opposite side of the argument can lead one to suggest that the tradeoff between equity and efficiency is overstated to the extreme. What if the drive toward equality opened opportunities to extraordinarily productive people who would have otherwise been shut out? What if programs that provide health care and nutrition for poor families actually broke the cycle of poverty, thereby increasing productivity and efficiency? Would not, then, operating the welfare state and incurring its expense be an investment in expanded human capital for the future?

10. a. List the following welfare-transfer programs in the order of their importance in the federal budget of 1989: Medicare; Medicaid; social security; unemployment insurance; food stamps and child nutrition; housing; aid to families with dependent children; and aid to the aged, blind, and disabled (consult Table 21-6 in the text).

(1) _____

(2) _____

(3) _____

(4) _____

(5) _____

(6) _____

(7) _____

(8) _____

b. The total amount budgeted for these programs in 1989 was $_____ billion. This is a large amount of money, but it should be noted that only $_____ billion (_____ percent of the total budget) is spent on programs designed to benefit the poor directly, with $_____ billion devoted to increasing poor families' incomes. This percentage is *(up / the same / down)* from the last pre-Reagan budget of 1980.

a. (1) social security **(2)** Medicare **(3)** Medicaid **(4)** food stamps and child nutrition **(5)** unemployment insurance **(6)** housing **(7)** aid to the aged, blind, and disabled **(8)** aid to families with dependent children **b.** 435.3, 101.1; 9.2; 23.3; down (from 8.8 percent in 1980, but up from 7.7 percent in 1984)

11. Consider a welfare system organized around the following rules of qualification:

1. Basic welfare support is $4000; $0.50 is deducted from that amount for every dollar earned up to $8000.

2. $3000 in food stamps is available for $1000 provided outside earnings do not exceed $2500.

3. $2500 in housing subsidy is granted, but that amount is reduced by $0.50 for every dollar earned over $2000.

4. $1000 per child in supplemental income is available to families with dependent children and outside incomes that do not exceed $3999.

Fill in the blanks of Table 21-5 to reflect the benefits received by each of four different families according to these rules. Assume that each family takes advantage of all four programs to the fullest extent possible (not, in reality, a good assumption). Family A has one child and no private outside income. Family B has no children and a private income of $2000. Family C has two children and an outside income of $2500. Family D has two children and an outside income of $4000.

Table 21-5

	Family A	Family B	Family C	Family D
1. Basic welfare				
2. Food stamps				
3. Housing subsidy				
4. AFDC				
5. Outside income				
6. Total				
7. Marginal tax rates:				
Last dollar earned				
Next dollar earned				

table columns: family A—basic welfare = $4000, food stamps = $2000 ($3000 net the cost of $1000 taken from basic welfare), housing subsidy = $2500, AFDC = $1000 (for the one child), outside income = $0, total = $9500, marginal tax rate for last dollar = not applicable (There is no "last dollar.") and for next dollar = 50% (the $0.50 in basic welfare lost on that dollar); family B—basic welfare = $3000 [$4000 −0.5($2000)], food stamps = $2000, housing subsidy = $2500, AFDC = $0, outside income = $2000, total = $9500, marginal tax rate for last dollar = 50% (the $0.50 lost in basic welfare) and for next dollar = 100% ($0.50 in housing subsidy lost, too); family C—basic welfare = $2750, food stamps = $2000, housing subsidy = $2250, AFDC = $2000, outside income = $2500, total = $11,500, marginal tax rate for last dollar = 100% (both welfare and housing reduced at $0.50 per dollar) and for next dollar = 200,100% (lost $2000 in net food-stamp payment for that $1 that is not even kept); family D—basic welfare = $2000, food stamps = $0 (exceed limit), housing subsidy = $1500, AFDC = $0 (just exceed limit), outside income = $4000, total = $7500, marginal tax rate for last dollar = 200,100% (lost $2000 in AFDC with the last dollar) and for next dollar = 100% (both welfare and housing reduced at $0.50 per dollar)

12. Table 21-6 identifies four different families by their potential earnings. This final question will investigate the parameters of a negative-income-tax system designed to guarantee a minimum income of $15,000.

a. Suppose initially that all four families work to their fullest potential; their resulting incomes are recorded in row 2 of Table 21-6. If all four were to receive an initial grant of $15,000, then a self-sufficient tax system would have to raise a total of $_____ to be distributed in equal parts. If the tax on earned income (income excluding the $15,000 grants) were to be proportional, then the marginal tax rate would have to be _____ percent. Now complete rows 3 through 6 by computing for each family the taxes paid, total after-tax earned income, total after-tax income including the transfer, and average tax rate. This negative income tax would, on average, be (progressive / proportional / regressive).

Table 21-6

	Family A	Family B	Family C	Family D	Total
1. Potential earnings	$10,000	$30,000	$60,000	$80,000	$180,000
2. Earned income	$10,000	$30,000	$60,000	$80,000	$180,000
3. Taxes	$3,333	____	____	____	____
4. After-tax earned income	$6,667	____	____	____	____
5. Total income	$21,667	____	____	____	____
6. Average tax rate	15.4%	____	____	____	____
7. Earned income	____	____	____	____	____
8. Taxes	____	____	____	____	____
9. After-tax earned income	____	____	____	____	____
10. Total income	____	____	____	____	____

Plot the initial, pre-tax distribution of income in Figure 21-6, and label the point A; plot the after-tax distribution of income in the same figure, and label this second point B. The after-tax distribution of income is (more equal / less equal) than before.

b. Now suppose that the families suffer disincentives to work in the face of proportional taxation and that the income they earn is thus equal to their potential divided by $(1 + t)$, where $t \times 100$ percent is the tax rate. The tax rate that must now be imposed is 50 percent. Why? Because the requisite $60,000 must equal $t \times 100$ percent of the total potential income of $180,000 divided by $(1 + t)$. Note that $60,000 = 0.5 \times [\$180,000/(1 + 0.5)] = 0.5 \times \$120,000$.

Complete rows 7 through 10 in Table 21-6 given the 50 percent tax rate and the work disincentive. Plot the resulting distribution of income in Figure 21-6; label this final distribution point C. The distribution of income is now (even more

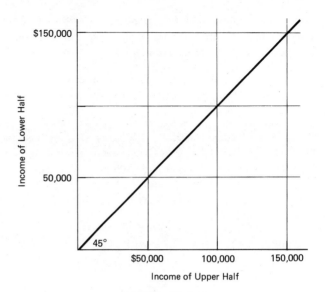

Figure 21-6

equal / even less equal), but the four families are sharing a smaller pie. Still, the two poorest families are (better / worse) off than they were without the negative income tax.

---

a. 60,000; 33.3 [(60/180) × 100]
table rows: 3—$10,000, $20,000, $26,667, $60,000; 4—$20,000, $40,000, $53,333, $120,000; 5—$35,000, $55,000, $68,333, $180,000; 6—28.6%, 36.4%, 39.0%, 33.3%
progressive; more equal (lying along a straight line through point A with slope equal to −1)   **b.** table rows: 7—$6667, $20,000, $40,000, $53,333, $120,000; 8—$3333, $10,000, $20,000, $21,667, $60,000; 9—$3333, $10,000, $20,000, $21,667, $60,000; 10—$18,333, $25,000, $35,000, $41,667, $120,000
even more equal; better (Point C is located below the AB line.)

REVIEW CONCEPTS

1. Income is measured as the flow of money to an individual during a specified period of time; major sources include labor earnings, rental payments, dividends, interest payments, and transfer payments. Wealth is a measure of the net dollar value of tangible and intangible assets, including homes, rental properties, other real estate, and motor vehicles, on the one hand, and cash holdings, bank accounts, business equity, stocks and bonds, on the other.

2. The Lorenz curve, plotting the percentage of income earned or wealth accumulated by x percent of the population, reflects the equality of income or wealth distributions. Comparing their position over time or across countries can suggest trends in equality.

3. Labor earnings vary because of differences in ability, differences in work intensity, and differences in occupation. Property incomes vary because of differences in wealth and inheritance. Only a small fraction of America's wealth can be accounted for by life-cycle saving; entrepreneurship is a dominant source of wealth for the richest Americans.

4. Political equality, equality of opportunity, and equality of outcome represent three distinct, but related, notions. Equality of outcome is the most contentious.

5. Movement toward equity generally involves efficiency losses—Okun's leaky bucket of disincentives and administrative costs.

6. The United States offers a wide array of programs designed to alleviate poverty (welfare, food stamps, Medicaid, aid to families with dependent children, etc.). They are frequently criticized for imposing high "benefit-reduction rates"—effective marginal tax rates on income.

7. The negative-income-tax idea is advocated by many as an alternative means of coping with poverty.

QUIZ: Multiple Choice

1. A Lorenz-curve chart is a graph on whose axes the following things are measured:
(1) the total amount of income in dollars on one axis and the total number of individuals or families receiving that income or a lower one on the other.
(2) the percentage of people (10 percent, 20 percent, etc.) on one axis and the percentage of total income received by the lowest 10 percent, the lowest 20 percent, etc., on the other.
(3) the number of individuals or families receiving a certain income on one axis and the percentage of the total population represented by that number on the other.
(4) the number of individuals or families in different occupations on one axis and the median income received in that occupation on the other.
(5) income classes (e.g., $0 to $1999 and $2000 to $3999) on one axis and the percentage of individuals or families in each such income class on the other.

2. Absolute or total equality in an income distribution would appear on a Lorenz-curve chart as:
(1) a curved line well bowed out from the diagonal.
(2) a curved line close to the diagonal.
(3) a right-angled line.
(4) a 45° diagonal line.
(5) none of the preceding.

3. Which alternative in question 2 would have been correct had that question referred to absolute inequality in income—i.e., a situation in which one individual or family gets all the income and the others receive no income at all?
(1).
(2).
(3).
(4).
(5).

4. From the mid-1970s to the late 1980s in the United States:
(1) the lowest 20 percent and the highest 20 percent of the income distribution became poorer relative to the middle 60 percent.
(2) the highest 20 percent became relatively poorer and the lowest 20 percent became relatively richer.
(3) the highest 20 percent became relatively richer and the lowest 20 percent became relatively poorer.
(4) both the highest and the lowest 20 percent of the income distribution became richer at the expense of the middle class.
(5) none of the above.

5. The average per capita weekly income in the United States in 1991 was:
(1) between $100 and $130.
(2) between $130 and $175.
(3) between $175 and $240.
(4) between $240 and $275.
(5) over $275.

6. Which of the following statements is an accurate description of the distribution of income in the United States?
(1) The mean is higher than the median, due to the presence of a large number of relatively low incomes.
(2) The median is higher than the mean, due to the presence of a small number of exceptionally high incomes.
(3) The mean is higher than the median, due to the presence of a small number of exceptionally high incomes.
(4) The median is higher than the mean, due to the presence of a large number of relatively low incomes.
(5) The median, which used to be lower than the mean, has recently become somewhat higher, due to the influence of progressive income taxation.

7. The "median" family income is:
(1) the figure obtained by listing all incomes from lowest to highest and taking the one exactly in the middle of the ranking.
(2) the income figure that would result if the total incomes received by all families were divided equally among those families.
(3) the income it is estimated a family must have in order to reach the "minimum-comfort" level of consumption.
(4) the level of income found at the exact midpoint of a Lorenz curve.
(5) none of the preceding.

8. Which alternative in question 7 would be correct had that question referred to the "mean" rather than to the "median" family income?
(1).
(2).
(3).
(4).
(5).

9. If there were any inequality at all in the distribution of income, then which of the following would be true of the group making up the lowest 20 percent in the income ranking?
(1) It is just as likely as not that it will receive more than 20 percent of this total income.
(2) It must receive exactly 20 percent of this total income.
(3) It will usually, but not always, receive less than 20 percent of this total income.
(4) It must have received less than 20 percent of the total income of all groups together.
(5) None of the above is necessarily true.

10. Differences in ability are commonly cited to explain differences in income. This explanation:
(1) covers only part of the reason because there are so many more instances of skewness in ability than there are of skewness in income.
(2) covers only part of the reason because the shape of the income distribution is significantly different from that of the ability distribution.
(3) covers only part of the reason because the measured range of individual ability differences is much wider than the range of income differences.
(4) gives a reasonably complete interpretation of income differences.
(5) is almost meaningless because there is no suitable way of comparing ability differences against income differences.

11. The poverty line, computed to reflect a minimum-subsistence income:
(1) grew from $3100 in 1962 to over $12,000 by the late 1980s.
(2) has been nearly stable in real terms since 1962.
(3) is roughly 3 times the minimum-subsistence food budget.
(4) saw its food component climb to more than $4000 in 1991.
(5) all the above.

12. The war on poverty, initiated by President John Kennedy and embodied in the Great Society of Lyndon Johnson:
(1) managed to reduce the percentage of American people below the poverty line from 22 percent in 1962 to 15 percent in 1971; it remains at 15 percent today.
(2) managed to cut the percentage of Americans below the poverty line from 22 percent in 1962 to 11 percent by 1970; it remained at 11 percent until 1981, when it started to climb back above 15 percent.
(3) had little or no effect on the percentage of Americans below the poverty line and thus warranted cancellation by the Reagan administration.
(4) had a small effect on lowering the percentage of people below the poverty line until participation requirements were tightened by the Reagan administration in 1982.
(5) none of the above.

13. Differences in education and training are considered to be major factors in determining the likelihood that an individual will find himself or herself in poverty. This link is reflected in the correlation of statistics about American blacks in the 1980s. While twice as many blacks as whites found themselves below the poverty line in 1989:
(1) the percentage of whites having completed high school was 8 points higher than the percentage for blacks.
(2) the percentage of blacks having completed college was roughly one-half the percentage of whites who completed college.
(3) the median income of white families, with which a college or professional education could be financed for white children, was 75 percent higher than the median income of black families.
(4) the median wealth of white families was more than 10 times higher than the median wealth of black families.
(5) all the above are accurate statements which support the correlation of education and training to poverty.

14. Which of the following is not a reason that might explain the incidence of poverty in contemporary America?
(1) Differences in education and training.
(2) The existence of noncompeting groups.
(3) Differences in economic environment, including the distribution of wealth.
(4) The asymmetric effect of recession on demographic groups.
(5) Differences in ability among all people.

15. The average income of the lowest 20 percent of the population has increased by more than 130 percent since 1929:
(1) so the need for antipoverty programs is a myth.
(2) but the percentage of total income that growth represents has held steady at 5 percent.
(3) but almost all that growth is explained by growth in total GNP.
(4) choices (2) and (3) only.
(5) none of the above.

16. Of all the children living in the United States in 1988, approximately:
(1) 1 in 10 were living below the poverty line.
(2) 1 in 20 were living below the poverty line.
(3) 1 in 5 were living below the poverty line.
(4) 1 percent were living below the poverty line.
(5) 1 million were living below the poverty line.

17. A poor family's employment earnings are supplemented by a negative income tax—in the amount, say, of $4000. Under this tax proposal, if family employment earnings were to rise by $1000, the income received from the negative tax would typically:
(1) fall by $1000.
(2) fall by more than $1000.
(3) fall by some amount less than $1000.
(4) fall by $4000.
(5) rise by some amount such as $500.

18. Referring to Figure 21-7, let point A represent some initial distribution of income between the indicated upper half and the lower half. Which point would represent the equal distribution of income if there were no leaks in the bucket?
(1) A.
(2) B.
(3) C.
(4) D.
(5) E.

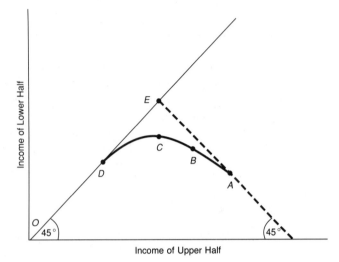

Figure 21-7

19. Which answer to question 18 would have been correct if it had asked for the point that would represent equality given the leaks that produce curve ABCD?
(1).
(2).
(3).
(4).
(5).

20. Which of the following is not likely to be a significant source of leaks in the equity-efficiency tradeoff?
(1) The administrative costs of running a welfare-income-redistribution program.
(2) The work disincentives of the progressive income tax.
(3) The disincentives against saving and investment that are produced by the progressive income tax.
(4) A change in attitude that makes cheating on taxes more acceptable.
(5) All the above could be significant, though there is little evidence to support choice (3).

21. In the 1989 budget, which of the following was the largest item targeted directly at helping the poor?
(1) Medicaid.
(2) Aid to families with dependent children.
(3) Food stamps and child nutrition.
(4) Aid to the aged, blind, and disabled.
(5) Housing assistance.

22. Despite its importance in explaining the incidence of poverty, spending on programs that support the education and training of the poor fell from 1981 to 1984, as did most of the spending targeted directly at helping the poor, by:
(1) less than 1 percent.
(2) about 5 percent.
(3) nearly 8 percent.
(4) almost 15 percent.
(5) more than 25 percent.

23. "Inefficiency" in income redistribution means:
(1) the reduction in total output caused by those unfavorably affected by redistribution and by their decision to pay less in income tax by working less.
(2) the administrative costs of redistribution and the burden it places on federal workers.
(3) the lesser skills of the gainers from redistribution.
(4) the total amount of income transferred from upper-income to lower-income groups.
(5) the resulting reduction in total taxes collected by the government.

SUGGESTED ANSWERS TO QUESTIONS IN THE TEXT: Chapter 21

1. Guess first, and see how close you are.

2. There is a large literature on the redistribution of income that takes work (dis)incentives into account. To make the income distribution more even, some people who work hard will have to pay higher taxes to subsidize the incomes of the less well-off. They may choose to work less, reduce the "pie" of total income, and make everyone worse off. This question goes to the heart of the tradeoff between equity and efficiency, and there is no right answer. It depends upon your "social objective function"; i.e., what you want for society.

3. a. No change; the tax reduces everyone's income at the same rate as the total.
  b. Moves in toward the 45° line; larger chunks taken from the higher incomes mean their share of the pie shrinks.
  c. Moves away from the 45° line; lower-income classes spend a larger proportion of their incomes and thus pay more tax as a fraction of their incomes.
  d. Moves away from the 45° line; recessions are hardest on the lower middle classes, whose jobs may be put in jeopardy.

4. The three types of equity are equality of political rights, equality of economic opportunity, and equality of economic outcome. State your view, again, but make sure that you specify precisely the type of equity you are addressing. Remember that you can conceptualize the inefficiency associated with programs designed to promote equity in terms of Okun's leaky bucket and graphs like Figure 21-5. Are the graphs the same for each type, or is the tradeoff for one type more severe than the tradeoff for another? Why? So what?

5. Cash is generally more efficient (it expands the utility possibilities of the recipients), but there is no guarantee that cash given to help pay for, e.g., food goes for food. Categorized benefits have such a guarantee (at least according to the law), but they are less efficient and spawn expensive bureaucracies.

6. *Absolute equality:* Gini = 0.
   Absolute inequality: Gini = [0.5(100)(100)]2 = 10,000.
   For text Figure 21-3, Gini for U.S. income is roughly 3200; Gini for U.S. wealth, roughly 8000.

7. Listing the people in order of income, they receive $1, $2, $3, $4, $5, $5, $6, $7, $8, $9. Their total income is $50. The 10-percentile intervals for population therefore collect, cumulatively, 2, 6, 12, 20, 30, 40, 52, 66, 82, and 100 percent of the income, respectively. (For the first two people, e.g., total income is $3, or 6 percent of $50.) Gini ≈ 740 × 2 = 1480.

8. The procedure is this: Get the population numbers; compute per capita incomes; rank the people according to per capita income; compute percentage of total population covered and income recorded for each per capita income cohort; and graph the resulting numbers in the cumulative fashion required in a Lorenz curve. The inequality should be enormous.

9. The efficiency argument in support of income grants is shown most clearly in indifference-curve analysis of the type presented in Appendix 6. An income grant moves a budget constraint out in parallel across the entire quadrant; the consumption of all goods can increase. Grants in kind achieve the same parallel shift, but only to the extent that people want the goods specified in the grant; the consumption of all goods may not be able to be increased.

To see this, consult Figure TQ21-1. There, line *AB* is a budget constraint between food and other goods without any welfare program; the individual in question has just $300 to allocate between the two each month. A program that gives this person $180 in food stamps each month shifts the budget constraint to schedule *A'CB*; the quantity of other goods possible is still bound by $300, but the maximum amount of food possible is now $480. Were the program simply to give the person $180, the resulting budget constraint would be *A'B'*—a straight line extending past point *C* to show that the maximum amount of other goods possible increased to $480.

Where is the increased efficiency? Suppose that this person is typical and wants to spend one-third of his income on food. Given the income grant and a resulting income of $480, he would want to spend $160 on food and $320 on

Figure TQ21-1

other goods (point *D*). With the food stamps, he would be constrained to purchase $180 of food and only $300 of other goods. His utility would therefore be lower with food stamps than with an income grant.

10. The equation of the tax is

$$T = -B + tY$$

where T represents tax liability, B represents the benefit payment, Y represents income, and t represents the tax rate (in percentage terms, $t \times 100$ percent). With $t = 0.5$ and $B = \$4500$, break-even occurs when

$$T = 0 = -\$4500 + 0.5Y$$

i.e., when

$$Y = \$4500/0.5 = \$9000$$

This conforms with Table 21-7 in the text. For $B = \$2700$, solving for t such that $9000 is the break-even income means solving

$$0 = -\$2700 + t(\$9000)$$

i.e., the appropriate tax is $2700/$9000 = 0.3 (30 percent). For $B = \$7200$, the same procedure produces a tax of 0.8 (80 percent). For $B = \$9000$, the tax is 1 (100 percent).

Higher rates associated with higher benefit payments certainly imply greater disincentives.

CHAPTER 22

THE WINDS OF CHANGE: THE TRIUMPH OF THE MARKET

Your attention has thus far been focused on the modern mainstream view of how a mixed economy like that of the United States works to solve the fundamental economic questions of *how*, *what*, and *for whom*. Your introduction to this type of structure is almost complete. Chapter 22 focuses on the economic alternatives to mixed capitalism, and it has been included at this point for two important reasons.

First, the profession did not arrive at its current state overnight. The mainstream view espoused by many economists in mixed economies is the product of an evolutionary process that has proceeded slowly over the course of more than two centuries. You should be aware of at least the broad outline of that evolution.

Second, not all the world's economies operate in a fashion that is best described by the mixed structure envisioned by mainstream economic thought in the United States. Over 1.5 billion people across the world live in societies whose economic structures are based on the principles of Marxism or socialism. Another 1 billion people live in countries whose economies are apparently in transition into a mixed capitalistic structure. You should therefore be aware of the major differences between these structures and the strains which transition will cause.

The general objectives of this chapter are thus easily defined; simply put, they prescribe your being exposed to different ways of looking for answers to the same fundamental questions. With your horizons broadened, you should have accomplished the following more specific objectives.

LEARNING OBJECTIVES

1. Recall Adam Smith's argument in support of laissez-faire: the market provides a self-regulating natural order even over the actions of people who are essentially self-motivated. Also note why Smith's book, *The Wealth of Nations*, was so well received by the business classes, who were happy to see intellectual justification of their purposes.

2. Delineate the rationale behind David Ricardo's forecast that rents would rise as land became the bottleneck to economic growth. Also explain his expectation that the future would make the capitalists the captains of economic order even as the world fell into a state of pervasive poverty. Given the gloom and doom, why were his ideas so popular with both the capitalists and the socialists?

3. Summarize the major contributions which the neoclassical school made to classical theory by recognizing consumer preferences and the demand side of a market. Also recognize the major objections raised by this school to the laissez-faire recommendations of the classicists.

4. Place the Keynesian revolution into its historical context, and describe the modern mainstream view of macroeconomic theory in terms of its historical antecedents.

5. Explain each of the major modern critiques of mainstream economic thought: the libertarian view of the Chicago School, the passive policy view of the rational-expectations school, the Galbraithian view of modern capitalism, the lessons of the Japanese experience, and the new left prescriptions of the radical economists.

6. Distinguish carefully between (a) pure market economy, (b) Marxism, (c) modern socialism, and (d) Soviet communism.

Use your experience and understanding of current events to place modern economies in their appropriate position in this spectrum.

7. Define what Marx meant by "the exploitation of labor by capital" and by "surplus value." Explain why Marx felt that capitalism was inevitably headed for a crisis generated by a failure of the purchasing power of labor to match the total value of goods produced.

8. Describe the Soviet economic structure, and compare its performance with that of the major developed economies of the West. Outline both the intent and the effect of the Gorbachev reforms.

Adam Smith's *The Wealth of Nations* occupies a unique place in the esteem of economists, less because it argued in favor of laissez-faire and more because it was the first coherent account of the working of a market system. Much of what is found in Chapters 2 and 3 of the text derives from Adam Smith: the law of scarcity, the role of prices, the need for competition, and the consequences of monopoly. Smith's argument is sometimes incomplete, sometimes confused, sometimes contradictory, but these are the inevitable shortcomings of a pioneer work of immense scope.

Two further points about the classical economists deserve mention. First, their work developed out of a lively and perceptive interest in contemporary issues. *The Wealth of Nations* is a frontal attack on the then-influential mercantilist philosophy of governmental interference in trade matters. Malthus and Ricardo dealt at length with issues arising from the Napoleonic Wars, notably war-induced price inflation and tariff protection. When Napoleon's power play ended and normal shipping was resumed, the British food-growing aristocracy found itself exposed to new competition from America and elsewhere. The English landowners contrived an increase in the grain tariff—the famous Corn Laws. Subsequently, and largely in consequence of the influential writings of the classical economists, the Corn Law rates were reduced and, in 1846, abolished.

Second, there is just enough unanimity of viewpoint among the English classical economists to warrant grouping them together as a school, and no more. Malthus and Ricardo conducted a lengthy correspondence on innumerable issues. Almost always, they disagreed. (These disagreements did nothing to destroy a touchingly warm and enduring friendship which terminated only with Ricardo's death at the age of 51.) For example, most of the classical economists accepted, at least in rough outline, Say's Law of full-employment purchasing power. Malthus did not, although he could not build an alternative theory. It was more than 100 years later that Keynes did construct such a theory.

1. The most prominent members of the early English "classical school" of economists were:

Adam Smith (1723-1790)

Thomas Robert Malthus (1766-1834)

David Ricardo (1772-1823)

Match these names with the following descriptions:

a. He sought, as a major part of his work, to discover the "laws of distribution"—i.e., the economic laws by means of which the national product was divided between three classes: laborers, landowners, and entrepreneurs (manufacturers and merchants). _____

b. He enunciated the doctrine of laissez-faire, which held that government should not interfere with human activity except in special areas such as the maintenance of law, police duties, and national defense. _____

c. Although best known today for his theory of population growth, he dealt, in fact, with a wide range of contemporary economic problems. _____

d. He developed the hypothesis that, in the long run, land was the crucially scarce economic factor, so economic growth would result in a continuing increase in the rental price per acre received by owners of land. (*Note:* Although one of the three economists cited is particularly associated with this hypothesis, it is implicit also in the reasoning of another of the three.) _____

e. He set out the doctrine of a self-regulating "natural order" of human affairs, and used the *invisible-hand* concept to illustrate this doctrine: each individual, pursuing his own self-interest within a market system, is "led by an invisible hand to promote an end which was no part of his intention." _____

f. Both relied heavily on the law of diminishing returns in their analyses (*Note:* Two of the three economists did so.) _____ and _____

a. Ricardo **b.** Smith **c.** Malthus **d.** Ricardo (or Malthus) **e.** Smith **f.** Malthus; Ricardo

2. The English classical economists had, so to speak, roughed out the general shape of economic analysis. Thereafter, one group—the neoclassical economists, still predominantly English until the early twentieth century—undertook to correct, refine, and enlarge classical ideas. Another group—Marx and his followers—attempted a more fundamental revision.

The classical account, perhaps because it felt impelled to emphasize the basic scarcity of productive factors (Chapter 2), stressed *supply* factors as the principal ingredient within commodity prices. Demand elements were not given much consideration. It is almost as though all classical supply curves were *(horizontal / vertical)*, so any shift in the demand curve *(would / could not)* change the price.

This classical supply-side account vacillated between a labor theory of value and a cost-of-production theory. (The latter asserts that the price of a commodity must be explained in terms of the expenditures on labor, land, and capital required for its production.) Both labor and cost-of-production theories may seem plausible at first; on closer inspection, though, they have proved to be after-the-event explanations.

Marx worked to solve this problem by adding his own notion of *surplus* value to the more widely held labor theory of value. Prices, Marx argued, *would* be equal to labor value in a properly functioning society. In a capitalist society, however, prices *would not* achieve this fundamental equality. The labor theory of value was thereby transformed into more of a description of "what should be" than a description of "what is."

By way of contrast, the neoclassical economists stuck (or tried to stick, at any rate) to descriptions of "what is." They recognized that labor cost, and costs of production generally, have a major part to play in price determination. At the same time, however, they added the element which had earlier been neglected, namely, _____ . The outcome—and here the work of Alfred Marshall (1842–1924) was most important—was the demand-curve and supply-curve approach of Chapters 4 and 5.

Demand and supply curves are graphs; therefore they have a mathematical background, whether that background is recognized or not. Economics was becoming more mathematical. The neoclassical introduction of "marginalist" concepts (marginal utility in Chapter 6, marginal product in Chapter 7, marginal cost and revenue in Chapter 8) illustrates the point. If you have had training in calculus, you will recognize that "marginal" signifies the taking of a partial derivative. It was as part of this more mathematical trend that the theory of general equilibrium (Chapter 17) was developed. Major figures were _____ , _____ , and _____ .

---

horizontal; could not; demand; Leon Walras; Stanley Jevons; Vilfredo Pareto

---

3. In the twentieth century, the major development in economics has been the development of Keynesian analysis; it will be discussed at length later in the text. Bitterly resented upon its introduction because it seemed to upset so many traditional beliefs, this analysis warned that the market system cannot be left to its own devices with assurance that a full-employment equilibrium will result in developed societies relying heavily on investment spending. In brief, Keynesian analysis banished *(the law of scarcity / the law of supply and demand / Say's Law / the law of diminishing returns)*.

Say's Law

---

4. a. The Chicago School of economists, including, _____ , _____ , and Milton Friedman, generally feels that markets *(work / don't work)* and that government intervention is *(necessary and beneficial / unnecessary and detrimental)*. The rational-expectations macroeconomics of the Chicago and Minnesota schools is simply a logical extension of this line of reasoning—a line of reasoning that traces its origins directly back to the *(invisible hand of Adam Smith / the lament of diminishing productivity of Malthus and Ricardo / the spending multipliers of Keynes)*. Lest anyone think that it abides only in the halls of academia, it should be emphasized that the *Economic Report of the President* prepared for President *(Nixon / Carter / Reagan)* by the Council of Economic Advisers in *(1972 / 1978 / 1982)* endorsed almost the entire philosophical picture of the Chicago School.

b. A second critique, made popular by John Kenneth Galbraith, also holds that mainstream theory is out of touch with reality. Circle each of the following statements that accurately reiterates either a contention of the Galbraithian view or a commonly held opinion of his work:

(1) His theory is basically Marxist both in its origins and in its conclusions.

(2) His work is more a criticism of existing theory than an outline of an identifiable and testable alternative theory.

(3) His argument presents a serious challenge to Keynesian economics.

(4) His reasoning is in large part a synthesis of other people's ideas; his role has been to merge these ideas and to present them in unusually persuasive fashion.

(5) Big business is not necessarily bad, though not necessarily good, either.

(6) Consumers are not the masters of their own fates; they are manipulated by advertising and salespeople to the point of not always knowing precisely what is in their best interest.

(7) The public sector seems to be starved for resources, while the private sector squanders enormous wealth that could otherwise be used to improve the welfare of all.

c. Radical economists come at the world from the new left.

They espouse many types of government intervention; list at least four in the spaces provided:

(1) _____

(2) _____

(3) _____

(4) _____

a. Frank Knight; Henry Simons; Friedrich Hayek; work; unnecessary and detrimental; invisible hand of Adam Smith; Reagan; 1982 **b.** (2); (4); (5); (6); (7) **c.** (1) Markets need democratic planning. (2) Price controls are needed to free resources. (3) Industrial policies are necessary. (4) Greater equity is essential.

The term **socialism** has been applied to a variety of political and economic movements. It is generally agreed that the characteristic common to most of these movements is a belief that the privilege of unlimited ownership of private property is not an inalienable right. In particular, socialists challenge the right of private ownership of productive resources in the form of land and capital goods.

While the origins of socialist thought can be traced back to the Greeks, the socialist movement developed its real momentum in the eighteenth and nineteenth centuries. The Industrial Revolution profoundly altered European economic and social conditions. It brought immense wealth to some members of the new entrepreneur class. It brought degradation and misery to many workers employed in the new industries. To people of conscience, it seemed that the cards were stacked in the new economy against anyone unlucky enough to be forced to try to earn his or her living from labor alone. Members of this "proletariat" class would inevitably be exploited by a small group of employers exercising power acquired through ownership of productive inputs other than labor.

However unanimous socialists may have been on the indignities of the new industrial society, they were far from agreement on the proper method of reform. The anarchists believed in total abolition of the state; later, anarchism came to be associated with the view that capitalism (and the state) could be overthrown only by violent means. In contrast, the "utopian" socialists hoped to reform society by establishing as seeds within that society small communal groups whose behavior would be governed by "high-minded" rules. Karl Marx regarded these utopian projects as fatuous diversions of the reform effort. He insisted on a socialism that would be "practical" in the essential sense of being based on a *scientific* analysis of human society. In 1848, to express these views, he and Friedrich Engels published *The Communist Manifesto*.

Marxism's intellectual foundation is "dialectical materialism," an adaptation of Hegel's "dialectical idealism." This Marxian system describes human history in terms of movement and change. Each stage of development within that history contains some inner contradiction which is the seed of its own destruction. Change is the process by which one contradiction is removed, only to produce another. The fundamental assumption in Marxism, as stated in *The Communist Manifesto*, is that "the history of all hitherto-existing society is the history of class struggles." In this history, the ruling class exploits one or more other classes. Feudalism was one stage in human history in which the ruling class consisted of landowning nobility. The inner contradiction within this system led to its overthrow by capitalism. According to Marx, the bourgeois ruling class of capitalists would in due course be overthrown by the proletarian laboring class. Marx thought this would be the final stage of the class struggle, since the overthrow of capitalism would result in a classless society. To enlarge his argument that capitalism carries within it an inner contradiction leading to its own destruction, Marx developed his theory of surplus value.

5. a. Karl Marx's principal work was his three-volume *Das Kapital*. Referring particularly to opinion among rebels and dissenters, *Das Kapital* is (*no longer* / *still*) considered Marx's major contribution to reform.

b. Marx's forecasts in this work included the following: The real wage of laborers would (*rise* / *fall*); the "reverse army of the unemployed" would (*increase* / *decrease*) in number; the rate of capitalist profit would (*rise* / *fall*); business cycles would (*grow* / *diminish*) in intensity; the capitalist system would collapse in response to (*an excess* / *a deficiency*) of purchasing power. Thus far, these forecasts (*have* / *have not*) been vindicated.

c. Interest in Marx is today turning toward other aspects of his thought. Two ideas in particular are emphasized. Record them in the spaces provided below.

(1) _____

(2) _____

a. no longer **b.** fall; increase; fall; grow; a deficiency; have not **c.** (1) alienation (2) the economic interpretation of history (the view that behavior is shaped by material interests or, in more Marxian terms, by the conditions of production)

6. Circle the statements below which accurately characterize the state of the Soviet Union prior to Gorbachev; put stars next to the statements which identify the intent of some of the Gorbachev reforms:

a. The state is relinquishing some of its ownership of the land.

b. The state owns almost all capital equipment.

c. Consumer goods are given money prices, and workers choose among the consumer goods according to these prices; the wages of workers are paid in money.

d. Central planners were once plagued with the problem of widespread piling up of consumer goods which could not be sold; now this problem is much less acute.

e. Workers have, in general, no choice as to the geographic area in which they may work.

f. Workers have very little choice as to the occupation they would like to enter.

g. Planners use prices to support and achieve their planning goals.

h. There are no important differences in wages or salaries; i.e., there are no significant departures from equality of income distribution.

i. Inequalities of income distribution exist to reflect political influence rather than special competence or skill in some occupation.

j. In the decision of what goods to produce, top priority is given to investment projects and defense production, consumer goods being produced to the extent possible after these requirements have been satisfied.

k. Industrial workers are now given a fair degree of freedom to bargain collectively with plant managers on wages and other terms of employment.

l. Industrial plants operate by being given a quota of output which they are expected to meet or exceed.

m. The quota system is presently used only to allocate productive resources, while consumer goods sell at competitive prices because markets are allowed to function to some degree.

n. Enterprise managers are rewarded for achieving quantity targets, and this system breeds poor quality, hoarding, and reluctance to take risks and pursue innovations.

o. Prices change frequently without warning because planning is an imprecise science.

p. Political control of economic planning has moved gradually, but steadily, away from centralization and toward decentralization.

q. Material balances help planners keep track of thousands of different goods and factors of production.

r. The state levies a tax on the sale of goods at each production stage, so consumer-goods prices considerably exceed wages paid to produce those goods.

s. Marxist concepts with respect to value are still employed with respect to relative prices set on consumer goods and on investment goods.

---

circle: **b, c, g, j, l, n, q, r;**   star: **a, p,** and, tentatively, **m**   (*Note:* Things are changing so quickly in the Soviet Union that these answers may be out of date as you read this.)

7. Circle the statements below which make accurate comparisons between the United States, the Soviet Union, and other economies:

a. The Soviet Union's rate of growth in GNP since World War II has exceeded that of all Western countries.

b. As the Soviet Union's output grows and, in consequence, turns more toward services, it is estimated that the USSR will grow more quickly because services require smaller investments in capital than manufacturing.

c. GNP in the Soviet Union is currently little more than one-half of U.S. GNP.

d. The Soviet Union has been able to imitate technologies already developed elsewhere. This fact has made it somewhat easier for the Soviet Union to maintain a high GNP growth rate.

e. The long-term rate of growth in real GNP in both the Soviet Union and the United States is fractionally above 5 percent annually.

f. The Soviet Union historically devoted a larger fraction of its GNP to military expenditure than did the United States, but both fractions are now declining.

g. Experience with GNP figures since World War II furnishes no clear answer to the question of whether collectivist societies or decentralized societies are better adapted to rapid rates of growth.

---

c, d, f (as of 1992), **g**

REVIEW CONCEPTS

1. Political economy evolved from the classicists' response to nationalism and protectionist mercantilism. Adam Smith (invisible hand, laissez–faire, etc.), David Ricardo (comparative advantage, etc.), and Thomas Malthus (diminishing returns, etc.) were major figures.

2. Neoclassical economics emerged to synthesize utility and costs, providing the marginalist underpinnings of modern theory. The Keynesian revolution added a macroeconomic synthesis with fiscal and monetary policy.

3. Alternative views to the mainstream theories have been offered by conservative libertarians (government action imperils personal freedom and economic efficiency), rational-expectations theorists (systematic policies cannot cure business cycles), Galbraithian iconoclasm (advertising power and the weakness of big business) and radical economists (denouncing pollution, inequity, and imperialism).

4. The periodic cycles of capitalism breed Marxism, socialism, and communism. Marx offered the laws of motion for capitalism—exploitation, pauperization, class struggle, and the ultimate proletarian victory. Socialism offered government ownership and planning as a compromise between capitalism and communism.

5. Eastern European planned economies are in transition. Reform toward market mechanisms is moving forward with mixed results from region to region within countries and from country to country across the continent.

QUIZ: Multiple Choice

1. The concept of a "natural order" is associated in economics particularly with the name of:
(1) John Maynard Keynes.
(2) Leon Walras.
(3) Adam Smith.
(4) Karl Marx.
(5) Alfred Marshall.

2. Which of the five economists cited in question 1 was the author of the statement, "People of the same trade seldom meet together, even for merriment and diversion, but the conversation ends in a conspiracy against the public or in some contrivance to raise price"?
(1).
(2).
(3).
(4).
(5).

3. An important part of David Ricardo's argument held that:
(1) the income or payment received by each productive factor or input would be governed by that factor's marginal productivity.
(2) economists relied to excess on the deductive process and neglected the requirement of verifying their conclusions empirically.
(3) supply and cost factors alone could not explain price or value, since demand was a factor of equal importance.
(4) the rate of business profit was bound to fall.
(5) profits would fall even as labor's wage fell.

4. Which alternative in question 3 would be correct had that question referred to Karl Marx (and to capitalist society) rather than to David Ricardo?
(1).
(2).
(3).
(4).
(5).

5. The contemporary economist whose name is most prominently associated with the principle of laissez-faire earlier advocated by Adam Smith is:
(1) Milton Friedman.
(2) Thomas Kuhn.
(3) Robert Solow.
(4) John G. Gurley.
(5) John Kenneth Galbraith.

6. The law of diminishing returns played a prominent part in:
(1) Leon Walras' theory of general equilibrium.
(2) the mercantilist theory of tariff protection.
(3) Adam Smith's principle of the invisible hand.
(4) David Ricardo's theory of income distribution.
(5) Karl Marx's theory of the business cycle.

7. The contributions of neoclassical theory to the advancement of economic analysis included:
(1) the development of a mathematical theory of general equilibrium and in the process brought marginalist concepts into use.
(2) the development of an econometric procedure to measure the significance of economic variables.
(3) the reversal of the classical emphasis on deduction, insisting that economists verify empirically the hypotheses on which they relied.
(4) a non-Marxist account of how the economy might reach an equilibrium which was substantially below the level of full resource employment.
(5) the first clear account of the significance of the law of scarcity on the supply side of the market.

8. The "economic interpretation of history" doctrine set out by Marx and Engels maintains that:
(1) the distribution of income by class is governed by the iron law of marginal productivity.
(2) the driving force behind entrepreneurial behavior is the maximization of profit.
(3) each class has its own economic interest, and beliefs and behavior are dictated by such economic interest.
(4) an authoritarian leader, thrown up by world revolution, is an imperative before any change in the conditions of production can be accomplished.
(5) the inescapable scarcity of land must lead to the progressive impoverishment of the growing body of laborers who must work on that land.

9. Marx's argument was that the output which requires labor effort is given a price which exceeds the money wage paid

that labor. The verdict of neoclassical economic theory on this argument is that it:
(1) may have some validity in labor-intensive production, but not in capital-intensive production.
(2) is entirely false.
(3) is correct, since inputs other than labor contribute to production.
(4) may have some validity as to capital-intensive production, but not as to labor-intensive production.
(5) is meaningless, since demand is a more powerful factor in price determination than is labor cost.

10. Marx's approach to the economic problem of values was that:
(1) the emphasis of the classical economists upon values was a distraction, the important thing being the exploitation of labor.
(2) the important thing is relative values—the valuation of one commodity against another.
(3) surplus value has to be measured altogether differently from labor value.
(4) there has to be an absolute measure of value, the measure being labor value.
(5) in capitalist societies, prices bear no consistent relationship to values whatsoever.

11. Socialism, as depicted in Great Britain, and communism, as formerly depicted in the planned economies of Eastern Europe, differ in which respect?
(1) Since World War II, the emphasis on public ownership of industry has been somewhat moderated in communism but not in socialism.
(2) Significant inequalities of income are accepted as necessary in socialist thinking but not in communist.
(3) Socialism accepts and encourages the trade-union movement; communism does not.
(4) Significant inequalities of income are accepted as necessary in communist thinking but not in socialist.
(5) None of the above.

12. In the Soviet Union, the decision of what to produce has historically been made:
(1) first on total consumer-goods production and then on defense, with the residual in total output being devoted to capital goods.
(2) principally through a pricing system, except for defense and defense-related production.
(3) according to a system of national priorities, among which consumer goods, capital goods, or defense may rank highest at any particular time.
(4) by the central authority, but there is no clear evidence as to the priority system.
(5) on defense and capital-goods production first, with consumer goods being caught in the residual in total output.

13. The distribution of income and privilege within the Soviet Union today is best described by which of the following?
(1) There are neither significant class distinctions nor differences of privilege; the only significant differences in income take the form of merit bonuses for exceeding production quotas.
(2) There are significant class distinctions, but these are based almost entirely on occupation, not on income, since differences in income and in privilege are minor.
(3) The income distribution is polarized; a few party members enjoy high income and privilege, while the remainder of the population receives low and approximately equal incomes.
(4) There are marked social classes and differences of privilege, and there is considerable inequality in income; party members may receive substantial incomes derived from property ownership.
(5) There are marked social classes and differences of privilege, and there is considerable inequality in income distribution between classes even though no significant amount of income is attributable to ownership of capital goods or other such property.

14. The Soviet government acquires much of the revenue needed for its operation through:
(1) levying an income tax, although it is not a progressive income tax.
(2) levying a turnover tax applied on goods at each stage of production.
(3) collecting payments made by each industrial plant in proportion to the cost of plant construction, much as a Western company might pay interest on a bond issue.
(4) levying taxes on privately owned property.
(5) levying a progressive income tax.

15. The best available estimates suggest that the U.S.S.R.'s total real GNP, compared with that of the United States:
(1) is slightly over one-half, but its per capita GNP is less than one-half.
(2) is approximately equal, and its per capita GNP is slightly higher.
(3) is about one-third, and its per capita GNP is perhaps less than one-quarter.
(4) is slightly higher, although its per capita GNP is still only about five-sixths.
(5) simply cannot be compared because commodities consumed in the two countries are so different as to make comparisons meaningless.

SUGGESTED ANSWERS TO QUESTIONS IN THE TEXT: Chapter 22

1. The market system supports laissez-faire capitalism; it was most closely approximated in nineteenth-century Britain. Marxism predicts the laws of motion of capitalism from the exploitation of labor through an ultimate proletarian victory—the last phase in social history; it influenced thinking in Europe, the Soviet Union, the People's Republic of China, and many parts of the developing world. Socialism calls for government ownership of the means of production, vigorous planning, and movement toward a welfare state; having evolved from a call for violence, it can represent one extreme in the market-command spectrum along which most mixed, developed economies find themselves. Soviet communism arose in Russia in 1917; the state owned (most of) the land and the capital and operated according to detailed, microlevel plans. The Gorbachev reforms started to move the system toward more decentralization, and the events of 1991 accelerated their pace.

2. The market-system solution to the questions is the topic of most of the text—dollar votes and profit incentives. The general answers generated in the command economies are outlined according to each question in the chapter.

3. Old thinkers would like little of the text—market prices, profit incentives, dollar votes, and all that. Contemporary thinkers would find it all very interesting as they search around in the reform process for thoughts that might work for them.

4. Succinctly, the libertarian argument is "If it is good for people, then they will do it on their own and the market will help them." There will be no lousy drugs, for example, because people will not buy lousy drugs. When constructing opposing arguments, think about externality effects and the information that people have when they buy things. What is good for one might not be good for all taken together (e.g., pollution, inflation, the fallacy of composition). Even harm that is apparently self-contained, like excessive injuries incurred by someone not wearing a seat belt in a car crash, can have wider social costs (lost productivity, higher insurance rates generally, etc.). These are not academic arguments; there are libertarians running in many congressional and senatorial races across the United States in every even-numbered year.

5. In general, the libertarian argument is that government attempts to solve a problem are ineffective, create other problems elsewhere, or both. Express your own views about Freidman's opposition to social security, flood insurance, food and drug quality regulation, free public schooling, the licensing of doctors, the establishment and maintenance of national parks, etc. Again, consider information, externality, and common effects.

The fundamental issue is this: Is economic freedom a social objective to be pursued universally, or should it be considered on a case-by-case basis? Even if it has not been assigned, read *Capitalism and Freedom* sometime soon—with a critical, questioning eye—while your recollection of this economics course is fresh. You may end up agreeing with all, none, or some of what Friedman argues; that is for you to decide. One thing is certain, though, you will *certainly* be a better citizen for having pondered the questions that he raises.

6. The United States is better at (b) and (d); the Soviet Union, probably at (a) and (c), although the road to reform has generated *both* inflation and unemployment. You may want to question whether Soviet full employment is really pervasive underemployment and whether administered prices hold inflation by removing all the informational content of those prices. You may want to worry about consumer tastes dictated by a distribution of income that may or may not be appropriately equitable.

7. Prices and profits indicate relative scarcity and provide incentives for firms to meet the demands of others. Remember dollar votes. In a command economy, planned quantities based on planned objectives dictate quotas for firms and enterprises. Increasingly, though, the incentive structure for managers includes profit in addition to quantity relative to target. *Perestroika* is struggling to bring price signals and profit incentives to bear on the Soviet economy, as effectively as possible within the constraints of continued planning from within government. Decentralization is happening, but not yet to the degree that is displayed by the mixed market system of the United States.

8. As is clear from Figure TQ22-1, MU does not equal MC unless the quantity target is carefully chosen. In the figure, X_m is the correct quantity with $MU = MC$. If, for example, X_p were selected as the total supply, then X_p would be supplied, sold at $P_p > P_m$, and the marginal utility generated by consuming or employing X_p would exceed the marginal cost of producing X_p. Welfare would be improved, in terms of consumer plus producer surplus, by an amount equal to the area of triangle ABE if output were to increase to X_m and price were to fall to P_m. The output of some other good would have to fall as resources were increasingly devoted to the production of X, but sorting that out is a general-equilibrium problem.

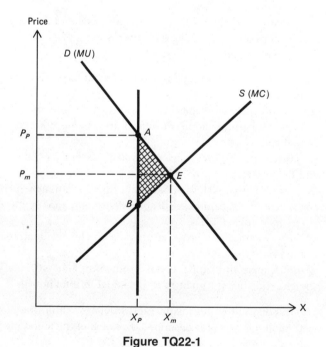

Figure TQ22-1

CHAPTER 23

INTERNATIONAL TRADE AND THE THEORY OF COMPARATIVE ADVANTAGE

Chapter 23 begins a four-chapter excursion into the fundamentals of international economics—the issues surrounding the conduct of international trade and finance and the sources of economic development. The first two chapters introduce the real factors involved in trade and describe how differences in resource endowments, tastes, and technology can generate the potential for gleaning substantial welfare benefits from trade abroad. The problems associated with that trade and the restraint of its proliferation by tariffs and quotas are thus central to the discussion. Chapter 24, in fact, focuses on these issues almost exclusively. In the meantime, the end of Chapter 23 presents a brief survey of how international trade accounts are kept. The details of the monetary mechanisms that support international trade, including exchange-rate determination and other current issues of international finance, occupy Chapter 26.

The details of international economics are extremely complex, and an introductory course can only scratch their surface. The fundamental welfare implications of international and interregional trade are nonetheless easily presented and understood. Chapter 23 starts the presentation and puts you on the way to achieving this general objective. In the process, you will also achieve the following more specific objectives.

LEARNING OBJECTIVES

1. Distinguish between absolute advantage and comparative advantage, the latter being defined in terms of the relative expense of producing a commodity; a country generally has a comparative advantage in goods which it can produce less expensively relative to other tradable commodities.

2. Explain, using a simple two-commodity model, how a country can increase its real income by specializing (for the purpose of export) in the commodity in which it has a comparative advantage and importing the commodity in which it has a comparative disadvantage.

3. Understand that the Ricardo model, in which exploiting comparative advantage is shown to improve welfare, is a classical, cost-based, full-employment model. Without the perfect markets that ensure full employment, the transitions required to take full advantage of the potential gains from specialization and trade can be costly, pushing an economy below its production-possibility frontier.

4. Explain why, assuming no transportation costs, the establishment of an international equilibrium price ratio common to both (all) trading partners is essentially a supply-demand problem of the sort studied in previous chapters.

5. Outline the basic accounting procedure with which the world keeps track of its international accounts. Define, in that outline, the four components of balance-of-payments accounting: current account, capital account, changes in official settlements, and statistical discrepancy. Note, as well, that a credit is recorded any time a transaction produces foreign currency and that a debit is recorded any time a transaction expends foreign currency.

6. Trace the usual evolution from young, debtor nation to mature, creditor nation. Notice, in passing, that the United States moved through that evolution to a new category—a mature nation whose low rate of saving has made it a debtor nation.

23 International Trade and the Theory of Comparative Advantage

The fundamental point of Chapter 23 is that foreign trade can improve welfare (i.e., the standard of living) of most nations, even if they are the most productive in producing everything. There are, of course, political problems that frequently stand in the way of countries' exploiting this potential: problems of reciprocal trade restriction in the face of "unfair" trading practices by trading partners, problems of national security and overreliance on foreign suppliers of critical commodities, and so on. There can, moreover, exist problems caused by the multiplicity of currencies across the world. Still, the welfare result that produces the potential gains from trade is robust and widely known. Chapter 23 produces it for you in the simple context of the Ricardo model, and the *Study Guide* explores it further. The numbers are different here, to provide variety and to avoid "puppeting" answers; but the point is the same: international trade has the potential to improve the welfare of everyone involved by expanding the consumption possibilities of everyone involved.

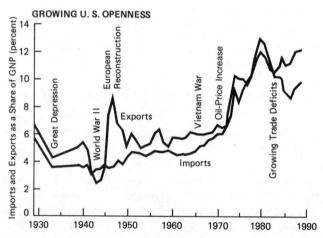

Figure 23-1 America has become more exposed to the winds of international competition. Like all major industrial countries, the United States has opened its borders to greater amounts of foreign trade over the last half-century. The greatest growth of the dollar value of imports came with the rise of oil prices and with the foreign penetration of American consumer markets.
(*Source:* U.S. Department of Commerce.)

1. As shown in Figure 23-1, the trend in the United States over the past half-century has been to *(open / close)* its economy to foreign trade. The usual measure of openness, the ratio of _____ and/or _____ to GNP has, in fact, *(risen / fallen)* to _____ percent. This is a percentage that is, however, *(higher / lower)* than the _____ percent which characterizes most of the economies of Europe.

It is important to note that although the simple Ricardo model implies complete specialization by bilateral trading partners, reality seldom achieves that extreme condition. The pattern of trade *(in fact shows that / does, however, show that)* the United States *(frequently / never)* imports and exports the same general commodity within the same year.

---

open; imports; exports; risen; 10; lower; 50; in fact shows that; frequently

---

If the United States had no domestic sources of tin, then it would surely have to import the tin it needed. What is not so obvious is why the United States, or any other country for that matter, should import a commodity which it could and does produce. The basic message of this chapter is that a nation should import some goods which it is capable of producing at home if it wants to use its resources to the best advantage. Each country should move toward specializing in the production of those commodities it is best equipped to make, given its own resources and those available to other countries. It should export part of what it has produced, receiving in exchange other goods (imports) which it is less well equipped to make.

The "model" used in this chapter is intended to drive home this point in the simplest possible form. Based on the model, most of the chapter concentrates on a critical review of some wrong ideas about international trade. One idea holds that profitable trade between two countries is impossible when one highly efficient country can outproduce another country in every line of activity; this is not true. Part of David Ricardo's great contribution to the study of international trade was to show that *relative* inefficiency in all lines of production would make a country poor, but it would not cause its trading opportunities to totally evaporate. Relatively efficient and inefficient countries can still trade to mutual advantage, provided there are some differences in their relative costs of production.

Before trying to understand why certain frequently held notions about international trade are incorrect, you must first grasp the basic notion of comparative advantage; it alone explains why, in terms of real income, it pays each nation to move toward specializing in the production of a specific good or goods, to export those goods, and to use the proceeds of that export trade to finance the import of other goods. The questions which follow immediately build toward an examination of the theory of comparative advantage by looking at economic conditions before trade begins. The idea is to start by identifying a country's before-trade position and standard of living and then to show how the initiation of foreign trade can increase real income.

The same simplifying assumptions are employed as in the text. There are only two regions: "America" and "Europe." Only two commodities are involved: food (F)

and clothing (C). All the costs of producing either F or C can be measured in hours of labor. For some reason, however, the yields from an hour of labor, in the making of both F and C, differ across international boundaries.

2. The quantities of F and of C resulting from 1 hour of labor in America and in Europe are given in Table 23-1. These data translate into the input requirements recorded in Table 23-2.

Table 23-1

Yield of 1 Labor-Hour	Units of F	Units of C
In America	20	6
In Europe	10	8

Table 23-2

	Minutes of Labor Required to Produce:	
	1 Unit of F	1 Unit of C
In America	3	10
In Europe	6	7.5

Assuming that "1 hour of labor" means the same thing in both countries, the figures indicate that America is more productive in (F / both F and C / C / neither F nor C). Europe is, meanwhile, more productive in (F / both F and C / C / neither F nor C). In an 8-hour day, therefore, a worker in America can produce either 8 × 20 = 160 units of F or (10 / 48 / 64 / 80) units of C. In Europe a worker can produce either 64 units of C or (10 / 48 / 64 / 80) units of F.

F; C; 48; 80

3. a. This chapter assumes that all the costs of producing either commodity in either region are labor costs and that all revenue from sale of the commodity goes to that labor. If the market price of a unit of F in America were $1, then the hourly wage earned by an American worker producing F would be $(0.05 / 0.10 / 1.00 / 10.00 / 20.00).

If, instead, F's price in America were $0.05 (5 cents), then the corresponding hourly wage for an F worker would be $(0.05 / 0.10 / 1.00 / 10.00 / 20.00). Similarly, if C's price per unit in America were $2, then the hourly wage of a C worker would be $(0.30 / 0.60 / 2.00 / 10.00 / 12.00).

b. If the price per unit of F were £1 in Europe, then the hourly wage of an F worker there would be £(1 / 4 / 6 / 8 / 10). If C's price in Europe were £1, on the other hand, then the corresponding hourly C wage would be £(1 / 4 / 6 / 8 / 10).

a. 20.00 ($1 per unit × 20 units per hour; labor is the only factor that is paid.); 1.00 (= $0.05 × 20 units per hour); 12.00 (= $2 × 6 units per hour)   b. 10; 8

4. a. Suppose that the prices of F and C in America are both $1. A worker, free to choose an occupation in either industry, would earn more by going to work in the production of (F / C). Specifically, earnings per hour would be $(1 / 6 / 8 / 10 / 20) in the production of F and $(1 / 6 / 8 / 10 / 20) in the production of C. Given freedom of labor to enter either occupation (and with no other preference between them), the prices noted above (both $1) (could / could not) characterize an "equilibrium" situation in America. If these prices did prevail—say, because the government tried to enforce them by law—then (only F / only C / both F and C) would be produced.

b. If the prices of both F and C were somehow £10 in Europe, then (again assuming no barrier to movement between occupations) (all the workers would move into production of F / all the workers would move into production of C / there would be no change in the production mix of F and C).

c. The point is that the supply of resources (here, the entire labor force) would shift away from production of the "underpriced" commodity unless the prices of F and C stand in the proper relation to one another, i.e., unless they reflect relative marginal costs. If the price of F were $3 in America, then the price of C would have to be $(1 / 3 / 8 / 10 / 12), if both F and C are to be produced. If the price of C were $2 in America, then the price of F should be $(0.30 / 0.60 / 1.00 / 1.50 / 2.00). Prices of $2.40 for F and $9 for C (would / would not) support an equilibrium.

It is relative prices that matter here. In America, the ratio between p_F and p_C must be (1:1 / 3:10 / 5:10 / 10:3) because only that ratio matches the underlying ratio of production costs, measured in labor time needed to produce 1 unit of each commodity. (The absolute level of prices would be governed by such factors as the quantity of money circulating within the country.) If prices of F and C somehow got stuck at $2.40 and $9, respectively, workers would move away from the production of (F / C) and into the production of (F / C).

d. In Europe the same requirement holds, except that the relationship must match productive conditions there. If the price of F in Europe were £4, then the price of C would have to be (1 / 2 / 3 / 4 / 5) to support an equilibrium in which both commodities were produced. More generally, Europe's price ratio (F to C) must be (3:10 / 5:10 / 4:5 / 5:4).

a. F; 20; 6; could not; only F   b. all the workers would move into production of F   c. 10; 0.60; would not; 3:10; F; C   d. 5; 4:5

The questions thus far have assumed that there is no international trade between America and Europe. Now assume that the opportunity for trade between the two regions suddenly materializes. Assume, for simplicity, that the costs of shipping goods from one region to the other are so small that they can be considered zero. The prices of F and of C in America are, respectively, 60 cents and $2.

5. a. You are a shrewd entrepreneur in America. To be more specific, you have $9000 in cash, and you are the first person to notice that the prices of F and C in Europe are £4 and £5, respectively. Given these prices, how can you convert your $9000 into $24,000? Describe the necessary operations in four steps (the first step is provided to get you on your way):

(1) Buy 15,000 F for $9000.

(2) _____

(3) _____

(4) _____

b. If you were an entrepreneur in Europe with a nest egg of £15,000 and a similar desire to improve your financial standing, what would you do to follow suit, and what would the result be? Construct another four-step process to turn your £15,000 into £40,000:

(1) _____

(2) _____

(3) _____

(4) _____

---

a. (2) Sell the 15,000 F in Europe for £60,000. (3) Buy 12,000 C in Europe with the £60,000. (4) Sell the 12,000 C in America for $24,000. **b.** (1) Buy 3000 C for £15,000. (2) Sell the 3000 C in America for $6000. (3) Buy 10,000 F in America with the $6000. (4) Sell the 10,000 F in Europe for £40,000.

6. a. Question 5 suggests that the two commodities will begin to move internationally as soon as someone realizes that relative prices are different on opposite sides of the trading border. Specifically, in this example (pick two alternatives), *(F moves from America to Europe / F moves from Europe to America / F moves in both directions / C moves from America to Europe / C moves from Europe to America / C moves in both directions).*

b. Had the prices of F and C in America been 30 cents and $1, respectively, rather than 60 cents and $2, then the results described in part **a** *(would / would not)* have changed. Had the prices of F and C in Europe been £8 and £10, respectively, rather than £4 and £5, then this *(would / would not)* have changed the results.

---

a. F moves from America to Europe and C moves from Europe to America
b. would not; would not

---

7. a. In America (and in Europe), opening trade would disrupt the pre-trade domestic "equilibrium." For example, in the United States, trade supplements domestic supplies of C. The price of C should therefore *(rise / remain unchanged / fall)*. This in turn means that the ratio of the price of F to the price of C (i.e., p_F/p_C) should *(rise / remained unchanged / fall)*.

b. We know from questions 3 and 4 that workers would leave the "underpriced" occupation if America's price ratio p_F/p_C were anything other than 3:10 (or 0.3). In this case, workers would move from the production of *(F / C)* to the production of *(F / C)* as the price ratio rose, and that would be good. Why? Because America's new export trade means that more workers are needed in the production of American exports—commodity F.

c. In Europe, which imports what America exports, there would *(be a / not be any)* corresponding change in domestic prices. There, the ratio p_F/p_C would *(rise / remain unchanged / fall)*. The price of F would fall as imports arrived from America. The price of C would rise, meanwhile, since there would now be a new and increased demand for European C in America. Workers would leave the production of *(C / F)*, moving instead to production of Europe's export—commodity C.

---

a. fall; rise   **b.** C; F   **c.** be a; fall; F

---

8. The before-trade price ratios were 3:10 in America and 4:5 (or 8:10) in Europe. Clearly, different price ratios allow people to make financial killings by simply buying and selling commodities. These *arbitrage* profit opportunities do not last, however. They are, in fact, a symptom of disequilibrium. As question 7 indicated, prices are affected when goods begin to move in volume between two countries. Specifically (to repeat question 7), America's before-trade price ratio of 3:10 would *(rise / fall)* and Europe's ratio of 4:5 would *(rise / fall)*. That is, the two ratios would move *(closer together / farther apart)*.

Suppose that America's ratio rises from 3:10 to 4:10 and that Europe's falls from 8:10 to 7:10. There would *(no longer / still)* be arbitrage profits to be made; they would persist as long as any difference at all existed between the two price ratios. As more and more people discovered this opportunity, though, the volume of trade would keep increasing; and this increase would, in turn, push the two price ratios even *(closer together / farther apart)*. In the case considered here (i.e., a case of zero transport cost), the two ratios must finally meet at a common ratio like 5:10. It could, in fact, converge to any ratio between 3:10 and 8:10, but we leave the matter of determination of the exact common ratio for a later question.

---

rise; fall; closer together; still; closer together

---

9. Both regions would enjoy an increase in real income as a result of this trade. Specializing in the production of F, America would have more F and more C available for consumption than it did before. The same result would apply to Europe if it concentrated its productive energies on C.

This point can be illustrated by looking at the labor cost to America of the two methods of getting C—domestic production, on the one hand, and trade, on the other. America can produce 6 units of C per hour; each unit costs 10 minutes of labor time. What would that unit cost if C were obtained by producing good F and exporting F to Europe in exchange for C? Assume, as in question 8, that the international price ratio, p_F/p_C, is 5:10. That is, assume that a unit of clothing costs twice as much as a unit of food, so 2 units of F exchange for 1 unit of C. America can produce 20 units of F in 1 hour. If this were sent to Europe (with transport cost still assumed zero), America could receive (5 / 6 / 10 / 20 / 40) units of C in exchange. Since 1 hour of labor effort was involved, each of those units of C would cost (5 / 6 / 10 / 20 / 40) minutes of labor. This is (not as good as / better than) obtaining C through domestic production.

10; 6; better than

International trade is thus seen as capable of producing, for America, a result equivalent to the development of a new technology which greatly improves labor productivity in the C industry. At the same time, a similar effect is felt in Europe, but for the F industry instead of the C industry. The introduction of transportation cost would reduce this real-income gain somewhat. If transportation costs were sufficiently high, in fact, then there would be no point in trade and no gain in real income.

10. The points of questions 2 through 9 can all be illustrated graphically. Take the input requirements listed in question 2 as given, and suppose that Europe and America are both endowed with 10 hours of labor (not very realistic, to be sure, but a convenient number around which to build some illustrative geometry). Suppose further that both regions start, in the absence of any trade, by dividing their labor resources equally between F and C.

a. Draw, in panel (a) of Figure 23-2, the production-possibility frontier for America, and identify the initial production mix as point A. Draw the corresponding frontier for Europe in panel (b), and identify the initial production mix as point B.

The slope of the American frontier, equaling _____ in magnitude, represents the relative domestic price ratio of food to clothing in America. The corresponding slope of the European frontier, equaling _____ in magnitude, is similarly the relative domestic price ratio in Europe. Start with America, which produces _____ units of F and _____ units of C; Europe begins producing _____ units of F and _____ units of C. Total "world" production of C is _____ units; total production of F is _____ units.

b. Suppose now, for the sake of argument, that America chooses to specialize in F in trade with Europe at the European domestic price ratio. In panel (a), draw a budget constraint (a consumption frontier based upon specializing in the production of F and trading to get C) indicating the possible points of consumption given this strategy. If America were to continue to consume the original 30 units of C, then it could increase its consumption of F from 100 units to _____ units by selling _____ units of F for 30 units of C. Welfare in America, assuming a smooth transition from a 50-50 labor split to 100 percent concentration in the production of F, would therefore necessarily (fall / stay the same / rise).

c. Now play the same game from the other side of the Atlantic. Assume that Europe decides to specialize completely in the production of C and buys as much F as it wants given the American price ratio. Draw the appropriate budget constraint in panel (b). If Europe were still interested in consuming 40 units of C, it could increase its consumption of F from 50 units to _____ units by selling 40 units of C for _____ units of F. European welfare would, in this second case, also (climb / remain the same / fall), again making the same assumption of continued full employment during the transition.

d. The world production frontier can now be constructed. Suppose, first of all, that both countries specialize in F; production of F would equal _____ units in America and _____ units in Europe, for a total of _____ units; total production of C would then equal _____ units. Plot this combination in panel (c) and label it point D. Now reverse the specializations of both countries. Total production of F would then equal _____ units, with the production of C climbing to a maximum of _____ units. Plot this second point and label it E.

Halfway between these extremes are two intermediate cases of mixed specialization. If Europe specialized in C and America specialized in F, then _____ units of F would be produced along with _____ units of C. Denote this point G and plot it in panel (c), as well. If the specializations were reversed, though, _____ units of F would be produced by Europe and _____ units of C would be produced in America. This point, plotted and labeled H in panel (c), (would / would not) be on the frontier because the production level(s) of (F is / C is / neither F nor C is / both F and C are) lower at H than at G.

The world frontier is now at hand. A straight line connecting points D and G would correspond to specialization by (America / Europe) in the production of (F / C) and some intermediate combination of F and C produced in (America / Europe). Similarly, points along a line connecting points

274 23 *International Trade and the Theory of Comparative Advantage*

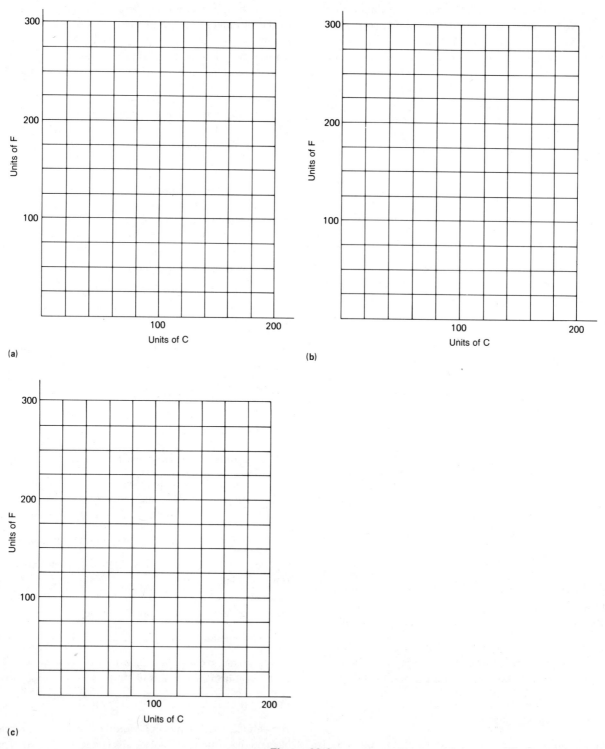

Figure 23-2

G and E would correspond to specialization in (America / Europe) in the production of (F / C) and some intermediate combination in (America / Europe). (*Note:* The frontier you just drew should look like the frontier shown in text Figure 23-3.)

e. Finally, plot the pre-trade initial production combination; it (*is / is not*) on the frontier. The point chosen by free trade outlined above would be (D / E / G / H). It (*would / would not*) be on the frontier, and it would, for both countries, be superior to the initial, pre-trade position.

a. the graphs: *(a)*—a straight line from (C = 0, F = 200) to (C = 60, F = 0), with point *A* at (C = 30, F = 100), and *(b)*—a straight line from (C = 0, F = 100) to (C = 80, F = 0), with point *B* at (C = 40, F = 50); 10/3; 5/4; 100; 30; 50; 40; 70; 150   **b.** graph *(a)*: a straight line from (C = 0, F = 200) to (C = 250, F = 0) (*Note:* C = 250 = 200 F times the European price ratio of 10/8); 162.5; 37.5; rise   **c.** graph *(b)*: a straight line from (C = 0, F = 266.67) to (C = 80, F = 0); 133.3; 133.3; climb   **d.** 200; 100; 300; 0 [Point *D* is (C = 0, F = 300).]; 0; 140 [Point *E* is (C = 140, F = 0).]; 200; 80 [Point *G* is (C = 80, F = 200).]; 100; 60 [Point *H* is (C = 60, F = 100).]; would not; both F and C are; America; F; Europe; Europe; C; America   **e.** (F = 150, C = 70); is not; *E*; would

The preceding questions have concentrated on an example in which Europe and America both held absolute advantages in the production of one good; America was more productive in food and Europe was more productive in clothing. The theory of comparative advantage stresses, however, that an even distribution of absolute advantage is not necessary for trade to be mutually beneficial. The next few questions will concentrate on this possibility—the real power of the Ricardo result.

11. Tables 23-3 and 23-4 show the effect of doubling America's yield per labor-hour in the production of both commodities, leaving the figures for Europe unchanged. Notice that American labor is now assumed more productive than European labor in the production of both commodities. We do not ask, "Why?" We simply accept the fact that there is now a "high-productivity" region and a "low-productivity" region so that we may ask the Ricardo question: Does there still exist the potential for mutually beneficial trade between Europe and America?

Table 23-3

Yield of 1 Labor-Hour	Units of F	Units of C
In America	40	12
In Europe	10	8

Table 23-4

	Minutes of Labor Required to Produce:	
	1 Unit of F	1 Unit of C
In America	1.5	5
In Europe	6	7.5

America's pre-trade price ratio p_F/p_C was 3:10 based on the data of Tables 23-1 and 23-2. That ratio would be *(higher / lower / unchanged)* given the revised data of Tables 23-3 and 23-4. With the changed productivity figures introduced now, the previously explored trading opportunity would *(no longer exist / exist exactly as before)*. Why? Because domestic, pre-trade prices would be unchanged. The dimensions of the transactions identified in question 5 might be different, but the directions of the trade discussed there are not.

---

unchanged; exist exactly as before (Relative prices have not changed.)

12. Let America be endowed with 5 hours of labor and Europe be endowed with 10; and suppose that the production possibilities of both countries are accurately described by Tables 23-3 and 23-4. Plot, in panels *(a)*, *(b)*, and *(c)* of Figure 23-3, the production-possibility frontier of America, Europe, and the world, respectively. Indicate, in panel *(c)*, the point toward which free trade would lead the two regions, if they could trade only with one another at some price ratio between 10:3 and 5:4. At that point, world production of F would equal _____ units and world production of C would equal _____ units because Europe would specialize in producing *(F / C)*, exporting *(F / C)*, and importing *(F / C)*; America would do the reverse.

---

the graphs: The required *PPF*s are identical to those in question 10, and the point is *G*, at the corner. 200; 80; C; C; F

13. The point, then, is that a low-productivity country should still be capable of trading profitably with a high-productivity country; both should gain in real income from international trade. The cost of low productivity is a low per capita income within that country, not an inability to cope with international exchanges. The essential factor is a difference in the pre-trade price ratio between the two countries.

a. Table 23-5 records three sets of pre-trade price figures (each quite different from anything used earlier). Indicate the proper conclusion, in the right-hand column, using this code:

1. America should export F, Europe C.
2. America should export C, Europe F.
3. No opportunity exists for gains from trade.

Table 23-5

America		Europe		
P of F in $	*P* of C in $	*P* of F in £	*P* of C in £	Answer
1	2	3	4	
1	2	3	6	
1	2	3	8	

b. It should now be clear why it was necessary to introduce such terms as "absolute advantage" (or "disadvantage") and "comparative advantage" (or "disadvantage"). America would have an absolute advantage over Europe in the production

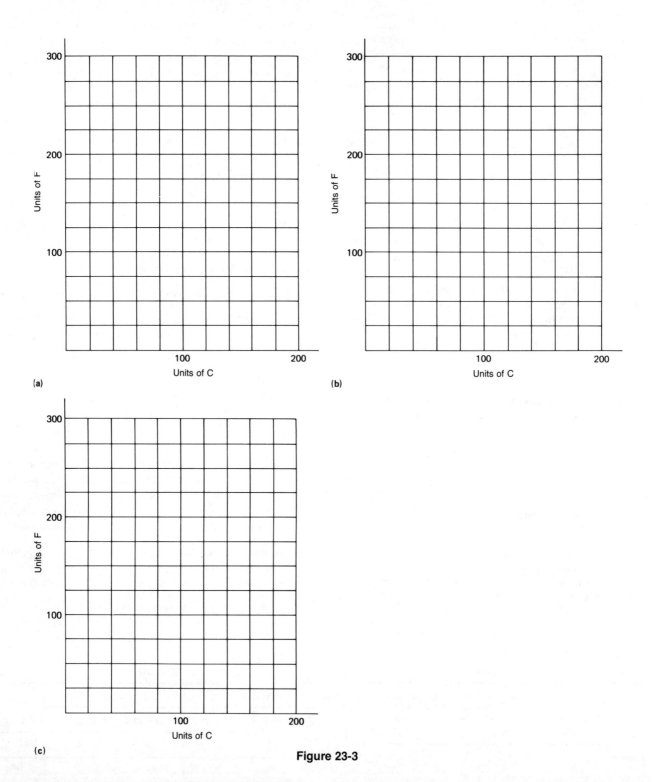

Figure 23-3

of some good if America could produce that commodity at smaller real cost (which in this chapter means simply labor cost) than could Europe. Look back at Tables 23-3 and 23-4. They indicate that America has the absolute advantage in (F alone / both F and C / C alone). Nonetheless, this circumstance should not prevent Europe from exporting good C. Regardless of its absolute disadvantage, Europe still has a comparative advantage in production of good (F / C). America is decidedly the high-productivity region according to the data in the tables, but its productivity shows up less prominently in the production of C.

In two-country, two-commodity examples (like the ones used here), it is necessary to examine and compare the prices of both commodities (in one country alone / in both coun-

tries) to determine who has a comparative advantage in what.

a. table column: 1, 3, 2   **b.** both F and C; C; in both countries

14. At what exact level will the common, post-trade price ratio be established once trade has been initiated between two countries? This is essentially a simple supply-and-demand question. The trading process is just an exchange of one good for another. Indeed, for purposes of understanding how the common intermediate ratio is reached, it's easiest to think of this trade as simple barter. The exact quantities exchanged are settled by working out a barter rate which both countries find, in terms of the amounts exchanged, satisfactory.

Start with the same pair of pre-trade p_F/p_C ratios used earlier: 3:10 in America and 4:5 in Europe. If the price of F in America were, say, $3, then the price of C would have to be $10. One unit of C would cost 3.33 times as much as 1 unit of F. In barter terms, it would take 10 units of F to match 3 units of C. Similarly, setting the p_F/p_C ratio equal to 4:5 in Europe means that *(4 units of F equal 5 units of C / 5 units of F equal 4 units of C)*.

When trade opens up, these two pre-trade ratios would be pushed closer together (recall questions 7 and 8). Consider any intermediate ratio picked at random—say, 1:2. At that ratio, there will be a particular quantity of F which America would wish to export and a corresponding quantity of C which it would want to import in return. If the desired quantity of export were 100 units of F daily, then the quantity of C that America would want in exchange (remember, the 1:2 ratio is expressed in p_F/p_C terms, as before) would be *(50 / 100 / 150 / 200 / 250)* units daily. At that same 1:2 ratio, there are also particular quantities of C and F which Europe would want to export and import daily, respectively, but these quantities may or may not match American desires. If they did not, then 1:2 would not be an "equilibrium" international price ratio. The intermediate and common ratio finally established is one at which the two regions' desires (expressed in terms of rates of exchange of F and C) do match. The better the barter terms America is offered, the *(more / less)* it will want to exchange. Europe, by contrast, will want to trade more extensively whenever the p_F/p_C ratio moves *(up / down)*. There should be a common price ratio that is mutually satisfactory somewhere between the two initial pre-trade price ratios.

5 units of F equal 4 units of C; 50; more; down

15. The principal basis for mutually profitable international trade is a difference in relative production costs and prices. The case in which a country imports a commodity which it cannot produce at all is simply an illustration of the extreme case of such differences-in-production-cost trade. It does not matter what factors account for these relative cost differences (e.g., climate, labor education and skill, capital equipment); they must simply emerge in the form of differences in relative prices.

Differences in "factor endowments" are usually cited as the principal source of such differences in relative production costs and prices (although this explanation is of the kind which may raise as many questions as it answers). Two other possible sources of mutually beneficial international trade are frequently identified. They are:

a. _____

b. _____

a. decreasing cost (*Note:* In this case, we can assume that the pre-trade cost ratio between commodities F and C is the same in Country A as in Country E. Given decreasing costs, though, Country A's specializing in the production of F may lower the per unit cost of producing F. Trade would then still be based on a difference in costs, but it would be a difference which could emerge only after trade had begun.)   **b.** differences in tastes between the two countries

16. The Ricardo analysis depends upon an implicit assumption of full employment. That is to say, when a country moves from producing a mix of goods toward specializing more heavily in a few goods, resources must flow freely from the production of one good to the other. Remember that Ricardo was a classical economist, and note that this is nothing more than the classical assumption of perfectly functioning markets. Labor *(must be / need not be)* included in this flow—labor which may or may not like the idea. If it does not, then serious opposition to free trade can arise, as labor asks its government for *(unemployment compensation / protection from foreign competition)*. Even though total welfare might improve with trade, it therefore is possible that some individuals would be forced to endure short-term pain sufficient to lobby against it. There could, moreover, be a long-term loss to some if the distribution of relative wages were to shift with the move toward specialization.

All is not barter and roses in the world of multilateral trade. The world is full of currencies and floating exchange rates that complicate international transactions almost beyond belief. The costs of foreign business offices, foreign exchange hedging, and insurance certainly lead to the conclusion that the Ricardo assumption of zero transportation (read "transactions") cost is far from reality. Profit margins have to be large to make international trade worth the effort.

must be; protection from foreign competition

17. a. A country's balance of payments is the official record of all its transactions with foreign countries for some specified period of time—usually 1 year. There are four main categories; list them in the spaces provided:

1. _____

2. _____

3. _____
4. _____

b. The key to entries in any of these categories is the effect that the transaction has on domestic holdings of foreign currencies. If a transaction generates foreign currency, then it is recorded as a *(debit / credit)*; if it costs currency because a foreign citizen (or institution) requires payment in his or her (or its) own currency, then it is a *(debit / credit)*.

---

a. (1) current account (2) capital account (3) statistical discrepancy (4) changes in official settlements   **b.** credit; debit

---

A less developed nation is typically one which borrows abroad to the full extent of its line of credit. A mature, developed nation is typically one which lends to other countries. As a nation develops over a long time period, it may change from borrower to lender, and this shift will affect its balance-of-payments position. The sequence outlined below—young debtor, mature debtor, new creditor, mature creditor—is an attempt to describe the likely balance-of-payments changes involved. In the 1980s, the United States moved from mature creditor into a new category. Greatly diminished saving caused heavy U.S. borrowing and turned the world's biggest creditor into the world's biggest debtor.

18. a. A less developed nation is likely to try to build up its stock of capital goods through sales of its IOUs to more developed countries. On its balance of payments, these security sales will be recorded as a *(credit / debit)*. The import of capital equipment or other goods purchased with security-sale proceeds will appear on the merchandise line as a *(credit / debit)*. This country has *(a favorable / an unfavorable)* balance of trade. These facts make it a "young debtor" nation.

b. As time passes, the country ceases to borrow, or borrows in smaller quantities. It still pays interest and dividends on earlier years of bond and stock financing, but its exporting capacity has increased. It now shows a surplus of merchandise exports over imports, or an excess of *(credits over debits / debits over credits)*. This *(favorable / unfavorable)* balance of trade is matched, or approximately so, by a surplus of debits on the investment income line of the balance of payments. The "mature debtor" stage has been reached.

c. Further down the road, the country may begin not only to repay its own earlier borrowings but also to lend to other countries. This means a surplus of *(credits over debits / debits over credits)* in the balance-of-payments capital account. If this is matched, or approximately so, by a surplus of merchandise exports over imports, the "new creditor" stage has been reached.

d. Ultimately, the "mature creditor" stage may be attained. At this point, the country may still be lending capital abroad, but its inflow of interest and dividend payments is more than sufficient to offset this lending. In the balance-of-payments merchandise account, therefore, there is a surplus of *(credits over debits / debits over credits)*, and the balance of trade is *(favorable / unfavorable)*. This balance is supported by the *(debit / credit)* balance in the investment income account.

---

a. credit; debit; an unfavorable   **b.** credits over debits; favorable   **c.** debits over credits   **d.** debits over credits; unfavorable; credit

REVIEW CONCEPTS

1. A country has an absolute advantage in the production of any good X if it can produce X at a smaller cost than a potential trading partner. It has a comparative advantage in the production of X if it can produce X relatively less expensively than it can produce some other tradable commodity.

2. The potential gains from trade are derived from comparative advantage. A country can collect these gains by concentrating its production efforts on goods in which it has a comparative advantage, exporting some or all of its output in exchange for goods in which it has a comparative disadvantage. A country with absolute advantages in the production of all goods can therefore still improve its welfare through trade if it concentrates on the production of goods in which its absolute advantage is largest.

3. The Ricardo model, which first described comparative advantage and the potential gains from trade, is a classical, full-employment model. Adjustment in the product mix designed to take full advantage of the potential can, however, be marked painfully by the short- to medium-term unemployment of displaced factors of production. Even when long-run equilibrium has been achieved with full employment, moreover, some people may be worse off than before. The idea is only that *aggregate* welfare has been improved.

4. Without transportation and other transactions costs, equilibrium in an international exchange market is the result of the usual mechanics of supply and demand. Countries supply their exports and demand their imports, and both markets must clear.

5. Balance-of-payments accounting notes four components: the current account (for goods and services), the capital account (for capital goods and services), official settlements, and statistical discrepancy (a catchall category). Any transaction which requires foreign currency (e.g., the purchase of a commodity produced in another country) is recorded as a debit; any transaction which generates foreign currency (e.g., the sale of a domestic product in a foreign country) is recorded as a credit.

6. Countries usually evolve through several stages in their balance-of-payments histories: young debtor nation, mature debtor nation, new creditor nation, mature creditor nation. The United States has recently "invented" a fifth category: low-saving, mature debtor nation.

QUIZ: Multiple Choice

1. In terms of comparative advantage, the most correct explanation of why bananas are imported instead of being grown commercially in the United States is that:
(1) bananas cannot be produced in the temperate zones.
(2) it would take a great deal of effort to produce bananas in the United States.
(3) bananas can be produced with less effort in other countries than they can in the United States.
(4) U.S. resources are better employed in producing other commodities, and tropical-country resources are better employed in banana production than in other things.
(5) the U.S. climate does not lend itself to banana production.

2. David Ricardo's theory of comparative advantage is intended to show that trade between two countries will be mutually beneficial. One assumption made in this analysis, to which some objection might be raised on the ground that it influences and perhaps alters the conclusions reached, is that:
(1) comparative advantage, not absolute advantage, is the important element in trade.
(2) each country, in consequence of such trade, will specialize in the commodity it exports.
(3) full employment is at all times maintained in both countries.
(4) no tariffs exist in either of the two countries.
(5) the pre-trade ratio of prices within each country has no part to play in the determination of trade flows.

3. Before international trade begins, a country will have an equilibrium ratio of prices (determined by relative production costs in the classical Ricardo model) between any two commodities. If trade involving these commodities begins with another country, then this price ratio will ordinarily be altered:
(1) only if a change in production costs results within the country.
(2) in all cases (except when the volume of international trade proves to be too small to affect it).
(3) only in cases where the volume of international trade is small.
(4) not at all, since it is an equilibrium relationship.
(5) only in cases where the volume of international trade is exceedingly large.

4. Table 23-6 records the output of labor (assumed to be the only input involved) in production of wine and of cloth in two countries, A and B. Comparing the two countries and contemplating trade between them on the basis of production advantages, it would be correct to say that Country A has:
(1) an absolute advantage in cloth production.
(2) an absolute advantage in wine production.
(3) a comparative advantage in cloth production.
(4) a comparative advantage in wine production.
(5) a comparative advantage in neither commodity.

Table 23-6

Production per Hour	A	B
Yards of cloth	5	15
Liters of wine	10	20

5. Suppose that there is no trade between the two countries of question 4. In Country A, the currency unit is the "donaro"; in Country B, it is the "gelt." The prices of cloth in A and B in their pre-trade situations are, respectively, 20 donaros and 60 gelts. For an equilibrium in which each country continues to produce both commodities, the corresponding wine prices would have to be:
(1) 5 donaros, 20 gelts.
(2) 40 donaros, 45 gelts.
(3) 10 donaros, 45 gelts.
(4) 10 donaros, 80 gelts.
(5) 40 donaros, 80 gelts.

6. If trading opportunities were to open, given the data of questions 4 and 5 (international transport cost assumed to be zero or negligible), then we should expect Country B to:
(1) import wine.
(2) export wine.
(3) import both commodities.
(4) export both commodities.
(5) neither export nor import, since its productive situation is such that there is no prospect of profitable trade with Country A.

7. Before the trading opportunity of question 6 emerged, each country had its own price ratio, reflecting domestic production costs. If trade develops between Countries A and B, this ratio—specifically, the ratio of the price of wine to the price of cloth—should:
(1) rise in Country A, fall in Country B.
(2) fall in Country A, rise in Country B.
(3) rise in both.
(4) fall in both.
(5) not change in either country, except perhaps during a short transitional period before equilibrium is reestablished.

8. Once international trade has been established, in the circumstances of questions 4 through 7, and a new equilibrium has been reached, then the ratio of cloth price to wine price (transport cost still assumed zero) might reasonably be:
(1) 1.2 in both countries.
(2) 1.6 in both countries.
(3) 1.8 in A, 1.5 in B.

(4) 2.1 in A, 1.3 in B.
(5) 2.3 in both countries.

9. Given the price ratio or ratios identified in question 8, if we know that the total of cloth exports was 500 yards daily, then the daily wine exports must be:
(1) 600 liters from A.
(2) 600 liters from B.
(3) 800 liters from A.
(4) 800 liters from B.
(5) 1150 liters from A.

10. The gain from trade can be illustrated by the position of the wine-importing country. Table 23-6 shows hourly output of wine if that wine is produced at home. If the country specializes in cloth production and imports its wine, then—at the price ratio of question 8, transport cost still assumed zero—the number of liters of wine resulting from 1 hour's labor would be:
(1) 16.
(2) 20.
(3) 24.
(4) 28.
(5) 32.

11. Differences in comparative production costs are usually cited as the principal basis for international trade. Another (and different) possible source of international exchange is:
(1) differences in climates.
(2) fixed foreign exchange rates.
(3) differences in transport costs.
(4) differences in labor skills.
(5) economies of mass production.

12. Trade between countries of comparable size but with different standards of living will be:
(1) profitable to the country of lower living standards at the expense of the one of higher standards.
(2) profitable to both as long as price ratios differ in the two countries, but of no profit to either once a common price ratio has been established.
(3) profitable in some degree to both, even after a common price ratio has been established.
(4) unprofitable to both because one country would be at an absolute disadvantage in all products.
(5) profitable to the country of higher living standards at the expense of the one of lower living standards.

13. A "favorable balance of trade" means:
(1) an excess of merchandise exports and other current account credits over merchandise imports and other current account debits.
(2) an excess of foreign currency received by the home country over domestic currency received by foreigners.
(3) an excess of merchandise exports over merchandise imports.
(4) an excess of total credits over total debits in the entire balance of payments
(5) a situation in which the value of total imports exceeds the value of total exports.

14. The five transactions listed below are all entries to be made on the U.S. balance of payments. For balance-of-payments purposes, four of the five are fundamentally similar. Which one is different?
(1) The Federal Reserve Bank of New York receives gold from the Bank of England.
(2) An American tourist on vacation spends francs in Paris.
(3) A South American government sells long-term bonds in New York.
(4) A British shipping firm is paid to carry an American export commodity abroad.
(5) An American investor receives a dividend check from a West German steel company.

15. A mature debtor nation is one whose balance of trade is:
(1) unfavorable, the import surplus being paid for by borrowing.
(2) unfavorable, thanks to the interest which is received from abroad.
(3) favorable, the interest on past borrowing being paid out of the surplus of exports.
(4) favorable, being made so by interest received from abroad.
(5) not correctly identified by any of these descriptions.

SUGGESTED ANSWERS TO QUESTIONS IN THE TEXT: Chapter 23

1. Not necessarily; it may be simply a statement of absolute advantage. Importing a good in which a country has an absolute advantage does not guarantee that welfare would improve.

2. **a.** Incorrect; it is a statement that the north has an absolute advantage in everything, but Mexico would help both itself and the north if it could export things in which it nonetheless has a comparative advantage (at least after factor markets adjust).
b. Correct; the point of Ricardo.
c. Incorrect; trade can increase aggregate income, though it may redistribute it.
d. Correct if it said the balance of payments, including not only the current account but also the capital account, changes in settlements, and any discrepancy.
e. Sure! Do what you do well.

3. Graph Table TQ23-1.

Table TQ23-1

Food	0	50	100	150	200
Clothing	150	112.5	75	37.5	0

4. With (1,2; 2,4), relative prices are 1 to 2 in both countries; neither has a comparative advantage, and neither can expand its consumption frontier through trade.

5. The gains come from specialization. Should Korea end up with the same technology as the United States, trade will disappear. The Korean standard of living will improve, but the American standard of living will decline with the decline in relative comparative advantage. Yes, there is a lesson here.

6. Those countries have the largest relative comparative advantages, and they are not diminished by international price adjustments as they enter the international market. Why not? Because their demand increment is too small to drive the price of the goods that they import up, and their supply increment is too small to drive the price of their exports down.

7. Newly discovered and unexploited land and resources should support relatively inexpensive food and resource supplies.

8. Refer to the definitions in the chapter. *Remember:* The flow of foreign currency determines whether a transaction is a credit or a debit. "Invisibles" are reflections of transactions for which there is no physical piece of material or commodity.

9. Again, apply the definitions, taking careful note of current and capital accounts. *Remember:* The overall balance of payments must balance.

10. Oil exports cause the current account surplus. The country can use the money to purchase foreign assets—debits in the capital account. Then, when it gets around to internal investment, it sells some of those assets to purchase the material required to supply the investment projects. The materials shipments turn the current account toward deficit; the sale of foreign assets produces foreign currency—credits that move the capital account toward surplus.

11. See Table TQ23-2.

Table TQ23-2

	Credit	Debit	Net
I. Current	$250	$250	$ 0
II. Capital	40	−50	−10
III. Stat. discrepancy			−20
IV. Official settlements			30

12. The first statement is the Ricardo result. Growth of competitors need not cause the standard of living in a trading country to decline. Growth that diminishes diversity, however, can.

CHAPTER 24

PROTECTIONISM AND FREE TRADE

The case for free trade has been made. The comparative-advantage results of Chapter 23 were produced in a simplified environment, to be sure, but they are strong and robust. It is now time to turn the coin over to look at its opposite side. If, in particular, free trade is so beneficial, then why do we see so many barriers to free trade in the real world? To answer this question, it is essential to see how trade barriers work. Only then can their effects be delineated and their merits evaluated. Chapter 24 tends to this task in its initial sections. With the effects of protection firmly in hand, the various arguments for and against protection are then critically reviewed. Having completed your work in this chapter, therefore, you will have accomplished the following objectives.

LEARNING OBJECTIVES

1. Use supply-and-demand analysis to outline the economic effects of protection. Show, first of all, that opening trade in a good drives its domestic price toward equality with its world price. Then show that a tariff can be expected to generate welfare losses by (a) promoting inefficient domestic production and (b) causing uneconomical reductions in domestic consumption even as it (c) generates some extra revenue for the government (unless it is prohibitive).

2. Outline a few non-economic arguments for trade restriction (protecting national interest, preserving national or regional culture, etc.), and evaluate their validity.

3. Outline a few traditional, false economic arguments for trade restrictions (pursuing favorable terms of trade in a mercantilistic spirit, reacting to special-interest lobbying, protecting domestic employment from cheap foreign labor; retaliating against the trade barriers of others, etc.), and indicate how they fall short.

4. Outline a few dynamic economic arguments for trade restriction (exploiting power over terms of trade with optimal tariffs in the absence of retaliation, protecting infant industries, preserving employment in special cases, etc.), and explain when they might apply.

5. List a few non-tariff barriers to trade that have been employed by the United States in the past few years (escape clauses, antidumping tariffs, etc.), and explain how they work.

Three principal reasons, often working together, explain the rationale behind most of the actual or proposed restraints of foreign trade:

1. A country fears unemployment and regards import competition as a potential source of that unemployment.

2. A country is short of foreign exchange reserves and sees increased tariffs as a potential source of new revenue.

3. The groups within a country who would benefit most directly from protection bring political pressure to bear for its imposition.

Much of this chapter will explore the validity of these reasons, but we must always be aware that they must be evaluated in the context of national economies which also have a multitude of nontrade policy options available. In a period of heavy unemployment, for example, it is hard to preach comparative advantage and free trade to legislators and businesspeople. They will argue that a reduction in imports would raise domestic employment at the expense of lower aggregate demand and correspondingly higher unemployment abroad, and so they might advocate an increase in protective tariffs. Such an attempt to "export unemployment" could, of course, be negated when other countries retaliate with similar tariff increases, but it would be wrong to insist that import restrictions can never reduce unemployment. The proper objection is that fiscal and monetary policies can be far more effective. Moreover, these policies avoid the dubious ethics of trying to foist off domestic unemployment onto other nations, and they do not incur the danger of retaliation.

Given reasonable assurance that unemployment can be handled by methods other than protection, many people in developed countries find it fairly easy to accept the free-trade principle; but people living in less developed countries tend to be more hesitant. They look at the world's most prosperous nations and hope that their own country might someday enjoy equally high standards of production and income. They wonder if some restriction on imports may not be needed in order to widen production and employment opportunities and to foster their nation's industrial growth. To evaluate the validity of these motives, it is essential to understand precisely how tariffs work. The first few questions explore their operation in a simple supply-and-demand model. Subsequent questions extend the discussion.

1. Consult Figure 24-1. Curve SS represents a domestic supply curve for some good X; if X is a competitive industry, then SS represents the horizontal sum of the marginal cost curves of many firms. Curve DD represents domestic demand for the same good. It is implicitly assumed that consumers do not care where the good was made; they simply want to buy the indicated quantities at the indicated prices.

Figure 24-1

a. The market-clearing price in the absence of trade is $_____; _____ units of X would be demanded and supplied domestically at that price. If the world price of $5 were allowed to prevail, though, then _____ units of X would be demanded, _____ units would be supplied domestically, and _____ units would be imported.

b. Now suppose that the domestic government has been convinced somehow to restrict imports by 50 percent. A tariff of $_____ per unit imported would do the trick, but it would raise the domestic price to $_____. At that price, _____ units would be demanded, _____ units would be supplied domestically, and _____ units would be imported. The effect of the tariff, therefore, is to (raise / lower) the price of X, (raise / lower) domestic production and employment, and (raise / lower) imports.

c. Given the tariff of part b, the government would collect $_____ in revenue; this is revenue that would be collected above and beyond the revenue that it collected from its domestic tax base. The higher domestic price would, however, promote (less / more) efficient production at home, and thereby produce an efficiency (loss / gain) of $_____. The marginal cost of producing X at home would, quite simply, increase to a level 50 percent higher than the marginal cost incurred by the rest of the world. The domestic economy would, in other words, be wasting resources in the production of X that would have been employed more efficiently somewhere else. Consumer surplus would, moreover, be (reduced / increased) by $_____. Total spending on X would, in fact, climb in the case drawn, so income effects on the demand for other goods across the economy should be expected.

d. If the government chose to impose a quota rather than a tariff, then it would award licenses to import up to _____ units of X. If these licenses were given away, then importers would earn excess profits of $_____ by buying X abroad and selling X domestically. If the government auctioned the licenses, though, the total revenue generated by the auction would be $_____.

e. If there were no tariff, but if it cost $2.50 per unit to transport X from the world marketplace into the domestic economy, then your answers to part b (would / would not) be altered. The revenue in part c identified as going to the government (would / would not) simply go to the transport company.

a. 10; 10; 20; 5; 15   **b.** 2.50; 7.50; 15; 7.5; 7.5; raise; raise; lower   **c.** 18.75; less; loss; 3.125 (= 0.5 × $2.50 × 2.5 = the area of the triangle above SS between $7.50 and $5.00 on the vertical axis and between 7.5 units and 5 units on the horizontal axis); reduced; 6.25 (= 0.5 × $2.50 × 5 = the area of the triangle above SS between $7.50 and $5.00 on the vertical axis and between 20 units and 15 units on the horizontal axis)   **d.** 7.5; 18.75; 18.75   **e.** would not; would

2. Often it is argued that a high tariff simultaneously (a) generates revenue for the government and (b) protects the domestic industry against competition. There is an inconsistency in using both of these arguments. What is it? _____

_____

_____

_____

Revenue can fall as protection increases. In the extreme, for example, a tariff sufficiently high to keep out all imports brings in zero revenue.

3. Several non-economic arguments for tariff protection have been advanced. One suggests that protection is necessary to preserve national security. The notion here is that foreign sources of supply are unreliable, so domestic production of certain strategic goods should be guaranteed even if it is inefficient. Protection, if it is awarded in response to this reasoning, should be (total / large enough to satisfy only minimum and essential needs / permanent and growing). If the commodity in question were a raw material, then perhaps _____ sufficient emergency supplies would be more efficient. If the commodity were a production good, then internal protection by _____ would be better than external protection by trade restraint.

A second argument is that protection is needed to preserve a way of life—a culture or a unique characteristic of an economy. _____ is again a more reasonable alternative than tariff protection.

large enough to satisfy only minimum and essential needs; storing; subsidy; Subsidy

4. a. The mercantilist approach to international trade argued that a nation should try to have (exports / imports) in excess of (exports / imports)—hence the phrase "favorable balance of trade." Any surplus so obtained would be used to acquire (merchandise / gold). The mercantilist position was thus strongly disposed toward (protectionism / free trade). It was a convenient argument for many (producer / consumer) groups seeking protection against foreign competition.

The underlying mercantilist philosophy was that a nation ought to apply the same principles of prudence appropriate for a family. It is prudent for a family to try to save part of its income. The nation, mercantilists said, is just the family on a larger scale. And they equated saving, at the national level, with the accumulation of gold.

The argument is not totally fallacious. Any nation will find it desirable to have reserves of gold (or foreign exchange) to cope with changing events which may produce balance-of-payments deficits. Even at the family level, though, the argument for "prudence" is wrong if interpreted as meaning that all families must hoard their money. Saving which is not allowed to flow into investment spending leads only to depression and to a fall in saving.

b. It would be (possible / impossible) for every nation to practice mercantilism successfully, since it is (possible / impossible) for every nation to have a surplus of exports. A general attempt to practice this philosophy, by trying to expand exports and restrict imports, would lead to a major (rise / fall) in (exports alone / imports alone / both exports and imports).

a. exports; imports; gold; protectionism; producer   **b.** impossible; impossible; fall; both exports and imports

5. a. In a country like the United States, a protariff argument sometimes advanced is that American producers cannot compete against "cheap foreign labor." The free-trade response to this argument is that (pick one):

(1) cheap labor is simply a particular illustration of international cost differences on which mutually profitable trade can, on the principle of comparative advantage, be based.

(2) protection from cheap labor is sometimes a valid reason to impose a tariff, but it has often been used to excess.

(3) the proper remedy is a subsidy or quota, not a tariff, when cheap foreign labor threatens a domestic industry.

b. If the United States were to impose a tariff on imported industrial goods, this would reduce U.S. exports of, say, agricultural goods if (pick one):

(1) but only if, foreign nations retaliated with a countertariff against such agricultural goods.

(2) foreign earnings of American dollars were reduced by this tariff to the point that other nations could no longer buy the agricultural goods, regardless of the imposition or nonimposition of a countertariff.

c. The "escape clause" provision in U.S. tariff legislation comes into play when import volume harms a domestic producer. A tariff imposed according to this clause is (pick one):

(1) valid where national security is involved.

(2) unfounded on economic grounds because the industry ought to be exposed to the competition even to the point of possible extinction.

d. If another country harms us by erecting a tariff against our goods, then our own position *(will / will not)* normally be improved if we impose a retaliatory tariff.

e. If an economically powerful country is also an important player in the arena of international trade, then it may find that a moderate tariff improves its real-income position, due to a change in the _____ .

---

a. (1) **b.** (2) **c.** (2) **d.** will not **e.** terms of trade

---

6. a. The "national-survival" argument for tariff protection for a particular industry may be valid, but it should be viewed with some skepticism. Why? Because it has so often been used by special-interest groups to support self-indulgent protection. Where concern for national survival (particularly in wartime) does seem to warrant protection for some domestic industry, then the best remedy may be a *(quota / tariff / subsidy)*.

b. There may also be a valid argument for imposition of tariffs in the case of the *(less developed / richer)* nations, because tariffs in that context *(may be one of the few sources of revenue for government that are administratively feasible / are almost the only effective means of protecting domestic employment in time of recession)*.

c. The "infant-industry" argument is one often invoked within the less developed nations. It holds that domestic industry needs protection when it is young, inexperienced, and unable to stand up to the competition of mature foreign producers. Economists generally agree that the infant-industry argument (circle one):

(1) has at least some validity in principle, although in practice many industries have proved to be perpetual infants, never able to survive without protection.

(2) has no validity at all, since international trade is founded on natural cost advantages.

Tariff arguments such as the infant-industry suggestion are based upon dynamic considerations. Chapter 23, on comparative advantage, was a good example of static analysis; it placed its emphasis upon equilibrium and the properties of equilibrium positions. Dynamic analysis deals with changes—e.g., with growth—and with the process of change. In general, *(static / dynamic)* economic arguments for protection are probably stronger.

---

a. subsidy **b.** less developed; may be one of the few sources of revenue for government that are administratively feasible **c.** (1); dynamic

---

7. Much has been made recently of domestic-content legislation for American-built automobiles. Under this idea, a fixed percentage of the parts used to produce a car built in the United States would have to be built in the United States. It is argued by labor that this sort of requirement would protect American jobs and increase employment in the United States. This question will explore the validity of that claim under the (reasonable) assumption that domestic-content restrictions would limit the quantity of parts imported from abroad (if that were not the case, why bother?).

Let some good Y be produced from some combination of inputs including both labor and good X of question 1. Content legislation would amount to placing a quota on imports of X, so Figure 24-1 shows that the price of X should *(rise / fall)* and quantities demanded should *(rise / fall)*. At the same time, though, domestic production of X should *(climb / fall)* and domestic employment in that industry should *(climb / fall)*.

It is now clear that the marginal cost of producing good Y should *(increase / decrease)*; illustrate this effect, assuming perfect competition, in Figure 24-2 by drawing a new supply curve for Y. The price of Y must therefore *(climb / fall)*, the output of Y must correspondingly *(climb / fall)* as the economy moves along the *(demand curve / old supply curve / new supply curve)*, and employment in the production of Y must follow suit—it must *(climb / fall)*, as well.

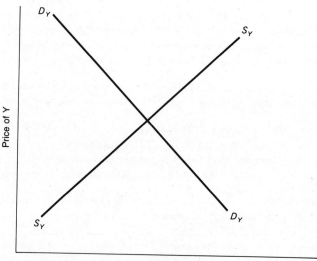

Figure 24-2

The result, if you add things up, is ambiguous. The claim that domestic-content legislation would help the employment picture in the United States is premature. Its employment effect will depend upon the elasticity of demand for automobiles (good Y), and it is by no means certain that it will be positive.

---

rise; fall; climb; climb; increase; the graph: new supply curve above and to the left of S_YS_Y; climb; fall; demand curve; fall

REVIEW CONCEPTS

1. Simple supply-and-demand analysis can be employed to show that protection strategies increase domestic prices and generate welfare losses by *(a)* promoting inefficient domestic production and *(b)* reducing consumption; the usual deadweight-loss triangle measures these losses. Unless the protection is prohibitive, however, it can also generate revenue for the government (tariff collections or import license auctions can be equivalent in this regard).

2. Non-economic arguments for protection are sometimes made: national interest and/or security, cultural and/or regional integrity, and so on. Domestic subsidy can be more effective in these instances.

3. Other economic arguments are false: protecting domestic employment, special-interest protection, and mercantilistic pursuit of favorable terms of trade. Alternative domestic policies can be more effective in these instances.

4. Dynamic arguments for protection are more attractive, but they can be risky. Optimal tariff barriers and infant-industry protection run the risk of retaliation, for example.

QUIZ: Multiple Choice

1. One argument for tariffs contends that they should be imposed to help a domestic producer to compete when the level of foreign wages is significantly below the level of domestic wages. This argument:
(1) is conceded by most economists to be correct, although sometimes exaggerated in order to justify some level of tariff protection.
(2) is fallacious because there are almost no instances in which there is any real difference between the levels of foreign and domestic wages.
(3) ignores the fact that differences in relative costs constitute the principal basis for international trade.
(4) may be correct with respect to money wages at home and abroad, but is not correct with respect to real wages.
(5) is not correctly described by any of the preceding.

2. Country A imposes a new tariff on Country B's products. Country B is considering a retaliatory tariff on A's goods. On economic grounds, B should:
(1) reject the idea of a tariff increase.
(2) make the retaliatory tariff less than A's tariff.
(3) make the retaliatory tariff more than A's tariff.
(4) impose the retaliatory tariff only if B is in a situation of full employment.
(5) adjust the price of its currency relative to B's currency.

3. The policy of the mercantilists with respect to foreign trade held that:
(1) imports should exceed exports—i.e., the country should "get more than it gives"—in order to increase real income at home as much as possible.
(2) exports should exceed imports in order to bring in gold.
(3) since this trade represented commerce, it should be encouraged to the greatest possible degree—i.e., there should be free trade.
(4) exports should be kept in balance with imports, and at the lowest possible level of both.
(5) trade in agricultural products was more important than trade in industrial goods.

4. The principal reason high-wage American labor should not require tariff protection from lower-paid foreign labor is:
(1) no American labor would be thrown out of work even if there were no tariffs.
(2) the high per-worker-hour productivity of American labor in many industries is an offset to the lower cost of foreign labor.
(3) American consumers tend to buy American-made goods in preference to foreign-made goods.
(4) a high-wage American industry can be presumed to have a comparative advantage over foreign competitors.
(5) none of the preceding reasons.

5. The argument by workers in a protected industry in the United States that free trade would worsen the income position of American labor is:
(1) not valid even for workers in that industry after allowance is made for the improvement in real income afforded by cheaper imports.
(2) not valid even for workers in that industry after allowance is made for the employment effect of increased exports.
(3) valid for workers in that industry but probably not valid for American labor as a whole.
(4) valid for workers in that industry and probably valid for American labor as a whole.
(5) probably valid for workers in that industry but unquestionably invalid for American labor as a whole.

6. From a purely economic point of view, the best level at which to set a tariff (under static assumptions) is:
(1) the prohibitive point.
(2) the amount needed to bring the level of foreign costs up to the level of domestic costs.
(3) zero.
(4) a level sufficiently low so that it is not likely to invite retaliation by other countries.
(5) the level at which revenues from the tariff will be at a maximum.

7. One argument for tariff protection contends that a tariff would improve the terms of trade in dealing with other nations. This argument:

(1) is a refinement of the mercantilist argument that a nation's exports should exceed its imports.
(2) may be valid if the tariff-imposing country is a relatively large one and the tariff is a relatively small one.
(3) is a refined version of the infant-industry argument and hence has no validity.
(4) may be valid if the tariff-imposing country is unimportant in world trade for the commodity or commodities involved.
(5) may be valid if it is applied to all the country's imports, without or almost without exception.

8. It may be argued that a tariff should be imposed on a commodity if that commodity is considered essential to material well-being and/or if it is suspected that the foreign suppliers thereof might use their supply control for purposes of political blackmail. Most economists hold that:
(1) the tariff is justified if the commodity is deemed really essential.
(2) a subsidy would be preferable to a tariff if the commodity is deemed really essential.
(3) the best remedy for threats of political blackmail is to insist on all-around free trade.
(4) although the imposition of a tariff might be used as a threat, political moves should be met by political countermoves (even to the threat of war), not by economic moves.
(5) its domestic production should be nationalized if the commodity is deemed really essential.

9. If we reduce the flow of import goods by imposing heavy tariffs, our exports are likely to be affected in which of the following ways?
(1) They will likely be reduced when other countries retaliate by imposing tariffs against those exports (as is likely), but not otherwise.
(2) There is little reason to expect that they will be affected at all, since retaliatory tariffs have usually proved ineffective.
(3) They will likely be increased, since other countries will find it necessary to buy more from us to compensate for the higher cost of the goods they sell us.
(4) They will likely be increased if the tariff raises the level of employment and national product at home, but not otherwise.
(5) They are likely to be reduced in all or almost all circumstances.

10. A valid counter to the argument that a tariff results in increased money wages in the protected industry is that:
(1) workers in that industry will in all probability suffer a loss in real wages.
(2) workers in other industries will suffer a loss in real wages.
(3) the increase in money wages in the protected industry will cause unemployment.
(4) tariffs cannot increase money wages in any industry.
(5) any increase in real wages is likely to lead to inflation.

11. Arguments cited in favor of a protective tariff frequently note that tariffs (a) protect domestic industry against foreign competition and (b) bring revenue to the government. In response to these arguments, it may be said that:
(1) the tariff reduces rather than increases the sales of the domestic industry.
(2) if the industry in question enjoys an absolute advantage in production, it stands in no need of such a tariff.
(3) the emphasis on government revenue may lead to a tariff per unit much higher than the domestic industry needs for protection.
(4) an effective tariff will actually bring in no government revenue at all.
(5) none of these statements is correct.

12. A difference between a tariff on an imported good and a quota on the same good is that:
(1) a quota can never be made to yield revenue for the government, whereas a tariff can.
(2) a tariff can never be made to yield revenue for the government, whereas a quota can.
(3) a quota can be used to shut off all, or virtually all, the inflow of the imported good, whereas a tariff cannot.
(4) a tariff can be used to shut off all, or virtually all, the inflow of the imported good, whereas a quota cannot.
(5) a quantity-equivalent quota will generate the same revenue only if import rights are auctioned.

SUGGESTED ANSWERS TO QUESTIONS IN THE TEXT: Chapter 24

1. You are on your own. Think of the difference between static and dynamic arguments, long-run and short-run effects, and the likelihood of retaliation to your proposal. Also, state carefully your objective in supporting protection, and look at the pros and cons carefully. Are you talking about protection in a small country or a large country? Finally, how do you feel about "beggar-thy-neighbor" effects that (e.g.) effectively "export" things like unemployment?

2. The same as above, with particular circumstances more clearly defined. Investigate both (either) industry and (or) its foreign competition. Think of the role of technological change. Note, as well, that all Japanese TVs except SONYs are now being made in Korea or Singapore. What does that tell you about the Japanese understanding of comparative advantage?

3. The infant-industry argument, in its proper context, is one of potential comparative advantage: "If we protect this industry, we will soon have a comparative advantage in its product, which will improve our standard of living." Infants still exist in manufacturing industries around the world (e.g., electronics).

4. You must argue whether or not this is really protection. It seems to be, even though it can be applied only after injury

has been felt; if no injury has been felt, why would anyone have suggested protection, anyway?

5. For trading partners, there must be at least two goods. There must, therefore, be two versions of text Figure 24-3, each showing two loss triangles. Each of these triangles, four in total, is a source of gain if the tariff were reduced.

6. **a.** This is an optimal-tariff argument, with the country having power over the terms of trade.
b. This is a short-run argument, and the problem might better be solved by domestic monetary or industrial policy. Maybe this domestic market should disappear?
c. This is a non-economic reason that illustrates the multiplicity of objectives in trade policy.
d. This one is awful, ignoring the notion of comparative advantage.

7. Everything is exactly the same, except that the revenue goes to the importers who buy or produce at the world price and sell at the higher domestic import price. When auctioned, these surpluses will be bid away and will flow to the government.

8. This is a national-defense argument. With inelastic supply, though, the tariff is borne entirely by the supplier.

CHAPTER 25

THE ECONOMICS OF DEVELOPING COUNTRIES

Twenty percent of the world's population, more than 1 billion people, live at or below the subsistence level. Only about 25 percent of the world's population earn the equivalent of $3000 per year or more. Nonetheless, the average per capita income of people living in the advanced market economies of North America and Western Europe exceeds $14,000 per year. A list of alarming statistics like this can be extended almost indefinitely, but the point is clear. There exists, across the globe, a disparity in standards of living that boggles the mind; and it is this observation that raises a litany of questions which could turn out to be *the* critical questions for survival through the twenty-first century. What, first of all, could possibly be the source of this disparity? Second, what can be done by the developing countries to correct it? And finally, is there anything that the developed world can do to help? Without some attempt to answer these questions, the growing gap between the wealthy and the poor nations of the world could foster economic, political, and military conflict that could wreak havoc across the planet.

These are the questions raised in Chapter 25. For our purposes, though, they will turn out to be, to one degree or another, almost unanswerable, and the text is modest in advancing solutions. The focus of the chapter is, instead, on pondering the ability of economic analysis to provide insight into possible answers. Only if we understand the sources of inequity can we begin to work to correct it, and only if we sort out false strategies from productive strategies will progress be made. The major objective of the chapter is, therefore, an understanding of the dimension of the problem. As you develop that understanding, you will also achieve the following more specific objectives.

LEARNING OBJECTIVES

1. Outline the modern theory of population through its four distinct stages (preindustrial, with high birth and death rates; early development, with diminishing death rates; later development, with further reductions in death rates and diminishing birth rates; and maturity, with low birth and death rates). Record its implications for economic growth, and relate it to its Malthusian antecedent.

2. Identify the four "wheels of development" (human resources, natural resources, capital formation, and technology), and explain the problems faced by less developed countries in getting any one of them "rolling uphill."

3. Describe the vicious circle of underdevelopment, and identify the means by which it might be broken. Relate how the applicability of these means depends upon the circumstance of the less developed country being considered (e.g., resource-rich or resource-poor; high population or low population, etc.).

4. Explain (a) the takeoff theory of development (b) the backward hypothesis applied to economic development, and (c) the balanced-growth theory of development. Indicate the path of development that each implies, and contrast each to the reality described by Simon Kuznets.

5. Explain several strategies for economic development (including emphasis on export goods, emphasis on import-competing goods, technology borrowing, etc.), and indicate the potential pitfalls associated with each. Explain the value of diversification.

The world's less developed countries are characterized by per capita income levels that are well below the worldwide average. Associated with low incomes are, moreover, human problems like poor health, widespread illiteracy, poor housing, poor diets, and demoralizing underemployment. Question 1 asks you to record quantitative measures of these problems.

1. Table 25-1 analyzes country groups according to key indicators. The data show that, compared with the high-income market economies, countries on the bottom of the development scale display the following characteristics:

a. Population growth rates that are *(twice as high / about the same / almost 3 times as high)*.

b. Per capita levels of GNP that are *(about 50 percent lower / about 90 percent lower / over 90 percent lower)*.

c. Adult literacy rates that are *(25 percent lower / nearly 50 percent lower / over 75 percent lower)*.

d. Life expectancies that are approximately *(20 percent lower / 33 percent lower / 50 percent lower)*.

e. Employment participation rates in agriculture that are *(5 times higher / 8 times higher / over 10 times higher)*.

---

a. almost 3 times as high **b.** over 90 percent lower **c.** nearly 50 percent lower **d.** 20 percent lower **e.** over 10 times higher

2. a. Compared with the Malthusian view of population growth, which predicted *(gradual / geometric / logarithmic)* growth in population and *(increasing / constant / decreasing)* growth in food production, modern population theory espouses a transition model of growth and development. Theorists identify four stages in the transition; list them in order in the spaces provided:

(1) _____

(2) _____

(3) _____

(4) _____

b. As countries proceed through the transitions, history suggests that high birth and death rates give way first to lower *(death / birth)* rates and second to correspondingly lower *(death / birth)* rates before converging to the final stage of *(growing / stable / declining)* populations. During the second stage, though, the birth rate *(exceeds / falls short of)* the death rate and the population can be expected to *(climb / fall / remain stable)*.

---

a. geometric; decreasing **(1)** preindustrial stage **(2)** early development stage **(3)** later development stage **(4)** maturity **b.** death; birth; stable; exceeds; climb

Table 25-1
Important Indicators for Different Groups of Countries

Country Group	Population		GNP 1985 ($ billions)	Per Capita GNP 1985 ($)	Adult Literacy 1980 (%)	Life Expectancy at Birth (years)	Percent of Employment in Agriculture 1980 (% of labor force)
	Level 1985 (millions)	Growth 1965–1985 (% per year)					
Low-income economies (e.g., China, India)	2,439	2.2	659	270	52	60	72
Middle-income economies (e.g., Brazil, Philippines, South Korea)	1,242	2.4	1,602	1,290	65	62	43
High-income oil exporters (e.g., Saudi Arabia, Libya)	18	5.0	180	9,800	32	63	35
European non-reporting, non-member economies (e.g., U.S.S.R., GDR)	363	1.0	2,258	5,900	99	69	22
High-income market economies (e.g., U.S.A., West Germany, Japan)	737	0.8	8,708	11,810	99	76	7

Countries are grouped by the World Bank into five major categories. In each, two or three important countries are listed. Note how well the indicators are correlated across most of the groups, with low-income economies having low per capita incomes, low literacy and life expectancy, and a very large fraction of the labor force in agriculture.

Source: World Bank, *World Development Report, 1987.*

The characteristics of a modern developed economy are well understood. A country in this category has a large supply of capital goods per capita. Members of its population accept the principle of division of labor, and they are trained in skills adapted to that principle. Money is almost universally employed in place of barter, and money is used for the hiring of labor. There is an active "entrepreneur class," and the making of money is not frowned upon or treated with scorn. There are well-organized money and credit markets. There is general acceptance of the authority and trustworthiness of a central government which passes laws, imposes taxes, and enforces execution of private contracts. The laws are in general obeyed, and taxes are generally paid. The developed economy accomplishes new things because of its entrepreneur class, its use of the money market mechanism, and its refusal to accept unquestioningly the dictates of tradition or custom as to how things should be done. As a result, it produces high material living standards for its members and a greatly increased life expectancy.

Since the characteristics described are common to most developed societies, it is agreed that they go a long way in explaining the relatively higher material living standards and increased life expectancy. The problem that remains is determining how these characteristics were acquired. This is the central problem for planners in less developed societies. It is also agreed that most citizens of less developed nations want the benefits of development. "The theory of development" is therefore charged with the task of explaining how the characteristics of developed societies emerged and how they can be fostered elsewhere.

3. a. Some of the explanations have emphasized wholly, or in the main, one single factor—for example, geography. The notion here is usually that a cool, temperate climate is conducive to vigorous activity and hence to growth. Most economists *(accept / accept with qualification / reject)* the view that geography is a vital consideration.

b. Another factor emphasized is culture. Most economists *(accept / accept with qualification / reject)* the view that some cultures have properties which impede growth.

---

a. reject   **b.** accept

Two questions are raised by the problem of cultures that seemingly oppose economic development:

1. Can established culture patterns be altered by planners for development?
2. Even if they can be broken, should they be?

There is a partial answer to the first of these questions. What appear on the surface to be well-established culture patterns sometimes break up quite easily, without evidence of any great distress appearing among the people involved. A more positive answer exists for the second question. No country can avoid the worldwide impact of economic development, so proposals to "protect" an established culture are becoming less popular. In their place are suggestions about how to integrate the essentials of a unique culture into a modern economy.

4. a. Max Weber did not agree that all determining forces in history were economic in origin. He certainly felt that cultural elements were of at least equal importance, and contended that religion had, in fact, been the critical element in Europe's economic development. The name given to summarize Weber's views is _____

_____

b. Many economists speak of the *preconditions* for economic growth—a kind of foundation that must be laid before any significant growth can begin. In general terms, this means the development of a reasonably well-knit and cooperative society, the establishment of tolerable stability in that society, and the acceptance of some degree of central authority.

We can be a bit more specific as to these preconditions. They find expression in external economies. These are economies which facilitate production (and so reduce cost) for the individual firm but are outside the control of any such firm (hence "external"). They would include such things as development in transportation facilities, health measures to improve the productivity of labor, and establishment of a system of law which makes contracts enforceable. The point about such external economies is that an individual firm *(can / cannot)* undertake them alone. They *(must / can, but need not necessarily)* be undertaken by government. Any individual firm which tackled such an external-economy project would find *(it worthless / that most of the benefit accrued to other firms that bore no part of its cost)*.

---

a. the "Protestant ethic"   **b.** cannot; must; that most of the benefit accrued to other firms that bore no part of its cost

---

5. Economists have identified four economic fundamentals which drive economic development: population, natural resources, capital formation, and technology.

a. Focusing for a moment on natural resources, which of the following statements or questions accurately describe a resources-related issue? (Circle as many as apply to the role of natural resources in development.)

(1) Many less developed countries appear to be resource-poor. How then are they to develop?

(2) Land reform is necessary for development in many countries, since individual holdings are too small to be used to their best advantage.

b. Turning now to capital formation, identify the statements that accurately record a development issue:

(1) Less developed nations find it very difficult to save (to refrain from consumption) to free resources for investment activity.

(2) The social customs in some less developed countries encourage rich people to hoard their savings or use them in nonproductive ways; they are not used to finance investment projects that would raise the national product.

(3) The desire for development and the example of the developed nations have noticeably increased the amount of saving out of income in many less developed countries.

(4) In many poor countries, investment expenditure tends to go heavily into housing, an investment form which does not have the highest priority in development.

(5) The amount of private lending for financing investment activity by citizens in developed areas is greater than it was in the nineteenth century, both absolutely and relatively; in less developed countries, it is not.

c. Finally, repeat the process one more time for the role of technology:

(1) Less developed countries have the advantage that imitation of techniques already worked out is easier than development of new and sometimes sophisticated techniques.

(2) Efforts by developed countries to export advanced "technological know-how" are frequently unsuccessful.

(3) Some advanced technologies are "capital-saving," and these are likely to be particularly well suited to adoption in less developed countries.

a. (1); (2) **b.** (1); (2); (4) **c.** (1); (2); (3)

6. Figure 25-1 illustrates the vicious cycle of underdevelopment. Identify the boxes of the cycle in the spaces provided. Box C is already identified for the purpose of providing perspective.

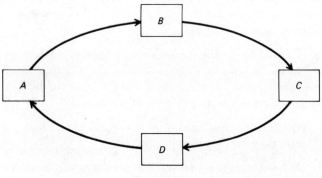

Figure 25-1

A: _____

B: _____

C: Low productivity

D: _____

A: low saving and investment   B: low rate of capital accumulation   D: low average income

7. a. Higher savings will be useless and productive investment will not take place in any country unless it has a class of vigorous, creative _____.

b. Sometimes it is said that the recurring problem with which a developed country must cope during recession is that of (too much / too little) saving and hence (too much / too little) demand for consumption. By contrast, the problem of the less developed country is that of (too much / too little) and hence (too much / too little) demand for consumption.

a. entrepreneurs **b.** too much; too little; too little; too much

8. Figure 25-2 displays the growth trends of three different countries (denoted I, II, and III) that are implied by the three different and modern theories of development. One is the takeoff theory, which envisions a leading sector catching fire, creating profits, encouraging investment, increasing the capital stock, increasing wages and incomes, and generally providing the initial momentum for consistent growth. The second is the backwardness hypothesis, which suggests that developing countries have it easier today than they did a century ago because technology and markets already exist. The third contemplates a balanced-growth approach that is slow but steady once it starts. Label each panel with the theory that it portrays. The Nobel Prize–winning work of Simon Kuznets suggests that the theory of _____ is the most accurate description of historical development trajectories.

the graphs: (a)—balanced growth, (b)—takeoff theory, (c)—backwardness hypothesis; balanced growth

9. Strategies for development must confront and answer at least three general questions if they are to be successful. First, is it more worthwhile to concentrate on industry or agriculture in initiating growth? Investment in industry might provide a few high-paying jobs, but investment in agriculture might support industrialization by (increasing the productivity of city workers / increasing the productivity of the farms and thereby releasing labor for industrial jobs / creating large agricultural surpluses that can replace imports).

(a): _____

(b): _____

(c): _____

Figure 25-2

Second, it is important to decide whether to promote exports to generate growth supported by the worldwide marketplace or to protect import-competing industries to generate growth in domestic markets. Care should be taken in considering the second alternative because protection can *(increase / decrease)* domestic prices, *(increase / decrease)* real incomes, and *(stimulate / retard)* investment at home and from abroad.

Third, many developing countries find themselves overspecialized and vulnerable to the whims of the world market for the few goods in which they have a comparative advantage. The key to avoiding this difficulty is

_____ .

increasing the productivity of the farms and thereby releasing labor for industrial jobs; increase; decrease; retard; diversification

10. a. One particularly troubling problem that beset the developing countries of the world in the late 1970s and 1980s was the debt crisis. Borrowing by developing countries from private banks had grown by $*(250 / 500 / 1000)* billion from 1972 to 1983. Many countries, particularly in Central and South America, began to have trouble meeting their debt obligations in the early 1980s because (pick as many as apply):

(1) American interest rates were so high.

(2) the value of the dollar was so high.

(3) the price of oil had climbed so high in the late 1970s that higher-than-expected debt was required.

(4) the crisis added risk premiums to the interest rates charged by private banks, particularly on refinancing agreements.

(5) the price of oil stopped rising, so the revenues that were expected to cover the debt were lower than anticipated.

b. The crisis seems to be under control, at least to some degree, but any disturbance that causes massive default *(could / could not)* create a major, worldwide banking crisis. To bail defaulting countries out with grants and income transfers would, however, dramatically increase the world's money supply and would therefore run the risk of causing significant worldwide *(deflation / inflation)*.

a. 500; all apply **b.** could; inflation

11. A less developed country is undertaking a large-scale development program and asks you to supply information on the points listed in parts **a** through **d**. What will you advise? (In each part, circle the number of the statement which you think furnishes the most likely scenario.)

a. Change in population to be expected:

(1) Both the birth rate and the death rate are likely to remain high for some time.

(2) Both the birth rate and the death rate are likely to remain low for some time.

(3) Both the birth rate and the death rate are likely to fall substantially in the next few years.

(4) The death rate is likely to fall, and the birth rate to remain at its present high level for some time.

b. Capital-formation policy:

(1) In view of the post–World War II experience, primary reliance can be placed on borrowing and aid from abroad.

(2) The primary problem will be achieving a better allocation of existing saving rather than increasing total saving.

(3) Historical experience suggests that the percentage of national product put into personal saving and into capital formation will have to be increased.

(4) "Borrowing technology" will enable development at existing levels of saving.

c. Investment allocation:

(1) The government should make sure that it is undertaking adequate investment in social overhead capital with external economies.

(2) Private entrepreneurs can be relied upon to properly allocate available saving.

(3) Although inflation tends ultimately to discourage saving, it also tends to better allocate available saving.

(4) Modern technology makes heavy use of capital in production and hence should be avoided.

d. Change in foreign trade:

(1) Imports are likely to fall as domestic manufactures replace foreign manufactures.

(2) Imports are likely to rise because of the need for foreign capital goods and possibly for food and fuel.

(3) Exports of primary products should be pushed, since this is where comparative advantage must lie.

(4) Exports should fall as the demand of developed countries for raw materials continues to decline.

---

a. (4)   b. (3)   c. (1)   d. (2)

REVIEW CONCEPTS

1. The modern theory of the link between development and population growth envisions four stages: preindustrial, with high birth and death rates; early development, with high birth rates and reduced death rates; later development, with reduced birth rates and low death rates; and maturity, with low birth and death rates.

2. Human resources, natural resources, capital formation, and technological advance are the four driving forces of development. Less developed countries typically have difficulty in exploiting all four.

3. The vicious circle of underdevelopment runs from low saving and investment through low capital accumulation, low productivity, and low incomes, and back again. It applies to many situations, but its general applicability varies from country to country depending upon the country's population, technology, resource, and capital base.

4. The work of Kuznets seems to suggest that the balanced-growth theory of development (with its deliberate and steady trajectories) explains more of our development experience than either of its two competing alternatives: the backwardness hypothesis (with its notion that development is easier now than before because technologies and markets already exist) and the takeoff theory (with its reliance on the profits of a single, leading sector which is the first to "catch on" internationally).

5. Strategies for promoting economic development abound. Some emphasize export goods; some emphasize import-competing goods; still others emphasize borrowing new technologies. Each has merit somewhere in the world, but none is universally applicable, especially in a world in which development must proceed with a cautious eye cast at its environmental consequences.

QUIZ: Multiple Choice

1. One area of economic development in which the country's government must take the initiative and also participate relates to:
(1) maintaining balanced growth.
(2) promoting heavy industry.
(3) transferring resources needed in the shift from agricultural predominance to industrial predominance.
(4) providing social overhead capital.
(5) none of the above, because there are no areas in which such government involvement is always needed.

2. The main reason population growth has spurted ahead so rapidly in many less developed countries in recent years is that:
(1) birth rates have increased sharply with improvements in nutrition.
(2) great strides have been made in keeping older people alive an extra 5 or 10 years.
(3) infant mortality and mortality due to epidemics have been drastically lowered.
(4) large-scale immigration has occurred into many countries since World War II.
(5) birth rates have risen markedly as the natural result of widespread reductions in the customary age of marriage.

3. Four of the following five statements identify a problem of economic development. One does not. Which one?
(1) Developing economies often have reasonable prospects of looking to "increasing returns to scale" as they expand their total output.
(2) Ordinarily, individual firms cannot undertake investment in social overhead capital, no matter how important such projects may be.
(3) Entrepreneurship and innovation are vital for the success of any developing economy.
(4) The principle of protecting import-competing industries is not necessarily a wise one for a developing nation to follow.
(5) In a probable majority of the less developed nations, excess saving is a significant problem.

4. "Disguised unemployment" refers to a situation in which:
(1) deficiencies in population statistics give a faulty picture of the labor force that is actually available.

(2) workers who actually are effectively self-employed claim to be in need of work.
(3) a country, having reached a certain stage in development, finds difficulty in recruiting workers for industrial jobs because of their reluctance to leave traditional occupations.
(4) the demand for finished consumer goods is insufficient.
(5) for most (or all) of the year, the marginal productivity of labor in agriculture is actually very low.

5. As a country develops economically and builds its own industry, one of the following usually does not occur. Which one?
(1) It imports less and less from other developed and industrialized countries.
(2) Its total exports tend to rise.
(3) It imports more and more from other industrialized, highly developed countries.
(4) It imports more from less developed countries.
(5) Its total imports tend to rise.

6. "Social overhead capital" is:
(1) the money investment required before any return is obtainable from a particular natural resource.
(2) a particular form of external economy.
(3) investment in those projects considered to have the highest net productivity.
(4) projects which must be financed by the nation itself, as distinct from those financed by external aid.
(5) any capital investment whose amount does not vary as the quantity of national output is increased.

7. An absolute precondition for growth is the:
(1) development of some excess of income over consumption.
(2) creation of a surplus labor force for employment in manufacturing.
(3) discovery and exploitation of some internal economies.
(4) cultural acceptance of free enterprise principles of economic behavior.
(5) development of manufacturing to the point where it can begin to supplant agriculture.

8. Four of the following five statements identify a problem of economic development. One does not. Which one?
(1) In some less developed countries, considerable investment takes place but goes into items that are of low priority or even are undesirable from the standpoint of national economic development.
(2) The development of adequate social overhead capital is usually essential if there is to be much economic development.
(3) In history, political revolutions have often taken place after some economic progress has been achieved.
(4) Most of the less developed countries are known to have substantial unexploited natural resources, if only the capital needed to bring them into effective use were available.
(5) In poor countries, especially rural ones, often a large part of the labor pool does almost nothing because there is nothing for it to do.

9. Less developed countries have lower per capita incomes than developed countries. Over the past several decades, that gap has been:
(1) diminishing between the "free enterprise" less developed countries but widening with respect to the socialist-oriented ones.
(2) almost incapable of measurement because of differences in cultures, tastes, and climates.
(3) perceptibly diminishing, evidently as the result of foreign-aid programs.
(4) diminishing with respect to those countries which have concentrated their investment upon social overhead capital.
(5) essentially stable, and in some areas may even be widening.

SUGGESTED ANSWERS TO QUESTIONS IN THE TEXT: Chapter 25

1. *Low-income countries:* early development (high birth and death rates)
Middle-income countries: later development (lower birth and death rates)
High-income countries: maturity (low birth and death rates)

2. Higher populations generate congestion and increase the need for more services. However, more people to choose from can increase the likelihood of finding extraordinary individuals. Think of finding the tall trees in a forest. The more acreage you survey, the more tall trees you will find, provided that you do not run out of good forest and have to survey over the tops of mountains.

3. The geometric series grows at a constant rate β; the arithmetic series grows at a declining rate that converges to zero.

4. The growth rate of the food-population ratio is equal to the growth rate of food minus the growth rate of population. This can be less than zero if food grows slower than population.

5. No, with increasing or decreasing frequency depending upon the national mood. Madonna's "Material Girl" would probably not have been a hit during the New Frontier and New Society days of the 1960s.

6. Human resources, natural resources, capital, and technology. The oil-rich countries got rich by exploiting their resource base into international currency with which they could finance internal capital investment and technology adoption. Bangladesh has a real problem, particularly if the Indian Ocean rises.

7. Consider the strategies outlined at the end of the chapter. Invest in capital that makes the farms more productive to release some time and people (e.g.).

8. Now, there is an increased opportunity for better education to increase the productivity of the human resources, perhaps a relatively depleted resource stock, more capital available in international markets, and more technology to adopt.

CHAPTER 26

EXCHANGE RATES AND THE INTERNATIONAL FINANCIAL SYSTEM

This concluding chapter focuses attention on the workings of the international financial system. Coverage begins with one essential fact of life: there exists, in the world today, a multiplicity of currencies that all function as money in one place or another. To conduct transactions on an international level is therefore to deal in foreign exchange markets. Flowing immediately from this fact of life is the necessity for the world community to prescribe some sort of standard of monetary exchange that sets down the rules of the game. Be it the old gold standard and its fixed-exchange-rate regime, the marketplace and its pure flexible-exchange-rate regime, or the intermediate managed-float mechanism and its goal to minimize inefficient exchange-rate variability, the rules of the game must be clearly understood by all the players. The first part of Chapter 26 reviews these issues.

The second part of the chapter provides a description of the evolution of the international financial system from the Bretton Woods agreement of 1945 to the managed-float regime of the 1980s and early 1990s. It sets the context for a critical review of the major issues of contemporary international finance. Significant here, of course, is the impact of recent wide swings in the value of the dollar on the United States and the rest of the world.

These are all complicated topics which draw on your understanding of much of what has gone before. Micro concepts are exercised as well as macro concepts. Having completed your work in this chapter, therefore, not only will you have accomplished the following objectives, but also you will have accomplished an integrated review of many of the fundamentals of economic analysis.

LEARNING OBJECTIVES

1. Define precisely what is meant when someone quotes an exchange rate, and describe the supply-and-demand framework through which exchange rates are determined.

2. Differentiate between devaluation and revaluation in a fixed-exchange-rate system; do the same between depreciation and appreciation in a flexible-exchange-rate system.

3. Contrast the fixed-exchange-rate system of the gold standard with the pure floating of a flexible-exchange-rate system. Describe the intermediate managed float that characterizes the contemporary international system.

4. Outline the worldwide effects of an overvaluation in the currency of a large economy like that of the United States and the various means by which an overvaluation might be corrected under a fixed-rate system (gold flows), a flexible system (market forces), and a managed system (official intervention). Explain why protectionism frequently accompanies overvaluation by noting that overvalued currencies make for relatively expensive exports.

5. Sketch a brief chronology of the evolution of the international financial system from the Bretton Woods fixed-rate system that was created following World War II through today's managed-float system.

6. Describe how the wide swings in the value of the U.S. dollar (down in the 1970s, up in the early 1980s, then down since the mid-1980s) have been caused by and have been the causes of major worldwide economic events.

7. Differentiate between the forced discipline of a fixed-exchange-rate system and the market-imposed discipline of a flexible-exchange-rate system.

8. Understand the economic interdependence created by international trade, and explain how policy coordination can help nations control and/or exploit the contractionary or expansionary spillover effects of various domestic policies.

The chapter begins with a thorough description of how equilibrium exchange rates are determined; it is a direct application of supply-and-demand analysis in which the only tricky part is identifying the determinants of supply and demand.

1. a. The earliest exchanges in human history were barters—goods exchanged for goods. These were succeeded by what we ordinarily call "money transactions"—those everyday swaps in which goods are exchanged for money. When we investigate international transactions, though, we are discussing transactions in which one type of money is exchanged for another type of money. In a sense, therefore, we are back to barter again. If we refer to the exchange market between dollars and German marks, we can speak equally well of the price of the mark in terms of (dollars / marks) and of the price of the dollar in terms of (dollars / marks).

b. Suppose, for example, that the rate of exchange between U.S. dollars and German marks is 2DM = $1. This would mean that (pick one or both):

(1) the price of the mark is $0.50.

(2) the price of the dollar is 2DM.

c. As a further consequence of the money-for-money property of foreign exchange transactions, note that the participants can be identified as "demanders" or as "suppliers" only by identifying which of the two monies is being bought and sold. If you want to buy marks because you want to buy a German car, then you could easily think of yourself as a demander of marks. It would, however, be equally correct to describe yourself as a (supplier of marks / demander of dollars / supplier of dollars).

---

a. dollars; marks **b.** (1) and (2) **c.** supplier of dollars

---

Left to its own devices, a foreign exchange rate will move up and down under the pressure of changes in supply and demand. The exchange rate is a price; it is subject to the same influences as any other price. Governments rarely leave the foreign prices of their own currencies entirely free to float, though; instead, they try to manage the exchange rates which reflect the value of their currencies, at least to some degree. Why? Because the value of their currencies affects directly the relative prices of their citizens' goods marketed abroad and the relative prices of foreign goods marketed at home. Until 1971, in fact, most governments tried to keep the prices of their own currencies in foreign monies fixed. Fixed rates were altered only under the strongest pressure for change. The great advantage of a fixed exchange rate was that everyone knew exactly what a foreign purchase would cost and what a foreign sale would bring in domestic money. Occasional calls for a return to a fixed-rate system (commonly heard among bankers and business firms, especially) are further bolstered by long memories of the days when nations relied on a particular technique for maintaining fixed rates: the gold standard. A country went on the gold standard by declaring that gold was the basis or standard for its currency unit. The United States might, for example, have declared that the gold "content" of its dollar was 1/100 of an ounce, but it then would have had to back this statement by a willingness to buy or to sell gold freely at $100 per ounce; it would have, in effect, specified *the* price of gold.

Taking the viewpoint of the United States for illustrative purposes, most international transactions fall into two categories: (a) export and exportlike items whose effect is to bring foreign money to the United States and (b) imports and importlike items whose effect is to send American money abroad. If the total money volume in category (a) exceeds that in (b), then under a fixed-exchange-rate system, U.S. reserves would tend to increase. Under a floating-rate system, though, the same excess of (a) over (b) would simply tend to drive the price of the U.S. dollar, expressed in any foreign money, up. Exports would then fall and imports would rise.

2. Assume a floating-rate system. For each of the following, indicate whether its effect would be to increase (I) or to decrease (D) the dollar's price in foreign-currency terms. Use the supply-demand framework reflected in Figure 26-1 to inform and illustrate your answers.

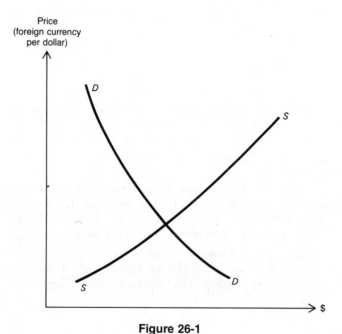

Figure 26-1

a. American demand for imports increases. .... (I / D)

b. Foreign demand for U.S. goods decreases. .... (I / D)

c. A recession in the United States results in falling GNP, employment, and imports. .... (I / D)

d. The rate of inflation in foreign countries is more rapid than that in the United States. .... (I / D)

e. Americans decide to invest less abroad—i.e., their demand for foreign assets decreases. .... (I / D)

f. Foreign firms increase their dividend payments, and some of the shareholders are Americans. .... (I / D)

g. Foreigners decide to hold fewer U.S. dollars. .. (I / D)

a. D (increases supply of dollars) b. D (reduces demand for dollars) c. I (reduces supply of dollars) d. I (increases demand for dollars) e. I (reduces supply of dollars) f. I (increases demand for dollars) g. D (increases supply of dollars or reduces demand)

3. A demand schedule for francs, at various dollars-and-cents prices, is outlined in Table 26-1. Convert it into a supply schedule for dollars, at various franc prices. [*Note:* This is not a simple problem. A "straight-line" demand schedule results in a supply schedule of quite unexpected shape. Convert in this way: If the price of 1 franc is 90 cents, then 1 franc = 90 cents, and so $1 = 100/0.90 franc (i.e., the price of $1 is about 1.1 francs). The schedule in Table 26-1 says that 100 francs will be demanded when the price of the franc is 90 cents; i.e., $90 will be supplied to buy them. In sum, then, $90 will be supplied when the dollar's price is 1.1 francs. Work out other points on the supply schedule similarly.] Plot both curves in the appropriate panels of Figure 26-2.

Table 26-1

P of Franc (in $)	Q of Francs Demanded	P of Dollar (in francs)	Q of Dollars Supplied
1.00	0	_____	_____
0.90	100	_____	_____
0.80	200	_____	_____
0.70	300	_____	_____
0.60	400	_____	_____
0.50	500	_____	_____
0.40	600	_____	_____
0.30	700	_____	_____
0.20	800	_____	_____
0.10	900	_____	_____

table rows (in ordered pairs of P and Q, respectively): fr. 1.00, 0; fr. 1.11, 90; fr. 1.25, 160; fr. 1.43, 210; fr. 1.67, 240; fr. 2.00, 250; fr. 2.50, 240; fr. 3.33, 210; fr. 5.00, 160; fr. 10.00, 90

Figure 26-2

4. Suppose that the exchange rate between U.S. dollars and French francs is floating. What effect, if any, is each of the following events likely to have on the price of the franc in dollars? Put (U) in the parentheses if the effect should be to push the price of the franc (in dollars) up, (D) if it should push the price down, and (N) if there is no reason why the price of the franc should be affected at all.

a. French corporations have a large interest payment to make, in dollars, to American bondholders. . . . . . . ( )

b. French corporations have a large interest payment to make, in francs, to American bondholders. . . . . . . ( )

c. France emerges from a recession, and with this increase in incomes, the French people want to buy more American merchandise. . . . . ( )

d. American residents decide to buy French bonds. ( )

e. The French government ships gold to the United States. . . . . ( )

f. French corporations sell bonds to Americans, borrowing in dollars and in New York because the interest rate is lower there. The proceeds of the bond issue are to be spent on French labor and materials. . . . . ( )

g. Foreign exchange speculators decide that the price of the dollar in francs is going to fall. . . . . ( )

h. The taste of American gourmets for French wine is replaced by a taste for California wine. . . . . ( )

i. The French government decides that American movies are immoral and refuses to admit them into France. . . ( )

j. An American citizen sends a package of merchandise to her French relatives as a gift. . . . . ( )

k. An American citizen sends a remittance of dollars to his French relatives as a gift. . . . . ( )

l. A French bank, in possession of a dollar bank account, decides to convert the dollars into gold. . . . . ( )

m. A French bank, in possession of a dollar bank account, decides to convert the dollars into francs. . . . . . . ( )

a. D b. D c. D d. U e. N f. U g. U h. D i. U j. N k. U l. N m. U

5. Suppose that a widespread taste for Scotch whiskey develops in the United States. This would create an increase in the demand for (dollars / pounds sterling). If the United States were on the gold standard and if this demand increase were sufficiently large, then there would be a flow of gold (away from / toward) the United States. If this demand increase persisted without a countering effect for a long time, then the United States might be drained of its entire stock of (gold / Scotch whiskey).

pounds sterling; away from; gold

The gold standard kept exchange rates steady by definition, but demand-and-supply forces were still at work. Why didn't some nations run out of gold while trying to maintain that standard? A nation did, indeed, have to "go off" the gold standard if it lost all or most of its gold because of a major rise in imports or a sufficient drop in exports. There were, however, some "equilibrating" forces that operated to brake any such overwhelming gold outflow. The first major attempt to describe an equilibrating mechanism was laid out by David Hume in the eighteenth century.

6. **a.** Suppose, as in question 5, that the U.S. demand for imports increases to a point where imports exceed exports. According to Hume's analysis, the resulting gold flow (out of / into) the United States (increases / decreases) the U.S. money supply, causing the price level to (rise / fall).

b. The (same / reverse) situation occurs in one or more foreign exporting countries. The gold which has left the United States flows into these countries, increasing their money stock and causing their prices to (climb / fall). Since American prices have gone down while foreign prices have gone up, (more / fewer) American goods will be bought by foreigners, while Americans will tend to buy (more / fewer) foreign goods. That is, in America, exports will (rise / fall), imports will (rise / fall), and the rise in the U.S. imports which began the process would be offset.

a. out of; decreases; fall **b.** reverse; climb; more; fewer; rise; fall

In rough outline, for sufficiently large movements, Hume's analysis may have some validity. There is today, however, almost no link between a nation's total gold stock and its total money supply. Moreover, Hume's analysis relies heavily on the quantity theory of money and its assumption of full employment. Both of these caveats leave the Hume analysis wanting as a description of modern-day responses to current account imbalance.

Although the old international gold standard and Bretton Woods system are both gone, their influence persists, particularly in two important respects. First, nations still consider their gold stocks as reserves for settling international balances. (But now they tend to regard gold as an "emergency" reserve; they do not part with gold unless events force them to do so.) Second, the desire for relative stability in exchange rates persists. The gold standard is not the only possible mechanism to this end. You can hold the price of your currency steady by simply maintaining a sufficiently large inventory of foreign monies.

7. **a.** Canada, for example, relies heavily on exports to, and imports from, the United States. Suppose that the Canadian

authorities (to whom the exchange rate is consequently important) decide that it would be desirable for trading purposes to keep the price of the U.S. dollar at $(Can.)1.15. If the price of the U.S. dollar begins to drift below this figure, then Canada could enter the foreign exchange market and support the price by *(selling / buying)* U.S. dollars. It would, for this purpose, supply (sell) *(Canadian / American)* dollars. If the U.S. dollar's price started to move above $(Can.)1.15, on the other hand, Canada could *(buy / sell)* U.S. dollars.

b. Alternatively, Canada might choose a modified version of the same plan, keeping the price of the U.S. dollar within a "band" of, say, $(Can.)1.12 and $(Can.)1.18. Canada could not, of course, keep the exchange rate indefinitely at a level not justified by supply and demand. If the price of the U.S. dollar kept trying to push above $(Can.)1.18, then Canada would *(accumulate too many / run out of)* U.S. dollars.

a. buying; Canadian; sell **b.** run out of (Use supply-and-demand geometry to see that these answers are correct.)

8. a. The word "devaluation" goes back to the days of the gold standard, in which the currency unit allegedly had a "gold content" and gold consequently had an "official price" per ounce. **Devaluation** meant a government-decreed *(reduction / increase)* in that gold content—i.e., *(a reduction / an increase)* in the official price. President Roosevelt's 1933 declaration that the dollar's gold content would be reduced from 1/21 to 1/35 of an ounce *(was / was not)* an instance of devaluation. With the dissolution of the gold standard, devaluations no longer take place. The U.S. government may still sell gold from time to time, but there is nothing "official" about the price it obtains.

b. Depreciation, in the context of foreign exchange, refers to a reduction in the price of a currency relative to other monies. Suppose that the price of the Canadian dollar is 90 U.S. cents. If this price were to drop to 85 U.S. cents, then the Canadian dollar would be worth, in U.S. funds, *(more / less)*; this would be an instance of depreciation. If the price were to rise from 90 to 95 U.S. cents, on the other hand, this would indicate *(a depreciation / an appreciation)* of the Canadian dollar.

c. Any depreciation of a foreign currency (relative to the U.S. dollar) makes that foreign country's goods appear *(cheaper / more expensive)* to Americans. To residents in that other country, in terms of their own currency, American goods appear *(cheaper / more expensive)*. When a country's currency is depreciated, therefore, this move tends to *(increase / decrease)* the volume of its exports and to *(increase / decrease)* the volume of its imports.

a. reduction; an increase; was **b.** less; an appreciation **c.** cheaper; more expensive; increase; decrease

9. At the close of World War II, the Western nations created two new international agencies: the International Monetary Fund (IMF) and the World Bank. The intended goal behind the IMF's formation was to maintain, to the extent possible, stable exchange rates. No nation would have to push itself deliberately into recession or depression just to maintain a steady international value for its currency, but each participating nation did deposit a supply of its own currency (and, in some cases, gold) with the IMF. These deposits established a "lending pool," from which any nation could borrow if it found itself temporarily losing reserves in its maintenance of a fixed rate. It was of course understood that persistent losses of reserves indicated some form of "fundamental disequilibrium" which could not be sustained by continual borrowing. A nation could then devalue its currency value by up to 10 percent if it wished. Further devaluation required "consultation with the fund"—in effect, international approval.

It became evident, over the course of time, that the IMF's lending pool of national currencies—dollars, pounds sterling, francs, etc.—was *(insufficient / excessive)* and in need of *(reduction / supplement)*. A new "international money"—one to be used only in settlements between governments or central banks—was created. It is called the

SDRs were and still are created just as money is created by commercial banks through their lending activity. The maximum amount of their creation each year is settled by vote of IMF members. The extent to which any nation can draw SDRs is governed by its quota participation in the IMF.

insufficient; supplement; special drawing right

10. a. The World Bank's task, in brief, is to channel money from richer nations to less developed ones. In slightly more detail, the bank's function is to *(make short-term loans / make long-term loans / provide foreign exchange for balance-of-payments shortages)* to the world's poorer countries. It provides funds for a less developed nation *(even if that nation can / only if that nation cannot)* borrow privately at a reasonable interest rate. The World Bank can make loans (pick one) :

(1) only from its capital, subscribed by member nations.

(2) either from its capital or by floating bond issues with principal and interest payments guaranteed by member nations.

b. In its early years, the bank was rather *(liberal / conservative)* in its loan policies. When Robert McNamara became its president (in 1968), however, it *(expanded / curtailed)* the scope of its activity. McNamara's plan for the World Bank in the 1980s was to focus especially upon the *(more rapidly developing / poorest)* nations.

a. make long-term loans; only if that nation cannot; **(2)** **b.** conservative; expanded; poorest

11. a. One of the most significant problems of international finance in the early 1980s was the overvalued U.S. dollar; estimated by some to have been *(10 / 25 / 50)* percent overvalued from 1981 into 1984. The scenario that produced this overvaluation began with the *(tight / loose)* monetary policy and *(stimulative / contractionary)* fiscal policy of the Reagan administration that drove real interest rates in the United States *(up / down)*. Foreign investment therefore flowed *(into / out of)* the United States, *(increasing / decreasing)* the demand for dollars and thus causing the dollar to *(appreciate / depreciate)* in money markets all around the world. Exports from the United States therefore became *(more / less)* expensive, while imports from abroad became *(more / less)* costly. Net exports *(expanded / contracted)* by nearly *($50 / $140 / $250)* billion, as a result, and created an enormous *(deficit / surplus)* in the current account. This discrepancy was, though, almost canceled by a *(deficit / surplus)* in the capital account, so the overvaluation persisted and drove interest rates abroad *(up / down)*. The result was a tendency for foreign economies to move into *(recession / boom)*, and *(depressed / overextended)* export- and import-competing industries called for *(free trade / protection and subsidy)* in the United States.

b. The only way to relieve overvaluation under fixed exchange rates is to endure a *(recession / boom)* to generate *(higher / lower)* domestic prices. Under flexible exchange rates, though, the correction is supposed to be automatic, but it can be retarded by capital account flows. The managed float of the type then in place (it still is, too) encouraged the government of the United States to help the exchange-rate correction along by *(selling / buying)* dollars in the world marketplace. The Reagan administration *(pursued this policy vigorously / claimed that the dollar was not overvalued and undertook little official intervention)*. The result was continued borrowing through the capital account, America's conversion into the world's largest *(creditor / debtor)* nation, and a *(further increase / plunge)* in the value of the dollar after 1985.

a. 50; tight; stimulative; up; into; increasing; appreciate; more; less; contracted; $140; deficit; surplus; up; recession; depressed; protection and subsidy **b.** recession; lower; selling; claimed that the dollar was not overvalued and undertook little official intervention; debtor; plunge

REVIEW CONCEPTS

1. An exchange rate is simply the price of some currency A in terms of some other currency B. It is determined by the interaction of supply and demand for currency A.

2. The supply of a currency is generated by any activity which releases that currency in exchange for another; e.g., the purchase of a foreign-made commodity first requires the exchange of the home currency for the currency of the manufacturing nation and thereby generates a supply of the home currency.

3. The demand for a currency is generated by any activity which requires that currency; e.g., the transaction noted in concept (2) generates a demand for the currency of the manufacturing nation.

4. Any increase (reduction) in the price of a currency, when exchange rates are allowed to float, is called an appreciation (a depreciation). The equivalent movements during fixed-rate regimes require official action and are called revaluation and devaluation, respectively.

5. Flexible rates allow market forces to determine exchange rates. Fixed rates must, on the other hand, be maintained by manipulation of the demand and supply of currencies by domestic fiscal and monetary policy. Managed floats try to allow the efficiency of flexible rates while limiting the volatility of their movement.

6. The economic interdependence bred by extensive international trade leads to the opportunity of coordinating domestic and international exchange policies across national boundaries.

7. Chronic or persistent overvaluation of a currency makes exports relatively expensive on the world market and imports relatively inexpensive at home. Both circumstances lead to calls for protectionism.

QUIZ: Multiple Choice

1. If we say that a country's currency has been devalued, we mean that:
(1) it has gone off the gold standard.
(2) the domestic purchasing power of its currency unit has fallen.
(3) its government has increased the price it will pay for gold.
(4) it is experiencing an unfavorable balance of trade.
(5) the prices of at least some foreign currencies, as expressed in that country's domestic currency, have fallen.

2. To be fully on the gold standard, the government of a country must:
(1) set a fixed price at which it is prepared to buy or sell gold in any quantity without restriction.
(2) be prepared to buy or sell gold at any time without restriction, but at a price which it is free to vary from day to day as it chooses, provided the same price (or almost the same price) applies to both purchases and sales.
(3) be prepared to buy gold in any quantity without restriction at a fixed price, but not necessarily to sell it.
(4) be prepared to sell gold in any quantity without restriction, but not necessarily to buy it.
(5) maintain a fixed gold content in its money unit, but not necessarily be prepared to buy or sell gold at any fixed price or without restriction.

3. In a stable exchange-rate situation, if the price of the French franc were 25 U.S. cents and the price of the U.S. dollar were 600 Italian lire, then the price of the French franc in Italian lire would be:
(1) 90 lire.
(2) 150 lire.
(3) 200 lire.
(4) 300 lire.
(5) 600 lire.

4. Suppose that the exports of Country A to Country B have increased substantially and that both A and B operate on the gold standard. According to David Hume's gold-flow mechanism:
(1) A's domestic price level will fall, but B's domestic price level may or may not change.
(2) A's price level may or may not change, but B's will fall.
(3) A's price level will rise, B's will fall.
(4) A's price level will fall, B's will rise.
(5) none of the above will happen.

5. If the exchange rate between Swiss francs and U.S. dollars were to change from Sfr. 4 to the dollar to Sfr. 3 to the dollar, then the franc's price must have:
(1) risen from 25 cents to 33 cents, and the dollar has appreciated relative to the franc.
(2) fallen from 33 to 25 cents, and the dollar has depreciated relative to the franc.
(3) risen from 25 to 33 cents, and the dollar has been devalued relative to the franc.
(4) risen from 25 to 33 cents, and the dollar has depreciated relative to the franc.
(5) fallen from 33 to 25 cents, and the dollar has appreciated relative to the franc.

6. If American corporations make large dividend payments (in dollars) to foreigners:
(1) the effect on the price of the U.S. dollar, if any, will be to depreciate it.
(2) the effect on the price of the U.S. dollar, if any, will be to appreciate it.
(3) gold will tend to flow into the United States to compensate for the U.S. money going abroad.
(4) imports into the United States will tend to increase to compensate for the U.S. money going abroad.
(5) none of the above will be true.

7. If the exchange rate between Canadian and U.S. dollars is a floating one, and if the demand for Canadian dollars increases, then:
(1) the supply of Canadian dollars has decreased or will decrease.
(2) the price of the Canadian dollar in U.S. currency will fall.
(3) the supply of U.S. dollars has decreased.
(4) the price of the U.S. dollar in Canadian currency will fall.
(5) the U.S. dollar has been devalued.

8. A substantial fall in the price of the dollar in foreign currencies (e.g., the price of the dollar in francs) could be expected to affect physical quantities of exports from the United States and imports into the United States in which of the following ways?
(1) It would increase both exports and imports.
(2) It would increase exports and decrease imports.
(3) It would decrease both exports and imports.
(4) It would decrease exports and increase imports.
(5) It would have no perceptible effect on either imports or exports.

9. If a country depreciates the foreign exchange value of its currency, the results will typically be that:
(1) its imports will seem cheaper (from the viewpoint of its own citizens), and its exports will seem more expensive (from the viewpoint of foreigners).
(2) its imports will seem more expensive (from the viewpoint of its own citizens), and its exports will seem cheaper (from the viewpoint of foreigners).
(3) both its imports and its exports will seem cheaper (from the viewpoint of both its own citizens and foreigners).
(4) both its imports and its exports will seem more expensive (from the viewpoint of both its own citizens and foreigners).
(5) none of the above will occur, since there is no reason why the prices of either imports or exports should be affected.

10. If GNP falls in the United States, and exchange rates are floating, then:
(1) imports will tend to decrease and the price of the U.S. dollar to increase.
(2) imports will tend to decrease and the price of the U.S. dollar to decrease.
(3) imports will tend to increase and the price of the U.S. dollar to increase.
(4) imports will tend to increase and the price of the U.S. dollar to decrease.
(5) none of the preceding statements will be true.

11. The principal task assigned to the International Monetary Fund at the time of its organization was to:
(1) serve as a partial substitute for the gold standard in maintaining stable exchange rates.
(2) try to maintain a high level of employment within member countries, so as to avoid any danger of competitive depreciation policies in the foreign exchange markets.
(3) make loans to private companies in any country where the funds could not otherwise be borrowed at any reasonable interest rate.
(4) facilitate the development of free-trade "regions" similar to the European Common Market.
(5) coordinate the views of the larger and more developed nations concerning exchange-rate and trade problems.

12. It could also be said that the principal task assigned to the International Monetary Fund was to:
(1) act as the world's banker in matters of both short-term and long-term credit.
(2) make direct long-term loans to less developed nations when necessary, so as to assist in their economic development.
(3) control international credit sufficiently to enable member nations to maintain their price levels at reasonably non-inflationary levels.
(4) help bridge short-run disequilibrium in any member nation's balance of payments.
(5) work toward the gradual reduction of tariffs and elimination of protectionist policies among nations.

13. Which alternative in question 12 would be correct had that question referred to the World Bank rather than the International Monetary Fund?
(1) ___.
(2) ___.
(3) ___.
(4) ___.
(5) ___.

14. A disturbance in its balance of payments may cause any nation to lose gold or foreign exchange reserves. This danger of loss is most acute whenever that nation:
(1) increases its exports.
(2) seeks to maintain a flexible exchange rate.
(3) seeks to maintain a fixed exchange rate.
(4) increases its borrowing from other nations.
(5) experiences a drop in GNP—i.e., whenever any recession or depression occurs.

15. A "managed float" means:
(1) an increase in the protectionist policies by some device other than a tariff increase.
(2) refusal by a nation to allow its currency to appreciate even though its reserves are large and increasing.
(3) a beggar-my-neighbor policy.
(4) introduction of a split exchange rate—a fixed rate for some transactions, a floating rate for others.
(5) periodic intervention by a central bank to check excessive fluctuation in an otherwise-floating exchange rate.

SUGGESTED ANSWERS TO QUESTIONS IN THE TEXT: Chapter 26

1. These are all definitions. Their significance is derived from our experience with them.

2. $1 = 0.54 pound = 5.72 francs = 126.74 yen = 740.74 won = 1.69 marks.

3. The demand for pounds comes from Americans who are supplying dollars at a rate equal to the (dollar-per-pound) exchange rate times the quantity of pounds demanded at that rate. The supply of pounds comes from Britons who are demanding dollars at a rate equal to the same exchange rate times the quantity of pounds supplied. Draw a graph with equilibrium at £/$ = 0.67.

4. It is a reflection of the need to protect against the disorder of excessive volatility. Volatility disrupts all sorts of markets, causes people to put too much effort into hedging, and may reduce the efficiency of international trade by inserting a "risk-premium" sort of transactions cost.

5. **a.** Increases the yen/$ exchange rate by intervening above the equilibrium. Why get 150 to the dollar when the government will give you 160?
b. Supply of dollars falls, and the yen/$ exchange rate climbs.
c. The demand for yen climbs, and so does the yen/$ exchange rate.
d. The supply curve of yen shifts out, so the yen/$ exchange rate falls.

6. Intervention by selling marks when the exchange rate tries to push above 1.60 marks per dollar and by buying when the exchange rate tries to fall below $1.50.

7. A crawling peg allows some flexibility, but it puts a limit on volatility.

8. An increase in the sale of oil should increase the demand for currency and thus push up the exchange rate. In anticipation of this, speculators may purchase the currency early, increasing its price early, and making other exports prematurely expensive.

9. Parts **a**, **b**, **d**, and **e** are straightforward. Relative prices move according to monetary theory under fixed rates; they move with the exchange rate otherwise.

10. All things equal, trade should bring prices to equivalent positions throughout the world; the exchange rate is the means to that end. If prices are higher for one country than they should be, then the demand for its exports will fall, the demand for its currency will fall, and its currency will depreciate.

11. You would want to increase aggregate demand in Britain and maintain it in the United States. If the value of the dollar were to rise (from a purchase, e.g.), then the price of British goods in the United States would fall and the price of U.S. goods in Britain would rise. In both cases, demand for British goods would increase—this would be the appropriate stimulus. If stimulative fiscal or monetary policy were undertaken in the United States, meanwhile, then aggregate demand there might be maintained.

By the way, congratulations for reaching the end of the book.

ANSWERS TO QUIZ QUESTIONS: MULTIPLE CHOICE

Chapter 2

1. (4) Definition.
2. (4) These questions are independent of the type of economic system employed.
3. (4) If there is no substitution possible between commodities, then there is no choice to exercise.
4. (3) The definition applies to all circumstances.
5. (2) The *PPF* is the "choice set" of the *what* decision.
6. (1) Refer to 5.
7. (5) Definition.
8. (4) Point *D* shows the largest value against the food axis.
9. (2) Shift to line 1 shows potential for more clothing but not more food.
10. (5) Shift to line 2 shows potential for more food but not more clothing.
11. (3) Shift to line 3 shows potential for more of both food and clothing.
12. (1) Only *A* shows smaller increments of wheat as labor employment climbs.
13. (3) Definition.
14. (2) Not on *PPF* means production of all goods can increase simultaneously; resources must be being wasted.
15. (1) Connecting the points is concave only for $X = 280$ and $Y = 270$.
16. (3) You net $1750 at home and $50 in France; the difference is opportunity cost.

Chapter 3

1. (1) Definition.
2. (5) Developing countries are typically too strapped to be able to forgo present consumption.
3. (2) The least-cost incentive answers *how*; specialization may be one way of cutting costs.
4. (3) The choice between present consumption and future consumption.
5. (5) None of the listed factors is "productive."
6. (3) A problem and an opportunity.
7. (2) Definition.
8. (2) Definition applied to deferred consumption.
9. (5) Capital "deepening" is growth in the mix of production opportunities.
10. (1) Definition.
11. (3) Definition.
12. (2) Definition.
13. (5) Capital is deferred consumption.
14. (5) This suggests a role for government.
15. (1) Directly, but usually affects "all the above."

Chapter 4

1. (4) Definition.
2. (4) Definition.
3. (1) This is the income effect.
4. (1) Only panel *(a)* shows any quantity being associated with one given price.
5. (2) Only panel *(b)* specifies a given quantity for any price.
6. (1) The store is committed to a constant price per unit.
7. (5) Demand curves assume fixed incomes; changing incomes mean at least two curves.
8. (4) Higher prices imply higher quantities supplied; only panel *(d)* shows the required positive slope.
9. (3) Only panel *(c)* shows the requisite negative slope.

307

10. (5) Only (3) identifies a change that might cause a shift, but it goes in the wrong direction.
11. (2) Only (2) does not identify a change in an "other things being equal" type of variable for demand.
12. (5) The price of X must change if you are drawing a demand curve for X.
13. (2) Higher costs of production contract supply.
14. (5) It is explained by an upward shift in demand.
15. (2) Supply contraction means a leftward shift in demand.
16. (3) Higher demand for pork means a rightward shift in demand.
17. (1) Excess supply puts downward pressure on price; one result is a reduction in the quantity supplied.
18. (3) Definition.

Chapter 5

1. (5) Constant revenue means that the percentage change in quantity equals the percentage change in price.
2. (4) Definition.
3. (2) Definition.
4. (3) Definition.
5. (5) Higher incomes imply that demand shifts up; equilibrium moves along the supply curve.
6. (1) Higher revenue with a lower price means that the percentage increase in quantity exceeded 10 percent.
7. (3) $E_D = 5/10 = 0.5 < 1$.
8. (2) Definition.
9. (4) The tax burden is shared with some price elasticity in supply and demand. Graph it.
10. (1) The tax means that supply changes; equilibrium moves along the demand curve. Graph it.
11. (1) Definition.
12. (1) Definition.
13. (4) Definition.
14. (1) Definition.
15. (3) Definition.
16. (5) Unit elasticity throughout implies a demand curve that is a rectangular hyperbola with revenue constant; the formula is $PQ = k$.
17. (2) Longer term means that the price elasticity of supply climbs; the price increase is therefore smaller. Graph it.
18. (2) Definition.
19. (4) Failure means a contraction in supply; quantity falls along the demand curve. Graph it.
20. (1) Contract supply; graph it.
21. (4) Definition of responsiveness.
22. (1) This is the only answer that maintains a constant ratio of percentage changes and the correct slope; (2) displays unitary price elasticity for demand.

Chapter 6

1. (4) Definition.
2. (1) Definition.
3. (2) Definition.
4. (5) The ratios of marginal utility to price must be equal.
5. (1) An increase in the price of a substitute or a decline in the price of a complement causes the quantity demanded to increase for each and every price; i.e., demand shifts up.
6. (3) $MU_A/P_A = 30/0.7 = 45 > 40 = 20/0.5 = MU_B/P_B$.
7. (2) Definition.
8. (5) Definition.
9. (4) $MU_X/1.5 = MU_Y/P_Y = 30/1 = 30$ means that $MU_X = 45$.
10. (5) Marginal utility figures are required, not total utility.
11. (1) Definition.
12. (1) $MU = 0$ means that more consumption does not cause total utility to increase further; total utility must therefore have peaked.
13. (2) Declining marginal utility for all goods means that consumption of all of them must be higher.
14. (2) Definition.

Chapter 6 Appendix

1. (5) Definition.
2. (4) Definition.
3. (4) The process described in this alternative leads to the requisite tangency; the others do not.
4. (5) Definition.
5. (5) Definition.

Chapter 7

1. (2) Definition.
2. (1) Debt service (interest payment) is a contractual obligation regardless of circumstance.
3. (5) Unlike the other things listed, dividends need not be paid.
4. (1) Debt service is still a contractual obligation.
5. (2) And so was formed the Harvard Business School.
6. (2) A step might be skipped, though.
7. (3) Depreciation is an accounting device to finance replacement capital.
8. (2) Personal taxes apply only to accrued income.
9. (1) Revenue net of business expense and interest is subject to the corporate tax.
10. (3) Definition.
11. (5) Diminishing returns can coexist with increasing, decreasing, and/or constant returns to scale; they measure different things.
12. (4) $MP < AP$ means that the contribution of the last unit employed is smaller than the previous average; that addition must therefore bring the average down.
13. (1) $AP = [TP(K = 3, L = 4)]/4 = 52/4 = 13$.
14. (4) $TP(K = 2, L = 5) = 40$, while $TP(K = 3, L = 5) = 62$. The MP of the third unit of K must therefore be $(62 - 40)/1 = 22$.

15. (5) Production displays diminishing returns throughout with respect to both K and L.
16. (3) IRS, because doubling the inputs yields more than twice the output.
17. (4) $TP(K = 2, L = 3) = 27$, so $TP(K = 4, L = 6)$ must equal 54.
18. (5) Answers 2, 3, and 4 are short-run responses, but anything possible in the short run is possible in the long run, too.
19. (3) Total productivity has increased an average of 1.5 percent per year since 1900, but it has averaged only slightly more than 0.5 percent per year since 1970.
20. (4) Technological progress means productivity must climb and output must be higher for any level of employment; the new curve must be higher and steeper at every level of employment (it is impossible to draw it higher and flatter for all levels of employment).

Chapter 8

1. (4) Definition.
2. (4) Definition.
3. (5) A change in fixed cost does not affect variable cost; marginal cost is thus unaffected.
4. (3) $MC = \$10$ while $AC(1000) = \$4.90$ and $AC(999) = \$4.88$.
5. (4) If $MC > AC$, then AC must be rising; if $MC < AC$, however, then AC must be falling. At minimum, where AC is flat, MC must therefore equal AC.
6. (1) $MC > AC$ means that the incremental cost is larger than the previous average, so the average must climb.
7. (4) Only constant AC means a constant MC, so AC must change. It may rise or fall depending upon whether MC is larger or smaller.
8. (4) The least-cost rule.
9. (4) Definition. Input prices are required to judge efficiency and/or compute costs.
10. (4) Definition.
11. (2) $MP_A/P_A = 60/4 = 15 < MP_B/P_B = 40/2 = 20$; minimum cost has not been achieved, so maximum profits are also not realized.
12. (3) Equal MP/P ratios guarantee minimum cost but do not necessarily guarantee maximum profits.
13. (3) Interest payments are a current expense.
14. (2) Depreciation should not exceed 100 percent of the cost of the machine.
15. (3) Definition.
16. (4) Net worth at the end of 1990 was $30,000; at the end of 1991, $40,000. Thus, net worth increased by $10,000 over the course of the year. Coupled with dividends of $15,000, total profits must have been $25,000.
17. (2) Profits are either distributed as dividends or held as retained earnings.
18. (3) An increase in net worth of $150,000[(\$550,000 - \$200,000) - (\$600,000 - \$400,000)]$ was financed by $100,000 in stock sales; profit must have contributed $50,000. Combine this fact with the recorded dividends of $50,000 to get total profit after taxes.

Chapter 8 Appendix

1. (3) Definition.
2. (4) Definition.
3. (4) Definition.
4. (2) Equal-cost line satisfies $C = P_X X + P_Y Y$ for two goods X and Y; that is $Y = -(P_X/P_Y)X + C/P_Y$.
5. (1) Given L-shaped isoquants, increasing the employment of either input by 1 unit causes no change in output.
6. (1) The B intercept is fixed, so P_B must be constant. A higher A intercept means that P_A must have fallen.
7. (5) Both intercepts' shifting out means that either cost went up or both prices declined.
8. (4) The A intercept is fixed, so P_A must be constant. A lower B intercept means that P_B must have risen.
9. (5) Definition.
10. (3) Definition.
11. (3) Definitions.
12. (2) Fixed proportions mean that a single combination of inputs exists for each and every output.

Chapter 9

1. (4) Definition, but profits are maximized when MC is rising.
2. (2) Specifically, the part above the shutdown point where $AVC > MC$.
3. (4) Information about MC is required to guarantee that the condition for maximizing profit is satisfied; knowledge of AC is not sufficient to judge.
4. (5) The cost of the marginal unit (unit 2001) is $\$19,010 - \$19,000 = \$10$. This matches the price, so $MC = P$ and profits are being maximized.
5. (4) Is it covering variable cost? Since there is no information about variable cost, there is no way of telling if the firm should shut down.
6. (2) It is now covering variable cost.
7. (5) A firm trying to maximize profit will produce a level of output such that MC equals P.
8. (3) Entry or exit of new firms or existing firms automatically drives pure economic profit to zero and P to the minimum of AC.
9. (5) Price information is required to guarantee that $MC = P$; the question provides only enough to guarantee that $MC = AC$.
10. (1) A tax applied to fixed costs shifts AC up along an unaffected MC curve; the profit-maximizing output for a (surviving) firm must climb along same MC.
11. (1) It is in long-run equilibrium.
12. (2) The firm's output maximizes profit, so $P = MC = \$10$; meanwhile, output $= TR/P = \$5000/\$10 = 500$ units.

13. (4) $AC = \$8$ and $AVC = \$5$; as a result, $AFC = \$3$. $FC = AFC \times$ output $= \$3 \times 500 = \$1500$.
14. (4) Price exceeds AC by \$2 for each unit produced; profit $= (P - AC) \times$ output $= \$2 \times 500 = \$1000$.
15. (1) Definition.
16. (3) Compare price and marginal cost. $P = \$7$ and $MC = TC(201) - TC(200) = (\$5 \times 201) - (\$4.99 \times 200) = \$7$.
17. (1) Profits would climb as MC rose toward \$1.90, so output must rise.
18. (5) Decreasing costs undermine perfect competition.
19. (5) The change in fixed cost leaves MC unaffected, so $P = MC$ at the same output and price. Nothing happens in the short run.
20. (2) The tax should cause minimum AC to climb; equilibrium price therefore climbs with the total quantity demanded falling correspondingly along the demand curve.
21. (3) The direction that output should move to (possibly) increase profits depends upon whether $P > MC$ (output should then climb), $P = MC$ (output should remain the same), or $P < MC$ (output should fall).
22. (1) $P > MC$ means that output should climb to get MC to move up toward P.
23. (3) The original \$5 price would fall to equal the minimum AC where $MC = AC$; the quantity demanded would therefore rise along demand curve.

Chapter 9 Appendix

1. (2) The definition of perfectly elastic demand applied to a shift in the supply curve (an "increase in supply"—remember the terminology which held that a change in "supply" denoted a shift in the supply curve while a change in the "quantity supplied" denoted movement along a supply curve).
2. (3) The definition of perfectly elastic supply applied to a shift in the demand curve (same terminology).
3. (1) Pure rent implies perfectly inelastic supply.
4. (1) The definition leads to a vertical line.
5. (3) Constant cost implies perfectly elastic supply; marginal cost is constant.
6. (1) The tax would increase (constant average and marginal) cost by the full \$1; the supply curve would shift by the entire amount of the tax, so the equilibrium price would climb up by \$1, too.
7. (3) Definition.
8. (4) Definition.
9. (2) Definition.
10. (1) Pure economic rent implies perfectly inelastic supply, so quantity cannot change.
11. (1) Perfectly elastic supply means that firms will produce any amount at the constant marginal cost indicated by the intercept of horizontal supply curves.
12. (1) Pure economic rent implies that a fixed supply will be offered at any price. The intersection of the resulting vertical supply curve and any demand curve therefore defines a fixed equilibrium price P^* paid by demanders regardless of whether or not some of that price goes to the government in recognition of some tax. The full burden of any tax T is thus paid by suppliers, who see the price which they receive reduced to $P^* - T$; i.e., diminished by the entire tax.
13. (1) Diminishing returns would apply to the productivity of other inputs, but not to the extent of fixing wheat output.

Chapter 10

1. (5) Application of the standard definition.
2. (3) Roughly 38 percent.
3. (1) $P > MR > MC$ means that output must increase to bring MC up toward either P (perfect competition) or MR (imperfect competition).
4. (3) Each (marginal) unit of increased sales increases revenue by exactly the price of the good sold with no associated reduction in the price applied to earlier output.
5. (1) Definition.
6. (3) Definition.
7. (3) For a monopolist, $MC = MR$ and $MR < P$; clearly, then, $P > MC$.
8. (5) Definition.
9. (1) Definition.
10. (3) $MR > P$ would mean that the sale of 1 more unit would allow the price of all the previously demanded units to increase; the marginal unit would bring in P, so the increment $(P - MR)$ must come from somewhere else—the prices earned by the previous units of output.
11. (2) The information provided holds that minimum $AC = \$1.75$. Since $MC = AC$ at the bottom of an AC curve, it must therefore be true that $MC < MR = \$2$. Output should therefore be increased (to move MC up toward MR), and this could happen only if the price were allowed to fall as output moves out along a demand curve.
12. (5) Information about marginal revenue is required.
13. (1) Definition.
14. (2) The rule for perfect competition is $P = MC$; $P > MC$ means output should increase. For the imperfect competitor, though, information about MR is required to make any judgment because profits are maximized where $MC = MR$, and $P > MR$ is possible.
15. (4) $P < MC$ means that the competitor should cut back to reduce MC. A monopolist or other imperfect competitor should do the same, since $MR < MC$ (because $MR < P$ in general along a demand curve and the specifics of the question describe a situation in which that $P < MC$).
16. (3) Economies of scale are major sources of market power.
17. (1) $MR > 0 (= 0, < 0)$ means that TR increases (stays the same, falls) as quantity increases and P falls. The percentage increase in Q must therefore be larger than (equal

to, smaller than) the percentage reduction in price; i.e., demand must be elastic (display unitary elasticity, be inelastic).

Chapter 11

1. (5) The answers trace out the characteristics of highly concentrated markets.
2. (2) Definition; focus on the word "legal." Tariffs are artificial, but they are still legal.
3. (4) Definition.
4. (1) Predatory pricing is illegal.
5. (2) Think of Saudi Arabia, which is generally the swing producer for the agreed-upon price, as well as all the other non-OPEC oil-producing nations.
6. (3) Lots of close substitutes are available.
7. (5) Lots of producers of identical products.
8. (4) The monopolistic competition long-run equilibrium shows $P = AC$, but above minimum AC.
9. (1) The firm should know more about its cost schedules than it does about the demand curve it might face under imperfectly competitive conditions.
10. (1) Definition of the hypothesis.
11. (5) A restatement of the modern view of market intervention.
12. (2) $MR = MC$ at 4 units; 4 units command a price of $6.
13. (3) $MC = MB$ (demand) at 8 units; 8 units command a price of $2.
14. (5) $MR = 0$ for maximum total revenue; 5 units at $5.
15. (4) The deadweight loss triangle has a base of $8 - 4 = 4$ units and a height of $\$8 - \$4 = \$4$.

Chapter 12

1. (4) Diminishing marginal utility means that the gain associated with any increase in consumption is smaller than the loss that would be incurred given an equal reduction in consumption.
2. (2) The marginal utility of consumption (the next unit) is equal to 2 in both regions when consumption in A equals 6 units of Y and consumption in B equals 3 units of Y.
3. (2) The transfer of 2 units from B to A increases welfare in region A by $4 (= \$2.67 + \$1.33$) and reduces welfare in region B by $2 (= \$0.67 + \$1.33$).
4. (5) The marginal utility of the next unit in A would be $2.67; the marginal utility of the first unit lost in B would be $0.67. The difference is $2.
5. (1) Equality of marginal utilities means that there exist no further beneficial transfers. This condition does *not necessarily* mean that total utility is equal across regions, nor does it mean that consumption is equal across regions.
6. (3) $U(1000) = 50$ utils and $U(900) = 30$ utils. As a result, the average utility across both states of nature is $40 [= 0.5(50) + 0.5(30)]$.
7. (2) Expected income is $950, and $U(950) = 45$.
8. (4) $U(925) = 40$ (expected utility given the variable income); the individual would therefore be willing to pay $25 of her constant $950 to avoid the risk.
9. (2) II shows the higher return or smaller loss, regardless of what B does.
10. (5) III is better when A plays I, but IV is better when A plays II.
11. (5) There is no dominant equilibrium because B has no dominant strategy.
12. (4) II is the dominant strategy for A, and B plays IV if A plays II.

Chapter 13

1. (5) All the statements are accurate descriptions of historical experience.
2. (2) Up from $42,000 in 1984.
3. (3) Definition.
4. (3) Definition.
5. (5) Definition.
6. (3) Apply the definition that $MRP = MR \times MP =$ price of the input.
7. (5) $MRP =$ price of the input.
8. (1) Monopoly power means that the price of output exceeds marginal revenue. As a result, $MRP_A < P_A$ follows from the data provided.
9. (1) Again, monopoly power means that the price of output exceeds marginal revenue; only $1 conforms to this fact.
10. (3) Given perfect competition, the price of output matches marginal revenue, so $MRP_A = P_A$.
11. (4) The single good serves as the "numeraire"; it is as if the price of output is $1, so $MP = MRP$.
12. (3) This follows from the definition of constant returns to scale.

Chapter 14

1. (2) Competition otherwise tends to equalize prices (wages, here).
2. (1) Definition.
3. (5) Anything that affects the quantity of labor supplied.
4. (3) Definition—identical people having different jobs with different characteristics.
5. (3) The "reserve army" of unemployed workers was Marx's explanation of the same idea.
6. (3) Inelastic product demand supports inelastic derived demand for labor; wages therefore can climb with little reduction in employment.
7. (4) Definition.
8. (3) Definition.
9. (5) Definition; the fallacy ignores possible creation of new jobs.
10. (1) Precisely when the need to create new job opportunities was most severe.

11. (3) D_1D_1 and D_2D_2 both intersect SS in its backward-bending, negatively sloped region—the region dominated by the income effect in which lower wages decrease leisure even though the opportunity cost of leisure has fallen.
12. (2) Quantity of labor supplied is unaffected; the two effects must cancel to achieve this, since they always push in opposite directions.
13. (1) Lower wage implies substitution toward leisure (its opportunity cost is down) that dominates the income effect.
14. (1) Direction does not matter; here, substitution out of leisure dominates.
15. (5) Definition of rent applied to people.
16. (2) Real wages rose from 1.5 (= 600/400) to 1.8 (= 540/300) for an increase of $[(1.8 - 1.5)/1.5] \times 100\% = (0.3/1.5) \times 100\% = 20\%$.

Chapter 15

1. (1) Union membership has fallen recently, but it still numbers more than 19 million—roughly one-sixth of the labor force.
2. (4) Definition—the genesis of the CIO.
3. (3) The local unions represent workers most directly; they do, however, gain support from their ties to national unions and federations of national unions.
4. (2) Definition (legal) from the Wagner Act.
5. (4) Gompers believed in federalism (of which this question speaks), voluntarism, and business unionism.
6. (2) The Wagner Act (National Labor Relations Act) established the right of workers to organize and bargain collectively.
7. (5) The NLRB, established before Taft-Hartley, validates the appropriate bargaining unit by election.
8. (3) The creation of the limited "cooling-off period."
9. (5) Supporting an aggregate production with a constant share of roughly 80 percent.
10. (2) Taft-Hartley, in general, started the pendulum moving away from legislative sanction of increased union power.
11. (4) The Clayton Act removed unions from the purview of the Sherman Antitrust Act.
12. (5) The "high-water" benchmark of pro-union legislation.
13. (4) Imperfections limit the market response to excess supply or excess demand.
14. (1) Shift the supply curve up.
15. (4) Shift the supply curve up.
16. (1) Draw a horizontal line above the supply-demand intersection; read new (employment,wage) pair from the demand curve. Unemployment is the difference between the quantity that *would be* supplied at that wage and the quantity that *is* demanded.

Chapter 16

1. (1) "Many alternative uses" means that the rental price received by suppliers is fixed; the entire tax is thus borne by the tobacco growers, even if they rent the land.
2. (1) A leftward shift of demand means that price falls—by more than it would if quantity could fall, too.
3. (2) Apply the definition of opportunity cost.
4. (4) Apply the definition of opportunity cost.
5. (1) Definition; price signals reflect social cost.
6. (5) Definition.
7. (2) Definition.
8. (3) Definition; highlight the word "net."
9. (2) The cost should include the cost of financing, if any; knowing the means associated with that cost is irrelevant.
10. (1) Definition—influencing the derived demand for capital.
11. (3) You need both sides of the market—demand (derived demand depending upon the rate of return) and supply (willingness to defer consumption).
12. (4) Definition—diminishing returns pushing rates so low that saving falls to zero.
13. (4) Technological change can push the demand out even as short-run supply shifts out to maintain a higher interest rate.
14. (2) Market value = present value = $100/0.08 = $1250.
15. (3) The interest rate appears in the denominators of the components of present value, with higher powers for more distant future returns.
16. (3) According to the formula for present value, $V = \$500/1.09 = \$459$.
17. (3) Definition.
18. (5) Just look at the $PV = \$N/i$ formula. Lower i means higher PV because future installments of $\$N$ are not discounted as strenuously.
19. (3) The rate of return depends on cost and revenue stream; a lower interest rate increases the likelihood that the assets in question might be constructed. (*Remember:* It will be considered if the rate of return exceeds the interest rate.)
20. (1) Real rate + inflation rate = nominal rate; if the inflation rate is negative, then real > nominal.
21. (1) Investors consider undertaking capital projects when their rates of return exceed (or just equal) the market rate of interest; otherwise, they can do better by lending their money to someone at the market rate.
22. (1) Definition.
23. (3) Profit is the justifiable reward for those who take risks, according to Knight; without those rewards, he argued, why would anyone take any risk at all?

Chapter 17

1. (1) The ratios of both marginal cost and marginal utility equal the same ratios of prices.

2. (5) The profit motive can move perfect competitors and imperfect competitors alike; profits are maximized by producing the output at which marginal revenue ($MR = P$ in perfect competition, remember) equals marginal cost.
3. (2) The competitive model provides a benchmark of efficiency against which other situations can be evaluated.
4. (4) Given any distribution of resources, and thus income, there exists a set of prices that will support competitive equilibrium.
5. (5) In long-run competitive equilibrium, $P = MC =$ minimum AC.
6. (4) Power over price distorts competitive equilibrium because $P > MC$.
7. (2) Definition.

Chapter 18

1. (3) The sum of the budgets of all governments in the United States has climbed from 10 percent of GNP prior to World War I to 35 percent now.
2. (2) Tax receipts nearly kept pace until the tax cuts of the 1980s.
3. (2) The only reference available that might apply is "securing the public interest."
4. (2) The ICC was the first (1887); regulation peaked in the mid- to late 1970s.
5. (5) Each choice identifies a role for government, and regulation is one possible tool.
6. (5) The general list is provided among the answers.
7. (2) The utilities of both people fall only in moving from A to C.
8. (1) The utility of II increases as the utility of I falls only in moving from A to B.
9. (4) Unanimity requires that the utilities of both people increase—a condition met only in moving from A to E.
10. (3) Majority approval requires that people of type I see their utilities increase—a condition met only by point D.
11. (5) Arrow proved that there exists no majority voting scheme that guarantees efficiency, respects individual preferences, and produces outcomes independent of agenda.
12. (5) All are consequences.
13. (1) Refer to your own experience; mine is indicated.
14. (2) The public nature of the good suggests that it is difficult to exclude; the fact that many can enjoy a public good simultaneously suggests that the cost of one more person (i.e., marginal cost) is small.
15. (5) Both have all the characteristics of externalities.
16. (4) Marginal social damage equals marginal cost of abatement at point D.
17. (3) The difference between marginal private cost and marginal abatement cost must be $2; it is too large for $2 at point D and just about right at C.
18. (1) Add the amount each would pay for the community demand curve.
19. (2) Some people stretch the result to "always"; most economists do not believe in the result that much, but admit to "may."

Chapter 19

1. (2) Defense has been particularly emphasized in the federal budget since the Reagan administration, though recently its share has begun to decline.
2. (5) It is an example of the government's providing a public good—in this case, physical infrastructure.
3. (2) Transfer payments increase the incomes of some people at the expense of the incomes of others.
4. (5) Corporate income is the sum of dividends paid and retained earnings.
5. (3) All explicit money income is subject to the personal-income-tax structure; some implicit income is (employer-subsidized mortgages) and some is not (housing services to homeowners).
6. (2) Money earned and retained would not be subject to any tax (save for capital gains, when realized) were it not for the corporation income tax.
7. (5) The personal income tax is applied to dividends generated by corporate income that has already been taxed.
8. (1) The federal government has long relied most heavily on the personal income tax.
9. (4) The increase in income is $2000. The increase in tax liability is $800. The marginal rate is thus $(800/2000) \times 100\% = 40\%$.
10. (2) The reason is given in the answer; answer (4) is a tautology.
11. (1) Definition.
12. (5) Definition.
13. (3) Definition.
14. (4) Definition.
15. (2) Property taxes (local governments) and sales taxes (state governments) tend to be regressive, particularly when compared with the personal income tax, which is designed to be at least mildly progressive, and the corporation income tax, which is effectively progressive if it is not shifted.
16. (1) $52.8 billion in 1988.
17. (1) The average rate paid by the top 10 percent increased by 2 percent; the next 10 percent saw rates fall, as did everyone else.

Chapter 20

1. (3) All the others are examples of social regulation.
2. (3) All the others are examples of economic regulation.
3. (2) Increasing returns to scale mean declining average costs; all the other answers are artificial sources of

monopoly power, though one might expect (perhaps incorrectly) that a government would create a monopoly only when it might exploit its natural monopoly production efficiency.
4. (5) $MR = MC$ at $Q = 4$.
5. (2) $MC = DD$ at $Q = 7$.
6. (3) $AC = DD$ at $Q = 5$.
7. (4) AC is approximately $2.25 at $Q = 7$ while $P = \$1$.
8. (3) Consumer surplus equals $0.5(\$5 - \$2)(4 + 7) = \$16.50$; the $1.25 subsidy is applied to 7 units, so $8.75 must be subtracted.
9. (4) AC pricing brings price down by $1 as it increases output from 4 to 5 units; consumer surplus is therefore increased by $0.5(\$1)(4 + 5) = \$4.50$.
10. (3) The Clayton Act specifically mentions price discrimination.
11. (1) The Sherman Act specifically makes the formation of a monopoly a felony.
12. (5) The Federal Trade Commission Act specifically forbids deceptive business practices.
13. (1) Horizontal mergers do the most to concentrate market power and sow the seeds for abuse.
14. (1) $MR = MC$ for profit maximization, but $P > MR$ whenever an increase in the quantity sold must be accompanied by a reduction in price.

Chapter 21

1. (5) All the statements are accurate descriptions of historical experience.
2. (2) Definition.
3. (4) The 45° line specifies that percentage of people always equals percentage of income.
4. (3) A line running along the horizontal axis until it reached 100 percent of the people, then climbing vertically to 100 percent of the income.
5. (3) The proportion of income received by the lowest 20 percent of the people was, e.g., 4.7 percent in the mid-1970s and 4.2 percent in the late 1980s.
6. (2) The distribution was skewed with an average that was somewhat higher than the median.
7. (5) $16,500 per year divided by 52 weeks is about $317 per week.
8. (3) Experience.
9. (1) Definition.
10. (2) Definition.
11. (4) Start with perfect equality: the lowest 20 percent get 20 percent of the income. Introducing any inequality means that the people who lose, relatively, must be in the bottom 20 percent of the population, and their cumulative percentage must fall below the original 20 percent of the income.
12. (2) The distributions do not match, so there must be something else going on as well.
13. (5) All the statements are accurate.
14. (2) It reached 15 percent in 1984 before falling slightly to 14 percent in 1988.
15. (5) All the statements are accurate; consult Tables 21-4 and 21-5.
16. (4) Recession has, recently, been fair—hitting most demographic groups equally.
17. (4) Poverty still exists, even though those in the poorest 20 percent of the population have seen their incomes grow in line with GNP.
18. (3) The exact percentage is 21.5 percent.
19. (3) The notion behind the negative income tax is that the marginal tax rate applied to the income earned by the working poor is small.
20. (5) No leaks means moving along the 45° line AE; equality occurs on the 45° line OE.
21. (4) Equality occurs on the 45° line OE.
22. (5) All are subjects for continued investigation.
23. (1) Medicaid was highest, followed by food stamps; see Table 21-6.
24. (5) Part of the Reagan agenda and reliance on the private sector.
25. (1) Work disincentives imply inefficiency.

Chapter 22

1. (3) The self-regulating natural order that Smith asserted would be provided by a freely operating market system.
2. (3) It was competitive markets to which Smith referred.
3. (5) Land would be the bottleneck of continued economic growth; profit falls while wage maintains a subsistence level.
4. (4) A decline in the rate of business profit would be the source of increased pressure on payment to labor that would lead to the proletarian revolt and ultimate victory.
5. (1) Milton Friedman has argued vigorously against many forms of government intervention in markets and society.
6. (4) Diminishing returns applied to land would make the capitalists more important.
7. (1) The notion of marginalism extended to all factors of production ultimately led to the development of a general-equilibrium view of economic systems.
8. (3) Other inputs must be paid out of the price that the product commands in the market.
9. (3) The Clark theory of distribution (e.g.).
10. (4) The labor theory of value described what should be.
11. (3) There are other differences, of course, but their distinctly different treatment of unionism is important.
12. (5) Consumer-goods shortages have plagued the Soviet Union for years; they have become more severe during the transition precipitated by reform.
13. (3) Gorbachev's reforms may change this to a degree.
14. (2) There are no income taxes in the Soviet Union.
15. (1) In 1985, for example, 52 percent and 44 percent, respectively.

Chapter 23

1. (4) All the other answers speak to absolute advantage; trade patterns are determined by comparative advantage.
2. (3) The Ricardo analysis is classical, assuming swift market adjustment to the changes created by trade.
3. (2) The demand for exported goods climbs, creating upward pressure on their prices; the demand for imported goods falls, tending to push their prices down.
4. (4) In A, each yard of cloth takes 12 minutes to produce; each liter of wine, 6 minutes. In B, each yard takes 4 minutes; each liter, 3 minutes. The wine-to-cloth ratio in A is thus 1:2; in B, it is 3:4. Country A therefore has a comparative advantage in wine even though B has absolute advantages in both goods.
5. (3) The prices of wine must preserve the 1:2 and 3:4 cost ratios in the Ricardo classical model.
6. (1) Country A has the comparative advantage in wine.
7. (1) It should move somewhere between 1:2 and 3:4.
8. (3) Without transportation costs, it must be the same in both countries. The wine-to-cloth price ratio must be between 0.5 and 0.75, so the cloth-to-wine ratio must be between 1.33 and 2.
9. (3) Each yard of cloth is worth 1.6 liters of wine; so 800 liters (= 500 × 1.6) must be exchanged—exported from A.
10. (3) B is the wine-importing country. Each hour devoted to wine there produces 20 liters; devoted to cloth, that hour could produce 15 yards, which, given the cloth-to-wine price ratio of 1.6, could be translated into 24 liters of wine.
11. (5) Decreasing costs (economies of scale) can produce gains from trade only after trade is begun and they can be exploited.
12. (3) This is the point of the Ricardo model; comparative advantage matters.
13. (4) Definition.
14. (5) Only this answer would be recorded as a credit because it produces foreign currency; all the others are debit transactions because they expend foreign currency.
15. (3) Definition.

Chapter 24

1. (3) It ignores the theory of comparative advantage.
2. (1) The second tariff would make Country B even worse off.
3. (2) The parallel view to personal saving, the mercantile position cannot be maintained by all countries.
4. (2) Higher productivity should give the United States a comparative advantage in some goods but not necessarily an absolute advantage in all goods.
5. (3) Protection makes domestic prices higher.
6. (3) Under static conditions, general welfare is maximized in long-run, full-employment, free-trade equilibrium.
7. (2) The optimal-tariff idea depends upon a country's ability to move the terms of trade without retaliation; its trading partner must, therefore, be small, and the volume of its trade must have no influence over the world price.
8. (2) Subsidy provides the effective encouragement without the price effects and the direct threat of retaliation.
9. (5) With other countries' exports reduced by our large tariffs, their ability to import our exports will be diminished if they are to maintain a reasonable trade balance even without retaliation.
10. (2) Protection increases domestic prices, and thus reduces domestic real income.
11. (3) Effective protection and revenue maximization are two different goals; they need not lead to the same policy.
12. (5) The right to import 1 unit will be sold for exactly the tariff in an auction.

Chapter 25

1. (4) Providing, essentially, public goods that promote development but for which there is insufficient gain to rely on private provision.
2. (3) They have moved into the "early development" demographic stage, with continued high birth rates and reduced death rates.
3. (5) Insufficient saving is one problem.
4. (5) People have work, but their productivity is minimal; in a developed economy, they would be called "underemployed."
5. (1) Imports rise as its markets open and its needs increase (e.g., for the capital that embodies the technology that the country is "borrowing").
6. (2) Definition.
7. (1) Saving required to finance the necessary investment.
8. (4) Some do, but many do not.
9. (5) There has been some widening since the early 1980s.

Chapter 26

1. (3) Definition.
2. (1) Definition.
3. (2) Four francs buy $1, which buys 600 lire; 1 franc must therefore buy 600/4 = 150 lire.
4. (3) B must pay for the exports with gold, increasing the money supply and prices in A and reducing both in B.
5. (4) Four francs to the dollar makes the price of 1 franc $0.25; three to the dollar, $0.33.
6. (1) Increase the supply of dollars.
7. (4) An increase in the demand for Canadian dollars increases the supply of U.S. dollars.

8. (2) Depreciation in the dollar makes U.S. exports less expensive and imports from abroad more expensive.
9. (2) Depreciation of a domestic currency makes imports more expensive at home and exports less expensive abroad.
10. (1) A decline in economic activity in the United States causes imports to shrink, the demand for foreign currency to fall, and thus the price of the dollar to fall.
11. (1) New rules were defined for maintaining exchange-rate levels.
12. (4) Some short-term, rate-sustaining borrowing was allowed.
13. (2) The World Bank was created to help developing countries with long-term loans.
14. (3) Without fixed rates, the exchange rate can move to ameliorate a balance-of-trade problem.
15. (5) Definition.